DOCUMENTA MISSIONALIA – 26

FACULTAS MISSIOLOGICA - PONT. UNIVERSITAS GREGORIANA

# CHRISTIAN THEOLOGICAL UNDERSTANDING OF OTHER RELIGIONS

## ACCORDING TO D. S. AMALORPAVADASS

JOHN BERCHMANS BARLA

EDITRICE PONTIFICIA UNIVERSITÀ GREGORIANA
ROMA 1999

IMPRIMI POTEST

Romae, die 18 martii 1999
R.P. Franco Imoda, S.J.
*Rector Universitatis*

IMPRIMATUR

Dal Vicariato di Roma, 22 marzo 1999
Sac. Luigi Moretti, *Segretario Generale*



ISBN 88-7652-819-9.

Editrice Pontificia Università Gregoriana
Piazza della Pilotta, 35 - 00187 Roma, Italia

ACKNOWLEDGEMENTS

Many are the persons to whom I owe my profound thanks for the completion of this thesis. While thanking God for his blessings and providence, I acknowledge my sincere thanks to Prof. M. Dhavamony, s.j., the moderator of this thesis. His long stay and expertise in the field of religions helped me complete this work in time. It would not have been possible to arrive at this stage without his encouragement, scholarly guidance and assistance in this work. I express my sincere thanks also to Prof. Philip J. Rosato, s.j., the second reader of the thesis, to Prof. Félix Pastor, s.j., and to all my professors at the Pontifical Gregorian University, Rome.

I am sincerely grateful to my confrères, especially, J. Prasad Pinto, ofm cap., my Minister Provincial, and his definitors, for giving me this opportunity to study in Rome. Thanks to Rev. Fr. John Corriveau, ofm cap., the Minister General, and the General Curia for the help I received for my stay and study in Rome. Thanks to the rector and the community of Collegio San Lorenzo for their assistance and fellowship during my stay at the college.

My special thanks goes to all my friends and benefactors, especially the parishioners of the *Heilige Familie* Church, Klinkum; friends from Wegberg and Rath-Anhoven; Rev. Fr. Laetantius Morskieft, ocarm., and the community of Karmeliterkloster, Wegberg, Germany; and Robert C. and Rose M. Nelson. I express my gratitude to them for their love and support, especially for their financial contribution for the printing of this book. I thank Sr. Teresa Geoghegàn and all those who helped me in different ways in this work.

Finally, I am greatly indebted to my parents, brothers and sisters, relatives, and all my well-wishers for their love and prayers, constant support and encouragement. May God be with them always.

# TABLE OF CONTENTS

## NOTE ON TRANSLITERATION

In this study the words taken from other languages which do not follow the Roman script, especially Hindi and Sanskrit, are written in the Roman letters with diacritical marks. However, we have avoided the diacritical marks for some of the names of persons, places and events which are popularly written in the Roman letters without diacritical marks. For example, the name of M. Gandhi which would have been written with diacritical marks as M. Gāndhī. Likewise, the word Ashram, whenever it refers to the names of some places or institutions (e.g., Anjali Ashram, Ramakrishna Ashram) then it is maintained as it is, otherwise written with diacritical marks as *āśram.*

The rest of the transliteration into Roman characters has been followed as it is shown below. Some of the Devanāgari characters are indicated because of their specificity. The characters within brackets with asterisks (*) are used for Greek or Hebrew; the rest, for Arabic, Hindi and Sanskrit.

*Vowels*

*a (')* * as in c*u*t
*ā* ........ c*a*lm
*ai* ........ t*i*me
*au* ........ c*ow*
*i* ........ b*i*t
*ī* ........ *ea*se
*u* ........ b*u*ll
*ū (û)* *....... r*u*le
*e (ĕ)* *....... *e*vidence
*(ē)* * ........ long *e*
*o* ........ g*o*
*(ō, ô, ó)* *... long *o*

*Consonants*

*b* ........ *b*oy
*bh* .... a*bh*or (hard sound of *b*)
*c* ........ *ch*urch
*ch* ........ (hard sound of *c*)
*d* ........ *th*is
*dh* ........ (hard sound of *d*)
*ḍ* ........ *d*ust
*ḍh* ........ (hard sound of *ḍ*)
*g* ........ *g*um
*gh* ........ dagger
*ḥ* ........ a*h* (Sanskrit :)
*h* ........ *h*oney

*j* ........ *j*ug
*jh* ........ (hard sound of *j*)
*k* ........ *c*ut
*kh* ........ as in German: Ma*ch*t
*l* ........ *l*ove
*m* ........ *m*ud
*ṁ* ..... to*n*gue (Hindi, Sanskrit ˙)
*n* ........ *n*urse
*ñ* ........ as in Italian: sig*n*ore
*ṅ* ........ ri*ng*
*p* ........ *p*ot
*ph* ... shep*h*erd (hard sound of *p*)

*r* ...... pu*r*ity
*ṛ* ...... like *r* (Devanāgari ऋ)
*s* ...... *s*ome
*ś* .... like *sh*eep (Devanāgari श)
*ṣ (š)** like *sh*ock (Devanāgari ष)
*(ṣ)** for *ts* sound in Heb. like *Z*ion
*t* ........ as in French: fê*te*
*th* ........ ma*th*ematics
*ṭ* ........ bu*t*
*ṭh* ........ (hard sound of *ṭ*)
*v* ........ *w*arm
*y* ......... *y*es

# ABBREVIATIONS

## *Vatican II Documents*

| | |
|---|---|
| *AA* | *Apostolicam Actuositatem:* Decree on the Apostolate of the Laity |
| *AG* | *Ad Gentes Divinitus:* Decree on the Church's Missionary Activity |
| *CD* | *Christus Dominus:* Decree on the Pastoral Office of Bishops in the Church |
| *DH* | *Dignitatis Humanae:* Declaration on Religious Freedom |
| *DV* | *Dei Verbum:* Dogmatic Constitution on Divine Revelation |
| *GS* | *Gaudium et Spes:* Pastoral Constitution on the Church in the Modern World |
| *IM* | *Inter Mirifica:* Decree on the Means of Social Communication |
| *LG* | *Lumen Gentium:* Dogmatic Constitution on the Church |
| *NA* | *Nostra Aetate:* Declaration on the Relationship of the Church to Non-Christian Religions |
| *OE* | *Orientalium Ecclesiarum:* Decree on the Catholic Oriental Churches |
| *OT* | *Optatam Totius:* Decree on the Training of Priests |
| *PO* | *Presbyterorum Ordinis:* Decree on the Ministry and Life of Priests |
| *SC* | *Sacrosanctum Concilium:* The Constitution of the Sacred Liturgy |
| *UR* | *Unitatis Redintegratio:* Decree on Ecumenism |

## *Other Abbreviations*

| | |
|---|---|
| *AAS* | *Acta Apostolicae Sedis,* the Vatican gazette, published a varying number of times each year. Carries the original text of the more important Vatican Documents. |
| AICU | All-India Catholic Union, the only officially recognized All-India Catholic organization, formerly, CUI, that is, Catholic Union of India. |
| BCC | Basic Christian Communities |
| BEC | Basic Ecclesial Communities |
| BG | Bhagavad-gītā |
| BIRA | Bishops' Institute for Inter-Religious Affairs |
| Bṛh. Up. | Bṛhadāraṇyaka Upaniṣad |
| CBAI | Catholic Biblical Association of India |
| CBCI | Catholic Bishops' Conference of India |
| CCC | *Catechism of the Catholic Church,* Doubleday, 1995. |
| CISRS | Christian Institute for the Study of Religion and Society |
| CRI | Conference of Religious in India |

| | |
|---|---|
| DFT | *Dictionary of Fundamental Theology,* edited by R. Latourelle and R. Fisichella, New York, Crossroad, 1994. |
| DM | "Dialogue and Mission" |
| DNC | Declaration of the Nagpur Conference |
| DP | "Dialogue and Proclamation" |
| DS | H. Denzinger-A. Schönmetzer (eds), *Enchiridion Symbolorum, Definitionum et Declarationum de Rebus Fidei et Morum,* Freiburg im Breisgau, 36th ed., 1976. (Collection of more important Church Documents). |
| DSA | D.S. Amalorpavadass |
| EATWOT | Ecumenical Association of Third World Theologians |
| *EN* | *Evangelii Nuntiandi* |
| *ET* | *Evangelica Testificatio* |
| FABC | Federation of Asian Bishops' Conference |
| FERES | The International Federation of Institutes for Socio-Religious Research, Louvain. |
| IAMS | International Association of Mission Studies |
| NBCLC | National Biblical, Catechetical and Liturgical Centre |
| NCLC | National Catechetical and Liturgical Centre. In 1971 it became NBCLC when the CBCI made it also the National Biblical Centre. |
| ND | J. Neuner and J. Dupuis (eds), *The Christian Faith in the Doctrinal Documents of the Catholic Church* (its 6th revised and enlarged edition, edited by J. Dupuis), Alba House, New York, 1996 by special arrangement with Theological Publication in India. |
| NT | New Testament |
| OT | Old Testament |
| *PP* | *Populorum Progressio* |
| *RH* | *Redemptor Hominis* |
| *RM* | *Redemptoris Missio* |
| SCNC | Special Committee of the Nagpur Conference |
| TNJBC | *The New Jerome Biblical Commentary* (student edition), edited by R.E. Brown and Co., London, Geoffrey Chapman, 1996 (reprint). |
| WCC | World Council of Churches |
| WCFBA | World Catholic Federation for Biblical Apostolate |
| WCT | World Congress of Theology (on the 'Future of the Church' Brussels, 1970) |

## GENERAL INTRODUCTION

### *1. Approaches to the Question of Religious Pluralism*

Religion[1] in some form or other is as old as humanity itself and religious pluralism is an ancient and universal phenomenon. But this religious plurality never posed a problem in the past as it is today.

The Church has always lived in a milieu that was religiously plural. From the earliest times, Christians, on encountering the followers of other religions, adopted diverse attitudes both in their theology and proclamation of the Gospel. In the early Apostolic Church we notice a predominantly apologetical approach to other religions. This approach can be well seen and summarized in Peter's and Paul's undaunted proclamations of Jesus as Christ the Messiah (both, however, using the concepts and categories of their hearers): Peter to the Jews (cf. Acts 2:14-36), Paul to the Gentiles (cf. to the Athenians, Acts 17:16-34; to the Lycaonians, Acts 14:8-18). This was a period of intense Christocentrism that saw the whole of reality in and through Jesus Christ, the risen and glorified Lord (cf. Col. 1:15-20). In traditional theological terms, this period referred to the understanding of Christ as the one and the only Lord and mediator of the world (cf. Acts 4:12; 1 Tim. 2:5).

In the Patristic period, though some of the Fathers discovered the 'seeds of the Word' in other religions (Clement, Justin, Origen, and others) as elements and points of contact between Christianity and other religions, one notices in this period in general an attitude of struggle and opposition.[2]

Though in the pre-Vatican II period there was an openness of the Church to the culture and value systems of other people, as can be seen in

---

[1] Belief in the supernatural or a phenomenon known as God or gods and all human activity relating to such a phenomenon constitute the essence of religion. Cf. Mariasusai Dhavamony, "Religion (I. Definition)", in: René Latourelle and Rino Fisichella (eds), *Dictionary of Fundamental Theology*, Crossroad, New York, 1994, pp. 819-821. (Henceforth this book will be cited as *DFT*).

[2] Cf. M. Dhavamony, "Theology of Religions", in: Sebastian Karotemprel (ed.), *Following Christ in Mission. (A Foundational Course in Missiology)*, Pauline Publications, Bombay, 1995, pp. 251-252; Jacques Dupuis, *Jesus Christ at the Encounter of World Religions*, (translated from the French by Robert R. Barr), Orbis Books, Maryknoll, New York, 1991, pp. 133-136.

the philosophical interpretation of faith (e.g., adoption of Greek philosophy), the symbolic systems of worship, spiritual categories of life and the administrative systems of the Church, in general a negative attitude towards other religions prevailed in the Church. In the medieval period, by now Christianity had become the religion of the majority by the conversion of Europe and their colonization programme, the encounter with Islam caused a radical change in the attitude of the Church towards other religions. Unlike other encounters it was a confrontation of two socio-political powers rallying around two religions. This led to religious antagonism and total rejection or exclusivism, designating others as "infidels". With this prevailing negative attitude the Western Church, under the protection of colonial powers, entered the Third World and confronted the great world religions. The evangelizing mission of the Church was marked by expansionism leading almost to the total rejection of other religions and their value systems and cultural forms till the *kairos* of Vatican II which recognized others as religions and broke the ground for dialogue and collaboration.

In short, the attitude of the Church can be seen in three phases: (i) apologetical (the early Church); (ii) ecclesiocentric (pre-Vatican II); and (iii) Christocentric, inclusive and dialogical (post-Vatican II).

The approach of theocentrism through Christ responds to the dialogical reality of the Church, emphasizing, thereby, the specificity and complementarity of all the religions. Theocentrism is thus an attempt to find a common theological platform in dialogue with adherents of other religions. It refers to the understanding of God as the source, the author, of all salvation. He is the creator of all humankind; he is the one who saves. He has manifold ways of saving man[3] in the unity and continuity (on-going) of the one salvation history directed towards its eschatological fulfillment in and through his Son Jesus Christ (cf. Heb. 1:1-2). Theocentrism through Christ or Christocentrism is also based on the fact that the Son, Christ himself, is centered in the Father (from the promise of salvation to its completion, cf. Heb. 1:1-2; 1 Cor. 15:28). Jesus proclaimed himself as the way to the Father (cf. Jn. 14:6). Therefore, the mystery of Jesus Christ cannot be interpreted except theocentrically.

---

[3] *Man/woman:* the language problem. When we say man or woman what we mean is human being (humankind). Henceforth we will be mostly using the term *man,* thereby, meaning *human person.* There is no sex discrimination or personal offence to anyone in anyway.

Though the encounter of the Church with the religions of the world is not a new phenomenon, in recent decades the issue has gathered great momentum in the theological thinking of the Church. While the Church is still trying to articulate her position with greater clarity, she is more and more entering in dialogue and mutual collaboration with others. The period of exclusivism, fanaticism and monologue seems to be over, although there are occasional backlashes in the form of fundamentalist and communalist eruptions. All religions are becoming aware of their particular historical, social and cultural contexts and limitations and of the consequent need of complementarity for the discovery of the entire religious heritage of humankind. It has also become clear that the mystery of God cannot be exhaustively and exclusively contained in any one particular historical form of religion. The all-pervading Spirit of God blows where he wills (cf. Jn. 3:8), sowing the seeds of love, joy, peace and fellowship (cf. Gal. 5:22). He cannot be "confined" to a particular historical form of religion. This view leads us to conclude that today we cannot accept either the view that "all religions are the same" or that "each religion is totally different from others" as true.

### 2. *Clarifying the Terms of the Title*

Since the title of the dissertation is *Christian Theological Understanding of Other Religions According to D.S. Amalorpavadass,* we proceed to say a word about D.S. Amalorpavadass and to briefly clarify the terms of the title.

#### 2.1. *D.S. Amalorpavadass (1932-1990)*

Doraisamy Simon Amalorpavadass (Amalor)[4] was born in Kallery near Pondicherry (Tamil Nadu) on 15 June, 1932. After his college education he became a student of St. Peter's Seminary, Bangalore. His weak health during his seminary life never deterred his zeal for serious studies

[4] Henceforth we will cite the name of D.S. Amalorpavadass in its short form as Amalor or as DSA. We find so in other books, too. See for example: Gerwin van Leeuwen, O.F.M., *Fully Indian - Authentically Christian. (A Study of the First Fifteen Years of the NBCLC -- 1967-1982, Bangalore, India -- in the Light of the Theology of its Founder, D.S. Amalorpavadass),* NBCLC, Bangalore, 1990; Cyril De Souza, S.D.B., *Catechesis for India Today. (An Appraisal of the Catechetical Proposal of D.S. Amalorpavadass),* Kristu Jyoti Publications, Bangalore, 1994.

and research. Already during his seminary studies he gave lectures to his fellow students and wrote seven booklets in Tamil,[5] his mother tongue. After his priestly ordination (1959) he was appointed as one of the staff members of the Regional Catechetical Centre at Tindivanam (1959-1965), where he soon revealed his extraordinary talent for animation, administration and organization.[6]

Amalor's interest in other religions dates back to his sojourn at the *Institut Catholique de Paris* (1962-1965) where he studied for his Master's degree in Catechetics and Doctor's degree in Theology. For his Master's degree he wrote *L'Inde à la rencontre du Seigneur* (published in 1964), a critical examination of the history of the Church in India, particularly its approach to evangelization. He obtained the degree of Doctor in Theology defending his second thesis *Destinée de L'Église dans l'Inde d'aujourd'hui* (published in 1967), in many ways a prophetic book, in which he clearly indicates the conditions for an effective evangelization in a multi-religious context. Apart from these two books, the list of his later publications of a multi-pronged approach is quite impressive.[7] His studies in Paris enabled him to follow the Vatican II Council very closely and as an accredited journalist he came into personal contact with prominent bishops and theologians.

After his return to India in June 1965 he became parish priest at Viriyur (1965-1966), a big parish with 63 villages. In October 1966 the Catholic Bishops' Conference of India (CBCI) appointed him Founder-Director of the National Biblical, Catechetical and Liturgical Centre (NBCLC), Bangalore, and Secretary of the CBCI Commissions for Catechetics and Liturgy (and of the Commission for Biblical Apostolate from 1971). As Director of the NBCLC (1966-1982), he did yeoman service in the implementation of the Vatican II theology in the Indian Church. He

---

[5] These are: *Why do I Suffer?* (the problem of evil), Pondicherry 1957; *The Royal Priesthood,* Madurai 1957; *The Heavenly Jerusalem* (the biblical theme 'temple'), Madurai 1957; *The Day of the Lord* (the biblical themes 'rest', 'joy' and 'hope'), Madurai 1958; *The Lord is my Shepherd,* Madurai 1958; *The Spouse,* Nagercoil 1958; *The Missionary Spirit in the Bible,* Madurai 1959.

[6] Cf. Gerwin van Leeuwen, "Fr. D.S. Amalorpavadass (1932-1990)", in: Paul Puthanangady, S.D.B. (ed.), *Church in India: Institution of Movement? (A Tribute to the Memory of Fr. D.S. Amalorpavadass, Founder-Director of NBCLC on the First Anniversary of his Mahasamadhi, 25th May, 1990--25th May, 1991),* NBCLC, Bangalore, 1991, p. xi.

[7] See in the bibliography.

worked very hard for the renewal and relevancy -- the indigenization of the Indian Church, keeping in mind the diverse religious, cultural and social situations of the Indian society. During his tenure at the NBCLC, to mention some of his important works, he organized with the International Federation of Institutes for Socio-Religious Research (FERES, Louvain) the Asian Seminar on Religion and Development in 1973, in order to use a reliable tool to critically analyze and reflect on the role of religion in the transformation of society. His organization of the Research Seminar on Non-Biblical Scriptures (1974) was in many ways a breaking ground of its kind: God's inspiration has been working in the scriptures of other religions. In 1974 he served as special secretary at the Episcopal Synod on Evangelization in Rome. His report, in which he strongly voiced the wholly different experience and approach of the Third World, was so different from that of the Roman (First World) secretary that for the first time an Episcopal Synod did not end with a final declaration.[8] A year later Paul VI published *Evangelii Nuntiandi* (1975). Besides his works and responsibilities at home, he had many assignments and commitments abroad. To mention a few: For several years he was a member of the executive committee of the International Commission for English in the Liturgy (ICEL) and *Pro Mundi Vita.* He belonged to the founding members of important international bodies like the World Catholic Federation of Biblical Apostolate (WCFBA) and the Ecumenical Association of Third World Theologians (EATWOT).

Amalor was the first one to start a Chair (1979) and a Department (1981) of Christianity in a secular state university in India. This Chair and the Department in Mysore University clearly manifest the secular character of the Indian nation. But for his vision, tact and perseverance this bold venture would never have been materialized. After the completion of his term as Director of the NBCLC and Secretary of the CBCI Commissions for Liturgy, Catechetics and Biblical Apostolate, Amalor went to Anjali Ashram (Mysore) in 1982, which he founded in 1979, and remained there, occupying himself mainly in spiritual animation and as professor of Christianity at Mysore University till his untimely demise in a road accident in 1990.[9]

---

[8] Cf. Gerwin van Leeuwen, "Fr. D.S. Amalorpavadass (1932-1990)", in: Paul Puthanangady, S.D.B. (ed.), *Church in India: Institution or Movement?*, op. cit., p. xii.

[9] Something more about DSA, but from a different perspective, will be seen while evaluating his theological stand in the general conclusion.

### *2.2. Other Religions*

The very adjective 'non-Christian', the term, which was earlier commonly accepted both in term and practice, with which Vatican II refers to religions other than the various Christian denominations and ecclesial communities, though negative, signifies positively other religions outside of Christianity.

God, the Tri-une (Father, Son and Spirit), is the creator of history and humankind; he is the author of the *one* salvation history of all humankind. God in and through his Word and Spirit has always been present and active among all peoples and religions. Only seen in this perspective can we justify Christ as the Lord of the universe and the saviour of all humankind.

However, it is not right to use the term 'Christian' for other religions, because, how do we then terminologically distinguish Christianity from other religions and, also, how can we call religions Christian, when their members do not like their religions being labelled 'Christian', afraid as they are to lose their own identity? Amalor concludes: "We decided to call them simply 'the religions', 'the world religions', 'the religions of the world' (Bombay Seminar) and 'the great religions of mankind' or 'the religious traditions of mankind' (Nagpur Conference)."[10]

Even today we do not have an adequate term, though the terms 'other religions' and 'other faiths' seem to get wider acceptance in spite of the weakness of the term 'other'. I have preferred to term them 'other religions'.

### *2.3. Christian Theology*

The particular objective of theology is the critical understanding of the content of faith so that the lives of believers may be fully significant.[11] Theology does not study God as he is in himself but as he reveals, relates

---

[10] See: DSA, *Approach, Meaning and Horizon of Evangelization. (The Theological Orientation Speech delivered at the All India Consultation on Evangelization at Patna, 3-8 October, 1973)*, NBCLC, Bangalore, 1973, p. 55. (Henceforth this work will be cited as *Approach*). Cf. also: Gerwin van Leeuwen, O.F.M., *Fully Indian - Authentically Christian,* op. cit., pp. 259-260.

[11] Cf. Rino Fisichella, "Theology (I. Definition)", in: *DFT,* p. 1061.

and communicates himself to humankind in creation and history.[12]

In spite of attempts made by adherents of different religions to unite and to bring harmony among religions, it is felt that besides similarities there are radical differences with regard to the experience and notion of God as well as the goal of religions and their ways of achieving this goal. Each religion has its own way of evaluating other religions. Each religion, we can say, has its own "theology of religions", dictating either total rejection of others or legitimization of all or equating all religions on the basis of one's own specific beliefs. In this regard ours is a Christian theology of other religions.

By 'Christian theological understanding' or 'Christian theology' we mean Catholic Christian theology. Since we are dealing with Christian theology of other religions *according* to Amalor who was a Catholic theologian, it is understood that we mean Catholic Christian theology of other religions. Amalor's theology of other religions is not a theoretical one, a speculation, but a very practical and pastoral one, proceeding from the Indian life-situation.

### *3. Choosing of the Theme: Its Relevancy*

The question of 'One and the Many' (religious pluralism) has always been a paradox in human existence. Philosophers, theologians and others have grappled with this problem in their own ways and have tried to offer certain explanations. The question is not only the concern of scholars, the learned and theologians. It is a question faced by any seeker after truth as it touches every sphere of life and at all levels.

Today people all over the globe are becoming more and more conscious of their historical, social, religious and cultural contexts; as a result there is religious and cultural renaissance and revival. However the same pluralistic trends have also given rise to narrow nationalism, fundamentalism and fanaticism.

While, with the rise and renaissance of religions and cultures, the Church must face the question of salvation in other religions which is the main problem in the theology of religions, she must face the challenges of other religions with their claims to unique and universal revelation and

---

[12] Cf. DSA, "Approach, Meaning and Horizon of Evangelization", in: *Light and Life We Seek to Share,* published by the Church Extension Commission (CBCI), Bangalore, 1973, p. 23. (Henceforth this work will be cited as "Approach").

ultimate truth.

The challenges of religious pluralism are real and they inevitably call for a serious study and reflection. It is a challenge not only to the Church but also to other religions and ideologies of the world.

Religious pluralism has always been in India but its recent manifestation calls for urgent attention. India, a land of many religious traditions and the cradle of diverse cultures, known for its tolerance and respect for other religions, is at cross-roads right now. It becomes all the more acute and it is imperative for all persons of good-will to face the rise of fundamentalist and communalist trends in recent times which is infecting and debilitating the whole nation, even to the verge of breakdown of the entire secular and democratic fabric. The communalist cancer is sapping India's energies, resources, culture and tradition of tolerance and active cooperation. The demolition of Babri Masjid at Ayodhya on 6th December 1992 and the recent attacks on religious priests and nuns[13] are shocking illustrations of the challenges to religious pluralism. Challenges of religious pluralism are signalling and shaping our theology today. What should be our attitudes and approaches to other religions? What is the role and responsibility, the contribution of the Church towards religious harmony, peace and progress in the society? The answer would depend much on the theology of religions.

*Our aim:* Various factors have brought us a clearer and profounder knowledge of the riches of other religions, dispelling much of the ignorance which in the past littered fear, suspicion and hostility. This new situation is particularly signalled and shaped by the development of inter-religious dialogue, collaboration, action in favour of the poor and struggle for a new society. These features call for a new theology of religions. The Church, in the world in general and India in particular, is challenged today to enter more and more deeply into the praxis of dialogue and collaboration in the struggle for a better society. This togetherness of religious communities and ideological movements will not only bring about greater

---

[13] For example, in September 1, 1994 Frs. Lawrence Kujur, Joseph Dungdung and Bro. Anup Indwar were murdered in Karondabera, Gumal; Sr. Maria Rani was stabbed to death on February 25, 1995 in Madhya Pradesh; on September 2, 1997 Fr. Christudas was paraded naked in Guhiajori, Dumka; on October 27, 1997 the beheaded body of Fr. A.T. Thomas was found in Chichi forest of Hazaribagh. Cf. *The New Leader* 111 (1998) 3, pp. 4-5. While these cases are still unresolved, the fear, mutual suspicion and mistrust among communal forces are on the rise.

and better understanding between the communities but it will also open new avenues to each other's world views, values and perceptions. It is at this stage that we choose the topic, aiming thereby also to contribute to the emergence of a genuine Indian Christian theology of religions which was one of the fondest desires and struggles of Amalor. India has a specially privileged position to take up this challenge of developing a new theology of religions, as all the major religions of the world existed in India side by side for centuries, and inter-religious harmony and fellowship (*sarva-dharma-samabhāva*) has always been part of the Indian ethos.[14]

Some studies on Amalor have already been done.[15] But a scholarly study of his theology of other religions has not been undertaken. Thus, ours is, to the best of my knowledge, the first attempt of its kind.

### 4. *Scope and Methodology*

As the title suggests, our study is the theology of other religions and, hence, the approach of our search is theological; and still, a modest answer to the questions of religious pluralism through the prism of Amalor's view.

There have been two major extremes in the theology of religions: either to reduce the many religions to the supremacy of one or to see the many as parallels that never meet. Both seem to be born of an exclusive view of religions.

A Christian theologian is called today to recognize and respect other religions in their own otherness. The call of the signs of the times is to understand deeply the significance and consequences of genuine pluralism of religions without compromise of any sort in a spirit of authentic dialogue and collaboration.

Religious pluralism is a fact today. But could pluralism be affirmed as a right? Are the many religions part of God's design and provision for

---

[14] Cf. DSA, "Meaning and Role of the Charismatic Renewal in India Today: Its Challenges", in: *Word and Worship* 10 (1977) 2, p. 90; also: Kuncheria Pathil, C.M.I. (ed.), *Religious Pluralism. An Indian Christian Perspective,* ISPCK, Delhi, 1991, pp. viii-ix.

[15] Such as: Gerwin van Leeuwen, O.F.M., *Fully Indian - Authentically Christian,* Bangalore (1990); Paul Puthanangady, S.D.B. (ed.), *Church in India: Institution or Movement?,* Bangalore (1991); Cyril De Souza, S.D.B., *Catechesis for India Today,* Bangalore (1994). See these works also cited above.

humankind? Does religious pluralism constitute a situation of grace? Is pluralism the outward expression of the infinite riches of the Absolute which no particular historical event, epoch, person or religious tradition can adequately and exhaustibly represent? What then are the deeper truths of pluralism?

We intend to answer directly or indirectly such questions in the course of the dissertation. Ours is an attempt to give a modest answer, limited to the thought and theologizing of Amalor. Our concern exposes his theology in such a way as to allow him to speak for himself, and, therefore, there are no comparisons nor much mention of other theologians, except when they are mentioned by Amalor himself or, in one way or the other, they have come into contact with him.

While presenting the theology of other religions according to Amalor, the thesis evaluates and examines its relevance, and at the end, besides making an evaluation of his theological stand and résumé of the chapters, it proposes some important points for a Christian theology of other religions in our multi-religious society, especially in the Indian context.

While, the Hindi and Sanskrit terms are written with diacritical marks, often in the quotations they are not found so, because we have kept them as they are written by the authors.

### *5. A Glance of the Divisions and their Content*

The dissertation is divided into three parts which are subdivided into six chapters, comprising the main themes of the Christian theology of religions.

We begin our theologizing basing ourselves on the biblical and the Conciliar sources. The first part is divided into two chapters. Chapter one mainly deals with the biblical world vision of Amalor -- God, man, the world, and the Church -- the vision of wholeness, revelation and inspiration, the on-going revelation of God in and through his Son Jesus Christ who is the supreme and definitive revelation of God, and some important biblical themes and texts.

Chapter two deals with Amalor's Vatican II vision of the Church and his renewal effort in all the ecclesial areas of life and activity, especially the relevancy of the Church and her theology with regard to other religions, indigenization and local theology. Christ came to save the whole man and every man. Evangelization which consists in bringing Christ to man and man to Christ aims at the realization of God's universal salvific plan in Christ (cf. 1 Tim. 2:4-6). This salvation consists in the fullness of life, which by nature is also eschatological. Salvation affects every aspect of human life. Thus even the issue of economic development comes under its purview. Christian mission must oscillate between its transcendent constants (*missio Dei:* Father - Son - Spirit) and its historical variants (the signs of the times). It is a mission accomplished with humble service and yet with the power of the Spirit, the power of the *missio Dei.*

Part two is divided into two chapters. Chapter three deals with the cosmic Christ. The one and universal salvific will of God (cf. 1 Tim. 2:4) is displayed to all humanity from the very beginning of human history. Human history is indeed salvation history which is one and is directed in its unity and continuity towards its completion. The authority of Christ comes from God himself. He is the Son of God, "the Word become flesh" (Jn. 1:14), and the risen and universal Lord to (re)unite and lead all things, all peoples and religions to God (cf. Eph. 1:20-21; Col. 1:15-20) so that "God may be all in all" (1 Cor. 15:28). The uniqueness and universality of Jesus Christ are the very universal salvific mystery of God: Christ's "historicity" (*incarnation*) and his "universality" (*resurrection*). Jesus Christ is "the way, and the truth, and the life" (Jn. 14:6), the inclusive way, not exclusive, the fullness of grace and truth (cf. Jn. 1:14). The Jesus Christ event is, therefore, "constitutive" of God's saving will and action in history.

Chapter four deals with the salvific value of other religions, seen in God's salvific providence for all. The Church, constituted as the universal sacrament of salvation (cf. *LG* 48), the sacrament of peace and unity, is the continuation of the saving mission of Christ on earth. She is the humble servant of Christ, his people and his kingdom on earth, who came to serve, not to be served (cf. Matt. 20:28).

Part three is also divided into two chapters. Chapter five deals with inter-religious dialogue in the common search for the fullness of truth and life. Today we are becoming more and more aware that man's personal and social life and religions themselves are dialogically structured. Dialogue here is understood as a mode of being and a way of life. It is a process of mutual sharing and mutual enrichment.

Chapter six deals with inter-religious collaboration in the common struggle for a new society, new heaven and new earth (cf. Rev. 21:1). The secularization of religion is another phenomenon of our times. No religion which preaches exclusively an other worldly salvation will be accepted by the modern man. All religions are becoming more and more committed to this world in transforming it into a better world, more human and just, marked by love, fellowship, peace and harmony. This vision of a better world, a new society, can be achieved only by the active collaboration of all religions and ideologies. Hence the urgent need for all religions of relating to one another in dialogue and common ventures.

Our age has presented a decisive challenge to the world religions. They must either relate themselves to the profound personal and social concerns of modern man or resign themselves to exist indifferently at the periphery of human concerns. Whereas many religions today continue to remain conservative and traditional, there is at the same time, at least among the serious thinkers, a sense of urgency to interpret faith and praxis, so that it would help people in dealing with the problems of contemporary living. Hence the interest of discussion in contemporary religious discussions has shifted from pure polemics to the constructive obligations of relevance to the actual life of man. This same situation challenges the Church, as it does every religion, to consider and formulate a theology of inter-religious dialogue and collaboration on the basis of the fundamentals of her own faith. The dialogical ecclesiology today has to recognize the presence and activity of the Spirit in other religions, bringing forth the fruits of love, peace, fellowship, justice and truth (cf. Gal. 5:22). The Spirit is certainly leading the Church and other religions to the fullness of truth and life and to their common unity in God (cf. Jn. 14:26; 1 Cor. 15:28).

# PART ONE

## SOURCES, ANALYSIS AND APPLICATION

The Bible, Patristic Tradition and Vatican II are the main sources of any Christian theology of other religions. While the Bible and Patristic Tradition are the ultimate norm of all Christian life and theologizing, hardly anyone can deny that Vatican II has been one of the most important ecclesial events (*kairos*) of the twentieth century, especially with regard to other religions. It was in Vatican II, especially *NA,* that the Catholic Church for the first time officially recognized the value and validity of other religions. The ecclesiology of Vatican II while recognizing others as religions, made a radical shift from the medieval pyramidal model of the Church to that of the People of God, which includes a fourfold shift: from institution to mystery, from hierarchy to people, from monarchical papacy to episcopal collegiality, and from the universal Church to the local. Since God has been the God of history, the Church cannot exist in a socio-cultural vacuum but, living in the world and for the world, she should work towards the total transformation of the world.

Since Amalor mainly based his theology of other religions on the biblical and Vatican II perspectives, we begin with the biblical and Vatican II sources and analyses, in so far as these sources and analyses go to serve his stand; and since the Conciliar theological points are also dealt under other chapters (e.g., salvation, dialogue, collaboration), in chapter two we will mainly dwell on the Conciliar vision of the Church and her evangelization, in so far as it serves our purpose.

## CHAPTER ONE

# ANALYSIS AND APPLICATION OF THE BIBLICAL SOURCES

### 1. Introduction

Bible is the source of Christian life, faith and theology. It is the word of God that he has spoken in history. Any Christian theology of other religions must be, therefore, solidly anchored in the word of God, the Bible, "which should be the soul, as it were, of all theology" (*Optatam Totius* 16).

God does not speak in the abstract. He always speaks to a concrete humanity in history. Therefore, to live our faith today in our history, in the signs of the times, hermeneutics of the Bible, the application and interpretation of the scripture, is important. One of the very obvious and unavoidable signs of the times today is religious pluralism and the recognition of other religions in the world by the Church. Amalor will base his understanding of other religions on the scripture.

God is an ineffable mystery. He reveals himself to all humankind, and in this he is sovereignly free. In and through his revelation, God comes to meet man. Man responds to this revelation in faith, and the meeting of God and man, salvation, takes place. Revelation is God's self-communication. It is not a communication of abstract truths and doctrines or intellectual ideas as such. It reaches our life and existence; it is a revelation of life in its fullness.[1] Revelation is the loving and free gift of God to his children, all human beings, in different times and manners, reaching its climax in the Jesus Christ event in the fullness of time (cf. Gal. 4:4; Heb. 1:1-2).

Amalor takes a positive attitude towards the religions of the world. He calls for constant collaboration and sincere dialogue with others in the common journey of all humanity towards its common goal. There is one

---

[1] Cf. DSA, *Theology of Evangelization in the Indian Context,* NBCLC, Bangalore, 1984 (4th print, its 1st print in 1971), p. 21. (This was originally an Inaugural Key-note address at the International Theological Conference on Evangelization and Dialogue in Asia, Nagpur, 6-12 October, 1971. Henceforth this work will be abbreviated and cited as *Theology of Evangelization*).

reality, one history of salvation and one common destiny of all humankind, namely, God (cf. *NA* 1).[2]

## 2. Overall World Vision of Reality: Traditional and Biblical

### *2.1. Why the World Vision at All?*

Amalor often points out the close connection of mind, heart, vision, structure and behaviour.[3] One never fails to see the importance of one's clarity of vision of reality and one's commitment, success and satisfaction in living that reality. Our theology and spiritual life are influenced and shaped, among others, by our world-view. "This world-view is itself a constitutive element of a culture and therefore, a characteristic of a people, of a time, and of a place. In short, the world-view determines the ethos of a people reciprocally."[4]

Clarity of vision is very much asked for in one's life and mission. One's understanding of oneself and of others, of one's religion and that of others, will always depend on one's image and understanding of God. Correct image of God leads to correct image of man and his mission. It determines one's life structure and behaviour. It is the vantage point from which one understands oneself and the whole of reality.[5] One must "know" God whom one loves and serves. Paul says, "... for I know the one in whom I have put my trust, and I am sure that he is able to guard until that day what has been entrusted to me" (2 Tim. 1:12). Jesus says to the Samaritan woman, "Woman believe me, the hour is coming ..., and is now here, when the true worshippers will worship the Father in spirit and truth, for the Father seeks such as these to worship him. God is spirit, and those who worship him must worship him in spirit and truth" (Jn. 4:21-24). Again, "And this is eternal life, that they may know you, the only true

---

[2] Cf. DSA, *Approaches in Our Apostolate Among Followers of Other Religions*, NBCLC, Bangalore, 1978 (4th print, its 1st print in 1970), p. 20. (Henceforth this work will be cited as *Approaches*).

[3] Cf. DSA, *Our Christian World Vision and Theological Synthesis*, NBCLC, Bangalore, 1980 (4th print), p. 3. (Henceforth this work will be cited as *Our Christian World Vision*).

[4] DSA, "Traditional Spirituality within Our Present Christian World Vision", in: Id. (ed.), *Indian Christian Spirituality*, NBCLC, Bangalore, 1982, p. 47.

[5] Cf. DSA, *Theology of Evangelization*, op. cit., p. 20.

God, and Jesus Christ whom you have sent" (Jn. 17:3). "I came to bring fire to the earth, and how I wish it were already kindled! I have a baptism with which to be baptized, and what stress I am under it until it is completed!" (Lk. 12:49-50).

For Jesus, we can say, the integral vision of the whole of reality consisted in these two key words: the correct image of God as *Abba,* and his mission of *God's kingdom.*[6] His vision differed from that of the religious leaders of his time in Israel. This is the reason why when Jesus preached God as Father and proclaimed his kingdom of "righteousness [or justice] and peace and joy in the Holy Spirit" (Rom. 14:17) in Israel, he had to face the opposition from the Pharisees and other religious leaders mainly because his faith-vision of reality did not coincide with theirs. The right interpretation of God, Law and religion, the *hermeneutical key* of Jesus, was different from that of the Pharisees and other religious leaders of his time in Israel. Even, in the beginning, John the Baptist had a doubt about Jesus and his hermeneutical key of the kingdom of God (cf. Matt. 11:1-6). But Jesus never deterred himself from his vision. For this vision he lived, suffered, and ultimately died, even accepting a shameful death on a cross.

Let us see the integral vision of Amalor in the following two main points: the four constitutive elements of reality, seen in their relationship in the traditional and the biblical world visions, and the vision of fullness (*pūrṇam*).

## *2.2 The Four Constitutive Elements of Reality: God, Man, the World, and the Church*

Amalor observes a difference of theological emphasis or priority among the various groups of the Fathers during the Synod of Bishops in Rome (1974) and attributes this divergence to "two clearly discernible theological approaches and ultimately ... to two different world-views."[7] These are: (i) the traditional world-view, and (ii) the biblical world-view.

---

6 Cf. John Fuellenbach, *The Kingdom of God. (The Message of Jesus Today),* Orbis Books, New York, 1995, (esp. pp. 174ff., 215).

7 DSA, "A Reflection and Summary of the Part Devoted to Theological Questions", in: Id. (ed.), *Evangelization of the Modern World,* NBCLC, Bangalore, 1975, p. 31. (Words and contents within brackets, [...], are and will be mine. While quoting DSA, at times, I will be italicizing some words to emphasize the theological thoughts there).

The global vision of reality referred to by Amalor comprises four elements which are constitutive of the one reality. These are: God, man, the world, and the Church.[8] This reality is not static, but it is seen in a process. Amalor's first exposition of this vision (1969), appears rudimentary and generic, with no mention of its constitutive elements (1970).[9] This was subsequently integrated with three components, namely, the Church, the world, and man,[10] and later modified to God, the world, and the Church (1971).[11] Finally, he presented these four elements: God, man, the world and the Church as the constitutive elements of the one single reality (1973).[12]

Reality is one. It is one single whole. *Wholeness* is the vision of Amalor. However, he does not fail to articulate here that a vision should not be identified with anarchy and confusion. It is not something nebulous and a man of vision is not a visionary. Our vision of reality should be total and integral.

> Vision is the *'vue d'ensemble'*. World-view is a comprehensive view of the whole reality or seeing all the realities in their relatedness within a single framework. It is a picture of the totality within a single glance.... It is a vision of reality, and *'this vision is structured'*. Now the *'major and basic realities which make this structure'* and constitute our life-milieu and which are to be related in our vision are: *'God and man, the world and the Church'*.[13]

Now, to make his stand clear, Amalor divides the Christian world vision into two models: Model I (Pre-Vatican II or the Old Christian World Vision) and Model II (Biblical or the New Christian World

---

[8] Cf. DSA, "Traditional Spirituality within Our Present Christian World Vision", and "Biblical World-View and a Renewed Holistic Spirituality" in: Id. (ed.), *Indian Christian Spirituality,* op. cit., pp. 47-63. Cf. also: Id.: *Theology of Evangelization,* op. cit., pp. 20-25; *Our Christian World Vision,* op. cit., pp. 7-8.

[9] Cf. DSA, *Approaches,* op. cit., p. 14.

[10] Cf. DSA, *Theology of Development,* NBCLC, Bangalore, 1979 (3rd print), p. 14.

[11] Cf. DSA, *Theology of Evangelization,* op. cit., p. 20.

[12] Cf. DSA, *Approach,* op. cit., pp. 23-25.

[13] DSA, "Traditional Spirituality within Our Present Christian World Vision", *op. cit.,* p. 47. (Long quotations are/will be cited in separate paragraphs).

Vision).[14] In the pre-Vatican II model, our reflexes and attitudes manifest the *static interrelationship* between these four "realities" or elements, while in the new biblical world vision, which Vatican II has rediscovered in its 'resources', we find that the same four realities are related, not as four separate and opposite realities, but as immanent to one another, forming, in spite of their distinctness, a single whole in a dynamic, synthetic and coherent relationship. This latter one is the world vision of Amalor. The former one is to be rectified and replaced by the latter. Each model can serve as a framework of reflection and action and as a tool of analysis. However, Amalor writes:

> In general none of us can pretend to have an entirely correct Christian vision. We shall be tending towards it as the heart changes and the society undergoes change. Inversely, a correct Christian world vision can challenge, facilitate and sustain both the heart change and the social change, attitudinal change and structural change. A very important point to be kept in mind constantly is that in these two models we are not evaluating individual behaviour, but relationship between two collectivities, structures or major realities, e.g. the relation between society as a whole and the Church as a whole. It is not interpersonal but interstructural relationship that is evaluated by this model.[15]

Let us now consider the vision of Amalor in the above mentioned models and see their implications in our approach to other religions.

### *2.2.1. Christian World Vision: Model I*

#### *2.2.1.1. God, Man, the World, and the Church*[16]

*(i) God:* God is considered in this vision as an abstract and distant Being, living up in the sky, away from the reality of life, world and history.[17]

---

[14] Cf. ibid., p. 47ff.

[15] Ibid., p. 48.

[16] Cf. ibid., pp. 48-49.

[17] One may see here a sort of deism where "God is supposed to have nothing to do after creating the world, as the latter is considered to be a finished product, needing no more God's presence and creative action." (See: Ibid., p. 48). However, deism has never been

Here one forgets to see God as *Emmanuel* who is always with us, guiding our life and history (cf. Matt. 1:23). Instead of discovering a God who unfolds his mystery, one forms different images of God and projects them on him. One attributes to him different roles to be played according to the needs of the people. Our different attitudes are determined thereby.

*(ii) Man:* Due to an over-emphasis laid on unchanging or static essence, man is considered as a *mould* producing the same kind of people, like a factory. Hence sufficient attention is not paid to the uniqueness of each man and his culture. One considers only what is applicable to all men, in all places, at all times and in all situations. One rarely considers man in his evolution, as one who constantly changes and grows, as one who is in a process of becoming in view of his self-realization.

Human beings are created in the image and likeness of God (cf. Gen. 1:27; 5:1). But here, in this model, man is considered before God as nothing, as dust and ashes. He is described as so insignificant to become a non-entity. He is often ignored as a reality in the structure of major realities. One is afraid to predict anything of him lest one should disparage God. If at all one attributes anything to him, it is sin. He is underlined in his sinfulness and as needing salvation.

*(iii) The world:* The world is thought of as a static and flat space. Once created, it is supposed to go on by itself like a machine. Due to sin it has become bad and a 'God-forsaken place'. Hence one should shun the world and work out one's salvation by fleeing from it and taking refuge in another world herebelow or hereafter.

*(iv) The Church:* In this vision, Christians imagine that they are not of this wicked world but they belong to another world of their own, the Church. This Church is considered to be constituted by institutions and premises, churches and chapels, convents and compound walls, structures of authority and forms of government, administrative set-ups and laws, in a pyramidal structure from top to bottom, from the pope to the laity. God is supposed to abide only in the Church and not in the world. His communication with the world is only through the Church.

---

accepted in the Catholic trend of theology.

### *2.2.1.2. Relationship among them*[18]

We can well sum up the relationship among these four realities in this vision in one sentence. That is: *Outside the Church there is no salvation.*

Accordingly, God, who is 'up in the sky', has communicated and entrusted to the Church what is necessary for the salvation of sinful mankind in this Godless world. God's revelation is found only in the Church. As a result, all truth, goodness, beauty, holiness, salvation and their source, God, are supposed to be found only within the confines of the Church. The Church and its realities are called holy, sacred, heavenly, supernatural, spiritual and christian, while the world is characterized by sin and evil, error and falsehood, wickedness and the absence of God. It is labelled, as 'secular', profane, worldly, natural, material, pagan, in the pejorative sense, and 'unchristian'. Christians are those who are baptized in the Church and their salvation is guaranteed because of their mere baptism. Outside this structural Church there is no salvation.

In this relationship the Church is supposed to fulfill her mission of salvation, as saving of 'souls', by transmitting to the world the revealed doctrines and dogmas, persuading the people to abandon the wicked world and take refuge in the Church. This Church is self-sufficient, self-complacent and clerical, and in her relation to the world she is triumphalistic and obsessed with a superiority complex. She is supposed to establish the kingdom of God by salvaging people from the sinking boat to the safety of 'St. Peter's bark'. Church is the kingdom of God.

This may seem to be a caricature and even disappointing. Amalor writes:

> This may appear to be a caricature. Yet one could ask oneself whether this is not more or less a vision of things, a type of relationship between the Church and the world, a manner of acting which is ours and in our case today whether this is not at the root of [theology and] spirituality by which we have been formed in the past and at present.[19]

---

[18] Cf. ibid., p. 49.

[19] Ibid., p. 50.

#### *2.2.1.3. Evaluation of this vision*[20]

Amalor's evaluation of the theological vision of this model can be seen in the following points.

*(i) A distant God above:* God's presence is very much limited to the Church and the 'sky', and in this vision there is no place for human persons as such.

*(ii) Sacred and profane:* There is a separation and opposition between the world and the Church, society and religion, culture and cult, Christianity and other religions. The Church is God-centered and its hallmark is theocentrism, while the world is man-centered. Man and humanistic ideologies are associated with the man-centered world. Man experiences a split-personality between the spiritual and the temporal.

*(iii) Church and other religions:* It is a denial of anything positive and the existence of any values in other religions. A lack of contact and dialogue between the Church and other religions is evident.

World history and the salvation history are seen as parallel. Revelation and salvation are seen as the monopoly of the Church. These are related only to Judeo-Christian traditions, thereby, excluding other people and religions in a narrow, 'linear', exclusivist, and particularist concept of salvation history. Revelation is regarded as merely a communication of abstract truths, and faith as an intellectual assent to the truths revealed and communicated.

*(iv) Church and the world:* All realities of the spiritual order are identified with the Church, for example, evangelization and catechesis, prayer and worship, spirituality and services of charity. Human life and various aspects of the temporal order, such as, sex and marriage, economic and political activities, science and technology, are identified with the world. It implies a non-recognition of the value and *raison d'être* of the temporal order, of its orientation and goal, of its consistency and autonomy. A pejorative and pessimistic attitude is fostered towards the world, other religions, the forms and movements of humanism and various ideologies.

The clergy and the religious, the élite group, are regarded as the real members of the Church. The laity belong to the "world" and have no specific role to play in the Church. Their attitude in the Church is passive

---

[20] Cf. ibid., pp. 50-52.

and un-involved.

*(v) Church and culture:* Christianity and European or Western culture belong to the Church, whereas other religions and the cultures of the third world countries are identified with the world.

*(vi) Mission and proclamation:* The mission and proclamation of the Gospel are looked upon as verbal and oral announcement of truths and moral precepts, doctrines and principles, made in schools or a church, in a stereotyped manner, mainly through formal instruction in absolute, essentialist and static terms, under the pretext of not adulterating God's word and for fear of betraying it.

The success of the Church is understood chiefly in terms of territory, number and quantity: statistics. It projects a conquering image and breathes a crusader spirit. The tendency of the Church appears to be to absorb the world and to subordinate the temporal order, in the name of her double jurisdiction: temporal and spiritual authority inherited from Christ for ushering in a spiritual reign.

*(vii) Its effect on the people of other religions:* From the standpoint of this vision, our missionary activity is viewed by people of other religions, by the audience:

a) as an act of *spiritual aggression*, ... as a confrontation between two opposite
parties, and a forced imposition of something unwanted or
b) as an act of *paternalism and condescension* on the part of the 'haves' towards the 'have-nots', as an attempt at bringing Jesus to where he is absent and as offering truth, light and life to those who are in error, darkness and death.
c) as an act of *pretended fulfillment* of the unfulfilled aspirations of people in other religions.
d) and more recently as a recognition and explicitation of the active presence of Christ in the religions and in the realities of the temporal order.[21]

*(viii) The missionary Church and conversion:* The missionary Church is considered as a foreign body, an alienating force, a state within state, a pressure group, a marginal group or as a ghetto whose main concerns are not directed towards their fellow citizens and the larger society but

---

[21] Ibid., p. 52.

towards themselves.

Conversion in this context implies a negation of the world, an evasion from one's commitment to the world, from one's task in the "secular" society. It implies a total break with one's whole past, abandoning all that one cherished most. The converts are to cut away from the mainstream of their national, political, cultural and social life. It means stripping oneself of everything old in order to accept unreservedly the Christian message with its Western cultural expressions, formulations, thought-patterns and systems, religious practices and forms of prayer and worship. Conversion means a change of religion by force or compulsion, by persuasion and allurement, by method direct or indirect. This is exactly what is called alienation.

As a result, people of other religions are apprehensive of missionaries and their mission work. Their normal response has been that of aversion and suspicion in various forms and degrees. For example, the 'Anti-Conversion Bills'(*Tyāgī Bills*) in general and the various atrocities committed against Christians in recent years in particular in some of the states of India only show their negative response towards the Church's mission work in India.[22]

The attitudes and approaches that emerge from the above world-view can be summed up in the following two conclusions and in three words each: "*Inside the Church:* complacency, self-sufficiency and clericalism; *outside the Church:* superiority complex, domination and triumphalism."[23] According to Amalor the theology and spirituality of this world-view will be evasive, abstract, isolating, dichotomic and dualistic, with a sense of self-righteousness, looking down upon the world and those involved in it.[24]

---

[22] Anti-Conversion Bill (*Tyāgī Bill*) in the 1970s/80s was very strong in India. Also, the gory incident at Karondabra, Gumla, Bihar, where a Brother and two Catholic priests were brutally murdered, at night, on September 1, 1994, and the broad-day light ghastly stabbing to death of Sister Maria Rani in front of people standing around on February 25, 1995 in Madhya Pradesh really shocked the Christians in general and the mission work of the religious and priests in particular. There might have been some other reasons for these trends and incidents, but the religious antagonism behind it cannot be denied.

[23] DSA, "Traditional Spirituality within Our Present Christian World Vision", *op. cit.*, p. 52.

[24] Cf. ibid.

## The Old World Vision: Model I[25]

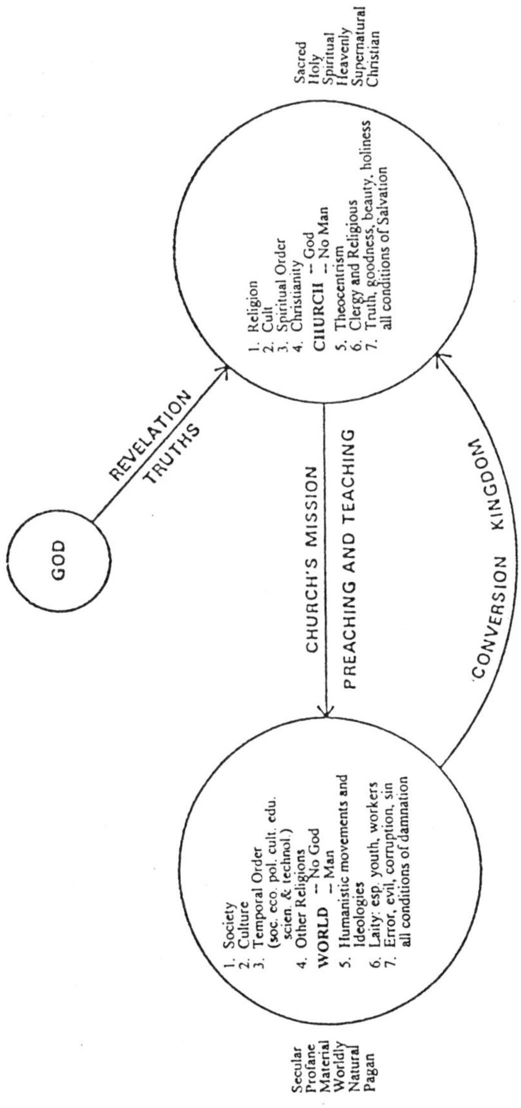


Figure: 1

---

[25] See: DSA (ed.), *Indian Christian Spirituality,* op. cit., p. 46.

## The New Word Vision: Model II[26]

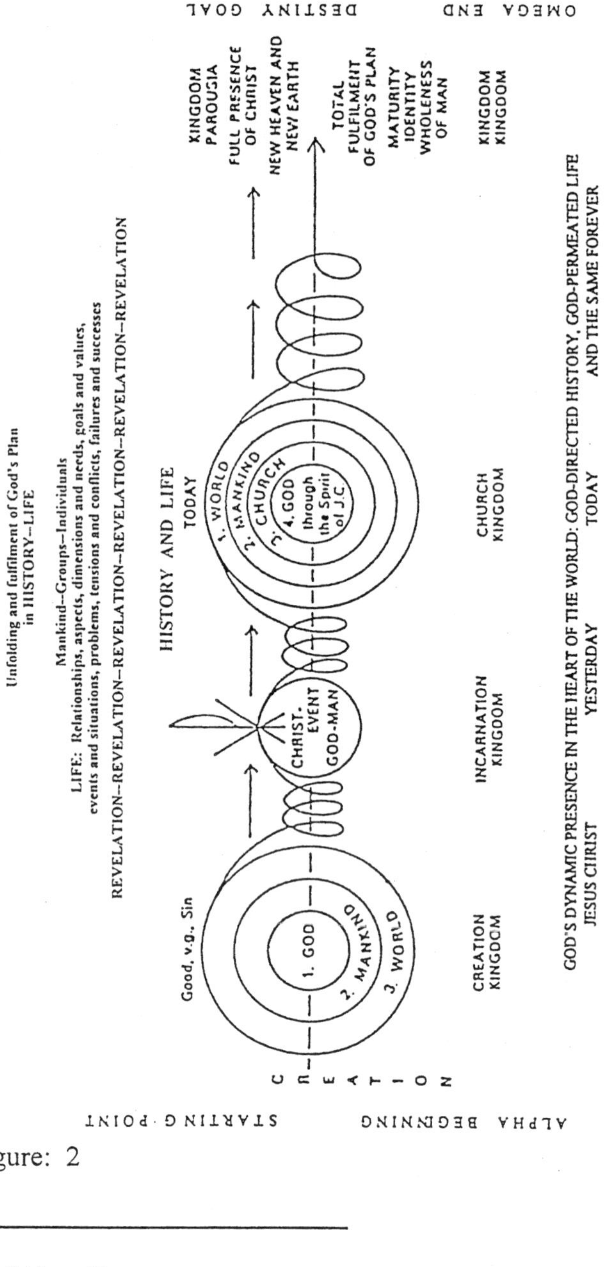


Figure: 2

---

[26] Ibid., p. 63.

### *2.2.2. Biblical Global Vision (Vue D'ensemble): Model II*[27]

The biblical world-view emerges from the prayerful reading of the Bible and its correct interpretation. It is a comprehensive view of the total reality and hence truly universal and holistic. It is "similar" to the Hindu world-view, not in the sense of pantheistic or monistic view of Hinduism but in which it calls for a *cosmic harmony,* universal community, fellowship and personal integrity, all making a single whole. Amalor writes:

> The world-view that one discovers and assimilates when one prayerfully reads through the Bible is comprehensive of the total reality and hence truly universal and holistic. It relates and integrates all realities. It takes everything in its stride; its dynamic character causing interaction among all and its movement towards the goal with specific thrust and objective make it purposeful. It starts from and ends with cosmic harmony, universal community, fellowship and personal integrity, all making a single whole. This is similar to the hindu world-view in which wholeness and all dimensional self-realisation and liberation are experienced at reaching the ultimate goal.... For the spirit is in the depths of one's being which is the ground of God and the ground of others. Like the current all realities can be inter-related in depth. Where the spirit is there is freedom and wholeness: *moksha and Shanti.*[28]

In the biblical world-view, God and man, the Church and the world -- the four realities -- are related not as four separate and opposite realities, but as immanent to one another and, thus, making a single whole, though

---

[27] In this section we do not intend to study any section of the Bible or any single Book in depth or make an exegesis and hermeneutics of all the important passages. That is not our purpose here. Here we only take DSA's basic thought-pattern with regard to his theology in general and the theology of other religions in particular from his lecture on "Biblical World-View and a Renewed Holistic Spirituality". His intention is seen here when he himself says, "In a single lecture it is next to impossible to study any section of the Bible or any single book in depth and make an exegesis and hermeneutics of all the important passages. Instead we intend making a bird's eye view of the Bible and capture the world vision and [theology or] spirituality that emerge from it and that were experienced and lived by the people of God." (See: *Indian Christian Spirituality,* op. cit., p. 54).

[28] DSA, "Biblical World-View and a Renewed Holistic Spirituality", *op. cit.,* p. 54.

they remain distinct and maintain their identity in openness and dialogue, interaction and transformation, solidarity and collaboration. This relationship is synthetic and coherent, dynamic and integrating.

Let us examine the interrelationship of realities in the biblical world vision.

*2.2.2.1. Creation: Man and the world, history and life*

Amalor sees in the whole act of creation a *gift* and a *task* for all humankind, received from a single common origin of all, God. There is only one God.

*(i) Creation, a gift and task:* In the beginning God created the heavens and the earth, the world. He created human beings in his own image and likeness, male and female, the human family, a community. God saw all that he made and found that it was good, indeed very good. He placed man in this world and made him master of everything to fill the earth, subdue it, and transform it (cf. Gen. 1:28). God thus shared with man his creative responsibility and treated him as a partner and collaborator (cf. Ps. 8; Heb. 1-2). A living man is indeed the glory of God![29]

*(ii) A common task of collaboration with God and with one another, commitment to life and history:* After the creation there began the historical adventure of mankind, indeed the whole of creation (cf. Rom. 8:22). It is a movement towards its consummation, in view of its total becoming. Even though man and the world exist, they are not finished products; they have to become -- they are in the process of growth. Man must reach his maturity, wholeness and integrity; the world must reach its destiny, goal, and become the kingdom of God. Man must move from where he is and reach where and what he should be. Amalor writes:

> Under the dynamism injected into the world and men by the creator, this human family [of all peoples and religions] has embarked on a journey towards its destiny both as persons, and as a community. This movement is what is called, 'life', 'history'.[30]

---

[29] Cf. ibid., pp. 54-55.

[30] Ibid., p. 55.

In this movement humankind is engaged in deploying its potentialities, exploiting its resources, actuating its faculties, developing its talents, inventing new tools for its evolution, mastering nature and transforming the world.

Man organizes his life at various levels: interpersonal, family, social, economic, political, cultural and religious. He wants to realize for himself and for all humankind a just and humane world -- a world of freedom, justice and peace.

> In short, this is all in view of its total *'devenir and avenir'*. In the course of this journey men realize that they have common aspirations and basic needs to be fulfilled, common life and events to be interpreted, common difficulties and problems to overcome, common values to live and die for, and above all one single goal, just as one single origin and history![31]

Amalor sees a purpose in the fast changing world and in the process of ever rapid and radical changes in all realities of life. Change or becoming is part and parcel of man's life and history.

> It is not baseless. It has *a long past and has a long way ahead. This history is neither cyclic nor rectilinear, but a combination of both, namely spiral,* hence it rises higher and higher and thus progresses in spite of ups and downs and zigzags.[32]

Amalor speaks of the evolving development of humanity, that is, the evolution of man and history, in line with Teilhard de Chardin. He writes:

> In this great historical drama all humanity -- nations and peoples, men and women, young and old -- are hurtling toward a final consummation under the dynamic impetus of creation. They are gathering their energies and resources and committing their whole being to make a better life and to create a better future. They know well that this can only be accomplished by *transforming* the world, which

---

[31] Ibid. Also cf. DSA, "The Apostolate to Non-Christians", in: *Foundations of Mission Theology*, edited by SEDOS (Rome, March 27-31, 1969), translated by John Drury, Orbis Books, Maryknoll, New York, 1972, p. 68ff.

[32] Ibid.

> necessarily involves transforming themselves as well. We must have the integral development of each individual and all men, so that they can take control over the universe they are to renew. Viewed thus, the drama of history comes down to the evolving development of humanity.[33]

*2.2.2.2. God in the world, history and life*

God's presence in creation and history is ever felt in the heart of the world, in the course of history and in the dense human existential realities. He is Emmanuel -- God in the world and history (cf. Matt. 1:23). He is in the world, yet he transcends it.

The God of creation is the master and the guide of history as well. "His universal presence and guidance to all people, is experienced everywhere and at all times. His *continued creation and revelation* are manifested and seen through events and men."[34] The reality of sin and evil in the world -- exploitation, oppression, injustice, hatred, conflict and war -- is the consequence of man's sin, that is, his pride, selfishness and disobedience to God (cf. Gen. 3:1-13; Rom. 3:23; 5:19). Still the world and men are good, though under an aspect the world appears to be opposed to God and his plan. In this perspective the *incarnation* of Christ Jesus is viewed as visiblization, intensification and totalization of God's already existing presence and action in the world and history. Thus, the historical movement is not chaotic just as the Exodus was not.

> God's guidance and leadership are present from within the world and life. For God through his *Creative Word* is at the centre of history, at the beginning and at the end. He is present to it by revealing himself and his plan of salvation for the world, by guiding mankind in the course of history towards the fulfillment of that plan.[35]

*2.2.2.3. The Church in the world, history and life*

Now, in this history of man's common adventure and in the process of God's revealing and saving action in the world, where does the Church

---

[33] DSA, "The Apostolate to Non-Christians", *op. cit.*, p. 70.

[34] DSA, "Biblical World-View and a Renewed Holistic Spirituality", *op. cit.*, p. 55.

[35] Ibid., p. 56.

come in? What is the unique experience of Christians, and how do they share this experience with others?

> There is but *one* world which God loves and *one* human family to which all men belong, including Christians. Christians are taken up in the same current of history and life as fellowmen, in total belonging and solidarity. Focusing on *man as centre and summit* they identify themselves with their cause as partners in the same projects. They are committed to the same tasks of liberation of man and realization of a just society.[36]

Though Christians are normal members of the human family, they have had, and are called to have, a unique experience of God in and through the Spirit of Jesus Christ.

> Christians ... have experienced God through the 'Spirit'[37] of Jesus Christ, in one another and in the world and in the midst of their life. They have had an inter-personal relationship with God and with one another in Jesus Christ. They feel reconciled and saved. They experience the joy and peace of fellowship with God which results in the fellowship with men. They yearn to realize this reconciliation and fellowship with all men. This is Christian experience.[38]

Church is the community of all those who have had this similar experience of God in the Spirit of Jesus Christ, both individually and collectively. The Church establishes her place in history and life by sharing with the world her special experience of God in Jesus Christ.

---

[36] Ibid.

[37] We make a note here that DSA does not simply say the experience of God through *Jesus Christ,* which for many means the Church, but through the *Spirit* of Jesus Christ. The implication is the same. However, when we say *in and through the Spirit* of Jesus Christ it immediately puts us in the broader understanding that the Spirit of Jesus Christ is not confined to the Church alone but people of other religions can also have the experience of God in the Spirit of Jesus Christ. People of other religions, like Mahatma Gandhi, have loved to follow the spirit of Christ, not necessarily being the members of the Church. Christ is present in other religions in and through his Spirit.

[38] DSA, "Biblical World-View and a Renewed Holistic Spirituality", *op. cit.,* p. 56.

> Now, this community of all those who have experienced God in the Spirit of Jesus Christ by word and faith, sacraments and service of love in the heart of their experience in the world is called *'the Church'*. The *'mission of the Church'* and every Christian consists in *sharing* one's Christian experience with other men in the course of one's experience in the world, in the very process of sharing with others, human existence in all its aspects and activities.[39]

### *2.2.2.4. What is common and unique in Christian experience: A Christian hope*

According to Amalor what is common and unique in Christian experience is the special experience of God in Jesus Christ, the risen Lord, both individually and collectively. However, this special experience of God in Jesus Christ does not separate the faith-community in Christ from the rest of mankind, forming a class apart and having to live in a world of its own. On the contrary, our experience of Christ in the very midst of individual and collective human existence, our sincere commitment to the process of mankind's historic dynamism and development, far from cutting us off from our solidarity with others, awakens and quickens us to our task in this world. What is our task? Our task is to share this special experience of God with others. It is to offer a Christian hope of liberation from sin, injustice and oppression. It is to offer hope to the world that "the ultimate remedy to those ills is salvation in Jesus Christ: openness and existence for others, by self-gift and self-sacrifice, in genuine love and humble service."[40] One who has encountered God in Christ cannot but do that. The encounter with Christ gives us a new stimulus to engage ourselves with renewed vigour and greater generosity to the realization of mankind's goal. It enables us to throw ourselves heart and soul into the adventure of mankind with deeper bonds that unite us with the rest of mankind. This gives us courage in a new and deeper level to join with others in rendering a relevant service to our fellowmen in creating a just and human society, a society willed by God.

> An encounter with Christ opens up a global vision of the world and God's plan. It gives us insight into our human existence. It shows

[39] Ibid.

[40] Ibid., p. 57.

the fuller meaning of our life. It indicates the unfailing means of fulfilling our aspirations. It enables us to live up to our ideals and values. It points out a clearer and surer orientation to the ultimate goal of our historical journey. And thereby it offers hope.[41]

Christian experience sheds light on all the data of human existence. It opens out its many dimensions, indicates its implications and spells out its exigencies in all directions. Therefore this faith-filled and hope-filled community, the Church, by the very force of its solidarity with other men and women, under the dynamism of its Christian experience, feels urged to share with others its fresh and special experience about liberation and reconciliation and the vision of the goal, route and means of our common pilgrimage.[42]

> We [Christians] experience the same joys and sorrows, the same problems and anxieties as our fellowmen. But as Christians we experience the joy and peace that come from *hope*, the hope that our present fellowship with God in man will one day find its perfect fulfillment. Now the community of those who have had this experience is the Church.[43]

### *2.2.2.5. Common pilgrimage and mutual sense of belonging*

Amalor says that in such an approach people from other religions will not look at Christianity as something 'foreign'. They will not consider Christians as aliens and resist them as harmful people. Instead, they will feel grateful to them for sharing this experience of God in the God-man, Jesus Christ. Through Christians they too will come to know Jesus Christ as one who has recognized their human dignity, elevated it marvellously and restored it to its wholeness. He will appear as the way, the truth and the life (cf. Jn. 14:6), as the one showing the way and giving the means to the *humanization* and *integral development*[44] of man. Impressed by the

---

[41] Ibid.

[42] Cf. ibid.

[43] DSA, *Theology of Evangelization,* op. cit., p. 23.

[44] DSA's concept of *salvation* implies at the same time liberation, humanization, Christianization and integral development of man, i.e., the kingdom of God *'already and not yet'* in the terms of Oscar Cullmann -- truly a salvation here on earth (*Jīvan Mukti*) and salvation here after (*Videha Mukti*). Cf. also: DSA, "The Apostolate to Non-

witness of these Christians they will want to establish an interpersonal relationship with Christ in faith. They may discover themselves in Jesus Christ, and in and through him, they will also discover the Father in the Spirit. They will realize that fellowship with God calls for greater fellowship with fellowmen and the removal of all the obstacles to it. "This in turn will realize the very goal towards which they have been tending, namely, to build a human community [*kutuṁbakam*] where man's dignity and equality will be recognized, where justice will prevail, where love will be the basis of relationship and where joy will reign."[45] Amalor continues:

> When this becomes the reality, we shall recognize the full presence of Christ (parousia) and the emergence of God's Kingdom. Mankind could have thus attained its destiny, the world its goal, history its omega point, man his wholeness. This is liberation, this is salvation, this is bliss. This is the new heaven and new earth that men have been struggling to create under the dynamism of the 'first creation'[46] and which God has made possible in Christ at the end of times. This is the fulfillment of God's plan, in the emergence of the *human, just and*

---

Christians", *op. cit.*, p. 73; id., *The Theology of 'Indirect Evangelization'*, NBCLC, Bangalore, 1970; id., *Theology of Evangelization*, op. cit., (in appendix: 'Declaration of the International Theological Conference on Evangelization and Dialogue in India', 1971, esp. nos. 30-37, pp. 37-39). The Declaration also appears in: M. Dhavamony (ed.), *Evangelization, Dialogue and Development*, Documenta Missionalia - 5, Università Gregoriana Editrice, 1972, pp. 8-11 (for nos. 30-37). DSA identifies himself with the declaration of the Nagpur International Theological Conference. This is well seen when Gerwin van Leeuwen writes: "DSA was entrusted with the task to share with the participants of the All-India Consultation on Evangelization in Patna, 3-8 October 1973, the insights, clarifications, conclusions and guidelines of the International Theological Conference on Evangelization & Dialogue in Asia, Nagpur, 6-12 October 1971. He [DSA] himself states: 'I am supposed to be their spokesman and faithful interpreter as I was involved both in the running of the Conference and in the formulation of the final statement as Chairman'." (See: Gerwin van Leeuwen, O.F.M., *Fully Indian - Authentically Christian*, op. cit., pp. 286-287, reference 15).

Another aspect of salvation with regard to other religions, i.e., the point of inter-religious collaboration, will be seen in chapter six.

[45] DSA, "Biblical World-View and a Renewed Holistic Spirituality", *op. cit.*, p. 58.

[46] ... *that men have been struggling to create under the dynamism of the first creation.* In this sense too DSA speaks of God's continuous creation and revelation that we have already mentioned earlier.

*free society as the Kingdom of God*,[47] and in the full appearance of the Lord, in luminous clarity, experiencing love, joy and peace.[48]

### *2.2.2.6. Evangelization and inculturation*

In this approach Amalor speaks of inculturation as an integral part of evangelization and mission of the Church. Evangelization becomes a task of the local Christian community, and the Church is then seen as an event, the continuation of the *Jesus Christ event* in the world, beginning with Israel, as inserting and "incarnating" herself into the historical movement in a given place, rendering her *diakonia* to the contemporary society, culture and religion.

> The aspect which sets in relief the Church as an *event* with significance is its innate dynamism towards incarnation, its need to be inserted into the historical movement and to be integrated into the contemporary society, culture and religion. It is *'kerygma and martyria, koinonia and diakonia'* in Christ made available and real in a particular place. It becomes thereby the *sign* and *instrument* of *God's kingdom*.[49]

In this model the proclamation of the *Good News* becomes relevant, welcome and really a good news. The proclamation becomes *good news* because this is what the world is in need of and has been looking for. It is relevant because the full growth of the individuals and groups within the society is a basic concern of man. It is welcome because it comes from those who are one with them in the realization of the same projects and goals; because it takes place in the course of a common journey, within a *dialogue* which presupposes rapport. This sharing of Christian experience brings new light and inspiration, new vision and insights, which the human community left to itself cannot discover without the experience of

---

47 The kingdom of God: DSA speaks of it as human, just and free society, of love and service, joy and peace, liberation, humanization, salvation, the kingdom as *already and not yet (Jīvan Mukti and Videha Mukti)*. See also the above footnote 43. More on this point will be seen in the last chapter.

48 DSA, "Biblical World-View and a Renewed Holistic Spirituality", *op. cit.*, p. 58.

49 Ibid., p. 59. Cf. also: DSA, *Approaches*, op. cit., p. 32.

this Christian community.[50] Here lies the importance, role and responsibility of the Christian community, the Church.

By *inculturation* or indigenization the Church is not only able to fulfill her mission but also to realize her catholicity or universality. The contribution of the local Churches consists precisely in this.

> The Church becomes universal not only when the Gospel is preached to all men and when all are saved but also when the spread of the Gospel *permeates and purifies, perfects and unifies the realities of the temporal order and all religions.* Thus, for example, for Indians, to be Catholic or ecumenical means also to be *fully Indian and Christian.*[51]

We make a note here that *inculturation* and *evangelization* should not be separated but should constitute a single whole. In the past many were, and even today many are, under the impression that at the first stage the Word is simply announced, celebrated and lived in the culture of the missionary, and only at the later stage these activities are to be adapted or acculturated to the mission country and its culture. "Historically there has been, by and large, a divorce between the two. In reality, however, both are so intimately connected that they should constitute a single whole. *'Inculturation should be part and parcel of the very process of evangelization'.*"[52] We do not announce the Gospel purely and simply in an abstract manner. The Word of God passes through a human word. This Word, to be a comprehensive and meaningful human word, should be expressed in a particular culture, that is, in the language, in the categories of thought, images and forms of speech, through the current means and techniques of communication and according to the pedagogy prevalent in the region and suitable to a particular human group.

Similarly, with regard to liturgy, Amalor says that we do not first celebrate an ethereal, other-worldly and "disincarnated" liturgy and then adapt it. No.

> In its very first act of worship the community gives expression to its aspirations and experiences regarding progress and struggles and its

---

50 Cf. DSA, "Biblical World-View and a Renewed Holistic Spirituality", *op. cit.*, p. 59.

51 Ibid.

52 Ibid.

relationship with God and men. The cultic forms must be such that they allow a people to use signs and symbols proper to their own culture to respond to God's *on-going revelation in Christ* and in witnessing to its beliefs and values. Indigenization [or inculturation] is thus simultaneous with every form of ministry. It is an integral part of the whole mission of the Church.[53]

### *2.2.2.7. True Christian identity: Fraternal charity, love and service*

Amalor shows his disappointment that in spite of the official teaching of Vatican II in its various documents, and in spite of the clear policy and sure guidelines given by the Sacred Congregation for the Propagation of Faith ever since its inception, there are still several bishops and priests, not to say lay people, who identify Christianity with Western culture. They think, speak and act as though the Church should be distinguished from other religions by its foreign character as though the Western *form* of Christianity should be preserved and perpetuated. They prefer *transplantation* of the Church to *inculturation* in a mission land. They seem to be afraid that the Church would lose its identity and originality if she set in motion a process of inculturation. Amalor writes that "they do not seem to remember that the only sign of Christ and his Church is *fraternal charity* [cf. Jn. 13:34-35] to the point of dying for others. It is by losing ourselves that we shall find ourselves, like the ferment that is lost in the dough in the process of transforming it."[54]

### *2.2.2.8. Meaning of conversion: By God and to God*

While accepting the meaning of conversion, in the sense of conversion from "non-Christian" faith to the Christian faith, that is, the faith, whether explicit or implicit in Jesus Christ the risen Lord through the mediation of the Church, conversion is first of all *by God* and *to God.*[55]

---

[53] Ibid., p. 60.

[54] Ibid.

[55] We make a note here that even today for many conversion means only external conversion of others into Christianity, winning the people over from other religious traditions. As a result, there is religious antagonism, hatred and jealousy. This sort of conversion has created many problems in India. Today we find a trend of 'anti-conversion', and 're-conversion' to Hinduism, especially from the side of Hindus with

It is a call to establish a new relationship with God and among men in Jesus Christ. It is to establish a new pattern of life that is expressed concretely through the medium of one's own family life, social organization, professional duties, economic system, religious and cultural heritage.

It is a transformation of one's basic attitudes and behaviour that is brought about by the *encounter with the risen Lord* and by the *reception of the Spirit.* It is the following of Christ Jesus in his self-emptying love and service of God and others (cf. Phil. 1:21; 2:5-8).

Ultimately, evangelization must be understood as an invitation to conversion, conversion to God, led by the Spirit. Conversion is for all, that is, both people of other religions as well as Christians themselves. "Ultimately, the conversion of anybody whether Christians or others -- is *'by God'* and *'to God'*, whatever be the 'medium or agent'[56] through which conversion takes place. Hence our task is evangelization and inculturation. Conversion is the work of the Spirit and the response in faith of the evangelized."[57]

### *2.2.2.9. Evaluation and characteristics of this world-view*[58]

*(i) One God, one world, one single history and one goal:* All men and women belong to the one world and a single history, with a common origin and common goal.

*(ii) Everything seen through God's plan and perspective:* Everything is situated in the total reality of life, with a global vision and an integrated

---

a ceremony, called *śuddhikaraṇa*, especially in many of the Northern states of India. For example, Dilip Singh Judev, the vice president of BJP unit in Madhya Pradesh, had his plan for 1996 to (re)convert some 100000 dalit and tribal Christians to Hinduism. He named the year, 1996, a "reconversion year". Cf. *The New Leader* 109 (1996) 5, p. 24.

56 Here we see religion itself, may it be Hinduism, Buddhism or Christianity, as a means or medium to an end, i.e., God, and not an end in itself. We apply here the axiom: *right means to right end* and say that as individual persons are called to conversion so are called the religions themselves to conversion. That is, religions themselves must be purified and perfected from their false religious customs and practices which result from the false notion of God.

57 DSA, "Biblical World-View and a Renewed Holistic Spirituality", *op. cit.*, p. 60.

58 Cf. ibid., p. 61. "DSA formulates himself 15 characteristics of his Christian world Vision, Model II, which confirm the broadness and dynamic catholicity of his theology." See: Gerwin van Leeuwen, O.F.M., *Fully Indian - Authentically Christian,* op. cit., p. 323. We have summarized his 15 points in some few short headings.

approach. There is no room for dichotomy, dualism, compartmentalism and split personality.

*(iii) Man as centre and summit, collaborator:* The focus is on man as centre and summit, as master of everything and co-responsible for it with God.

*(iv) Individual and communitarian evolution:* In this world-view there is concern for interpersonal relationships and group belonging among Christians and others, dynamic process and movement of history. Everything is done by a group process, with all men and women of different communities. Interaction and transformation of both persons and society take place from within.

*(v) Society and the Church:* Emphasis is laid on the common function of all and yet distinction is made of the specific role of each; especially that of society and the Church.

Solidarity and partnership, involvement and contribution, collaboration and common pilgrimage are obvious. All need to work for the common cause, each one with his or her specific contribution. Yet the uniqueness of the *Church's mystery*[59] and the necessity of her mission shine out. Her goal-directed and not self-centered involvement becomes evident.

*(vi) Universal and specific revelation of God:* The universal and on-going revelation of God in the whole world and in the entire history becomes evident.

Yet the specificity of Judeo-Christian revelation and the total, definitive and once-and-for-all character of the revelation of God in Jesus Christ is acknowledged.

*(vii) The mystery of God's salvific love, immanence and transcendence:* The immanence and transcendence of God are related in dialectics. God's presence/guidance/leadership in our world and history is from within. This has to be sought and discerned, interpreted and manifested

---

59 The uniqueness of the Church's mystery lies in the uniqueness of Jesus' mystery, i.e., God's mystery in Jesus Christ. Here, DSA says -- *the uniqueness of the Church's mystery* rather than the uniqueness of the *Church*. Some language problem may arise in the latter sense. Even today, some religious and priests, not to say lay people, see the uniqueness of Christianity only in the Church's "externality", forgetting thereby the mystery of Jesus Christ.

by the Church from within as part of its prophetic mission.

*(viii) Mutual sharing in dialogue:* Through dialogue and mutual sharing, the Church offers society inspiration and orientation.

*(ix) Respect for other religions:* Respect for the freedom of all is assured at all stages and in every activity.

*(x) The kingdom of God:* In the whole process of history, the kingdom of God is present from the beginning till the end, in all realities and groups. The Church is at the service of the kingdom which is already present here and now and which will emerge one day in its fullness.

In this world vision we find that God, man, and the Church, all are involved in one and the same world. They are involved in the movement of life and history, trying to establish the kingdom of God here on earth where God will be all in all (cf. 1 Cor. 15:28) and where people of different languages, sex and religions "may have life, and have it abundantly" (Jn. 10:10; cf. 1 Cor. 7:19-20; Gal. 3:28; 5:6).

> This is the faith response in the Spirit of those to whom God reveals in the totality of history and in the totality of their life through Jesus Christ. Such a [theology or] spirituality will be human, *secular* and *worldly* in the correct sense (with involvement in all the happenings in the temporal order, respecting its autonomy and value for its own sake), ecclesial and communitarian, personal and cosmic, unique and universal with a dialectic of immanence and transcendence, reflecting the holiness of God and thus it also be divine. In short such a [theology or] spirituality will be the *work of the Spirit.*[60]

### *2.3. Fullness: Wholeness, Harmony, Integrity and Totality (Is. 11:5-9)*

*Fullness there, Fullness here! Fullness comes from Fullness.*
*When Fullness has come from Fullness, Fullness remains.*
*Om! Peace! Peace! Peace!*[61]

---

[60] DSA, "Biblical World-View and a Renewed Holistic Spirituality", *op. cit.,* p. 62.

[61] This prayer is an invocation preceding the *Īśā Upaniṣad.* Cf. also Michael Amaladoss, S.J., *Towards Fullness - Searching for an Integral Spirituality,* (Lectures in Memory of Fr. D.S. Amalorpavadass - 1932-1990), NBCLC, Bangalore, 1994, p. 1. This was a favourite prayer of DSA. He used to recite it very often, especially in the beginning

### 2.3.1. *Three dimensions of fullness or wholeness*

"Integration, wholeness, harmony, all-round development -- these were popular themes of Fr. Amalor."[62] Amalor speaks of the wholeness within and wholeness without, that is, peace and integrity within oneself and with others, with the whole of reality. He writes:

> This wholeness is realized at three levels: cosmic, communitarian (social) and personal. To live a life of the Spirit and to experience him ... one must first of all unify one's own self at the core of one's being. One must transcend all forms of dualism (body-soul duality) or the distinction of subject-object. One must really integrate one's own self from within. One should make into one the many elements, parts, senses, 'levels and layers [*koşas*]'[63] of which one is composed. In other words, one should be an integral person, not a split personality. This is necessary for one's total health and all-round well-being. For this one should really gather oneself and make a totality of oneself, an integrated whole.[64]

Once one realizes one's personal integrity, one must enter into a deep-level communion and extend this wholeness to one's relationship with all people. This is the second dimension or level of wholeness. Wholeness is in our solidarity with others; it is to be experienced in a communitarian dimension. "At least attitudinally one should be open to

---

and end of prayers and lectures in Anjali Ashram, Mysore. Once I was there with him for a prayer retreat for two weeks and I experienced the same. His vision was Fullness and Peace, and he tried to apply it in his theology, spirituality and life.

62 Michael Amaladoss, S.J., *Towards Fullness - Searching for an Integral Spirituality,* op. cit., p. 2 (Preface).

63 DSA speaks of the analysis of human personality in terms of Indian Philosophy and says, "Our self is composed of five layers (koşas) just as the world (cosmos) consists of five elements. This alone is enough for us to understand the complexity of our self and how many factors determine our wholeness, and how going to a state of consciousness is to penetrate and transcend these five sheaths." See: DSA, "A Synthesis of Basic and Constitutive Elements of Indian Christian Spirituality", in: Id. (ed.), *Indian Christian Spirituality,* op. cit., p. 232.

64 DSA, "A Synthesis of Basic and Constitutive Elements of Indian Christian Spirituality", *op. cit.,* p. 230. While speaking about the three levels of wholeness, DSA does not say that this is a matter of succession, i.e., one following or preceding the other. Rather he sees it as three dimensions of wholeness.

all people and sincerely seek and yearn for a deep-level communion with them all, as a part of one's effort and movement towards total wholeness."[65]

The third dimension of wholeness is ecological balance, environmental condition or cosmic harmony. Amalor says that it is only lately that the Western countries have come to realize the damage done to our environment by various forms of exploitation and pollution. Cosmic harmony (*ṛta*) and social order (*dharma*) are indispensable factors for personal wholeness.

> Life on earth is not merely social but also *cosmic*. Total human health is affected by community health and total environment. But the people of India had from the dawn of history a great intuition and from the Vedic times were conscious of the various dangers that threaten human wholeness and paid great attention to cosmic harmony (*ṛta*) and social order (*dharma*) as indispensable factors for personal wholeness. So here we combine the modern concern for *ecology* with the age-old Indian concern for cosmic harmony.[66]

Our wholeness is also connected with the animal and vegetative kingdom. It represents the interacting relationship between man and his environment. Amalor quotes here the famous passage of the 'Peaceful Kingdom' from Isaiah: "Integrity is the loincloth round his waist, faithfulness the belt around his hips. The wolf lives with the lamb.... They do not hurt ... for the country is filled with the knowledge of Yahweh as the waters swell the sea" (11:5-9).[67] He describes this passage as a nostalgic recall of the original harmony that prevailed in paradise and the vision of the new heaven and new earth where man will be fully himself in freedom and fellowship even with the so called wild animals.[68]

This universe belongs to us as part of our being. If God made it and "saw everything that he had made, and indeed it was very good" (Gen. 1:31), then it is all the more for us a gift and a task to find our wholeness and peace in the cosmic harmony.

---

65 Ibid., p. 231.

66 Ibid.

67 See in: Ibid.

68 Cf. ibid., p. 232.

Personal integrity, community fellowship, social solidarity and cosmic harmony are levels and dimensions of the wholeness we need. It is at the depth of this multiple wholeness that we experience the mystery of being, whether in God, in oneself, in others (community) or in nature. In short, it is an experience of unity, communion and harmony. All these five constitute a single process of arriving at a state of wholeness. Where there is integration there is wholeness; where there is all-level wholeness there is the multiple and integrated consciousness; and where there is awareness, there is peace and harmony.[69]

### *2.3.2. Wholeness and holiness*

The origin of Amalor's vision of the fullness of life, the all-round development (*sarvodaya*) or inculturation,[70] and his theology and spirituality are based on the *fullness of God* and God sharing his fullness in history and the whole of creation in love (*līlā*). Wholeness is holiness. Man fully alive is the greatest glory of God. 'Fullness there, Fullness here; Fullness proceeds from Fullness; when Fullness has proceeded from Fullness, Fullness remains.' "Fullness is the symbol of ultimate mystery in the Indian tradition.... The Ultimate Reality is Fullness."[71] This Reality is not static. It is full of life and creativity -- where God is *OM,*[72] where history becomes mystery and movement, the mystery of eternity is seen in the historical movement or evolution, where history gets a definite

---

69 See DSA quoted by M. Amaladoss in: Id., *Towards Fullness - Searching for an Integral Spirituality,* op. cit., p. 2 (Preface).

70 By *inculturation* DSA does not mean a liturgical inculturation in a peripheral sense but an all-round development in its deeper meaning. "Fr. Amalor himself would have described it (inculturation) as all-round development", writes M. Amaladoss, in: Id., *Towards Fullness - Searching for an Integral spirituality,* op. cit., p. 1 (Preface).

71 M. Amaladoss, S.J., *Towards Fullness - Searching for an Integral Spirituality,* op. cit., p. 3.

72 *OM* is God's Word -- *Ādi Śabda* -- in Hinduism, in and through which God creates and sustains the universe. "This (in the beginning) was only the Lord of the universe. His Word was with Him . He contemplated. He said, 'I will deliver this Word so that she will produce and bring into being all this world (TMB, XX, 14,2)." See as quoted by F. Vineeth, C.M.I., "Theology of Adisabda and OM" , in: DSA (ed.), *Indian Christian Spirituality,* op. cit., p. 125, and for theology of *OM,* in the same, pp. 125-131. See also the 'logos' in John 1:1-4a.

direction towards its fulfillment in the mystery of God's plan. God is never absent from the world. He is always with us.

> Thus the whole history becomes salvation history. Besides, eternity as God's realm is not something that comes after history, but is contemporaneous with it, transcending it, however. History is real, but relative -- it is related to the mystery that transcends it. The eschaton is not the future but a different level of the present.[73]

Thus, one is, along with his or her particular social, religious, economic and political life, in constant collaboration with God in the process of salvation, liberation, humanization and "Christianization". One is in the process of establishing the kingdom of God here on earth (cf. Rev. 21:1). One is in cosmic harmony and peace with all -- God, self, fellow human beings, the world, and the religions. The individual self is in the process of union (*yoga*) with God. In short, one is in the

> Mystery of Being, ... [experiencing] the Mystery of Being in oneself ... in others and in God, all the three united and identified at the same depth.... Only a person who has an experience of being in himself can experience the Mystery of Being in others and in God. So it is not a question of penetrating the mystery of God and that of others without first experiencing in oneself the Mystery of Being.[74]

Then, in such a wholeness, one can, in the sense of the fullness of relationship with God, truly say: *aham Brahmāsmi.*[75] This is fullness (*pūrṇam*), harmony (*lokasaṁgraha*), peace (*śānti*) and bliss (*ānanda*). This is salvation (*mokṣa/mukti*).

---

[73] M. Amaladoss, S.J., *Towards Fullness - Searching for an Integral Spirituality,* op. cit., pp. 50-51, where M. Amaladoss interprets the mind of DSA.

[74] DSA, "A Synthesis of Basic and Constitutive Elements of Indian Christian Spirituality", *op. cit.,* p. 222.

[75] We make a note here that the notion of union (yoga) in Hinduism: *aham Brahmāsmi,* which embodies a monistic view, is not the same as the notion of union with God through Christ in Christianity. Christianity believes in a personal God.

## 3. Revelation and Religions: Truth, Faith and Salvation

### *3.1. What is Revelation?*

Revelation (Lat."taking away the veil") means "the disclosure of God of what was previously unknown."[76] Revelation is a theological concept and it implies something to be revealed. The meaning of revelation is determined by a particular religious tradition as well as by a particular school of thought within a tradition.[77]

The Old Testament records the divine revelation communicated primarily through words (cf. Jer. 23:12.22) and events of history (cf. Ex.15:1-21) and secondarily through the created world (Ps. 19:2; Wis. 13:1-9). As major mediators of God's revelation, the classical prophets also spoke of the saving revelation to come (cf. Is. 40:1-11; Jer. 31:31-34). In and through his incarnation, life, death, resurrection and sending of the Holy Spirit -- the whole Jesus Christ event (cf. *DV* 4, 17) -- Jesus has become the climax of God's revelation in history (cf. Jn. 1:14; Heb. 1:1-2), being simultaneously the *revealer* and the *revelation* itself, that is, the agent and the content of revelation, salvation. "The act of God's supreme revelation is located in history; i.e., the incarnation and redemption [in Jesus Christ]."[78] In and through Jesus' preaching and behaviour, his conflicts and denunciation of self-righteousness, legalism, injustice and finally in his resurrection, God has concretely and definitively spoken to mankind.[79] With Christ and the apostolic age the foundational revelation is completed, and we await only the final, glorious revelation of the *parousia* (cf. Tit. 2:13; 1 Jn. 3:2; *DV* 4).

The Second Vatican Council understood revelation as primarily God's personal self-manifestation that invites man's personal response of faith (cf. *DV* 2, 6) and secondarily as the communication of divine truths (cf. *DV* 7, 9, 10, 11, 26). It recognized the essentially salvific and

---

[76] Gerald O'Collins, S.J. and Edward G. Farrugia, S.J., *A Concise Dictionary of Theology*, Paulist Press, New York, 1991, p. 206.

[77] Cf. Avery Dulles, *Revelation Theology*, Herder and Herder, New York, 1969, p. 171. Here we do not go into detail to see the 'revelation' in different religious traditions. That would be beyond our scope.

[78] M. Dhavamony, "Indian Christian Theological Method", in: *Studia Missionalia*, vol. 45, Editrice Pontificia Università Gregoriana, Roma, 1996, p. 92.

[79] Cf. M. Dhavamony, "Indian Christian Theology", in: *Studia Missionalia*, vol. 45, op. cit., p. 111.

sacramental nature of God's self-revelation, mediated through events, deeds and words (cf. *DV* 2, 4, 14, 17).

God's revelation is basically God's entry and his continuous saving and life-giving presence in the human history, in the historical happenings and trends of the world.[80] Thus, the human history becomes the salvation history. Salvation history and the history of revelation are inseparable. They are two sides of the same reality. However, God is an ineffable mystery. God's revelation is, therefore, God's symbolic self-communication which human beings experience in different faith-communities and cultures. Christian revelation, because of the special revelation of God in Christ, as we have seen above, is termed the special revelation; and because God has been, in a general way revealing in and relating himself to other religions (cf. Heb. 1:1-2), we call it general revelation. Our theology recognizes that the Holy Spirit is mediating revelation and salvation beyond institutional Christianity.[81]

### *3.2. Why Revelation At All?*

God has created the human beings in his image and likeness. He has created them to love him and serve him. The human nature is essentially and constitutively oriented towards God.

Ever since the creation of the world humankind has "known" God, either by reason, conscience or faith. God's eternal power and his divine nature, invisible though they are, have been understood and experienced by humankind in and through the things he has made (cf. Rom. 1:19-20). However, God is an ineffable mystery. We cannot grasp the mystery of God or "know" him 'as he is' and give him the true worship; neither can we know his will 'as it is' and do it unless he reveals himself and his will and thereby gives us the 'grace' to follow him 'as he wills'. God says, "You cannot see my face; for no one shall see me and live" (Ex. 33:20). Reason alone is not enough to fully grasp the mystery of God; man needs reason as well as faith, he needs the revelation of God. Therefore, it is God who takes the initiative to reveal himself to mankind. "Revelation is the divine initiative in its object and finality. It is dialogue. It is a mani-

---

[80] Cf. DSA, *Approaches,* op. cit., p. 24.

[81] Cf. G. O'Collins, S.J. and E.G. Farrugia, S.J., *A Concise Dictionary of Theology,* op. cit., pp. 206-207.

festation of the concrete plan of God."[82] Revelation is dialogue between God and man. It is a continuous and constant dialogue of life and salvation.

### *3.2.1. Quest for God*

From the beginning of the human race, man has been constantly engaged in solving an important and somewhat inevitable question in life: 'What or where is the ultimate meaning of life?' Different philosophies and ideologies of the world, for example, Epicureanism and *Cārvākas* (*enjoy life*), Friedrich W. Nietzsche (*death of God*) and Jean-Paul Sartre and Albert Camus (*absurdity of life and death*), have tried to answer this question in their own way. However, man has not been satisfied with all these answers. He has come to realize that left to himself he cannot find the true meaning and fulfillment in life, and so he opens himself to someone beyond himself, to the "Other". This "Other" is God who reveals himself in his self-gift to man as an answer to man's question of the ultimate meaning of life and death.

Religion in its variety of forms and expressions consists of a fellowship with the sacred, with God. It includes a reciprocal relationship between God and humankind and involves a belief that the divine plan and power affect human affairs, happiness and salvation. In the history of religions, humankind has sought the divine will manifested in the cosmic or natural order (*ṛta*) as hierophany, or in the positive revelation from God, where it is not man who discovers what belongs to the order of the divine but God himself personally, in history, takes the initiative to reveal and communicate to humankind his plan and truths concerning its nature and operations for the happiness and salvation of all humankind.[83]

### *3.2.2. God's response*

It pleased God, in his goodness and wisdom, to reveal himself and to make known the mystery of his will (cf. Eph. 1:9; 2:18; 2 Pet. 1:4; *DV* 2). God wills the universal salvation of all mankind (cf. 1 Tim. 2:4). He is the

---

[82] M. Dhavamony, "Indian Christian Theological Method", in: *Studia Missionalia*, vol. 45, op. cit., p. 64.

[83] Cf. M. Dhavamony, "Revelation in the History of Religions", in: *Studia Missionalia*, vol. 20, Gregorian University Press, Rome, 1971, pp. 9-15.

God of all. Nobody is outside God's plan. God has been continuously revealing himself to all humanity in different times and manners. In this he is sovereignly free. Paul writes: "O the depth of the riches and the wisdom and the knowledge of God! How unsearchable are his judgements and how inscrutable his ways!" (Rom. 11:33; cf. Ps. 115:3; Is. 40:13).

### *3.2.3. Double revelation*

God's revelation is always salvation-centered. Man sees and seeks in God's revelation the answer to his quest for God and the meaning of his existence. In this, there is a double revelation: revelation of God as well as revelation of man. Amalor calls this the anthropological aspect of revelation. He quotes H. Bouillard and says, ".... Therefore God's revelation would have no meaning for us if it were not at the same time the revelation of the meaning of our existence."[84]

When man responds to God's revelation in faith and lives this faith-experience in the context of a community, it becomes a religion that puts him in the life-giving relationship with God and with his fellow beings.

### *3.2.4. Realization of God's plan*

Amalor stresses that the primary concern in revelation is the *realization* of God's plan in the world.[85] Revelation is the medium of God's self and salvific communication with humanity. Reflecting on the revelation and faith in a post-Conciliar perspective, Amalor holds that the very personal communication of God is social and communitarian. God's revelation may come through individuals, but it is not meant for individualism or isolationism. It is basically addressed to a living *community* of people for the realization of his kingdom, the salvation of mankind here on earth. God communicates himself to a community and, in turn, makes this community *communicating* to others the salvation that is revealed. This is the mission of the community. God is a God of communion and interpersonal

---

[84] DSA, *Approaches*, op. cit., p. 22.

[85] Cf. DSA, *Purpose and Motivation of Missionary Activity*, NBCLC, Bangalore, 1970 (reprinted in 1976), p. 12. (Henceforth this work will be cited as *Purpose*). Cf. also *AG* 9.

relationship.

> God relates himself to men in communion and communication as members of a living community so that the inter-personal relationship between God and man may be the source and climax, the pattern and model of the inter-personal relationship among men, so that the human community in which revelation takes place may gradually be liberated from all forms of slavery and alienation, from isolation and division, and be built up and transformed into a community of faith and love, witness and service, a community of salvation.[86]

Amalor firmly rejects all individualism, isolationism and ecclesiastical egoism. Instead, the Church is the servant, witness and instrument of God's design for all humanity. Quoting here *Lumen Gentium,* Amalor says that the Church has to be "a sure and enduring germ of unity, hope and salvation for the whole of mankind" (9b).[87]

### 3.3. *Revelation, Faith, Salvation: Initiation by God, God's Freedom*

#### 3.3.1. *Revelation as God's self-communication and self-gift*

To understand the theology of God's revelation according to Amalor, let us first see Amalor in his own words.

> Revelation is an inter-personal *relationship* between God and man; God unveiling the mystery of his person and his designs for mankind in an act of *self-communication* and *self-gift.* It gathers persons and builds up *community* by breaking down barriers, liberating and reconciling people. God relates himself to men in communication and communion, as members of a living community so that the relationship between God and man be the source and climax, the pattern and model of the relationship among men, so that the human community in which revelation takes place may gradually be built up into a community of *faith* and *love,* witness and service, a community of *salvation.* All this takes place concretely and really in our existence

---

[86] DSA, *Approach,* op. cit., pp. 26-27; see also: Id., *Purpose,* op. cit., pp. 10-11.

[87] See: DSA, *Purpose,* op. cit., p. 41; id., *Approaches,* op. cit., p. 16; also: Id., *Poverty of the Religious and the Religious as Poor,* NBCLC, Bangalore, 1984, p. 39. (Henceforth this will be cited as *Poverty of the Religious*).

> through the *events of history,* in the midst of *life-situations.* Thus humanity [people of all religions] stands at no time outside the process of revelation, but always *within* it. Hence it becomes relevant to every human group. Its relevance and dynamism make an impact on the audience and bring about change of attitudes in persons and *transformation* of society.[88]

The purpose of God's revelation is the fullness of life, the salvation of all peoples and religions. God takes the initiative to reveal the mystery of his person and his salvific design for mankind in an act of self-communication and self-gift and in that he is sovereignly free. "According to Christian understanding of Revelation and Faith the *initiative* belongs to God and He is sovereignly *free.*"[89] It is God's plan and choice to reveal himself in the time and manner that is appropriate and pleasing to him (cf. Heb. 1:1-3).

In this comprehension, we see that God's revelation has a definite direction and a definite goal, that is, the salvation of all. God has revealed himself to all humankind, to people of all religions. Now he continues to reveal himself in our history in and through his Son Jesus Christ and his Spirit. "God in Jesus Christ, wills to *re-generate* in every human being a son or daughter and to *re-inspire* in them or *breathe* into them his Spirit of love, which is a spirit of sonship and daughterhood."[90] This is our Christian faith and task. This is the task of the Church to follow Christ and to pursue his cause of love, peace and unity in the whole world.

### *3.3.2. Faith as response to revelation: Salvation*

We have already seen that God and man always meet in history, in a historico-cultural context. History becomes the location of God's revelation; and the purpose of revelation is man's salvation. Salvation comes from faith. Faith is man's response to God's revelation. Thus revelation implies a double way process: God's Word and man's response in faith.

Revelation, as we have seen above, is God's self-communication, and

---

88 DSA, "Approach", *op. cit.,* p. 28.

89 DSA, "Initiation to Basic Christian Prayer or Biblical Prayer", in: Id. (ed.), *Indian Christian Spirituality,* op. cit., p. 293.

90 René Latourelle, "Quest for Meaning and Gift of Meaning", in: *DFT,* p. 650.

the very word "communication" needs at least two intelligible parties to understand and to be understood: God and man. God is person. He is *Abba* -- Father (Matt. 5:48; 6:9; 22:32; Rom. 8:15). God's revelation and his salvific plan are to be understood and lived. For this, revelation will need the process of inculturation, that is, God's revelation and man's response in a particular place, culture and history. That is to say in other words that God's revelation needs its 'anthropological infrastructure'.[91] One might say that the whole of creation is God's revelation or manifestation and, thus, there is no culture, no sign, no medium needed for God's revelation. But creation itself is not without any purpose. Man is created in the image and likeness of God to control and give meaning to this creation and direct the course of history according to God's will (cf. Gen. 1:26-28; 5:1).

God freely reveals to all, and man responds to this revelation in faith and freedom. However, the modality and intensity of revelation and man's response may vary from one community to another (cf. Heb. 1:1-3). Jesus is the fullness of revelation. He is "full of grace and truth" (Jn. 1:14). He is so because of the mystery of *incarnation.* Jesus is the incarnation of God's Word in the fullness of time (cf. Gal. 4:4). The mystery of incarnation is the Christian answer to the human longing for a direct experience and perception (*pratyakṣa anubhava*) of God. "Jesus is the empirical grounding of our knowledge of God."[92] The historical "revelation of God in Jesus Christ is the supreme Christian norm (*pramāṇa*) of the divine testimony."[93] It gives history a value. It gives revelation the character of actualization.

In the mystery of the incarnation God has positively willed to intervene personally in history in order to reveal the mystery of his person and his designs for mankind definitively and to complete it fully. Because of this special revelation and intervention of God in history in the mystery of the God-man in the person of Christ, the Christian revelation (OT and NT) is termed as "positive" or "specific" revelation of God; thereby the

---

[91] The term is taken from: Franz Jozef van Beeck, *God Encountered: A Contemporary Catholic Systematic Theology. Vol. 2/1 - The Revelation of the Glory. (Introduction and Part I: Fundamental Theology),* M.G. Book, The Liturgical Press, Minnesota, 1993, p. 295ff.

[92] M. Dhavamony, "Indian Christian Theological Method", in: *Studia Missionalia,* vol. 45, op. cit., p. 93.

[93] Ibid., p. 92.

"general" revelation of God in other religions, that is, God's will revealed in various ways in the past (cf. Heb. 1:1-2), have been fulfilled in Christ and they are oriented to this specific revelation in Christ for their fulfillment.[94]

God manifests himself in and through a culture. However, he transcends all cultures and manifestations. We cannot *identify* the medium of revelation with God, with the *totality* of God. We cannot say that Hindu revelation or Judeo-Christian revelation *is* God. "God is spirit" (Jn. 3:24). He reveals himself as well as "conceals". Unfortunately, for some people, at the exclusion and condemnation of others, 'seeing God and living in him, with him and through him' means the *identification* or *equalization* of God with the culture, the medium, in which God reveals himself. Such a comprehension of God causes a lot of havoc in the world. As a result, God becomes a point of contention and religion a sign of contradiction. In the Christ event, "God's revelation took place in a specific culture, but from the beginning it was destined for all cultures."[95] Martin Buber writes, "We cannot ascribe finality to any one of his [God's] revelations, nor to any one revelation the character of the *Incarnation*. Unconditionally, that futuristic World of the Lord points to the Beyond at every moment of passing time; God transcends absolutely all of his manifestations."[96]

In and through the mystery of incarnation Jesus has become the supreme medium of God's revelation. Jesus is also, representing mankind, the perfect response of mankind to God. Amalor writes:

> If God's word and self-gift is revelation, man's word and his self-surrender to him is faith. The signs of inter-communication between God and man through revelation and faith are *'Words'* and *'Deeds'*. There is an inner unity between them. In Jesus Christ the word and deed tally, since he becomes the *total* language and *perfect* communication, the greatest *sign* and supreme *medium* of revelation. He is the meeting point between God's revelation and man's faith,

---

[94] The incarnation of Jesus and his mediation in the salvation history will be dealt in detail in chapter three.

[95] M. Dhavamony, "Indian Christian Theology", in: *Studia Missionalia,* vol. 45, op. cit., p. 97.

[96] Statement of Martin Buber, quoted by Dan Cohn-Sherbok in: Id., *On Earth as it is in Heaven. (Jews, Christians, and Liberation Theology),* Orbis Books, Maryknoll, New York, 1987, p. 3.

between God's Word and man's word. Since he is the revelation of the Father, there is nothing new or more *outside* Jesus Christ; in this sense revelation is said to be *closed* with the early Church and the last apostle. But in the Church there is a gap between word and deed. This explains her pilgrim character and imperfection; this calls for on-going reform, renewal and conversion on her part.[97]

### 3.3.3. *The biblical 'dabar', the deed-word: Making history, pedagogy of revelation*

God's Word (*dabar*) is a creative force. It is dynamic. "God said, 'Let there be light'; and there was light...." (Gen. 1:1-2:4a). The Jews in the course of their history discovered God and understood his designs for themselves and for all humankind from the way in which Yahweh intervened in their history and acted on their behalf. They saw God acting in and through his word (*dabar*). That is why the Hebrew *dabar* is not a mere sound, a mere message or doctrine. It refers more to persons, events and things than to words. It is a word that activates response from man in deed. It is both word and deed. It makes history.

> History comprising a series of events, orientations and a goal, involves man fully in his tension towards that goal and in his concrete effort to attain it both as individual and as a member of his community. It also serves as the milieu and medium of God's self-revelation and communication. The Jews in the course of their history discovered God and understood his designs for themselves and mankind from the way God intervened in their history and acted on their behalf. It is by reflecting on God's successive interventions in their favour, in the course of history that they discovered him and themselves. That is why the Hebrew *'dabar'* refers more to persons, events and things than to words, in the sense that persons, things and events are eloquent by themselves. Through the deed God expresses Himself, and man likewise. The word is not a mere sound, *flatus vocis,* a mere message or doctrine, it is dynamic, transforming and productive. It is not merely uttered; but when uttered it becomes creative. Hence revelation is not handing down of a doctrine or

---

97 DSA, "Approach", *op. cit.*, p. 28.

> infusing of ideas, but God acting in historical events, meeting man in his life-situations and revealing and communicating Himself to him in a personal and community relationship. The *'dabar Yahweh'* is therefore something concretized in the events of history, nay it makes history itself.[98]

This concretization of God's word reaches its climax in the incarnation of Jesus. The word of God becomes a human person (cf. Jn. 1:14): Emmanuel, 'God with us'(Matt. 1:23). In the mystery of his Son Jesus, God has entered into the historical process of revelation and salvation in a climatic and final way.

> That is why none can be more eloquent and reveal God better than Christ, the Word of God. He is indeed the definitive, ultimate, total and supreme revelation of God; He is so more by His deeds than by His words; the very deeds of the Word are words. Likewise, there is no better and more fruitful encounter between God and man than the person of Jesus Christ, the Word Incarnate.[99]

Amalor, after pointing out the relation between the word and deed in God's revelation, continues to say that the function of the word is also to proclaim the deed, to clarify it by removing all ambiguity and forestalling false interpretations.

> That is why God's action even in our contemporary history has to be interpreted in the light of His word, in the light of His past interventions narrated in the Bible and interpreted by the Church. Thus both word and deed are equally important.[100]

---

[98] DSA, *The Theology of 'Indirect Evangelization'*, op. cit., pp. 9-10. (Originally this was a lecture delivered by DSA at the Second Missionary Consultation held in Bombay from 20th-23rd September, 1969. It was so well received by both missionaries and theologians assembled there that the wish was expressed to publish it, and thus made available to all).

[99] Ibid., p. 10.

[100] Ibid.

On this point he quotes the dogmatic constitution on Divine Revelation (*Dei Verbum*):[101]

> God's plan of revelation is realized by deeds and words having an inner unity: the deeds wrought by God in the history of salvation manifest and confirm the teaching and realities signified by the words, while the words clarify the mystery contained in them (no. 2).

### 3.4. *Jesus Christ: The Greatest Sign of Revelation in the Unity and Continuity of God's Salvific Action in the One Salvation History*

"The self-communication of God is not confined to the Judeo-Christian tradition, but extends to the whole of mankind in different ways and degrees in the same divine economy."[102] But God's self-communication reaches its climax in the Jesus Christ event (cf. Heb. 1:1-4). "Jesus Christ is the greatest sign and medium of revelation."[103] Jesus is the perfect model of God's communication. For he is "the meeting point between God's revelation and man's faith, between God's Word and man's word."[104] The concretization of God's word reaches its climax in the incarnation of Jesus when the *dabar Yahweh* becomes a human person: *Emmanuel,* God-with-us.[105] The Jesus Christ event is seen, not as something additional or outside the *one* salvation history, but within it, within the unity and continuity of God's saving action and as its climax.

Amalor's basic understanding of God's self-communication is Christocentric. He considers all revelations, whether past or present, as deriving their significance from Jesus Christ, in whom they find their unity, value and reliability.[106] In Jesus Christ "the Father reveals Himself and His designs for us, whether in the past, or in the present or in the

---

[101] See quoted in: Ibid.

[102] See: DSA, *Theology of Evangelization,* op. cit., p. 32. Here DSA agrees with and is influenced by the Declaration of the Theological Conference on Evangelization, Nagpur, India (no. 14).

[103] DSA, *Theology of Development,* op. cit., p. 14. See also above footnotes 97 & 99.

[104] DSA, *The Church's Mission as Prophetic and Hermeneutical,* NBCLC, Bangalore, 1982 (4th edition), pp. 5-6. (Its 3rd edition appeared in 1978, earlier editions are not found).

[105] Cf. DSA, *Theology of Development,* op. cit., p. 15.

[106] Cf. Cyril De Souza, S.D.B., *Catechesis for India Today,* op. cit., p. 335.

future."[107]

Jesus is not merely the word of God, but the very deed of God; not just a medium of revelation, but the revelation itself. To see Jesus Christ is to see God (cf. Jn. 14:9-11); to meet Christ is to meet God; to hear Christ is to hear the word of God; to be united with Christ is to be in communion with God.[108] As such, Jesus Christ is the definitive, total and supreme revelation of God both by his deeds and his words. "In Jesus Christ the word and the deed tally."[109] Since the revelation or the covenant of God with man in Jesus Christ is definitive, and which will never pass away, no new public revelation, contrary to the truth and content of the revelation in Jesus Christ is to be expected before his glorious manifestation at the end of time (cf. 1 Tim. 6:14; Tit. 2:13; *DV* 4). This is our Christian faith.

Jesus is not only the revelation of God, he is also the revelation of man, the perfect response of man to God. Thus we speak of the double revelation in Jesus: revelation of God as well as the revelation of man. Amalor, in consonance with *Ad Gentes* 8 and *Gaudium et Spes* 3, 4, 11, concludes saying that "Jesus Christ will not be the revelation of God unless and until he is also the revelation of man."[110] Thus we can say here with someone who has rightly said: "Jesus is what man understands by *God* and what God understands by *man*."

In the Christ event, God's mystery is conclusively unveiled and penetrated. The Christ event is the "coming down" of God himself to the aid of man in the mystery of his "Son" Jesus Christ in the fullness of time (cf. Jn. 1:14; Gal. 4:4; Heb. 1:1-3). This is the loving and saving mystery of God. Humanly speaking, this is the perfect response of God to man's longing and seeking for him. Now he continues to respond and reveal himself to mankind through his Son Jesus Christ, that is, God continues to call and save all humanity in the life of divine participation in the fullness[111] of truth in and through the person of Jesus Christ and his Spirit.

---

[107] DSA, *Theology of Catechesis*, NBCLC, Bangalore, 1973 (first print in 1971), p. 27.

[108] Cf. ibid., p. 20.

[109] DSA, *The Church's Mission as Prophetic and Hermeneutical*, op. cit., p. 6. See also above footnote 97.

[110] DSA, *Approaches*, op. cit., p. 24.

[111] When we speak of the fullness of *truth* in Jesus, we speak in the sense of a "qualitative" fullness of truth, not quantitative. Jesus is the source of all grace and truth. The rays of truth that are found in other religions proceed from him.

Consequently, the revelation is said to be closed with the apostles, in the sense that there is nothing new and nothing more outside the saving mystery of Jesus Christ (cf. 1 Cor. 1:22-25). This does not exclude God's love and freedom from revealing himself in other religions, other cultures, other times and manners (cf. Heb. 1:1-2). God's saving act is not limited to the Judeo-Christian historical vehicle of God's revelation in Israel. His salvific will is universal, now definitely revealed and realized in his Son Jesus Christ. The historicity of Jesus has its own place in the history of salvation because the revelation of God who is Spirit (cf. Jn. 4:24) and an ineffable mystery, to be a revelation, a sign, needs to be concretized and historicized.

In the revelation of God in Jesus, we like to make a note of the following two points. *Firstly,* in the historicity of the Word becoming flesh in the person of Jesus, Jesus becomes the greatest *sign,* the *sacrament* of God. We cannot do away with this *historicity* of what God who, in his love, freedom and wisdom, has accomplished his universal salvific design for the world in the mystery of the *person* of Jesus Christ. *Secondly,* the historical "setting" of Israel, that is, the socio-cultural milieu of Israel, that served as the vehicle of God's revelation in Jesus Christ cannot limit or hinder the truth and grace of Christ from reaching to others. It cannot confine within itself the Spirit of the risen Christ. Jesus Christ has truly become universal and all-inclusive in his Spirit.[112] It is to this truth that the Church has to proclaim to the world, has to instil the Spirit of Christ in others, has to *recognize* the "general" revelation of God in others and *share* with them the experience of her "specific" Christian revelation, the saving mystery of God in Jesus Christ. In other words, she has to carry out the 'mission mandate' of Christ to the whole world (cf. Matt. 28:18-20), not by "sword", exclusivism and condemnation, but by recognizing, sharing and living the life-giving and eternal Spirit of Christ in the context of religious pluralism today. The risen Christ is constituted the Lord and saviour of all peoples and religions (cf. Phil. 2:9-11). In this sense, it is said that the general revelation of God in other religions is oriented towards the specific revelation in Jesus Christ.[113]

---

[112] Cf. DSA, *The Church's Mission as Prophetic and Hermeneutical,* op. cit., p. 21. We will be dealing with the historicity and universality of Christ in detail in the following chapters.

[113] Cf. DSA, "Biblical World-View and a Renewed Holistic Spirituality", *op. cit.,* p. 61.

### *3.5. On-Going Revelation: God's Manifestation, Economy of the Spirit*

"All over the world the Spirit is moving, and there's a mighty revelation." It is a song, and it is a reality for Amalor.[114] Amalor holds that, on the one hand, revelation is closed with the death of the last apostle, for there is nothing new and nothing more outside the saving mystery of Christ; on the other hand, revelation, ultimately an interpersonal relationship, is an on-going process in history and life. Hence God continues to reveal himself through Christ who is the same yesterday, today and forever. The risen Christ transcends time and space and is present and active in the whole universe and hence also in our own life-situations today. We can listen to the *eternal Word* of God *today,* in every twist and turn of history, and accordingly organize our society towards its goal and project of building a just and human community of fellowship, peace and unity among the people of different religions and cultures.[115]

God's on-going revelation means God's on-going self-communication and self-gift, his on-going presence and assistance in mankind's on-going "becoming" in history, in the evolution of man and history.[116] The revelation of God in the Christ event, in so far as it refers to us, demanding our commitment and response in our actual life-situations, has to be a continuous and an on-going process.

> Revelation is an actual, ever-present reality and *on-going process.* The revelation in Israel, in Jesus Christ and in the Church understood in terms of inter-personal relationship is not and cannot merely be something of the past but also of the *present* in a certain sense. If, on the one hand, God reveals himself to us through the events of our life and history, and if, on the other hand, revelation as inter-personal relationship involves our presence and commitment in the process of communication, then revelation must take place *in our life itself now.* Though the Christ-event is a happening once for all, still revelation is, in a certain sense, an on-going process involving each one of us personally. For the *Christ* of *yesterday is the same today and forever.*[117]

---

114 DSA, "Foreword", in: Id. (ed.), *Indian Christian Spirituality,* op. cit., p. 5.

115 Cf. DSA, "Approach", *op. cit.,* pp. 27-28.

116 Cf. DSA, *Approaches,* op. cit., pp. 15 & 19.

117 DSA, "Approach", *op. cit.,* p. 29. Cf. also: Id., *Destinée de l'Église dans l'Inde*

The fact that Jesus Christ is the perfect revelation of the Father would normally lead one to view the Christ event not only as definitive, but also as past. But, given the new perspective wherein revelation and faith are understood in terms of an interpersonal relationship, involving our response today, there is a dimension of the *mystery* of Christ, which is present and also future.[118]

Granted that the total and definitive revelation of God in Jesus Christ should be preserved in its integrity, and authoritatively transmitted to successive generations,[119] yet there is no gainsaying the fact that God is to be found in the heart of the world, in the events of man's history and in the midst of human life. It is man's duty to seek him, listen to the Word, receive the message, interpret it and understand his designs in life and history.[120] The Spirit that Christ communicated through his resurrection, as the greatest gift of Easter to mankind, is present everywhere, especially in the Church, transcending time and space. "God continues to give Himself to us through Jesus Christ in the midst of our life and history."[121]

God has been always interested in the history of mankind, and he continues to do the same. This is the anthropological approach of revelation. Today God continues to reveal himself in and through the Spirit of Christ Jesus, the risen Lord. Thus we say that

> after the coming of Christ no new revelation is to be expected concerning the fundamental situation of humanity in relation to its salvation. In and through Christ God has made fully known his universal plan of love. This revelation is regarded as having ended with the death of the last apostle. But during the present stage in the economy of salvation there is still room for divine revelations intended to enlighten the faithful about the way they should behave in the circumstances of their lives and to guide them in their practical, social, spiritual, and religious activities.[122]

---

*d'aujourd'hui*, Fayard-Mame, Paris, 1967, p. 99. (Henceforth this work will be cited as *Destinée*); id., *Approaches*, op. cit., p. 30.

118 Cf. DSA, *The Church's Mission as Prophetic and Hermeneutical*, op. cit., p. 6.

119 Cf. DSA, *Theology of Catechesis*, op. cit., p. 21.

120 Cf. DSA, *The Church's Mission as Prophetic and Hermeneutical*, op. cit., p. 7.

121 DSA, *Theology of Catechesis*, op. cit., p. 22.

122 See Pierre Adnès, "Revelations, Private", in: *DFT*, p. 950.

It is the *Spirit*, the gift and the power of God to mankind in Christ Jesus (cf. Jn. 20:22; Acts 2:38; Heb. 2:4), who will teach humanity everything. He will teach us the fullness of truth (cf. Jn. 14:26) and he will give us the life in its fullness, the eternal life (cf. Rom. 8:11; Eph. 1:19-20; 1 Cor. 6:14; 2 Cor. 13:4; Lk. 11:13). Thus we see here another aspect of God's on-going revelation to mankind, that is, man's constant seeking for the fullness of truth, the 'discovery of God', and God's gradual and on-going revelation and sanctification of the world in and through his Spirit.[123]

Amalor likes to stress the 'economy of the Spirit',[124] that is, the role and activity of the Spirit, in the universal salvific plan of God. The Spirit was present there at the very beginning of creation (cf. Gen. 1:2). The presence and the power of the Spirit is more intensely manifested and experienced in the "new creation" (2 Cor. 5:17), in the creation of "a new heaven and a new earth" (Rev. 21:1; Is. 65:17; cf. Is. 66:22; 2 Pet. 3:13), in Jesus Christ. The power of the Spirit in the whole Jesus Christ event -- the promise and incarnation, life and ministry, death and resurrection, cf. Matt. 1:18; 3:16, 4;1; 12:18; Mk. 1:8; Lk. 23:46; Jn. 19:30; 1 Cor. 6:14; etc. -- is very much manifest in the Bible. Christ's greatest resurrectional gift of the Spirit to his disciples (cf. Jn. 20:22), the Pentecostal grace and mission (cf. Acts 2:1ff.) and the outpouring of the Spirit in abundance in the last days (cf. Acts 2:33-36), make us recognize our age as the "golden age of the Spirit".

We must recognize the Spirit of God working in other languages and religions as on the day of Pentecost the disciples, filled with the Holy Spirit, began to speak in other languages, as the Spirit gave them ability (cf. Acts 2:4). However we make a note here that the presence and activity of the Spirit in the Church, because of her special relationship with Christ, is "different" from that of in other religions. The Holy Spirit is the soul of the Church (*anima ecclesiae*);[125] this is not so in other religions though there is presence and activity of the Spirit in other religions.[126] The Spirit

---

[123] Cf. DSA, *Approaches*, op. cit., p. 42.

[124] 'Economy of the Spirit': cf. *Catechism of the Catholic Church*, Image Book, Doubleday, New York, 1995, 685-689 (nos.). (Henceforth this work will be cited as *CCC*).

[125] The Spirit is the quasi formal cause of the Church; Christ, the efficient cause.

[126] Cf. DSA, *Approaches*, op. cit., p. 10.

of Jesus Christ is always with his disciples. God creates, recreates and saves the world with his on-going revelation and presence with us in and through his Son Jesus Christ and his Spirit (cf. Gal. 4:6; Rev. 2:7).

While Jesus reveals God as the mystery of the 'Holy Trinity',[127] he makes all the more evident and inevitable the activity of the Spirit in the world (cf. Jn.7:39; 14:26; 15:26; 16:14). Paul calls the Spirit of God as the Spirit of Christ (cf. Rom. 8:9.14; 15:19; 1 Cor. 6:11; 7:40; 2 Cor. 3:17-18). It is the Spirit of the promise (cf. Gal. 3:14; Eph. 1:13), the "Spirit of adoption" (Rom. 8:15; cf. Gal. 4:6). In the words of Peter, it is the "Spirit of glory" (1 Pet. 4:14). It is the Spirit of God, the Holy Spirit, the Paraclete, the "Advocate" (Jn. 14:16), the "Spirit of truth" (Jn. 14:17) whom the Father now sends in Jesus' name, who will teach humanity the fullness of truth and peace of God (cf. Jn. 14:26-27); and "all who are led by the Spirit of God are children of God" (Rom. 8:14).

> Experience of the Spirit is very intense today both in the East and in the West, in spite of the rampant materialism and practical atheism. There is a yearning for the Spirit and for the continuous experience of Him.
>
> In Christian understanding one can say that more people are becoming aware of God's on-going revelation and want to discern His abiding presence in all realities of life. They also want to respond to this revelation by an ever growing awareness of His presence. They are looking to interpret His designs, discern His will and engage themselves in various activities and areas of life in a contemplative attitude while remaining in mystic communion with God and others.[128]

### *3.6. Revelation and Evangelization*

If the Christ event is the supreme and definitive revelation, Amalor sees in it the task of evangelization by the Church. He says:

> Now, evangelization is a ministry of the Church by which the process of revelation is to continue in our history and in which the encounter

---

[127] Cf. *CCC*, 243-248 (especially 244). Here we do not go for the exposition of the Trinity or *filioque*. That would be going beyond our scope.

[128] DSA, "Foreword", in: Id. (ed.), *Indian Christian Spirituality*, op. cit., p. 5.

of man with God must take place, resulting in a deep interpersonal relationship. If the designs of the Lord for mankind are to be communicated to the men of our days -- which is the mission of the Church -- then the economy or the pedagogy to be followed in it is the same as what was used by God in the whole history of salvation which embraces also our own times.[129]

This contemporary awareness -- which constitutes the theological basis for the 'new' thrust for evangelization -- should characterize the pastoral action of the Church and its mission to the whole world, both mission of conversion and of transformation of the world.[130]

### 3.7. *Revelation and Inspiration: Holy Spirit and the Ineffable Mystery of God*

"The inspiration of the scripture is closely linked to the content of revelation, in addition to being an important matter in its own right."[131] What we mean by the biblical inspiration? It is the special impulse and guidance of the *Holy Spirit* through which the books of the scripture were composed and so can be called the word of God and so that we may come to believe in God and have life, life in its fullness (cf. Jn. 20:31; 2 Tim. 3:16; 2 Pet. 1:19-21; 3:15-16; also Jer. 18:18; Neh. 8:1).

God, in his love and goodness and in order to reveal himself to human beings, speaks to them in human words.[132] What God has to say is found in scriptures in human oral words or in the words of human writers who were *inspired* by God. They "were genuine authors and not mere stenographers copying down what God dictated" (cf. *DV* 11; DS 3006, 3629).[133] However, there lies another and no less important principle of correct interpretation, without which scripture would remain a dead letter. Sacred scripture must be read and interpreted with divine authorship, in the light of the same Spirit by whom it was "written" (cf. *DV* 12 para. 3).

---

[129] DSA, *Theology of 'Indirect Evangelization'*, op. cit., p. 10.

[130] The point the Church's mission and her collaboration with others will be dealt in detail in the later chapters (especially in chapters two and six).

[131] See: R. Fisichella, "Inspiration", in: *DFT*, p. 515.

[132] Cf. *CCC*, 101.

[133] G. O'Collins, S.J. & E. G. Farrugia, S. J., *A Concise Dictionary of Theology*, op. cit., p. 107.

In fact, the Holy Spirit is the interpreter of scripture.[134]

Scripture is a privileged expression of God's witness through the means of human communication, oral or written. However, "human language is never up to the task of expressing the fullness of divine reality."[135] "Indeed the words of God, expressed in the words of men, are in every way like human language, just as the Word of the eternal Father, when he took on himself the flesh of human weakness, became like man"(*DV* 13).

There is no doubt that the biblical scripture is inspired by God. God is the author of the Bible. However, we cannot hinder or limit God inspiring other scriptures. The Spirit moves where he wills. Man is a social being. Since men who are saved attain their salvation in the context of their religious tradition, the different sacred scriptures and rites of the concrete religious traditions of the world can be, in various degrees, expressions of a divine mystery and can be conducive to salvation. Amalor says that other scriptures can be read and reflected, all towards the pleroma of Christ who is the fullness of revelation. This in no way undermines the uniqueness of Christian economy of salvation, the mystery of Christ and the Church. Other scriptures cannot replace the Bible.[136]

### *3.7.1. A fact and a problem: A new experience of non-biblical scriptures*

"By this you know the Spirit of God: every spirit that 'confesses' that Jesus Christ has come in the flesh is from God, and every spirit that does not confess Jesus [or does away with Jesus][137] is not from God." (1 Jn. 4:2-3). "All scripture is inspired by God and is [or every scripture inspired by God is also] useful for teaching, ... and for training in righteousness" (2 Tim. 3:16).

Today a great turning point has taken place in the history of the Church, that is, a new relationship has been established between the Church and other religions. This is partly the result of a renewed Christian biblical world vision which in turn has brought about a change of relation-

---

[134] Cf. *CCC,* 109.

[135] See: R. Fisichella, "Inspiration", in: *DFT,* p. 515.

[136] Cf. DSA, *Approaches,* op. cit., p. 38. Also cf. "Declaration of the International Theological Conference on Evangelization and Dialogue in Asia (Nagpur 6-12 October, 1971)", no. 16, in: DSA, *Theology of Evangelization,* op. cit., p. 33.

[137] Other ancient authorities read *does away with Jesus* (Gk. *dissolves Jesus*). See Bible (New RSV, NT), p. 240.

ship between the Church and other religions. Today the Church does not entertain the attitude of condemnation against other religious communities. She recognizes them as 'religions' and looks forward to dialogue and mutual collaboration in reaching our common destiny in God. It is in this change of relationship that many aspects of the Church's life are understood, renewed and lived today, whether one is conscious of it or not.

One of the Church's new approaches towards others is concerned with the issue of revelation and inspiration, that is, the formation of scriptures in every religion, their origin and character and their function and role in the life of a religious community. Above all, in the context of the changed and renewed relationship of the Church with others, the experience of God in other religions, especially their scriptures, the non-biblical scriptures, have assumed great importance in the life and worship of the Church in general and the Indian Church in particular which has acquired urgency among all the Churches of Asia.

Amalor deals with the issue of revelation and inspiration with a pragmatic outlook. The problem here is not a mere theoretical speculation. It is not only a theological problem but practical and pastoral. It is also, in a sense, altogether a new problem for the solution of which we need to break new grounds, besides profiting by the tradition of the Church. Can we use texts from other non-biblical scriptures in our liturgy? How far can we use them in our preaching, worship and catechism? Are they inspired at all? Today, besides, scholars and students,

> several Christians, bishops, priests, brothers, sisters and a few lay people-students, etc., do read the non-Biblical Scriptures as a source of *spiritual nourishment,* as inspiring as the object of *meditation* and as helpful to *prayer.* Whether we like it or not, whether we agree or not and whether it is right or wrong, this is a fact; and this practice is widely spreading. It seems to be part of the actual experience of the Church in India and in a few other countries.... This experience ... is due to a new awareness and a new vision of God's *universal active presence* in the whole world, in the *entire* course of history and in the *totality* of our life. They are not only considered to be inspiring texts, but are also given more or less the value and authority of the word of God. One wonders whether these Scriptures are not inspired and whether they are not bearers of the divine revelation, like the Bible, though in an *analogical* sense.... On the one hand some sections of the Church go ahead with the inclusion of readings from other Scrip-

tures as part of Christian worship, and on the other hand the vast majority of the Church with their traditional formation and mentality maintain a negative attitude, react adversely to such a practice and emphasize possible danger to our faith as undermining the uniqueness of the Christian Revelation, and as equating the Bible with other Scriptures.[138]

The problem touches our life and it is a challenge before us. One could obviously make a distinction between their use in private prayer and in public worship, among inter-religious prayer services, para-liturgical celebrations, the Office of Readings, the Sacraments, and chiefly the Eucharist. But the problem is not solved by a juridical consideration of what can be allowed and what cannot be. The issue goes deeper. The problem needs to be discerned and interpreted with the help of a theological reflection and pastoral decision. This is altogether a new and unprecedented problem in the history of the Church. The Church cannot draw very much from her past tradition. This question was not explicitly envisaged and studied by Vatican II. The Church in India, which is in the very midst of other religions with their age old scriptures, has therefore to make a unique contribution both for the solution of her special problem and for the common good of the universal Church.[139]

The issue becomes more clarified as we proceed further.

### *3.7.2. The term: Why 'non-biblical' and not 'non-Christian' scriptures?*

Amalor deliberately likes to use the phrase 'non-biblical scriptures' rather than the phrase 'non-Christian'. The phrase 'non-Christian scriptures' "can be an expression of our unchristian attitude."[140] Because then we will be limiting the Spirit of the ineffable mystery of God that 'moves where he wills' (Jn. 3:8; cf. Is. 40:13) to the periphery of the Church

---

[138] DSA, "Non-Biblical Scriptures in Christian Experience", in: Id (ed.), *Non-Biblical Scriptures - Theological Understanding, Liturgical Role and Pastoral Use,* (reprint of the *Word and Worship,* March, 1975), NBCLC, Bangalore, 1976, p. 11. (Henceforth this work will be cited as *Non-Biblical Scriptures - Theological Understanding*).

[139] Cf. ibid., p. 12.

[140] Ibid., p. 13.

structure. We will be confining the all-inclusive Spirit of the risen Christ, who is the Lord of all (cf. Col. 1:15-20; Phil. 2:9-11; Matt. 28:18; Jn. 1:1-5), to the boundaries of the Church. Instead the phrase 'non-biblical scriptures' applies and extends to all scriptures, to scriptures other than the Bible.

Finally, before explaining his position on this issue, Amalor poses before us this problem:

> Scriptures in other religions normally refer to those which these religions consider as in some way revealed and or divinely inspired. For example in Hinduism these would be the sacred books regarded as *Śruti* and also as *Smṛti*. Granting that sects and *saṁpradāyas* may differ as to the extent of both śruti and smṛti, one can also include under this title scriptures which are neither śruti nor smṛti. Here again it is not a theoretical speculation. Experimentally people find them revealed and inspired.... Do these two terms mean the same thing in every religion? If different, can we understand them in a broad sense or analogically? In Christianity itself there is a new understanding of the notion of revelation and inspiration. If so, which christian notion of revelation and inspiration do we take as term of reference while studying the same in other religions? Can we, for example, compare the Hindu understanding of revelation and inspiration with the inadequate notion of the same in Christianity that prevailed some years ago?[141]

God is always present in the history of mankind. He is always present in the history of religions. Therefore this history becomes a salvation history. Amalor even calls this a "*holy* history."[142] He calls us to be open to God's Spirit because "what makes anything the word of God is the *Spirit.* We are assured by Christ that His Spirit will lead us to the full truth, to the total reality in luminous clarity [cf. Jn. 14:26].... The Father will reveal it all to us, not in our capacity ... but as little children, open and docile to him."[143]

---

[141] Ibid., pp. 13-14.

[142] Ibid., p. 16.

[143] Ibid.

### *3.7.3. Theological understanding and statement on revelation and inspiration*[144]

#### *3.7.3.1. The one history of salvation:*[145] *Different manner of revelation*

We have already seen the underlying Spirit of God in every religion. 'This does not imply, however, that God has revealed himself in every religion in the same way' (no. 15).[146] The biblical manner of articulating

---

[144] For this point we refer to the "Statement of Research Seminar on Non-Biblical Scriptures (NBCLC, Bangalore, 11th-17th December, 1974)", in: DSA (ed.), *Non-Biblical Scriptures - Theological Understanding, Liturgical Role and Pastoral Use,* op. cit., pp. 17-52. Cf. also the published book form of the Seminar: DSA (ed.), *Research Seminar on Non-Biblical Scriptures* (December 1974), NBCLC, Bangalore, 1975. We take up this point here in so far as DSA, as its organizer-director, contributes his understanding and is influenced by the Statement of the seminar. As Gerwin van Leeuwen, in his book *Fully Indian - Authentically Christian* (1990), writes: "As Organizer-Director of the Research Seminar on Non-Biblical Scriptures ... DSA also bears a particular responsibility for the 'Final Statement'.... Hence we may also find an echo of DSA's theology in that Statement" (p. 324). Added to it, we obviously see here the use and importance of *Local Theology* that one talks of so much today. DSA had understood its use and implication quite well. The above seminar itself, that he convened, confirms to the fact.

While urged by the exigency of the crucial issue of revelation and inspiration in other religions with regard to the Church's approach to other religions in general and the Indian context in particular, DSA, in the capacity of the Director of the National Biblical, Catechetical and Liturgical Centre (NBCLC), Bangalore, and the Secretary of the CBCI Commission for Liturgy, convened and organized a Research Seminar on Non-Biblical Scriptures. He was its first organizer-director. It was held at the NBCLC from 11th to 17th December, 1974. It was a research seminar by a broad panel of experts in the various disciplines. Several bishops and priests were also invited who could bring to the research seminar the riches of their pastoral experience. Since the subject has a bearing on the theology in general and Liturgy in particular also outside India and on the whole Church, and since it affects the relation between the Church in India and the Apostolic See, the Cardinal Prefect and the Secretary of the Sacred Congregation for Divine Worship, the Secretary of the Sacred Congregation for the Propagation of Faith and the President and Secretary of the Vatican Secretariat for non-Christians were invited. Only one of them could attend it. The members of the seminar had the chance of heartily welcoming Mgr. Pietro Rossano, as Secretary of the Secretariat for non-Christians amidst them.

[145] The point - one history of salvation - will be dealt in detail in chapter four.

[146] The numbers within brackets in this section refer to the Statement of the Research Seminar on Non-Biblical Scriptures (Bangalore 1974). See: DSA (ed.), *Non-Biblical Scriptures - Theological Understanding, Liturgical Role and Pastoral Use,* op. cit., pp. 17-49.

these differences is to set them in the context of a history of salvation. Jesus is the supreme and definitive revelation of God. He is the Word become flesh. He is the term towards which the whole of human history is moving.

The revelation in Jesus Christ is not an additional gift of God outside and above the common destiny of the entire human race. Rather it is the climatic manifestation of the one order of salvation that comprises all men and of all times (no. 16). God has created the world through Christ and made him Lord of all (cf. 1 Cor. 8:6); the whole universe has been reconciled to God through Christ (cf. Col. 1:20); God wants to recapitulate all things in Christ (cf. Eph. 1:10).

### *3.7.3.2. Meaningful talk about inspiration: God - individual - community*

#### *(i) Divine origin, Holy Spirit, faith-experience and institutional role*

Holy Spirit is the guarantee of the divine inspiration in the scriptures of the faith-community, the Church. Paul's statement that "all scripture is divinely inspired" (2 Tim. 3:16) does not say much more than affirm the divine origin. Peter may throw more light on the question by remarking that "no prophecy of the scripture is a matter of one's own interpretation, because no prophecy ever came by human will, but men and women moved by the Holy Spirit spoke from God" (2 Pet. 1:20-21). We see here the Spirit inspiring not only the individuals but the community as a whole. The men and women 'moved by the Holy Spirit spoke from God', should be understood, not on the strength and will of individual interpretation but with the guidance of the Spirit as the Spirit lives in the Church, the faith-community. Thus we see here the institutional role of the community. 'Alonso-Schökel, McKenzie, Karl Rahner and other modern theologians have underlined the internal connection between the Church and inspiration. Not only was it the Church who selected the canon in view of her inner awareness of the Spirit, the Old and New Testaments came about as books within the community of believers and were inspired in function of it. Behind the Old Testament there was the inspired Hebrew nation. Behind the New Testament, the inspired Christian community' (no. 25).

This link between the sacred writings and the inspired community explains the remarkable phenomenon of a *re-authoring* and *re-reading* of inspired passages in the Bible. An Old Testament text was not a static entity with a fixed unchanging meaning. Rather it was continually reinterpreted and given new meanings in new situations. For example, the oracle of Isaiah 7:14 (the sign of Emmanuel), first promised merely the birth of a son to Ahaz in the context of the Syro-Ephraimite war. After its fulfillment it was given a new meaning by Isaiah himself as a promise to the Davidic dynasty. Still later, as part of the present Book of Isaiah, it acquired an eschatological meaning. Now the most thorough re-reading is done by the New Testament community which re-interprets many Old Testament passages in a totally new Christological sense (no. 26).

Thus when a Christian says that the scriptures are inspired he is speaking within the linguistic 'form of life' or 'language game' (no. 12), which is the Christian community. He refers to a *role* that the scriptures have within this form of life. He does not refer to the immediate effect they have on him. Neither does he refer primarily to the manner of their composition. How can we specify this role? The Scriptures are the "objectification" of the faith-experience of the community during the period of its constitution as such. As an objectification they acquire an institutional role with regard to its faith-experience, which is no longer an absolute creation, but an actualization, a recreation. It is to this *institutional role* that talk of inspiration refers (no. 12).

Thus Amalor sees in the Bible its three constitutive elements: God who inspires, man who responds to this inspiration in faith, and the community that serves as an *institutional role.* It "is the Word of God as *revealed, enshrined* and *communicated* in the Bible."[147] The word 'inspiration' with reference to any scripture 'cannot be used as a term of descriptive-object-language'(no. 11). Inspiration is not describable. It is basically a faith-experience of an individual in a community. 'This is meaningful only in the faith-experience of the one who is speaking. This reference to the faith-experience of the speaker does not make his perception and affirmation regarding inspiration purely subjective. For a person is always speaking within a social institution which defines and situates his assertion.... Every social group, affirms, lives and manifests its belief and value systems through symbols. Such self-expression of social group, when it is primordial, is absolutely creative and unique and constitutes an institution. This structure then is handed down from age to

[147] DSA, "Initiation to Bible Meditation", in: Id. (ed.), *Indian Christian Spirituality,* op. cit., p. 296.

age. The individual and the group assume this pre-existent structure and *re-actualize* it rather than create it. It is from within such a structure that a community or an individual operates' (no. 11).

The Christian community can speak meaningfully of the inspiration of the scriptures of other religions only in so far as its experience of itself is no longer that of a closed group but of a community that is open and moving towards the formation of a new, wider community that would be as wide as God's economy of salvation. Talk about inspiration can have a meaning only within the *context* of faith-experience. Therefore the extension of the term "inspiration" to the scriptures of other religions always bears a primary reference to the "inspiration" of the Christian scriptures (no.13). The New Testament is the fulfillment of the Old Testament. We cannot understand the New Testament *text* without the *context* of the Old Testament. Even so we will not be able to understand and talk about the inspiration of other religions without the *context* of the Bible, that is, the Christian revelation and inspiration. Hence the Christian revelation, inspiration and scriptures cannot be done away with, or cannot thereby be replaced outrightly by the scriptures of other religions. Instead we talk of the *fulfillment* of the revelation and inspirations of other religions in the context of our Christian revelation and inspiration.

*(ii) The letter and the spirit*[148]

We should not reify scripture. Scripture is the embodiment of God's living Word, in which the Holy Spirit is active and which comes alive when it is proclaimed in the context of a believing community. Hence the text of scripture must always be understood in the context of the experience of the believing community. The language of the scripture is always symbolic, leading beyond itself to the reality that is mediated through the symbol. It is self-involving and it is read in the context of a God-man dialogue and demands faith and commitment.

This idea of scripture as leading man to God and not mere dead letter is characteristic of Hinduism and of Islam. The scriptures of other religions must be approached, not from outside, as it were, but from inside in the context of a living and experiential dialogue, that does not overlook differences. For differences can be signs of the richness of an underlying

---

[148] Cf. the Statement of the Seminar, no. 14.

*mystery* of God; they can be complementary, mutually enriching and point to the ground and goal beyond. However, no scripture can be *identified* with God himself. All scriptures are historically conditioned, and hence none can contain the totality of God's self-manifestation. They are also the response of man to God's Word and in this sense share in the human limitations of that response. Therefore the language here is always symbolic. In this sense, 'not even the historical Jesus of Nazareth [i.e., his earthly life] can be said to be simply the totality of God's revelation' (no. 14). But he is *the* sign of the Eternal Word speaking to man through signs.

Jesus Christ is the supreme sign, the fullness of God's revelation; he is the fullness of truth. The Holy Spirit will teach us the fullness of truth in Christ. Meanwhile, in dialogue with others, we strive to attain the pleroma of Christ: the fullness of his salvific mystery and his universal Lordship.

### *3.7.3.3. The inspiration of the scriptures of other religions*

#### *(i) The positive value of non-biblical scriptures*

First of all, Amalor sees a positive value of non-biblical scriptures 'since they manifest with their own specific character, the universal salvation offered by God to mankind and which we have received in Jesus Christ' (no. 5).[149]

Today the attitude of mutual recognition, dialogue and collaboration among religions 'has led the Christians to the discovery that the Scriptures of other religions not only help them to discover aspects of the divine mystery hitherto unknown to them but also makes them capable of a wholly new penetration into the mystery of Christ' (no. 10).

#### *(ii) God manifests himself to all: His underlying Spirit in all religions*

God's salvific will extends to all men as individuals and as grouped in communities. The Holy Spirit is present and active in every personal experience of God. In the order of divine-human relationships,

---

[149] This is the Christian interpretation and follows from the special universal salvation in Christ.

the Holy Spirit is God becoming personally present to man. It is in the *Spirit* that man's religious experience becomes truly personal. Hence we can say that 'every genuine experience of God is the experience of the Spirit' (no. 15).

The action of the Spirit of God, however, is not confined to the personal dimension but includes also the social manifestations of religious experience. The scriptures, as we saw above, are communal, institutional expressions of this experience. In this sense they are manifestations or signs of the action of the Spirit of God in them and are not mere human words. Thus we can say that the saving self-manifestation of God is not confined to the Christian community and its scriptures but can be extended to every other religious community and its scriptures (no. 15 & no. 54).

*(iii) The inspiration of the scriptures of other religions: Analogical*

We have already seen the historic and progressive self-manifestation of God to mankind. Now in the light of this we can say that the scriptures of other religions are inspired, though this quality is to be attributed *analogically*[150] (no. 17). 'If inspiration is taken in the *strict sense* of the witness given by the Spirit to the eschatological action accomplished by God in Jesus of Nazareth and in the history leading immediately up to Jesus [OT], it cannot be said that the Scriptures of other religions are inspired. But if inspiration is taken in the *broader sense* of witness in the Spirit to the action of the Spirit leading mankind to Christ, the Scriptures of other religions may have this inspiration' (no. 17).

'An analogical predication of inspiration to the Scriptures of other religions would be easier if we realize that biblical inspiration itself is deeply analogical' (no. 18). The Spirit must have been as much active in the oral traditions anterior to the scriptures as in the writer who put them down in writing. Therefore there must be a prophetical or apostolic inspiration anterior to scriptural inspiration. These prophets or apostles reacted to facts and those facts were brought about and shaped by the

---

[150] We distinguish the biblical inspiration from the inspiration of other scriptures. The Bible (OT and NT) is the "Word" of God. God is the principal cause in biblical texts; whereas other scriptural texts are principally the word of men, of course helped by God. Human author is the principal cause in other scriptures. More about the distinction between the Bible and other scriptures, see in further points in this section (3.7.3.), especially point: 3.7.3.7.

Spirit. Thus a factual inspiration precedes prophetical or apostolic inspiration. After the biblical inspiration, there is the ecclesial inspiration, the role of Tradition or Magisterium, by which the Spirit in the Church leads her to fulfill her hermeneutic function. 'Such being the case, among these analogies of inspiration, there is a place for an inspiration through the cosmic covenant' (no. 18).

The analogical inspiration of the scriptures of other religions can be also understood, if we have a more clear idea of the relationship of the Old Testament to the New as far as inspiration is concerned. In recent theology this relationship has been conceived in various ways, three of which are particularly significant. First, the *Law-Gospel Model* which looks upon the Old Testament not as God's Word, but as prepaedentic to the New Testament. Scriptures of other religions too could be inspired for the pre-understanding of the Gospel which emerges under the Old Testament. The Gospel can emerge as well within other historical embodiments of divine law. Second, the *Salvation History Model* which sees the Old and the New Testaments as inter-locking parts of a single history of salvation. Every genuine religious experience or religion must form part of this history if it is to be truly the history of God's saving deeds. As records of such experiences scriptures of other religions can also be inspired. Third, the *Tradition History Model* in which the Old and the New Testaments are related to each other as parts of a single, living, continually *developing* tradition. Inspiration, so conceived, could be more easily extended to the scriptures of other religions (no. 19).

The term *inspiration,* therefore, does not cover exactly the same reality at the various stages of the continuity and graduality of the history of revelation and salvation. This history is one... But it bears in different manners the imprint of the influence of the Spirit of *providence* who directs the destiny of mankind to its appointed goal through all the stages of his self-revelation (no. 20).

### *(iv) The difference of the canon, the cultural content and historical context*

Considering the above deliberations on the scriptures of other religions, we say that the initiative of revelation, faith and inspiration belongs to God and in that he is sovereignly free. Where would then the main difference between the Bible and the non-biblical scriptures lie? The visible difference lies in the canon, the cultural content and the historical context. In other words, firstly, we make the difference with regard to the Church's canon,[151] the Tradition and Magisterium, which may be absent in the case of other scriptures; and secondly, the Judeo-Christian cultural content and the historical context,[152] which is not the same in other religions. 'Of course, the biblical writings are of their very nature linked to a specific, limited and time-bound community. As such they are *inward-looking* and do not claim to be exhaustive' (no. 22).

Considering the above points, can we say that other scriptures have something to say to us? What should be our attitude to these scriptures? Do biblical scriptures have an exclusive claim on inspiration?

### *3.7.3.4. The attitude of the biblical scriptures*

#### *(i) Biblical inspiration: Not exclusive*

Do the Old or the New Testament writings themselves give any positive judgment about God's Word in non-biblical scriptures? The Bible nowhere explicitly deals with the question in the specific way in which it has arisen in our own days. But form the way in which the sacred authors approach other religious writings of their own time we may infer that they do not exclude God's revelation in them (no. 21). The New Testament books emphatically proclaim the universal salvation brought through Christ, but they do not thereby deny that God had communicated aspects of that salvation to other people in other writings. Paul cited stoic texts in his sermon to the people of Athens (cf. Acts 17:28). While the Old Testament mainly affirms God's special commitment to the Jewish people through the covenant, it readily acknowledges that God speaks through non-Jewish prophets also, such as Balaam the Ammonite (cf. Num. 22:2-24:25), and that he has special message for non-Jews like Cyrus, the king of Persia, to proclaim liberty for the Jewish exiles. These messages reach them through their own oracular media (cf. 2 Chron. 36:22-23).

---

[151] Cf. The Council of Trent, 1546, see: ND 210-213. (*The Christian Faith in the Doctrinal Documents of the Catholic Church,* edited by Jacques Dupuis, Alba House, New York, 1996. This is the sixth revised and enlarged edition).

[152] Here when we speak of the cultural content and historical context we mean the particular historical and cultural setting of the Bible, i.e., the time and culture of the OT and the NT (its externality) and not *the* content and context of the Bible, i.e. the *salvation* and the *salvation history* respectively.

In this context it is of special importance to note that *'many non-Jewish writings have been incorporated into the Old Testament'* (no. 23). Among such insertions we find historical texts, prayers, laws and instructions of wisdom. In some cases much re-editing has been done, but in other instances, such as in Psalm 29, the complete non-Jewish texts was taken over with no more than minor modifications. 'Presumably Inspiration also extended to the original non-Jewish community and author' (no. 23). It is also interesting to observe that next to and apart from the Old Testament books *other writings existed which were referred to as co-extensive with the inspired texts* (no. 24). For the Hebrews the laws of God were sanctioned by the covenant and some of these laws found explicit mention in the Bible. From an internal analysis of the texts and external comparison with ancient Middle Eastern literature we can deduce with certainty, however, that the Hebrews were actually using the ancient Canaanite law books in the covenant. The norms of justice accepted under the sacred covenant (cf. Josh. 24:25-26) and imposed under divine sanction (cf. Deut. 16:19) were for the greater part *mishpatim* previously sanctioned and written down under Canaanite religion. Paul's preaching too presupposes the active presence of Hellenistic exegetical texts (cf. 1 Cor. 15:45.54). The point is that the dividing line between inspired texts and non-inspired texts was not always very clear. That some texts were included and other ones excluded seems frequently to have been due more to accidental reasons than to real internal difference in status (no. 24).

*(ii) A Christian re-reading of other scriptures*

'If we accept the presence of the Word which "enlightens all men" as active also in other religious scriptures, if we affirm that the Holy Spirit has been at work in their coming about, it is natural to think of the possibility of a Christian re-reading of these scriptures in the light of the resurrection' (no. 27). The Church is related to all religions on the basis of the one, common economy of salvation for the whole of mankind. The Christian is therefore able to read these texts of other religions in a *fuller* sense, that is, to place this text beyond its immediate context into a wider perspective. They should be interpreted in the Christian faith. Vedic and Upaniṣadic references to *vidyā* (knowledge), to the desire to overcome death, to spiritual food, to vision, etc., can be understood by the Christian in the light of the Gospel (no. 27).

In conclusion we may say that, from a biblical point of view, the scriptures of other religions should not be disregarded as channels of God's revelation. The Church should rather recognize in them whisperings and enunciations of the Word, initial and hidden words of God, but truly divine words (no. 28). Although the precise modality of inspiration would still need to be refined from the point of view of the New Testament, the inspiration of non-biblical scriptures is a distinct possibility. The least we can say is that, following the pattern set by the Bible itself, the Church can legitimately read and study the scriptures of other religions in theology, religious instructions, and other para liturgies. The reading of non-biblical texts, such as the *acta martyrum,* in the Early Church may confirm the validity of this conclusion (no. 28).

*(iii) Special and central place of biblical scriptures*

After the re-reading of other scriptures, we say that the biblical scripture has a central place in our Christian life and worship, especially in the liturgy of the Eucharist. The Christian liturgy is a representation of the Lord's Passover until he comes. Its language has not just 'an informative function but rather a *performative* one which creates what it says' (no. 58a). It makes us relive the mystery expressed in them. The liturgy may be described as a symbolic action of a community. At its core it is an action and the meaning of this action is specified by word. Word and action together constitute the *text* to which the faith-experience of the community, the Church, serves as the context.

Thus, *firstly,* the biblical scripture is based on the Church's faith-experience of God's mystery in the historical Jesus Christ event. *Secondly,* the religious signs and symbolic actions have no meaning without or outside the faith-experience of the community. *Thirdly,* and the most important point here is the word which, as we have already pointed out, together with action constitutes the text of the liturgy. As we relive and celebrate our life and salvation accomplished by Jesus Christ in the liturgy, the liturgy of the word (Reading/s) must relate itself to Christ and the faith-experience of the community. Thus Amalor would say with the participants gathered in the Seminar: "The element that makes the Christian Scriptures [OT and NT] basically irreplaceable is the existential fact that God's redemptive intervention was expressed in and through them.... [Therefore] the prophetic message demands a hearing not by the inherent beauty or wisdom of its content, but by the authority of God [himself]."[153] Thus the biblical scripture occupies a special place in our life and worship, especially in the liturgy of the Eucharist.

However, this does not mean that the mystery of Christ is limited to the Judeo-Christian faith-experience of the Church alone. With regard to the various expressions of the ineffable mystery of God in the 'economy of the Spirit', that is, the Spirit speaking in other religious experiences and in their sacred books, the Church is not exclusive. Today the Church seeks to be inclusive and truly *catholic*. The Holy Spirit is, as we have seen above, the soul and the quasi formal cause of the Church, the guiding principle of our ecclesial life, leading all peoples and religions to the fullness of truth in Christ (cf. Jn. 14:16-17,26). Thus, in short, we say that non-biblical scriptures can find place in the life and worship of the Church in so far as they fulfill the function in the overall actualization of the faith-experience of the Church in Jesus Christ (cf. nos. 42, 58, 60).[154]

#### *3.7.3.5. Other scriptures read in the context of Christ, the Word, the Alpha and the Omega (Rev. 22:13)*

Jesus is the Word become flesh. The mystery of God is conclusively unfolded to us in the Jesus Christ event. In him is the fullness of God's revelation, fullness of grace and truth.

Christian tradition has always professed that the unity of the scriptures is to be found in Christ. Behind the Old and New Testaments Christ Himself is the "One Book" (no. 29, cf. no. 53). As Hugo of St. Victor says, *'Omnis scriptura divina liber unus est, et ille unus liber Christus est'* (no. 29). In the words of Rupert of Deutz, Christ is the 'condensed word, so that in Him any word that works for salvation finds its consummation' (no. 29). Thus the Old Testament was completely predicated of Christ by the New Testament and the Fathers (no. 29).

The traditional Christian theologian may almost instinctively apply the same thought to his interpretation of non-biblical scriptures. However, the path of instinct does not help us in doing Christian theology of other religions. Christ is the Word in the sense of John 1: the Word of creation,

---

153 DSA (ed.), *Research Seminar on Non-Biblical Scriptures (December 1974)*, NBCLC, Bangalore, 1975, p. 79.

154 Here we do not intend to see in detail as to which scriptural passages of other religions and where exactly in the Liturgy of the Eucharist they can be used. This treatment would be beyond our scope.

of revelation, of incarnation and glorification. Christ is the unifying principle, the norm by which all scripture is read. Just as the Old Testament did not show *who* Christ is, but *what* he is, may so the non-biblical scriptures not tell us *what* Christ is? 'As Jesus Christ is both judge and fulfiller of all religions, the Christian finds in Him the norm to reject whatever in the scriptures of other religions would detract from obedience to God.... In Jesus Christ he would positively see the recognition and guarantee of the fulfillment of whatever truth, goodness and genuine aspirations for men and human society are found in them' (no. 30). If Christ is the *Alpha* and the *Omega* of history and if he is its guiding principle and moving force, the Christian and his partner from other religious community who are deeply involved in an inter-personal dialogue of life and worship are bound to find a convergence in their religions, 'especially as far as their *Christ content* is concerned' (no. 30).

*(i) Christ and Hindu scriptures (Śruti and Smṛti)*[155]

We find in the Ṛg Veda a continuous quest of man to reach the Divine and to relate everything back to the Divine. But 'in ultimate analysis it seems that the Ṛg Vedic theologians have not fully realized this quest' (no. 31). At this point Christ can give an answer to this quest because he has revealed 'to us in history the true and Divine ... and the real nature of the relation of this man-inhabited world to the Divine' (no. 31). Śankara teaches that *Śruti* (revelation) has its sole purpose to urge men to seek with relentless desire the supreme goal of human existence. If this is so and if 'Christ died for all men, and the ultimate vocation of all men is in fact one (*Gaudium et Spes,* no. 22), then *Śruti* is *de facto* urging man to enter into that great mystery of return to the source which we call the Paschal Mystery of the Lord, of which the Eucharistic celebration, the heart of Christian liturgy, is the daily showing forth' (no. 31).

The Hindu scriptures give us many openings into the mystery of Christ. The Upaniṣads make *OM* the fundamental divine affirmation, the

---

155 See M. Dhavamony, *Classical Hinduism*, Documenta Missionalia - 15, Università Gregoriana Editrice, Roma, 1982, p. 5. [For Hinduism, we refer to this scientific & masterly work of M. Dhavamony who is an authority in Hinduism. It is also used so by others, e.g., see: John Monis, *"Liberated Society": Gandhian and Christian Vision. Comparative Study,* Documenta Missionalia - 23, Editrice Pontificia Università Gregoriana, Roma, 1996, (cf. p. 38, footnote 1)].

centre of meditation. In this they come close to the theology of the Word, the *Logos,* which is Christ. The insistence of the Upaniṣads on the supremacy of loving God with all the powers of our ears, our mind and our pondering heart (cf. Bṛh. Up. 2.4.5), resembles closely to the central demand of the Old Testament that one should love God with all one's might, one's heart and one's mind, that is, loving God with the totality of one's personality (cf. Deut. 6:5). The mystical love in the Bhagavad-gītā may truly be said to foreshadow the love by which Christ embraces man. It reads:

> You are my desired, my friend; therefore I will tell you your salvation. Bear Me in mind; love Me and Worship Me, sacrifice, prostrate yourself to Me; so will you come to Me, I promise you truly, for you are dear to Me.
>
> BG 18.64.65 (no. 32).

In these examples we may see God's *preparatio evangelica* or a kind of inspired "pre-understanding". One may even incline to equate in this the function of the Old Testament and that of other non-biblical scriptures (no.32). However, the Old Testament, because of its special relationship to Christ and serving as the immediate context of the New Testament, is, we say, the proximate preparation of the New Testament, while other scriptures are remote preparations. Thus, the inspiration of other scriptures is not the same as that of the Old Testament. We do not equate the Old Testament with other scriptures. The Old Testament is the foreshadowing of the New Testament; the New Testament is the fulfillment of the Old Testament.

### *(ii) Jesus Christ and Qur'ān*

We have a real point of contact between Christian and Muslim faith. The Qur'ān is related to Christ but in a different way. Many points of doctrine from the New Testament have been incorporated into the Qur'ān, not only about God and man, but particularly about Jesus Christ. In Islam Qur'ān (Arabic), a "recitation", is God's revelation to Muhammad[156] and Jesus is God's Word (*kalimat Allāh*).[157] If we can speak

---

[156] Cf. Ary A. Roest Crollius, S.J., *The Word in the Experience of Revelation in Qur'ān*

of the 'unknown Christ of Hinduism', we have to speak also of the 'half-known Christ of Islam'.

Christ has communicated himself as the light that enlightens the world. 'Some of this communication is partially recorded in the Qur'ān which is acknowledged by Muslims as normative in Islam' (no. 33). There are traces of divine influence in the Qur'ān. Qur'ānic verses such as the one that describes Christ as the "sign of the hour" unite Islam and Christianity drawing us to our common destiny in God (no. 33).

### *3.7.3.6. A final word on this point: Pinpointing the historicity*

Reading the above points, one may be inclined to conclude that Amalor and others there at the Research Seminar are giving a resemblance to or equating the Hindu scriptures or Qur'ān, or for that matter any other scripture, with the Bible. Of course, not. They only talk of the *openings* into the *mystery* of Christ in these scriptures. "The Veda does not in the least resemble the Christian Bible. It is not an account of God's dealings with man in *history.*"[158] The sacred account in the Veda, unlike the historicity of Jesus Christ event in the Christian scripture, is not historical. Indian thought has conceived of reality more as 'a rotating wheel in which the movements are endless and ultimately meaningless, and in which one can find more possible ways of reaching the centre which is motionless' (no. 35).

It is characteristic of the Judeo-Christian world view that God's saving action is experienced in historical events. In this life it is a journey, a pilgrimage, a goal- directed road with many historical windings and curves leading to its destiny. 'Jesus Christ is seen as the definitive, eschatological event putting for all time the seal of finality [of God's revelation] on history' (no. 35).

The participants see in the reflections and findings of the Seminar a new vision in the 'wonderful works of God' wrought by the Spirit in the religious traditions of the world in general and of India in particular. They state: "We have recognized as never before in the sacred books of other

---

*and Hindu Scriptures*, Documenta Missionalia - 8, Università Gregoriana Editrice, Roma, 1974, p. 80.

157 Cf. ibid., p. 50ff.

158 M. Dhavamony, *Classical Hinduism*, op. cit., p. 30.

religions the dynamic presence of the Spirit leading our fellow countrymen ever deeper into that ineffable Mystery which is revealed to us in Christ. We have realized too the grave responsibility this recognition lays upon us of allowing ourselves to be led by the same Spirit, in a new and perhaps unforeseeable ways, to live out the full implications for our country of the *universality* of the Risen Lord, still largely hidden from us in the *mystery* of God" (no. 78).

The final word of Amalor on the Statement of the Research Seminar on this subject is this:

> This Statement is not the last word on the subject, nor do the participants consider it as an adequate, rigorous and fully satisfactory theological formulation. But they hope, pray and wish that this will pave the way for other Seminars, promote further study and deeper research, and serve as a catalyst for a new and on-going effort in faith-reflection [i.e., theology] on their Christian experience of non-Biblical Scriptures.
> Likewise, in the awareness of their limited role in the Church and in their loyal obedience to the authorities of the Church both at the level of the Church in India and of the universal Church they do not intend their document to be a call for implementation of their proposals. But they submit them to the consideration of the Hierarchy of India and request them to take relevant decisions in this regard. They also offer this as their contribution to the Church in India for deepening and enriching its experience of the *ineffable mystery of God* as revealed to us in Jesus Christ and as understood and lived by the people of other religions and enshrined in their Scriptures among others.... It seems that the Church in India is destined by Divine Providence to contribute as its specific share, to the theology of the Religious traditions of mankind, more specially to that of non-Biblical Scriptures.[159]

The inspired books teach us the truth. However, "the Christian faith is not a *'religion of the book'*. Christianity is the religion of the *'Word'* of God, *'not a written and mute word, but incarnate and living'*."[160]

---

[159] DSA, "Editorial", in: Id. (ed.), *Non-Biblical Scriptures - Theological Understanding*, op. cit., p. 7.

[160] St. Bernard, *S. missus est hom.* 4, 11: PL 183, 86. See cited in: *CCC*, 108.

Christian faith is based on the mystery of the Word become incarnate in the person of Jesus Christ. Therefore, "If the Scriptures are not to remain a dead letter, Christ the eternal Word of the living God, must, through the Holy Spirit, *'open [our] minds to understand the Scriptures'* [cf. Lk. 24:45]."[161]

### *3.7.3.7. Pointing the difference*

After exposing the mind of the Seminar on revelation and inspiration above, we now briefly see how Amalor would differentiate the biblical revelation and inspiration from that of the others.

#### *(i) The Bible: God's Word, God speaking through his Son*

For Amalor other scriptures could be said to be, as we have seen above, in a certain or broader sense and in the mystery and providence of God, "revealed" and "inspired". But the Bible is *the* inspired book of God. What do we mean? It is God's own word and deed, his definitive salvific intervention in the world in and through the Jesus Christ event, enshrined and expressed in the Old and the New Testaments. Thus, in the strict sense, we say that it is God himself who is the "author" of the Bible. "Long ago God spoke to our ancestors in many and various ways by the prophets, but in these last days he has spoken to us by a Son ..." (Heb. 1:1-2).

The Bible is God's salvific Word, definitively "spoken", revealed, and fulfilled in his Son Jesus Christ. Thus the Bible is the Word of God primarily, principally and intrinsically. Other scriptures are primarily the words of men, mythical or historical, and secondarily word of God in the sense that God has helped or inspired them to formulate their scriptures, either oral or written in the various stages of salvation history -- all pointing to Christ for their fuller meaning, content and perfection.[162] Thus the basic difference would lie in the *authority:* that is, whether the one who is "speaking" in and through the scriptures is God or mere man; whether the scriptures themselves are real and historically fulfilled by God's power and grace, as in the case of the Bible, or they are mythical

---

[161] Ibid.

[162] Cf. DSA, *Approaches,* op. cit., pp. 37-38.

depictions of the sincere aspirations of man for salvation in God, as in the case of Hinduism.[163]

*(ii) Church: The community constituted by Christ and led by his Spirit*

We have already seen the special intervention of the Holy Spirit in the whole Jesus Christ event. Likewise, there is the special intervention of God in the Church in Christ. The Church is constituted by Christ and led by his Spirit. Because of her special relation to Christ we say that the Church is and should be the Spirit-filled community.[164] If it is so then the special *inspiration of the Spirit* on the biblical scriptures and the Spirit inspiring the *community* as a whole, cannot be denied. Analogically we can speak of inspiration of the scriptures other religions which form part of the one progressive salvation, to be consummated in Christ.

In agreement with the final Statement of the Research Seminar on Non-Biblical Scriptures, Amalor would say:

> In the religions of the world God reveals himself through a variety of signs and symbols (16). Analogically we can speak of inspiration of the Scriptures of other religions, because they may be record of authentic religious experiences, which form part of the one progressive salvation history; hence also through them people may be led to Christ by the Spirit (17-19).... This does not mean that everything in these Scriptures is adequate, but 'that this action of the Spirit brings to these Scriptures an overall religious authority for these communities as God-given means, leading them to their ultimate destiny' (54).[165]

Thus Amalor does not identify or equate the scriptures of other religions with the biblical scriptures. The Bible cannot be replaced by

---

[163] Cf. ibid., pp. 36-42.

[164] Cf. DSA, "Biblical World-View and a Renewed Holistic Spirituality", *op. cit.*, p. 56ff.

[165] See: Gerwin van Leeuwen, O.F.M., *Fully Indian - Authentically Christian,* op. cit., p. 287 (reference 17). He writes this to show the agreement of DSA with the Statement of the Research Seminar. The ciphers in the quote refer to the articles of the Statement.

other scriptures. The texts from other scriptures cannot replace the biblical texts, especially the word of God in the liturgy of the Eucharist. However, Amalor, recognizing and respecting the universal salvific mystery of God and his providential ways in other scriptures, always encourages their reading especially in the para liturgical services: prayers, meditations, etc.[166] What is required is due discretion and careful selection of the texts from other scriptures. These texts must conform themselves to God's universal salvific plan fulfilled in the mystery of his Son Jesus Christ. Amalor also encourages their study in seminaries and research seminars in order to foster inculturation[167] and mutual collaboration among religions and, above all, for deeper understanding of God's universal salvific mystery in Christ.

> Christians benefit from the Indian Scriptures for a deeper understanding of the biblical Word and the Hindus benefit by the biblical Word to re-interpret their Scriptures and to discover the unknown riches and facets. In Mahatma Gandhi we have a beautiful example of one who made not only an intellectual synthesis of Bhagavadgita and the Gospel (especially Sermon on the Mount) but also an inspirational synthesis for social reform, religious renewal and struggle for political independence on the rock of authenticity of personal renewal and holiness.[168]

As such there should not be comparison, condemnation and counter-condemnation among the religions and scriptures of the world. That has never been the aim of Amalor. What is needed is a Christian re-reading of these scriptures in the light of the resurrection of Christ.

> When their various forms and experiences of prayer, ways of worship are integrated into the Christian liturgy, when the religious literature of other religions can be read, understood and lived with reference to

---

[166] Cf. Antony Mookenthottam, M.S.F.S., *Indian Theological Tendencies. (Approaches and Problems for Further Research as Seen in the Works of Some Leading Indian Theologians)*, Peter Lang, Berne, 1978, p. 94.

[167] Inculturation was one of the favourite topics of Amalor. However we will not be dealing this topic in detail. This is beyond our scope.

[168] DSA, *The Bible in Self-Renewal and Church-Renewal for Service to Society*, NBCLC, Bangalore, 1984, p. 15.

the Sacred Scriptures of Christianity, then we can say that all these have been consecrated to God and thereby have their fulfillment and consummation in the pleroma of Christ.[169]

## 4. Some Relevant Biblical Texts Applied

At the first glance, the Bible may seem to condemn other nations and religions. It may seem to consider other nations as enemies. The Bible, especially the Old Testament, may seem to adopt the attitude of exclusivism and contain "judgements against the nations" (cf. Gen. 15:14; Ex. 23:23-24.32-33; Deut. 7:2; Judg. 5:31; Ps. 59:5; 72:9; 92:9; Esth. 9:22; Jer. 1:16; 46-51; Joel 3:2; Mal. 2:11; 1 Cor. 10:20; etc.). But the scientific study and the objective hermeneutics of the Bible show us that the Bible does not condemn religions as such nor the imperfection and religious deficiency of peoples. Rather, the condemnation falls on certain social and religious evil practices, for example, the anti-social and homicidal practices of sin, sorcery and human sacrifices, especially to Molech, by the Canaanites and Ammonites (cf. Lev. 18:21; Deut. 18:9-14; 2 Kgs. 23:10; Wis. 12:3-6), the sexual degeneration (cf. Ex. 18:2-3; Rom. 1:18-25), the worship of self or of State, in that they either favour syncretism or constitute an alternative to Yahweh (cf. 1 Kgs. 11:7-8).

These judgements and condemnations of the socio-religious evil practices of other nations and religions signify in their final analysis the true worship of God. For example, in Psalm 95:3, God is seen as *El*, who was the head and the supreme deity of the Canaanite pantheon. *El* was also the "Great King", a title borne by emperors in the ancient Near East.

---

169 DSA, *Approaches*, op. cit., p. 38. This thought -- the theology of the 'economy of the Spirit' -- has been shared by many others in the Church today. For example, in *Jesus Christ at the Encounter of World Religions*, (1991), p. 177, J. Dupuis, referring to Amalor and others, writes:

'Certain aspects of the divine mystery may actually be given more emphasis in other sacred scriptures than in [the Old and] the New Testament. We need only think of the deep sense of the divine majesty and the holiness of the divine decrees on every page of the Qu'ran, or the sense of the immanent presence of God and the interiority in which religious experience is steeped in the sacred books of Hinduism. Paradoxically as it may appear, a prolonged contact with the nonbiblical scriptures -- practised with their own faith -- can help Christians to a more in-depth discovery of certain aspects of the divine mystery that they behold fully revealed in Jesus Christ.'

For the Israelites *El* applied to Yahweh meant that Yahweh was the true, supreme, and only creator God and gods of the other nations were idols, nothings (cf. Ps. 96:5).[170]

Jesus summarizes the whole Bible and gives the ultimate meaning of all religions as the 'love and service of God and neighbour', our salvation (cf. Mk. 12:30-31). 'Love of God and one's neighbour' implies that peoples and religions acknowledge and repent of their failures, their socio-religious aberrations and imperfections (cf. Jon. 3:5; Wis. 11:23; 12:8-11.22; 13:6ff. Lk. 11:32). It means loving and serving the One, true God who, in and through Jesus Christ and the mediation of the Church, wills to gather "as a hen gathers her brood under her wings" (Lk. 13:34) all nations and religions, both "Jews" as well as "Gentiles" (Gal. 3:28), into one fold in peace and unity, in the one human family and fellowship of all God's children (cf. Jn.11:52; Eucharistic Prayer III).

With this above perspective, we try to see Amalor's thoughts and theology on the Bible and other religions in the following points.

### *4.1. From Chaos to Creation to Collaboration (Gen. 1:1-2:4b-9; Ps. 136; Sir. 16:24-17:24; Jn. 1:1-5)*

God is the creator of all. He is the creator of the world and history.[171] Though the "creation account"[172] may be different and varied from one to another, all the religions of the world in one way or the other attribute the origin of the universe to God.

---

[170] Cf. Raymond E. Brown and Co. (eds), *The New Jerome Biblical Commentary*, Geoffrey Chapman, London, 1996 (reprint, student edition), 34:112, 113. (Henceforth this book will be cited as *TNJBC*).

[171] Cf. DSA, *Gospel and Culture. Evangelization and Inculturation,* NBCLC, Bangalore, 1985, pp. 29-30. (Henceforth this work will be cited as *Gospel and Culture*).

[172] 'Creator/creation': When we say God as creator here, we mean God as the 'Origin' of creation. Christian principle of 'creation' as *creation out of nothing (Ex Nihilo)* may not be agreeable to other religious and philosophical thoughts. Some philosophies, e.g., Greek, may explain the origin of the universe with the principle of *Emanation,* and not *Ex Nihilo.* Hinduism may see the creation of the universe as the work of *Viśva-karman(Maker of all things)* or *Prajāpati (Lord of all creatures)* or see it in the principle of *Hiraṇyagarbha (Golden Seed)* or in the sacrifice (*yajña*) of the *Puruṣa.* Zoroastrianism may see it as the work of *Ahura Mazda*, the Supreme Lord above all other gods and the creator of heaven and earth and of man. (Cf. M. Dhavamony, *Classical Hinduism*, op. cit., pp. 47ff.).

The creation accounts in the scriptures of the world are primarily books of theology, books of faith, rather than a scientific explanation of the origin of the universe.

> The [creation account in the] Bible does not stand or fall by the accuracy of its information, because it is not a text book of science, or history or archaeology. It stands or falls by what it has to say about the purpose of life, the meaning of the world we live in, and the reality that lies beyond it. It claims to provide the clue to the mystery that surrounds our existence, to tell us who we really are, where we should be going, what we ought to be doing, and how we can do it.[173]

"In the beginning when God created the heavens and the earth, the earth was a formless void and darkness covered the face of the deep, while a wind from God swept over the face of the waters" (Gen. 1:1-2). What do we mean by the word when we say a wind from God or the Spirit of God swept over the 'formless void' and 'darkness' in the text? It is *creation* from *chaos* or "nothingness", from a 'formless void' (Heb. *tōhû wābōhû*). It is God giving life and order to chaos, the disorder, the formless waters. It is the life and order over the disorder, the rough sea waters, which the Hebrews in the Book of Genesis saw and experienced.

> Gen 1 stays within the categories of the 'science' of its time and attempts to see in those categories divine power and purpose, and the unique place of humans.... Creation follows effortlessly from mere God's word.... Because Gen 1 is a portrait of what God intends, it is also an eschatological statement. This serene, beautiful world, in which all is ordered to humans, and humans are ordered to God, is how it will be at the end of time. The stories of human sin ... cannot permanently disfigure the original divine intent; God's world will triumph.[174]

---

173 William Neil, *One Volume Bible Commentary*, Hodder and Stoughton, London, 1973 (second edition), p. 13.

174 *TNJBC*, 2:4.

In Hinduism (Ṛg Veda 10.82.5-6), we say it is chaos, the primeval waters, 'giving birth' to Viśvakarman, the 'Maker of all things'.[175] There is no life without 'creation', no life without harmony, unity, peace and order among all and different creatures of God. God is the origin of life and order (*ṛta*). He is the Lord of the whole creation.

While the theology of chaos to creation shows God as the origin of life and order, it demands man's cooperation and collaboration in the creation of God. Thus here we speak in term of a 'continuous creation'. The creation account in Genesis suggests that the Israelites thought of creation as a 'finished product', completed in six days. But in other Old Testament accounts

> creation is represented as a continuing process that endures as long as the world itself endures. The victory of Yahweh over the monster of chaos is sometimes spoken of as a victory that constantly recurs; the monster is said to be bound and restrained rather than killed (Ps. 89:10; 104:6-8; Job 26:12; 38:8-11). Thus Yahweh sustains and defends the material universe against the forces of disintegration; without the uninterrupted exercise of his saving power, the world will relapse into chaos.[176]

In the Old Testament the continuing creative activity of Yahweh was well recognized in these areas: (i) *Fertility*-- where unlike the gods of fertility of the ancient Near East, Yahweh bestowed the blessings of fertility without himself being involved in the process (cf. Lev. 26:4; Deut. 7:13; 11:13-15; Is. 30:23; Jer. 5:24; 31:12; Hos. 2:10ff.). (ii) *God's wisdom and order in nature* (cf. Job 5:23; 38-39; Prov. 3:19; 8:22ff.; Is. 28:23-29; Jer. 5:24; Hos. 2:18; 8:7; 9:14; Joel 2:1-11; Amos 4:7). (iii) *God's control over nature* (cf. Is. 13:3-10; 24:3.19.23; Joel 3:3; Jer. 4:23-26), God over the *storm* (cf. Ex. 19:16.19; Judg. 5:4-5; Ps. 18:8-16; 29:3-9; Is. 30:27.30; etc.), and his *wonder* in nature and *punishment* (cf. Job 4:8-10; 9:5-10; 26:5-14; etc.). It is in this perspective, the deluge (cf. Gen. 7:11ff.) was seen in the past, according to P version, as a return to chaos as a sign of God's punishment to man for not obeying God's command.[177]

---

[175] Cf. M. Dhavamony, *Classical Hinduism,* op. cit., p. 48.

[176] *TNJBC,* 77:55.

[177] Cf. ibid., 77:56-60.

It is in this perspective of doing God's will lies the role and responsibility of man towards God (faith, *śraddhā*) and towards his fellow men (social duties, *dharma*), to collaborate with God and with one another because man is created in the 'image and likeness' of God. He is to 'subdue' the earth according to God's plan (*ṛta*).

Amalor speaks of man's double duty (*karma*), the twofold action of man. *First,* man's *karma* towards the *cosmic order (ṛta)* in creation, the plan of God; and *second,* his *karma* towards the *social order (dharma).* In this twofold *karma* of man lies his liberation, *mokṣa* (cf. Hinduism in the period of Vedas, *c.* 1500 B.C. and Brāhmaṇas, *c.* 1200 B.C.).

> The whole world is in perfect harmony [*cosmic order*]: the universe is an integrated totality; this is due to *ṛta,* which is a perfect law inscribed into the universe. This cosmic harmony must be reflected in the *social order,* and this is possible only when *dharma* is followed. The function of man is to perform *karma,* or do his actions as prescribed by the *dharma....* By performing them man enters into this double order: he becomes part of them and thereby attains *Mokṣa.* Man has also to safeguard and maintain this order which can be disturbed or broken. It is also his responsibility to contribute to it. All this function is filled by his performing *karma* according to the various forms of *dharma* [social duties]: marriage and family *dharma*, professional *dharma,* social *dharma,* etc.[178]

From the beginning of the Hindu tradition -- from the Vedic times (*c.* 15th to 10th century B.C.) -- this order is seen as comprising three orders: "cosmic, social and human."[179] This order is seen as an integrated whole. This vertical and horizontal world-view is the basis of life and liberation, the ultimate concern of every religion. "We are called upon to discern the meaning of the signs of the times and participate with all men of good will in the building up of a universal brotherhood of love."[180]

---

[178] DSA, "Karma Marga and Spirituality of All-Round Presence and Awareness - Solution to a Problem both Ancient and Modern, Hindu and Christian", in: Id. (ed.), *Indian Christian Spirituality,* op. cit., p. 171. (Numberings of the text have been omitted in the quote).

[179] Ibid.

[180] DSA, *Theology of Evangelization,* op. cit., p. 29. (Cf. also *Declaration of the international Theological Conference on Evangelization and Dialogue in India,* 1971, no. 2).

In this above perspective of creation Amalor calls for dialogue and collaboration among the religions of the world. People of various religions are called to consciously collaboration with God and with one another in the transformation of man and his society. God is not exclusively Christian. He is the God of all, Christians as well others; he is the creator of all humanity. He is the God of peace (cf. Heb. 13:20; 1 Cor. 14:33; Prov. 11:30), not of war (cf. Ps. 46:9; Is. 2:4).

The Pauline concept of 'new creation' in Jesus Christ is very important in the concept of chaos, creation and reconciliation. Paul sees the creation and consummation of the world in Jesus Christ. He sees Christ as the light of the world. He sees God's creation of light in and through Christ (cf. 2 Cor. 4:6). Jesus Christ is the light that shines in the darkness of the world; he gives life and order to the chaos of the world; he enlightens and strengthens every heart and every religious tradition to know the one true God, to obtain unity and peace in the one true God, and to love and serve him and, thus, have life and salvation.[181]

### 4.2. *One Human Family and the Pleroma of Christ*[182] *(Gen. 1:27; Ps. 2:8; Lk. 8:19-21; Gal. 3:28; Eph. 2:11-22; Col. 1:15-20, 2:10)*

"So God created humankind in his image ... male and female he created them" (Gen. 1:27).

In the theology of other religions it is very important to see the whole world, the whole of humankind, that is, all people of different religions and ideologies, as belonging to the one human family (*manuṣya jāti*). This is the family of Adam and Eve, 'the mother of all living' (Gen. 3:20). The word for *Adam* (Heb.) is *Ādi-Puruṣa* or *Ādamī* (Sanskrit and Hindi) which signifies the *first* man or woman in the order of humankind. All are children of God.

> In the beginning God created heavens and earth.... He placed man in this world as its master, 'to fill the earth and subdue it'. Under this dynamism, the human family [*manuṣya jāti*] embarked on a journey

---

[181] Cf. *TNJBC*, 82:13 & 37.

[182] The *pleroma* of Christ will be dealt in detail in chapter three. We see this point here in brief.

towards its destiny, on a journey that enables man to reach his fulfillment both as person and as a community. Engaged in mastering nature ... man tries to create for himself a world of freedom, justice and peace. During the course of this journey men realized that they are a *community* -- they share common aspirations, common life-situations, common difficulties and one life goal.[183]

Since all humanity owes its origin to God, naturally, it longs for God. God is the origin and end of all. Therefore, all humanity, nay the whole creation, cries out "Abba! Father!" (Gal. 4:6; cf. Rom. 8:21-23), and the Father has responded to this 'cry' of creation in a very special way in Jesus Christ his Son (cf. Col. 1:15-20; 2:10). God has confirmed the oneness of human family with his everlasting covenant with mankind in his Son Jesus Christ. People of different religions, "circumcised" or "uncircumcised", are *one* in Christ Jesus (cf. Eph. 2:11-22) in whom all are "built together spiritually [in the Spirit] into a dwelling place for God" (Eph. 2:22). This is the family of "those who hear the word of God and do it" (Lk. 8:21).

### *4.3. Need of Liberation:[184] From Adam to Exodus to the Paschal Event in Jesus Christ (Gen. 3:1-24; Ex. 1-14; Ps. 62:1; Jn. 15:5; Rom. 1:17-32, 5:12-21; 1 Cor. 15:45)*

The world is to be liberated from sin; it needs a liberator. Jesus says, "I am the vine, you are the branches ... apart from me you can do nothing." (Jn.15:5).

What is sin? We can define sin as "any thought, word or deed that deliberately disobeys God's will and in some way rejects the divine goodness and love."[185] Sin in Hebrew in the Old Testament is called *haṭṭa* ("missing the mark"), *pesha* ("transgression of orders or revolt against superiors") and *'awôn* ("guilt stemming from iniquity").[186] That is to say

---

183 DSA, *Theology of Evangelization*, op. cit., p. 22.

184 The point of *salvation/liberation* will be dealt in detail in the later chapters when we will be dealing with salvation in Jesus Christ and the salvific value of other religions.

185 G. O'Collins, S.J. and E.G. Farrugia, S.J., *A Concise Dictionary of Theology*, op. cit., p. 222.

186 Cf. ibid.

sin signifies something *away from* God. In the context of the Last Judgement, Jesus speaks of the sin of commission as well as of omission. Whatever one does or does not do to one's brothers and sisters in need, one does or does not do it to Jesus himself (cf. 25:31-46; Lk. 10:25-37).

Starting from the sin of Adam and Eve (cf. Gen. 3:1-24), the Old Testament tells a story of human sin, repeatedly denouncing, thereby, idolatry, injustice, social as well as personal sinful acts and failures (cf. Jer. 31:29-30; Ezek. 18:1-4). The sin of Adam and Eve which we call the 'original sin' signifies that: (i) In the first man, Adam, all humankind, both "Jews" as well as "Gentiles", is somehow or other fallen into sin (cf. Rom. 1:18-32). It has become a victim of sin. It experiences a sinful situation in the world. (ii) Left to himself man cannot save himself and his situation. For God says that apart from him man can do nothing (cf. Jn. 15:5). Without the creator, the creature vanishes (cf. *GS* 36). (iii) Man needs salvation. He needs a saviour.

The opposite of sin is salvation which would imply a state of being *with* God, being in *union* with God, which in turn results in communion (*koinonia*) with one's fellow beings (cf. 1 Jn. 2:9-11; 4:7-8). In Hinduism we rightly call it *yoga*, union of *self* with Brahman here on earth (*jīvan mukti*) and hereafter (*videha mukti*).

The central message of the Bible is salvation, the kingdom of God (cf. Mk. 1:15), to which Jesus came to proclaim here on this earth so ardently. He said, "I came to bring fire to the earth, and how I wish it were already kindled!" (Lk. 12:49). This is the kingdom of God which is "not food and drink but *righteousness* and *peace* and *joy* in the Holy Spirit" (Rom. 14:17). It is the kingdom of a "a new heaven and a new earth" (Rev. 21:1; cf. Is. 65:17). This was the vision of Jesus which he wished as already burning on this earth. For the cause of this vision he lived even at the risk of a sword and separation (cf. Matt. 10:34-39) and died, accepting even a "death on a cross" (Phil. 2:8).

The need of liberation and of a liberator is seen from the very first man, Adam, to the Exodus event, culminating in the Paschal mystery of Christ. This is the vision of liberation, a liberation of all, "where on the basis of equality, justice and love, peace and joy will reign. This is the new heaven and new earth that men [of all religions] have been struggling to create under the dynamism of the first creation and which God has made possible through Christ at the end of time."[187]

The very same notion of the need of deliverance and the deliverer is found in other religions too. For example, we read in the Bhagavad-gītā:

> For whenever the law of righteousness withers away, and lawlessness raises its head, then do I generate myself on earth (4.7).
> For the protection of the good, for the destruction of evil-doers, for the setting up of righteousness, I come into being, age to age (4.8).

The need of humankind of a deliverer is beautifully depicted in Genesis: "And the Lord God made garments of skins for the man and for his wife, and *clothed* them" (3:21).

### *4.4. 'On Earth As It is in Heaven': The Person-centered Law, Justice and Love (Matt. 6:9-13; Jn. 4:34; 8:55; Rom. 14:17; 1 Jn. 2:9-11; 4:20)*

Jesus says: "My food is to do the will of him who sent me and to complete his work" (Jn. 4:34, cf. 5:30, 6:38; Matt. 26:42; Heb. 10:7).

(i) What was the will of God for Jesus? It was to save the world. "For God so loved the world that he gave his only Son, so that everyone who believes in him may not perish but have eternal life" (Jn. 3:16). Jesus is God's love, "the Word become flesh" (Jn.1:14). He is "full of grace and truth" (Jn. 1:14). God "desires everyone [every human person of any religion] to be saved and to come to the knowledge of the truth" (1 Tim. 2:4; cf. also the Book of Jonah). Jesus came on earth to do his Father's will. In other words, God has fulfilled his will and his promise to save all humankind in his Son Jesus Christ (cf. Gen. 3:15; Matt. 18:11*h*; Gal. 4:4; 1 Jn. 4:9; Lk. 3:6; Is. 40:3-5; 1 Tim. 1:15) from sin, Satan and the wages of sin, death (cf. Rom. 6:23).

(ii) What is the will of God for us? It is our salvation and sanctification, the fullness of life, our wholeness and holiness (cf. 1 Thess. 4:2-7). Jesus has taught us to pray: "Your will be done, on earth as it is in heaven" (Matt. 6:10). In the prayer of the 'Our Father' (Matt. 6:9-13),[188]

---

[187] DSA, *Theology of Evangelization,* op. cit., pp. 24-25.

[188] We do not go for paraphrasing the 'Our Father'; it would be beyond our scope here.

Jesus shows us what is the will of God for us and he calls us to live the will of God on earth with one another, which we are to work out, not in the power of the law but in *faith* and *love* (cf. Matt. 17:20; Acts 26:18; Rom. 5:1; Gal. 2:16; Eph. 2:8; Heb. 11:33). God calls us to do his will and he gives us the necessary strength to fulfill it.

The question may arise here as to how the people of other religions come to know God and his will. How are they to know the truth and do what is right and just? A sincere search for God is an essential and constitutive dimension of humanity. It springs from the very human nature that is created in the image of God. From the very beginning of the world and history mankind has been longing for God, for truth and life. Thus, even without knowing the specific revelation of God in Jesus Christ, people have known how to turn themselves to the true God (cf. Sir. 17:1-8; Gen. 4:25; Ps. 14:1-2; Wis. 13:11; Rom. 1:19-20).

There are various laws and regulations in the world. But all these human laws and regulations are well summed up in the words of Jesus: "You shall love the Lord your God with all your heart and with all your mind.... And ... you shall love your neighbour as yourself" (Matt. 22:37-39). The love of God is reflected in the love of one's neighbour and vice versa (cf. 1 Jn. 2:9-11). In summing up the Decalogue (cf. Ex. 20: 2-17), Jesus emphasizes the love of neighbour and brings down, so to say, the "notional" love of God of the Pharisees, the law, to the practical love of one's neighbour. His is, therefore, a *person-centered* law, the law of love. In other words, the love of God asks for the love and service of man. For, "Those who say, 'I love God', and hate their brothers and sisters, are liars" (1 Jn. 4:20). Human laws must, therefore, "'gaze upon the world which is the theatre of man's history' (*GS* 2). Undoubtedly 'the human person deserves to be preserved, human society deserves to be renewed.' Hence the pivotal point ... will be 'man himself, whole and entire' (*GS* 3)."[189]

For Paul the kingdom of God, the kingdom of justice and peace, consists in the life-giving relationship of "righteousness and peace and joy in the Holy Spirit" (Rom. 14:17). Justice is in living in right relationship with others. It is the relationship of love and humanization -- a relationship which demands to take the human person, history and society seriously in line with the act of creation itself (cf. Gen. 1:27-28). This is the kingdom Jesus came to proclaim to the world (cf. Mk. 1:15), and he

---

[189] DSA, *Approaches,* op. cit., p. 21.

established the Church as the nucleus and the sacrament of this kingdom. In this kingdom God is glorified and man is humanized and sanctified. This is the 'anthropological'[190] or 'person-centered' approach of following the Lord upon this earth, his discipleship.

## 5. Conclusion

The God of salvation is the God of history. God always reveals his plan in history, in the signs of the times. His universal salvific plan is to be discovered and lived in the "contingent data"[191] of our historical zig-zags, especially in the context of religious pluralism today.

Amalor differentiates the Vatican II world-view or what he calls the biblical or the new Christian world-view of other religions from the pre-Vatican II or the traditional Christian world-view. The Vatican II world-view is an inclusive view. It recognizes the presence of God in other religions, and looks for dialogue and collaboration with others in all sincerity and truth. The traditional Christian world-view is instead an exclusive view. It looks for condemnation of others, rather than collaboration. It should be rectified and replaced by the biblical world-view.

God wills the salvation of all mankind (cf. 1 Tim. 2:4). In the fullness of time, he has definitively revealed himself in the historical event of Jesus Christ, his Son, the Word become flesh in history. The mystery of this 'historicity', the 'humanity' of God in the person of Jesus Christ, makes the Christian revelation a "positive" and specific one in the history of salvation. God's specific revelation in the historical Jesus Christ event is enshrined in the Bible. The Bible is the living word of the living God.

God now continues to reveal himself and to "gather up all things in him, things in heaven and things on earth" (Eph. 1:10) in and through

---

190 'The law is for man and not man for the law' - this is in short the 'anthropological approach' of DSA. In this approach he speaks of liberation and salvation or evangelization in the process of 'humanization', 'human justice and peace'. Cf.: DSA, *Approaches*, op. cit., p. 20ff; id., *The Theology of 'Indirect Evangelization'*, op. cit.; id. (ed.): *The Indian Church in the Struggle for a New society*, NBCLC, Bangalore, 1981; id. (ed.), *The Kingdom of God. Jesus' Vision of a New Society* (by George Soares Prabhu), NBCLC, Bangalore, 1981; etc. The anthropological approach of the kingdom will be seen in chapter six.

191 The term is taken from J. Fuellenbach, S.V.D., *Hermeneutics, Marxism and Liberation Theology*, Divine Word Publications, Manila, 1989, p. 32.

Christ (cf. Rev. 12:10). In Christ there is "the new life of the Spirit" (Rom. 7:6), a new society, a new humanity, a new Jerusalem (cf. 2 Cor. 5:17; 1 Cor. 8:6; Rev. 21:1-2). The Bible says: "How very good and pleasant it is when kindred live together in unity" (Ps. 133:1). In Christ all "are one" (Gal. 3:28). All peoples and religions of the world are united and oriented to God in and through Christ. The Church is the instrument of this unity. She is the sacrament of the universal salvation, the sacrament of Christ on earth.

## CHAPTER TWO

## ANALYSIS AND APPLICATION OF THE VATICAN II SOURCES

### 1. Introduction

Catholic theology has been, right from the very beginning, taught and done "in the light of faith and under the guidance of the Church's authority" (*OT* 16). However, it is only in the Council of Vatican II (1962-1965) for the first time, the Church officially recognized and accepted other religious traditions as "religions".

The Church's theological application of *Extra Ecclesiam nulla salus*[1] in the Council of Florence (1439-1445), which was originally meant for the Copts (Jacobites) for the "reunion" with the Roman Catholic Church, has been reinterpreted and clarified today.[2] The Jansenist proposition that said that "no grace is granted outside the Church" had already been condemned by Clement XI in 1713 (cf. DS 2429).[3]After the Second Vatican Council, the Church concedes more and more to the recognition of other religions and the principle of religious liberty. The Council recognizes the moral, spiritual and salvific values of these religions and urges the Church not only to enter into friendly dialogue with their adherents but also in a more open attitude to learn from their traditions in mutual respect and collaboration in our common search for truth and salvation. The Council recognizes the presence of the Holy Spirit in other religions. In the conciliar ecclesiology, the Church is no longer described as a society on a par with structures like the state but as the mystery of God's presence in the world, as a sign and sacrament of God's kingdom on earth.[4] In short, the Church "examines with great attention what is her relation to non-Christian religions" (*NA* 1).

In her sincere desire to implement the theology of Vatican II the

---

[1] *Extra Ecclesiam nulla salus:* The Council of Florence took it from the Treatise on Faith of Fulgentius of Ruspe (457-533), an African bishop and disciple of St. Augustine.

[2] Cf. ND, pp. 284-285.

[3] Cf. ibid., p. 378.

[4] Cf. David Bosch, *Transforming Mission. Paradigm Shifts in Theology of Mission,* Orbis Books, Maryknoll, New York, 1991, pp. 371-373.

Church has been now explicitly and inevitably involved in her contact and deliberations with other religious traditions and cultures of the world. The population statistics today shows that in the enormous span of human history the Judeo-Christian event fills only a tiny fraction, and that those who profess Jesus Christ as the Lord are a diminishing minority in the world. This naturally leads the Church to a more intense theological reflection in her contact and deliberations with other religions. The Church's various conciliar documents, propositions and papal pronouncements with regard to other religions[5] only show her contact with them in her constant search for truth and life.

## 2. Vatican II and the New Missionary Approach

According to Karl Rahner Vatican II is the Church's first official self-actualization as a world Church with a world-wide participation and, thereby, the emergence of a universal and catholic theology.[6] Amalor too sees Vatican II as one of the many marvels God has done in our age, a *kairos* in our history. His theology is very much influenced and supported by the new theology ushered in by Vatican II. He calls for sincere implementation of the new vision of Vatican II. He says:

> One such marvel is the neo-pentecostal event of the II Vatican Ecumenical Council of 1962-1965! God has done *magnalia* and *mirabilia* in this *kairos* of history! *Kairos* has something unrepeatable in it, hence it contains a specific revelation and demands of us a unique response. If we miss it, we miss it forever. There is something ineluctable and irrevocable about it. Some people bemoan the present, regret what has happened and are getting upset at the way the world is going and the trend history is taking, with certain pessimism

---

[5] For the conciliar and papal documents with regard to other religions in detail see: ND 1001-1065.

[6] Cf. John Fuellenbach, S.V.D., *Hermeneutics, Marxism and Liberation Theology*, op. cit., pp. 2-9. K. Rahner (1979) divided the history of the Church into three periods: (i) the short period of Jewish Christianity, (ii) the period of Hellenism and of European culture and civilization, and (iii) the period in which the sphere of the Church's life is in fact the entire world (Vatican II).

> and negative attitude. As for us let us rejoice that we are people of this century and this age! Citizens of this world and this country! It is worth living just for the unique event of the Ecumenical Council and its impact on our life![7]

Amalor's studies at the *Institut Catholique de Paris*[8] enabled him to follow the Second Vatican Council very closely and "as an accredited journalist he came into contact with prominent bishops and best theologians. This shaped him more than his academic studies. His stay in Europe from 1962-1965 enabled him to absorb the spirit of Vatican II. That in particular prepared him to spearhead the Vatican II renewal in India."[9] In both his books: *L'Inde à la rencontre du Seigneur* (1964) and *Destinée de l'Église dans l'Inde d'aujourd'hui* (1967), the focus of his reflection is the Church's contact with other religions and her missionary activity in India. Amalor attributes the missionary crisis, among others and above all, to missionary's prejudice or misunderstanding of other religions. He calls for the sufficient reading and implementation of Vatican II. He writes:

> It is everyone's knowledge that there is today a crisis in the missionary vocation, missionary motivation and missionary activity of the Church. This is due, on the one hand, to the new attitudes towards non-Christian religions and better appreciation of them as formulated by recent theological research and affirmed by the documents of the Vatican Council II. This partly condemns the earlier attitudes towards the world religions and widens the missionary aims and motivation as understood hitherto. On the other hand, the doctrine of Vatican II on the mission of the Church, ... and its relation with other religions as taught in three important documents (*Ad Gentes, Lumen Gentium, Nostra Aetate*) and the new insights and trends in mission theology

---

[7] See as quoted by Gerwin van Leeuwen, in: Id., *Fully Indian - Authentically Christian,* op. cit.,
p. 17 (reference 1). Amalor speaks in his key-note address on the occasion of the 20th anniversary of the NBCLC. (Only available in cyclostyled form).

[8] DSA's studies in Paris show his interest in other religions. His study there took the form of two books: *L'Inde à la rencontre du Seigneur* (1964), and *Destinée de l'Église dans l'Inde d'aujourd'hui* (1967).

[9] Gerwin van Leeuwen, "Fr. D. S. Amalorpavadass (1932-1990)", in: Paul Puthanangady, S.D.B. (ed.), *Church in India: Institution or Movement?,* op. cit., pp. xi-xii.

as expounded by some theologians have not only not been sufficiently understood, but often enough misunderstood.[10]

As Director of the NBCLC, Amalor took part in various discussions and seminars dealing with the Church's role, her approach and attitude towards other religions.[11] He was called upon to clarify the new approach outlined by the Council with regard to other religions and to explain its basis, that is, to expound the 'new' global or the Vatican II vision of reality and ecclesiology in contrast to the commonly held 'old' or the pre-Vatican II vision of reality.

Amalor bases his theology of other religions on the 'new' global vision. We have already seen in chapter one the interrelations and the theological implications of the four elements that go to make up the reality: God, man, the world, and the Church. In the 'old' vision, the four elements engender a pejorative attitude towards other religions and ideologies.[12] Whereas, according to the Vatican II vision of reality, the whole of the human society is caught up in the movement of history towards its destiny. All human beings, Christians and others, are fellow pilgrims in genuine belonging and vital solidarity, identified with the common cause, committed to liberation, development and the realization of a just human society.[13] Seen in this perspective Christians are called to become "a most sure seed of unity, hope and salvation for the whole human race" (*LG* 1). Then Christianity will be relevant to others, inasmuch as it brings them hope and inspiration, light, truth and salvation.[14]

Unlike the pre-Vatican concept of the Church's mission and missionary activity, often understood in terms of imperial conquests, Amalor refers to the mission today in an integrated approach of words and deeds, love and service,[15] that is, in its wider significance of the kingdom of God,

---

10 DSA, *Approaches,* op. cit., p. 7. Cf. also: Id., *Theology of Evangelization,* op. cit., p. 12 where he gives the numbers of Vatican II: *LG* 16, *AG* 7, *GS* 22.

11 Cf. DSA, *Theology of Evangelization,* op. cit., pp. 10-11.

12 Cf. DSA, *Our Christian World Vision,* op. cit., p. 10; id., *Approaches,* op. cit., pp. 15-16; id., *Approach,* op. cit., pp. 24-25.

13 Cf. DSA, *Approach,* op. cit., p. 25. Cf. also: *NA* 1.

14 Cf. DSA, *Our Christian World Vision,* op. cit., p. 19.

15 Cf. DSA, *Approach,* op. cit., p. 91; also: Id., *Theology of Development,* op. cit., pp. 25-26.

the kingdom of justice, peace and joy in the world.[16] It is "everything that the Church does in service of the Kingdom of God."[17] Today mission is

> no more to be understood in terms of imperialist conquest, geographical expansion, territorial limits, numerical additions, but by the all-round, ever-ready presence through the spirit of Christ which is one of humble and loving service, losing, so to say, one's identity in order to live in a new way to make others live.[18]

Amalor describes his understanding of the Church, which he frequently repeats, as "taken up in the tension between the first and the second coming of the Lord, between his Pasch and Parousia, the Church, the community of Christ's disciples, has to fulfill her eschatological mission."[19] The missionary activity of the Church finds its meaning, origin and end in God's salvific action in the paschal mystery of Jesus Christ.[20] The Church is to continue the universal salvific mission of Christ on earth, and thus work for the realization of his eschatological pleroma.[21] Amalor sees the mission of the Church based on the mission-mandate of Christ to his disciples: "You will be my witnesses ... to the ends of the earth" (Acts 1:8); and, "Go therefore and make disciples of all nations" (Matt. 28:19).[22]

---

[16] Cf. Cyril De Souza, S.D.B., *Catechesis for India Today*, op. cit., p. 51.

[17] William McConville, "Mission", in: Joseph Komonchak and Co. (eds), *The New Dictionary of Theology*, Glacier Inc., Wilmington, p. 664.

[18] DSA, *Preaching the Gospel Today. Main Problems in Mission Lands*, NBCLC, Bangalore, 1973, p. 8.

[19] DSA, *Theology of Catechesis*, NBCLC, Bangalore, 1973 (reprint), p. 9; see also: Id., *L'Inde à la rencontre du Seigneur*, op. cit., p. 13.

[20] Cf. François-Xavier Durrwell, *La résurrection de Jesus, mystère de salut*, Éditions Xavier Mappus, Le Puy, 1954, p. 315, as referred to by DSA in: Id, *L'Inde à la rencontre du Seigneur*, op. cit., p. 13.

[21] Cf. DSA, *Destinée*, op. cit., p. 15 where regarding the history of salvation and the present time of the Church, DSA refers to: Oscar Cullmann, *Christ et le Temps*, Delachaux & Niestlé, Neuchatêl, 1957, pp. 103 & 110.

[22] Cf. DSA, *L'Inde à la rencontre du Seigneur*, op. cit., p. 13; see also: Id., *Destinée*, op. cit., p. 17. DSA describes the enthusiasm of the early Christians to fulfill the mission-mandate of Christ with the hope of his second coming with a variety of expressions: 'to take the Gospel', 'to announce the Gospel', etc., taken from St. Paul: Rom. 1:14; 15:22-29; 1 Cor. 9:16, 18, 22-23; 2 Tim. 4:6-7; etc. (Cf. *L'Inde à la rencontre du Seigneur*, pp. 13-15).

The Church's mission is, therefore, to preach the Gospel. "All of us should redouble our zeal to fulfill this task."[23]

The Church fulfills her unique mission by exercising her triple ministry: the prophetic (word), the liturgical (worship), and the directive (guidance).[24] These three ministries of the Church are the three dimensions of the one holistic saving mission of Christ -- the king, the priest and the prophet -- and hence they are complementary.[25] The Church's mission is, therefore, basically the mission of the Word which became flesh and life for all mankind (cf. Jn. 1:1-18).

The ministry of the Word embraces different functions in the Church: (i) the *magisterium* as the guardian, transmitter and interpreter of the deposit of faith; (ii) theology and theologizing as a reflection on faith and Christian experience or as a systematic treatment and scientific investigation of the truth of faith; and (iii) pastoral ministry of the Word through evangelization, catechesis and homily.[26]

Vatican II has widened the Church's attitude towards other religions and deepened her commitment to them. Hence, there arises the need for a post-Conciliar theology of religions, which necessarily includes the consideration of these points: evangelization, inculturation, inter-religious dialogue and collaboration, the universal and the local Church, the hierarchy, etc.[27]

---

[23] DSA, *Vision, Thrust and Policy for Evangelization,* NBCLC, Bangalore, 1985, p. 5. Here the words of Amalor are directed to the CBCI Commission for Proclamation, Ecumenism, Dialogue & Social Communication (1983).

[24] Cf. DSA, *L'Inde à la rencontre du Seigneur,* op. cit., p. 45. T. Groome, like Alberich, refers to four ministries of the Church: word, community, worship, and service; see: Thomas Groome, *Sharing Faith. A Comparative Approach to Religious Education & Pastoral Ministry. The Way of Shared Praxis,* Harper-Collins Publishers, New York, 1991, pp. 301-303, as cited by Cyril De Souza, in: id, *Catechesis for India today,* op. cit., p. 56 (footnote 31). Amalor instead always referred to the triple dimension of the Church's mission.

[25] For further explanation of the complementary relationships among these three ministries of the Church, see: Cyril De Souza, S.D.B., *Catechesis for India Today,* op. cit., pp. 58-63.

[26] Cf. DSA, *Theology of Catechesis,* op. cit., p. 10. Cf. also: *GCD (General Catechetical Directory)* 17, as cited by Cyril De Souza, in: Id., *Catechesis for India Today,* op. cit., p. 67. Our treatment here will be focused on theology and evangelization or theology of evangelization.

[27] Cf. DSA, *Preaching the Gospel Today. Main Problems in Mission Lands,* op. cit., pp. 25-26; id., *Destinée,* op. cit., pp. 210-211; Antony Mookenthottam, *Indian*

We proceed to examine some of these points here in this chapter while other points are or will be dealt in other chapters.[28]

## 3. Evangelization: The Indo-Asian Scenario

### *3.1. Theology of Evangelization*

#### *3.1.1. Evangelization: Sharing a unique experience of God in Jesus Christ*

The Church, by her very nature, is missionary (cf. *EN* 14). To effectively carry out her missionary call for salvation, the Church needs theology. This point of the theology of evangelization is very much stressed in Vatican II (cf. *AG* 1; *Ecclesiae Sanctae* 1).

Evangelization is the proclamation of the Good News, the good news of salvation in Jesus Christ addressed to men, in order to enable them to have faith and life in him and to have full fellowship with all men.[29] Amalor defines evangelization in line with the Special Theological Committee at Nagpur as "the proclamation of the good news of salvation in Jesus Christ by the Church to men who do not know him in order to bring them to the faith and to fellowship in him."[30]

Before going into further detail, Amalor likes to briefly explain the constituent elements of evangelization found in this above definition. These are: (i) Jesus Christ, (ii) salvation in Jesus Christ, (iii) Evangelium, the Good News, (iv) through word and deed, (v) by the Church, (vi) to lead men to the response of faith, (vii) in the Spirit.

##### *3.1.1.1. Jesus Christ*

Evangelization is Christocentric. Jesus Christ is everything in evangelization. He is the source and substance, object and end of it. "If Christ is absent, all our activity however relevant to man and his life, which does not spring from and orient toward Jesus Christ, is not

---

*Theological Tendencies,* op. cit., pp. 84-85.

28 However, to treat all the above mentioned points in equal length and intensity is beyond our scope here.

29 Cf. DSA, "Approach", in: *Life and Light We Seek to Share,* op. cit., p. 18.

30 Ibid., p. 78.

evangelization. Any activity which does not share our experience with him and lead others to an encounter and fellowship with him in *faith* will not be evangelization."[31]

> Evangelization is a process in which there are stages. Men's relationship with Jesus ranges from total ignorance to explicit knowledge of him. In between there are many who follow him implicitly, led by his Spirit, incarnating his love through service, translating his values through lives, and working for his cause.[32]

Amalor, referring to the Declaration of the Nagpur Conference, says that evangelists will have to look carefully into each situation what aspect has to be explained or brought home to the audience. At one stage or other, Jesus Christ should be explicitly proclaimed as the one sent by the Father to inaugurate his Fatherly rule by which he wants to unify mankind and to create a new world freed from sin and enslavement of the forces of evil (DNC 18).[33]

#### *3.1.1.2. Salvation in Jesus Christ: Existential and eschatological*

Salvation is the result of God's loving and eternal plan unfolded through the ages, definitively revealed and realized in the historical event of Jesus Christ who in his death and resurrection is constituted Lord and head of the new community of faith and salvation.

> The content of this salvation is the liberation of the *whole* man and the whole of mankind from the fetters of law, sin and death and leading them to intimate union with God and with one another. This saving activity of God has physical and spiritual, this-worldly and other-worldly, existential and eschatological dimensions.[34]

This liberating and life-giving action of God corresponds to the "basic aspiration of India today towards liberation from every form of

---

[31] Ibid.

[32] Ibid., pp. 78-79..

[33] Cf. ibid., p. 79.

[34] Ibid.

oppression and servitude so that her children may realize their basic vocation to be truly and fully human (SCNC; DNC 18)."[35]

*3.1.1.3. Evangelium, the Good News: Gift of salvation*

The universal salvation in Jesus Christ should be proclaimed and presented to people of other religions as *good news,* something they do not have, but to which they aspire and which they get now. It should be a message which raises an echo in their hearts, makes them vibrate with enthusiasm and corresponds to their innermost yearnings.

The Good News of Jesus Christ is God's gift of salvation for all men in Christ through whom they are reconciled with God and their fellowmen, and led to the fulfilment of their destiny in God (SCNC).[36]

*3.1.1.4. Through word and deed: Task of collaboration*

The good news of salvation in Jesus Christ is communicated through words and deeds. The oral proclamation must be accompanied by deeds, by a witnessing of Christian life, an existence lived in the Spirit. It means embodying Christian values, witnessing to the saving love of God in Christ, collaborating with him in creating and radiating the fellowship of a community of all men and religions, and thus, creating a new heaven and a new earth of justice, peace and joy in the Holy Spirit.[37]

*3.1.1.5. By the Church: How and why?*

It is the privilege and duty of the Church, the Christian community, to proclaim Christ, to bear witness to him and to announce the salvation realized in him. The Church has a double reason to do so: (i) intrinsically, due to the saving experience she has had with the risen Lord, which urges her to share this experience with others; (ii) extrinsically, because Christ has commissioned her to proclaim: "All authority in heaven and on earth has been given to me. Go therefore and make disciples of all nations, baptizing them in the name of the Father and of the Son and of the Holy Spirit" (Matt. 28:18-19).

---

[35] As quoted by DSA, in: Ibid.

[36] Cf. ibid.

[37] Cf. ibid., p. 80.

> The Church is the dynamic agent within the world and the historical expression of the new humanity liberated and re-created in Christ through the Spirit (DNC 19). She is not only the agent, but also the sign, in the sense that she contains what she announces and wants to share. She is a sacrament; a universal sacrament of salvation must be an effective sign for all men. Hence the exigency to be and to appear as a group of people who are reconciled, united, who live the Gospel, who are happy and saved, who manifest fellowship with God and man. Being in pilgrimage she is subject to weakness and temptation, but her witness is precisely in the struggle to be what she should be.[38]

In this above comprehension of the Church one immediately sees her nature and task in the world. "The Church is in the last period of history; time is short; salvation must reach the whole of mankind; so the Church experiences an urgency to share her Christian experience."[39] The missionaries are at the service of the Good News. They have to run from place to place to proclaim the Word, in spite of their inadequacy and obstacles, risking their life at the service of the Word.[40]

*3.1.1.6. The aim: To lead men to the response of faith in Jesus Christ*

The aim of evangelization is to lead man to salvation in Christ, that is, to lead him to a living, active and conscious faith in Jesus Christ.

> This is the aim of evangelization. Those who hear the proclamation of the Good News should be enabled to open themselves, to accept the self-gift of God in Jesus Christ and to surrender to him unreservedly by a total gift of themselves and a commitment to live according to his word. This is Faith. Hence it is not sufficient that a man be saved in his own religion or life-situation through an implicit and unconscious faith in Christ. He should be led to an explicit knowledge of, and conscious faith in Christ; for no other name has been given under the sky by which man can be saved (Acts 4:12).[41]

---

[38] Ibid.

[39] Ibid.

[40] Cf. ibid., pp. 80-81.

[41] Ibid., p. 81.

Evangelization must also be addressed to Christians themselves so that they know Christ more clearly, love him more deeply and follow him more closely and faithfully.

> Evangelization, let it be well noted, is also addressed to Christians: (1) so that our dormant faith may be awakened; (2) so that our theoretical, verbal and oral faith must be transformed into a practical, living and active faith, shown by deeds, by a life of Christian witnessing; (3) so that our immature faith may be purified of childish fixations and go into the full stature of Christ (cf. Eph. 4:13).[42]

*3.1.1.7. In the Spirit: Source and inspiration*

Evangelization is not purely human activity. It is the work of Christ, led by his Spirit and man is called to cooperate with him.

> It is the Spirit abiding in the Church who gives her a paschal experience of Christ; it is the Spirit who urges her to go forth and to proclaim; it is the Spirit who inspires her to say what, when, where and how. It is the Spirit who gives missionaries courage and zeal, who shows them the way, and directs their way, to go here or there, to Asia or Europe (Acts 16:6-10), to tribals or to Hindus, to Buddhists, to Muslims, to Harijans or caste people.... In short, the Spirit blows where he wills (Jn. 3:8), and distributes charisms to those whom he wills (Rom. 12:4-8; 1 Cor. 12: 4-11; esp. 1 Cor. 12:11); and the work of the Church in evangelization can be styled as a response of the Church to be at the *service of the Spirit*.[43]

Evangelization is an event of the Spirit. It is the Spirit who inspires and gives courage and strength for the apostolate to build up the Church of Christ here on earth (cf. Eph. 4:12). On the part of man, evangelization needs a careful planning, technical organization and efficient implementation.

The Spirit is active and operative in the world, in the religions of the world. No one can dare quench the Spirit for he cannot be quenched (cf. 1 Thess. 5:19). The Church stands for the outpouring of the Spirit in a new

---

[42] Ibid.

[43] Ibid., pp. 81-82.

Pentecost (cf. Acts 2) for a new apostolic endeavour of country-wide, nay, world-wide evangelization! "Jesus Christ is Lord, to the glory of God the Father" (Phil. 2:11).[44]

After considering what is evangelization, we pass on to the hermeneutics of evangelization.

### *3.1.2. Locus of theological reflection on evangelization: Hermeneutics*

A successful and effective evangelization will always need its hermeneutics. One's attitude to and success in evangelization will very much depend upon one's understanding and interpretation of Christ and his Gospel, the Church, the world and history, revelation and salvation in other religions, religion and society, the understanding and interpretation of the particular reality and tools of analysis and assessment of it, and one's point of departure in a particular socio-religious and cultural context. This is in short the hermeneutics of evangelization.

Amalor considers this subject under these headings:[45]

(i) approach to understanding of the reality as basis for theological reflection.

(ii) Jesus Christ and the Church.

(iii) the Church's role in the context of the Indian reality.

(iv) the Church in India to be evangelized, to be fit for evangelization.

#### *3.1.2.1. Approach to understanding the reality: Basis for theological reflection*

Evangelization is the proclamation of the universal liberation of God in Christ. Christ came to liberate all mankind from all forms of sin, slavery and alienation. How to define the mission of the Church with reference to God's definitive revelation in Christ to people of other religions? What is our point of departure? Is the word that we proclaim meant for today?

---

[44] Cf. ibid., pp. 82-83.

[45] Cf. ibid., p. 20. These five points will not be dealt in five separate headings as DSA has done (see ibid., p. 21ff.). We will explain the points in different numberings and titles. Because of its importance the point of Jesus Christ with regard to other religions will be dealt in detail in a separate chapter.

Is it a word meant for India, for the world and its religions? Does its significance change when the realities are viewed as a whole in the context of India, the world and history?

The word that the Church announces in evangelization is God's word addressed to mankind. It will become a message only if it becomes a human word, meaningful to each group at a particular moment of life and history, related to the dynamics of human existence today. The word has to be, therefore, deciphered, translated and interpreted in reference to a particular context. Is our theology then an inculturated theology? What are the conditions, criteria and processes of an authentic and relevant interpretation?

When the Word is interpreted in order to be intelligible and relevant to varied and changing situations, shall we not arrive at pluralism in theology, language and communication? If pluralism is tolerated, is there no danger of unity and orthodoxy of faith in the Church? Is there then a way to combine orthodoxy and relevance, unity of faith and plurality of interpretation? Is such a combination possible without freedom and confidence, critique and support, creativity and originality? These are some of the important questions we intend to see in this point.

*(i) The type of theology we follow: Reality, the point of departure*

The Church's proclamation of the Gospel is not to be reduced to a simple act of preaching. For the relevant proclamation of the Good News, the Church must take into account these factors: the *text,* the *context,* and the *interpreter* or the prophet-agent, each of which requires a triple experience: an encounter with the Word (text), an active experience of the reality (context) and an experience of a Christian community (prophetic Church).[46]

An adequate evangelization presupposes an adequate theology. "Our approach to reality, our understanding of it, our critique of it, our discovery of God's revelation and our formulation of its message, are all determined very much by the type of theology that we follow."[47] It is indispensable, therefore, to have a correct understanding of the theology

46 Cf. DSA, *Vision, Thrust and Policy for Evangelization,* op. cit., pp. 5-8; see also: Id., "Evangelization in the Context of India", in: *Indian Theological Studies* 17 (1980) 2, pp. 98-100.

47 DSA, "Approach", *op. cit.,* p. 22.

of evangelization.

> The theology of evangelization, which is meant to make present God's saving power in this world to re-create a just and free human society and which is meant to be normative for the Church's work of evangelization, should be one that receives, understands, lives, formulates and proclaims the word starting from the reality of the world and society.[48]

*(a) Approach of theology: Reflecting the reality*

To clarify his stand on the approach of theology in relation to reality, Amalor quotes the Resolution of the World Congress of Theology on the Future of the Church (WCT), Brussels, 1970:

> Theology is a reflection of Christians upon their faith and their Christian experience in a particular time and culture. Hence, only Christian communities, involved in the life of the contemporary world and taking active responsibility within their society can fashion the theology of the future (no. 2).[49]

The above definition consists of three elements: (i) to be involved in the reality of life and society: *the world;* (ii) to be conscious members of the Christian community: *the Church;* and (iii) to do an action-reflection in faith on their experience as Christians in the world: *the word.* Here we limit ourselves to the first element: to be involved in reality, in the world. To be involved in reality is the prerequisite for any theology.[50]

Theology is a faith seeking understanding (*fides quaerens intellectum)* of God who is involved in the historical realities of the world. It is a critical faith-reflection as well as faith-praxis in a particular situation, in the signs of the times. Any theology that does not critically reflect on itself and the given reality easily falls prey to ideology. It runs the risk of falsifying and destroying reality. Theology does not study God as he is in

---

[48] Ibid., pp. 22-23.

[49] Ibid., p. 23. (The World Congress of Theology on the Future of the Church, Brussels, 12-17 September 1970, Resolution no. 2).

[50] Cf. ibid., pp. 22-27.

himself but as he reveals, relates and communicates himself to man in creation and history. Therefore, theology must be interested in the reality of God's self-communication to man, which takes place in the existential reality of the world and history, different cultures and religious traditions.

> Theology studies and is interested in the reality of God and men, in the reality of their relationship, in the reality of God's self-communication to men, which takes place in the reality of the world and history, society and life.... God is dynamically present in the reality, revealing and fulfilling his plan of salvation for mankind. Theology does not study God as he is in himself but as he reveals, relates and communicates himself to men in creation and history. Likewise man also is interested in the reality of this world and his life. He is taken up in triple dynamics of his personality development, group life and common historical adventure towards its ultimate destiny. Nothing is relevant to him that is not connected in some way with this triple dynamism.[51]

Thus, theology cannot be separated from reality. In fact, "reality becomes a theological source -- *Locus theologicus* -- for its reflection, formulation, interpretation; and if there is no reality, there will be no theology or no *raison d'être* for it."[52]

*(b) Function of theology: Interpretation*

The function of theology is to discover, interpret and express reality (cf. *GS* 3, 10, 22, 40, 42, 62). Theology has also to make a permanent critique of society and the Church and thus powerfully change the reality. For this purpose theology has to interpret the Gospel message in a meaningful way in every context, especially in the context of religious pluralism today. Its normative and dynamic function towards reality is determined, to a large extent, by its hermeneutic function and validity of its hermeneutics.[53]

---

[51] Ibid., pp. 23-24.

[52] Ibid., p. 25.

[53] Cf. ibid., p. 24.

In this connection, Amalor, quoting W. Kasper, says that we have to assert that the reality of today or the signs of the times "are endowed with hermeneutic ... function so as to disclose the hitherto undiscovered and only partly discovered aspects of the faith."[54] Again, quoting *Gaudium et Spes,* he says that the Church has to interpret the signs of the times: "*The signs of the times* which the Church has the duty of scrutinizing and interpreting in the light of the gospel, in order to respond to the perennial question which men ask, in language intelligible to each generation" (no. 4).[55]

If God continues to reveal himself and his divine plan to all humanity in the various religious traditions of mankind here and now, in life and history, how can we recognize, discern and interpret it? "This is precisely the mission of the Church. Today the Church and every Christian community animated and inspired by the Spirit ... must render a service of interpretation."[56] For this, the Church must hear, scrutinize, distinguish, decipher, judge and interpret the designs of God in our world and history (cf. *GS* 4, 11, 44) in the light of the Gospel and discover God's presence and purpose in the midst of religious pluralism and share it with others, by a relevant formulation and intelligible language.[57] Prophetism or religious pedagogy of the Church,[58] is a service of recognition, reflection on and interpretation of the signs of God's on-going revelation in view of discovering God's presence and his designs for our life and thus transform ourselves, history, society and nature. This is the Church's mission (*diakonia*) of interpretation.

The theological hermeneutics is seen in the very process of the composition of the Bible itself.[59] The Old Testament tells us how the people of Israel, reflecting in faith the reality of their history and experience under the guidance of its prophets, discovered who God is, what his plan is and what is the meaning of his interventions in their life and history. Likewise, the gospels contain the theologies of the Apostolic Churches, the fruit of their reflection and interpretation of Jesus' life and

---

[54] Ibid. DSA quotes W. Kasper from Kasper's Conference 'What is Theology' at the WCT.

[55] See as quoted in: Ibid.

[56] Ibid., p. 29.

[57] Cf. ibid.

[58] Cf. ibid., 30.

[59] Cf. ibid., pp. 24-25.

teaching in the context of their own Christian life and missionary problems. Paul interpreted the Christian message in the context of his audience, the "gentile" world. He preached Christ within the experience of the Churches to which he belonged, using their concepts and categories.

*(c) Theologizing and interpreting: A common concern of the whole Christian community*

Theology and theologizing should be a concerted effort of all the members of the whole Christian community: the magisterium, priests and religious, theologians and the laity. Each group of members in the Church has its specific role to play.[60]

> Theology is not only a specialized and professional science.... It is also a common and popular science, as it is the property and function, right and duty of the whole Christian people. Every member of the Christian community is supposed to theologize, namely to reflect together in faith on the reality of their involved experience in the world; ... thus it becomes action-reflection process in faith.... 'The major source of reference for theology today is those communities of Christians that stammer out this experience', the Christian experience as lived in the heart of this world and in this age of history.[61]

The interpretation of God's word for our times, his on-going revelation, is the prophetic function of the Church, the People of God. This prophetic function belongs to the whole Church. Before interpreting the word, the Church must hear it. Hearing the word, proclaiming it, witnessing to it and giving it a relevant interpretation is a common task of the Church. Hence anyone who does this service must belong to the community, carry out his function in dialogue and communion with it and in its name. Magisterium is to be understood within the Church as related to it and not as separate from and outside of it (cf. *LG* 9).[62]

Interpretation is a service to the Spirit who is the author of all charisms. There are different charisms, given to different groups of members

---

[60] Cf. ibid., p. 30.
[61] Ibid., p. 27.
[62] Cf. ibid., p. 30.

in the Church but coming from one and the same Spirit (cf. 1 Cor. 12:4ff). Since interpretation is the common task of the whole community,

> all the charisms, given to different groups of members in the Church for the fulfillment of its mission must be recognized, pooled together and enabled to be operative. It is for the magisterium to recognize their charisms, bring them together and to profit by them; it is a service to the Spirit, the author of the charisms.[63]

Since God's word is a living one and revelation is on-going, we are not to make of today the absolute and categorical in our language. It means that there is always the need to be open to the movement of history and change in society, to new manifestations, aspirations and challenges of the Spirit. For the Spirit only gradually leads his Church into the full truth till the Lord appears in full light.[64] The community and the magisterium within it are at the service of God and his people of different creeds, castes and cultures. In interpreting God's word, they must, as the prophets, be in full communion with God. Thus, receiving and bearing his word afresh, they may speak in his name.[65] Their language can be relevant to the world only if they are involved in the concrete reality of the world and inserted in its dynamism and history.[66] When the Church is so involved in interpreting and witnessing the word of God in different socio-religious contexts, she genuinely becomes a local Church. In this perspective, Amalor likes to assert the importance of the Indian local Church, her theology and her involvement in society. He writes:

> Theologizing is a function of Christian communities of local Churches. The Indian Church will never start theologizing unless and until she becomes genuinely a local Church. She must be incardinated in the soil, identified with the life of the Indian society, and be adult to take up full responsibility to re-think in an original way her message in the context of the particular human group and to

---

[63] Ibid.

[64] Cf. ibid., p. 31.

[65] Cf. ibid.

[66] Cf. ibid.

> reformulate her message in order to make it relevant and meaningful to them.[67]

In the Indian context theology of evangelization has to study and encounter other religions, especially Hinduism, as they constitute the vast majority of the Indian population. The real theology of evangelization can be spelt out normally only after a social and situational research and critical analysis of the reality. India is a vast country with its different social strata, religious, economic and cultural variance. Evangelization in India must take an account of its historical, anthropological and sociological data. "To start with at least a socio-religious research is called for as an imperative need for a relevant plan of evangelization.... It is a plain fact that hitherto no research has been made on the Church itself, on its role in the India of today."[68]

*(d) Theology in dialogue with society and other social human sciences*

Theology, as we have seen above, is a faith seeking understanding of God and the interpretation of reality, using the resources of reason and assisted by other sciences, chiefly human or behavioural sciences, like psychology, anthropology, sociology, economics, politics, history and philosophy.[69] To be a relevant science today, theology must get the data from these sciences and dialogue with the reality of society, that is, it has to take into consideration different cultures, arts and sciences, ideologies and religions.

> Theology today has become a partial science, along with and together with other sciences. Hence theology must get the data of reality from other sciences: physical sciences, but chiefly, human sciences or behavioural sciences like psychology, anthropology, sociology, economics, politics and history. In order to function, it should dialogue with other sciences. This dialogue is with regard not only to method and technique, but also to the very content of theology.[70]

---

67 DSA, *Approach,* op. cit., p. 17.

68 DSA, "Approach", p. 26.

69 Cf. ibid., p. 25.

70 Ibid.

Amalor likes to stress the point here with the theologians gathered at the Brussels World Congress (WCT):

> The gospel message, to which the Church gives witness to the world, cannot be articulated without taking seriously the bearing of the world on this message. Therefore, the work of theology is to be carried on in the light of both the gospel message and society, i.e. the contribution of various cultures, their sciences and arts, literature and religions. Christians must recognize that the philosophies and humanisms of our cultural environment contain indispensable elements for Christian proclamation and theology.[71]

It follows then that theology must not only end in reality by way of application, but must also *start from and permanently remain in reality* so that the word that is announced may be understood from within one's life situation and be articulated in all its freshness, vitality and challenge.

> Hitherto, our theology has been starting from principles, abstracted from reality, speculated in laboratory and thus became an arm-chair theology. Proceeding from principles to reality, it will distort and falsify reality and lead to illusion. Above all it can be a normative science only on the basis of an analysis and knowledge of the reality. Otherwise it could become a deviation instead of being an orientation of human existence and history.[72]

*(e) Church: Institution or movement? Ambiguous image and latent role of the Church in Indian history to·be studied*

There is no doubt that for the last twenty centuries, especially during the last four centuries in an ambiguous situation of colonialism and foreign rule, the Indian Church has played some roles in the socio-religious movements; at times open and recognized, at other times latent and unknown. With the best of intentions, she has also given meaning and

---

[71] See as quoted by DSA from the WCT, Resolution nos. 3, 7, 8, in: Ibid., p. 36-37 (footnote 3).

[72] Ibid., p. 25.

legitimization to oppressive regimes and unjust situations.[73] The three week 'Asian Seminar on Religion and Development on the Social Function of Religion' organized by the NBCLC at Bangalore from July 16 to August 4, 1973, in collaboration with FERES, Louvain, is very revealing and challenging in this regard. It states:

> The Church is part of society and in it she has to spell out her mission. She has therefore, to be aware of how society is functioning and of her role in it. We were particularly sensitized to the latent functions of the organized religions in the course of history and realized how with the best of intentions, while rendering innumerable services, the Churches consciously or unconsciously have often upheld a situation of injustice.... Likewise, theology as a systematic reflection of Christian communities on their faith and on their involved experiences in the world, and in its function to discover and interpret, criticize and change reality, needs to know and start from reality. In this it [the Church] should profit by the analysis and knowledge of the social phenomena ... should take immediate steps to prepare men and women who would help in this scientific analysis (Statement no. 5).[74]

What is the Church's social involvement in India? Amalor would still pose the challenging question before us: Is the Church in India an institution or movement?[75] Paul Puthanangady answers:

> Well, what has happened during this 25 years of post-Vatican II renewal is precisely this: the Indian Church has slowly begun to change its physiognomy: from institution it is gradually trying to become a movement. It is true that there is a long way to go. But ... the process has already started. Certainly Fr. D.S. Amalorpavadass has had a very important role to play in this.[76]

---

[73] Cf. ibid., p. 26.

[74] See quoted by DSA, in: Ibid., p. 37 (footnote 5).

[75] Cf. Paul Puthanangady, "Foreword", in: Id. (ed.), *Church in India: Institution or Movement?*, op. cit., p. vii.

[76] Ibid.

The Church is an event, a movement, historical and dynamic. Amalor has had a very important role to play in implementing the Vatican II renewal and its theology in the Indian Church. Some of the theological research conferences and consultations, like the Nagpur Theological Conference (1971), Patna Theological Consultation (1973), and Bangalore Theological Research Seminar (1974), which he convened or in which he played an important role, bear witness to this fact.[77]

*(ii) Theology of faith and revelation[78] and reality*

The theological basis for the relation between theology and reality "is to be found not in human sciences alone but chiefly in the theology of revelation and faith."[79]

We have already seen that revelation is an inter-personal relationship between God and man. God reveals and relates himself to men in communication and communion with the purpose of liberating and reconciling them and building a community of faith and love, service and salvation. Thus, the end, the source and climax, the pattern and model of relationship among men and the world religions should be based on the pattern of loving and liberating relationship, the revelation-response pattern, that exists between God and man.

Faith is response to revelation. If God's word and self-gift is revelation, man's word and his self-surrender to him is faith. Revelation and faith take place concretely and really in our existence through the events of history, in the midst of life-situations. Revelation, the encounter between God and man, is an actual, ever-present reality and an on-going process. God constantly meets man in life and history. Thus humanity stands at no time outside the process of revelation, but always within it.

Now, if God meets man in his concrete situation, it follows that our theology should meet reality, it should be relevant to the reality. Theology requires reality. It must start from, dwell in and end in reality.[80]

---

[77] Cf. DSA, "Approach", *op. cit.*, p. 27.

[78] We have already seen what is revelation and faith in the first chapter. Here we deal with it in short to show how it is related to reality.

[79] DSA, "Approach", *op. cit.*, p. 28.

[80] Cf. ibid., pp. 27-29. See also: DSA, *The Church's Mission as Prophetic and Hermeneutical,* op. cit., p. 5f.

### *3.1.2.2. Pluralism in theology and unity of faith: Orthodoxy and orthopraxis*

What makes pluralism in theology is our approach to and involvement in reality. "Theology stands in that inner inevitable tension between the once-for-all transmitted faith and the every-newly-acquired understanding and actualization of the faith here and now."[81]

#### *(i) Pluralism in theology*

The Church should be present everywhere; she is sent to proclaim Christ to all people of all cultures and traditions. To be relevant to these different cultures and traditions of the world, the Church needs pluralism in theology; she cannot limit herself to one single theology or to one form of message. "Pluralism in theology, in pastorale and hence in evangelization is an accepted principle today and it will assert itself more and more with our involvement in reality."[82]

On the one hand, there has never been a uniform human society. Given the diversity of social, cultural, politico-economical, religious and ideological pluralism in the world, pluralism in theology is inevitable. On the other hand, "this pluralism is inevitable if theology has to be relevant, and has to explore all the possibilities of faith for the present and for the future, for each and every situation, for each and every human group. This calls for a vigorous theological activity and a bold prophetic thrust within the Church and outside."[83]

In this regard, Amalor aims at the convergence of efforts and pooling together of resources and services. This is not a question of toleration, but respect for others and openness to the Spirit who is ever guiding the Church towards the fullness of truth. Amalor actively encourages pluralism of approaches and emphases in the Church's involvement in society, in the formation of its members, in the theological research and teaching, in worship and spirituality and in the diversification of pastoral activity.[84]

---

[81] Ibid., p. 32.
[82] Ibid.
[83] Ibid.
[84] Cf. ibid.

### *(ii) Unity of faith: One faith, plurality of interpretations*

Pluralism is not against unity of faith and unity of faith does not exclude pluralism in theology. Pluralism must abide by the *perpetual confession of faith* and of the Church in the obedience of faith. Such a unity of faith is necessary.

> The unity of the Church is constituted by its common confession [of faith] and not by its technical organization for satisfying religious needs. A Church can necessarily be a Church only if it can say what unifies and animates it; for, service rendered by the Christians to the world can only be so if they can show how their service springs from their conviction of faith and thereby if the world can be enabled to measure their common action against their common faith.[85]

The content of our faith is God's salvific mystery in Jesus Christ. How do we unfold it, especially in our context of religious pluralism today? The spelling out of the content of the Christian message must include at least these points: (a) a statement about God in a way intelligible to people; (b) a statement about the salvific intervention of God in the world and its historical culmination in Jesus Christ and that, from the very start, within the framework of a universal history of salvation; (c) a statement that Jesus is not merely the messenger, but the very content of the Christian message; (d) a statement about the Church as the community of those who believe in the message of Jesus. It must be shown: (a) that such a community must be a socially *institutionalized* reality, due to the *nature* of man and due to the exigency of *witness* to be given; (b) that such a society, though historically contingent in many aspects, has to be recognized and accepted for what it is; (c) that the greatest possible clarity of its *continuity* in history vouches for its origin from Jesus.[86]

> Such a statement of common and original confession need and should not be brought under an absolutely common formula, but can be pluriform, starting from different starting point of departure and from very different basic aspects, but corresponding always to the

---

[85] Ibid., p. 33.

[86] Cf. ibid., pp. 33-34. Here DSA refers to Karl Rahner's Conference on 'What is the Christian Message' at the WCT, Brussels, 1970 (footnote 7).

audience's concrete situation which is historically conditioned and constantly changing, both individually and collectively. This implies again that the Christian message must essentially take into account the concrete situation of the hearers and can do so without any ultimate danger to itself.[87]

*(iii) Orthodoxy and dialogue*

Today the concept of orthodoxy has been given a new understanding. It is to safeguard and verify faith and theology in a new and dialogical way.

> The concept of orthodoxy should be thus less static, materialistic and individualistic and hence dynamic, spiritual and dialogical. Orthodoxy is not to be assured by one against the other, but by all in the community, all the charisms, status, functions and groups in a frank dialogue and in an effort to have a correct and relevant understanding of the faith in the present time.[88]

Amalor, quoting Karl Rahner, continues saying:

> The important criterion for the true and life-giving orthodoxy of our Christian message is whether it can go beyond a monotonous repetition of the old formulas. This monotony will prove that it has not taken into account the historical change in the situation of the hearers.[89]

It follows, therefore, that the message of salvation in Jesus Christ, to be relevant to different cultures and religious traditions, "has to be reinterpreted and re-formulated today in such a way that it may become a fresh word, a warm word, a word for today, a word related to the thought and life of our contemporaries."[90] Regarding this, Amalor once again likes to

---

[87] Ibid., p. 34.

[88] Ibid.

[89] Ibid. DSA quotes Karl Rahner from his Conference on 'What is Christian Message' at the WCT (footnote 8).

[90] Ibid., p. 35.

quote the thought and theology of the two hundred theologians gathered at the WCT, Brussels in 1970. They emphasized this point in their conclusions:

> The great Christological confessions and definitions of the past have a lasting significance for the Church of today. But they cannot be interpreted without taking into account their historical context. To speak to men of different ages and cultures [and traditions] the Christian message must find really new formulations (no. 6).[91]

*(iv) Orthopraxis and witness*

There should be a balance between orthodoxy and orthopraxis. Orthodoxy must lead to orthopraxis, to the living witness of faith in life. Amalor says:

> The media of communication and signs of revelation ... are both words and deeds. Likewise ... evangelization is done in a total language of proclamation of the word and witness of Christian life. So also here, it is harmful to emphasize unilaterally orthodoxy. We must come to the original balance between orthodoxy and orthopraxis. Both are equally important and they are dialectically related, one calling for the other. With reference to evangelization and Christian witness, perhaps orthopraxis is even more important and needs to be stressed.[92]

To conclude we say that sincere involvement in human realities calls for originality and creativity in theology. The pluriformity in theology is not something to be tolerated, much less a luxury which we cannot afford to have, "but a necessity for its orthodoxy and universality, on the one hand, and for its pastoral relevance and efficacy, on the other."[93]

---

[91] Ibid., p. 37 (footnote 9).

[92] Ibid., p. 35.

[93] Ibid.

### *3.1.3. Some practical problems connected with the Church*

Though at the level of theological reflection all may agree with what we have said hitherto, Amalor does not like to pass over in silence some practical problems connected with the Church with reference to evangelization, especially in the context of other religions. We proceed to see them in brief.

#### *(i) Universality of the Church: Universality of Jesus Christ*

There is, first of all, the reaction against the "condescending" attitude or the *pretension* of the Church.[94] The Church pretends to bring others salvation, development, libération, while she herself may be in sin, enslaved and underdeveloped.[95] At the same time,

> all that the Church wants to announce and effect by her evangelization is already found as much outside the institutional Church as inside it if not more at times, e.g. openness, concern for others, selfless service, justice, fellowship, peace and joy. On the one hand, the Church does not manifest to others what she wants to offer, namely, Christ, his Spirit, a life according to the gospels; and on the other hand, she fails to recognize honestly in others the presence of these realities. Instead she wants to convert them and bring them to the very community which does not witness to Christian values. Hence the conclusion that the theological formulation of the qualities proper to the Church are notional and illusory and do not wholly respond to reality and that Evangelization itself is thus a mere pretension.[96]

It is deplorable to see at times that some Christian groups, chiefly youth organizations, have more in common with Marxists and Communists than with the Church, regarding their commitment to a cause; more in common with Hindus and Protestants in questions of prayers, meditations and experience of God; more friendship with people in society at large than in convents, religious houses and parish communities, and they get better collaboration from private agencies and government offices

---

[94] Cf. ibid., p. 42.

[95] Cf. ibid.

[96] Ibid.

than from religious authorities.[97] What is our answer? The answer is that the Church is part and parcel of the world. She is for this world.

> In answer to these we would say that the Church is not a separate entity beside the universe or parallel to the historical process of mankind; it is part and parcel of it. Moreover, although it contains the full mystery of the Church, it does not *exhaust* all its possibilities, since the reality of the Church is to be found in the whole world and in the whole of human history, outside and beyond her visible structures just as Christ himself cannot be limited to the Palestine of the first century, nor his Spirit imprisoned in any person or institution.[98]

The universality of the Church follows from the universality of Christ himself. It follows from this, therefore, that far from diminishing the entity and importance of the Church, it impels her to go forward, to open herself out, to recognize the elements of truth in other religious traditions and ideologies of the world, and thereby realize her true catholicity (cf. *NA* 2; *GS* 22; *LG* 16). Amalor, quoting the Nagpur Declaration, says: "Animated by the Spirit of God, who knows no limitations or barriers, the Church is called on to search out, acknowledge and ennoble everything that is true and good in the world and in human history" (no. 7).[99] Or better still, quoting *Lumen Gentium,* he says:

> This Church, constituted and organized in the world as a society, subsists in the Catholic Church ... although many elements of sanctification and of truth can be found outside of her visible structure. These elements, however, as gifts properly belonging to the Church of Christ, possess an inner dynamism towards Catholic unity (no. 8b).[100]

In other words, "the Church's action is universal in all time and space, so much so the work of the Spirit and the fruits of his action can be at times more evident outside Church structures and institutions than within them."[101]

---

[97] Cf. ibid., pp. 42-43.
[98] Ibid., p. 43.
[99] See quoted in: Ibid.
[100] See: Ibid.
[101] Ibid.

*(ii) The uniqueness of the Church: Uniqueness of Jesus Christ*

If the Holy Spirit is active also outside the peripheries of the Church's structures, then the question arises: What is the *uniqueness* of the Church? The problem of the uniqueness of Christianity vis-à-vis other religions creates a lot of misunderstanding. All the religions assert their uniqueness.

The uniqueness of Christianity "is precisely Christ. As we have said above, *Christ means a total openness to all,* an existence for others, and consequently, a total gift of himself to others by becoming one with others to the point of dying for them."[102] According to Amalor, the uniqueness of Christ cannot be understood apart from his universality. Christ is open to all. The uniqueness and universality of Christ are, if we can say, the two sides of the same coin. The uniqueness of Christ does not imply exclusivism, instead inclusivism. Likewise, the uniqueness of the Church or Christianity does not imply exclusivism but inclusivism and universality.

Jesus says: "By this everyone will know that you are my disciples, if you have love for one another" (Jn. 13:35). The Church is truly a community of all those who have identified themselves with Christ and want to realize this reality of Christ's love in every human group and religion.

> Wherever this openness and self-gift are evident, wherever one's life is genuinely dedicated to the point of dying for others, there we have the Church. The institutional or visible Church is nothing else but the sign and instrument of this process of gathering men and unifying all of them with God by this process of openness and self-sacrifice. Thus many possibilities are opened before us for more universal communion [and] joint action among men, whether we be Christians, Muslims, Marxists or Atheists.[103]

*(iii) The Church's institutional character: Sign, the historicity of Jesus*

We have already seen that because of the human nature in general and the communitarian witness of the Christian community in

---

[102] Ibid., pp. 43-44.
[103] Ibid., p. 44.

particular, the Church needs institutions and structures. We must beware of the risk of depreciating the value of institutions and structures or of doing away with them. Some people like to belittle or ignore the institutional Church. They may speak of two Churches: institutional and charismatic, even at times separating the Church from Christ. Some do not even see the need and importance of the historicity of Christ, and, thereby, shirk their responsibility and give up all efforts at reform and renewal of the Church from within. However, in doing so, in the final analysis, they only clamour for new structures.[104]

> The sinfulness of the institutional Church is a challenge to us its members to be first of all what we should be; and secondly, to see that the visible realities contain the realities they signify. Moreover, visible and external signs are necessary for men who are soul and body and who live in society. The very service of witnessing which is the mission of the Church calls for visible signs which are embodiments of the spirit. Finally, the reality of the Church as reconciliation and relationship of persons, as liberation and salvation has to be expressed in tangible and experiential terms if the Church is to be real and authentic as fellowship among men. Jesus wanted his followers to be one body, one community, a visible society, so that people might recognize in them in a visible way his saving presence.[105]

It would, therefore, be an illusion to think that we can dispense with structures and institutions. One who says that they can be dispensed with, simply creates other structures and institutions. Clamouring for new structures need not be the solution of the problem. Sometimes, indeed, structures must be changed if they are unjust, oppressive or have become countersigns. But no structure is final or perfect. The new ones have to be constantly criticized and evaluated in terms of their functions to *contain, make visible* and *effect* the reality. In any case, no sign can be identified with the ultimate reality, namely, the kingdom of God. The visible or the institutional Church is not the ultimate reality; she is the sign of the ultimate reality, the kingdom of God ushered in by Christ on earth.

---

[104] Cf. ibid.

[105] Ibid., pp. 44-45.

> All signs are more or less adequate. They are signs, *not simply as signs but as signs of Christ* due to his active presence through the Spirit. Only in Christ do the sign and the reality tally. When the sign of the Church and the reality will tally, the kingdom of God will emerge. Till then we are on pilgrimage; in pilgrimage we have to be humble, to be detached while using things (1 Cor. 7:29-31) and transcend all things while being incarnate in them.[106]

The Church in spite of her infidelity and sinfulness is still, on the whole, the sign and instrument of the movement ushered in by Christ for the total liberation, fellowship and communion of all men.[107]

> She [the Church] is the divinely appointed animator and vanguard of this movement, pointing to and gathering up all efforts at openness, commitment and self-sacrifice, within or without the structure. It is in this way that she can be called the universal sacrament of salvation.[108]

*(iv) No Church apart from Christ*

The Church has no existence apart from Christ. But can we *identify* the Church with Christ? No. Christ lives in the Church (cf. *LG* 8b). The Church is the sacrament of Christ.

> On the one hand, to identify the Church with Christ, is to exalt her above the earth and to indulge in triumphalism; on the other hand, the Church will be no Church without Christ. All that she has and is and does is due to Him, who is in her, acting in her and giving her all she needs and making of her the universal sacrament of salvation. Thus, far from being self-complacent or pharisaical about this universality, she rather tends towards it; it is precisely this tension that gives her elan in this movement and impels her to what we call *'Evangelization'*.[109]

---

106 Ibid., p. 45.

107 Cf. ibid.

108 Ibid.

109 Ibid., pp. 45-46.

The Church's existence and activity, seen in this perspective, will not tend towards domination but *diakonia* (service). The Church is called to render her humble *diakonia* to people of all cultures and religions, nay, to the whole of creation itself, orienting it towards its creator. Then evangelization will be seen in the context of love and service, dialogue and collaboration with the world and its religions, recognizing, thereby, the salvific values in other religions and joining all in the fellowship of one God and one humanity in and through Christ. The Church is called to share with others the design of God for the world revealed in Christ. Thus, "this [evangelization] will not be an effort at domination against which all react; it will rather be a spiritual animation and leadership in humble and universal diakonia."[110]

*(v) No two Churches: No alienation*

Belonging to the Church does not mean one's alienation from the mainstream of national or social life. When people criticize or oppose the structure of the Church, it is not against her internal and constituent structures they react but rather to the historical and social expression of them.

> The structures of the Church should not be such as to be in opposition with those of society in such a way that belonging to the Church would mean alienation from the mainstream of national and social life, from one's religious and cultural heritage, one's family, social and professional milieux. One's commitment to the Church should in no way cause a split personality, imply a double loyalty or cause any kind of alienation.[111]

This challenges us today to visualize a new Church which, starting from her constitutive elements and renewing the faithful in her inner structure, will be able to work out all her other external organization, social set up, institutions and structures, laws and regulations, forms of authority and partners of relationship. These should be such that they can be constantly changed to enable the Church to fulfill her mission in each place, locally, in each culture and historical period in terms of social change, concrete

---

[110] Ibid.

[111] Ibid.

situations, people's needs and aspirations. Thus there arises the need for the local Church.[112]

With regard to the missionary activity of the Church, Vatican II defines the Church as "the universal sacrament of salvation" (*AG* 1; cf. *LG* 48).[113] According to the plan of the Father, the Church has her origin in the mission of the Son and the Holy Spirit (cf. *AG* 2; *LG* 1). The Church, in deep communion with Christ, becomes the bearer of his mission to all people and religions. As the visible community she becomes the prolongation of Jesus's life and mission on earth, the sign, the sacrament, the servant of Jesus and his dynamic agent of salvation in the world and history. "The mystery of Jesus is thus embodied and kept alive in the world by the mystery of the Church."[114] This mystery of Jesus subsists in the Catholic Church (cf. *LG* 8b).

> Thus, in the Spirit, the Church gathers and reconciles the people from the four winds, forms and guides them and becomes a community of those reconciled to God and to others. Rightly, therefore, *Lumen Gentium* opens with this crucial statement that the mission of the Church concretely consists in effectively bringing about and signifying the union of all men with one another and of all men with God (no. 1).[115]

The Church is called to be the leaven of human society. She is at the service of God and people, Christians as well as others. She is called to render her service of salvation to individuals as well as religions themselves. She is the universal sacrament of salvation for all people and religions, infusing in them the Spirit of Christ and perfecting them in God through Christ. Striving to be what she should be and yearning for the day when the universal fellowship of all human beings with one another and with God in the unity of the Spirit will be realized, she is carried forward by a new dynamism to announce the word to all people, to celebrate the Eucharist and to make herself the servant (*minister*) of all. "The Church

---

[112] Cf. ibid., pp. 46-47.

[113] Amalor frequently uses the expression for the Church as 'the sacrament of salvation'. See: DSA, *Theology of Catechesis,* op. cit., p. 9; also: Id., *Approach,* op. cit., p. 46.

[114] DSA, "Approach", *op. cit.,* p. 40.

[115] Ibid., pp. 40-41.

is thus the beginning and the foreshadowing of God's kingdom to emerge at the end of times, when Christ will lead the whole redeemed universe to His Father and God will be all in all (1 Cor. 3:23; 5:28)."[116]

> In a word, she is in urgent necessity for continual conversion and reform, so that both in word and in deed, she might proclaim ever more efficaciously God's liberating and unifying love in Christ Jesus. In spite of her infidelity and in her very struggle to convert herself fully to him and to respond to the exigencies of the world, the Church belongs to Christ as his spouse, as his own Body.[117]

### *3.2. Contextualizing the Commission: Indo-Asian Reality*[118]

Before delivering his inaugural key-note address at the International Theological Conference on Evangelization and Dialogue in Asia, Nagpur, 1971, Amalor introduces his speech to the theologians gathered there, saying:

> The hour of the Lord has struck his Church in Asia! We have now become participants and witnesses in an historic event. We need only faith and vision to discern its significance: we need distance and time to assess its impact and consequences; we need courage and perseverance to meet its challenge.[119]

What is the reality of Asia in general and of India in particular vis-à-vis theology and evangelization? The total world population today (1995) is 5.750 in millions, of which Christians are 1.937 and Catholics, 1.056 million.[120] Nearly sixty percent of the world population lives in Asia and

---

[116] Ibid., pp. 41-42.

[117] Ibid., p. 41.

[118] For this topic see in general: DSA, *Theology of Evangelization,* op. cit., pp. 5-25. See also: M. Dhavamony (ed.), *Evangelization, Dialogue and Development,* op. cit., pp. 21-39.

[119] DSA, *Theology of Evangelization,* op. cit., 3.

[120] See: David B. Barrett, *Annual Statistical Table on Global Mission: 1995,* in: *International Bulletin of Missionary Research,* vol. 1, 1995, pp. 24-25, as it is cited by Sebastian Karotemprel, "The Shape of Christian Mission in the Third Millennium", in: *Indian Missiological Review* 18 (1996) 2, pp. 65-66.

Christianity here is a minority. What is the significance of evangelization amidst the vast majority of other religious traditions in Asia, in India?

### *3.2.1. The religious scene of Asia in general: Characteristics and challenges*[121]

Evangelization in the Asian continent presupposes that the Asian trends, situations and realities are taken into consideration. However, for our purpose, we limit ourselves only to the religious characteristics and challenges of Asia.

#### *3.2.1.1. Homeland of the world religions and the challenge of religious pluralism*

Asia is the homeland of ancient and living world religions like Hinduism, Buddhism, Jainism, Sikhism, Christianity and Islam. It is also a homeland of prestigious millenary civilizations.

The dawn of political independence has facilitated the renaissance of local cultures, the development of vernacular languages and literature, the reform and revitalization of old religions and the rise of new religions, especially in Japan.

The Christians in Asia are a minority, *pusillus grex*. How can the Church's presence and action have an influence on the vast masses of humankind in the continent of Asia? What should be the proper approach and method of evangelization to meet the various needs and situations of different ethnic, socio-cultural, religious and ideological groups? How can the Church establish dialogue of life and collaboration in nation-building and solving modern problems of society amidst the pluralism of religions?

#### *3.2.1.2. Movement of liberation and revolution: Secularization and materialism*

In addition to the traditional cultural and religious values, a new materialism is having its sway in the Asian scene. However, by and large, the moral and religious values have still their appeal and expression. Religion and politics are not seen as opposing realities. The secular values,

---

[121] Cf. DSA, *Theology of Evangelization*, op. cit., p. 5ff.

like man's personality, his dignity, thirst for social justice, economic and religious freedom, are incorporated in religions. The Asian problem is not either of preserving the traditional cultural and religious values or of accepting the modern, technological and secular values, but of appropriating the latter without abandoning the former, and of finding a new synthesis and equilibrium.[122]

After the political independence from the hegemony of European nations, the leadership of the élite of each country is conscientizing the masses towards its new war of revolution and liberation from poverty and misery, illiteracy and ignorance, exploitation and enslavement, social, political and economic injustice and inequalities, uneven trade agreements and exploitative foreign aids, etc. In this crucial period of history people look for a tool of analysis and ideologies, the interpretation, orientation and application of their policies and programmes for a bright future. It is here that all forms of ideology, humanism, socialism, Gandhism, Communism and Marxism have an appeal, especially to the youth. These ideologies nourish their imagination, meet their needs and inspire their action. Can the Church give meaning and orientation, critique and fulfillment to these movements? Can the Church remain indifferent and isolated or should she work in alliance with other religions to safeguard, uphold and propagate religious and moral values against the onslaught of materialism and secularism in order to inspire and guide the religious forces and projects towards peace and progress? How can the Church's *good news* of salvation in Christ be made meaningful to people engaged with heart and soul in the process of integral human development? Does the Church know to present the Gospel as a motive force and ideal blueprint for the new society? Does her act of evangelization appear as an act of human promotion and creation of a new, just, human and fraternal society, an act of hope for the realization of the kingdom of God here on earth? Amalor says: "Unless the Church is aware of this multiple challenges that modern Asia or India poses, her theology of evangelization or her ministry of preaching will be totally irrelevant, not to say, meaningless."[123]

Formerly the West was considered as the centre of the world, both materially and spiritually, at least, as regards Christianity. Today there is a great drift of the axis of history from the West to the Asia-Pacific and

---

[122] Cf. ibid., p. 7.

[123] Ibid., p. 9.

other continents. Amalor says that if the axis of history is poised in Asia and the Pacific then the *kairos* of Asia must be recognized, its significance should be noted and the leadership of Asia should be played. "In what way does the Gospel or the Church inspire and facilitate such a leadership role?"[124]

Some of the Asian traits that we have indicated above pose several challenges to the religions in general and to the Church and evangelization in particular. From this glimpse of the Asian scene, we can narrow down to each country and in each country to each region and group of people. We proceed to consider the Indian context.

### *3.2.2. The Indian context: Religious pluralism*

If India is the home of more than 400 million out of nearly two billion people of other religions in the world, is it surprising that the Church has an absorbing interest in this country? India has often been considered the hope and despair of the missionary endeavours of the Church. Hope because the consuming concern of India from time immemorial has been spirituality; despair, because in this subcontinent comparatively only a tiny minority has come to know and accept Christ, in spite of 19 centuries of missionary toil, sweat and tears.

> The progenitor and custodian of admittedly one of the finest cultures in human history, India has been a hard missionary nut to crack. But crack it must in God's good time; for India needs Christ and Christ needs India, but the two have hardly met. The question agitating many a missionary mind is: Is Post-Independent India anywhere near God's good time?[125]

India is a land of ancient culture and the cradle of many world religions. The vast majority is that of Hindus. We give a bird's eye view of the figure of religious percentage in India, out of its total population of nearly 666 million in 1981 general census, and 846.3 million in

---

[124] Ibid., p. 8.

[125] See: Introductory address of Herman D'Souza, Secretary of the CBCI Commission for Church Extension, during the All India Consultation on Evangelization, Patna, 3-8 October 1973, in: *Light and Life We Seek to Share*, op. cit., p. vii (Preface).

1991.[126]

| Religions | Percentage: 1981 | 1991 |
|---|---|---|
| Hindus | 82.6 | 82.8 |
| Muslims | 11.4 | 11.7 |
| Christians | 2.4 | 2.3 (Catholics, *c.* 1.71) |
| Sikhs | 2.0 | 2.0 |
| Buddhists | 0.7 | 0.8 |
| Jains | 0.5 | 0.4 |
| Other | 0.4 | ....... |
| Total | 100.0 | 100.0 |

Such being the case, when we talk about Indian scene vis-à-vis Christianity, we generally refer to Hinduism. Christians here are a minority. Christ seems to be unheard of and unknown to the majority; though understood and accepted by a few, he is quite often misunderstood by many. The *good news* of Christ has to be preached to all.

*3.2.2.1. A context of meetings and seminars: Other religions and missions*

*(i) The 38th International Eucharistic Congress and the Theological Seminar, Bombay (1964):* Amalor refers to the Theological Seminar held in Bombay in December 1964 during the 38th International Eucharistic Congress. The four papers read then by eminent theologians and the discussions that followed in the meeting, and above all what spilled out into the press and subsequent meetings, though sometimes controversial in tone, stimulated fresh reflections in the country with regard to the role of world religions in the economy of salvation and fostered positive and

126 For the 1981 figure, see: *Manorama Yearbook 1994,* K.M. Mathew (chief ed.), Malayala Manorama, Kottayam (issue, yearly), p. 463. For the 1991 figure, see: *Manorama Yearbook 1997,* K.M. Mathew (chief ed.), Malayala Manorama, Kottayam, p. 456. (Today, 1998, the total population of India is nearly 980 million, cf. *International Herald Tribune,* May 28, 1998, p. 1). For the figure of population by religion, see: *Manorama Yearbook 1997,* p. 460.

optimistic attitude towards them.[127]

During the Congress, Paul VI himself showed great interest and a favourable attitude towards other religions. While addressing to the representatives of various religions gathered there, he stressed the need for mutual respect, acceptance and collaboration among religions. In this and other Bombay speeches he quoted approvingly from the sacred books of Hinduism. He said:

> This visit to India is the fulfillment of a long cherished desire. Yours is a land of ancient culture, the cradle of great religions, the home of a nation that has sought God with a relentless desire.... Rarely has this longing for God been expressed with words so full of the spirit of Advent as in the words written in your sacred books many centuries before Christ: *From the unreal lead me to the real; from darkness lead me to light; from death lead me to immortality* [*Bṛhadāraṇyaka Upaniṣad* 1.3.28]. This is a prayer which belongs also to our time. Today more than ever it should rise from every human heart.[128]

Again, towards a universal communion and collaboration, the Pope said:

> Therefore, we must come close together, not only through the modern means of communication ...; we must come together with our hearts, in mutual understanding and love. We must meet ... as pilgrims who set out to find God ... in human hearts. Person must meet person, nation meet nation, as brothers and sisters, as children of God. In this mutual understanding and friendship, in this sacred communion, we must also begin to work together to build the common future of the human race. We must find the concrete and practical ways of organization and cooperation ... towards achieving a true communion among all nations. Such a union cannot be built on universal terror or fear of mutual destruction; it must be built on a common love that embraces all and has its roots in God who is Love.[129]

---

[127] Cf. DSA, *Theology of Evangelization,* op. cit., pp. 10-11.

[128] See: ND 1031. See also the text quoted in: AAS 57 (1965) 132-133.

[129] See: ND 1032.

The Pope's speech much favoured the Indian theologians in their approach, understanding and theologizing towards other religions.

Then came the Declaration on the relationship of the Church to non-Christian religions (*Nostra Aetate,* 28 Oct. 1965), the Vatican II Decree on missionary activity of the Church (*Ad Gentes,* 7 Dec. 1965), supported by other documents, especially the Dogmatic Constitution on the Church (*Lumen Gentium,* 21 Nov. 1964) and the Pastoral Constitution on the Church in the modern world (*Gaudium et Spes,* 7 Dec. 1965).

*(ii) The All India Seminar (1969) and the Evangelization and Adult Catechumenate, NBCLC (1970):* The next event for the quest for understanding the mission of the Church and evangelization in India was the All India Seminar on 'The Church in India Today' in 1969. Its workshops on evangelization, dialogue with other religions and Indian culture emphasized practical and organizational matters rather than the theology of evangelization and dialogue, though some inspiring passages and approaches towards an Indian theology are found in the preamble (Report, pp. 331-351).[130]

According to Amalor, the subject was dealt with in greater depth in the three zonal consultations on Evangelization held in Sitagarah, Bombay and Ootacamund, and above all in the fortnight-long VII National Seminar organized by the National Catechetical and Liturgical Centre, Bangalore, in May-June 1970 on Evangelization and Adult Catechumenate.[131]

*(iii) The Symposium in Rome (1969) and the World Congress of Theology, Brussels (1970):* Amalor makes a significant reference to two more International Theological Congresses:

(a) The Symposium on 'Mission Theology for our Times' held in Rome in March 1969. It treated two questions: "Non-Christian Religions and the Mission" and "Development and Missionary Activity".

(b) The World Congress of Theology on 'the Future of the Church' held in Brussels in September 1970 took as one of its four topics, "What is the Christian Message?".[132]

---

[130] Cf. DSA, *Theology of Evangelization,* op. cit., pp. 10-11.

[131] Cf. ibid., p. 11.

[132] Cf. ibid.

### *3.2.2.2. The context of crisis*

The Church in India faces the question of religious pluralism mainly from these two counts: (i) the context of religio-political crisis; and (ii) the missionary crisis.

We proceed to consider the above points, situating the Church mainly in a Hindu context.

#### *(i) The religio-political crisis: Seeking the saviour in the crisis*

*(a) Sanātana dharma and tolerance:* The Indian attitude towards religions is one of tolerance or respect. Tolerance reflects India's social and political structure, psychology and religious convictions.[133]

Hinduism (*sanātana dharma*) has no human founder, no dogmas and no infallible, central, controlling authority. Consequently in Hinduism subjective religious experience has primacy and it relativizes truth. The ultimate Reality (*Brahman*) or the Absolute (*Ātman*), without name and form (*nirguṇa Brahman, arūpa*), is contemplated under its different aspects by devotees and called *Īśvara* by Hindus, Yahweh by Jews, *Allāh* by Muslims, heavenly Father by Christians, and in similar ways by other religions. The Absolute manifests itself in different names and forms (*saguṇa Brahman, sarūpa*). The Truth or Reality is One but it is called in different names (*ekam sat vipara bahudā vadanti*). For example, one and the same substance *water* (English, Christians) is called *jala* by Hindus, and *pānī* by Muslims.[134]

Accordingly, though revelation is seen as an on-going process, religion is seen as man's initiative in his self-realization. Religion, therefore, has to adapt itself to the individual, society and nation. Since man is at the origin of religion, no religion is adequate, or exclusively perfect. All are more or less identical in their usefulness and inadequacy. All religions lead to the same goal.

These are some of the principles which govern the Indian attitude towards religions and on which is based the principle of tolerance. The conclusion drawn from these principles is that "since all religions are equally good and necessary, equally lacking in power and inadequate, all

---

[133] Cf. DSA, *Destinée,* op. cit., pp. 95-102. (No special reference is given unless quoted).

[134] Cf. ibid., p. 103.

deserve an equal tolerance."[135]

Though as old as India and Hinduism itself, the theory of tolerance was developed during the last hundred years from the time of Ramakrishna Paramahamsa (1834-1886), and with Mahatma Gandhi (1869-1948) it became an axiom.[136] A number of Hindu reformers, like Vivekananda (1863-1902) and Radhakrishnan (1888-1975), while remaining attached to the principle of tolerance, claim universal validity for Hinduism side by side with Christianity.[137]

Though there is tolerance, there have been cases of intolerance.[138] However, there is every reason to hope that the tradition of tolerance continues.[139]

These are some of the elements of Hinduism which are favourable and also unfavourable to the Church's evangelization in particular and her relation with other religions in general.[140]

*(b) Traditional value crisis:* Modern India seems to be passing through a crisis of the system of traditional religious values owing to an evolution in every domain of her life.[141] The English education of a secularist, materialist, positivist and rationalist type, though fruitful, was generally instrumental in weakening the spiritual equilibrium of the country and her fidelity to ancestral customs.[142] Has this education and modern ideologies brought about a radical change in the outlook of the people? Do they reject traditional values and adopt new ones? How does this crisis affect evangelization?[143]

---

135 Ibid., p. 102: (La conclusion s'impose naturellement:) "puisque toutes les religions sont également bonnes et nécessaires, également impuissantes et inadéquates, toutes méritent une tolérance égale." (Translation mine).

136 Cf. ibid., pp. 102-103.

137 Cf. ibid., pp. 103- 106.

138 Cf. ibid., p. 117. Here DSA cites an incident of a village Church in Vardhaman Nagar, Bihar, which was profaned by the members of the Hindu Maha Sabha during the Mass in October 1955. For some other incidents see ibid., pp. 115-119. The similar incidents continue to happen even today.

139 Cf. ibid., pp. 111-124.

140 For favourable and unfavourable factors arising from Hinduism, see: Ibid., pp. 140-144.

141 Cf. ibid., pp. 42-64.

142 Cf. ibid., p. 44.

143 Cf. ibid., pp. 45-46.

Several answers have been given. According to the opinion termed, "idealist", the changes in India are only superficial. The country remains faithful and deeply rooted to her traditional religious values, and consequently monasticism and mystical witness are the best way to lead India to Christ.[144]

From the realistic point of view, India is as materialistic as the Western countries. Religious indifference, indiscipline and criminal tendencies bear evidence to it. In such a situation, the best path of action might be the entrance of the Church into the movement of the nation, heralding the message of the Gospel through promoting national welfare, without neglecting at the same time the witness of Christian life.[145]

A more balanced view is possible. Nearly eighty per cent of Indians live in villages. An analysis of the actual situation shows that modern thought and socio-economic evolution have not profoundly changed or modified Indian mentality, rhythm of life and traditional culture of the rural population nor affected their religious traditions, though there might be exceptions. Religious traditions are not the principal obstacles to progress.[146]

There are three kinds of reactions that seem to be prevalent among the educated class and in urban milieu: the orthodox and conservative reaction of defence, an abrupt break with the past in favour of the material value of Western civilization, and a search for a balanced synthesis of the spiritual heritage and new values.[147]

Amalor writes that this crisis calls for a harmonious synthesis of what is durable and transcendental in the spiritual tradition of India and what is necessary and valuable in world civilization; it is this synthesis which the whole world expects from India.[148]

> Today India is perhaps in the melting-pot, but she has to harmonize the durable and transcendental element in her spiritual tradition in an organic fashion with what is profitable and necessary in world civilization. India's soul cannot live without the spiritual; her body

---

[144] Cf. ibid., p. 46.
[145] Cf. ibid., pp. 47-49.
[146] Cf. ibid., pp. 50-57.
[147] Cf. ibid., p. 57. For a detailed explanation of these reactions, see: Ibid., pp. 57-64.
[148] Cf. ibid., pp. 65-66.

> needs the material to subsist. When India will live body and soul -- soul above the body, but to animate it -- then she will present the living and original synthesis which the entire world is expecting from her.[149]

*(c) A saviour awaited in the crisis:* Who will achieve this relevant and much needed synthesis? In spite of its renaissance, its power of integration and assimilation, Hinduism does not seem to be capable of resisting the onslaught of materialism and communism for lack of organisation, unity and direction and clarity of doctrine concerning modern problems and many other similar factors.[150] Communism presents itself as a saviour. But India has not given herself to communism though the danger is not past.[151] The government of India makes an effort at integrating the spiritual with the material but it is based on vague religiosity, subordinating the spiritual values to the material. Who will be her saviour? Amalor says that the saviour is Christ. India is waiting for Christ.

> There is another Saviour for India: Christ. We know that he is not an 'imposter' like others (Matt. 27:63), but the true Redeemer, the unique Saviour of the universe, of the whole humanity. His message of salvation, the Gospel, his instrument of salvation, the Church, can give India a perfect remedy for all her ills. The void created in the spirit by the destruction of ancient gods, the vanity they discover in the new idols, make them turn precisely, not to atheistic communism, but to Christianity. The struggle of the Indian soul to implant a spirituality at the very roots of the secular structures imposed by a technico-material civilization is an evident appeal to a religion which, by its very nature, is an incarnation of the spiritual in the material, an appeal to the God incarnate and to the Church, his body.[152]

---

[149] Ibid., p. 66: ".... L'Inde est peut-être aujourd'hui dans le creuset (*melting pot*), mais elle doit harmoniser de façon organique l'élément durable et transcendant de sa tradition spirituelle avec tout ce qui lui est profitable et nécessaire dans la civilisation mondiale. L'âme de l'Inde ne peut vivre sans le spirituel; son corps a besoin du matériel pour subsister. Quand l'Inde vivra corps et âme -- l'âme au-dessus de corps, mais pour l'animer -- alors elle présentera la synthèse vivante et originale que le monde entier attend d'elle." (Translation mine).

[150] Cf. ibid., pp. 73-78.

[151] Cf. ibid., pp. 78-81.

[152] Ibid., pp. 85-86: "Reste à l'Inde un autre Sauveur: le Christ. Nous savons qu'il

Amalor writes that "Christ has indeed saved not only India but also Hinduism; but Hinduism [as a religion], as Hindus [as individuals], must, at first be 'baptized' in the baptism of Christ Himself (Lk. 12:50)."[153] Christ saves individuals as well as religions. He saves all peoples and traditions through his living and life-giving Spirit and through the evangelization of the Church.

*(ii) The missionary crisis*

The crisis in the "mission world" touches profoundly the missionary vocation, motivation, attitude and activity of the Church. The crisis is not a superficial passing one; it has deep roots and raises fundamental issues which have serious repercussions on the life and activity of the Church, of each person and community.[154] Amalor explains the reason for this crisis:

> First of all, it is due to *'the new attitude towards non-Christian religions and a better appreciation of them'* as formulated by recent theological research and affirmed by the documents of the II Vatican Council (*LG* 16, *AG* 7, *GS* 22). This partly condemns the earlier attitude towards the world religions, widens the missionary aim as hitherto understood, and deepens the missionary motivation.... Formerly one thought that the followers of non-Christian religions were not saved. A missionary was fired with zeal to rush to their

n'est pas comme d'autres un 'imposteur' (Mat. 27,63), maïs le vrai Rédemteur, le Sauveur unique de l'univers, de toute l'humanité. Son message de salut, l'Evangile, son instrument de salut, l'Eglise, peuvent apporter à l'Inde le remède parfait à ses maux. Le vide creusé dans les esprits par la destruction des dieux anciens, la vanité q'ils décourent dans les nouvelles idoles, les inclinent précisément non pas au communisme athée, mais au christianisme sauveur. La lutte de l'âme indienne pour implanter une spiritualité aux racines profondes dans les structures profanes imposées par la civilisation technico-matérielle est un appel évident à une religion qui est, par sa nature même, une véritable incarnation du spirituel dans le matériel, un appel au Dieu incarné et à l'Eglise qui est son corps." (For translation see: A. Mookenthottam, M.S.F.S., *Indian Theological Tendencies*, op. cit., p. 83).

153 Ibid., p. 144: "Le Christ a, certes, sauvé non seulement l'Inde mais aussi l'hindouisme; mais l'hindouisme, comme les Hindous, doit d'abord recevoir le baptême dans le baptême du Christ Lui-même (Luc 12, 50)." (Translation mine).

154 Cf. DSA, *Theology of Evangelization*, op. cit., p. 12.

> rescue and save them. Today he is told that Christ is at work by his saving presence and action among the non-Christians and that the latter can be saved in the very socio-religious milieu of their own religions.[155]

As a result, when one studies the insights and trends in the modern theology of evangelization, the motives which formerly inflamed the zeal of a missionary and enabled him to spend himself in the service of the Gospel are found overnight as baseless. He finds himself in crisis.

*(a) Tension between theologians and missionaries:* Due to the above theological teaching on mission today one could notice a tension between theologians and some mission workers and bishops. Missionaries seem to see theologians as theoreticians. They say that theologians do not know the realities of mission work. Their teaching and publications are harmful to the missionary cause. They accuse them saying that they take away the motivation and zeal that animated the missionaries in the past, and condemn the methods employed by them in evangelization. Amalor cites an example of protest of a missionary at the Bombay Theological Seminar in 1964 as symptomatic of the pre-Vatican II missionary attitude and motive all over the world:

> You, theologians, are taking away from us what has all along been the main motive of our apostolic zeal. You tell us that non-Christians are being saved outside Christ's Church and that their religions are for them channels of grace; why then disturb their good faith? And what have we come to do? To preach Christ or to make Hindus better Hindus and Muslims better Muslims -- For me, I will go on converting, baptizing and, from today, I will also pray for the conversion of theologians.[156]

Another missionary wrote: "If non-christians are saved without Christianity what is the use of missionaries going all over the world ... to sacrifice their lives."[157]

---

[155] Ibid.

[156] DSA, *Approaches,* op. cit., pp. 7-8. DSA cites it from *The Clergy Monthly Supplement* 7 (1965) 6, p. 229.

[157] Ibid., p. 8. DSA cites it from: *Christ to the World,* 1965, p. 450.

Theologians may get the impression that missionaries are not open enough to accept the light and are not willing to change their ideas, attitudes and approaches in the light of the new theology proposed by Vatican II. Thus a certain mutual distrust and crisis characterizes the relationship between the pre-Vatican and Vatican II attitudes towards other religions.

What is needed is that one creates an atmosphere of openness and dialogue between theologians and mission workers. To tide over the crisis is to spell out the comprehensive aim of the mission, thereby, offering a convincing missionary motivation and reconciling in a new doctrinal and vital synthesis the possibility of salvation in non-Christian religions, yet affirming the necessity and urgency of the Church's mission.[158]

*(b) Dialogue misunderstood:* Vatican II suggests a new approach to and a new relationship with other religions. This is called "Dialogue".[159] Here again many are disturbed. They feel that inter-religious dialogue is a poor substitute for evangelization and an evasion of its exigencies. Amalor says:

> The question is one of *'relating evangelization and dialogue'.* Within the wider context of meetings of minds and hearts, of discovering God wherever he is present and active, of mutual respect for and acceptance of each other's integrity and commitment, of the acts of communion in understanding truths and sharing religious experience (dialogue), there is certainly room and possibility for the sharing of Christian experience and the communication of the good news of the Christ-event.[160]

*(c) Evangelization and development:* The relation between evangelization and development is another source of trouble and confusion. Connected with it is the theology of liberation. This is a burning problem all over the world, still more in a developing country like India where it gets accentuated. On the one hand, the dilemma is expressed as either evangelization proper or development, Christianization or humanization. On the other hand, people in India, by and large, still esteem the traditional

---

158 Cf. DSA, *Theology of Evangelization,* op. cit., p. 12.

159 Ibid. The point of inter-religious dialogue will be dealt in chapter five.

160 Ibid., p. 13.

spiritual and moral values. Spirituality means for many only prayer and contemplation and so is seen as something incompatible with action and development. How to reconcile action and contemplation? Amalor says:

> Like the Church, the missionary is expected to embrace both of them as integral parts of the mission [for an integral liberation].... What is evangelization if it is not a sharing of one's Christian experience, of one's experience of God in Jesus Christ in the very midst of one's human involvement?[161]

*(d) Dialogue: New theology and preparedness for a change:* The mistake evidently is not with the documents of the Council, nor even with the new theological trends and approaches. We can list some of the reasons for the crisis as: (i) lack of preparedness on the part of missionaries, (ii) their lack of serious effort to read carefully the documents of Vatican II and the writings of theologians, (iii) lack of proper presentation of the new theology and theories to the general public in the pastoral perspective.[162]

> Theology... like ... all the rest is at the pastoral mission of the Church; and when it is not approached in the pastoral perspective and when it is not presented according to pastoral pedagogy, it may end in creating confusion and distrust instead of enlightening, guiding and encouraging the pastoral and missionary activity of the Church.[163]

Today theologians owe it to the Church -- to the missionaries and to the hierarchy in particular -- to render a relevant service and to tide over the current crisis by clarifying and spelling out more carefully the new discoveries on evangelization and mission theology. It is the task of everybody, of the whole Church.[164]

It is true that mission theology is still in the making; particularly the theology of other religions is in its infant stage. The last word has not been said on the matter. Theology is an on-going process and a never ending venture to understand God's inexhaustible revelation. All the same we

---

[161] Ibid., pp. 13-14. The point of man's integral development will be dealt in detail in chapter six.

[162] Cf. DSA, *Approaches,* op. cit., p. 8.

[163] Ibid.

[164] Cf. ibid., pp. 8-9. DSA refers to Motu Proprio (*Ecclesiae Sanctae,* August 6, 1966).

must admit that the doctrinal foundation of the theology has been laid by Vatican II and the main elements are available. Therefore in order that theology may fulfill its function of pastoral diakonia for the benefit of the magisterium and the missionaries and of the Church at large, it should be able to state less ambiguously and more coherently the acquisition of the recent research on particular realities in a dynamic synthesis where conflicts and opposition are solved and reconciled.[165] The various changes and revolutionary movements which the Indian Church faces today constitute as many signs of the times and signs of the Lord. The Lord who is present in this process of change and revolution challenges his Church to be relevant to the reality.[166]

Evangelization or the relevant role of the Church in this context would imply that the Church accepts the fact and phenomenon of change in the world, in Asia, in Indian society and in all aspects of Christian life. Does the Church discern the designs of the Lord for our countries and for our times and does she have the courage to meet the challenges and to go forward with the rest of mankind, in full solidarity and unreserved commitment?[167] Evangelization must touch the total man and the whole reality he is in touch with: religion, politics, the whole gamut of society. This applies chiefly to politics where decisions are made. Amalor deplores the fact that the Church in India has been mostly apathetic to participation and involvement in politics. He says:

> The absence and silence of the Church has nowhere else been so conspicuous as in the political field, that means her non-involvement in the process and institutions that make decisions for oppression or liberation! It is precisely and first of all in the realm of the affairs of the *'polis'* that the prophetic voice of the Church must ring out and must be heard. It is here that she must be more engaged. Evangelization in this revolutionary situation implies that the Church is ready *'to renew herself by a radical metanoia, announcing the word first of all to herself.'* Unless the Church understands the word in this context she cannot proclaim it meaningfully to others.[168]

---

165 Cf. ibid.

166 Cf. DSA, *Theology of Evangelization,* op. cit., pp. 16-17.

167 Cf. ibid.

168 Ibid., p. 17.

To be relevant to the reality, the Church must constantly review her mission and re-formulate her relationship with the world, recognize the values of truth in others and thus enlighten, sustain and orient all peoples and traditions to their final destiny in God. To do this effectively, the Church must be inculturated to every reality, every society. When she does that then she cannot but be a local Church.

### *3.2.3. Inculturation and the Indian local Church in a setting of religious pluralism: Relevancy*[169] *(AG 19-22; LG 26)*

The importance of inculturation and of the local Church is well seen when Amalor writes:

> The living Gospel lived by the Church in a living culture with all the transformations and realities it entails is what is called inculturation. Then there will be an authentic local Church in which the full mystery of Christ will be at work and in which the whole and universal Church will be present. Hence there is no preaching of the Gospel (evangelization) without inculturation. There is no Church without being localized, concretized and visibilized. There is no salvation without the incarnation of the word of God![170]

To contextualize the reality of the Church, as we have seen above, Vatican II speaks of the need and importance of the local Church (cf. *AG* 19-22; *LG* 26; *SC* 41-42). Amalor says that "the Church in India [is] to be evangelized [first] to be a fit instrument for evangelization."[171] The Church's self-evangelization means her renewal in her divine call to be a relevant agent of evangelization, dialogue, development and fellowship in the world. This is the very entity and purpose of her existence.

Time and again Amalor returns to the subject of the local Church which, for him, is of vital importance for the Church's relevant evangelization. The local Church is the concrete realization in a place of the whole mystery of the Church. It is the "incarnation" and localization of all

---

169 We are not going to see the point of inculturation and local Church in detail. We will see it only in regard to the Church's evangelization in the context of other religions.

170 DSA, *Gospel and Culture,* op. cit., p. 32.

171 DSA, "Approach", *op. cit.,* p. 64.

that we mean by the Church in a particular place, in a concrete historical context and culture, and in that it becomes an event.

> The Local Church is precisely that realization by which the full mystery of the Church will be incarnated in each place, time and people.... The Local Church is a dynamic process by which a Christian community shares its Christian experience with its contemporaries, from within, fully integrated into their socio-cultural-religious milieu.[172]

The local Church is the microcosm[173] of the mystery of the universal Church, for "she alone has the unique possibility of appearing as a microcosm of herself in a place."[174] It is an indigenous Church which, becoming conscious of her mystery and mission, is taken up by the dynamism of her diakonia of salvation to all.

When the Christian community in a place becomes conscious of its being the Church and fulfills the main task of its diakonia, the Church cannot but become indigenous. If she is not so, it is because she did not discover her own identity, did not understand her mystery and was not taken up by her own dynamism. As a general rule, indigenization concerns every aspect of the Church's life and mission.

> The process of evangelization is the very process of founding a Local Church.... This process goes on continuously till the universal community is realized. It is when the Church will be incarnated all over the world that the Church will appear missionary in character and her universality will be realized.[175]

---

172 Ibid., p. 65.

173 Microcosm here in the context of a local Church does not mean a mere administrative portion or territorial subdivision of the universal Church, but the actualization of the whole mystery of the Church in a particular place, cultural and historical context. See: DSA, *Theology of Evangelization,* op. cit., p. 18.

174 Ibid.

175 DSA, "Approach", *op. cit.,* pp. 65-66.

### *3.2.3.1. Why the Indian local Church? Relevancy*

Why should there be an Indian local Church? Amalor would answer this question in the following three points:

> First, that we have an experience of contemporary life in full solidarity with all Indians. Secondly, we have an experience of God in the Risen Christ who is the very centre of this life. Thirdly, we know how to communicate with all sectors of Indian life both our contemplative unity with God and our involvement with Bharat [India].[176]

The Indian Church will never start theologizing, will not know her mission to re-interpret the designs of God in concrete historical contexts unless and until she becomes a genuinely local Church.[177] For Amalor, among many others, mainly these two following factors appear as the signs of the times and call the Church in India for a sincere action and involvement. These are:

(i) India is the cradle of great religions which are ancient, alive and have a long following.

(ii) India is in the process of liberation and development yearning to weld her vast population into a well-integrated nation and create a just and human society.[178]

Amalor writes that it is at this juncture that the Catholic Church in India, in the wake of Vatican II is engaged in an all-round renewal movement, which necessarily includes her becoming the Indian local Church, thereby, integrating into her theology the rich elements from Indian culture and religious traditions.[179] The Church should be involved and should take an active responsibility in the concerns and tasks of the contemporary society and that she, as a community, must reflect on her faith and Christian experience.

---

176 Ibid., p. 68.

177 Cf. DSA, *Theology of Evangelization,* op. cit., p. 18.

178 Cf. DSA, "Approach", *op. cit.,* p. 48. These two points will be dealt in detail in the later chapters: point (i) in chapter four when we deal with the salvific value of other religions, and point (ii) in chapter six when we deal with inter-religious collaboration for a new society.

179 Cf. DSA, "Foreword", in: Id. (ed.), *Indian Christian Spirituality,* op. cit., p. 5.

> This is the reason why an Indian theology cannot be developed or formulated by non-Indians, living abroad however competent and eminent they may be in theological erudition, however much we may profit by their insights and contributions. Ultimately it is the members of the local Church who can solve their problems, by being conscious of constituting the Church in a locality and period, by getting involved in the tasks of the society, and by making a reflection in faith. We have therefore, (1) to be a real local Church, (2) to be involved in the life of the contemporary society, and (3) to reflect on our Christian experience.[180]

*3.2.3.2. Seminary formation and other religions (OT 15-16, 19-20)*

To realize the emergence and stay of the Indian local Church amidst other religious traditions in India, Amalor, among others, focuses his attention on the seminary formation.

For dialogue with other religions and with our contemporaries, the revision of ecclesiastical studies by the Council encourages and exhorts the students to have recourse to the studies of other religions, their scriptures and values (cf. *OT* 15). The Council states:

> They should also be introduced to a knowledge of whatever other religions are most commonly encountered in this or that region, so that they may recognize more clearly how much goodness and truth they possess through the Providence of God, and learn how to refute their errors and bring the light of truth to those who are without it (*OT* 16 last para).

Amalor deplores to see the situation that though 98 per cent of Indian population is that of non-Christians, the majority of Indian priests are absorbed in the care of Christian communities. They are unwilling to go to "mission" areas and work among the people of other religions. What is still more deplorable is that even with a handful of priests in vast regions like North India, some of the priests and missionaries have no work and hence undergo an identity crisis simply because there are no Christian

---

180 DSA, *Theology of Evangelization,* op. cit., p. 18.

communities to keep in contact.[181]

There are many reasons for this. *Firstly,* our dioceses and parishes are anything but apostolic and all-round pastoral communities. Most of our seminarians and priests hail from closed-in-Christian ghettos with bias attitude towards other religions. *Secondly,* most of our training has been geared to serving Christian communities.[182] What is needed is more openness towards God and his ever-guiding Spirit in the understanding of other religions, his providential ways of loving and saving mankind. The fear of risks should be overcome. Amalor continues:

> It is easy, but evasive, to lay all the blame on seminaries: yet, something radical and urgent must be done to transform our seminary set-up, the approach to studies, means of formation, the life-style and the attitudes and habits of this generation. The experience of the last few years has shown two formidable obstacles: first, the needed change calls for pioneers, specially gifted and competent men; there is a great dearth of them: e.g. for the project of *pilot seminaries.* The second obstacle is the freedom and confidence that is required for such a venture. These can only be given by the bishops concerned. Barring a few exceptions, the Bishops are not prepared to take a risk. They are afraid of failures and counter effects.[183]

Amalor suggests that the present large size of seminaries should be cut into small groups so that the students could have a living contact with the normal reality of the people's lives, either in an *āśram* set-up (*gurukula*) or in a parish set-up. The theology taught there should be a reflection on Indian reality, so that theology does not become an ideology, devoid of everyday realities.

In seminary formation a basic course on the analysis of reality and a course on sociology of religion are imperative. In major seminaries the main course could be preceded by introductory lectures by specialists in the various aspects of the social situation. A basic knowledge of sociology and religions should be imparted to them if they are to analyse and

---

[181] Cf. DSA, "Approach", *op. cit.*, pp. 73-74.

[182] Cf. ibid., p. 74.

[183] Ibid.

understand reality and if their service is to be relevant to the people.[184]

The same, what we have said for the seminary formation, may apply to the religious life. Their life should be oriented not to themselves but to others, to the society where people of different castes, creed and status live together.[185] The religious communities must renew and adapt themselves to the modern times (cf. *PC* 2; Paul VI, *Evangelica Testificatio* 5, 6).

What we have said so far is not detrimental to the contemplative communities. These communities are not closed to themselves. They are basically led by the love of God and his people. They are oriented towards the realization of the kingdom of God here on earth by the witness of their lives with a 'hidden apostolic fruitfulness' (cf. *ET* 8; *PC* 7). Amalor says, "The role of contemplative communities is of paramount importance for witnessing to the gospel. The perplexing lack of appeal to the contemplative life in India calls for serious study and effective action."[186]

### *3.2.3.3. Inculturation, evangelization and religious pluralism*

The new theological reflection on the subject of inculturation was recognized and confirmed by Vatican II. However, the debate on inculturation reached its climax and the issues got clarified further and the implications and consequences were articulated during the Synod of Bishops on Evangelization of the modern world in September-October 1974. This came in the wake of a deeper and original understanding of the local Church, seen as essential and ever urgent mission of evangelization.[187]

We proceed to briefly dwell on this topic in so far as Amalor understood the importance of inculturation in relation to other religions and tried

---

[184] Cf. ibid., pp. 73-74.

[185] Cf. *Word and Worship* 13 (1980) 8, pp. 237-249.

'Religious life' when lived in love and service of God and his people, crossing the boundaries of creeds and castes, is well accepted by non-Christians. This can be well exemplified in the life and activity of Mother Teresa of Calcutta (1910-1997). Her burial ceremony was well attended also by the people of other religions and their religious heads as a sign of respect and recognition of her religious life and activity. Hers was the *evangelization* which can truly be said in the words of DSA a sharing of the paschal experience of Christ with others.

[186] DSA, "Approach", *op. cit.*, p. 73.

[187] Cf. DSA, *Gospel and Culture*, op. cit., p. 9.

to apply it to the Indian Church. The NBCLC in Bangalore and Anjali Ashram in Mysore show his keen interest in the theology and praxis of inculturation.

*(i) Inculturation: Immediate consequence of Christ's incarnation*

Amalor sees inculturation as the immediate consequence of Christ's incarnation. In its true and deeper meaning inculturation implies a total "incarnation", the total contextualization, of the Church in the culture of a particular human group, in its needs, aspirations and daily struggles.

In a pluri-religio-cultural society, inculturation will include religious dialogue and collaboration among various religious traditions. Lack of inculturation in a pluri-religious society would mean lack of religious dialogue which, in turn, will hamper effective and relevant mission of the Church in the land. While assessing the Church's mission in India in 1964 Amalor said that the Church in India has failed in her missionary work because of insufficient inculturation and an almost total lack of dialogue with Hindus, and so he proposed inter-religious dialogue as a new method of missionary approach.[188]

Since "inculturation deals with the interaction between religion and culture,"[189] we cannot compartmentalize religion and culture. Religion and culture go hand in hand. God reveals himself in and through a culture in history, and religion is always practised in a culture. The Gospel will become abstract and notional unless and until it is manifested in history and culture. As Paul VI states, "For the Church, evangelization means bringing the good news into all strata of humanity, and through its influence transforming humanity from within and making it new" (*EN* 18). However, "What matters is to evangelize man's culture and cultures not in a purely decorative way as it were by applying a thin veneer, but in a vital way, in depth, and right to their very roots, in the wise and rich sense which these terms have in *Gaudium et Spes*" (*EN* 20).[190]

---

[188] Cf. DSA, *Destinée,* op. cit., pp. 141, 231. Cf. also: Jose Kuttianimattathil, S.D.B., *Practice and Theology of Interreligious Dialogue,* Kristu Jyoti Publ., Bangalore, 1995, pp. 31-32. The point of inter-religious dialogue will be dealt later in chapter five.

[189] DSA, "Theological Reflections on Inculturation", in: *Studia Liturgica,* 20 (1990) 1, p. 45.

[190] See *EN* 18 & 20 quoted in: DSA, *Gospel and Culture,* op. cit., p. 33.

> The living Gospel lived by the Church in a living culture with all the transformations and realities it contains is what is called inculturation.... Hence there is no preaching of the Gospel (evangelization) without inculturation. There is no Church without being localized, concretized and visibilized. There is no salvation without the incarnation of the Word of God! It is good to note that the Incarnation of the Word, the localization of the Church and indigenization [or inculturation] should not be understood as referring only to externals. The humanity of Christ is the total and integral human nature with all its faculties and properties both internal and external [cf. Jn. 1:12; *DV* 4].[191]

The Church continues Christ's mission of recapitulating, reconciling and unifying all persons and things in God, and in the process, purifying and redeeming them (cf. *EN* 14). "This mission of recapitulation includes not only all men but also all the cultures and religions."[192] It includes not only all persons and individuals, reaching them one by one, but also their cultures and religions, in their collectivity. Thus culture itself becomes a field of evangelization (cf. *EN* 19).

The inculturating attitude of the Church of "borrowing" from cultures and religions is no danger to her universality. For, "the 'Christian culture' as such does not exist anywhere,"[193] neither can we say that the Church is beyond cultures. Instead, by inserting herself into each culture where the seeds of the Word are already planted by God prior to the preaching of the Gospel (cf. *AG* 18), enables her to become an ever-widening and all-inclusive fellowship with all. Thus Amalor writes, "Inculturation implies and brings about not one single universal Christian culture, but many particular 'Christian cultures'."[194] In doing so the Church vibrantly moves towards her universality and realizes the fullness of her catholicity,[195] in due respect for her sound tradition (cf. *AG* 22).

Inculturation is no danger to the tradition of the Church. Amalor

---

191 Ibid., p. 32.

192 Ibid., p. 34; cf. also: Hervé Carrier, "Evangelization of Culture", in: *DFT*, p. 283.

193 DSA, *Gospel and Culture*, op. cit., p. 42.

194 Ibid.

195 Cf. DSA, "Theological Reflection on Inculturation", *Studia Liturgica*, op. cit., pp. 51-52.

writes, "Inculturation should be in continuity with the healthy and venerable tradition of the Church and in discontinuity with the recent and ambiguous tradition."[196] He feels happy that today Vatican II has re-affirmed and re-launched the process of inculturation, based on the principle of incarnation of the Word. He continues:

> Vatican II far from teaching a new doctrine and instead of initiating a new tradition re-affirmed the age-old Christian principle of incarnation. In so doing it re-launched the process of inculturation, which had been impeded during the last four centuries of colonialization and political expansion of the West. Thus Vatican II has facilitated the earlier and authentic Christian tradition to continue from now on, in spite of the break of four centuries and more.[197]

Religion is always practised and fostered in a particular culture which includes such elements as: the world-view, value-system, social organizations, forms of government and authority, way of life, spirituality and religious experience of a particular community.[198] An isolationist Christianity, therefore, which splits the Gospel and culture and which is closed to the local culture, runs the risk of being alienated from that culture. Quoting Paul VI, Amalor calls it "the drama of our times" (*EN* 20).[199] A lop-sided and unilateral understanding of theology which exclusively emphasizes religion beyond culture, or sees culture as something external and peripheral to religion is not Christian.[200] Then, it would, in its final

---

[196] DSA, *Gospel and Culture,* op. cit., p. 39. Identification of Christianity with the American or European, or for that matter with any single culture and tradition at the exclusion of others, is not the sound tradition of the Church. Unfortunately sometime it was so in the past and even for some in the present. The tradition of the Church in this perspective, is seen as including as its essential parts, the unhealthy and ambiguous elements of a particular culture (cf. ibid., pp. 41-42).

[197] Ibid., p. 43.

[198] Cf. DSA, "Theological Reflection on Inculturation", in: *Studia Liturgica,* op. cit., p. 166; see also: Id., "Final Statement", in: Sergio Torres and Virginia Fabella (eds), *The Emergent Gospel,* Orbis Books, Maryknoll, 1978, pp. 269-270.

[199] Cf. DSA, *Gospel and Culture,* op. cit., p. 16; cf. also: Id., *Our Christian World Vision,* op. cit., pp. 11-12.

[200] Cf. DSA, "Theological Reflections on Inculturation", in: *Studia Liturgica,* op. cit., pp. 118-119. Cf. also: Joseph Komonchak and Co. (eds), *The New Dictionary of Theology,* op. cit., p. 511.

analysis, amount to diminishing the very historicity of Christ, his redemptive incarnation in history.

Denial of God's revelation in other religions and the understanding of Christianity, expressed exclusively in Western or European culture, loses the perspective of the universality of God's self-communication, and the importance of inculturation is denied thereby.[201] Indian culture or rather the cultures of India have been influenced by different religions, chiefly Hinduism. Indian religions, in their turn, have been influenced and shaped by Indian culture. Hence, any process of inculturation in India necessarily includes religious traditions as a dimension of the total reality.[202]

### *(ii) Pinpointing some salient theological implications and conclusions*[203]

#### *(a) Inculturation -- yes! but Hinduization -- no!*

Inculturation does not mean Hinduization in the Indian context. Hinduism, though predominant, is one of the religions in India. Besides, broadly speaking, culture is not limited to religious thoughts and its liturgical practices alone, but includes under its umbrella the whole dynamic and integrating complex of the total reality, both secular as well as spiritual.

The purpose of inculturation is not to become a Hindu in a Hindu culture, or for that matter, a Muslim in an Islamic culture or a Buddhist in a Buddhist culture. Hinduism is not the end, but Hindu culture, the culture of the people, is a medium or vehicle, an effective and relevant medium for an effective and relevant proclamation of the Good News as well as its praxis in and through this culture. Then, one will be called for a double heritage and double fidelity, not either Hindu or Christian but Hindu *and*

---

201 Cf. DSA, "Theological Reflection on Inculturation", in: *Studia Liturgica,* op. cit., pp. 118-119; cf. also: Id., "Church and Culture", in: J. Komonchak and Co. (eds), *The New Dictionary of Theology,* op. cit., p. 204.

202 See: Cyril De Souza, S.D.B., *Catechesis for India Today,* op. cit., p. 319, he interprets the mind of DSA.

203 Cf. DSA, *Gospel and Culture,* op. cit., pp. 45-67; id., "Inculturation is not Hinduization but Christianization", in: Id. (ed.), *Indian Christian Spirituality,* op. cit., pp. 107-114.

Christian, fully Indian and fully Christian.[204]

Inculturation is not Hinduization but Christianization. When Hindus are incorporated into the Church at the end of a process of evangelization, conversion, catechumenate and baptism and other sacraments of Christian initiation, we do not call it Hinduization. A Hindu becomes a Christian. In the same way when some elements from Hinduism are taken and purified, given a new interpretation and integrated into Christian worship of life, we should call it Christianization of Hindu elements and not Hinduization.[205]

### *(b) Inculturation includes religious traditions as part of the total reality*

We do not talk of compartmentalization in inculturation. The scope of inculturation extends to all realities, including religions. It follows the pattern of the redemptive incarnation of Christ and finds its meaning in the very universal salvific plan of God for the whole of creation. In Christ Jesus "all things hold together" (Col. 1:17).

> Through the mystery of Incarnation he assumes the whole creation in order to redeem it and unify it. Nothing is saved unless it is assumed; and everything that has been created must be saved; and so everything created was assumed by Christ. On the cross he destroyed hostility, broke down the barriers and reconciled God with man, and men among themselves (2 Cor. 5:17-21; Eph. 2:11-22; Col. 1:20).[206]

If God has submitted everything under Christ, if the saving action of Christ extends to the whole of humanity and creation, and if the Spirit of the risen Lord fills the universe and permeates everything then the Church has no right to exclude anything -- especially religions -- from the object of Christ's saving action. We cannot "call profane what God has made clean" (Acts 10:15). "God does not have favourites but that anybody of

---

204 Cf. DSA, *Gospel and Culture,* op. cit., p. 17; id., "Indian Culture: Integrating cultural elements into our spirituality", *op. cit.,* p. 92. See also: Gerwin van Leeuwen, O.F.M., *Fully Indian - Authentically Christian,* op. cit. (the whole book in general).

205 Cf. DSA, "Inculturation is not Hinduization but Christianization", *op. cit.,* 109-110.

206 DSA, *Gospel and Culture,* op. cit., p. 46.

any nationality who fears God and does what is right is acceptable to him" (Acts 10:34-35). The Holy Spirit is poured out even on the so-called pagans like Cornelius (cf. Acts 10:45). If so, Hinduism and other religions are not outside the plan of God but take their place and come within God's *one* plan of salvation which is centered in Christ through whom all things and all human beings are led to their fulfillment.[207]

> The Church like Christ cannot save anything unless she assumes it even before transforming it.... Truth, goodness, beauty, purity and holiness -- wherever found -- originate in God and belong to God. They have God for author and goal. They should be recognized by the Church as gifts of God and inheritance of Christ (Ps. 2:6).... The Church cannot disown them as alien, as 'theirs'. Everything belongs to us, we belong to Christ; and Christ himself belongs to God (1 Cor. 3:23), so that God may be all in all. This is the goal and fulfillment of creation, this is the full effect of Christ's redemptive work, and this is the total mission of the Church to be carried out.[208]

*(c) The Church's attitude towards other religions*

Basing himself on the Vatican II documents, Amalor says that the Church and all her members should "prudently and lovingly, through dialogue and collaboration, acknowledge, preserve and promote the spiritual and moral goods found among these men, as well as the values in their society and culture" (*NA* 2). We are expected "to learn by sincere and patient dialogue what treasures a bountiful God has distributed among the nations of the earth" (*AG* 11d). We are supposed to save "whatever truth and grace are to be found among the nations, as a sort of secret presence of God" (*AG* 9).[209]

Thus, inculturation means "that young Churches in imitation to the plan of Incarnation, rooted in Christ take to themselves in a wonderful exchange, all the riches of the nations which were given to Christ as an

---

207 Cf. ibid., pp. 46-47; also: Id., "Inculturation is not Hinduization but Christianization", *op. cit.*, p. 108.

208 Ibid., p. 47; *Indian Christian Spirituality,* op. cit., p. 109.

209 See these Vatican II documents as cited by DSA in: Id., "Inculturation is not Hinduization but Christianization", *op. cit.*, p. 109.

inheritance (cf. Ps. 2:8)" (*AG* 22a).[210]

Concluding the point here, Amalor emphasizes once again the need and importance of inculturation. He writes:

> With this clear statement and teaching of Vatican II none can say that elements from other religions cannot be integrated into Christian theology, worship, prayer life and spirituality provided, of course they can all be christianized.... So inculturation includes, in this correct sense some kind of 'hinduization'.[211]

*(d) Inculturation supposes participation in the paschal mystery*

Christ, through his paschal mystery, has redeemed humanity form sin and death (cf. 1 Cor. 15:4; 2 Cor. 5:21). The Church as the body of Christ (cf. Eph. 1:23) should continue to live and present to the world this paschal mystery and mission of Christ as an on-going reality today, that is, purifying the religions and cultures from error and falsehood in the light of the Gospel.[212] For

> the words of Christ are at one and the same time words of judgement and grace, of death and life. For it is by putting to death what is old that we are able to come to the newness of life. This fact implies, first of all, to persons, but it holds good also for the various goods of this world which bear the mark of both man's sin and of God's blessings (*AG* 8).

If the purpose of the Church's mission is to gather everybody and everything to God through Christ then "only those have been Christianized and who conform to Christ can be taken up in the unity and fellowship of the Church."[213] The same must hold good for inculturation.

> We do not indiscriminately admit anything and everything from the doctrines and practices of other religions into the Church whether in liturgy, theology or spirituality, etc., nor can we indiscriminately

---

[210] Ibid.

[211] Ibid.

[212] Cf. ibid., p. 110.

[213] Ibid., p. 110.

> assume them as they are. They should be first brought to the touchstone of Christ and his paschal mystery. They should be first made to pass through Christ's death and resurrection.[214]

Likewise, nothing can be integrated into our theology, liturgy or spirituality from other religions unless they have values in them, unless they can survive a prophetic critique, unless they acquire a Christian meaning through a Christian interpretation and unless they are oriented towards a Christian goal under the guidance of the Spirit. This is an important and indispensable condition for inculturation.[215] The process of inculturation in fact frees religion from all taint of evil and restores it to Christ its maker. Thus, whatever good is found in other religions and cultures is not lost. Instead, "it is healed, ennobled and perfected for the glory of God, the shame of the demon and the bliss of men (*AG* 9c; cf. *AG* 11d; *LG* 17)."[216]

*(e) God's kingdom is bigger than the Church*

The Church is the universal sacrament of salvation. For many this amounts to the self-sufficiency of the Church. For them inculturation would be, therefore, even harmful as it might show indirectly that the Church does not have the fullness.

Amalor distinguishes between God and Christ and between Christ and the Church. Even though Christ is the total, ultimate and definite revelation of God, and even though Christ is present in the Church, one cannot and should not *identify* Christ with the Church, nor can one limit his presence to the Church alone. He is present always and everywhere as the word of God, as the risen Lord and saviour of mankind. Likewise, the one true Church of Christ subsists in the Catholic Church (cf. *LG* 8) but is not exhausted by it. The saving action of Christ extends beyond the visible boundary of the Church.[217]

> The Church is a contingent, historical, temporary and relative realization: its period is between the Pasch and the Parousia. Like every other sign it is less than the reality. The Kingdom is present in the

---

[214] Ibid., pp. 110-111.
[215] Cf. ibid., p. 111.
[216] See as quoted in: Ibid.
[217] Cf. ibid., p. 112.

Church, but the Church and the Kingdom are not identical. [The Kingdom is bigger than the Church]. That is why the Church is in continuous pilgrimage and tends towards fullness and total consummation.[218]

*(f) The Church can and should "borrow" from other religions*

Vatican II asks the Church, therefore, to realize her pilgrim nature and to borrow from other religions without the least hesitation or shame or complex. *Ad Gentes* states, "From the customs and traditions of people, from their wisdom and their learning, from their arts and their sciences, these churches borrow all those things which can contribute to the glory of their creator, the revelation of the Saviour's grace, or the proper arrangement of Christian life" (no. 22).[219] Further we read in the same, "Particular traditions, together with the individual patrimony of each family, and of nations can be illuminated by the light of the Gospel, and then be taken up into Catholic unity" (no. 22).[220]

Everything belongs to Christ; and in fact there is no borrowing as such by the Church from others. Amalor writes:

> In fact, there is no borrowing; all that she appears to borrow is in fact what already belongs to Christ by creation, and by resurrection and hence what the Church should *'claim and gather as her own!'* As Indians, we can claim all that is hindu and Indian as our own; as Christians we can state that whatever belongs to Christ belongs to us. So we borrow nothing.[221]

*(g) Towards realizing the Church's universality, fullness and unity*

Inculturation leads the Church to realize the plenitude of Catholic fellowship, the ecclesial communion between the universal Church and the particular Churches in their variety and uniqueness, and also fellowship between the Church and other religious traditions (cf. *AG* 22).

---

218 Ibid.

219 See as quoted by DSA, in: Id., *Gospel and Culture,* op. cit., pp. 51-52.

220 See as quoted in: DSA, "Inculturation is not Hinduization but Christianization", *op. cit.,* p. 113.

221 Ibid.

> The greatness and uniqueness of the Catholic Church will be set in evidence not by setting up barriers between the Church and other religions, not by speaking a 'we'-and-'they' language, ... Christian and non-Christian. Her uniqueness can only be shown by the universal Christian vision, by dynamic and persevering effort ... and to integrate all traditions and values within her Catholicity. *Ad Gentes* advises the Church to be Catholic. In this sense the prophecy of Isaiah is fully applicable to the Church: 'To this people it was said in prophecy: enlarge the space of your tent, spread out your tent cloths unsparingly (Is. 54:2)' (*AG* 9a).[222]

Though all this may be correct in theory many Catholics find it difficult in practice to accept customs, practices, signs and symbols of other religions. Amalor says that this is due to their earlier training and erroneous judgements, emotional and psychological blocks and prejudices against other religions. They find difficult to accept the new theological understanding brought about in the Church by the Vatican II theology. This difficulty can be overcome only with the passage of time, supported by on-going education, dialogue and experiential participation in indigenous forms of prayers and worship.[223] Thus it will be more clearly seen in what ways Christian faith can seek for understanding in the philosophy and wisdom of peoples from other religious traditions. Then

> a better view will be gained as to how their customs, outlook on life, and social order can be reconciled with the manner of living taught by divine revelation. As a result, avenues will be opened for a more profound adaptation in the whole area of Christian life. Thanks to such a procedure, Christian life can be accommodated to the genius and the dispositions of each culture (*AG* 22).[224]

Amalor took great care to always keep a *vue d'ensemble* and spoke of inculturation on variety of issues from the theological and anthropological point of view. For him inculturation meant a total inculturation of *life* and *worship*. In his radical commitment to radical inculturation, he seems to have focused his attention mainly on liturgy, catechetics and the

---

222 Ibid., p. 114.

223 Cf. ibid., pp. 113-114.

224 See as quoted by DSA in: Id., *Gospel and Culture*, op. cit., p. 57.

development of an Indian Christian spirituality.[225] The 'liturgical inculturation' (worship) is one of the aspects of the Church. His focus on the aspect of 'liturgical inculturation' was only a step towards the actualization of his deeper thought and theology of the total inculturation of life and worship. His concern was the total inculturation of the Church, her mission, theology and liturgy.[226] Thus when we speak of inculturation, we do not speak in terms of changing some liturgical garbs and rituals but the inculturation of the total life and worship.

### *3.2.3.4. Inculturation and the National Centre (NBCLC)*[227]

After a theological survey about inculturation and evangelization in the light of Vatican II, we proceed to briefly deal with the National Biblical, Catechetical and Liturgical Centre (NBCLC), Bangalore, India. Amalor was its first Founder-Director (1966/67-1882), appointed by the Catholic Bishops' Conference of India (CBCI).[228]

The National Centre which was decided upon by the CBCI in October 1966 and was founded in February 1967, tries to embody and spread the vision and the spirit, the values and the ideals, the objectives and the goals of the *Church-in-renewal* ushered in by the Vatican II Council (1962-1965).[229] Amalor defines the aim of the Centre as follows:

> To plan and implement on a national level under the guidance of the hierarchy a programme of biblical, catechetical and liturgical renewal in India, within the overall framework and movement of Church Renewal in India and according to the spirit and programme of II

---

[225] Cf. Gerwin van Leeuwen, O.F.M., *Fully Indian - Authentically Christian,* op. cit., p. 238.

[226] Though important in itself, we do not deal with the 'liturgical inculturation'. This would be beyond our scope. Our main concern here is the inculturation of the Church, her mission and theology, and that too, with regard to other religions.

[227] In 1971 the National Catechetical and Liturgical Centre (NCLC) became NBCLC.

[228] Cf. Cyril De Souza, S.D.B., *Catechesis for India Today,* op. cit., p. 2; Gerwin van Leeuwen, O.F.M., *Fully Indian - Authentically Christian,* op. cit., p. 12, he says that in 1966 the CBCI appointed DSA as the Founder-Director of NBCLC, but DSA actually took charge of the office on 6th February 1966. The National Centre was decided upon by the CBCI in 1966 and founded in 1967.

[229] Cf. DSA, "The NBCLC Campus a Living Synthesis of Indian Christian Theology and Spirituality", in: Id. (ed.), *Indian Christian Spirituality,* op. cit., p. 237.

Vatican Council and the exigencies of the Post-Vatican period. Thus it is to be an agency to promote and coordinate renewal at the national level in collaboration with regional and diocesan agencies.[230]

Amalor describes the spirit of the Centre in three key words: *national, pastoral* and *diaconal.* Thereby the Centre would maintain a comprehensive vision of the country; its pastoral action would reflect the community character with the hierarchy and the faithful, pooling together all the charisms for the common good of building up the Church. Every pastoral activity would be guided by the diaconal spirit in love and humble service of God and his people in imitation of Christ himself, the servant of God.[231] The Centre is to be an animating -- not dominating -- organism of pastoral action; and one of its policies, among others, is to create an atmosphere of freedom and fellowship for all, fellowship and harmony among Christians as well as people of other creeds and ideologies in dialogue, sharing and life.[232]

Amalor formulated the task and mission of the Centre in four main thrusts for the overall Church's renewal in India. These are the following:

> First, commitment to *social justice* and struggle for liberation in view of creating a new society: free, just, human, fraternal, egalitarian, sharing and participatory.
> Secondly, to raise the above through an all-round *inter-religious dialogue, and cooperation* with people of all religions and ideologies.
> Thirdly, *inculturation* of all aspects of Christian life and all activities of the Church.
> Fourthly, an *authentic Indian Christian Spirituality* to be developed, lived and promoted as a source and climax of the three other concerns. This will make the Church in India authentic and relevant.[233]

---

230 See: *The National Biblical Catechetical Liturgical Centre of India,* NBCLC, Bangalore, 1979 (5th edition), p. 3 as cited in: Gerwin van Leeuwen, O.F.M., *Fully Indian - Authentically Christian,* op. cit., p. 12.

231 Cf. ibid., pp. 3-6. (*The National Biblical Catechetical Liturgical Centre of India*).

232 Cf. DSA (ed.), *Post-Vatican Liturgical Renewal in India,* vol. 1 (1963-1968), NBCLC, Bangalore, 1968, pp. 72-73.

233 DSA, *NBCLC Campus. Milieu of God-Experience. An Artistic Synthesis of Spirituality,* NBCLC, Bangalore, 1982, p. 6. These four points were the final formulation of the fourfold task and mission of the NBCLC.

From the very beginning the aims and objectives of the Centre are being carried out both in letter and spirit. The Centre is open to all people from different walks of life. On the one hand, the Centre provides research work and seminars. For example, (i) the Asian Seminar on Religion and Development (1973), (ii) the Research Seminar on Non-Biblical Scriptures (1974), (iii) Research Seminar and Pastoral Consultation on Ministries in the Church (1976), (iv) Interdisciplinary Research Seminar on 'The Indian Church in the Struggle for a New Society' (1981), and (v) Research Seminar on Sharing Worship (*Communicatio in Sacris*) (1988). On the other hand, the common people benefit themselves from the animation, meetings and various programmes of the Centre.[234]

The NBCLC building reflects Amalor's overall theological vision and synthesis, his psychological insights and spiritual experience and his concrete planning and execution. The whole atmosphere of the campus agrees to the tone of the Centre and facilitates its purpose in inculturation, in Church-renewal and self-renewal. Its chapel, *Saccidānanda* (Reality, Awareness and Bliss), with its Indian art and architecture, signs and symbols, prayer forms and worship, philosophy and spirituality, obviously breathes the air of inculturation.[235] It stands as an example of the Church's "incarnation" in a Hindu philosophico-religious ambient; thereby, recognizing the seeds of the Word in it, it is trying to purify and perfect the Hindu culture, religion and society as a whole -- all in an atmosphere of mutual sharing, dialogue and respect.

After the expiry of his term as Director of the NBCLC, Amalor continued his radical commitment to inculturation and evangelization in Anjali Ashram, Mysore, which he founded in 1979. This is yet his another contribution to the Indian Church in particular and the whole universal Church in general.

---

[234] For the NBCLC animation, meetings, seminars and other programmes, cf. Gerwin van Leeuwen, O.F.M., *Fully Indian - Authentically Christian,* op. cit., pp. 19-189.

[235] For further explanation of *Saccidānanda*, cf. DSA, "The Chapel 'Saccidananda' Unique Place of God-Experience", in: Id. (ed.), *Indian Christian Spirituality,* op. cit., pp. 246-256e; id., *NBCLC Campus. Milieu of God-Experience. An Artistic Synthesis of Spirituality, op. cit.,* pp. 6-7; id., "The NBCLC Campus a Living Synthesis of Indian Christian Theology and Spirituality", *op. cit.,* pp. 237-245; cf. also: Gerwin van Leeuwen, O.F.M., *Fully Indian - Authentically Christian,* op. cit., pp. 14-17.

## 4. Conclusion

Gerwin van Leeuwen writes, "The struggle to embody and incarnate the vision of Vatican II characterizes the life of D.S. Amalorpavadass (DSA) and the history of the NBCLC. Although not officially a Council peritus, DSA became acquainted with the spirit that moved the Council even before it started."[236]

The Church is missionary by her very nature (cf. *EN* 14; *AG* 3, 7-9, 11). The purpose of her mission is salvation of the whole man and the whole of mankind. Her mission must be an incarnated mission modelled on the redemptive incarnation of Christ, assuming and redeeming all peoples, cultures and religions. Every religion and culture should be put on the anvil of the Gospel of Jesus Christ (cf. Col. 1:16; 2:15).

Theology, to be relevant to the reality, must be involved in the reality. "The Church is the formal dimension of the knowledge of faith (...). Were theology not to proceed from an ecclesial awareness and as contributing to the growth of the community, it would be only an esoteric sort of knowledge producing no results."[237] The Church must take the socio-cultural and religious data of the people seriously, that is, she must announce the *good news* of Christ to all peoples, religions and cultures in the unity of faith and pluriformity of theology. "This unity of faith is based upon the unity of the Spirit, and the unity of the Spirit is revealed in the unity of the Word which the Spirit-filled witnesses proclaim."[238]

Today the proclamation of the Gospel, especially amidst the world religions, poses a great challenge to the Church. It is a challenge of the Spirit. Amalor, in his radical commitment to implementing the spirit of Vatican II took many initiatives and bold steps towards inculturation and evangelization, dialogue and collaboration, unity and peace, amidst the challenges of the great world religions and ideologies in the Asian and particularly in the Indian context. Among others, his two great contributions towards inculturation and evangelization of the Church are worth mentioning. These are: (i) The NBCLC, Bangalore, and (ii) Anjali

---

236 Gerwin van Leeuwen, O.F.M., *Fully Indian - Authentically Christian,* op. cit., p. xv.

237 Rino Fisichella, "Meaning, Ultimate, in Jesus Christ (I. The Meaning of Revelation)", in: *DFT,* p. 647.

238 M. Dhavamony, "Indian Christian Theology", in: *Studia Missionalia,* vol. 45, op. cit., p. 95.

Ashram, Mysore, which today continue to further his effort and inspire others towards the contextualization of the Church's theology and her salvific message. In and through these institutes "thousands and through these thousands lakhs of people have been initiated into the spirit of Vatican II."[239]

Paul Puthanangady writes, "I wish that they [others] may come to know what it means to respond to the challenges of the Spirit [today]. May Amalor inspire them to go forward in radical commitment and uncompromising option for the Kingdom of God."[240]

---

[239] Gerwin van Leeuwen, O.F.M., *Fully Indian - Authentically Christian,* op. cit., pp. 340-341.

[240] Fr. Paul Puthanangady, "Foreword", in: Id. (ed.), *Church in India: Institution or Movement?,* op. cit., p. viii.

# PART TWO

## JESUS CHRIST AND RELIGIONS

Jesus Christ is the Son of God and the saviour of the world. In his kenotic condition the Son of God became the "historical" Jesus, the Word become flesh in a particular time and place (cf. Jn. 1:14; Gal. 4:4); and in his resurrection he is constituted the "cosmic" Christ, the saviour of all (cf. Eph. 1:20-22). In and through this event (the whole Jesus Christ event) Christ is seen as the ultimate and definitive figure in all of God's dealings with the human family, on whom the destiny of every person and history itself depend. Through the saving mystery of this event Christ assumes into himself all creation, reconciling and bringing all things, things in heaven and things on earth together (cf. Eph. 1:10), so that he will be all in all (cf. Eph. 1:23; Col. 3:11) and that through him God will be all in all (cf. 1 Cor. 15:28). Now, while the Church is constituted the universal sacrament of salvation on earth (cf. *LG* 48), Vatican II (*NA*) clearly points out to the unique mediation of Christ spilling over the limits of the visible Church and to the action of the Holy Spirit working outside the boundaries of the visible Church.

# CHAPTER THREE

# THE COSMIC CHRIST
# HIS PLEROMA, CENTRALITY AND UNIVERSALITY

## 1. Introduction

"And the Word became flesh and lived among us, and we have seen his glory, the glory as of a Father's only Son, full of grace and truth.... From his fullness we have all received, grace upon grace" (Jn. 1:14-16).

The above quotation from John well contains, in short, the content of this chapter. Jesus is the incarnation of God in history in the "fullness of time" (Gal. 4:4). The incarnation of God in the person of Jesus is the culmination of God's continuous revelation, that is, God's greatest act in the one and continuous salvation history, in the unity of his saving activity (cf. Heb. 1:1-3). Jesus is the Son of God and, therefore, the supreme medium of revelation and the most decisive intervention of God in the history of salvation. He is the visible image of the invisible God (cf. Col. 1:15), the sacrament of God and his kingdom on earth. The Johannine *Logos:* "the Word became flesh" (Jn. 1:14), the *Abba-experience* of Jesus on earth: "The Father and I are one" (Jn. 10:30; cf. 8:23-24,28,58; 10:38; 12:50; 14:9), his life, ministry, death and resurrection, that is, the mystery of the whole Jesus Christ event goes to make Jesus -- the *cosmic Christ,* the fullness, the plenitude (*pleroma, pūrṇam*)[1] of history and salvation. The authority of Jesus, the *Son,* is that of God, the *Father* (cf. Jn. 5:19-30). The fullness of grace and truth dwells in Jesus, and God continues to dispense the fullness of grace and truth, fullness of salvation, in and through his Son Jesus Christ. In his on-going revelation, God continues to save the world and bring all people and religions to their fulfillment in and through his Son Jesus Christ. Jesus Christ, therefore, becomes the source and centre of history, life and salvation. Peoples and religions are ordained to God, to the fullness of life and salvation, in and through the person of Christ Jesus. Now the Church, the mystical body of Christ, continues the universal saving action of Christ on earth. The Church is the sacrament of

---

[1] DSA often speaks of the *pleroma* of Christ and his Spirit. See, e.g., id., *Destinée,* op. cit. p. 144; id., *Approaches,* op. cit, p. 36.

Christ on earth, and because of her special relation to Christ she is the special and universal sacrament of salvation.

In and through his life of obedience to the saving will of the Father to the point of death on the cross, Jesus is proclaimed by the Father the universal saviour of the world (cf. Phil. 2:6-11). The universality of Jesus Christ does not mean an attribution of an abstract universal concept which is predicated of many individuals, such as the concept of humanity to all and different human beings everywhere, nor does it mean that truths common to other religious personages are also found in Christ.[2] "It means that Jesus Christ is the concrete universal, the historical God-man who is the plenitude of all perfections, who is the universal saviour of all peoples, not exclusive of the other religious personages who have appeared in human history but inclusive of all that is found true and good in them."[3]

The incarnation of Christ Jesus is very central in Amalor's thinking.[4] Some see Jesus only in ontological categories, forgetting thereby Jesus' incarnational approach to life and salvation, his humanity and life-behaviour on earth. Today, the basic stress of Christology, especially, from Asian and Latin American countries, is incarnational, that is, the following of the historical, human and socially involved Jesus who was often accused by the Jewish leaders as false prophet, blasphemer, law-breaker, causing religious and political unrest. This socially involved Jesus, dead and risen, has established the new covenant between God and human beings. Jesus is seen, thereby, as creating a new relationship between God and man: a new worship of God in spirit and truth, a new socio-political and religious system, structures and institutions, based on love and service.

Paul sees the fullness of creation and salvation in the mystery of Christ Jesus. In his person Jesus has inaugurated and revealed in its fullness the compassionate God and his kingdom of "righteousness and peace and joy in the Holy Spirit" (Rom. 14:17), and now through the sacra-

---

2 Cf. J. Ratzinger, "Der Christliche Glaube und die Weltreligionen", in: *Gott in Welt,* II Festschrift Karl Rahner, 1964, pp. 287-305, as cited by M. Dhavamony, "Theology of Religions", in: Sebastian Karotemprel (ed.), *Following Christ in Mission,* op. cit., p. 252.

3 M. Dhavamony, "Theology of Religions", in: Sebastian Karotemprel (ed.), *Following Christ in Mission,* op. cit., pp. 252-253; cf. also: Id., "The Cosmic Christ and the World Religions", in: *Studia Missionalia,* vol. 42, Editrice Pontificia Università Gregoriana, Roma, 1993, pp. 179-225.

4 Cf. Gerwin van Leeuwen, O.F.M., *Fully Indian - Authentically Christian,* op. cit., p. 308.

mentality of the Church, his body (cf. Eph. 1:23; Col. 1:18; *LG* 7)[5] and bride (cf. 2 Cor. 11:2; Eph. 5:29,32; Mk. 2:19),[6] he continues to work for the kingdom, bringing all peoples and religions, ideologies and principalities to the peace and unity and the fullness of salvation. This is the pleroma (*pūrṇam*) of the mystery of Christ (cf. Rom. 11:25; 16:25-27; Col. 1:26; 2:2), the mystery of the Gospel (cf. Mk. 16:15-16; Eph. 3:4-6; 6:19).

## 2. Jesus Christ Event: The Centre of Salvation History

Jesus is the way, the truth and the life par excellence. He is the norm of human existence, the pattern of salvation: life and salvation here on earth 'already' (*jīvan mukti*) and hereafter, 'not yet', the resurrection (*videha mukti*).[7] Since he is the Word become flesh, the living person, he is the fullness of God's revelation and the fullness of salvation.[8] Hence, the history and religions of the world, whose final goal is salvation, must turn to Christ Jesus for salvation.[9]

Christ is the fullness of grace and truth (cf. Jn. 1:14); he is the cosmic saviour, the centre of salvation history.[10]

### *2.1. The Cosmic Christ: The Logos, the God-Man and His Redemptive Cross*

God has left traces of himself and of his salvific plan in other religious traditions (cf. Heb. 1:1-2).[11] Though other religions may contain

---

[5] Cf. also: *CCC*, 779, 789, 805.

[6] Cf. also: Ibid., 796, 808.

[7] Cf. DSA, *Approaches*, op. cit., pp. 20-24.

[8] Cf. DSA, *Theology of Development*, op. cit., p. 15.

[9] Cf. DSA, *Approaches*, op. cit., pp. 36-37.

[10] Cf. DSA, *Approach*, op. cit., pp. 44-45.

[11] The traces of God, his revelation and salvation in other religions are verified by the very definition of religion itself. R. Otto defines religion as the numinous experience of the holy; M. Eliade considers religion as the manifestation of the sacred hierophanies through signs and symbols. The most sublime hierophany known to history is the incarnation as realized in Jesus Christ. Cf. M. Dhavamony, "Religion: Definition", in: *DFT*, op. cit., pp. 819-827.

a partial realization of God's revelation and salvation, this in no way puts them contrary to Christ or Christianity; rather, what is partial must be led to its fullness. The partial revelation must be oriented to and fulfilled in Christ who is the fullness of God's revelation. In other words, the theology of religions, being a normative science, has the right to judge in the light of Christian revelation what is of value and necessary for salvation. It is in this sense that Christ fulfills other religions' aspirations and their partial realization of God's revelation and salvation. Amalor writes:

> Thus the religions of the world and all that is religious, we may say, are in a state of vocation to salvation; they implicitly yearn for Christ to have their meaning and fulfillment; they tend towards Christ like the rest on the historical movement; they constitute an ensemble to be permeated and transformed by the ferment of the gospel; they fall within the universal sovereignty of God.[12]

Jesus Christ not only fulfills the law and the prophets, he, being the eternal Logos, Reason or Truth, also fulfills the philosophies and ideologies of the world which reflect the ray of that truth which enlightens all men (cf. *NA* 2).[13] The religions of the world implicitly yearn for Christ and find their meaning and fulfillment in him. For example, Kṛṣṇa in Hinduism and Buddha in Buddhism, that is, the need and aspiration of a God-man in Asian religions, or their concept of *avatāra* or *Bodhisattva,* that is, the need and aspiration for resurrection, the desire of union with the Absolute or God, are fulfilled in the person of Christ Jesus, "the Word *incarnate,* the God-man",[14] who *lived, died* and *rose* from the dead. In short, *it is because of the definitive divine salvific mystery in the incarnation, life, death and resurrection of Jesus that Jesus becomes the Christ of all times -- past, present and future -- and religions, the central figure, the fullness of all religions and ideologies.* It is in this sense that other religions are considered as preparation for Christ or as oriented to Christ. This is the centrality and the universality of Jesus Christ.[15]

---

[12] DSA, *Approaches,* op. cit., p. 33.

[13] Cf. ibid., p. 34.

[14] See: DSA, *Theology of Catechesis,* op. cit., p. 20.

[15] Cf. DSA, *Theology of Development,* op. cit., p. 15; id., *Approaches,* op. cit., pp. 33-35.

The religious figures of other religions are either only mythical and ahistorical *avatāras,* like Kṛṣṇa and Rāma or only human and historical, like Gautama Buddha and Muhammad. They are not fully human and fully divine.[16] But Jesus Christ is fully human and fully divine. For he is the God incarnate. It is this incarnate God in the saving mystery of the person of Jesus Christ who saves all men. Christ is the universal saviour. However, what we have to keep in mind always in this chapter in particular and in the whole Christian theology of religions according to Amalor in general is that, as we have already seen, *there is no comparisons of religions. Comparisons are useless, odious and harmful. The Church is called, not to compare and condemn others, but to share her unique experience of the risen Lord with others.*[17]

The whole of humanity partakes in the Logos through creation (Logos Christology). The cosmic Christ is related to all peoples and is at work in their religions, calling them to perfection. In the person of Christ the two religious traditions, namely, the prophetic and the mystical, meet together and are reconciled.[18] That is to say, Jesus Christ in his person comes to fulfill the world religions (fulfillment theology).[19] Aurobindo would interpret the evolution of the world, history, human beings and their religions in and through his theory of 'cosmic consciousness' (Super Man or Super Consciousness, i.e., the evolution of consciousness rather than a biological evolution which is by now complete). Amalor, in line with Teilhard de Chardin, sees the evolution of the 'cosmic consciousness' in the process of Christification.[20] Consciousness or knowledge (*jñāna*) does not exist in itself; to be real, it must exist in somebody. Or rather, we speak of the consciousness of somebody, a person. In this context Aurobindo would speak of 'Super Man' or 'Super Consciousness' which, if it has to be real, must exist in a person. This person is Christ Jesus, the Word become man, the Logos, the supreme consciousness (*jñāna*) of God who fully and perfectly unites man with God in the supreme consciousness

---

[16] Cf. DSA, *Approaches,* op. cit., p. 40.

[17] Cf. DSA, "Biblical World-View and a Renewed Holistic Spirituality", *op. cit.,* p. 56ff.

[18] Cf. DSA, *Approaches,* op. cit., pp. 39-41.

[19] Cf. ibid., p. 15. DSA sees the world, history and religions in the thought of P. Teilhard de Chardin, oriented towards Christ for their fulfillment, i.e., evolution of the cosmos from the simple cell to plant life, to animal life and then to the human life, putting Christ at the centre, the Omega point. Cp. the creation story in the Bible.

[20] Cf. ibid., p. 18.

of the union (*yoga*) of the *self* with Brahman as: *aham Brahmāsmi* (*Bṛhadāraṇyaka Upaniṣad* 1.4.10) and *tattvamasi* (*Cāndogya Upaniṣad* 6.8.7). In this evolutionary process of Supreme Consciousness in Christ, the Omega point, the creation and history, human beings and their religions are oriented to Christ for their fulfillment and liberation (*mukti*). It is the process of cosmic Christification, that is, the convergence and consummation of the entire humanity with its religions into God in and through Christ (cf. 1 Cor. 15:28; Eph. 1:9-10; Col. 1:18). This is the plan of God from the beginning of the world: the unity, the fullness of union or reconciliation (*yoga/mukti*) of humankind with God, which proceeds from the 'unique' and individual person of Jesus Christ through the collectivity of his body, the Church, to a unity in diversity of religions -- all centered on the cosmic Christ and oriented towards his pleroma.[21] God, in and through Christ, has been reconciling everything to himself. The religions of the world "fall within the God's universal plan of salvation [in Christ] and are subjected to the eschatological sovereignty of God."[22]

Christ is the goal of the whole cosmic process, both religious as well as secular. That is why we say that Kṛṣṇa, Rāma and the Bodhisattva not only prefigure Christ; Christ is not only the true Tao (Way) of Taoism or the hope of Yudhiṣṭhira in Mahābhārata or the fulfillment of Nirvāṇa in Buddhism or the aspirations of the prophetic traditions of Judaism and Islam; they all converge to Christ in a cosmic process of the whole universe. The unity or convergence of religions in Christ does not in any way suppose any kind of universal syncretism; on the contrary it stresses the transcendence of Christ and his rule over all races and religions, rulers and principalities. Christ is the Lord of all and his Spirit must permeate everything. All the religions are called to embody the Spirit of Christ.

Amalor always likes to stress the incarnational economy of salvation in Christ. He writes:

> The humanity of Christ is the enfleshment of God's self-gift.... This humanity is the visible sign, efficacious instrument, permanent agency of the Word in his work of salvation according to the present dispensation which is an incarnational economy. Likewise the Spirit

---

21 Cf. ibid., pp. 34-35; DSA, *Gospel and Culture,* op. cit., pp. 46-47.

22 DSA, *Approaches,* op. cit., p. 34.

of Jesus ... is invisible but becomes embodied and is manifest in the visible community of Christ's disciples.[23]

Now the humanity of Jesus Christ continues to be the sacrament of God's self-gift and salvation in and through the mystery of his body, the Church, the social and historical continuation of Christ's presence and action in the world,[24] thereby, Christ being the head always. Christ has constituted the Church as his body for the continuation of his life and mission. The Church is then the sacrament of Christ on earth, and she must serve as the central *axis* of universal convergence of the world religions under one God, and one Lord, Christ Jesus, the life giving Light that must enlighten and inform all peoples and religions in their search and worship of the true God, real life and salvation.[25]

### *2.1.1. Meeting of religions in God in the paschal mystery of Jesus Christ*

All the religions of the world are oriented to God and have their foundation in God.[26] If it is so then in the theology of religions the solution of strict segregation is to be excluded since it favours egoism and isolationism. The substitution of one religion for another is also inadmissible as it is unchristian in so far as it undermines the foundation on which the religions rest. A solution which proposes an eclectic unity and upholds that all religions are same and ultimately one and equal, overlooks the socio-historical context, the concrete historical religious situation of real people, and disregards the real conflict that exists among religions. Again, a "passive co-existence"[27] or passive tolerance of religions is, according to Amalor, not the solution, for it would mean overlooking the sins and failures, errors, imperfections and superstitious practices in other religions, and thus be a negation of the call to the fullness of grace and truth in Christ. Christ has come to fulfill the laws and the religions of the world (cf. Matt. 5:17). What is required, therefore, is "a universal charity and all-

---

23 DSA, *Gospel and Culture,* op. cit., p. 31.

24 Cf. the Declaration of the Nagpur Conference, no. 6, in: DSA, *Theology of Evangelization,* op. cit., p. 30.

25 Cf. DSA, *Approaches,* op. cit., pp. 33-44.

26 Cf. DSA, *Destinée,* op. cit., p. 300.

27 DSA, *Approaches,* op. cit., p. 16.

embracing concern and an active pro-existence in the midst of the world and its religions by means of whole-hearted and humble service"[28] towards the realization of the fullness of truth, life and salvation in Christ. This means that the religions are called to be purified from their "imperfections" and be perfected in the light of the Gospel. This is what Amalor calls as dying to sin and rising to the fullness of life in Christ, the paschal mystery or Christification.[29] He writes: "Every religion, like every man must pass through this death to the resurrection [i.e., purification and transformation in Christ] in order to be saved."[30] The role and the responsibility of the Church in this context is very obvious in the realization of the cosmic Christ amidst the world religions, aiming at their unity and fullness in Christ (cf. *LG* 9).

### *2.1.2. Why Christ and not others?*

The world needs a saviour. Our question here is, why Christ and not others? Why Christ should be the centre of the meeting point between God and man and the religions? We have already briefly dealt this point above.

God wants to save all human beings. There is no salvation without God's grace, all need the grace of God. Since Christ is the Word become man, and, therefore, the fullness of truth and grace, he is the greatest possible oneness with God. There is a new creation in Christ. The Spirit of Christ must permeate everything and make everything new. It is the saving presence and activity of the Spirit of Christ in all the religions of the world, in accordance with the saving will and the saving "power" of God in his Son, which makes Christ the universal saviour. Christ is God's salvific will and action become flesh in history. To see Christ, therefore, is to see God; to meet Christ is to meet God; to hear Christ is to hear the Word of God; to be united with Christ is to be in communion with God (cf. Jn. 10:30; 14:9).[31] This is the reason why we say that the religions of the world are oriented to Christ and in and through Christ to the Father, so that God may be all in all. Paul writes: "When all things are subjected to him [the Son, Christ], then the Son himself will also be subjected to the

[28] Ibid.

[29] Cf. ibid.

[30] Ibid., p. 36.

[31] Cf. DSA, *Theology of Catechesis*, op. cit., p. 20.

one who put all things under him, so that God may be all in all" (1 Cor. 15:28).

In following Christ and faithful to his command (cf. Matt. 28:18-20), the Church must take initiative to meet other religions.[32] Christianity and other religions have to meet each other in a reality which partakes of the *divine* and *human;* that is, in him whom Christians call Jesus Christ. This theandric reality is Christ Jesus, the Lord, the embodiment of divine will and divine grace, the "incarnation" of salvation in the world, the perfect *mārga* (way) and the fullness of *yoga* (union) between God and man. Because of this fullness of salvation in Christ, the perfect *mārga* and *yoga,* we say that there is no other way but through Christ, that is, there is no way that is as perfect or more perfect than Christ, nor is there anything qualitatively more or outside of Christ Jesus (cf. Acts 4:12). This does not mean that other religions are wrong and should be abrogated thereby. Other religions can be channels of grace for their followers in so far as they accept Christ, the truth of the Father, the way to the Father, and in so far as they are led by the Spirit of Christ in their life and worship of God. Other religions may be seen as tributaries, always seeking to join Christ who will lead them to the Truth, the Father, the Source and the End of all.[33]

The major difficulty occurs when Christians identify Christ with Jesus, the son of Mary. Jesus is the Christ, the Lord of all. He is the culminating point of God's self-disclosure. He is the embodiment of the Absolute. He is the embodiment and actualization of God's saving will. He is the saving power of God. He has finally displayed the saving will and the saving power of God through his life, death and resurrection and now has become the source of all salvation. Through his resurrection he has transcended the temporo-spatial factor of mere man. God has constituted him the Lord of all times and generations. He embodies the Spirit of God in his person. The Spirit of God is the Spirit of Christ.

The personal identity and unity of Jesus with the Father as "the Father and I are one" (Jn. 10:30) is seen from the very beginning of creation to its consummation. It is an identity and unity of a triple order:

---

32 As the servant and sacrament of Christ on earth, the Church has to meet other religions and render her *diakonia* (service) to them. It is a diakonia of orienting them to Christ, to the pleroma of Christ. This point will be dealt in detail in the next chapter.

33 Cf. DSA, *Approaches,* op. cit., p. 33.

*ontological, historical,* and *eternal.* "In the beginning was the Word, and the Word was with God, and the Word was God" (Jn. 1:1) (ontological). "And the Word become flesh and lived among us" (Jn. 1:14). Jesus lived on this earth, fulfilling the Father's will (historical). He died and rose, and lives and reigns forever in his Spirit (eternal). It is this triple union of Jesus with the Father, that is, the saving mystery of God in the Jesus Christ event, which makes Jesus, unlike Rāma or Kṛṣṇa in Hinduism or Muhammad in Islam or Buddha in Buddhism, the Lord and the Messiah of all, the cosmic Christ.

Now, how do other religions relate to the cosmic Christ? Or, what should be the Church's theological attitude towards other religions?

We can shortly say that it should be the relation and interaction between the Church and other religions that is based on the Vatican II's comprehension of the "seeds of the Word" in other religions (*AG* 15; cf. *NA* 2).[34] Jesus Christ is the one mediator, the one universal saviour. However, in the mystery of God's universal salvific will in Christ and in his universal salvific providence, people of other religions too can attain salvation, who "through no fault of theirs are still ignorant of the Gospel of Christ and of his Church, yet sincerely seek God and, with the help of divine grace, strive to do his will as known to them through the dictates of their conscience..." (*LG* 16). The Holy Spirit calls all human beings and all religious traditions to Christ through the recognition of the "seeds of the Word" and the preaching of the Gospel and awakens in their hearts an obedient acceptance of faith (cf. *AG* 15). The Church has to proclaim and share with others the fullness of redemption brought about by Jesus Christ and recognize in them the "seeds of the Word". She has to accept in other religions whatever is of the cosmic Christ and reject whatever is inimical to the Word of God. The seeds of the Word of God in other religions must grow and bear fruit. That means to say that the Church has to reverently seek to uncover the convergent lines of the action of the Holy Spirit in the aspirations and anticipations in other religions, however confused, to which the answer is Christ. In the prophetic religions the transcendent God speaks and intervenes through his messengers in human history; in the mystical religions God is obscurely perceived as immanent in the soul of

[34] Here we do not go to elaborate the Church's recognition of the "seeds of the Word" in other religions or the presence of the cosmic Christ in other religions as the "seeds of the Word". This point has already been dealt in the foregoing chapters.

man and in the universe. Both can be, through the power of the Holy Spirit and preaching of the Gospel, led to the encounter with the cosmic Christ.

### *2.1.3. Christ uniting all peoples and religions in one body: A new humanity*

Jesus' death is not an isolated event to which God has attached many extraneous consequence.[35] There is an inner link between the passion and death of Jesus and the future of humanity. According to Paul, Jesus' passion and death, even when it is participated in by his disciples in their suffering, has a vital influence on others. Paul writes: "... so that the life of Jesus may be made visible in our mortal flesh. So death is at work in us, but life in you" (2 Cor. 4:11-12). Jesus' dying on the cross and his resurrection signify the death of death, that is, the victory over death, the birth of a new humanity, its hope, unity and salvation. For Christ in his person has preached peace and unity among peoples and religions, breaking down the dividing wall and hostility among them, reconciling man with God and man with man (cf. Eph. 2:14-16). "In him [Christ] the whole structure is joined together and grows into a holy temple in the Lord ... a dwelling place for God " (Eph. 2:21-22). The New Man, the Son of Man, is the prototype of the new humanity that God recreated in the person of Christ, the second Adam, after destroying the sin and the sinful nature of all Adam's race in the crucifixion. This is the cosmic function of the death of Jesus on the cross in the rebirth of the world, rebirth of a new humanity, new creation.[36] The faith in Jesus as "the Word became flesh and lived among us" (Jn. 1:14) means that Jesus expresses absolutely all that God has wished to reveal and relate himself to all human beings.[37]

The new creation in Christ is the new life, lived in fellowship with God through Christ in the Spirit. This new life means life in Christ the Lord or the life in the Spirit. "The Lord is the Spirit" (2 Cor. 3:17). Though Christ and the Spirit are distinct persons but are experienced together (cf. 2 Cor. 17-18; Jn. 4:24). The whole Christian life comes from the Spirit who is the source of new life. Our living, suffering, praying,

---

[35] Cf. DSA, *Approaches,* op. cit., pp. 36-38; id. (ed.), "Inculturation is not Hinduization but Christianization", *op. cit.,* p. 110.

[36] Cf. DSA, *Gospel and Culture,* op. cit., pp. 29-30.

[37] Cf. ibid., pp. 30-34. Here DSA deals with the theology of redemptive incarnation.

hoping, all is guided, promoted and nourished by the Spirit of God in Christ. The sphere in which this new life is lived is the Church. This corporate Church is the new people of God, reconstituted by Jesus' death and resurrection, empowered by the Spirit, and called to universal mission for the consummation of the whole history and creation in Christ.[38]

### *2.1.4. The corpo-cosmic personality of Christ and other religions*

The Pauline Christology indicates that Christ is an "inclusive personality" (cf. Gal. 3:28; Rom. 16:7; 1 Cor. 15:22; etc.).[39] The all-inclusive personality of Christ and his all-pervasive presence includes all, Christians as well as others. Again, even if the whole Christ dwells in each believer, it is the corporate and conscious whole of believers, the Church, which dwells in Christ.[40] Corporate personality does not imply, however, the mere mutual interpenetration of two individuals nor does it imply a union of identity but an organic relationship between the head and the members.

Now let us apply this individual personality of Christ and the corporate personality of Christ, the Church, to the case of other religions. Christ is present in other religious believers and they are present in Christ. Between Christ and others there is the mutual interpenetration of two individuals in intimate relationship. However, more than this relationship, in the case of Christians there is also the incorporation of all believers in Christ; namely, the relationship of corporate personality between Christ and the Christians through baptism and other sacraments.[41] In other words, Christ is the head of the universe and of the Church; but it is only the Church that is his body (cf. Col. 1:18), not the universe as a whole. But the entire universe and, *a fortiori,* other religions are oriented towards the corporate Christ; namely, to the incorporation in *Christ* in and through the mystery of the *Church* which is his mystical body, the people of God, led

---

[38] Cf. DSA, "Biblical World-View and a Renewed Holistic Spirituality", *op. cit.,* pp. 56-57.

[39] Cf. DSA, *Approaches,* op. cit., pp. 10-11.

[40] Cf. DSA, "Approach", *op. cit.,* pp. 23, 40-44; id., "Biblical World-View and a Renewed Holistic Spirituality", *op. cit.,* pp. 54-55.

[41] Cf. DSA, "Biblical World-View and a Renewed Holistic Spirituality", *op. cit.,* p. 56; id., "Approach", pp. 39, 44-45.

and animated by the Spirit of Christ (cf. *LG* 9; 1 Pet. 2:9-10).[42] This also explains how Christ is active in and through the sacramentality of the Church for the entire humanity.[43] That is to say that the cosmic Christ is oriented to the corporate Christ. Other religions are oriented to the corporate Christ and his mystical body, the Church. There are no two Christs but only one Christ, both cosmic and corporate. There is only one head, one Lord. It is the same Christ who is the head of the universe as well as of the Church. The Church as the body of Christ is the sacrament in and through which the corporate life of the living Christ must operate. She is an organism in which and through which God in Christ is found and worshipped. Corporate Christ signifies that one cannot have Christ without the Church, for the Church is Christ's organ of communication.[44] Thus we see more clearly the presence of Christ in the Church, which is distinct from the presence of Christ in other religions. Yet Christ must not be judged by the Church's performance; she is in herself under the judgement of Christ (cf. 1 Cor. 15:28). Christ's grace is at work also outside the visible Church. The salvation of others is, therefore, possible but always in and through Christ Jesus.[45]

When we speak about the cosmo-corporate and inclusive personality of Christ, we reject the exclusive theological position which holds Christ and Christianity to be the truth *exclusively*. The central figures of other religions, such as Buddha and Kṛṣṇa are deemed false thereby. We hold the inclusive theological position in accordance with the New Testament teachings. In the inclusive sense, whatever may be found true in the religious personages of other religions, that is, the "seeds of the Word" in other religions, is included and transcended in Christ. Although both exclusive and inclusive positions reject equality of religions, they vastly differ between themselves.[46]

Jesus Christ is the unique character, the embodiment of whatever at any time may be called God's utterance (Moses, Muhammad, Buddha,

---

[42] Cf. DSA, *Approaches*, op. cit., p. 33.

[43] Cf. DSA, *Gospel and Culture*, op. cit., p. 31; id., "Biblical World-View and a Renewed Holistic Spirituality", *op. cit.*, p. 56ff.

[44] Cf. DSA, "Approach", *op. cit.*, pp. 40, 45-46.

[45] Cf. ibid., pp. 38-47.

[46] We do not elaborate the point here. This has already been dealt in the foregoing chapters.

Kṛṣṇa).[47] He is the embodiment and accomplishment of what God has been all along saying and doing in fragments in Abraham, Moses and the prophets.[48] This in no way implies that we have nothing to learn from other religious geniuses. Intensively all is summed up in the mystery of Christ; extensively we have also to learn from other religious figures. The study of other religions can throw light on the part of the Christian to understand the mystery of God in Christ more comprehensively and universally.[49]

### *2.2. The Uniqueness of Jesus Christ Fullness of Revelation and Salvation*[50]

After dealing with the corpo-cosmic Christ, which in itself shows his uniqueness, we now proceed to explain the word "unique" or "uniqueness" with regard to Christ and other religions. The word "unique" seems to have created much misunderstanding in the theology of religions. Today each religion considers its religious figure as unique. Where does Christ stand?

The uniqueness of Jesus Christ lies in his saving mystery: the mystery of the incarnate love that permeates *all* and saves *all*. Jesus is "the Word become flesh" (Jn. 1:14), the Emmanuel, God with us (cf. Matt. 1:23).[51] He is the fullness of God's saving revelation in the fullness of time (cf. Heb. 1:1-4). "Jesus Christ is the greatest sign and the supreme medium"[52] of God's revelation in the life and history of mankind. He is "the meeting point between God's revelation and man's faith, between God's Word and man's word."[53] In him "the word and the deed tally."[54] Thus, Jesus Christ is not just a medium of revelation, but Revelation itself. He is the perfect

---

[47] Cf. DSA, *Approaches,* op. cit., p. 34-35.

[48] Cf. DSA, *Theology of Development,* op. cit., p. 15; id., *The Theology of 'Indirect Evangelization',* op. cit., pp. 9-10.

[49] Cf. DSA, *Approaches,* op. cit., pp. 10-12, 38; id., "Approach", *op. cit.,* pp. 43-44.

[50] We have already seen the revelation of God in Jesus Christ in chapter one. Hence, we very briefly touch upon this point here so as to explain in short the relation between the uniqueness and fullness of God's revelation and salvation in the Jesus Christ event.

[51] Cf. DSA, *Theology of Development,* op. cit., p. 15.

[52] DSA, *Theology of Catechesis,* op. cit., p. 20.

[53] DSA, *The Church's Mission as Prophetic and Hermeneutical,* op. cit., pp. 5-6.

[54] Ibid., p. 6.

'Amen' of humankind to the Father.[55]

In the Jesus Christ event, God's mystery is conclusively unveiled and penetrated. Consequently, revelation is said to be closed with the apostles, in the sense that there is nothing new and nothing more outside Jesus Christ. Jesus is the fullness of God's revelation.[56]

Jesus Christ is God's positive and definitive revelation. He is the saving mystery of God that comprises the past, present and the future -- the 'fullness of time' (cf. Heb.1:2) and the 'fullness of things, creation'(cf. Col. 1:15-20). In other words: "God continues to give Himself to us through Jesus Christ in the midst of our life and history."[57] Hence, it follows that this fullness of revelation must be not only of the past but also of the present and the future -- an on-going revelation in creation and history wherein all peoples and religions must find their orientation and fulfillment. Christ is the "the same yesterday and today and forever" (Heb. 13:8). The Spirit that he communicated through his resurrection is present everywhere, especially in the Church, transcending time and space. Thus God in Christ is "present and active in our world and history, not limiting his saving presence to the Judeo-Christian tradition alone, but extending it to the whole of humanity, to all religions and to all temporal realities."[58]

The uniqueness of Jesus Christ does not imply exclusivism. His uniqueness signifies the fullness of God's revelation in him in history for the fullness of salvation of all peoples and religions.[59] Judaism may look for a unique Messiah, the "Son of Man", in the future; Hinduism may see this saviour personified in God's *avatāras* like Rāma and Kṛṣṇa; or in Buddhism, uniqueness may be accorded to Buddha, the deified man by men. The uniqueness of Jesus Christ lies in the historicity of God's definitive revelation and response to mankind's search for salvation in and through the mystery of the whole Jesus Christ event: the incarnation, life, death and resurrection, his cosmic Lordship, the sending of the Spirit and the mystery of the Church. The uniqueness of Christ includes all peoples and religions. The Church therefore has to lead all peoples and religions to the full stature of Christ (cf. Eph. 4:13) and through Christ to God (cf.

---

55 Cf. DSA, *Theology of Catechesis,* op. cit., p. 20.

56 Cf. DSA, *The Church's Mission as Prophetic and Hermeneutical,* op. cit., p. 21.

57 DSA, *Theology of Catechesis,* op. cit., p. 22.

58 DSA, *Approach,* op. cit., p. 26.

59 DSA, *Our Christian World Vision,* op. cit., p. 21; id.,"Approach", *op. cit.,* pp. 38-40.

1 Cor.15:28).[60]

### *2.2.1. The term 'uniqueness' misunderstood*

Gerwin van Leeuwen writes, "DSA has hardly brought out the theological issue of Christ's uniqueness and has never worked out a systematic and complete Christology; however, all his theologizing is based upon and oriented towards the one inexhaustible Christ mystery: the mystery of the Incarnation, the mystery of his Pasch and the sending of his Spirit, and the mystery of his cosmic Lordship."[61]

Amalor does not seem to use the traditional term "unique" which easily betrays apologetic as well as superiority pretensions and exclusivism. It causes a lot of misunderstanding among other religions. Gerwin van Leeuwen too writes on this point: "I have the impression that DSA is not very anxious to use the traditional term 'unique', because it easily betrays apologetic as well as superiority pretensions."[62] The uniqueness or superiority of Christ is that of a servant, servant of God, the God of truth and justice, mercy and compassion, love and service, peace and unity (cf. Is. 42: 1ff; Mk. 10:45; Jn. 12:26; Matt. 23:11; Eph. 1:10; Lk. 13:34). His is the service of 'holding together' all peoples and religions in the unity of faith (cf. Col. 1:17; Eph. 4:13).

### *2.2.2. Jesus Christ the universal saviour: Incarnational approach*

In every religion we find these three structural concepts: the *ideal,* the *need,* and the *deliverer.*[63] These elements should be regarded as the religious dimension of human experience. The ideal is the central element in all religions; it is the *goal* and *ground,* the destiny of man that offers man reason and strength in his final fulfillment of life -- salvation, happiness, *mukti, nirvāṇa.* Religion lives in the conviction that the natural existence of life in day to day experience is separated from the ideal by some flaw or sin and unsatisfactory situation. All religions acknowledge

---

60 Cf. DSA, "Approach", *op. cit.,* pp. 38-47.

61 Gerwin van Leeuwen, O.F.M., *Fully Indian - Authentically Christian,* op. cit., p. 319.

62 Ibid., p. 320.

63 Cf. John Fuellenbach, S.V.D., *Hermeneutics, Marxism and Liberation Theology,* op. cit., pp. 12-13.

the need of deliverance and a deliverer; and thus, there is in every religion the concept of a deliverer, human or divine.

Man is both body and spirit. He needs the integral deliverance of his body and spirit. Amalor sees the salvation of man in the struggle for a new and living synthesis of the material and the spiritual. Our scientific and technological age is in its struggle to synthesize the spiritual and the material. Amalor sees this world-struggle well typified with the Indian situation today.[64]

As we have already seen, in *Destinée de l'Église dans l'Inde d'aujourd'hui,* Amalor sees India passing through a crisis: a crisis of synthesizing the spiritual and the material. He poses the question: 'Who/what will save India?' 'Is India waiting for Christianity?'[65] He first shows that neither Hinduism with its renaissance, nor communism that is making its pretence felt especially in Kerala and West Bengal, nor the Indian government with its five-year plans, is capable of offering to India a real future, a real saviour. He then affirms that the only true redeemer of India is Christ, the unique and universal saviour of the universe. Only his salvific message, the Gospel, and his instrument of salvation, the Church, can bring to India the perfect remedy for all her ills. Christ alone can fill the emptiness, caused by the destruction of the old gods and the vanity of the new idols.[66] Therefore, Amalor holds (to quote again):

> The struggle of the Indian soul to implant a deep-rooted spirituality in the profane structures imposed by the technical-material civilization is a clear appeal to a religion which is, by its very nature, a true incarnation of the spiritual in the material, an appeal to the God incarnate and the Church which is his body.[67]

---

[64] Cf. DSA, *Destinée,* op. cit., pp. 35-64; id., *Theology of Evangelization,* op. cit., pp. 15-17.

[65] Cf. DSA, *Destinée,* op. cit., p. 65ff.

[66] Cf. ibid., p. 85.

[67] Ibid., pp. 85-86: "La lutte de l'âme indienne pour implanter une spiritualité aux racines dans les structures profanes imposées par la civilisation technico-matérielle est un appel évident à une religion qui est, par sa nature même, une véritable incarnation du spirituel dans la matériel, un appel au Dieu incarné et à l'Eglise qui est son corps." (For the English translation see as quoted by Gerwin van Leeuwen, O.F.M. in: Id., *Fully Indian - Authentically Christian,* op. cit., p. 318). See also chapter two, footnote 152.

Like the rest of the world, India's concern for the material is on the increase. The world is looking forward to India for a new synthesis of the spiritual and the material. Up to now India lacked spiritual poverty, thinking she could save herself. Now, after many *avatāras* (ahistorical figures) who came and went, she feels the need for a true *incarnation* of God in history. Jesus, as the incarnate Word in history, fulfills this aspiration. It is the providential hour of the incarnate Word. Salvation, therefore, is in the new synthesis of the matter and the spirit. It is in the incarnational approach of Jesus, the Christ. Hence,

> the Church can now show herself to India as the one which takes the material world seriously and is at the same time able to fill her with a spirit, the very Spirit of the Son of God, whose mystical body she is. The Church has been founded precisely to continue the incarnation of Christ in time and space till the end of the world. When the technical civilization is born [rampant] in the West, the Church has undertaken its redemption; she has given this civilization a soul through her Gospel and her institutions. What she has done and continues to do for the West, the Church can and must do for India. The situation of this country launches a pressing appeal: without India the procession to the parousia of the Lord will not be complete: one of the precious stones of the heavenly Jerusalem will be missing.[68]

Amalor likes to take the material world rather seriously. The Spirit of Christ must guide and fulfill the material world. There is no running away from the world, no negation of the body, the matter. In fact, spirituality does not exist in itself. It is lived in this material world and it

---

[68] Ibid., 86-87: "L'Eglise peut maintenant se montrer à elle comme celle qui prend au sérieux le monde matériel et qui est capable de l'animer d'une esprit, de l'Esprit même du Fils de Dieu dont elle est le Corps mystique. L'Eglise est été fondée précisément pour continuer l'incarnation du Christ dans le temps et dans l'espace, jusqu'à la fin du monde. Quand la civilisation technique est née en Occident, c'est l'Eglise qui a entrepris sa rédemption, qui lui a donné une âme par son Evangile et par ses institutions. Ce qu'elle a fait et continue de fair pour l'Occident, l'Eglise peut et doit le fair pour l'Inde. La situation de ce pays lui lance un pressant appel: Sans l'Inde, le cortège vers la parousie du Seigneur ne serait pas complet, il manquerait une de ses pierres précieuses à la Jérusalem céleste." (Translation mine; cf. also: Gerwin van Leeuwen, *Fully Indian - Authentically Christian,* op. cit., pp. 318-319).

is for this world. Salvation is in the living synthesis of the spiritual and the material, the spirit incarnated in the matter. This is the incarnational approach of salvation wrought by Jesus Christ.

Amalor sees the present Indian situation, especially its religions, as waiting for Christ to be truly set free.[69] Referring to several texts of Monchanin's *Ermites du Saccidananda,* he writes:

> India waits in hope 'to discover the effusion of the trinitarian love' which becomes flesh in the unique Christ ... (through the Church we are working and waiting for the parousia where) God will be all in all for all eternity. Indeed, Christ has saved not only India, but also Hinduism; but Hinduism, like the Hindus, has first to receive the baptism in the baptism of Christ himself (Lk. 12:50).... Hinduism has to undergo a circumcision of the heart, a noetic crucifixion and a christic resurrection to become a new creature (2 Cor. 5:17). Till this becomes a reality, India will have to wait with patience and hope, continuing its vigil through the centuries.[70]

Amalor continues to write that though

> Christ was born in a determined time and place, He is the Redeemer of all times and of all the peoples of the world. He is the universal Saviour of the world.... Christ has recapitulated everything, saved everything, marked everything with the sign of the cross, led everything to its fulfillment, integrating everything in the march of the

---

69 Cf. ibid., p. 144; Gerwin van Leeuwen, O.F.M., *Fully Indian - Authentically Christian,* op. cit., p. 319.

70 See: DSA, *Destinée,* op. cit., p. 144: "Pourtant, elle [l'Inde] attend, dans l'espérance 'de découvrir l'effusion de l'Amour trinitaire' qui s'incarne en l'unique Christ, qui sanctifie dans le Paraclet et qui achève en l'Eglise eschatologique, au jour désiré de la Parousie, l'homme et toute chose en l'unité du Plérôme du Christ et du Paraclet: Dieu 'tout en tous' et pour l'éternité. Le Christ a, certes, sauvé non seulement l'Inde mais aussi l'hindouisme; mais l'hindouisme, comme les Hindous, doit d'abord recevior le baptême dans le baptême du Christ Lui-même (Luc 12,50).... Bref, l'hindouisme doit subir une circoncision du cœur, une crucifixion néotique et une résurrection christique pour devenir une nouvelle créature (2 Cor. 5,17). Jusqu'à ce que celles-ci se réalisent, l'Inde attendra avec patience et espérance, continuant sa veillée à longueur de siècles." (See as translated by Gerwin van Leeuwen, O.F.M., in: Id., *Fully Indian - Authentically Christian,* op. cit., p. 319).

> redeemed humanity to the Father, through the Son and in the Spirit....[71]

As we have already seen, Amalor's theology of inculturation is an immediate consequence of Christ's incarnation. The unique place of Christ in the history and mystery of salvation also receives a great emphasis in his theology of inculturation.[72] India will not reach its fulfillment without Christ, while the Church will never be fully one, holy, catholic and apostolic, till she has integrated all the pieces of manna spread over the whole world.[73] However, Christians are not to boast or claim any superiority. Comparisons are useless and odious.

> The only thing that we have -- for no merit of our own, and that in order to be given to others -- is the *Word of God,* is Jesus Christ. Christianity or the Church is the Risen Lord and the Spirit whom he communicates. This is the newness of the Gospel, the originality of the New Testament, the uniqueness of Christianity, the purpose of our mission.[74]

Amalor returns again and again to the centrality, the key role, of Christ in the salvific economy. Referring to the well-known texts of the New Testament (Acts 4:12; 1 Tim. 2:4-5) and Vatican II, especially *AG* 8, and after quoting R. Panikkar who holds that a *bona fide* Hindu is saved by Christ and not by Hinduism,[75] he writes: "Salvation is always of Christ, from Christ and through Christ even if men do not know Him; any saving

---

[71] Ibid., pp. 258-259: "Le Christ s'est fait homme dans un temps et un pays déterminés, mais Il est le Rédempteur de tous les temps et de tous les peuples du monde, le Sauveur universal.... Le Christ a tout récapitulé, a tout sauvé, a tout marqué du signe de croix, a tout amené à son achèvement en intégrant tout dans la marche de l'humanité sauvée, vers le Père, par le Fils et dans l'Esprit, dans le courant de la charité trinitaire." (Translation mine).

[72] Cf. ibid., pp. 258-261; see also: Gerwin van Leeuwen, O.F.M., *Fully Indian - Authentically Christian,* op. cit., pp. 238-245.

[73] Cf. ibid., pp. 259-260; Gerwin van Leeuwen, O.F.M., *Fully Indian - Authentically Christian,* op. cit., p. 319.

[74] DSA, *Purpose,* op. cit., pp. 20-21; see also as cited by Gerwin van Leeuwen, O.F.M., in: Id., *Fully Indian - Authentically Christian,* op. cit., p. 319.

[75] See: Raymond Panikkar, *The Unknown Christ of Hinduism,* London, 1964, p. 54 as cited by DSA, in: Id., *Approaches,* op. cit., p. 11.

grace belongs to Christ."[76]

The universality of salvation is well seen in the life-behaviour of Jesus.[77] In the Old Testament, at least in the thinking and practice of the purity and priorities of the Pharisees and the scribes (cf. Mk. 7:1-23), salvation was reserved to these, so called the "righteous" (Pharisees, scribes, rabbis). The so called "sinners", "outcasts", "poor", and the Gentiles were outside the reach of salvation. It was not a universal salvation. Who could save these people who are now outcast from the "chosen" race, from the Mosaic Law, the temple and the kingdom? Who could hear their cry? Jesus "revolutionizes" the whole intent and outreach of salvation. He makes it a universal salvation -- salvation reaching out to the poor and the weak, the sinners and the outcasts, the 'faith-full' of the Lord, who repent and believe, not so much in the 'law' but in God's 'grace' and the Gospel (cf. Mk. 1:15) and do the will of God. In this sense Jesus says:

> Truly I tell you [chief priests and scribes], the tax collectors and the prostitutes are going into the kingdom of God ahead of you. For John came to you in the way of righteousness [Law] and you did not believe him, but the tax collectors and the prostitutes believed him; and even after you saw it, you did not change your minds and believe him (Matt. 21:31-32; cf. id. 5:3; 9:13; Lk. 7:36-50; 13:1-5; 14:15-24; 15:1-7, 11-32; etc.).

Jesus condemns the hypocritical practices of the Pharisees and the scribes and says, "Therefore I tell you, the kingdom of God will be taken away from you and given to a people that produces the fruits of the kingdom" (Matt. 21:43). Again, "Not everyone who says to me, 'Lord, Lord,' will enter the kingdom of heaven, but only the one who does the will of my Father in heaven" (Matt. 7:21; cf. 23:1-36). Jesus foresees the coming of the nations from east and west and participating in the kingdom proclaimed by him (cf. Matt. 8:11; Is. 2:2-3). In Jesus, in his words and deeds, the nations will come to know the true God and worship him in spirit and truth (cf. Jn. 4:24); for he is the definitive and supreme revelation of God; he is the truth, the way and the life for all (cf. Jn.

---

[76] DSA, *Purpose,* op. cit., p. 25. See also: Gerwin van Leeuwen, O.F.M., *Fully Indian - Authentically Christian,* op. cit., p. 319.

[77] Cf. John Fuellenbach, *The Kingdom of God,* op. cit., pp. 144-148.

14:6).[78] He is the saviour of all. One is saved in Christ, "not by the works of the *law* but through *faith* in Christ" (Gal. 2:16) and his Gospel. "For the gospel is 'the power of God saving *all who have faith*' (Rom. 1:16)."[79] "For in Christ Jesus neither circumcision nor uncircumcision counts for anything; the only thing that counts is faith working through love" (Gal. 5:6).

### *2.2.3. Proclaiming the uniqueness of Christ His centrality and universality*

Our God is an eternal God as well as the God of history. He *creates, sustains* and *saves* everything -- things in heaven and things on earth -- in and through his eternal Word (*Vāk* or *Vāc, Śabda*)[80] and his Spirit hovering over the whole of creation (cf. Jn. 1:1-5; Gen. 1:1-2:4a). The concept of God as creator, sustainer and saviour is well symbolized in the concept of *trimūrti*[81] or 'trinity' in Hinduism as *Brahmā, Viṣṇu, and Śiva - A, U, M or OM.*[82]

Jesus is the Word of God, the Word become flesh, the incarnate Word, who took the human form and assumed human nature in history to save man in his integrity. Jesus of Nazareth, in his love and service of God and humanity, in and through his humble obedience to God even to the point of freely accepting a death on a cross and his resurrection (cf. Phil. 2:6-11), has become the "Lord" of all (Phil.2:11). "The historicity of Jesus is not confined to the fact of his having lived on earth; it implies something more -- his awareness of *who* and *what* he was [as 'the father and I are one', Jn. 10:30] and the way he conveyed this to others."[83] God has

---

[78] Cf. DSA, *The Theology of 'Indirect Evangelization'*, op. cit., pp. 9-10; id., *Approaches*, op. cit., p. 33; *TNJBC*, 15:9.

[79] See cited by DSA in: Id., *Approaches*, op. cit., p. 31.

[80] Cf. M. Dhavamony, *Classical Hinduism*, op. cit., pp. 13-19.

[81] *Trimūrti* is generally translated as "Trinity". Let us note that the Hindu understanding of "Trinity" is not the same as the Catholic doctrine of Trinity. For a detailed study on the same, see: M. Dhavamony, *Classical Hinduism*, op. cit., pp. 63-68. Cf. also: Id., "The Holy Spirit in Hinduism", in: *Credo in Spiritum Sanctum, Atti del Congresso Teologico Internazionale di Pneumatologia*, Estrato, Libreria Editrice, Vaticana, 1982, pp. 1426-1435.

[82] See: M. Dhavamony, *Classical Hinduism*, op. cit., pp. 63-64.

[83] Rino Fisichella, "Meaning, Ultimate, in Jesus Christ (I. The Meaning of Revelation)",

taken the initiative and opened himself to the world in order to give himself to all men in love and, thus, establish a saving relationship with them. In Jesus this openness of God has been made permanent, once for all, irrevocable. So Jesus is the incarnation of God's love and self-gift; in him God's power of saving men is operative. He is the Father's love for the world in his Son (cf. Jn. 3:16). The fullness of salvation is found in Jesus Christ, wrought through the salvific mystery of his incarnation, passion, death and resurrection.[84] This is the marvellous work and the wisdom of God: "'What no eye has seen, nor ear heard, nor the human heart conceived, what God has prepared for those who love him' -- these things God has revealed to us through his Spirit ... no one comprehends what is truly God's except the Spirit of God" (1 Cor. 2:9-11).

Now we proceed to see in brief the many ways in which Amalor confesses and affirms the key role of Christ and Christianity in the economy of salvation.

### *2.2.3.1. Christification of history, religions and the universe*[85]

Amalor writes, "Like everything else, all that is religious and the religions themselves are called to salvation, tend towards Christ, *the author of salvation,* and implicitly yearn for Christ to find in Him their meaning and fulfillment; like everything they must be assumed in the *Christification* of the universe."[86] He sees the whole creation recapitulated in Christ and restored to God.

in: *DFT,* p. 647.

[84] Cf. DSA, "Approach", *op. cit.,* pp. 38-39.

[85] See: DSA, *Approaches,* op. cit., p. 15, where DSA refers to Teilhard de Chardin who sees the whole of humanity and the universe in the unity of Christ, the Omega point, and calls the whole of history and creation as 'one vast phenomenon of Christification'. Cf. also: Ibid., p. 33; id.: *Purpose,* op. cit., p. 16; *Towards Indigenization in the Liturgy,* op. cit. (1975), p. 16. In: Id., *Theology of Development,* op. cit., p. 5 and 31 DSA uses Christianization, distinguishing it from humanization, but he himself holds that all authentic humanization is Christianization, and we could say, Christification. [Cf. Gerwin van Leeuwen, O.F.M., *Fully Indian - Authentically Christian,* op. cit., p. 335 (reference 14)].

[86] DSA, *Towards Indigenization in the Liturgy,* op. cit., p. 16.

> On the one hand everything *yearns for Christ,* tends towards Christ and *needs Christ to be saved and fulfilled.* On the other hand, everything *belongs to Christ,* because everything was made through the Word, everything has to be *recapitulated* in Christ, according to the designs of God (Eph. 1), and everything that was given to Christ as inheritance (the riches of the nations, Ps. 2:8), must be *restored* to Christ, so that when Christ Himself will be submitted to the Father, God may be all in all (1 Cor. 15:28).[87]

*2.2.3.2. Jesus: The 'dabar Yahweh', the incarnate Word, the definitive revelation*

Jesus is the *dabar Yahweh* (God's word). God creates and saves the world through his word. In the mystery of the *incarnation* the *dabar Yahweh* becomes a human person: *Jesus, Emmanuel,* God with us (Matt. 1:23). That is why none of the figures of other religions can be more eloquent and can reveal God better than Christ Jesus. Jesus Christ is indeed the definitive, ultimate, total and supreme revelation of God. He is so more by his deeds than by his words; the very words of God are deeds. Likewise, there is no better and more fruitful encounter between God and man than the person of Jesus Christ, the Word Incarnate.[88]

> In Jesus Christ, the Word Incarnate, word and deed tally and He becomes the *total language, the perfect communication and the greatest sign and supreme medium of revelation.* He is the meeting point between God's revelation and man's faith, between God's Word and man's word. As such, he is the *total, ultimate and definitive revelation* of the Father; so there is nothing new or more outside Jesus Christ.[89]

As we have already seen in chapter one, Amalor holds that, on the one hand, revelation is closed with the death of the last apostle, for there

---

87 Ibid., p. 17; cf. DSA, "Inculturation is not Hinduization but Christianization", *op. cit.*, p. 108.

88 Cf. DSA, *The Theology of 'Indirect Evangelisation',* op. cit., p. 10; id., *Theology of Development,* op. cit., p. 15.

89 DSA, *Approach,* op. cit., pp. 27-28; id., *The Church's Mission as Prophetic and Hermeneutical,* op. cit., p. 21.

is nothing new or more outside the revelation in Jesus Christ; on the other hand, revelation, ultimately an interpersonal relationship, is an on-going process in history and in our own life. Hence God continues to reveal himself and save the world through Christ who "is the same yesterday and today and forever" (Heb. 13:8). In and through his Spirit, the risen Lord has transcended time and space and is present and active amidst all peoples and religions, in all creation and history. We can listen to the Word of God, receive the message, interpret it and understand his designs for our times. Accordingly, we can orient the history, the religions, nay the whole of creation to God in and through Christ.[90]

> Through His Son, God has *communicated Himself to us totally and definitively.* But Jesus does not only reveal the Father. In Jesus Christ (wo)man has once again come to know him/herself and his/her human existence fully.[91]

In Jesus Christ we have the perfect dialogue and the deepest fellowship between God and man.[92]

*2.2.3.3. Jesus the SON and the sacrament of GOD, the ineffable mystery*

We see in the Jesus Christ event the epiphany and the actualization of a double love in its maximum expression and sign:

(i) God's love for mankind -- the coming down of God himself according to his promise of salvation (cf. Gen. 3:15; Jer. 32:42; Gal. 3:16) by sending his *Son.* "For God so loved the world that he gave his only *Son,* so that everyone who believes in him may not perish but may have eternal life" (Jn. 3:16).

(ii) Jesus' double-dimensional love for God and for men.

The highest form or medium or sign in which the Israelites, or for that matter any religious tradition, could "see" or meet God, the Absolute, the ineffable mystery (cf. Ex. 33:20,23; 1 Cor. 13:12; 1 Jn. 3:2; Gen. 16:13)

---

[90] Cf. DSA, *The Church's Mission as Prophetic and Hermeneutical,* op. cit., p. 7; id., *Theology of Catechesis,* op. cit., pp. 21-22.

[91] See so quoted by Gerwin van Leeuwen, O.F.M., in: Id., *Fully Indian - Authentically Christian,* op. cit., p. 320.

[92] Cf. DSA, *Theology of Catechesis,* op. cit., (1973), pp. 20-21.

"face to face" was/is best conceivable in and through his *Son (offspring)* in the *human form* (cf. Ps. 2:7; Is. 4:17; 9:6; Mk. 1:11; 9:7; Lk. 20:13; Jn. 8:36; Acts 13:33; Gal. 1:16, 4:4; Col. 1:13; Heb. 1:2; 1 Jn. 1:3; 4:9,14; cp. *avatāras*[93] in Hinduism, the coming Messiah in Judaism, God's Word and Jesus at the Last Day of Judgement in Islam, the deification of Gautama Buddha in Buddhism, etc.). Thus, we say that the cosmic or general covenant of God with the whole of humankind in Adam and Noah has been fulfilled in the historical covenant of God in the Jesus Christ event. The longing of the nations to see God 'face to face' has been fulfilled in the mystery of his *Son* Jesus, the Word become flesh. The Jesus Christ event is the definitive salvific intervention of God in the world in history. It is the culminating event in the unity and continuity of God's saving will and action in the one history of salvation.

> In Jesus' death and resurrection, the climax of his life, we see *the supreme epiphany of double love in its maximum expression and sign:* the Father's love for the world in his Son ('God so loved the world....' Jn. 3:16), and Jesus' love for the Father and for men is the sign of his total gift to his Father and to his brethren ('A man can have no greater love....' Jn. 15:13).[94]

Again,

> Next to creation of the world *the incarnation of the Word* together with *the death and resurrection of Christ* is *the most dynamic expression of God's Word, the greatest intervention of God's power in human history, and the most decisive event in the life of mankind....* Incarnation is the most dynamic and most personal encounter between God and man.[95]

As Amalor is greatly responsible for the Nagpur Declaration on

---

[93] The Hindu concept of *avatāra* ("incarnation") is different from the Catholic doctrine of Incarnation. For 'incarnations' in Hinduism, see: M. Dhavamony, *Classical Hinduism,* op. cit., chapter three, pp. 69-111.

[94] DSA, *Approach,* op. cit., p. 38.

[95] DSA, *Our Christian World Vision,* op. cit., p. 21.

Evangelization and Dialogue and since he identifies himself with it,[96] we also quote the following:[97] "[The ineffable mystery of God] is *definitively* disclosed and communicated in Jesus of Nazareth" (no. 13). "Through faith the Christian knows that ... salvation is union with Christ, his *liberator* and *saviour*" (no. 15). The fact that other religious traditions, their scriptures and rites may also manifest the divine and help people to attain salvation "in no way undermines the *uniqueness* of the Christian economy to which has been entrusted the decisive word spoken by Christ to the world and the means of salvation instituted by Him" (no. 16). "The recognition of the positive relation of the religious traditions of mankind to Christ does not in any way lessen the urgency of the Christian mission; rather it is recognized as more meaningful, more human, more universal" (no. 17).

*2.2.3.4. Christ the supreme norm of existence for all peoples and religions*

> Christ is *the supreme norm of existence,* an existence for God and in God; and consequently when other existences [other religions] come into contact with the supreme norm they get verified by this norm; thus every encounter [with Christ] brings about judgement.[98]

Christ judges no one; but under the light of the Gospel, men feel judged in what they are. "'The words of Christ are at one and the same time words of judgement and grace, of death and life.... This fact applies first of all to persons, but it also holds for the various goods' and the *religions* of this world 'which bear the mark both of man's sin and of God's blessings'" (*AG* 8).[99]

The centrality and universality of Jesus Christ is not established by men, rather by God himself (cf. Phil. 2:9-11; Heb. 1:1-4). God continues

---

[96] See: *Approach,* op. cit., p. 11. Cf. also: Gerwin van Leeuwen, O.F.M., *Fully Indian - Authentically Christian,* op. cit., p. 261, 320. We have already seen this point in chapter one, footnote 44.

[97] See the nos. in: DSA, *Theology of Evangelization,* op. cit., pp. 32-33; M. Dhavamony (ed.), *Evangelization, Dialogue and Development,* op. cit., pp. 4-5; also cited by Gerwin van Leeuwen, O.F.M., in: Id., *Fully Indian - Authentically Christian,* op. cit., p. 321.

[98] DSA, *Approaches,* op. cit., pp. 36-37.

[99] See as quoted in: Ibid., p. 37.

to save all mankind in and through Christ. Christ is the *"Fulfillment and Saviour"*[100] of all peoples and religions. "Even Christians are not saved by 'Christianity' as a religion but by God, by Jesus Christ, the only Saviour."[101] He saves all in and through his Spirit, that is, the life lived according to his Spirit. The salvation in Jesus Christ is a process of a new way of being and becoming, the process of "incarnating" and witnessing the Spirit of the risen Lord, anywhere and by anybody, Christians or others.[102] This is the pleroma of Christ and of his Spirit, the Paraclete.[103]

Our resurrection is 'a new way of being and becoming in Jesus Christ'. When we look at Jesus, the God-become-man, who is fully God and fully human, we realize that he is the revelation of God as well as the revelation of man. He has given meaning, orientation and purpose to human existence. Salvation is a life- process; and the process of becoming truly and fully human in the spirit of Jesus Christ is a movement towards one's freedom, resurrection and salvation.

> Jesus ... who is fully and authentically human ... has given meaning, orientation and purpose to human existence ... *to be in existence for others....* This is the meaning of *resurrection as a new way of being and becoming....* The *process* of becoming human is a movement towards freedom [liberation, salvation], *to be imbued with the Spirit of Christ, to love the values of the Gospel to the core, to manifest its radicality through our life-style [mission, witness], to move towards the vision and good news of the Kingdom, and thus to offer hope.* This is the most basic aspect of a Christian spirituality for all.[104]

As we have already noted that as Organizer-Director of the Research Seminar on Non-Biblical Scriptures (Bangalore 1974), Amalor also bears a particular responsibility for the Final Statement of the Seminar, and

---

100 Ibid., p. 43.

101 Ibid., p. 11.

102 Cf. ibid., p. 32.

103 Cf. DSA, *Destinée,* op. cit., p. 144.

104 DSA, *Social Communication and Christian Communion. Reality, Theology, Pedagogy and Spirituality of Communication,* NBCLC, Bangalore, 1984, pp. 29-30. (Henceforth this work will be cited as *Social Communication*).

hence lies an echo of his theology therein.[105] In the synthesis of the papers we read:

> In Jesus Christ the Word becomes flesh. Christ is *the ultimate and final Word.* He is the *term* towards which the whole of human history is moving. The revelation in Jesus Christ ... is *the climatic manifestation* of the *one order* of salvation that comprises all men of all times. Christ is *the one Lord* through whom the whole universe comes from God and returns *to him* (cf. 1 Cor. 8:6); the whole universe has been reconciled *towards him* (cf. Col 1:20); God wants to *recapitulate all things in Christ* (cf. Eph. 1:10) (no. 16).[106]

In the Statement proper in part III of the whole document, after the affirmation that the presence and expressions of the *one ineffable mystery of God* may be recognized in other religions, no. 48 states:

> In this new perspective of our faith we wish to affirm *the centrality of Jesus Christ for us.* In Him we see the mystery of God realized as *self-emptying creative love.* We know Him as the Son who in his words and deeds, life and death, identified himself with the sovereign freedom of God reversing the judgement of mankind, bringing liberation to the oppressed. In Him God is beginning to make all things *new.* In Him we are beginning to call God, *Father.* In His *resurrection* God has shown the significance of Jesus as *Christ, the sacrament of universal salvation* even though this universality remains itself involved in *God's own mystery.*[107]

### *2.2.3.5. Uniqueness in witnessing the identity of Christianity*

After indicating that many of the Church's pretensions are false, because many, so-called, characteristics of Christianity are found also and

---

[105] See chapter one, footnote 144.

[106] See: DSA (ed.), *Non-Biblical Scriptures - Theological Understanding,* op. cit., pp. 24-25.

[107] See: Ibid., p. 36.

even more pronounced elsewhere,[108] Amalor himself raises the question: "What is the originality of Christianity?" He then formulates the answer:

> It is precisely *Christ.* Christ means ... a total openness to all, an existence for others, a humble service and consequently, a total gift of oneself to others up to the point of dying for them, losing oneself so that others may exist. *'By this love you have for one another, everyone will know that you are my disciples'* (Jn. 13:35). The Church is therefore nothing else but a community of all those who have identified themselves with Christ and want to realize this reality of Christ in every human person and every human group ... wherever this openness and self-gift are evident, *wherever one can identify this pro-existence for others by the loss of one's identity, there we have the Church.*[109]

Thus, the best way of proclaiming the pleroma of Christ is through practising the *fraternal charity,* which is the only sign of Christ and his Church. The relevant praxis of this fraternal charity demands the inculturation and contextualization of the Church, her life and message, amidst the world religions. As we have already seen, at the International Missionary Conference (Lyons 1972) Amalor was upset and even scandalized by the 'foreign' character of the Church and Christianity because of the lack of commitment to indigenization even after the clear policy of the Sacred

---

[108] Cf. DSA, *Approach,* op. cit., pp. 42-44. Here DSA refers to the Nagpur Declaration, no. 7: "Animated by the Spirit of God, who knows no limitations or barriers, the Church is called on to search out, acknowledge and ennoble everything that is true and good in the world and in human history." He then quotes from *LG* 8: "This Church ... subsists in the Catholic Church ... although many elements of sanctification and of truth can be found outside its visible structure." Finally he cites from St. Augustine's *De Baptismo Contra Donatistas* (Book V, ch. 27, no. 28): "There are many who are outside but indeed inside, and there are others who are inside but in fact outside." [See: Gerwin van Leeuwen, O.F.M., *Fully Indian - Authentically Christian,* op. cit., p. 335 (reference 28)].

[109] Ibid., pp. 44-45; see also: Id., "Inculturation is not Hinduization but Christianization", *op. cit.,* p. 110, where DSA calls the Church "a community of those who have died and risen with Christ by being identified with his body."

At times the quotations may seem to be repeated in our dissertation. This is because: *firstly,* DSA writes about the same or the similar subjects in various books and articles at times with little change of words; *secondly,* to bring out and see his theology in consequence in a particular topic, some of his writings may be found repeated.

Congregation of the Propaganda Fide and the recent official teaching of Vatican II. He said, "Some are afraid that the Church would lose its identity and originality if it adapted itself, if it started a process of acculturation, ... *the only sign of Christ and His Church is fraternal charity:* 'By this everyone will know that you are my disciples if you love one another as I have loved you' (Jn. 13:35)."[110]

The Spirit of Jesus Christ, the spirit of love and service, is not bound to a particular society, time and culture. It is universal and must be "incarnated" and inculturated in all times, cultures and religions. It is the Spirit of Christ that gives us life. It is in and through his Spirit Christ becomes the Lord of all.[111] It is in this sense that the Gospel becomes the message of universal salvation in and through the life of interpersonal relationship, unity and peace -- peace in right relationship with God and men, among nations, religions and ideologies of the world.

> The gospel is Jesus Christ and a life of loving relationship with him and all men. It is a relationship among persons, an interpersonal relationship of communion in love with God the Father through Christ in the Spirit and among men with one another. This life of love in community should be realized and expressed by the testimony of Christians, the disciples of the Lord. 'By this all men will know that you are my disciples if you *love one another*' (Jn. 13:35).[112]

Then we say that "evangelization communicates the explicit knowledge of Christ and a deeper union with him, who is *the central event of the history of salvation.*"[113] The Church is the sacrament of Christ; she is the universal sacrament of the universal salvation in Jesus Christ. "This [the Church] is a historical, positive and divine institution."[114] She is "*the sign and instrument of salvation for all men: universal sacrament of*

---

110 DSA, *Preaching the Gospel Today. Main Problems in Mission Lands,* op. cit., pp. 11-12. Cf. also: Id., *Our Christian World Vision,* op. cit., p. 20; id., "Biblical World-View and a Renewed Holistic Spirituality", *op. cit.,* pp. 56-60.

111 Cf. DSA, *Gospel and Culture,* op. cit., p. 15.

112 DSA (ed.), *Evangelization of the Modern World,* op. cit., 42.

113 DSA, *Approach,* op. cit., p. 58.

114 DSA, *Our Christian World Vision,* op. cit., p. 26.

*salvation.*"[115] But this should not be understood exclusively: the pilgrim Church has to become again and again universal and "catholic". Self-sufficient and truly Catholic and universal are only God and Christ.[116] The greatness and 'uniqueness' of the Catholic Church is set in evidence not by condemning and excluding others, by setting up barriers between the Church and other religions. Her uniqueness can only be shown by "the universal Christian vision, by *dynamic persevering effort and by relentless and unbroken movement to embrace everything, to claim everybody as her own, to integrate all traditions and values within her Catholicity*" (cf. *AG* 9a).[117] The uniqueness or universality of the Church follows, therefore, from the uniqueness of Christ. It is the special *experience* of the transforming encounter with the risen Lord to which the Church cannot but share *universally.* While speaking to Christian journalists Amalor, because of their special experience of God in Christ, distinguishes them from others. He says that their task as Christian journalists is to communicate to others their *Christian experience* in the very process of sharing with others human existence in all its aspects and activities.[118]

Christians have to be fully and whole heartedly involved in all that affects human existence and be totally sensitive to and be imbued with the spirit and power of the Gospel. The Church has to *instil* the Spirit of Christ in the vicissitudes of the world; the Gospel is to be proclaimed 'in' and 'for' this world.[119] Jesus Christ has come in and for this world to establish the kingdom of God, the kingdom of the *Spirit* amidst peoples and religions. The Church has to become the model for other religions of the Spirit-filled community of Christ on earth. Then we can say that other religions are oriented towards God through the Church, imitating the Church as their model, which in turn looks on Jesus for her model and means.

The world ever needs the Gospel for its 're-creation', orientation and fulfillment (cf. Gen. 1:1ff.), because one of the realities that humankind

---

[115] Ibid., p. 39.

[116] Cf. Gerwin van Leeuwen, O.F.M., *Fully Indian - Authentically Christian,* op. cit., p. 322.

[117] DSA, *Our Christian World Vision,* op. cit., p. 41; see also: Id., "Inculturation is not Hinduization but Christianization", *op. cit.,* p. 114.

[118] Cf. DSA, *Social Communication,* op. cit., p. 25.

[119] Cf. DSA, *Approaches,* op. cit., p. 32.

is painfully experiencing is 'sin' and destruction (cf. Rom. 3:9,23; 8:12; Ps. 14:1-3).

> The experience of Christ in the faith-community also makes us aware of the humankind's unknown needs, chiefly liberation form sin, from all its forces and consequences, and from various kinds of alienation and frustration. Sin is the root cause of its difficulties and problems, of its struggles and tensions and of its state of injustice and oppression. *It also reveals to us that the ultimate remedy to all ills is salvation in Jesus Christ: openness and existence for others, by self-gift and self-sacrifice, in genuine love and humble service.*[120]

The *specificity* of Christ and Christianity in the history of salvation and amidst the world religions can also be seen, as we have already seen in Amalor's formulation of the fifteen characteristics of his Christian world vision, Model II, in chapter one, "which", writes Gerwin van Leeuwen, "confirm the broadness and dynamic catholicity of his theology."[121] The following are important in this context:

> The universal and on-going revelation of God in the world and in the entire history becomes evident. Yet *the specificity* of Judeo-Christian revelation and the total, definitive and once-for-all character of Christian revelation is acknowledged (7).
> Solidarity and partnership, involvement and contribution, collaboration and common pilgrimage are obvious. All need to work for the common cause each one with his specific contribution (10).
> Yet the uniqueness of the Church's mystery and the necessity of its mission shine out. Its *goal-directed* and not self-centered *involvement* becomes evident (11).[122]

---

[120] DSA, *Our Christian World Vision,* op. cit., p. 18.

[121] See: Gerwin van Leeuwen, O.F.M., *Fully Indian - Authentically Christian,* op. cit., p. 323.

[122] DSA, *Our Christian World Vision,* op. cit., pp. 22-23; id., "Biblical World-View and a Renewed Holistic Spirituality", *op. cit.,* p. 61. See also as cited by Gerwin van Leeuwen, in: Id., *Fully Indian - Authentically Christian,* op. cit., p. 323. The ciphers in brackets refer to the numbers that DSA gives to the fifteen characteristics.

Almost fifteen years later (20-25 January 1988)[123] during the Research Seminar on 'Sharing Worship' (*Communicatio in Sacris*) with other religions Amalor made a major intervention on 'Christian identity' which almost literally found place in the final Statement of the Seminar:

> Our Christian identity is derived from Jesus Christ by *our sharing in the experiences of Jesus' relationship with his Father.* An Individual or a community participates in the Paschal Mystery by reliving the Resurrection-Pentecost event.
> This implies:
> a) to be filled with the Spirit of Christ, the spirit of selfless and self-sacrificing fraternal love, humble service to all and identification with the poor and the least;
> b) to live the Gospel values, to take them as the ultimate criteria for Christian witnessing and to commit oneself to the Kingdom of God.[124]

### *2.2.3.6. Celebrating in the liturgy*[125]

The centrality of Jesus Christ in the economy of salvation is also celebrated in the liturgy. It is difficult to make out whether we have in this case 'lex orandi est lex credendi' or 'lex credendi est lex orandi'.[126] The Research Seminar on Non-Biblical Scriptures states:

> The whole of the liturgy of the Word leads to the Gospel or proclamation of Jesus Christ, making his action and word present in the community. This presentification of the person of Jesus, who is

---

123 After the Non-Biblical Research Seminar, Bangalore, in 1974.

124 See: Paul Puthanangady (ed.), *Sharing Worship: Communicatio in Sacris,* NBCLC, Bangalore, 1988, Final Statement, no. 13, p. 18 as cited by Gerwin van Leeuwen, in: Id., *Fully Indian - Authentically Christian,* op. cit., p. 324.

125 As we have seen that from 1966 to 1982 DSA was the Founder-Director of the NBCLC, Bangalore, and also the Secretary of the CBCI Commissions for Catechetics and Liturgy and of the Commission for Biblical Apostolate from 1971. He organized and or participated in many meetings, conferences, research seminars, etc., and, among others, has very much contributed towards the initiatives, adaptation and indigenization in the liturgy, esp. the Indian Rite/Prayers.

126 See: Gerwin van Leeuwen, O.F.M., *Fully Indian - Authentically Christian,* op. cit., p. 324.

himself *the core of the Christian faith* leads, immediately when assimilated in homily and silence, to the liturgical action of the breaking of the bread. Like all other elements of the Liturgy of the Word, it seems that the reading of SOR [Scriptures of other Religions] would also be *dynamically directed to the proclamation of Jesus Christ* in the Gospel, but with its proper function and intrinsic value.[127]

In the structure of the Indian Anaphora, the composition of which was welcomed by the Consilium (Rome, April 25, 1969),[128] Stanza VII occupies a central place. It proclaims the centrality of the Jesus Christ event in the economy of salvation and highlights the Son's divine origin, his great teaching and his love for the poor, his selfless death, his resurrection, and finally, the sending of the Spirit to fill the world with hope, joy and peace:

> O God invisible,
> at the favourable time
> you were pleased to become visible to us.
> Your Word, your only-begotten Son, took on our human condition and was born of the Virgin Mary.
> As Supreme Teacher and Master,
> he imparted the words of the eternal life
> to the poor and humble of heart.
> He went about doing good.
> When his hour had come,
> of his own accord he laid down his life
> as sacrifice for our sin.
> Raised from the death by you, Father,
> he became for us the source of life
> and sent the Holy Spirit
> to fill the world with joy and peace.[129]

---

127 See: DSA (ed.), *Non-Biblical Scriptures - Theological Understanding,* op. cit., p. 42, no. 61i.

128 See the official approval of the 12 Points of Adaptation in: DSA, *Gospel and Culture,* op. cit., pp. 87-88; also cited by Gerwin van Leeuwen, in: Id., *Fully Indian - Authentically Christian,* op. cit., pp. 95-96 (reference 15).

129 DSA, *Towards Indigenization in the Liturgy,* op. cit., p. 91; see also cited by Gerwin

Finally, we may conclude saying that, although Amalor rarely uses the traditional term "unique", he confesses this uniqueness of the Jesus Christ event in the history of salvation whenever an opportunity offers itself.[130] This uniqueness is a *faith-experience* rather than a logical conclusion.[131]

### *2.2.4. The Pauline pleroma of Christ as paradigm for proclaiming the uniqueness and unity of God's action in the history of salvation*

> '[God] desires everyone to be saved and to come to the knowledge of the truth. For there is one God; there is also one mediator between God and humankind, Christ Jesus, himself human, who gave himself a ransom for all -- this was attested at the right time' (1 Tim. 2:4-6).
>
> 'For in him [Christ Jesus] all the fullness was pleased to dwell, and through him God was pleased to reconcile to himself all things,

---

van Leeuwen, in: Id., *Fully Indian - Authentically Christian,* op. cit., p. 325. Every line and certain terms refer to footnotes that show how the text of this anaphora has been inspired by both the biblical and the Indian tradition. For the footnotes, see: DSA, *Towards Indigenization,* op. cit., pp. 97-98.

Regarding the structure of the first part of the Eucharistic Prayer we observe the following: first we have three stanzas on God's creative activity, the stanzas that follow briefly proclaim salvation history

> "with its progressive unfolding in three successive covenants. First comes the cosmic covenant with all men (stanza IV), where reference is made to Noah, Job and Melchizedek. Stanza V applies the cosmic covenant to the Indian context. After the search for God as Power present in nature in the animistic religions, mention is made successively of the Hindu religion with its three characteristic *margas* (*karma, jnana, bhakti*), of Buddhism, Jainism and Islam. Stanza VI is devoted to the historical covenant which God made with Israel through Abraham and Moses. He spoke to Israel and saved it; He instilled in his chosen people a longing for the Messiah. Stanza VII ends with the proclamation of the Christ-event as the fulfillment of salvation-history. The longings of the nations and of Israel are fulfilled in Christ, the God-man. In the narration of Christ's public life, special reference is made to his role as Teacher and Master, in view of the *Guru-chela* relationship in the Indian religious tradition. Christ's earthly career culminates in the Paschal Mystery, by which He becomes the source of life and fills the world with joy by sending the Holy Spirit." (See: *Towards Indigenization in the Liturgy,* op. cit., pp. 67-68).

[130] Cf. Gerwin van Leeuwen, O.F.M., *Fully Indian - Authentically Christian,* op. cit., p. 325.

[131] Cf. DSA, *Approaches,* op. cit., p. 11.

whether on earth or in heaven, by making peace through the blood of his cross' (Col. 1:19-20; cf. Eph. 1:10).
'For in him the whole fullness of deity dwells bodily, and you have come to fullness in him, who is the head of every ruler and authority' (Col. 2: 9-10; cf. Eph. 3:19).

Paul is generally known as the apostle of Gentiles. His Jewish background on the one hand and his contact and familiarity with the Gentile world on the other, with its "pagan" philosophies and religious beliefs and practices helped him, we could say, start a Christian theology of other religions for the first time in the history of the Church. The Pauline soteriology as -- Jesus, the universal Lord -- is inevitable[132] in proclaiming the pleroma of Christ in the history of salvation. Hence it seems appropriate here to see in brief the Pauline theology of salvation: his concept of Christ, creation and its consummation, and the salvation of all in Christ. It must serve as a paradigm for proclaiming the pleroma of Christ and as background for the Christian theology of other religions. It has to be applied to our times and exigencies.

### *2.2.4.1. From Law to Christ*

The polemical passages in which Paul reacts against the Mosaic law should not be allowed to obscure the fact that even the Christian Paul looked back with pride on his life as a Jew of the Pharisaic tradition (cf. Phil. 3:5-6; Gal. 1:14; 2 Cor. 11:22). This strong Jewish background accounts for the fact that he thinks and theologizes in the Old Testament categories and images. He often quotes the Old Testament to stress the unity of God's action in both dispensations and often as announcing the Christian gospel (cf. Rom. 1:2) or as preparing for Christ (cf. Gal. 3:24). Even if he contrasts the "letter" of the law and the "Spirit" (cf. 2 Cor. 3:6; Rom. 2:29; 7:6), the Old Testament is still for him a means through which God speaks to humanity (cf. 1 Cor. 9:10; 2 Cor. 6:16-17; Rom. 4:23;

---

132 As we have been seeing throughout our dissertation, DSA, or for that matter any one, in dealing with 'Christ, religions and salvation' has to depend upon the Scripture, especially, the Pauline writings for its basis. See the picture DSA draws about the biblical world vision on 'history and life', in: Id. (ed.), *Indian Christian Spirituality,* op. cit., p. 63. See this also in chapter one, p. 48 (figure 2). The picture clearly shows and confirms the Christology of Paul.

15:4).[133]

However, "Paul's theology was influenced most of all by his experience near Damascus and by his faith in the risen Christ as the Son of God that developed from that experience."[134] Paul speaks of this experience as the revelation of the Son accorded him by the Father (cf. Gal. 1:16). The revelation of the crucified "Lord of glory" (1 Cor. 2:8), now the Lord who is the Spirit (cf. 2 Cor. 3:17-18), not only turned Saul, the Pharisee, into an apostle Paul but also made him the first Christian theologian.[135] He spoke of it as an event in which he had been "seized" by Christ Jesus (cf. Phil. 3:12) and in which a "necessity" had been laid upon him to preach the Gospel to the Gentiles (cf. 1 Cor. 9:16; Gal. 1:16). He compares the experience of the revelation of the Son to God's creation of light in and through the Son, Jesus Christ. Paul says, "For God who said, 'Let light shine out of darkness,' has shone in our hearts to give the light of the knowledge of God's glory on the face of Christ" (2 Cor. 4:6).[136] Paul's response to the revelation is one of vivid *faith,* in which he confesses with the early Church that "Jesus is Lord" (1 Cor. 12:3; cf. Rom. 10:9; Phil. 2:11). Now he finds himself compelled by the divine *grace* to dedicate his life and energy to the service of Christ. His mind is illumined by the insight of "the mystery of Christ" (Eph. 3:4).[137]

### *2.2.4.2. Salvation and the mystery of Christ*

The cursed and rejected Jesus in the sense of Deuteronomy 21:23, that is, the crucified Jesus, "hung on a tree", a "stumbling block to Jews and a foolishness to Gentiles" (1 Cor. 1:23), becomes in Paul's eyes the "the power and the wisdom of God" (1 Cor. 1:24). The vicarious, soteriological, and messianic value of the death of Jesus makes Paul accept

---

[133] Cf. *TNJBC,* 82:10.

[134] Ibid., 82:13. Paul bases his life and theology on the *resurrectional experience* -- an encounter with the risen Christ. Likewise, for DSA too, as we have seen, the Church or Christianity is the community of those who have experienced *the risen Christ* both personally and collectively. This experience is so powerful that one cannot but share it with others. Cf. DSA, "Biblical World-View and a Renewed Holistic Spirituality", *op. cit.,* pp. 57-58.

[135] Cf. *TNJBC,* 82:13.

[136] See: Ibid.

[137] Cf. ibid.

the crucified Jesus as the "Lord of glory" (1 Cor. 2:8), the exalted Messiah.[138]

Before the encounter with the risen Christ, Paul saw human history divided into three great periods: (i) from Adam to Moses -- the period without the law; (ii) from Moses to Messiah -- the period of the law; and (iii) the messianic age -- the period when the law would be perfected or fulfilled. The experience near Damascus (cf. Acts 9:3-19; 22:6-16) now has taught him that the messianic age is already begun in the mystery of Christ. Now Paul introduces a new perspective into salvation history, that is, the *eschaton,* "end-time", which so vividly awaited before has already been inaugurated by the death and resurrection of Christ Jesus (cf. 1 Cor. 10:11), although the definitive stage will be realized at the end of time at the second coming of Christ in the fullness of his power and presence, the parousia.[139]

Jesus Christ is the fullness of the promise that the God of "the covenants" (Rom. 9:4) had made to Israel and to the world (cf. Rom. 1:2; 4:13-14; Eph. 1:13; 3:6; Is. 52:7). God is the "Father of our Lord Jesus Christ" (2 Cor. 1:3; Rom. 15:6), and he saves the world through the power of the Spirit and the Gospel of his Son, Jesus Christ (cf. Rom. 1:16).

### *2.2.4.3. Three qualities of God:[140] Personified and perfected in Christ*

All the qualities of God that are contained in the world religions could be summarized in the three qualities of God that are prominent in the Pauline theology. These are the following.

(i) "The wrath of God" (*orgē theou*) (Rom. 1:18; cf. 1 Thess. 1:10; 2:16; 5:9; Col. 3:6; Eph. 5:6; etc.): This quality is inherited by Paul from the Old Testament (cf. Ps. 78:31; Is. 30:27-28), where it expresses not so much a divine emotion or, anthropologically speaking, an angry frame of mind as God's reaction against evil and sin. "The wrath of God" is the Old Testament way of expressing God's steadfast reaction as a judge to Israel's breach of the covenant relation (cf. Ezek. 5:13; 2 Chr. 36:16) or the nations' oppression of his people (cf. Is. 10:5-11; Jer. 50:11-17).

Related to "the Day of Yahweh" (Zeph. 1:14-18), the wrath of God

---

138 Cf. ibid., 82:14.

139 Cf. ibid.

140 See: Ibid., 82:38-40.

was often conceived of as God's eschatological retribution. For Paul it is either already "manifested" (Rom. 1:18) or still awaited (cf. Rom. 2:6-8).

(ii) "The uprightness" or "the righteousness of God" (*ṣedeq, 'ĕmet, ḥesed*): In contrast to "God's wrath" there stands the "righteousness of God" (Rom. 1:17; 3:5,21-22,25-26; etc.). In 2 Corinthians 5:21 it is rather conceived of as a gift given to human beings. This quality of God is also inherited by Paul from the Old Testament, even though the phrase itself is not found as such. The closest one that comes to the Pauline phrase is *ṣidqat YHWH (ṣedeq),* "the just decree of the Lord" (Deut. 33:21). At times the Old Testament scholars see a cosmic dimension of God's righteousness: the creation of the world and its salvation, that is, his justice in the whole creation. In the post-exilic period, however, *ṣedeq* as a quality of God acquires an added nuance; it becomes the quality whereby he acquits his people, manifesting towards them his gracious salvific activity in a just judgement (cf. Is. 46:13). His act of judgement is seen as non-judicial, a salvific act (cf. Is. 51:5,6,8; 56:1; 61:10; Ps. 40:9-10).

The other non-judicial or covenantal qualities of God are his: *'ĕmet,* "fidelity" (Gen. 24:19; Josh. 24:14; 38:19), and *ḥesed,* "steadfast mercy" (Gen.19:19; 20:13; 21:23). These latter qualities are a mode of translating that reflects the post-exilic nuance of *ṣedeq* from its original denotation.

In virtue of this Old testament understanding of "God's uprightness" Paul sees God providing a new mode of salvation for humanity as a justification, not by the law as such, but by *grace through faith* in Jesus Christ as the salvific mystery of his plan for the world.

(iii) "The love of God": Paul sees the saving power and wisdom of God finally and fully displayed in the Jesus Christ event. Jesus is the saving "power", the saving "love" of God.

Though this divine quality does not appear as often as "God's righteousness", it is an important concept for Paul. It pervades the second section of the doctrinal part of the Letter to the Romans. Jesus, the love of God, "is poured out into our hearts" (Rom. 5:5; cf. 5:8; 8:31-39; 2 Cor. 13:11,13; 2 Thess. 3:5). In virtue of this quality Paul sees the Church and Christians as "brethren beloved by God" (1 Thess. 1:4). Salvation comes from faith in Jesus Christ, the faith working through love and service. God in his love and wisdom has created and saved the world in his Son Jesus Christ. This is the mystery of the pleroma of Christ.

## 3. The Mystery of Incarnation and Resurrection Historico-transhistorical

Amalor's theology is an incarnational-resurrectional theology. He sees in the mystery of the incarnation and resurrection, the decisive intervention of God, the supreme sign and the fullness of God's love and revelation. Human experience shows sin to be so radical in the world that left to himself man cannot redeem himself. Evil can be overcome only by the mighty intervention of God. God has definitively and ultimately intervened so in the person of Jesus Christ.[141]

In the mystery of the incarnation Jesus becomes a 'unique' person, God-man, God in history in the mystery of his Son Jesus Christ (cf. Jn. 1:14), a historical man like us except sin (cf. Jn. 8:48; 2 Cor. 5:21; 1 Pet. 2:22; 1 Jn. 3:5,9). In his resurrection he becomes the transhistorical and universal Lord, the Lord of the universe (cf. Acts 2:36; Rom. 14:9; 1 Cor. 15:27-28,57; Phil. 2:10-11). In the incarnation Jesus embraces the whole of humanity, assuming and perfecting thereby, its religious traditions and ideologies. The religions and ideologies that are not against the Spirit of Christ are for Christ, for the Church. They are with the Church. When the apostles try to stop a man who is outside their community and who casts out demons in Jesus' name, Jesus says to them: "Do not stop him; for whoever is not against you is for you" (Lk. 9:50). In and through his life, death and resurrection Jesus becomes the source of every man's life and resurrection. He says, "I am the resurrection and the life" (Jn. 11:25). Salvation is, therefore, in following the example of Jesus himself, in living a life of faith, love and service, truth, endurance and unity (cf. Jn. 13:14-15; 1 Tim. 1:16; 1 Cor. 11:1; 1 Pet. 1:21; 5:3). It is to live in "the law of the Spirit of life in Christ Jesus" (Rom. 8:2).

### *3.1. Centrality of Religions: Incarnation, Pasch and Parousia*

With the Pasch of Christ, the last period of the History of Salvation has been ushered in and everything tends towards the Last Day of his total presence -- Parousia. Meanwhile the plan of God for the world is to be fully realized. His sovereignty is to be fully realized, mani-

---

[141] Cf. DSA, *Approach,* op. cit., pp. 27-28. See this point already dealt above.

fested and acknowledged by all peoples [and religions] gathered together in peace and unity and become the disciples of Christ.[142]

The pasch and parousia of Christ Jesus show the reality of his total and permanent presence in the world. The mystery of the incarnation, pasch and parousia of Christ is the reality that, as we have seen above, truly and fully fulfills the longings of other religious traditions, expressed through, for example, *saṁsāra* (cycle of 'rebirth') and *mokṣa* (release), or seeing their gods in different mythical forms and figures, the *avatāras,* like Rāma and Kṛṣṇa in Hinduism, or eternalizing and deifying their human religious figures, like Gautama Buddha in Buddhism. The mystery of the incarnation and resurrection is a fact, not a myth.[143] For "the Word became flesh and lived among us" (Jn. 1:14).[144] However, the primary concern of Jesus in his life, as the gospels show us, was not to show or prove that he was God but rather what it means to be human. In the mystery of Christ Jesus we see the "humanization" of God and the divinization of man, the incarnational salvation of man.

In the mystery of the incarnation we also see the 'right to human life', the 'sacredness of human life', as opposed to death or a demand of some human sacrifices in some religious beliefs and practices. We see God's love and concern for this "secular" world. God has created the world and given us life. He is interested in it (cf. Jn. 3:16); it is a purposive creation, founded on God's redemptive mystery of his Being, the wonders of his love and self-gift. God gives it life, life in its fullness, the fullness of grace and truth and salvation, in and through his Son Jesus Christ (cf. Jn. 1:14).

Christ Jesus is a unique historical person, who lived on this earth, died and rose from the dead and now as the risen Lord, with his all-pervading Spirit, continues to live and reign forever and ever. The very

---

[142] DSA, *Approaches,* op. cit., p. 13.

[143] A myth or a mythical story may, under the mythical forms and figures or symbols, be used to explain the supernatural realities. The mythical forms and figures, thereby, are not facts, not real, not historical; e.g., Rāma, in Hinduism, is a mythical figure, not a historical fact, unlike Jesus who is a historical fact. Rāmāyaṇa is a mythical story, not factual or historical. For explanation of myth and mythical salvation, see: M. Dhavamony, *Phenomenology of Religion,* Documenta Missionalia - 7, Università Gregoriana Editrice, Roma, 1973, chapter six, pp. 137-157; see also: Id., "Indian Christian Theological Method", in: *Studia Missionalia,* vol. 45, op. cit., pp. 73-74.

[144] Cf. DSA, *Towards Indigenization in the Liturgy,* op. cit., p. 168; cf. also: Gerwin van Leeuwen, O.F.M., *Fully Indian - Authentically Christian,* op. cit., p. 308.

basis and source of Christianity and the goal and aspiration of every religion, therefore, is the mystery of Jesus' incarnation and resurrection.[145]

"By his [life], death and resurrection Christ became the Lord of the universe, saviour of mankind and supreme norm of human existence and history."[146] Therefore, the historical life of Jesus, that is, *history* in Christianity, is very important. However, Jesus does not ask one to follow his external Jewish culture and history in which he came, that is, to be baptized as a Jew, but to "incarnate" his spirit in one's own culture and history. To follow Christ is, therefore, to live the life-giving *Spirit* of Christ in every culture and historical set-up. Salvation in Christ comes not from the circumcision of flesh but from the spiritual circumcision of "heart and ears" (Acts 7:51; cf. Rom. 2:29; Col. 2:11). Paul writes: "Circumcision indeed is of value if you obey the law; but if you break the law, your circumcision has become uncircumcision" (Rom. 2:25). Again, "For in Christ Jesus neither circumcision nor uncircumcision counts for anything; the only thing that counts is *faith working through love*" (Gal. 5:6; cf. Phil. 3:3). In Jesus Christ one's salvation is to be attained not through witchcraft or magic[147] or miracle, but faith working through love and service. Salvation in Jesus Christ comes from seeing and recognizing the historical Jesus as the *RISEN CHRIST* (cf. Jn. 20:18),[148] thereby, transcending and transforming, not negating, the earthly life into spiritual life, death into resurrection.

The fullness of life begins here on earth. As Gerwin van Leeuwen, interpreting the mind of Amalor, writes: "We have been saved by both the death [i.e., earthly life] and resurrection of Christ, neither by the latter nor by the former alone, but by both, or rather by the passage of the one to the other."[149] Resurrection or salvation, thereby, is a consequence (*karma,*

---

145 Cf. DSA, *Approaches,* op. cit., pp. 33, 36-37.

146 DSA, "Inculturation is not Hinduization but Christianization", *op. cit.,* p. 108.

147 Some primitive, tribal, or animistic religions had or still may have recourse to magic or to a "magical salvation", especially in controlling and directing the supernatural powers, and thus obtaining health, happiness and prosperity in life. For details on magic and religion, see: M. Dhavamony, *Phenomenology of Religion,* op. cit., especially chapter two, pp. 31-48. Even in our age this sort of obtaining salvation is seen practised here and there, e.g., "New Age" religions and witchcraft.

148 Cf. DSA (ed.), *Non-Biblical Scriptures - Theological Understanding,* op. cit., p. 36 (Statement no. 48).

149 Gerwin van Leeuwen, O.F.M., *Fully Indian - Authentically Christian,* op. cit., p. 283.

*saṁsāra*)[150] of one's life lived in the spirit of Christ (cf. Col. 2:12). It is the life lived in and by the power of the spirit of Christ that really sets one free from sin and *saṁsāra*. Salvation is therefore in encountering and experiencing the risen Christ in one's life-vicissitudes and history, creating thereby a new relationship with God and others, a new humanism, a new "race" and "religion" in Christ.[151]

The living of the Spirit of Christ throws a new challenge to the Church today as she lives amidst the world religions and sees the Spirit of Christ active and at times more pronounced in them. The Nagpur Conference states the challenge in its Declaration:

> This new humanism in Jesus Christ -- of living in God, of giving himself completely to his fellowmen, of losing his life in order to find it -- becomes the pattern of the new humanity. His disciples, baptized in him and united in and through the Eucharist, become his Body, i.e. the social and historical continuation of his own presence in the world and of his mission for all men.... They are sent to keep this mystery of Jesus Christ alive in this world, and to become the leaven of this society in all ages, the vanguard of a new race (no. 6).[152]

### *3.2. Christ Constantly Saving the World: A Process*

Looking at the world where there is sin and suffering, crime and injustice, hatred and war, division, suspicion and insecurity, religious and ethnic genocides, one easily inclines to ask: Has Jesus really saved the world? Has he really destroyed sin? How?

Viewed from a broader perspective, sin is an objective situation which conditions human beings and leads them to commit further sin. Sin is a social, even a cosmic event, rather than merely an individual problem. Sin seems to leave its long mark in the experience of humankind from the

---

150 Here we are not concerned with the exposition of the doctrine of *saṁsāra* (doctrine of the cycle of rebirth) in Hinduism. What we want to show is that salvation in Hinduism is seen also as a *consequence* of one's life-behaviour and actions (*karma*). For more on *saṁsāra*, see: M. Dhavamony, *Classical Hinduism*, op. cit., esp. pp. 443-445.

151 Cf. DSA, "Biblical World-View and a Renewed Holistic Spirituality", *op. cit.*, pp. 57-58.

152 See in: DSA, *Theology of Evangelization*, op. cit., p. 30.

very beginning when Adam and Eve committed sin against God (cf. Gen. 3:1-19; Rom. 5:12). Yet, another aspect of sin and salvation, as we have already seen, is seen in the act of "(re)creation" from chaos, that is, God, in and through his spirit, creating the world and giving it life and order from *tōhû wābōhû,* from sin, disorder and darkness (cf. Gen. 1:1-2). God has defeated sin or chaos; he has saved his 'original creation', creation without sin,[153] when it was tainted by the consequences of sin. God has destroyed 'sin' but its consequences are still experienced in the life and history of mankind. Since the consequences of sin are constantly experienced in life and history, the saving act of God must be constantly effective. It must be an on-going process, at least as regards the *response* or obedience of man to the saving act of God is concerned. God has saved the world from chaos and he continues to save it in history till man, history and the creation itself, in the process of evolution, reaches its full stature, its consummation, in God in and through Christ (cf. 4:13; Rom. 8:21-22).[154] "In these last days he [God] has spoken by a Son, whom he appointed heir of all things, through whom he also created the worlds" (Heb. 1:2). The creation which was "subjected to futility" (Rom. 8:20) is "set free from its bondage to decay" (Rom. 8:21) in Jesus Christ. God creates and re-creates a new heaven and a new earth in and through his Son (cf. 2 Cor. 5:17; Rev. 21:1). God is all in all in and through his Son Jesus Christ.[155] Christ "must reign until he has put all his enemies under his feet. The last enemy to be destroyed is death" (1 Cor. 15:25-26). "When all things are subjected to him, then the Son himself will also be subjected to the one who put all things in subjection under him, so that God may be all in all" (1 Cor. 15:28).

---

153 Here we do not enter into a philosophical debate as to when exactly sin entered into creation, or whether 'sin' or evil is an eternal principle vis-à-vis with God, the principle of goodness. This is beyond our scope. I have used the term the 'original creation' and '(re)creation' in the context of the creation story in Genesis to explain the presence of 'darkness and disorder', and to show, in short, that sin is not the creation of God. God who is 'all good' cannot create sin or evil. When he created everything - everything was good, without sin. In this sense, if at all we can call the 'chaos' in the creation story as 'sin', then it would mean that God's original creation was tainted by 'sin', chaos, and hence the word, '(re)creation'.

154 Cf. DSA, *Gospel and Culture,* op. cit., pp. 29-30; id., *Approaches,* op. cit., p. 33.

155 Cf. DSA, *Approach,* op. cit., pp. 27-28.

### *3.3. Salvation in Christ: Gift and Task*

Salvation in Christ is an incarnational economy; Christ has saved the world through his life, death and resurrection. Salvation in Jesus Christ is, therefore, patterned on Jesus' life-behaviour, his death and resurrection, the paschal mystery. Jesus is the pattern *par excellence* of our life on earth. Paul says that if we share in the life and death of Jesus, we shall share in his resurrection (cf. 1 Cor. 15:20-23). Accordingly, man's love for God and his neighbour, both individually and collectively as a religious community, is to be patterned on the life-example of Jesus and led by his Spirit.[156] A true religion then is to be found in the discipleship of Christ. This is what the religion means in gist: loving God and one's neighbour (cf. Matt. 22:37-40). It is to live as "the salt of the earth" (Matt. 5:13), "the light of the world" (Matt. 5:13-14) and as the leaven in the flour (cf. Lk. 13: 20-21), bearing witness to the truth to the end (cf. Matt. 10:22).

In the following we give a glimpse of Jesus' life-behaviour, his "religion": the deliverance of the suffering in and through his 'identification' with and 'representation' of the poor, the weak and the innocent. We will briefly see the life-behaviour of Jesus, summarizing everything in two main points: the right notion of God and the right notion of man, society and religion, that is, his vertical and horizontal relationship with God and man respectively. These two notions of Jesus, which are complementarily connected, make him live and die for the cause of truth, even accepting a death on a cross.

#### *3.3.1. The notion of God: Loving the world, not judging*

The God of Jesus is neither a mythical god nor a 'wooden god' (Hos. 4:12); he is not a God in the "sky", far above, nor a God of condemnation. The God of Jesus is the God of love and life, mercy and compassion -- "Abba! Father!" (Rom. 8:15; Gal. 4:6; Mk. 14:36). Jesus reveals this notion of God to the world religions; he lives for it and dies for it; and in this God is "well pleased" (Matt. 3:17; 17:5; cf. Jn. 8:29).

When Jesus came to this world he came not to condemn or abolish the existing laws and religions. He came to fulfill them (cf. Matt. 5:17). He came not to condemn this world as sinful but to love it and save it: "For God *so loved* the world that he gave his only Son... Indeed, God did

---

[156] Cf. DSA, *Approaches,* op. cit., pp. 36-37.

not send the Son into the world to condemn the world, but in order that the world might be *saved* through him" (Jn. 3:16-17). Jesus came, he lived and died for this world. He hated the sin in the world, not the world that is created by God. He came to *reconcile* it to the Father.

> In Jesus of Nazareth, who died and rose from the dead, God has spoken the irrevocable *'yes'* to our world. Having completely inserted himself into our human existence he gives to this existence a new meaning: its radical openness to God and universal brotherhood. Completely united with his Father he pours out his life for his brothers in a total self-gift, knowing that it is only in losing life that he can really live.[157]

In Jesus, God becomes a personal God, a God-with-us, who "situates" himself with the human beings, "lives and dies" with them and thus saves them and their situation, thereby the human life, nay, the existence of the whole creation is ratified in Jesus. Have the religions of the world understood this revelation of God in Jesus Christ? Since this revelation and response in Jesus is an on-going process,[158] to understand this best is to live it. It is, therefore, to be put into life-perspective and practice. It is to be concretized and manifested in life and history, religious beliefs and practices.[159]

#### *3.3.2. The notion of man, society and religion: Hope and salvation of the poor*

To understand the life-behaviour of Jesus it is important to know the constitution of the Jewish society and its social communication among its members prevalent at the time of Jesus. For our purpose here, we could generally divide the Jewish society of Jesus' time into two groups: (i) the rich -- the élite, the religious leaders (Pharisees, scribes, rabbis - the keepers and administrators of the law) who were socially, economically and politically powerful, who looked for their help in the law, and (ii) the poor -- sinners, the "law-breakers", and outcasts who were materially

---

[157] See the Declaration of Nagpur Conference (DNC), no. 5, in: DSA, *Theology of Evangelization,* op. cit., p. 30.

[158] Cf. DSA, *Theology of Catechesis,* op. cit., pp. 6, 21-22.

[159] Cf. DSA, *The Theology of 'Indirect Evangelization',* op. cit., pp. 9-10.

impoverished, economically and politically powerless, who were cognizant of their own weakness, looking for help in God for they could not find anywhere else.[160]

> A sinner in the Old Testament is not someone who *has committed an offence against God.* Rather, to be a sinner means to be someone *who breaks and disregards the Law....* The Law defined the boundaries of the People of God; breaching the Law meant living outside the boundary marked by the Law, outside the [chosen] people who by definition are those who live within the Law. Sinners were, therefore, first of all Gentiles who lived outside the Covenant; and second, all those Jews who did not keep the Law.[161]

In the Old Testament the law and the prophets especially made it clear that social responsibility for the poor and oppressed belonged to the covenant and took priority over worship (cf. Deut. 24:10-15; Is. 1:11-17). The concept of the "Sabbatical Year" or the great "Jubilee Year", the year of release, restoration and liberation (cf. Lev. 25; Is. 27:13; 61:1-2), is best understood in this context. However, the law was monopolized by the powerful. It is here that Jesus denounces the evil practices of the élite: the extortion of the law and confiscation of properties of widows and the weak (cf. Matt. 23:13-36).

Jesus himself was regarded as a sinner because he did not follow the strict observance of the law which the élite demanded. They criticized Jesus. They said, "How can a man who is a sinner perform such signs" (Jn. 9:16; cf. Matt. 9:11; Mk. 3:1-5; Lk. 7:34; etc.). Jesus accepted the criticism hurtled against him. He turned it around and made it a statement of positive intent, forcing his opponents to realize that he had come precisely for this group -- the poor and the ostracized.[162] Against this background we must place Jesus' words: "I have come to call not the righteous but sinners" (Mk. 2:17).

Jesus came to save all -- the poor as well as the élite, that is, the whole of Israel; nay, the whole world, from Satan, sin and the wages of sin, death. He hated sin, not the sinner. He hated injustice, untruth, the

---

160 Cf. John Fuellenbach, *The Kingdom of God,* op. cit., p. 144.

161 Ibid., p. 145. Cf. also: Benedict T. Viviano, *The Kingdom of God in History,* Michael Glazier, Wilmington, Del., 1988, p. 26.

162 Cf. ibid., pp. 145-146 (J. Fuellenbach, *The Kingdom of God*).

hypocrisy of the Pharisees, scribes and the religious leaders of his time and not the Pharisees and the religious leaders themselves. He preached God's justice and mercy, repentance and salvation to all (cf. Mk. 1:15; Jn. 8:24). His salvation reached beyond the boundaries of caste, creed, sex and social status (cf. Lk. 7:1-10) and the religious taboos of ritual purity-impurity codes (cf. Lk. 11:37-41). His is a universal salvation. What counts for him beyond all these man-made social and religious laws and taboos is the law of God: love and service.

In Jesus, the human person, no matter of what faith and sex, who is created and called in the image of God is to be saved. Traditional taboos give way to reason and true faith-practices. In his "table fellowship" with the sinners and outcasts Jesus breaks the law of "racism and untouchability" (cf. Lk. 5: 27-32). The law of 'clean and unclean food' is broken (cf. Acts 11:2-9; 1 Cor. 10:27; cp. 1 Macc. 1: 62-63). Thus, we could say that the evil of the caste system in Hinduism would not be compatible with Jesus.

Women from the beginning had a low profile in the Jewish society and religion. Sin and impurity were easily associated with them. Eve was accused of "eating the forbidden fruit" (Gen. 3:12). But unlike all these prejudices women were found among the closest followers and friends of Jesus (cf. Mk. 15: 40-41; Lk. 8:1-3; 10:38-42). He preached justice and equality of all in the society. This is well seen in his teaching on divorce applied to both partners (cf. Mk. 10:11-12; cp. Gen. 1:27).

Do our religious laws and customs help us live fully human lives in our societies? Whom does our religion serve: the rich or the poor, or both? Above, we have pinpointed a few incidents from the life-behaviour of Jesus to show his notion of God, man, society and religion in general. We have already seen earlier that we cannot separate religion from society.[163] Religion does not exist in the air. Instead religion must help individuals and societies attain peace, prosperity and unity with God and with fellow beings. Jesus, the 'God-with-us', is the living standard of individual persons and religions.[164] Peoples and religions must be constantly put on the anvil of the salvific word and spirit of Christ.[165]

Though, as a result of the contact with Christ and Christianity, the

---

[163] Cf. DSA, *Gospel and Culture,* op. cit., pp. 14-16.

[164] Cf. DSA, *Approaches,* op. cit., pp. 36-37.

[165] Cf. ibid., p. 36.

*sati prathā* (widow-burning) and other socio-religious evil practices in Hinduism[166] have been abolished they still continue in different forms and intensity. The low status and secondary role of women in Islam is still deplored all over the world. Still in many parts of the world, backed by religious laws and customs, women have less opportunities to life and liberation. There is no equality; often it seems that they have to be doubly liberated: liberation from the 'sin' of humankind, the original sin, and the sin of male chauvinism, the enforced sin.

Liberation in Christ calls for the liberation of '*every* man and the *whole* man',[167] that is, the liberation of the whole humankind and whatever is related to it, including all the religious traditions of the world. Individuals and socio-religious laws and customs must conform themselves to the spirit of Christ.

The note we make in the incarnational approach of Jesus is that he has proclaimed salvation to all, especially to the poor, the weak and oppressed, the sinners and outcasts, through repentance and purification. It is the purification of persons as well as of their religious traditions themselves from *within.* His is the law of love and service in every context and culture. His is the reign of the 'servant-king' of Yahweh (cf. Is. 9:6-7; 42:1ff.). This is the incarnational approach where Amalor is much fascinated in the continuing mission of Jesus for the salvation of the world. Jesus' identification with the poor was well seen by Amalor and others at the Nagpur Conference. The Conference states:

> In the face of Christ disfigured in the suffering poor and oppressed, our religious leaders will have to change their style of life which associate them with privileged groups. Divested of all superfluities they will not only be identified with the poor around them but this will also bc apparent to others. They will then be able to discern the revolutiotionary implications of evangelization for changes in socio-economic structures that are an insult to God, the loving Father of all men. Then the power of the Word can transform the Eucharistic assemblies to radiate in the form of relevant service to society.[168]

---

166 As a result of their contact with Christianity, *sati prathā* (widow-burning) has been abolished by Hindu reformers, like Raja Ram Mohan Roy (1772-1833) and M. Gandhi (1869-1948).

167 Cf. DSA, *Theology of 'Indirect Evangelization',* op. cit., p. 6.

168 See: DSA, *Theology of Evangelization,* op. cit., p. 38 (Statement no. 33).

The most needy of God are the poor, the poor in the spirit, who turn to God for their help and strength. The Bible shows that God has been saving the world through "the mystery of the poor". In Hinduism, too, especially by M. Gandhi, the God of the poor is well understood. M. Gandhi called the poor, the outcastes, the untouchables, *harijans* (the people of God),[169] and God, among other names, as *Daridranārāyaṇa* (God of the poor).[170]

In and through his life, death and resurrection Jesus has become, the Lord of all peoples and religions, the hope and salvation of all humankind, the norm of human existence *par excellence* in history. In short, human beings and their religions find their basis, direction and fulfillment in the mystery of the incarnation and resurrection of Jesus Christ.

## 4. Conclusion

We summarize this chapter in the following two points.

### *4.1. The Jesus Christ event, the centre of salvation history*

The historical event of God's becoming flesh in Jesus marks the deepest and the most decisive engagement of God with mankind. Christ Jesus is the redemptive mystery of God realized as self-emptying creative love.[171] He is the unifying love of God with all humankind (cf. 1 Cor. 3:23; 5:28).[172] Peoples and religions, from the beginning of creation to the end, are oriented to God in and through his Son Jesus Christ (cf. Heb. 1:1-3), because he is the beginning and the end of creation and the central event of the history of salvation.[173]

---

169 See: M.K. Gandhi, *The Removal of Untouchability*, Navajivan Publishing House, Ahmedabad, 1954 (reprinted in 1959), p. 1.

170 See: R.K. Prabhu and U.R. Rao (eds), *The Mind of Mahatma Gandhi*, Navajivan Publishing House, Ahmedabad, 1969 (reprint), p. 196.

171 Cf. DSA (ed.), *Non-Biblical Scriptures - Theological Understanding*, op. cit., p. 36 (Statement no. 48).

172 Cf. DSA, "Approach", *op. cit.*, pp. 41-42.

173 Cf. DSA, *Approaches*, op. cit., pp. 14-15; id., "Approach", *op. cit.*, p. 81; id., *Theology of Evangelization*, op. cit, p. 35 (DNC 22).

### *4.2. The mystery and sacramentality of the Church*

In the Christian economy of salvation the community, the Church, remains a sacramental bearer of the kingdom.[174] The Church is the "body", the sacrament of Christ on earth, animated and led by his Spirit (cf. 1 Cor. 12:27; Eph. 1:23; 5:30). She is the chosen servant and sacrament of the kingdom of God here on earth (cf. *LG* 48).[175] Jesus Christ is the ultimate source of the Church's service and sacramentality.[176] Following the spirit and example of Christ, "the Church is, therefore, to gather from the four winds the various nations into one Family, one People of God, one Body of Christ and one Temple of the Spirit (cf. *AG* 17; *LG* 9a, 13a; *GS* 32; Priestly Ministry 1)."[177]

The Church is the new People of God, a new community, found everywhere wherever two or three who are "gathered" in Christ's name (cf. Matt. 18:20).[178] All human beings are, or rather called to be, members of Christ (cf. 1 Cor. 6:15). "There is one body and one Spirit" (Eph. 4:4) and Christ is "the head of his body, the Church [his disciples]" (Col. 1:18); he is also the "bread" (Jn. 6:35), the life-giving Spirit of this body, the Church.

Amalor sees the mystery of Jesus Christ as universal, open to all. Jesus Christ is the fullness of God's revelation, yet this universality, the fullness, the pleroma of Christ, is at present realized only partially by the Church. The Church has to be open to continuous sharing and enrichment in dialogue with other religions and ideologies of the world in view of the fullness of the mystery of the cosmic Christ that is to be revealed and realized at the end of time.[179]

---

174 Cf. DSA, "Approach", *op. cit.*, pp. 44-45.

175 Cf. DSA, *Theology of Catechesis,* op. cit., p. 9; id., *Approach,* op. cit., p. 46.

176 Cf. DSA, *Approaches,* op. cit., p. 50. More about the sacramentality of the Church will be dealt in chapter four.

177 Ibid., pp. 14-15.

178 Cf. DSA, "Approach", *op. cit.*, pp. 80-81.

179 Cf. ibid., p. 55.

# CHAPTER FOUR

# SALVIFIC VALUE OF OTHER RELIGIONS
# GOD'S SALVIFIC PROVIDENCE

## 1. Introduction

### *1.1. Salvation: The focal and final goal of every religion*

Salvation or liberation is the end of every religion. Salvation is the fundamental desire of every human person, even those so-called unbelievers, humanists and atheists;[1] nay, the whole creation has been groaning to be set free from its bondage and decay to life and liberation in God through Christ (cf. Rom. 8:21-22).

Since, today in our multi-religious society, each religion claims the salvific value within itself and equality with others, there is no outright negation or condemnation of this fact without involving some sort of risk.[2] What is our Christian outlook and approach? Amalor says that it is an extremely delicate task and even a dangerous one to assess the salvific value of other religions. It is a question of "judging" a religion by the Gospel, the word of God, especially at the time today when each religion claims within itself the fullness of truth and salvation.[3] Proper assessment of other religions demands a proper study and knowledge of them as well as of one's own tradition. Religions are best 'criticized' from "within", not from outside. Amalor, at the very outset, likes to drive home that criticism of other religions is not a criticism of a person. It is not a personal attack.[4]

---

[1] Cf. DSA, *Approaches,* op. cit., pp. 41-42.

[2] Cf. M. Dhavamony, "Today's Challenge: Salvation Offered by Non-Christian Religions", in: *Studia Urbaniana,* vol. 34 (1989), pp. 81-100.

[3] Cf. DSA, *Approaches,* op. cit., p. 37.

[4] Cf. ibid., p. 39.

### *1.2. The point of departure: Recognizing the reality of other religions*

The point of departure for a more open theology of religions is based on God's universal and efficacious will for salvation (cf. 1 Tim. 2:4-5; *AG* 7). People from other religions live outside the visible boundaries of the Church and may not have existentially encountered the Gospel of Jesus Christ; yet, since God's salvific will and action is operative and effective in history before the foundation of the Church (cf. Heb. 1:1-2), other religions come under the purview of God's one and universal salvific plan which is centered in Christ.[5] "The revelation and realization of God's universal plan of salvation for mankind is older and longer than the Church; wider than the narrow, linear and limited Judeo-Christian history of 4000 years."[6]

Vatican II rightly recognizes the reality of other religions as seekers of God, truth and salvation.[7] To recognize them as religions means, therefore, to recognize them as seekers of God, truth and salvation; and to deny them would mean denying the very sincere search of God in them. In Hinduism, for example, men contemplate the divine mystery and express it through an inexhaustible abundance of myths and through philosophical inquiry. They seek freedom from the anguish of our human condition either through ascetical practices or profound meditation or a flight to God with love and trust. Buddhism in its various forms realizes the radical insufficiency of this challengeable world; it teaches a way by which human beings in a devout and confident spirit, may be able either to acquire the state of perfect liberation or attain, by their own efforts or through higher help, supreme illumination. So too other religions of the world attempt in their own ways to calm the hearts and minds of their followers and secure them salvation (cf. *NA* 2)

The Catholic Church rejects nothing of what is true and holy in these religions. She sees the providence of God and recognizes the possibility of salvation in them. Yet she proclaims that all truth, grace and salvation come through Jesus Christ who is "the way and the truth and the life" (Jn.

---

[5] Cf. DSA, *Gospel and Culture,* op. cit., p. 47.

[6] DSA, *Approach,* op. cit., p. 54. These concepts were expounded at the Nagpur Theological Conference (1971); see: DNC, nos. 12-17, also found in DSA, *Theology of Evangelization,* op. cit., pp. 32-33; cf. also: Cyril De Souza, S.D.B., *Catechesis for India Today,* op. cit., p. 336.

[7] Cf. DSA, *Approaches,* op. cit., 43.

14:6). In other words, she believes and is duty bound to proclaim, without fail, the universal salvific mystery of God in Jesus Christ. The whole of humanity and creation is assumed and saved by Christ. The salvific Spirit of Christ permeates all, assumes all and saves all (cf. *NA* 2). All the religions of the world are included in the one salvific plan of God. God's grace is also operative and effective in other religions. If it is so then the Church has no right to exclude other religions from the object of Christ's salvation. They are God's providential ways of salvation.

> If God has submitted everything under Christ, if the saving action of Christ extends to the whole of humanity and creation, if the *Spirit* of the Risen Christ fills the universe and permeates everything, we have no right to exclude anything -- especially religions -- from the object of Christ's salvation.... If so Hinduism and other religions are not outside the plan of God but take their place within God's *one plan of salvation* which is centered in Christ through whom all things and all men are led to their fulfillment.[8]

## 2. Basic Suppositions

### *2.1. Revelation and Salvation in Other Religions*[9]

Amalor writes:

> With St. Paul (1 Tim. 2:4-5) and Vatican II (*AG* 7), we start from God's universal and efficacious will of salvation. Since the gospel even today is far from being preached everywhere and the vast majority of men live outside the boundaries of the visible Church, the universal plan -- gradually revealed and realized through human history -- is both older and wider than the Church and necessarily includes the Non-Christian religions.
> True, the Church holds a special place in this history of salvation and has the fullness of the message of salvation; but she cannot either

[8] DSA, *Gospel and Culture,* op. cit., pp. 46-47.

[9] Here we do not proceed to deal with the point of general revelation in other religions and the specific revelation in Christ. The point has already been dealt in detail in chapter one.

> limit God's saving presence in Christ. His presence and action as Saviour and Light are universally operative and effective before the foundation of the Church and outside the visible Church today.[10]

From this above statement, Amalor draws the following basic suppositions on the salvific value of other religions.[11]

### *2.1.1. Religions under the purview of God's one and universal salvific plan and his providence*

Amalor puts the religions of the world under the umbrella of God's universal plan and providence in and through Jesus Christ. God's universal and efficacious will of salvation is fully revealed and realized in Jesus Christ.

Admittedly the Church, the bearer of the fullness of the Good News, has a special place in the history of salvation. But God's saving presence is not limited to the Church alone. God's saving presence and action in and through the saving mystery of the cosmic Christ and his all permeating Spirit are universally operative and effective before the foundation of the Church and outside the visible Church today.[12] This is made clear once again in Vatican II when it takes up the Patristic phrase the "seeds of the Word" (*AG* 11; cf. *NA* 2) and explains the possibility of salvation in other religions.

> The Non-Christian Religions come within God's plan of salvation for mankind in Jesus Christ. From this point of view, religions cannot be opposed to the Church, but must be understood and evaluated in reference to it. This universal active presence [which] is expressed in the Patristic phrase [as the] *seeds of the Word* [is] taken up again by the Council (*AG* 11).[13]

---

[10] DSA, *Approaches,* op. cit., p. 10.

[11] From 1 Tim. 2:4-5 and *AG* 7 DSA briefly draws his basic suppositions on revelation and salvation in other religions in eleven points (a, b, c, ... k). Cf. ibid., pp. 10-12. I have followed a different numbering system and put the points under different headings.

[12] Cf. ibid., p. 10; also: DSA, *Approach,* op. cit., p. 54.

[13] Ibid. While citing the numberings have been dropped.

Other religions of the world fall within God's plan and are recipients of the general revelation. The specific revelation in Christ Jesus and in the Church is the fulfillment of the general revelation in other religions.[14] Since the destiny of all the religions of the world is one and the same, which is divine, (cf. *GS* 22), other religions are related to the Church, and the Church must play an important and decisive role in the realization of the universal salvific will of God fulfilled in Christ.

> The religions of the World are not empty rooms to step into or voids to be filled in or heaps of rubbish to be removed. We are to be aware that God is present not only in the followers of religions but *in the religions themselves.* They fall within God's universal plan of salvation and are subjected to the eschatological sovereignty of God. They are partners to the covenant of Noah and recipients of the cosmic revelation. Their structures and elements are reached by the saving grace of Christ and are related to the Church, the universal sacrament of salvation.[15]

Amalor views other religions as being animated by God in his providence. They are in a state of expectation, searching for the true God.[16] Quoting *Ad Gentes,* he writes: "Through the kindly workings of Divine Providence, [they] may sometimes serve as a guidance course towards the True God, or as a preparation for the Gospel" (no. 3).[17] Seen in this perspective the proclamation of Christ and his Gospel does not come as a bolt from the blue; Christ does not come as a stranger, but "as one whom they have always sought for: *'quod ignorantes quaeritis, hac ego annuntio vobis'* --'He whom without knowing you have been seeking, he it is whom I proclaim to you' (Acts 17:23)."[18]

The other religious traditions in which their followers have been born and brought up are the means Providence has provided them to relate to

---

[14] Cf. *CCC,* 845.

[15] DSA, *Approaches,* op. cit., p. 34. In this context, on the same page, see DSA giving many references to the teaching of Vatican II: *AG* 4, 11, 15, 21; *GS* 92d; *NA* 2.

[16] Cf. ibid., p. 35.

[17] See as quoted in: Ibid.

[18] See: Ibid., p. 48.

'the One without a Second'.[19] This in no way undermines the uniqueness and universality of the Christian economy of salvation and of the Church as the universal sacrament of salvation for the world, instituted and entrusted by the decisive word spoken by Christ.[20]

*2.1.2. Saved in their own religions: 'Because of it', not 'in spite of it'*

Here it is important once again to note that religions are not the end in themselves but means to the end, God. People are saved not by a 'religion' as such but by God, by his Word -- Jesus Christ, the Word become flesh, the saviour of the world. Basing himself on the Petrine and the Pauline theology as well as on *Ad Gentes,* Amalor states:

> Indeed, even Christians are saved not by 'Christianity' as such but by God, by Jesus Christ the only saviour: to this doctrine of Peter (Acts 4:12) and Paul (1 Tim. 2:4-5) upheld by the Council (*AG* 8) correspond some acknowledgements, e.g., that 'the good *bona fide* Hindu is saved by Christ and not by Hinduism.'[21]

Amalor firmly holds the view that the believers in other religions are saved in their own religions. He writes:

> It is a fact that some non-Christians are saved in their own religions outside the boundaries of the visible Church (*LG* 16; *GS* 22; *AG* 7c). Not only are non-Christians *'saved',* but saved *'in their own religions',* for it is within their framework that God's grace reaches them: men do not live in isolation, but as members of a given social group and members of a given religion -- all of which have an influence on their formation (cf. *AG* 10). Hence, the universal plan of salvation implies that God's grace reaches men in their life situation and, that their (non-Christian) religions are for them channels of grace, and *providential ways of salvation, and milieus of God's saving action.*[22]

---

[19] Cf. DNC 12, 14, 16 published as appendix in: DSA, *Theology of Evangelization,* op. cit., pp. 32-33; Statement of the Research Seminar on Non-Biblical Scriptures (11-17 December 1974), nos. 15-19, 54, in: DSA (ed.), *Non-Biblical Scriptures - Theological Understanding,* op. cit., pp. 24-26 and 38.

[20] Cf. DNC 16.

[21] DSA, *Approaches,* op. cit., p. 11.

[22] Ibid., pp. 10-11.

God's grace works in an unseen way in the hearts of all men of good will. *Gaudium et Spes* states: "For, since Christ died for all men, and since the ultimate vocation of man is in fact one, and divine, we ought to believe that the Holy Spirit in a manner only known to God offers to every man the possibility of being associated with this paschal mystery" (no. 22). Vatican II has made it clear that persons who through no fault of their own do not know the Gospel of Christ or his Church, but who nevertheless seek God with a sincere heart, and moved by grace, try to do God's will as they know it through the dictates of their conscience, can be saved (cf. *LG* 16). It is because our God is a God of salvation and life, and human history is a history of salvation.[23] By God's intervention in history, especially by his openness to the world through the historical event of his becoming man in Jesus and his rising from the dead, the whole Jesus Christ event, thereby assuming the whole man and every man, the whole earth has simply become a place of salvation, the world's history is simply salvation history and time is simply a veritable moment for man's encounter with God -- salvation is available at the very heart of the world.[24] Hence the responsibility of the Christian community is that of a global vision and global concern, universal charity, an active pro-existence in the midst of the world and its religions, that is, the salvation of the world.

### *2.1.3. The mystery of faith: Mystery of salvation*

If indeed people are saved by God through Christ, the next question that emerges is: *How* does the grace of God in Christ reach people of other religions? Or, how do people of other religions respond to God in and through Christ? For Amalor it is basically a mystery of faith. It is this faith, not law, says Paul, that brings salvation to the Christians and others, 'the Jews as well as the Gentiles' (cf. Rom. 4:16; 5:1; Gal. 2:16; 3:28-29; Eph. 2:8). "Any explanation on *'how'* this grace reaches all men and how they respond to it, can be only a groping attempt, for it is *a mystery of faith.*"[25]

---

[23] Cf. DSA, *Purpose*, op. cit., p. 24.

[24] Cf. DSA, *Approaches*, op. cit., pp. 15-17. For this point DSA refers to H. Urs von Balthasar, *Théologie de l'Histoire*, Paris 1960, pp. 44, 52, 53. See this as cited in: Ibid., p. 15.

[25] Ibid., p. 11.

### *2.1.4. No parallelism of religions*

If God has revealed himself to people in and through their different socio-religious contexts (cf. Heb. 1:1-2), and if the final goal of all religions is one and the same, that is, God or salvation, can we say that all religions are equal or same?

The content and intensity of faith in religions are not the same. For Amalor the Christian revelation is the supreme, definitive self-revelation of God in his Son Jesus Christ. Christ Jesus is the Word become flesh in the fullness of time; he is the fullness of revelation. He is the saviour long waited for; and the Church is the universal instrument of salvation, instituted by Christ himself. Therefore, "non-Christian religions are not equal or parallel to Christianity, which is by divine positive institution, the universal sacrament of salvation."[26]

### *2.1.5. "Ordinary and extraordinary ways", "natural religions" refuted*

Vatican II acknowledged the possibility of salvation in other religions, yet much of its explanation was left to theologians. There arose the controversy: Are these other religions the 'ordinary' or 'extraordinary' ways of salvation for those born in them?

A number of theologians, precisely because God reaches out to people in their own historico-socio-religious milieux, may be in favour of calling the religion in which one is born and bred, the 'ordinary' or 'normal' way and Christianity, because of Christ, the 'extraordinary' way (H. R. Schlette).[27]Amalor considers this "an exaggerated conclusion, going far beyond the conclusion of the Council."[28] He also refutes the position of putting the other religions under the term, "natural religions". He writes: "We should not speak of the other religions as *natural religions* as the term would imply an exclusion of grace, thus putting these religions outside the ambit of Christ's universal saving action."[29]

The universal plan of God implies that the salvific grace of God in Christ encounters men in their own life situations and religious traditions. This leads Amalor to the conclusion that other religions can be God's

---

[26] Ibid.

[27] See DSA referring to H.R. Schlette, in: Ibid.

[28] Ibid.

[29] Ibid.

providential means or channels of grace for their followers, and thus, are salvific; and hence these religions are not to be considered as 'natural', that is, devoid of grace. Gerwin van Leeuwen writes: "Though he [Amalor] attaches great importance to the recognition of Christ's active presence in and working through these religions, the Indian theologian finds it difficult to justify the thesis that for believers of other faiths Christianity is the 'extraordinary way'."[30] Instead the fact, that they come within the covenant of Noah and that they are depositories or recipients of the cosmic covenant and that they contain the 'seeds of the Word', does not lead us to such a statement.[31] Other religions have a place within God's universal plan of salvation, "for they do contain some authentic spiritual and supernatural values which are the fruits of God's active and universal presence [and action]: in their framework, God's grace reaches and saves men."[32] In his speech at the Patna Consultation, Amalor again considers calling Christianity the 'extraordinary way' for followers of other great religions an excessive and unwarranted conclusion.[33]

The stand of any religion is not concluded or compared from its quantitative strength. Amalor ultimately bases the position of the Church, as the fully adequate means of salvation, on the authority of Christ. The Church has been positively and historically instituted by Christ as the universal sacrament of salvation.

> The criterion is not the number of people in a religion or the presence of spiritual and supernatural values, but [as regards the Church it is] the positive and historical institution of the Church by Christ *as the fully adequate means of salvation, as the universal sacrament of salvation,* as the animator and leader of the spiritual movement launched by Jesus Christ for the renewal and unification of mankind.[34]

---

30 Gerwin van Leeuwen, O.F.M., *Fully Indian - Authentically Christian,* op. cit., p. 265.

31 Cf. DSA, *Purpose,* op. cit., p. 26.

32 DSA, *Approaches,* op. cit., p. 12; id., *Purpose,* op. cit., p. 26.

33 Cf. DSA, *Approach,* op. cit., pp. 57-58.

34 Ibid.

### *2.1.6. Service to the world religions: Diakonia and dialogue*

While proclaiming the Gospel of Christ in the context of world religions, Amalor emphasizes the twofold task of the Church, which may also be seen as two forms of evangelization: diakonia and dialogue.[35]

On the one hand, the Church is called to render her service of purifying the other religions from "their ambiguous character and defects inherent in their very structure and signs [which] prevent them from being certain and reliable means of salvation, namely, the sign and instrument of all the salvation realized within and outside the institutional limits of the Catholic Church."[36] On the other hand, if the Church is to purify and perfect the religions, she can best do so, not by judging and condemning them from outside but through dialogue. Added to it, as Vatican II states, the Church subsists in the Catholic Church but does not exhaust all the realities of the Church (cf. *LG* 8). God is also present and active outside the confines of the visible Church. The Church should, therefore, recognize the ray of 'truth' in other religions, and promote and facilitate interreligious dialogue towards attaining the fullness of truth and life in Christ, in common search and mutual collaboration.

We find a fine summary of Amalor's view on the issue when he cites a part of the conclusions of the Bombay Seminar[37] from *The Clergy Monthly Supplement* (1965):

> 'To understand well the meaning of the world religions, they have to be considered from the theocentric point of view: the whole of mankind is embraced by the one salvific plan of God which includes all the world religions. They are not just natural theology, natural piety, natural morality, but are sharply ambiguous.... For the man who is not confronted in an existential way with the gospel of Jesus Christ, they can be the channel of Christ's saving grace. Christian faith represents radical universalism. *Every human being and every world*

---

[35] The point of diakonia to the world religions will be dealt in this chapter; dialogue with other religions will be dealt in the next chapter.

[36] DSA, *Approaches,* op. cit., p. 11.

[37] The International Theological Conference at Bombay was organized at the occasion of the Eucharistic Congress in 1964, at which Hans Küng, F. Masson, P. Fransen, and R. Panikkar were the main speakers. See: J. Neuner, S.J., (ed.), *Christian Revelation and World Religions,* London, 1967.

> *religion is under God's grace. But Christian universalism is grounded and centered in Christ.'* ... the way in which saving grace can reach the individual man is as follows: (there are) 'only two fundamental and contrary positions of an adult before God: self-centered love or openness to man and acceptance of God. Man is called by God in this life to a personal commitment that will determine the basic orientation of his religious and moral life.'[38]

God is the maker of every people and tradition (cf. Acts 17:23; *AG* 9). He now responds to people and fulfills the traditions of the world through his Son Jesus Christ and his Spirit. The Spirit is at work in the heart of every man and in the midst of every people.[39] The "seeds of the Word" have already been sown by God in other religious traditions (cf. Jn. 4:35-38). They wait for their fulfillment; they are in expectation of a true God and true worship. The Church has to recognize the "seeds of the Word" in other religions and fulfill them in Christ, not alone, unilaterally, but in dialogue and collaboration with others who have been working and waiting for salvation in their religious traditions.[40]

### *2.2. The Concept of Salvation: New Creation, New Humanity*

#### *2.2.1. Realizing the Jesus Christ event*

The concept or content of salvation is the *realization* of God's loving and eternal plan, both individually and collectively, for the whole human race and creation unfolded through the ages and now definitively revealed and realized in the historical event of Jesus Christ. It is, in few words, as we have already seen earlier, the total transformation, the Christification, of nature and society, that is, the unification of the whole humankind and creation with God through Christ in the Spirit; it is the realization of the fullness (*pleroma*) of Christ, the fullness of grace and truth in Christ. Basing himself in particular upon the texts of the Nagpur Theological

---

[38] See DSA quoting from *The Clergy Monthly Supplement,* June 1965, pp. 238-239, in: DSA, *Purpose,* op. cit., pp. 26-27.

[39] Cf. DSA, *Approaches,* op. cit., pp. 37, 46-48.

[40] Cf. ibid., p. 35.

Conference (1971), Amalor writes:

> The content of this salvation is the 'liberation of the whole man and the entire mankind from the fetters of law, sin and death and leading them to intimate union [*yoga*] with God and with one another. This liberation and saving action of God has both physical and spiritual, this-worldly [*jīvan mukti*] and other-worldly [*videha mukti*], existential ['already'] and eschatological ['not yet'] dimensions. This liberation takes place in this life for everyone who submits in faith to Jesus Christ; it is perfected finally in the sharing of his glory.' This liberating action of God corresponds to the 'basic aspiration of India today towards liberation from every form of oppression and servitude so that her children may realize their basic vocation to be truly and fully human ... by transforming human society it enables it to develop forms of life and fellowship in which the oneness of our race is expressed with the ultimate purpose of the building up of the fullness of Christ.[41]

*2.2.2. Liberation and freedom: Individual and communitarian*

What does liberation or freedom mean? How does Jesus see it? It is to turn from one's evil way and live: repentance, love and service to God and neighbour, as it was for Zacchaeus (cf. Lk. 19:1-10). It is a holistic approach to life and liberation, individual and communitarian. Amalor writes:

> Freedom is not only an ability for self-determination but also an ability to respond to self, to the Other and others: responsiveness and responsibility.... Freedom is ultimately the dynamism and ability to respond: a) to respond to one's yearning and movement to realize oneself and work for one's personal development; b) to respond to others by giving oneself totally and accepting others unconditionally, and finally c) to respond to God, the Other. It is a triple ability to respond to self, others, and the Other.[42]

---

[41] DSA, *Approach*, op. cit., p. 90; DSA refers both to the Special Committee's Statement (SCNC) as well as the Declaration of the Nagpur Conference (DNC), no. 18.

[42] DSA, "A Synthesis of Basic and Constitutive Elements of Indian Christian Spirituality", *op. cit.*, p. 229.

One cannot be aware of self, others and the Other, that is, God, nor can one respond to God and others by giving oneself totally and unconditionally except when one is whole. A total and universal giving and receiving, the all-round relationship and fellowship, becomes complete only in wholeness and inner freedom. It is through this triple response to self, others and to God that one becomes whole, universal, free and authentic. This concept of total liberation, wholeness or freedom, is shared by Christianity as well as by others. It is the integral liberation of the matter and the spirit brought about by the Word and the Spirit of God.

> Both in Christianity and Hinduism, freedom is in fact wholeness, integrity, totality on the one hand and non-attachment and renunciation on the other [i.e., the *kenosis* and the cross of Christ].... One has to attain liberation (*moksha*) as ultimate goal and one can become free already in this life (*jivanmukti*).... The Spirit is connected with the movement (*yatra*) and freedom. Where the Spirit is, there is freedom.... In some traditions of Hinduism freedom may at times be wrongly interpreted as a kind of liberation of the soul from the matter. But Hinduism as a whole and in general follows a holistic approach, taking everything as a whole and totality. So there is no separation of matter and spirit.[43]

In the late 1960s, when the discussion on the relationship between missionary activity and human development was at its zenith, Amalor addressed various zonal consultations on evangelization in India.[44] In these speeches he very much stressed on the holistic approach to missionary activity which calls for a firm anthropological basis, whereby, man is envisaged as an integral personality. The once commonly-held missionary attitude of saving individuals, specifically their souls, and thereby, viewing the development work as something secular and profane of the temporal order should be avoided at all costs.[45]

---

[43] Ibid., p. 230.

[44] The lectures at these zonal missionary consultations at Bombay (1969), Jamshedpur (1969), and Ootacamund (1970) were published as: *Theology of Development* and *Purpose and Motivation of Missionary Activity*. See: Cyril De Souza, S.D.B., *Catechesis for India Today*, op. cit., pp. 161-162.

[45] Cf. DSA, *Approaches*, op. cit., pp. 14-16.

> It is not a question of man's soul alone but of the integral man: 'man whole and entire, body and soul, heart and conscience, mind and will' (*GS* 3). What matters is not only integral men as 'individuals without mutual bonds' and removed from their spatial-temporal context: but as social beings and members of groups marked 'by permanent cultural ties, by ancient religious traditions and by firm bonds of social necessity' (*AG* 10), namely, men as belonging to their social, cultural and religious ensembles. Nay more, it is the whole human race and creation that has to be brought together in unity.[46]

This objective freedom or salvation (*mukti*) calls for the development and salvation of *every* man and the *whole* man in *all* his dimensions -- be they personal or communitarian, Christian or as held by others.[47]

> Salvation in Jesus Christ is not only a liberation from sin and all its forces but positively it is the realization of a new creation, leading a new kind of existence, learning a new way of being man, having deeper and fuller unity, and reaching total fulfillment in wholeness and harmony: peace and bliss.[48]

The previously held lop-sided soteriology of pre-Vatican II might have restricted salvation to the "saving of souls". Amalor instead, in keeping with Vatican II (*GS* 3), holds that in the holistic anthropological approach,[49] "salvation or integral development of man means the total liberation of man from sin and all its forces and consequence."[50] The entire history of man is a continuous struggle for freedom from social, political, economic and cultural oppression. The deliverance of man, both individually and collectively, from social injustice and inequality, economic oppression and stark poverty falls equally within the purview of the liberation effected by Jesus Christ. It affects the whole ambience of man.[51]

---

46 Ibid., p. 14.

47 Cf. DSA, *Theology of Development,* op. cit., pp. 10 and 14.

48 DSA, "Inculturation is not Hinduization but Christianization", *op. cit.,* p. 110; id., *Gospel and Culture,* op. cit., pp. 48-49.

49 More about the anthropological approach to liberation will be seen in chapter six.

50 DSA, *Theology of Development,* op. cit., p. 9.

51 Cf. Cyril De Souza, S.D.B., *Catechesis for India Today,* op. cit., pp. 162-163 where

### *2.3. The Notion of the One Dynamic History Evolution and Consummation*

In chapter one, we have already seen the on-going revelation of God in Christ in the one history of salvation. In Christ the history of the world has indeed become the salvation history. What does it mean? It means that the human history -- past, present and future, from creation to its consummation -- is a dynamic history, tending towards its destiny, that is, its consummation in Christ. There is only one salvation history with its many phases and turns, and the Church is not outside this history but within it. Neither the followers of the great religions of the East, as some thought or still think, are outside the history.[52] There is one appointed saviour and Lord, Christ, and one salvation in God in and through Christ. All salvific grace of God is now referred to Christ -- it is centered in Christ, flows from Christ and must return to Christ.

We may distinguish the salvation history in the following three stages:

(i) Creation (the theology of creation: one God, one creation in evolution)

(ii) Election of Israel and the Incarnation, the Word in the flesh (the theology of redemption: one God, one saviour)

(iii) Resurrection and Recapitulation: Easter, Pentecost and the Parousia (the theology of the Church or her missionary apostolate: the time to realize the salvific plan of God for all peoples and religions).[53]

#### *2.3.1. One God, creation and history in evolution, salvation a process*

Amalor likes to base his holistic vision of history and salvation on the theology of creation.[54] God created everything through his Word, Jesus Christ, the Word become flesh (cf. Jn. 1:1-3) and "saw everything that he had made, and indeed, it was very good" (Gen. 1:31). This basic and fundamental oneness and goodness of creation came into existence by

---

Cyril links Amalor's thought on the issue with the tenor of *Populorum Progressio.*

52 Cf. DSA, *Approaches,* op. cit., p. 17.

53 Cf. Gerwin van Leeuwen, O.F.M., *Fully Indian - Authentically Christian,* op. cit., p. 195.

54 Cf. Ibid.

God's Word under the hovering of the Spirit (cf. Gen. 1:2); it revealed God's features and never lost his stamp. The same Word through whom he created everything is also the purpose of his creative activity: "all things have been created through him [Jesus Christ] and for him" (Col. 1:16). Hence Jesus Christ is the firstborn of creation and he holds all things in unity (cf. Col. 1:15-17).[55]

God's universal plan of salvation that began with the very act of creation has never been cancelled or given up. It is a continuous saving act of creation and history in and through his living Word, for he "desires everyone to be saved and to come to the knowledge of the truth" (1 Tim. 2:4).

Amalor emphasizes the goodness and the dynamism in God's creation. Creation is not a finished product. The world and the human beings are in the process of growth, becoming. He writes: "Man must reach his maturity, wholeness and integrity; the world must reach its destiny, goal, and become the Kingdom of God."[56] With creation,

> there began the *'historical adventure of mankind'*, a movement towards its consummation, in view of its total becoming.... This movement is what is called, 'life', 'history'. In this movement humankind is engaged in deploying its potentialities, exploring its resources, actuating its faculties, developing its talents, inventing new tools for its evolution, mastering nature and transforming the world.[57]

The fullness of the evolution of the world and mankind is in and through Christ. It is the Christification of history and the universe;[58] it is the Christification, the full flowering in Christ of the 'seeds of the Word' (*semina verbi*) in other religions, which are such an abundant manifestation of God's universal presence and his universal kingdom.[59]

"The God of creation is the master of history as well."[60] When man installs himself as "king" of creation and history, aspiring to be God (cf.

---

55 Cf. DSA, *Gospel and Culture,* op. cit., pp. 29-30.

56 DSA, "Biblical World-View and a Renewed Holistic Spirituality", *op. cit.*, p. 55.

57 Ibid. See this point also in chapter one.

58 Cf. ibid.; DSA, *Approaches,* op. cit., p. 15.

59 Cf. *AG* 9, 11, 15; *NA* 2.

60 DSA, Biblical World-View and a Renewed Holistic Spirituality", *op. cit.*, p. 55.

Gen. 3:5), the reality of sin stultifies the sense of God's presence, hampers the kingdom or salvation process. Then man is responsible for the reality of sin and evil, selfishness and greed, exploitation and oppression, injustice and hatred, conflict and war. However, the will of God is the salvation of all. Time and again, he has been appealing to his partners, humankind, to collaborate with him in the consummation of creation, that is, the realization of his plan of universal salvation. In the past he has done so in many and various ways through the prophets and now through his Son Jesus Christ (cf. Heb. 1:1-3; Matt. 21:33-43).[61]

*2.3.2. One God, one Christ, one saviour*

Amalor writes:

> Though the world is affected by sin and bears its imprint in all realities, the first creation through Christ's work of reconciliation and redemption has become good again.... The same Word has been present in the whole of creation and throughout human history revealing himself in various ways to various peoples. The seeds of the Word are found in all religions and temporal realities.[62]

Amalor is fascinated by the broadness of Paul's cosmic vision: the global understanding of God's plan, creation and redemption in the mystery of the Christ event. He repeatedly refers to Eph. 1:9-10; 2:11-22, and Col. 1:15-20.[63] Christ has revealed and fulfilled the great saving plan of God's love, at work from the beginning but hidden from our eyes. God's hidden plan was to bring everything under Christ as head (cf. Eph. 1:10).[64] It is in this context that Amalor speaks of the incarnation of Christ as the visibilization, intensification and totalization of God's already existing presence and action in the world.[65] When the Word became flesh in Jesus,

---

61 See also the IV Roman Eucharistic Prayer. God reaches out to mankind again and again.

62 DSA, *Gospel and Culture,* op. cit., pp. 29-30.

63 See: Ibid., p. 30, 46; DSA, *Approaches,* op. cit., 19; id., *Purpose,* op. cit., 22; id. (ed.), *Indian Christian Spirituality,* op. cit., pp. 107-108.

64 Jesus Christ is the fulfillment of the OT. Here we do not go into detail in explaining the history of Israel in the theology of redemption.

65 Cf. DSA, *Our Christian World Vision,* op. cit., p. 15; id. (ed.), *Indian Christian*

he entered human history, assuming all that is human and the whole created world in order to redeem and unify it. Christ assumed everything in order to save everything which includes

> not only the salvation of souls, but also of the whole man and all men, not only all men but all that is human, not only cultures but also religions, all that is religious and cultural; in short, everybody and everything in the whole of creation (Rom. 8:18-25). That is why by his death and resurrection Christ became the Lord of the universe, saviour of mankind, supreme norm of human existence and history. All authority is given to him in heaven and on earth (Matt. 28:17). He is constituted judge of the living and the dead (Acts 10:42).[66]

Through his life, death and resurrection, that is, through his paschal mystery, Christ has became the Lord of the universe, the saviour of all mankind -- Christians as well as others, reconciling everything to God. This reconciliation work is a process. The reconciliation in Christ must go on, for Christ has reconciled us and all humanity with the Father and made us ambassadors of this reconciliation (cf. Rom. 8:14-16; Eph. 2:13-18; 2 Cor. 5:18-20).

> This [reconciliation] is to be shown and extended to the point of dying for another.... Each one giving himself to others to make the others exist... is the basis of the resurrection [or salvation] of others.... The resurrection of others and ourselves in this way and this change of order is the dawn of a new creation, the process by which we can build up a truly human community. This is the new humanism, revealed by Jesus Christ, in which we find a new meaning to human existence, a new orientation to history and a new means to fulfill all men's aspirations, and through which this process of reconciliation, liberation and relationship of man is realized.[67]

---

*Spirituality,* op. cit., p. 56.

[66] DSA, *Gospel and Culture,* op. cit., p. 46.

[67] DSA, *Approach,* op. cit., pp. 38-39; see also cited by Gerwin van Leeuwen, in: Id., *Fully Indian - Authentically Christian,* op. cit., pp. 197-198.

### *2.3.3. From resurrection to return: One Spirit, one Church, one plan*

"With the Pasch of Christ, the last period of the History of Salvation has been ushered in and everything tends towards the Last Day of his total presence -- Parousia."[68] The period between the resurrection and the parousia may be called the period of the Holy Spirit, the golden age of the Spirit. It is the Spirit that brings us to the fullness of truth in Christ. Christ now continues to save all and everything in and through the power of his Spirit.

The Church, according to Amalor, as we have already seen, is first of all 'a community of the Spirit, a Spirit-filled community,' that is "in all openness and docility, gathered, united, animated and led by the Spirit, experiencing the Spirit and living under his constant influence."[69] Amalor is not very much concerned about the juridical definition of the Church, though he acknowledges its validity and usefulness.[70] He stresses the presence of the Spirit of Christ in the Church as the nucleus of the Church's existence and mission.[71] "A Christian community is nothing else but a

---

[68] DSA, *Approaches,* op. cit., p. 13; id., *Purpose,* op. cit., p. 12.

[69] DSA (ed.), *Evangelization of the Modern World,* op. cit., p. 44; cf. id., "Biblical World-View and a Renewed Christian Spirituality", *op. cit.,* p. 56.

[70] Cf. Gerwin van Leeuwen, O.F.M., *Fully Indian - Authentically Christian,* op. cit., p. 198.

[71] DSA (ed.), *Evangelization of the Modern World,* op. cit., p. 44. This does not mean, as Gerwin van Leeuwen writes, that Amalor underrates the visibility of the Church nor does he accept two churches -- a visible, and a charismatic one. He stands by the Council's definition of the Church as the universal sacrament of salvation; better still, as 'the sacrament or sign and instrument of the intimate union with God and of the unity of the entire human race' (*LG* 1).

At the Patna Conference (1973) he is more elaborate and states under the heading of 'The Church is a Community': 'All those who meet Jesus in faith through word and sacrament and reconcile themselves to him and to others by total self-surrender and continue to live and die for him according to his Word, modelling their life according to his normative existence -- word become deed or living word -- are bound together into a community of disciples, become his Body and experience Communion.' He continues: 'What basically makes the Church a Church is a paschal experience, a work of the Spirit,' and then he shows his agreement with the Declaration of the Nagpur Conference (1971): 'The Church is the presence of the risen Christ at the heart of the universe, renewing and transforming it from within by the power of the Spirit' (no. 38).

Also in *Our Christian World Vision* (p. 16), he states: 'Christians ... have experienced God through the Spirit of Jesus Christ, in one another and in the world and in the midst of their life.... Now, this community of all those who have experience God in the Spirit

group of people imbued with the Spirit, transformed by him, and led by him. That is why we say 'where the Spirit is, there the Church is.' Likewise there is no Church if there is no Spirit."[72] Yet the Church cannot imprison the Spirit of Christ within herself. The Spirit blows where he wills. The Church is at the humble service of the Spirit. Gerwin van Leeuwen writes:

> When we define the Church in terms of being gathered, united, animated, energized and led by the Spirit, it is high time that we acknowledge that this does not mean that the Church 'owns' or 'possesses' the Spirit, still less that it is able to imprison the Spirit within its own frontiers. It still holds good that the Spirit blows where he wills (Jn. 3:8) and that the very life of the community itself is the first sign of the Spirit's presence in the community.[73]

The Spirit blows beyond the frontiers of the structures of the Church. "The Word [or the Spirit] has become flesh today and the incarnation continues to take place beyond the frontiers of the Church."[74]

As Christ was sent by the Father to accomplish his universal salvific plan in the world, Christ, in turn, sends the community of his Spirit, the Church, in continuation of the realization of the same salvific plan in him and through him till his return in the fullness of glory. "The period between the resurrection and the return of the Lord is the period of the Church and the time for missionary activity. During this period what is primary is not so much the salvation of individuals and the way it is worked out, as the plan of God for the world to be fully realized [in Christ]."[75] The Church always needs to read the 'signs of the times', interpret the plan of God in the historical zigzags and, thus, direct the course of history towards its final goal, God. The Church is sent forth to act as a nucleus and the source of God's salvation in Christ and the diffusion of

---

of Jesus Christ by word and faith, sacraments and service of love in the heart of their experience in the world is called *the Church.*' (See also: *Indian Christian Spirituality,* op. cit., p. 56). For this footnote see: Gerwin van Leeuwen, O.F.M., *Fully Indian - Authentically Christian,* op. cit., pp. 217-218 (reference 31).

72 DSA, *Gospel and Culture,* op. cit., p. 31.

73 Gerwin van Leeuwen, O.F.M., *Fully Indian - Authentically Christian,* op. cit., p. 199.

74 Ibid., p. 198.

75 DSA, *Purpose,* op. cit., p. 12.

his Spirit in the whole of creation and history. It is the hermeneutic task and responsibility of the whole Christian community to interpret history in which it is involved in the light of God's word in order to discover the Christian response in history.

### *2.3.4. A dynamic history tending towards its destiny: Consummation in Christ*

This history is a dynamic history. "This history ... rises higher and higher and thus progresses in spite of ups and downs and zigzags."[76] This sense of history is also found in Hinduism today. Referring to Radhakrishnan and Aurobindo, Amalor writes:

> History in Hinduism ... may be considered, according to classical interpretation, as a cyclic movement; consequently time may be considered as deprived of any creative activity and as having no goal, possessing no ultimate significance and leading to no consummation. But today this notion is questioned as over simplification and unqualified. Hindu philosophers and religious leaders do claim a sense of history in Hinduism, e.g., Radhakrishnan and Aurobindo.[77]

The modern and wider interpretation of history in Hinduism which proposes a purposeful history and holds an optimistic attitude towards the world comes much closer to the Christian concept of history. At the same time it corresponds to the material and spiritual needs and exigencies of the people. This is what is called the special concept of history. Gerwin van Leeuwen writes:

> When we listen to DSA or read his writings, it strikes us that he puts almost every issue or problem in the perspective of salvation history, asking himself and his listeners or readers: what does the Lord tell us at this moment (kairos) of history through this or that situation? I feel that this is the main reason why he considers it providential to finish his book [*L'Inde à la rencontre du Seigneur,* 1964] on

---

[76] DSA, "Biblical World-View and a Renewed Holistic Spirituality", *op. cit.*, p. 55.

[77] See: S. Radhakrishnan, *Eastern Religions and Western Thought,* Oxford, 1940, p. 128, and Aurobindo, *The Human Cycle,* as cited by DSA in: Id., *Approaches,* op. cit., p. 18.

> Epiphany, because the liturgical celebration of the first Manifestation of the Magi, representing all humankind, invites us to look forward to the last and final Manifestation at the glorious return of the Lord. That will be the fulfillment of the hidden plan made in Christ from the beginning: 'to unite all things in him, things in heaven and things on earth' at the fullness of time (cf. Eph. 1:10).[78]

It is very important to see the world religions within the *one* saving plan of God, in the unity of the *one* history of salvation centered in Christ. The whole of humankind is embraced by the one salvific plan of God which includes all the world religions which, in turn, look for God's grace for their consummation. Christ is the fullness of God's grace and truth (cf. Jn. 1:14). There is one God, one origin, one creation, one history and one and the same destiny. This history is perennially on the movement or process till it reaches its total transformation, the Omega point in Christ. Here Amalor expresses his agreement with the conclusions of the Bombay Theological Seminar. He writes:

> To understand well the meaning of world religions, they have to be considered from a theocentric point of view: the whole of mankind is embraced by the one salvific plan of God which includes all the world religions.... Christian faith represents radical universalism. Every human being and every world religion is under God's grace.[79]

### *2.4. Universal Salvation and Cosmic Concern*

In chapter one we have seen that the reality is comprised of four basic elements: God, Man, the Church, and the World. Dialogue, interaction and collaboration among these basic elements of the reality contribute to the fulfillment of history: the fullness of life for all mankind in God (cf. 1 Cor. 15:24-28).

The fullness of God's grace and truth is found in Jesus Christ (cf. Jn. 1:14). Humankind has veritably encountered the fullness of God's grace and truth in the Jesus Christ event, and the whole earth has simply become

---

[78] Gerwin van Leeuwen, O.F.M., *Fully Indian - Authentically Christian,* op. cit., p. 193.

[79] See as quoted by DSA in: Id., *Purpose,* op. cit., p. 27 from *The Clergy Monthly Supplement,* June 1965, pp. 238-239. See also: Gerwin van Leeuwen, O.F.M., *Fully Indian - Authentically Christian,* op. cit., p. 216 (reference 6).

a place of salvation.[80] Salvation is available to all -- Christians as well as others -- who respond to God's grace. God desires the salvation of all humankind. This is in short the global vision (*vue d'ensemble*) of Amalor and his cosmic concern. It is the global vision of the unification of the world and religions with God in and through the saving mystery of Jesus Christ. In other words, salvation is the process of Christification of the entire creation. In this perspective, quoting Teilhard de Chardin's intuition on Christian unity of man, of humanity and of the universe, Amalor writes, "The essence of Christianity is nothing more or less than the belief in the unification of the world, through the Incarnation. The whole history of the world is, in my eyes, one vast phenomenon of Christification."[81]

This integral vision of salvation is re-affirmed in Vatican II. Vatican II repeatedly rejects a dualistic or dichotomic view of salvation, both at the level of the individual human person,[82] that is, not only his or her soul but the whole human person: body and soul, and at the level of human society, the whole humankind, that is, all men and women of all religions and religions themselves are to be saved. Quoting Vatican II in *The Theology of Development* (1979),[83] Amalor writes: "We are interested here not only in integral man but in every man and Vatican II affirms it: 'When we say man, we mean every man whatsoever, and every group of men, of whatever race and from whatever part of the world'" (*GS* 64). "It has not pleased God to call men to share His life merely as individuals without any mutual bonds. Rather, He wills to mould them into a people in which His sons, once scattered abroad, can be gathered together" (*AG* 2).

Such a vision, before theologizing about other religions, first recognizes the reality of other religions. The number of men and women continues to increase and "these [men and women] are formed into large

---

80 Cf. DSA, *Approaches*, op. cit., p. 15.

81 See as quoted in: Ibid.

82 The preface of *GS* puts it with great emphasis: "The human person deserves to be preserved ... the pivotal point of our presentation will be man himself, whole and entire, body and soul, heart and conscience, mind and will." See: Gerwin van Leeuwen, O.F.M., *Fully Indian - Authentically Christian*, op. cit., p. 216 (reference 13). In *Theology of Development* (1979, p. 11), Amalor quotes *AG* 3: "The object of God's creative and redemptive love, the one for whom Christ died and rose again, the one to whom the Paschal message is to be proclaimed is the whole man, not some disembodied 'soul'."

83 See as quoted in: DSA, *Theology of Development*, op. cit., p. 11. See also: Gerwin van Leeuwen, O.F.M., *Fully Indian - Authentically Christian*, op. cit., p. 216 (reference 14).

and distinct groups by permanent cultural ties, by ancient religious traditions, and by firm bonds of social necessity" (*AG* 10). In order to be able to offer all of them the life and salvation brought by God in Christ, the Church must become part of all of these groups for the same motive which led Christ to bind himself, in virtue of his incarnation, to the definite social and cultural conditions of those human beings among whom he dwelt (cf. *AG* 10).

The vision of Vatican II places the mission of the Church in a cosmo-historical context. It calls for a cosmic concern for the future of mankind, nay for the whole of creation. It stresses that the future of the Church is inseparably linked with the destiny of humankind.

In considering the above salvific global vision, we arrive at these following two points: salvation on two counts and one human race or human solidarity.

### *2.4.1. Salvation on two counts*
### *Individual and communitarian, Christians and others*

According to this global vision salvation must be achieved, above all, in the order of the whole --universal -- without, of course, forgetting salvation in the order of the individual. If the universal concern for transforming and saving the whole is absent, the Church will only look after the salvation of the individuals, centered on the sole security of a private, selfish possession of salvation, reducing her apostolate to a numerical addition of individuals. Such a concern will also lead the Church to discouragement, considering the small number of Christians vis-à-vis a vast number of non-Christians in the world today. More still, according to the present trend, there is every possibility that Christians will become ever more a minority as a result of the current demographic explosion amidst the people of other religions.

The communitarian salvation in Christ does not in any way imply collectivism or depersonalization. The Church must always be aware of the dangers of religious individualism and spiritual selfishness that is so contrary to the spirit of Christ, and thus harmful to the Church's apostolate. The care for individual salvation must be situated at the very heart of salvation for all. "All peoples compose a single community and have a single origin. One also is their final goal" (*NA* 1).[84]

*2.4.2. One human family, human solidarity*

Further, writing about the universal salvific concern of the Church, Amalor refers to H. de Lubac, *Catholicisme* (Paris, 1952, pp. 184, 200):

> The human race is one ... and we are members of the same body. How then, could there be salvation for the members if by an impossibility the body was not saved?... In such a doctrinal context it looks as if the Christian watchword can no longer be 'evasion' but 'collaboration'. It is on condition of tending towards it with everyone instead of pursuing one's own selfish game that we can hope to share in the final triumph, to have our place in the common redemption: *in redemptione communi.* The City of the Elect does not welcome profiteers.[85]

*Gaudium et Spes* states: "United in Christ and guided by the Holy Spirit, [Christians] press towards the kingdom of the Father and are bearers of the message of salvation intended for all men. That is why Christians cherish a feeling of deep solidarity with the human race and its history" (no. 1). The Church does not exist for herself, but for others; she is an instrument for the redemption of all and her "missionary activity is nothing else and nothing less than a manifestation or epiphany of God's will, and the fulfillment of that will in the world and in world history"(*AG* 9).

## 3. The Issue of Salvation Outside the Church: A Bird's Eye View

If God has chosen the Church as the universal sacrament of salvation, that is, to dispense the universal saving grace wrought through Christ to all human beings, then the question is: How can she reach this salvation in Christ to followers of other religious traditions?

---

[84] DSA, *Approaches,* op. cit., p. 16.

[85] See quoted in: Ibid., pp. 16-17.

There are three main theological positions or the "change of paradigms" in answer to this question: ecclesiocentrism, Christocentrism, and theocentrism or regnocentrism,[86] and in parallel with these, the three basic positions respectively designated are: exclusivism, inclusivism, and pluralism. While the first position has been generally abandoned, the position between the second and the third are hotly discussed. The theocentric approach seems to be gaining momentum, but it raises a host of theological problems concerning the role of Christ in the history of salvation and his personal role in the salvation of humankind. We can briefly see the burning issue of salvation outside the Church in three periods: pre-Vatican II, Vatican II, and post-Vatican II.[87]

### *3.1. Pre-Vatican II: Predominantly Ecclesiocentric*[88]

Since the Patristic age the issue of the salvific value of other religions was dominated and discussed between these two fundamental theological positions:

(i) God's universal love and desire to save all human beings. This view is well expressed by the Council of Arles (473): "God does not want anyone to perish, Christ died for all."

---

[86] Cf. John Fuellenbach, *The Kingdom of God,* op. cit., p. 149; Jacques Dupuis, *Jesus Christ at the Encounter of World Religions,* op. cit., pp. 104-110. Some would, e.g., J. Peter Schineller, "Christ and Church: A Spectrum of Views", in: *Theological Studies* 37 (1976), pp. 545-566, reprinted in: Walter J. Burghardt and William G. Thompson (eds), *Why the Church?,* Paulist Press, New York, 1977, pp. 1-22, put the issue of salvation outside the Church in four major categories: ecclesiocentric universe (exclusive christology), Christocentric universe (inclusive christology), theocentric universe (normative christology), and theocentric universe (nonnormative christology). Others like to discuss the issue in the 'salvation model' perspective, e.g, Paul Knitter, *No Other Name? (A Critical Survey of Christian Attitudes Towards the World Religions),* Orbis Books, Maryknoll, New York, 1974, while many recent authors put the issue in three main perspectives: ecclesiocentric (exclusivism), Christocentric (inclusivism), and theocentric (pluralism). See J. Dupuis in ibid.; M. Dhavamony, *Christian Theology of Religions. (A Systematic Reflection on the Christian Understanding of World Religions),* Peter Lang, Berne, 1998, pp. 43-61.

[87] Cf. John Fuellenbach, *The Kingdom of God,* op. cit., pp. 149-154.

[88] For this see also the pre-Vatican II world vision by DSA, which we have already dealt in chapter one: DSA, "Traditional Spirituality within Our Present Christian World Vision", *op. cit.,* pp. 47-52.

(ii) The necessity of the Church for the salvation of all. This view finds its traditional expression in the axiom: "Outside the Church, there is no salvation", which was originally intended and applied to the heretics and schismatics (Copts) by Fulgentius of Ruspe (457-533), and Cyprian of Carthage (d. 258) and was later, for the first time in the official document, through misinterpretation, applied to non-Christians or "pagans" by the Council of Florence (1442).[89] It stated:

> [The Holy Roman Church] ... firmly believes, professes and preaches that 'no one remaining outside the Catholic Church, not only pagans,' but also Jews, heretics and schismatics, can become partakers of eternal life; but they will go to the 'eternal fire prepared for the devil and his angels [Matt. 25:41],' unless before the end they are joined [*aggregati*] to it.... 'And no one can be saved, no matter how much alms one has given, even if shading one's blood for the name of Christ, unless one remains in the bosom and unity of the Catholic Church.'[90]

It has never been easy to strike a balance between the above two positions in the Church. In the first three centuries the Fathers were more open to the issue. We find the expressions like 'the seminal Word' (*Logos spermaticos*) of which all humankind partake (Justin, Origen), and the 'natural Christian Soul' (Tertullian). Even Augustine held that true religion existed from the very beginning of humankind and that the saving grace of this religion had never been refused to anyone who was worthy of it.[91] However, when Christianity became the official state religion under Theodosius (emperor, 379-395), and later when it was threatened by the Islamic invasion, 'the necessity of the Church for salvation' was once again stressed. Added to it, the Creed of the Fourth Lateran Council (1215) and the Bull *Unam Sanctam* (1302) of Boniface VIII clarified the position of the Church and stressed the supremacy of the papacy. The

---

[89] Cf. ND, pp. 284-285, 381; cf. also: Fulgentius of Ruspe, *De fide liber ad Petrum*, 38:79 & 39:80 - *PL* 65:704AB; Cyprian of Carthage (d. 258), *Epist. (73) ad Iubaianum*, chap. 21 (*PL* 3:1123AB), where "Salus extra Ecclesiam non est" is applied to the heretics. (See: J. Dupuis, *Jesus Christ at the Encounter of World Religions*, op. cit., p. 97; J. Fuellenbach, *The Kingdom of God*, op. cit., pp. 149-150).

[90] See: ND 1005 (DS 1351).

[91] Cf. Paul Knitter, *No Other Name?*, op. cit., pp. 120-144.

temporal order was put under the spiritual order, the Church, and submission to the Roman Pontiff was seen necessary for salvation.

After the discoveries of the "new worlds", the Church suddenly realized that there were millions of people who had never heard of the name of Jesus. The question was: Are these people automatically designated for hell, though no fault of their own? The Church had to take a different position. The Council of Trent, facing up to the new situation, proposed the famous distinction of baptism in *re* and baptism in *voto.* At least the "implicit desire" for baptism sufficed for salvation for the one outside the Church.[92]

What really had happened over the centuries was a development from an *exclusive* to an *inclusive* understanding of the Church as the sole channel of grace. But the problem remained. No one dared say that this grace could reach the person through the practice of his or her own religion. Other religions were still regarded not as carriers of grace but as instruments of the devil. The vexing question, therefore, was this: How does grace reach the followers of other religious traditions? It seemed that such people could be saved, but only by renouncing their own religions and making a decision for God, or rather Christianity, through a grace that came like an inspiration from nowhere.

### *3.2. Vatican II: God's Universal Plan, Universal Providence*

Vatican II, in the *Declaration of the Relationship of the Church to Non-Christian Religions (NA),* was the official turning point. The Council's position can be summarized in the following points:

(i) The Council strongly stressed the universality of grace available everywhere in the history of humankind. God's universal salvific will was placed in the forefront, as opposed to the prior emphasis on the necessity of the Church. It emphasized God's universal salvific plan and his universal providence in other religions (cf. DNC 12).

(ii) Although Vatican II did not state explicitly that other religions are *ways* of salvation, it acknowledged the *possibility* of salvation in other religions.[93] It taught that "authentic religious experiences" take place *in*

---

92 See: ND 855.

93 Cf. DSA, *Inter-Religious Dialogue in India,* NBCLC, Bangalore, [1977], p. 7; cf.

and *through* these religions. However, the fullness of the means of salvation is found in the Church. The Council maintained the other axiom: "The Church is necessary for salvation." It stated:

> The Church, a pilgrim now on earth is necessary for salvation ... which men enter through baptism as through a door. Hence they could not be saved who, knowing that the Catholic Church was founded as necessary by God through Christ, would refuse either to enter it, or to remain in it (*LG* 14).

With the possibility of salvation in other religions, most Catholic theologians take it for granted that grace does reach the hearts of men and women through the visible, experiential signs of various religions. In the 1960s Karl Rahner laid the foundation for this Catholic position. He started with the axiom that God wills the salvation of all. In his thesis of "anonymous Christians" he argues that God's grace through the gift of his self-communication reaches to all human beings. Every human being, every believer of other religions, is a recipient of God's grace which makes him or her capable of knowing and loving God .[94] Since salvation is not possible without grace, grace must be offered to all human beings in an effective way. Rahner explores first the "existential openness" to the supernatural with his theory of the "supernatural existential", that is, human beings are, by nature, open to the "supernatural horizon". Secondly, we are by nature socio-historical beings. If grace is to be universally available, it needs to be grounded in socio-historical reality. It must become body, flesh, event and symbol. This happens in history, in the various religious traditions which visibly contain the grace that leads to salvation. Hence the conclusion: God's saving grace reaches the person not from outside of his or her religion but from within it.[95]

(iii) The kingdom of God is bigger than the Church. The Church has no monopoly of the kingdom of God. She is the "universal sacrament" of salvation, the servant of the kingdom. Other religious traditions are

---

also: *GS* 22; *LG* 16.

[94] See: Karl Rahner, "Anonymous Christians", in: *Theological Investigation*, vol. 6, Darton, Longman and Todd, London, 1969, pp. 390-398; also id: "Anonymous Christianity and the Missionary Task of the Church", in: Ibid., vol. 12, 1974, pp. 161-174.

[95] See: John Fuellenbach, *The Kingdom of God*, op. cit., p. 151.

acknowledged as bearers of God's saving grace, which in effect means that one does not have to be a member of the Church in order to be saved. The saving grace in other religions is seen within the context of God's larger plan for the whole world, whole of creation, the plan expressed in the Bible with the symbol, 'the kingdom of God'. The position of ecclesiocentrism is replaced by the kingdom of God to which all the religious traditions are called in their common journey to realize it in common endeavour, mutual collaboration, dialogue and service.[96]

### *3.3. Post-Vatican II: Christ and the Economy of the Spirit*

The former ecclesiocentrism or exclusivism has been overcome in the Catholic Church. Today the question is no longer whether the Church is constitutive for salvation, but the issue is:

(i) How constitutive is Christ for the salvation of all, of Christians and of the followers of other religious traditions? The saving mystery of Christ is present and active in other religions. This is the saving mystery of God's universal plan through Christ in the Spirit.

(ii) Is it possible to perceive the kingdom of God as detached from the historical person of Jesus of Nazareth? Most New Testament scholars would say no. One cannot separate the kingdom of God preached by Jesus from the person of Jesus; there is an identification between the message and the messenger (cf. *RM* 18).

(iii) The 'economy of the Spirit' in the kingdom of God is being much emphasized.[97] God's universal saving grace is present and operative in the whole of creation in and through the mystery of his Son Jesus Christ. Christ permeates everything in and through his Spirit (inclusive Christology). The Church is the servant of the Spirit. After the resurrection Christ continues his saving work in and through the Church. The Church, as the "universal sacrament of salvation", continues the kingdom work of Christ, orienting and re-orienting everything, the world, religions

---

[96] Cf. DSA, *Approaches*, op. cit., pp. 28-29.

[97] Cf. DSA, "Approach", *op. cit.*, pp. 81-83; Jacques Dupuis, "The Kingdom of God and the World Religions", in: *Vidyajyoti* 51(1987) 11, p. 530-544; J. Dupuis, *Jesus Christ at the Encounter of World Religions*, op. cit., pp. 152-177; M. Dhavamony, *Christian Theology of Religions*, op. cit., pp. 213-215; DNC 21 and 40.

and the whole of creation to God through Christ, that is, theocentrism in and through Christocentrism.

We can well succinctly see the position of Amalor on the issue. In agreement with the Nagpur Declaration, he writes:

> The Nagpur Declaration rightly recognizes in other religions Christ's active presence and says that the mystery of Christ in them is a reality (DNC 12). We see at work in them Christ and his grace. An ineffable mystery ... which is called by different names, but which no name can adequately represent, is definitively disclosed and communicated in Jesus of Nazareth. As there is a universal providence leading all men to their ultimate destiny and since salvation cannot be reached by man's effort alone, but requires divine intervention, the self communication of God is not confined to the Judeo-Christian tradition, but extends to the whole of mankind in different ways and degrees within the one divine economy (DNC 13-14).[98]

Everything considered we can say that God wants the salvation of all human beings. God's saving grace will permeate all and radiate effectively to all, in their respective religious traditions or otherwise. His grace will reach all human beings no matter what their faith or confession. But all saving grace is linked to Christ and his Spirit, regardless of how difficult it may be to explain it theologically.

In the next point we attempt to understand and explain the universal saving mystery of God as fully realized in and through the mystery of Jesus Christ and now being continued through the Church.

### 4. All Salvation by God in and through the Mystery of Christ

It is God who saves all and everything in the saving mystery of his Son Jesus Christ whom Vatican II calls the Model, Mentor, Liberator, Saviour and Source of all life (*AG* 7; *GS* 10).

> He [Christ] who is the 'image of the invisible God' (Col. 1:15), is himself the perfect man who has restored in the children of Adam that likeness to God which had been disfigured ever since the first sin....

---

[98] See: DSA, "Approach", *op. cit.*, p. 50.

This holds true not for Christians only but for all men of good will in whose hearts grace is active invisibly. For since Christ died for all, and since all men are in fact called to one and the same destiny, which is divine, we must hold that the Holy Spirit offers to all the possibility of being made partners, in a way known to God, in the paschal mystery (*GS* 22; cf. *LG* 16; Rom. 8:32).

### *4.1. A Mystery of Faith*

How does Christ save people in their own religion? We have seen in his basic suppositions that Amalor admits that the issue of the universality of Christ and his salvation in other religions is, first of all, a mystery of faith and any explanation of it is only a groping attempt.[99] The incarnational economy of salvation is very important for Amalor. All human persons, Christians, believers of other religions as well as so-called 'unbelievers' are saved by God who invites them to make a so-called 'fundamental option'.[100] Man always needs the *grace* of God. Now, the incarnation of Christ, the mystery of the Word, is the culmination and visibilization of God's saving grace. It is the mystery of God's supreme, total, definitive and yet on-going salvific self-revelation in and for the world.[101] "The grace of God becomes intensively visible -- and only in visibility it can really touch us; that is why God works with an incarnational economy -- in Jesus of Nazareth who after his passion, death and resurrection has been established Lord of all people and creation."[102]

In and through the paschal mystery Christ, in his person, has become the primordial sacrament of God and his salvation, and now anyone, whether Christian or follower of other religion, is saved by his or her participation in this paschal mystery of Christ. In other words, salvation reaches to human persons through signs and sacraments which signify the various historical salvific interventions of God, culminating in the paschal mystery of Christ, and they re-act mystically the same realities for salvation for men today who believe in them.

---

[99] Cf. DSA, *Approaches,* op. cit., p. 11.

[100] Cf. ibid., p. 38ff.

[101] Cf. DSA, *The Theology of 'Indirect Evangelization',* op. cit., pp. 9-10; id., *Theology of Catechesis,* op. cit., p. 27. This point has been elaborately dealt in chapter one.

[102] Gerwin van Leeuwen, O.F.M., *Fully Indian - Authentically Christian,* op. cit., p. 262.

### *4.2. The Sacramental Economy of Salvation: The Church, the Universal Sacrament of Salvation*

The uniqueness of Jesus Christ is also found in his sacramental presence, especially in the Eucharist. The establishment of the Eucharist, that is, his presence in it and his encounter in and through the sacraments make him something unique and universal. Christ is *really* and universally present and operative in and through the sacraments. This is the sacramental economy of salvation in Christianity, instituted by Christ himself, which we do not find in the "sacramentality" (*saṁskāras*) of other religions, at least, in the actuality and extent as it is believed and found in the Christian sacramental economy of salvation.

Jesus is the same yesterday, today and forever. In the sacramental economy of salvation he transcends the temporo-spatial coordinates. If Jesus were actually *only* what the temporo-spatial coordinates yield, no Christian could speak of the real presence of Christ in the sacraments, nor accept that whatever one does to the least of one's brothers and sisters one does unto Christ (cf. Matt. 25:40); neither will one accept that Christ is "the same yesterday and today and forever" (Heb. 13:8) and much less admit that Christ was before Abraham (cf. Jn. 8:58), not to say anything of the cosmic Christ of the Epistle of Paul (cf. Eph. 2:11-22; 4:4-6; Col. 1:15-20; 2:9; etc.) and of many of the sayings of John (esp. Jn. 1:14-18). If Christ were only that, that is, a mere external event bound to the temporo-spatial order, who existed only at a certain time in history and had a certain place in geography, then the whole of the Christian faith would collapse. No Christian will say that the living Christ of his faith is only a man of the past and no Christian will affirm either that when he or she receives Christ in the Eucharist, for instance, he or she is eating the proteins of Jesus of Nazareth who was walking in Palestine some twenty centuries ago.

The whole Christian sacramental economy of salvation is seen in the salvific providence of God. It flows from his universal salvific will. God's universal salvific will is "sacramentalized" at the fullness of time in the Jesus Christ event, and now continues to be so in and through the sacramentality of the Church on earth. Since God is an ineffable mystery man encounters God in and through signs and sacraments. "God acts normally through the physical and historical order. That is to say, he makes use of means which are natural, normal and ordinary."[103] The importance of the incarnation of Christ is established here. Gerwin van Leeuwen writes: "The incarnation has taught us the integration of the divine and the human. Even God will not and cannot reach out to us except through the medium of his creation, the human, the visible, because only visible signs, sacraments of the visible, existentially touch human persons."[104] In and through the mystery of the Jesus Christ event, Jesus has become the *sacrament* of God for all humankind, humanly speaking the best encounter between God and man. This is the salvation or union (*yoga*) of humankind with God in Christ Jesus.

The sacramental economy of salvation becomes corroborated and more clear in the Christian revelation. The Christian message is essentially one of supernatural salvation which is a sacramental encounter with God in the person and event of Christ Jesus, which God himself has planned it to be so (cf. Heb. 1: 1-3). Christ Jesus is the sacrament of God for the world, because "through him God was pleased to reconcile to himself all things, whether on earth or in heaven, by making peace through the blood of his cross" (Col. 1:20).

Just as Christ Jesus in his visible humanity was the sacrament of God on earth so also the Church as a visible society and as the mystical body of Christ is the sacrament of Christ on earth today. She is the universal sacrament of the universal salvation in Christ. Jesus, in his earthly life and ministry, was the visible and effective, definitive and supreme sign of the mercy of God, the visible image of the invisible God. After his resurrection Christ in his Spirit continues his saving work visibly through the sacramentality of the Church. Today the Church is the visible "image" of the invisible Christ. Between the resurrection and the parousia, the Church continues the saving mystery of Christ, led by his Spirit.[105]

### *4.3. Sacraments: Participating in the Person and Action of Christ Jesus*

Amalor asks these questions: If the ordinary means of grace and salvation in the Church are the sacraments, what are the means provided by God for the salvation of other believers in their religions? We have

---

[103] DSA, *Approaches*, op. cit., p. 39.

[104] Gerwin van Leeuwen, O.F.M., *Fully Indian - Authentically Christian*, op. cit., p. 203.

[105] Cf. DSA, *Approaches*, op. cit., p. 13.

referred above to the way in which the grace of God could reach the people of other religions in the very framework of their religions, then what have we to say about the signs and the means of salvation in these religions? What is the value and efficacy of the signs in the religions of the world? Are the rites and rituals, *saṁskāras,* ethical regulations, doctrinal teachings of other religions, for example Hinduism, salvific?[106] What is our answer? In a word, Amalor would answer: "This efficacy [the efficacy of the sacraments or *saṁskāras* in Christianity or other religions] comes not simply from the signs but from the action of Christ."[107] The efficacy, therefore, of the signs and sacraments of religions, including Christianity, comes from the words and actions of Christ, from the person behind the action; or with regard to other religions, their openness and conformity with the person and Spirit of Christ who is the source and the fullness of all grace and truth (cf. Jn. 1:14-16). Amalor makes a small comparison between the signs and means of salvation in Christianity and those supposed to be in other religions. He writes:

> How does the grace of Christ reach us in the Church and save us? It is by words and signs, by the Gospel and the Eucharist, by the preaching of the word of salvation and by the celebration of the signs of salvation (the Sacraments, especially the Eucharist) (*AG* 5, 9) which are diverse aspects of the one basic and primordial sacrament which is the Church and ultimately Christ.[108]

We are saved, in short by our participation in the Paschal Mystery which is proclaimed by the word and re-presented by the sacraments, chief of which is the Eucharist. These signs of Christianity are instituted by *God himself,* endowed with significance and efficacy, and operated by the presence of Christ himself. Sacraments are thus the actions of Christ. They signify the various historical events of salvation which are all God's interventions in human history to save humanity, culminating in the Paschal event of Christ. They re-act mystically, symbolically and substantially the same realities for the salvation of men today who believe in them. In virtue of the divine institution and the presence of Christ recalled

---

106 Cf. ibid., pp. 38-39.
107 Ibid., p. 39.
108 Ibid., p. 38.

by the words on the one hand and the disposition of the recipients on the other, salvation is communicated to them through the signs. This efficacy comes not simply from the signs but from the action of Christ.

Now, if the ordinary means of grace and salvation in the Church are the sacraments, what are the means provided by God for the salvation of non-Christians in their religions?

First of all we must admit that though grace or salvation is a free gift of God, God acts normally through the historical order. That is to say, as we have seen above, he makes use of means which are natural, normal and ordinary. Secondly, even in Christianity, signs are not efficacious by themselves; they become so due to the person behind it perceived through faith, who gives them meaning and efficacy; this function is fulfilled by the word that is proclaimed when the sign is performed. In other religions, religious signs are *natural signs,* in the sense that these rites and *saṁskāras* are "created" by men and signify activities of man; for example, the *saṁskāras* of the process of reproduction, manifestation of natural phenomena and movement of the cycles of nature (seasons) in which even the gods are caught, so to say. Rites in general are closed on themselves and are magical; they are not salvific in themselves. They will be salvific only if they become *prophetic,* if they refer to a *person* beyond them, if they open themselves to transcendence and are disposed for the intervention of God.[109] They should be signs of a good, free and transcendent Being, a Person, who takes the initiative of coming to man to save him. But these religions lack even the notion of creation and person, creation understood as the first intervention of God in history.[110]

If we consider other religions, for example, Hinduism, as religious systems and structures, their elements are ritualistic, closed on themselves and immanent. This holds good for mysticism[111] as well. However when we observe the practices of Hinduism as lived in concrete men and women in their concrete situations, they appear to be prophetic, open, leading the devotees to communion with a Person, God. In this respect, says Amalor, "they may [or can[112]] be salvific."[113] Here Amalor is rather cautious about

---

[109] Cf. ibid., p. 39.

[110] Cf. ibid.

[111] Here DSA refers to his book: *Destinée,* op. cit.: 'La mystique naturelle à la lumière de la théologié catholique', pp. 315-324, see cited in: Id., *Approaches,* op. cit., p. 39.

[112] See: DSA, "The Apostolate to Non-Christians", in: *Foundations of Mission*

affirming the value of the rites and practices of other religions.[114] What he says in other words is that God *de facto* uses non-Christian rites as ways of grace but *de jure* only the Christian sacraments are the means of grace and salvation. We see here emerging a positive evaluation of the rites of other religions. The rites and sacraments of other religions are seen as God's providential ways of salvation. This positive evaluation of the rites of other religions received the collective approval of the theologians gathered for the Theological Conference at Nagpur (1971).[115] We see it in the declaration of the Conference which states that "the different sacred scriptures and rites of the religious traditions of the world can be in various degrees, expressions of a divine manifestation and can be conducive to salvation."[116]

Though other religions may lack a historical person behind their signs and *saṁskāras,* their actual practice by concrete men and women has always been a worship of a personal God. Let us take the example of Hinduism. Though the *advaita* philosophy with its non-dualistic, 'non-personal' and 'mystical' character -- which sees the ultimate reality as one, infinite, eternal Being, which is immanent in the nature and to the soul of every person and which is experienced in the depths of one's being -- has been inspiring and dominating the religious tradition, there has also been the *bhakti mārga* with its devotion to the personal God like the cult of Śiva, or the worship of Viṣṇu and his *avatāras,* like Rāma and Kṛṣṇa. Whatever may be our critical assessment of some of the Hindu ritualistic structures and systems, millions of devotees have entered through them into communion with the liberating God, whatever be his name.[117]

> There has always been a worship of a personal God in Hinduism and perhaps less in Buddhism and Confucianism...., there has been also

---

*Theology,* op. cit., p. 82 where DSA writes: 'they *can* be'. See this also cited by Jose Kuttianimattathil, S.D.B. in: Id., *Practice and Theology of Interreligious Dialogue,* op. cit., p. 403.

113 DSA, *Approaches,* op. cit., p. 40; cf. also: id., *Destinée,* op. cit.: 'La religion [l'hindouism]: une initiative de l'homme', pp. 100ff.

114 Cf. Jose Kuttianimattathil, S.D.B., *Practice and Theology of Interreligious Dialogue,* op. cit., p. 403.

115 Cf. ibid.

116 Declaration no. 16, see in: DSA, *Theology of Evangelization,* op. cit., p. 33.

117 Cf. DSA, *Approaches,* op. cit., p. 40.

> a bhakti current -- which developed into a remarkable movement all over India according to which the reality is a personal God with a real relationship with the world and the soul. *Bhaktimarga* is the way of loving devotion to the personal God like the cult of Siva, Vishnu and his avatars, Rama, Krishna, etc.... This personal God is love itself, shows mercy to his devotees and bestows grace on them; the devotees pour out their soul in devotion and total surrender. Though at the philosophical level the *advaita* system dominates, at the popular level it is *bhakti* that is the current form of religion for most Hindus. When we go to temples or centres of pilgrimage and observe the *puja* (worship) performed, their expressions of *bhakti* (piety), the ecstatic experience of devotees in the presence of their God, the moving cry for mercy and forgiveness and the genuine acts of adoration, love and surrender, we wonder how we can brand them as superstitious, magical acts or simple natural rites.[118]

Amalor then points out that also some Christians perform their devotions, for example, novenas and litanies, and even receive the sacraments, for example, confession, with little reference to the person of Christ and in a total or partial lack of faith, expecting thereby some magical or mechanical effects. Though at times even in the Church there seems to be an ambiguity, a mixture of paganism and faith, Amalor holds that there is a basic difference between the signs of salvation in the Church and those in other religions, like Hinduism. He writes:

> In Christianity the signs are in themselves (*per se*) salvific, because they are essentially prophetic and dynamic; but here and there they may become merely ritualistic and magical. Whereas in Hinduism, they are not salvific in themselves, due to its lack of inherent prophetism, dynamism and openness to transcendence; but existentially, in some concrete persons and cases they may become prophetic, open out to a personal God and respond to his interventions and invitations. So the source of the trouble is in the system itself and the system as such cannot be baptized.[119]

---

[118] Ibid.

[119] Ibid., pp. 40-41.

What we observe here is that for Amalor the celebration of signs and sacraments is not a 'sacramentalism' or ritualism. That is to say, a mere performance of the sacraments and *saṁskāras* does not bring salvation but a sincere faith in and the following of the person behind the sacraments; and this *person* behind the sacraments is Jesus Christ, the historical reality of the God-man on earth. The mythical figuration or deification of such a personality in other religions is oriented towards and fulfilled in the Jesus Christ event. Salvation is indeed in the doing of God's will (cf. Matt. 7:21) and, in turn, the celebration of sacraments, especially the Eucharist, is the celebration of one's life in God, the celebration of the universal salvation wrought by Christ Jesus.

It is because of God's action, that is, God in the historical person of Christ Jesus who himself institutes and effects the sacraments of the Church, there lies a difference between the sacraments of the Church and the rites and signs of salvation in other religions which basically lack a historical divine person, the God-man, behind them. The sacraments in the Church are in themselves (*per se*) salvific, because they are essentially prophetic and dynamic, but here and there they may become merely ritualistic and magical and may not bring salvation in some cases; whereas the "sacraments" in Hinduism do no have salvific power in themselves, essentially, but in some concrete persons and cases, existentially, they may become prophetic, open to a person, and salvific for their believers. Some would object to this assessment as insufficient and hold that in some literature of "systematic" Hinduism and formulated traditions some of its elements are said to be prophetic and salvific. But what is more true, says Amalor, is that often enough there is no magisterium or competent authority in these traditions to distinguish what is authentic and what is false, what is prophetic and what is ritualistic. Above all, the intervention of God cannot be verified historically in other religions as it can be done in Christianity.[120]

Amalor always holds and stresses that the elements of Hinduism or of any other "non-Christian" religions, unlike the sacraments of Christianity, cannot be in themselves *means* of salvation. All the same, we may suppose that in certain cases there could be an intervention of God and the openness of the religious man and there could be, as Vatican II holds, the possibility of salvation in other religions (cf. *GS* 22). In such a case, the

[120] Cf. ibid., p. 41.

religious man basically, not explicitly perhaps, opens himself to the intervention of God in the saving mystery of the person and the Spirit of Jesus Christ. Man should open himself to the free intervention of God in Christ and should not make *saṁskāras* magical rites, thereby trying to manipulate even God. It is here, Amalor once again quotes R. Panikkar: "It is through the sacraments of Hinduism, through the message of morality, good life, through the *Mysterion* that comes down to him through Hinduism that *Christ* saves the Hindu normally."[121]

Amalor states that a person -- believer or so called non-believer -- is ultimately saved because of the fact of what the traditional theology calls 'the fundamental option', and the mystery of God's providence. The grace or salvation of God reaches everyone by the fundamental option that one is supposed to make in one's existential framework, whether one is Christian, Hindu, Muslim, or one who adheres to a particular secular or atheistic ideology. One may either shut oneself in selfish love, refuse existence and thereby refuse the 'others' -- God, fellow human beings and creation -- or open oneself out in selfless love, in the acceptance of existence and thereby in the acceptance of the 'others'. This total and unreserved openness to everything, the act of otherness, is actually a 'yes' to God's invitations and interventions in life and history. One is saved through this authentic 'yes' in the spirit of love and service to God and one's fellow beings.[122]

In his orientation speech at Patna Amalor briefly returns to this question of salvation in other religions, frequently referring to what was discussed earlier at the Nagpur Conference:

---

[121] See: R. Panikkar, *The Unknown Christ of Hinduism,* Darton, Longman and Todd, London, 1964, p. 54, quoted by DSA in: Id., *Approaches,* op. cit., p. 41. Here we must make a note that the theological Christ content for DSA and Panikkar is not exactly the same. For DSA the historical Jesus is the Christ, that is, he sees Christ in 'the incarnational economy of salvation'; while Panikkar tries to see Christ beyond the historical Jesus of Nazareth; for him Christ is one of the many expressions of Brahman. Panikkar is basically inspired by the *advaitic* philosophy of Śankara for whom the absolute reality is the *Absolute* or *Īśwara (Brahman).* This Brahman expresses himself in different religions as Jesus in Christianity, Kṛṣṇa in Hinduism, etc. This leads to "pluralism" in the theology of religions, i.e., all religions are equal. Cf. also: R. Panikkar, *Salvation in Christ: Concreteness and Universality. The Supername,* Santa Barbara, California, 1972. DSA does not accept such "pluralism".

[122] Cf. DSA, *Approaches,* op. cit., p. 42.

> Man having a body and living in society, can come into contact with God and respond to Him and thereby attain salvation *only through the historico-socio-religious phenomena,* 'in the context of their religious traditions' (Nagpur Declaration, 16). In other words, the beliefs and practices should have their origin in God. Hence we logically conclude that the reality of *Revelation* is possible in their religions and life-situations; their Scripture must be *inspired* in some way or other ... and their religious practices (cf. the *samskaras* in Hinduism) may be visible means of *salvation:* Revelation, Inspiration and Salvation should be granted and recognized in them in some way or other, if we are open and logical with the Vatican II statements. This is what we declared in Nagpur: 'The different *sacred scriptures and rites* of the religious traditions of the world *can be in various degrees,* expressions of a divine *manifestation* and *can be* conducive to *salvation*' (Nagpur Declaration 16). The workshop report on the subject was more categorical in its statement: [these can be] 'expressions of divine *revelation* and *means* of salvation' (Nagpur Workshop Report V).[123]

Amalor feels that the time is not yet ripe for the general agreement on the way we express the active presence of Christ in other religions nor on the ambiguous character and defects in the 'structures, signs and formulations in a religion'. However, we cannot deny the reality of Christ's saving action through the socio-religious phenomena of any religion.[124]

Finally, we make a note here that Amalor does not accept these two positions on the issue: (i) that other religions are equal or parallel to Christianity, and (ii) that other religions are for their respective believers the 'ordinary' or 'general' ways of salvation, which makes Christianity for them an 'extraordinary', 'exceptional' or 'special' way.[125]

---

[123] See as cited by Gerwin van Leeuwen, O.F.M., in: Id., *Fully Indian - Authentically Christian,* op. cit., pp. 264-265.

[124] Cf. ibid., p. 265.

[125] Cf. DSA, *Approaches,* op. cit., 11; id., *Approach,* op. cit., pp. 57-58; id., *Purpose,* op. cit., p. 26.

## 5. Diakonia to the World Religions: Salvific Approach

Amalor sees the aspect of diakonia (service) to other religions as closely connected with the Church, especially when we consider the Church as 'the universal sacrament of salvation'. Why should there be diakonia? What should be the Church's approach and attitude towards it? What are the tasks and stages of diakonia? These are some of the important points which we will be seeing in this topic.

### *5.1. Why Diakonia? Church's 'Universality' in Action*

Christ is the author of salvation. He came to save both individuals as well as religions. He came to save and to recapitulate to the ends of the earth (cf. Acts 1:8), up to the end of time (cf. Matt. 28:20) not only man and all that is human, not only what is religious but all the religions of the world. Whether men are aware of it or not, the historical venture is oriented towards Christ; the whole of creation is in the process of its evolution, transformation and Christification. Everything has a forward thrust towards Christ, that is, everything tends towards Christ and everything, including the religions of the world, must be assumed in the process of Christification of the universe. Amalor writes:

> The religions of the world and all that is religious, we may say, are in a state of vocation to salvation; they implicitly yearn for Christ to have their meaning and fulfillment; they tend towards Christ like the rest on the historical movement; they constitute an ensemble to be permeated and transformed by the ferment of the gospel; they fall within the sovereignty of God, subject to his judgement, which is one of condemnation and salvation.[126]

The religions of the world have to enter into the paschal mystery of Christ, that is, they have to be tested on the anvil of the Gospel of Christ. In their religious behaviour men may display the limits and errors that disfigure the image of God in them (cf. syncretism in 1 Kgs. 11:7-8; idolatry in Rom. 1:18-25).[127] This fact is well noted in *Lumen Gentium.* It

---

126 DSA, *Approaches,* op. cit., p. 33.
127 Cf. *CCC,* 844.

states:

> Very often, deceived by the Evil one, men have become vain in their reasonings, and have exchanged the truth of God for a lie, and served the creature rather than the Creator (cf. Rom. 1:21,25). Or else, living and dying in this world without God, they are exposed to ultimate despair (no. 16).

Therefore, errors and superstitions in other religions are to be removed. The Church which is constituted the universal sacrament of salvation by Christ has the responsibility towards other religions to render the diakonia in the process of their paschal event, the death and resurrection, in Christ. In other words, in order to be saved, every religion, like every person, has to die to what enslaves it and rise to a newness or fullness of life in Christ. For

> the words of Christ are at one and the same time words of judgement and grace, of death and life. For it is only by putting to death what is old, that we are able to come to newness of life. This fact applies first of all to persons, but it also holds [good] for the various goods *and the religions of the world* which bear the mark both of man's sin and of God's blessings (*AG* 8).[128]

Amalor says that Jesus made love and service to others --'the washing of feet' (cf. Jn. 13:12-20,34-35) -- *the* characteristic of being-Christian, of Christian discipleship, the most important mark of the Church of Christ. For: "By this all men will know that you are my disciples if you love one another" (Jn.13:35).[129] The Church's diakonia to other religions is a diakonia of salvation, in keeping with her universal mission of salvation,[130] that is, the realization of the pleroma of Christ. However, this diakonia is extremely delicate and even dangerous, "for it is a question of judging a religion by the gospel, of proving a culture in the furnace of the Word of

---

[128] See as quoted in: DSA, *Approaches,* op. cit., p. 37; DSA inserts 'and the religions of the world' in the quotation *AG* 8.

[129] See: DSA, *Approach,* op. cit., p. 44; id., *Approaches,* op. cit., pp. 27-28; id., *Purpose,* op. cit., 14; id. (ed.), *Evangelization of the Modern World,* op. cit., p. 42; id., "Biblical World-View and a Renewed Holistic Spirituality", *op. cit.,* p. 60.

[130] Cf. DSA, *Approaches,* op. cit., p. 33.

God. It is a question of distinguishing the good seed from the cockle, truth from error, openness from closure, grace from sin, real values from the false ones...."[131] Hence Amalor first speaks about the right attitudes and approaches the Church should have in her mission of diakonia to other religions.

### *5.2. Approaches and Attitudes*

#### *5.2.1. Recognition and reverence*

As God is present in other religions and in their followers, the Church has to approach them with reverence and delicacy. Any attitude of superiority or condescension is out of place. It is a humble diakonia, a participation in the very double-dimensional diakonia of Christ -- to God the Father and to the world.[132]

Diakonia (service) is essentially humble. Yet, Amalor sees a deeper reason for approaching other religions with great humility, delicacy, respect and reverence. It is because of the mystery of God and the "mystery" of the human being. As every human being is a mystery when we consider him or her as a person, endowed with freedom and will and God working in him or her, so also other religions are not any devil's creation or a heap of rubbish to be removed or voids to be filled in. We are to be aware that God is present not only in the followers of other religions but in their religions themselves. The religions of the world fall within God's cosmic plan of salvation and are subjected to the eschatological sovereignty of God. The saving grace of the Word has been reaching and perfecting the elements and structures of these religions and so these religions are related to Christ and his universal sacrament of salvation, the Church.

To substantiate his stand on the status of other religions in this context Amalor once again refers to the documents of Vatican II: before Christ was glorified, the Holy Spirit, anticipating the Apostles' action, was already present and at work in the world and in the religions of the world (cf. *AG* 4), in which "the seeds of the Word lie hidden in their national and religious traditions" (*AG* 11); through these seeds of the Word the Holy Spirit calls people to Christ in their own religions (cf. *AG* 15). Thus "the

---

[131] DSA, *Purpose,* op. cit., pp. 17-18.

[132] Cf. DSA, *Approaches,* op. cit., p. 34.

truth and grace are found among the nations" (*AG* 21) that the bountiful God has distributed among the nations of the earth (cf. *AG* 11) and "the precious elements of religion and humanity are preserved in their traditions" (*GS* 92d). Their ways and conduct of life, the rules and teachings, though differing in many particulars from what the Christian holds and sets forth to them often reflect a ray of that Truth which enlightens all men (cf. *NA* 2).[133]

### *5.2.2. God's activity preceding ours: Our collaboration*

The second important attitude in the Church's diakonia to other religions Amalor touches upon is that the Church must not consider other religions as a virgin soil where we are the first ones to work, starting from scratch, or see them as *tabula rasa,* pretending to start from zero. We must be aware that the world and history have been from the beginning the field of God's revelation, his presence and action. We only enter a place where others are present and have been working for their salvation, namely, God and men animated by his Spirit.[134] That is to say, 'the seeds of the Word' have already and generously been sown by God in these religions. God calls for our collaboration in his 'vineyard' to work for his kingdom on earth. Taking a clue from John 4:35-38, Amalor writes: "Yes, 'the seeds of the Word' have already been sown by God there and we have to do the rest, not alone but with others."[135]

### *5.2.3. Other religions in sincere search for the true God*

The third aspect of our approach is the fact that other religions and their followers or the persons belonging to no religion, whether they are aware of it or not, are in real need and in sincere search for the one true God. They are in a state of expectation.[136] We must remember that those whom we approach are expecting us, expecting for the proclamation of the Gospel, though thy may not be fully aware of it. This expectation or their authentic religious quest is expressed in their religious elements and

---

[133] See these Vatican II documents referred to by DSA, in: Ibid.

[134] Cf. ibid., p. 35.

[135] Ibid.

[136] Cf. ibid.

structures, rites and practices, and through their multiple endeavours, "by which", writes Amalor, referring to Paul at Athens (Acts 17:27), "men search God, groping for him that they may by chance find him (though he is not far from any one of us)."[137] *Ad Gentes* 3 rightly recognizes in these multiple endeavours the workings of divine providence, an authentic religious quest for the true God and sees them as a preparation for the Gospel.[138]

### *5.2.4. A relevant service*

Finally, our service must be relevant, and relevancy is determined by the needs and requests, aspirations and desires of those whom we want to serve. Sometimes, religions as well as people, whether they be followers of religion or atheists, may not be aware of their real needs. In such a case, it is incumbent on the heralds of the Good News to make them aware of their religious quest for the true God, deeply hidden in them. Otherwise our diakonia is irrelevant. Christians are challenged "to exert themselves lest modern man, overly intent on the science and technology of today's world, become a stranger to things divine. Rather, let them awaken in him a fiercer yearning for that truth and charity which God has revealed [in Jesus Christ]" (*AG* 11).[139]

### *5.3. Tasks and Stages of Diakonia*

Once we approach other religions with proper attitude and in the right spirit, we ask: What is our task or what is the content of diakonia towards them? This diakonia comprises several tasks and stages, ultimately aiming at the realization of the pleroma of Christ, that is, the unity, fulfillment and consummation of all peoples and religions in Christ. For this Amalor distinguishes three stages, for which three Christological mysteries stand as models. These are: the mystery of the Incarnation, the paschal mystery of Death and Resurrection, and the mystery of consummation, Ascension and Parousia.[140]

---

137 Ibid.

138 See *AG* 3 referred to by DSA, in: Ibid.

139 See *AG* 11 as quoted by DSA, in: Ibid.

140 Cf. ibid., p. 36. These three stages DSA formulated for the first time in: Id.,

### *5.3.1. Incarnation, assumption and identification*

The first stage of the diakonia to other religions is *incarnation.* Incarnation supposes presence and assumption. As Christ assumed everything, the whole of our nature except sin, to save everything (*AG* 3), so also following the spirit of Incarnation, the Church should incarnate herself in every culture and religion, penetrating them gradually and totally as a leaven in the mass and become one with them.

The Good News that is a person -- Jesus Christ -- rather than a message must become "flesh" in every nation and culture. The Church has to identify herself with every culture and become part of the society in which she enters, and thus become a local or indigenous Church. This will translate itself in the Church's true sympathy for the human, cultural and religious values, customs, art forms, ways of thinking, praying and worshipping, etc., found in other religions and cultures. Otherwise we will fall into another form of docetism and the *good news* will no more be experienced as such. In this context Amalor refers to the exhortation of *Nostra Aetate* and writes that Christians have to "prudently and lovingly, through dialogue and collaboration with the followers of other religions, and in witness of Christian faith and life acknowledge, preserve and promote the spiritual and moral goods found among these men, as well as the values in their society and culture" (no. 2).[141]

'Incarnation' immediately implies 'assumption' or 'identification', that is, things and religions to be saved, as it was with Jesus, are to be assumed first. Without this assumption the salvation which the Church may so ardently try to bring to these religions will be seen, from the part of the giver as well as receiver, as 'replacing' of one religion with the other. It will be seen by the receiver as the Church's making inroads into his or her religion. Then the Church will appear as pretending to give salvation from outside, as an outsider, to the one who does not have it. The Church is called and commissioned, not so much to "give" salvation to other religions from outside but rather to *"make"* these religions "salvific" from within. Making other religions salvific does not mean their termination or replacement but their transformation, purification and

---

*Destinée,* op. cit., pp. 263-266. They are also found in: Id., *Towards Indigenization in the Liturgy,* op. cit., pp. 16-17; id., *Purpose,* op. cit., pp. 16-17. We follow mainly *Approaches.*

[141] See as quoted in: DSA, *Approaches,* op. cit., p. 36.

perfection, in and through the power of the Spirit of Christ. This is what we call the process of 'Christification' of religions and the universe through the process of incarnation, assumption and identification.

### *5.3.2. Purification and transformation*

The second stage is purification and transformation, which Amalor bases on the model of Jesus' death and resurrection. To quote again, Amalor says, "Every religion, like every man, must pass through this death to resurrection in order to be saved."[142]

Christ came not to judge the Law and religions but to fulfill them. Christ, who through his life, death and resurrection has become the supreme norm of existence,[143] judges no one, but men and religions feel judged when they come into contact with this supreme norm. The Gospel which is proclaimed throws light on everything, on religious doctrines and practices and points out their value. Thus the religions of the world are purified and perfected in the light of the Gospel. All peoples and religions stand in "need of Christ who is the model, master, liberator, saviour and giver of life" (*AG* 8).[144]

As Christ became man to save humankind, the Church has to assume the cultures in order to save them by purifying and transforming them; she has to recognize the truth and remove what is sinful, false, idolatrous, superstitious, and ambiguous in other religions in the light the Gospel. Amalor writes: "Hinduism, and for that matter any other religion, must undergo 'a passion of the spirit', 'a noetic crucifixion' in order to pass on to Christic resurrection."[145] The judgement of religions involves a process of rupture and continuity, rejection and assumption, death and resurrection, that is, a process of perfection or liberation in Christ. This is an extremely delicate task where often emotions seem to take precedence over reason and the spirit and attitude of Christ. It is not a question of rash judgement from outside, but the judgement of a religion must be perceived from inside under the light of Christ that falls on it. For that the Church should look at the religions from inside. That is why incarnation precedes

---

142 Ibid.

143 Cf. ibid., pp. 36-37.

144 See cited in: Ibid., p. 37.

145 Ibid.

this stage.

We can well summarize this stage, saying that the Church has to render the diakonia of freeing "from all taint of evil whatever truth and grace is to be found among the nations", "preserving, healing, ennobling and perfecting whatever good is to be found to be shown in the hearts and minds of men, or in the rites and cultures peculiar to various peoples" and "restoring them to Christ its maker" (*AG* 9).[146]

### *5.3.3. Fulfillment and consummation*

Amalor takes the mystery of Christ's ascension and glorification as model for the third stage of diakonia to other religions. This is the stage of the fulfillment and consummation of everything in Christ, the pleroma of Christ.

Christ did not come to destroy but to fulfill. He came to lead all cultures and religions, ideologies and philosophies to their goal and consummation and constituted the Church as the universal sacrament of salvation to continue this mission of consummation of all peoples and religions in his pleroma. By enriching and fulfilling other religions and indigenous cultures then the Church, in turn, enriches herself. In this context, paraphrasing *Ad Gentes,* Amalor writes:

> When all the riches of the nations which were given to Christ as an inheritance (Ps. 2:8) are taken up by the Church in an integral exchange, when the customs and traditions ... are assumed and lived by the Christians, when Christians seek for understanding of the faith in the philosophy and wisdom of the new people, when their customs and attitude on life and social order can be reconciled with the manner of Christian living (*AG* 22), ... when the religious literature of other religions can be read, understood and lived with reference to the Sacred Scriptures of Christianity, then we can say that all these have been saved and consecrated to God, and thereby have reached their fulfillment and consummation in the pleroma of Christ.[147]

---

[146] See: Ibid.

[147] Ibid., pp. 37-38; DSA, *Purpose,* op. cit., p. 18; id., *Towards Indigenization in the Liturgy,* op. cit., p. 17; cf. id., *Destinée,* op. cit., p. 226.

### *5.4. The Diakonia of Interpretation: Christocentric Interpretation of God's Design for History, Mankind and Religions*

"The Church's mission is basically a prophetic function consisting of a service of interpretation."[148] If God continues to reveal himself to us here and now and shares his plan for mankind in our own life and history in the various religious traditions of mankind, then how can the Church recognize, discern and interpret it? This is precisely the mission of the Church amidst the world religions and ideologies, the mission of docility to the Spirit of Christ, seeking the fullness of truth and salvation in and through Christ.

Vatican II often speaks about the importance of this prophetic task of the Church:

> The people of God believes that it [history and destiny of man] is led by the Spirit of the Lord who fills the whole world. Moved by that faith it tries to discern in the events, the needs, and the longings which it shares with other men of our time, what may be genuine signs of the presence or of the purpose of God (*GS* 11).[149]

*Gaudium et Spes* uses a great variety of words to describe the prophetic responsibility of the Christian community: "to scrutinize the signs of the times", "to interpret these in the light of the gospel", "to decipher authentic signs of God's presence and purpose in the happenings, needs and desires" of the people of today, "to assess the values most highly prized today", "to hear, distinguish, and interpret the many voices of our age, and to judge them in the light of the Divine Word".[150]

The Spirit of Christ guides the Church and history. Therefore the authentic interpretation of history will depend upon the docility to the Spirit. The following elements play an important role in the process of the Church's authentic interpretation of history.[151]

---

[148] DSA, "Approach", *op. cit.*, p. 29.

[149] See also: *GS* 4, 44.

[150] See: *GS* 4, 11, 44 as cited by Gerwin van Leeuwen, in: Id., *Fully Indian - Authentically Christian*, op. cit., p. 200.

[151] See: DSA, *The Church's Mission as Prophetic and Hermeneutical* (4th ed.), op. cit., pp. 8-12; id. (ed.), *Evangelization of the Modern World*, op. cit., p. 45; id., *Approach*, op. cit., 29-30; id., *Theology of Catechesis*, op. cit., pp. 29-38; id., *Social Communication*,

### *5.4.1. Service to the Spirit: Church's responsibility towards others*

In and through his Son, God has ultimately and fully communicated his universal salvific design for the world to the Church. The Church, in turn, has to interpret or communicate this salvific plan of God to the world, to other religions and ideologies. The Church's service of interpretation and communication of God's plan and revelation in history is therefore to be always in communication with the world, its religions and ideologies.

Since the purpose is to discern God's will in the concrete reality of today amidst the world religions and ideologies, the prophetic function can only be exercised by those who are involved in the world and speak its language. Relevant interpretation of God's universal salvific act in and through the mystery of Christ in our time will, therefore, call for dialogue with the world, especially with other religions and ideologies.

God reveals himself in history. History is the medium and milieu of God's on-going revelation, the meeting ground of God and man. God's will is to be deciphered and done in history so that one sees one's place in history and enables others to experience God's presence, action, consolation and challenges in today's world, and thus, to deepen one's own and others' commitment to constant self-renewal and transformation of the human society.

Since the Word is a living one and revelation is on-going, the Church, in her task of interpretation, needs to be open to the movement of history and changes in society, to new manifestations and challenges of the Spirit. For the Spirit leads his Church, the world and history only gradually into the full reality till the Lord appears in the full light.[152] Amalor, quoting H. Bouillard, writes:

> In order to interpret Christian message, we must envisage it from the point of view of its having a meaning for all men, that is to say, as it gives an answer to the questions of the meaning of human experiences. Therefore God's revelation would have no meaning for us if

---

op. cit., pp. 19-27; id., *The Bible in Self-Renewal and Church-Renewal for Service to Society,* op. cit., pp. 7-10. See also: Gerwin van Leeuwen, O.F.M., *Fully Indian - Authentically Christian,* op. cit., pp. 200-203.

152 Cf. DSA, *The Church's Mission as Prophetic and Hermeneutical,* op. cit., p. 11; see also: Id., "Approach", *op. cit.,* p. 31; Gerwin van Leeuwen, O.F.M., *Fully Indian - Authentically Christian,* op. cit., p. 201.

> it were not at the same time the revelation of the meaning of our existence.[153]

*5.4.2. Christocentric interpretation*

The origin and fulfillment of creation and history is in Christ. Therefore, the Church's interpretation of the whole creation, history and salvation is a Christocentric one.

> Christ [is] hailed by the faithful as 'the expected of the nations and their Saviour' (*AG* 8). If Christ, his Gospel and his Church are to transform the world, orient history and lead them to fulfillment, they should enter INTO this process, into this adventure, into this historic movement. What we say about mankind in general holds good for each country, people and nations.[154]

Christ is with the Father from the very beginning of creation and history. For "all things came into being through him, and without him not one thing came into being" (Jn. 1:3). "All things have been created through him and for him" (Col. 1:16). God has been reconciling the world in his Son (cf. Col. 1:20). God has been working for the creation of a new heaven and a new earth, that is, the total transformation of history, mankind and creation led by the Spirit of his Son Jesus Christ. The Church is the agent of this transformation in Christ and the instrument of the kingdom of God that is immediately linked with mankind and history. Therefore, "in their journey to the kingdom of the Father united with Christ and led by the Spirit, this community [the Church] should realize that it is truly and intimately linked with mankind and its history."[155] Amalor continues:

> Christ does not come only at the end; namely, where we pass from the human to the religious or spiritual; he is present and operating from

---

153 See: H. Bouillard, S.J., "Human Experience as Starting point for Fundamental Theology", in: *Concilium,* no. 1, vol. 6, pp. 40-49 as quoted by DSA in: Id., *Approaches,* op. cit., p. 22.

154 DSA, *Approaches,* op. cit., pp. 19-20.

155 Ibid., p. 21.

> the beginning. When we converse with men about any of their problems and difficulties, their desires and aspirations, we must see God operative through them. We must see God's presence in the secular world and his saving operation in human activities.[156]

The salvation of God in Christ does not enter human history from outside. Jesus, in the mystery of the *incarnation,* has made God visible and present in the very midst of us and he calls us to take man and history seriously. Because, "Just as history serves as the milieu and medium of revelation for God, so also the 'human' could be the milieu and medium of understanding the word of God, faith and supernatural salvation."[157]

The Christocentric or incarnational interpretation of history calls us to join hands with all people of good will in dialogue and collaboration in building the kingdom of God on earth and the realization of his universal salvific plan which includes all men and women of all castes and creed, all times and turns of history, the whole creation.

### *5.4.2.1. Encounter of change and challenge*

Any encounter with Christ challenges persons as well religions. It brings change. It perfects, fulfills and saves them. The Church continues this saving and fulfilling mission of Christ through her diakonia to the religions of the world.

Though this diakonia is a vast and delicate task, even at times dangerous and difficult one, Amalor is very optimistic about it. He cites the example of Hinduism. The spread of Christianity in India was both a challenge to Hinduism and a source of inspiration for reform. As a result of its contact with Christianity a renaissance of Hinduism started a century and a half years ago and in the process of it, it got itself purified and revitalized, shedding much of its magical, mythological and superstitious elements. The Hindu worship and way of life have been gradually influenced by Christianity; there is a notable trend towards prophetism or faith in a personal God. Amalor writes:

> The Hindu worship and way of life have been gradually influenced by Christianity: there is a notable trend towards prophetism; personal

---

156 Ibid., p. 22.

157 DSA, *Theology of Development,* op. cit., p. 26.

> and real relationship between the personal God and his devotees has been evident, the ritualistic element is diminished. There is a certain elan in which Hindu worship and life is carried forward.... There is a change for the better. The one-sided 'mystical' or 'ritualistic' character is balanced by the growing prophetism or 'bhakti' character.[158]

In addition to the discovery of a personal God, the need to meet the challenge of technological culture and the exigencies of the developing nation, Hinduism has also inculcated the necessity of love and service to fellow human beings and its commitment to the temporal tasks as part and parcel of religion.

*5.4.2.2. Openness to Christ*

Amalor attributes the renewal and progress of Hinduism partly to the dynamic element of Hinduism itself and partly to its encounter with Christianity.[159] That is to say that other religions are not the work of the devil. The 'seeds of the Word' are shown by God in them. They are not opposed to Christ. There is an inherent openness in them to truth, to the Gospel, to Christ. This openness to and acceptance of Christ and his Gospel makes them prophetic and salvific. Amalor writes: "The ferment of the gospel has been active all these hundred of years. It has not only saved Hindus ..., it has somewhat saved Hinduism to the extent of making it a little more prophetic and thereby a little more salvific."[160]

The truth and grace are found among other religions (cf. *AG* 21), but they may be bleared by insufficient knowledge, superstitions and ambiguous nature in their culture and religious practices. The diakonia of the Church to other religions falls exactly here:

-- to acknowledge the grace and providence of God, the universal saving mystery of Christ, in the very framework of other religions: *recognition by the Church*,

-- and to help them acknowledge the fullness of truth and salvation in God in and through the mystery of the Gospel, the mystery of Christ: *openness of other religions* to Christ.[161]

---

158 DSA, *Approaches,* op. cit., p. 42.

159 Cf. ibid.

160 Ibid., pp. 42-43.

161 Cf. ibid., p. 33.

The diakonia that is expected of the Church in this regard is precisely to recognize the all-permeating presence and action of Christ in other religions, collaborate with them and serve them as a factor to open their doctrines and practices towards a transcendent and personal God and towards the love and service of fellowmen. Any effort towards this end in the Church's relationship and her dealings with followers of other religions, for example, moral instruction, classes at schools, literature, dialogue or collaboration, will contribute to their salvation.[162]

### *5.4.3. Avoiding illusions*

Though Amalor is very optimistic about the Church's attitude and appreciation of other religions, he likes to have no illusions about it, lest one falls in a false situation. He is well aware of the difficulty and delicacy of the matter; namely, making Hinduism or other religions more prophetic and salvific is not that easy. Though the Church may lay emphasis on the power of God and the efficacy of his Word and though she believes in the goodness of man, she cannot afford to forget the sinful tendency and state of fallen man, the centuries-old closure and rigidity of religions and the little prophetic élan that is inscribed in their very nature.

> It is not simply a question of ambiguity, a mixture to be separated or an impurity to be removed. The difficulty is not so much perceived when we deal with persons as with religions as systems and structures. For example, 'saving Hinduism' and 'making it more prophetic and salvific' are not so easy in fact as they appear in words, however agreeable it may sound. Hinduism needs a deeper metanoia; it is not simply one of purification and fulfillment but also one of rejection and rupture. There is no possibility of new life without real death. Christ will then be a sign of contradiction, whether we like it or not: the scandal of the Cross cannot be avoided in any case. Perhaps Hinduism needs to be provoked and challenged; this may serve as a better way to discover Christ as the Fulfillment and Saviour.[163]

---

[162] Cf. ibid., p. 43.

[163] Ibid.

Amalor likes to corroborate what he theologizes above with an example. He quotes the example of Fr. Johanns in envisaging an Indian Christian Theology.[164] A lot of discernment is needed in this delicate task of diakonia. It is not a question of declaring a pantheon, the Church of All Saints by a ceremony of dedication nor of baptizing, for example, the system of Śankara into the Indian Christian philosophy or theology. If we compare each Hindu system to a Hindu temple and if we want to build a Christian cathedral out of it, we have first of all to dismantle it completely. Then with the heap of stones thus removed, rejecting some of them and taking some from Christianity we have to reconstruct them into a cathedral. For other religions or their metaphysical systems lack in one way or other corner stones, for example, the right interpretation of creation, history, salvation, without which no Christian construction can exist.

The diakonia to other religions is the task of the whole Church. It should not be restricted to an élite group or scholars but should become the concern of the whole rank and file of the Christian community. For this Amalor likes to give a tremendous importance to the formation programmes of Christians at various levels. It is the mission of the Church which she is commissioned by Christ to conscientiously fulfill in the "tension" between the 'already' and 'not yet' of the universal salvation in Christ. On the one hand, in virtue of the creation through the Word everything already belongs to Christ and the religions of the world bear the stamp of Christ; on the other hand, everything and every religion is oriented towards Christ for their unification and fulfillment in God. The Church should be really and truly involved in the dynamics of history, that is, everything must be restored to Christ who will then turn over everything to the Father so that "God will be all in all" (1 Cor. 15:28).[165] On that day the Church will be truly Catholic and universal. Till then she has to do much effort, but "no effort is too much and no effort should be spared for fulfilling a task which is the very *raison d'être* of the Church."[166]

While interpreting God's design for the world and history in Christ

---

[164] See: P. Johanns, S.J., *To Christ through Vedanta (Light of the East series)*, Ranchi, India (1943), no. 4, Part I: *Sankara, introduction,* referred to by DSA, in: Id, *Approaches,* op. cit., p. 44; also in: Id., *Destinée,* op. cit., pp. 302-303.

[165] Cf. DSA, *Towards Indigenization in the Liturgy,* op. cit., p. 17.

[166] DSA, *Approaches,* op. cit., p. 44.

Jesus, the Church is called to bear witness to the unity of humankind. "The love overflowing from the Trinitarian fellowship and made visible in Christ, must reach all men through the living testimony of all Church members, a testimony which is at the same time an invitation to communion [of all humankind] (cf. *AG* 2-6)."[167] The Church is then seen as the place where humanity must discover its unity and salvation. She has to be 'the world reconciled', the bark which 'in the full sail of the Lord's cross, by the breath of the Holy Spirit, navigates safely in this world'.[168]

> In the Spirit the Church gathers and reconciles the people from the four winds, forms and guides them, and becomes a community of those reconciled to God and to others in mutual acceptance and self-gift. This gathering of Christian community is nothing else than the visible expression of the reconciliation which Christ accomplished in his body on the cross and which his Spirit continues to realize.... As promoters of a new relationship of brotherhood of all men in Jesus Christ, it tries to realize peace and harmony among men and with God.... Therefore *Lumen Gentium* opens with this crucial statement that the mission of the Church concretely consists in effectively bringing about and signifying the union of all men with one another and of all men with God (no.1).[169]

## 6. Conclusion

### *6.1. All salvation in and by God: Father - Son - Spirit*[170]

When we say that all salvation comes from God, we immediately understand by God the triune God as revealed to us by Christ. The grace or salvation of God reaches to all peoples and religions through Christ and his Spirit. "God's ways are mysterious and unfathomable, and no one can determine the direction of divine grace."[171]However, the grace of God

---

167 Ibid., p. 13.

168 See: *CCC,* 845.

169 DSA, *Approach,* op. cit., pp. 40-41.

170 Cf. DSA, *Approaches,* pp. 46-47.

171 See: *BIRA* II quoted by Stephen Bevans, "Inculturation of Theology in Asia", in: *Studia Missionalia,* vol. 45 (1996), p. 14. (*BIRA* is the Bishops' Institute for Inter-

received by the members of Christian tradition and of others is distinct in its modality. It is different in kind and degree. In others it is implicitly present in a concealed manner; in the Christian tradition, because of Christ, it is present overtly and explicitly. In the former it is a preparatory mode of mediation; in the latter it is the fullness of mediation.

> In fact no religious relationship can equal that which is brought about in Christ in whose person mankind and the living God are united.... Again, in the case of the Buddha Amitābha, we have to note that the entrance into Buddha's Paradise is only a preparatory goal of salvation, a gateway to *nirvāṇa*. But Christ is himself salvation; his whole existence is the means for salvation, ... a movement of man towards God and of God towards man.... It belongs to the realm of faith to see that Jesus Christ was none other than God himself.[172]

Amalor does not only see the possibility of salvation in other religions but also their value and role in the whole economy of salvation.[173] Even if other religions may contain a mixture of errors and deviations, nonetheless these religions do contain authentic values and constitute a true preparation for the Gospel. Purified and elevated by grace, these authentic values may constitute a means of salvation for the followers of these religions, drawing them to the act of 'faith and charity' which is necessary for salvation.

### *6.2. Other religions: An ordering unto Christ*

The existence of other religions, far from rendering useless the proclamation of the Gospel, really provides a new argument which justifies its abiding importance. To state that these religions may serve as preparation for the Gospel, is to state that "there exists in them an ordering unto Christ -- a thrust towards Christ -- which only the proclamation of the Gospel can bring into fulfillment."[174]

---

Religious Affairs, a working committee of FABC: Federation of Asian Bishops' Conference, 1974 onwards).

[172] See: M. Dhavamony, "Mediation in the History of Religions", in: *Studia Missionalia*, vol. 21, Gregorian University Press, Rome, 1972, pp. 19-20.

[173] Cf. DSA, *Theology of Evangelization*, op. cit., p. 14.

[174] See the "Conclusions of the Symposium on Mission Theology for our Times" by

The Church is not the end, she is the sacrament of Christ between his Pasch and Parousia to lead all people and religions to Christ and through Christ to God where God will be all in all (cf. 1 Cor 15:28). Her diakonia towards other religions is that of the realization of the pleroma of Christ. "She must be present everywhere as the sign, witness and instrument of God's design for mankind, and as 'a sure and enduring germ of unity, hope and salvation for the whole mankind' (*LG* 9b). It is here then that we ought to recall the images of the light of the world, the salt of the earth and the leaven in the dough whose influence is universal and within."[175]

If the providential grace of God given to followers of other religions for their salvation ordains them to Christ, the Church in her service to others must allow, orient and lead them as well as their religions to the fullness of truth in Christ. The Church has to recognize the salvific value of other religions in the light of the Gospel and work for the kingdom of God that waits for its eschatological fulfillment. This needs sincere dialogue and mutual collaboration among the religions of the world.

---

SEDOS (Rome, 27-31 March, 1969), in: DSA, *Approaches,* op. cit., pp. 46-47.

[175] DSA, *Approaches,* op. cit., p. 16.

# PART THREE

## CHURCH AND RELIGIONS

The affirmation that God is one and has one and the same salvific plan for all humanity implies that religions are oriented to a unity -- a unity that is rooted in God and that it has to be achieved through dialogue leading to mutual enrichment and fulfillment. The question of one and many is no more a mere theoretical one. It challenges all people of good will to affirm that the bond that unites us is stronger than the walls that divide us. In fact, it is in building up a human community of freedom, fellowship, peace and justice that religious persons should discover themselves in dialogue. Religions come together in dialogue for not to form 'one religion' but to effectively become what each religion understands by God and man, and that too, not in isolation but in mutual collaboration in a common search for the fullness of truth and life. Till recently, the unjust situation of the world was considered exclusively a socio-economic condition of nations. As such, religion was seen to be a hindrance to social change. Today it has become clear that religions together should play the role of the other pole that keeps challenging actual structures and proposing a vision for a new society. The 'social' is no more secular in the sense of being outside God's plan but is involved intimately with the dynamic of the kingdom of God. Therefore faith and justice are bound closely together. Change of heart (individual, spiritual or moral conversion) will have to go along with change of structures (socio-economic and political conversion).

# CHAPTER FIVE

# INTER-RELIGIOUS DIALOGUE
# SEEKING THE FULLNESS OF TRUTH AND LIFE

## 1. Introduction

### *1.1. Dialogue: Essential part of human nature*

Dialogue is an essential part of human nature. It is not something novel to the human race. However, the word dialogue has assumed new dimensions of meaning in the context of religious pluralism today where the word is used in relation to the world religions and ideologies.

Some sort of dialogue was going on between religions from the time immemorial. But this need not be an inter-religious dialogue. A real dialogue presupposes an openness to the other person, an attitude of mutual recognition and respect, that is, the recognition of truth and goodness in other religions and mutual enrichment. This is what is new to the word dialogue when it is used in the context of religious pluralism today.

Today mankind is approaching the phenomenon of religion as the outpouring of a divine mystery than a ready made answers to its problems. A mystery is something to be lived than to be intellectually analyzed and answered. In spite of its modern tendencies of secularism and humanism, something great is happening in this world today. The religions and ideologies are giving up their exclusive claims of truth or God, while remaining open to the mystery of divine self-communication. There is a growing dialogue and collaboration among the religions of the world in view of reaching their common destiny in God.

### *1.2. Dialogue: Towards realizing the fullness of truth*

All the religions of the world are seekers after truth and salvation. The truth that makes all humankind free is the common end of all the religions of the world. To achieve this common destiny, what is needed is not confrontation but communication and communion among the religions of the world. They are called to communion with God and with one another in and through dialogue.

Dialogue is the positive attitude of Vatican II towards other religions that suggests a new relationship of the Church with other religions. It is a positive effort of two or more persons or groups of different religious traditions as religiously committed persons to arrive at a deeper understanding of truth in mutual engagement and enrichment, mutual respect and recognition of the spiritual and moral values found among religions with an awareness and sincerity of one another's convictions and mutual witnessing (cf. *NA* 2).[1]

The term "dialogue" could be applied to the means and techniques that may be used in any form of collaboration among the religions of the world towards reaching and realizing their common destiny. Dialogue, then, will become an inevitable means of religions in their common seeking and sharing of truth and life. Dialogue, by Christians, is to be understood as "a response of Christian Charity to the fact of religious pluralism, wherein the partners seek for the fullness of Truth; it praecipeposes the religious concern, respect for the convictions of others and fraternal openness."[2]

Since the Council of Vatican II, the Church has begun to accept the plurality of religions (cf. *NA* 2) and with ever increasing clarity begun to understand that her 'being' is "*to be in dialogue* with others, with the world, because She is the Sacrament of God's dialogue with Man in Christ Jesus."[3] Dialogue which makes us aware of the omnipresent mystery of God's salvific love urges us to proclaim and make manifest the Christ still hidden and unknown to others as the one in whom the whole world, with its religions, is to be reunited and consummated.[4]

However, a genuine dialogue is possible only between two persons who encounter each other in their concreteness. Two religions in dialogue means two religions encountering each other in their different personality,

---

[1] Cf. The Patna Workshop Report no. III -1 on "Evangelization and Dialogue with Unbelievers", in: *Light and Life We Seek to Share,* op. cit., p. 315; DSA, *Theology of Evangelization,* op. cit., pp. 12-13; also: M. Dhavamony, "The Christian theology of interreligious Dialogue", in: *Studia Missionalia,* vol. 43, Editrice Pontificia Università Gregoriana, Roma, 1994, p. 62.

[2] See: The Patna Workshop Report no. III -1 on "Evangelization and Dialogue with Unbelievers", in: *Light and Life We Seek to Share,* op. cit., p. 315.

[3] Felix Machado, "Dialogue in the Year 2000: From Discussion to Dialogue", in: Paul Puthanangady, S.D.B. (ed.), *Church in India: Institution or Movement?,* op. cit., p. 127.

[4] Cf. the Patna Workshop Report no. III-3 on "Dialogue with Hindus and Other Religions of India", in: *Light and Life We Seek to Share,* op. cit., p. 325.

where there is no attempt of reducing the one to the other or considering the one as a preparation or accessory to the other. It is just like two individuals meeting in their individuality, integrity and openness. God is an ineffable mystery; and the other religion, like other person, is a revelation to be admired than something to be intellectually grasped by abstraction or controlled by categories and concepts that one has formed. The other is then considered as an unveiling of another truth-dimension of *reality* which one cannot comprehend in its totality. One would like to know more. Hence one holds oneself open to the concrete presence of its being in front of the other. It is in this sense that we speak of dialogue among the religions of the world today.

## 2. Theological Bases of Dialogue

A genuine dialogue will always look for its theology. We can speak of the basis of dialogue at different levels, basing ourselves, mainly, on the life and nature of the trinitarian God and our active participation in it. We proceed to see them in the following points.

### *2.1. The Trinitarian Basis*

The trinitarian basis for dialogue lies in the fact that the Trinity is a community of persons, always in communion and communication, in dialogue. Jesus Christ has revealed to us that God is the triune God -- the Father - the Son - and the Holy Spirit. The three persons in the trinity are in a continuous *communication* and *communion* among themselves and with the world. In other words, there has always been a united will and action of the trinity from the very beginning of the creation of the world by the Father, its salvation through the Son and its sanctification in the Holy Spirit.

Created in the image and likeness of God and called to participate in the divine life, our life on earth ought to be a reflection of the unity of the trinity, that is, a "dialogical" life -- a life in communion, communication, peace and salvation among the religions of the world.[5]

---

[5] Cf. DSA, *Approaches,* op. cit., pp. 25-29.

### *2.1.1. God's continuous divine-human dialogue through Christ in the Spirit: Will and action*

We derive from the theology of creation and its consummation that God is in constant dialogue with the world. The Pauline theology of Christocentric creation and consummation (cf. Col. 1:15-20; Eph. 1:9-10; etc.) and the Johannine testimony of the Word (*śabda*) "become flesh" (Jn. 1:14) confirm to the fact that God is now visibly and fully speaking or dialoguing with the world through Christ and his Spirit.

#### *2.1.1.1. The Father's universal salvific will*

God wills the salvation of everyone, every religion, culture and community. He "desires everyone to be saved and to come to the knowledge of truth" (1 Tim. 2:4). The truth is this: that there is one God, and there is one mediator who brings God and mankind together in the fullness of relationship, Christ Jesus, the Word become flesh at the fullness of time, who lived and died and rose again to redeem every human being of any religious tradition or society (cf. 1 Tim. 2:5-6; *AG* 3; *LG* 16).

God's will is at one and the same time action, for God is Act, Will and Person at one and the same time. He has been saving humanity from the very beginning of the world. The Holy Spirit has been "hovering over the waters", that is, hovering over the world to give it life and liberation in accordance with the divine will (cf. Gen.1:1-2). In and through the mystery of the God-man, Christ Jesus has become the centre, the means of grace and the fulfillment of all divine intention and action. He has become *the* mediator between God and humankind, to unite and save the whole of humanity. Before his incarnation he was the Word, in his life on earth he was the God-man and in his death and resurrection he became the Lord, the "life-giving spirit" (1 Cor. 15:45). At the fullness of time, the universal salvific will of God has become visibilized in its fullness, in the mystery of the God-man, Jesus Christ. Christ now continues his saving mission among all people and religions through the Church, led and animated by his Spirit. The Spirit has been especially given to the Church which is the mystical body of Christ on earth. The Church has been empowered by the Spirit of Christ to continue the will and action of God in Christ on earth till his parousia. Here we see the eschatological dimension of the completion of God's will in Christ among all peoples and religions of the world. The Church, therefore, cannot but relate herself to other religions to realize the will of God on earth; and this she does best in dialogue with the world and its religions.

This is, in short, what we mean by God's salvific-intentional basis of dialogue.

*2.1.1.2. Christological basis*

Dialogue between God and human beings which started from the very beginning of human history (cf. *DV* 3) has become visible and tangible in the incarnation of the Word in Jesus. In Jesus "the divine-human dialogue is fully revealed. He is dialogue in flesh."[6] By becoming human, the Word "has in a certain way united himself with each man" (*GS* 22); in and through him, God has "reconciled us to himself and to one another" (ibid.). The creation of the universe and its salvation in and through Christ form the basis of the unity and destiny of all peoples and religions. Our God is the God of life, love and truth, unity and community. Jesus in his person is the complete breakthrough of this reality. In his 'birth' all peoples and religions are included, for he was born for all (cf. Lk. 1:33; 2:30-32), and in his 'death' none is excluded, for he died for all (cf. 2 Cor. 5:14-15).

The subordination of creation, which is longing for its liberation (cf. Rom. 8:19-22), to Christ constitutes the theological foundation of his expectation, return and redemption. In the depth of human freedom there is alive an expectation, a hope, a waiting for the full realization of one's being, one's destiny. This hope of humanity has been fulfilled in the mystery of Jesus Christ. How? The longing of humanity for the coming of Christ, the Messiah, has been fulfilled in the incarnation of the Word in the person of Jesus Christ; and in his resurrection, the realization of the future hope, the "finality", of humanity has been established. Though the decisive event for the actualization of the future is already fulfilled in the resurrection of Jesus who has assumed all humanity and its religions in his incarnation, what is needed on the part of humanity and religions for their eschatological fulfillment of God's salvific mystery in Jesus Christ, is the appropriation of this salvific mystery in history, that is, their participation in the fullness of God's grace and truth in Christ (cf. Jn. 1:14). In this,

---

[6] CBCI Commission for Dialogue and Ecumenism, *Guidelines for Inter-Religious Dialogue*, CBCI Centre, New Delhi, 1989 (2nd revised edition), no. 28. Henceforth this work will be cited as *Guidelines for Inter-Religious Dialogue* (1989).

humanity is not left alone; God, in his Spirit, is constantly present and active in the world, in all religions. The historical phenomenology of religions testifies to the fact of how God is constantly committed to the world and humanity, constituting the mystery of the Jesus Christ event as the fulfillment of all hope.[7]

As sharers in the mission of Christ (cf. Jn. 20:21), the Church is sent forth to gather and unite all peoples and religions in the unity and peace of God's kingdom (cf. Jn. 11:52; Matt. 12:30; Lk. 11:34; *Communio et Progressio* 122). She has been sent forth to recognize the mystery of Christ's presence and his workings in them,[8] cooperate with them and gather them all to the one paternity of God through Christ (cf. *GS* 22). The Church is the people of God from all peoples.[9] She is called to further this divine-human dialogue of God in Christ among all peoples and religions. One way of doing this is through dialogue with them. This is the Christological basis for dialogue.

*2.1.1.3. The pneumatological basis: The Spirit, the principal agent and the meeting ground*

The pneumatological basis for dialogue is: (i) the all-pervading presence and action of the Spirit of God in the whole of creation and in the religions of the world (cf. Gen. 1:3; Jn. 3:8; 1 Cor. 2:10-11; Ps. 104:30; *GS* 22), as it were, the Spirit making the religions his home;[10] and (ii) the promise of Jesus that the Spirit will guide all people and religions "into all the truth" (Jn. 16:13). Hence the Church is called to recognize the presence and activity of the Spirit in others, listen to him in her common seeking with other religions after the fullness of truth and life in dialogue and collaboration.[11]

---

[7] See the centrality of Christ in the history of salvation in chapter three.

[8] Christ is present and active in other religions. For whatever truth and justice, goodness and grace are found in other religions are from God, dispensed through Christ who is the fullness of God's grace and truth (cf. Jn. 1:14). See this point already dealt in earlier chapters.

[9] Cf. DSA, *Approaches,* op. cit., p. 33. Cf. also: M. Dhavamony, "The Christian theology of interreligious Dialogue", in: *Studia Missionalia,* vol. 43, op. cit., pp. 67-75.

[10] Cf. R. Antoine, "Dialogue", in: *All India Seminar: Church in India Today, Bangalore, 1969* (Catholic Bishops' Conference of India), CBCI Centre, New Delhi, n.d., p. 107.

[11] Cf. DSA, *Approaches,* op. cit., pp. 28-29.

The all-pervading presence of Christ and his Spirit implies that truth can be better perceived in relation with others rather than in isolation. It signifies a truth "together with", not a truth "against" one another. Truth is one and the same. It is a universal truth -- the truth of God as revealed and lived by Jesus Christ; it is for Christians as well as for others. Dialogue, then, becomes a means of *seeking* after truth and *sharing* it with others.[12]

The Spirit is constantly at work in building the body of Christ on earth, the "Church", the new people of God who follow the Spirit of Christ, and so belong to the kingdom proclaimed by Christ. The Holy Spirit is ever present and active in the world beyond the visible frontiers of the Church. But this activity is related to Christ because of the mystery of the trinity and to the Church because of her special relation to Christ. The Church is the sacrament of Christ and his salvation for the world.

Since the Holy Spirit, "who fills the whole earth" (*GS* 11) and "who with wondrous providence directs the course of time and renews the face of the earth" (*GS* 26), is present and active in other religions and is working for the unity and completion of creation, history and religions, he becomes the common ground of inter-religious meeting and dialogue.[13] We must first remember that the principal agent of inter-religious dialogue is the Spirit of God who animates the partners. The Spirit is at work on both sides, the Christian and the other. Thus, dialogue cannot be a monologue. The Christian partner, then, will not only give but receive as well. The "fullness" of revelation in Jesus Christ does not dispense Christians from listening to others. Christians do not have the monopoly of the Spirit. They must rather allow themselves to be possessed by the Spirit, who will teach them the fullness of truth in Christ. Indeed, the other partners or interlocutors in dialogue, even without having heard of God's revelation in Jesus Christ, may be more deeply submitted to this truth because the Spirit of Christ has been working and spreading the rays of truth in them (cf. *NA* 2). One can, then, in all sincerity say that in dialogue Christians and others walk together towards truth.

In listening and witnessing to the Spirit, the Church has to recognize the voice of the Spirit present and active in others and collaborate with

---

[12] Cf. ibid., p. 44. DSA refers to Bede Griffiths and Swami Abhishiktananda.

[13] Cf. DSA, *Destinée,* op. cit., pp. 308, 319ff.; also: Id. (ed.), *Evangelization of the Modern World,* op. cit., p. 100.

them in saying and doing what it implies in calling God -- "*Our* Father" (*AG* 7). A genuine dialogue, then, will call for the communion of the Holy Spirit among the religions of the world, and their "listening" to him in communion will comply them for collaboration among themselves in realizing the kingdom of God on earth. In the communion of the Spirit the religions of the world have to, first, recognize the Spirit in others, and, secondly, in dialogue, give and receive part of that reality which is God's gift, that is, his Spirit, in all of them. This mutual giving and receiving has within it the essential life of communion of all people and religions with God and with one another. Such a communion through dialogue has its source in the basic covenantal relationship with all humankind in Adam (cf. Gen. 1:26-27).

When seen in the perspective of this basic theandric covenant of God with all humankind in Adam, all distancing and dividing elements, prejudices and antagonism among different races and religions of the world are resolved through dialogue that leads them to mutual understanding and collaboration. This basic covenantal relationship of God with all humankind has been broken by Adam. He has sinned, failed and fallen (cf. Gen. 3). But God in his love and mercy has never left man in his sinfulness; he has renewed the covenant all through the history of humankind (cf. Heb. 1:1) and, in the "fullness of time" (Gal. 4:4), established an unbreakable covenant in Jesus Christ, his Son (cf. Heb. 1:1-3). This is the salvation history accomplished in Jesus Christ. Thus, different religions, different "covenants", "revelations" and "responses", of the world today are not to be considered as mutually exclusive, but they are to be led to Christ who is the fullness of truth and revelation and through Christ to their unity in God.[14]

Just as Christ who searched the hearts of men and by a truly human dialogue led them to the divine light, so also the Church, profoundly penetrated by the Spirit of Christ, should know the people among whom she lives and should establish contact with them in sincere dialogue and collaboration (cf. *AG* 11).[15]

---

[14] Cf. DSA, *Approaches,* op. cit., p. 33.

[15] Cf. ibid., p. 28.

### *2.1.2. The Church and the kingdom-call basis*

The kingdom-call basis and orientation of dialogue is centered in Christ.[16] Christ has proclaimed the kingdom of God to all; he calls all peoples and religions to this kingdom. It is a universal kingdom. The kingdom of God is not an abstract notion but a reality to which all are called. Jesus in his person is the complete breakthrough of this kingdom.

Christian revelation holds that God is tri-une -- Father, Son, Spirit -- three persons in one Godhead. The kingdom of God is, therefore, the kingdom of the Father, the Son and the Spirit. The person of Christ Jesus cannot be excluded from the kingdom of God. Christ will bring this kingdom to its eschatological completion and hand it over to the Father at the end of time (cf. 1 Cor. 15:27-28).

The Church is the sacrament of Christ and the sacrament of the kingdom on earth. She is sent in the world not to condemn others but to call them to the kingdom and communion in Christ.[17] Dialogue is a step towards the kingdom.[18] The Church is in the world and for the world to continue the saving plan of God in Christ till all things and all religions are subjected to Christ. Then, Christ himself "will also be subjected to the one who put all things in subjection under him, so that God may be all in all" (1 Cor. 15:28). Till then, and because of this, religions are called to continue their double-directed dialogue: (i) horizontally or horizontal dialogue among religions themselves in their common seeking after truth, mutual sharing and mutual growth, and (ii) vertically or vertical dialogue between God and religions, both individually and collectively.[19]

### *2.2. God's Christocentric Dialogue and the Dialoguing Church*

The Church has been constituted and commissioned by Christ to continue his universal gathering mission of all peoples and religions in God. She is the salvific instrument of Christ's continuing dialogue for the reunion of the entire humanity with God. Therefore the Church, as the body of Christ on earth (cf. Eph. 1:23), must play an important and active

---

[16] Cf. DSA, *Gospel and Culture,* op. cit., pp. 46-47.

[17] Cf. DSA, *Theology of 'Indirect Evangelization',* op. cit., p. 10; id., *Theology of Evangelization,* op. cit., p. 12.

[18] Cf. *Guidelines for Inter-Religious Dialogue* (1989), no. 28.

[19] Cf. DSA, *Approaches,* op. cit., pp. 25-29.

role to gather all things under the rule of Christ, the head, "the fullness of him who fills all in all" (Eph. 1:23). For this the Church, under the guidance of the Holy Spirit, has to find her own ways and means to carry out this "dialoguing" mission amidst different religious traditions and cultures of the world. Paul's "dialogue" with the pagans in Athens (cf. Acts 17:22-31) could be seen as an example of how and why the Church should be involved in inter-religious dialogue with other religions.[20] God is one; he is the God of love, truth and communion -- communion of all religions with God and with one another. This is the basis of the Church's dialogue with other religions.

In searching for more effective methods of evangelization, writing in 1964, Amalor held that the Church in India had failed in her missionary work because of insufficient inculturation and an almost total lack of dialogue with Hindus or Hinduism, and so proposed dialogue as a new method of missionary approach.[21]

In the thirteenth chapter of *Destinée* Amalor first remarks the general negative attitude of the Indian Church leaders towards other religions in general and dialogue with them in particular.[22] Even after India's independence (1947), dialogue with other religions did not begin until the wake of Vatican II. However, Amalor does not fail to note here that some sort of dialogue with Hinduism in the Indian soil, though unofficially and on an individual model or life style, had started already four and a half centuries earlier. The name of the famous Italian Jesuit missionary, Robert de Nobili, deserves special attention. During the first half of the seventeenth

---

[20] Cf. John J. Kilgallen, "Acts 17, 22-31: An example of interreligious Dialogue", in: *Studia Missionalia,* vol. 43, op. cit., pp. 43-60.

[21] Cf. DSA, *Destinée,* op. cit., pp. 141, 231; cf. also: Jose Kuttianimattathil, S.D.B., *Practice and Theology of Interreligious Dialogue,* op. cit., pp. 31-32.

[22] See: DSA, *Destinée,* op. cit.: chapter 13, pp. 274-286, in which DSA mentions the report of Mgr. O. Sevrin (Ranchi) and Mgr. Bouter (Nellore) on indigenization, Indian culture and the foreign appearance and outlook of the Indian Church to the CBCI in 1946. Mgr. Bouter presented another report on the link between evangelization and adaptation in 1951, in which he wrote that in spite of the so many directives of the Holy See the Church in India did not seem eager to study Indian culture and give up its foreign appearance. However, in 1953 there was a commission on Indian Christian art and a few Catholics took up Indian architecture, painting, music, dance, etc. in the Church's life and expressions. After the Council Cardinal Gracias took the initiative to organize a meeting (24-26 April 1966) of rectors and professors of major seminaries and scholasticates, where directives were evolved for a progressive indigenization of priestly formation.

century he lived for years in India (1605-1656) as a Brāhmin *sannyāsi* and was highly respected also by high caste Hindus. Amalor mainly looks at the last twenty years that show him that the providential hour of dialogue with Hinduism has now come; what his predecessors often sowed in tears can now be harvested. The climate has really changed; dialogue should neither be considered an empty dream nor a deviation from Catholic orthodoxy.[23]

Besides some sporadic and individual attempts, dialogue on an organized level with other religions in India, in particular with Hinduism, had already started at the wake of Vatican II.[24] In the 1960s there were several colloquia, seminars and symposia on various aspects of Hinduism and the way they might contribute to the enrichment of Christianity, the fullness of Christ. Especially the three ecumenical colloquia (Almora 1961, Rajpur 1962, Nagpur 1964) organized by Dr. Cuttat, the then Swiss ambassador in India, are well known. These colloquia were blended with both theological and practical nature. Their outcome and fundamental message to the world was: "Hinduism represents ... one of the most important religious pedagogies (in the Pauline meaning) of humankind and hence that, if we take this as an historical fact, it must have a place in the economy of salvation."[25]

We may distinguish three stages in the dialogue with Hinduism at this time:[26] (i) studies on Hinduism made by both Catholics and Protestants,

---

[23] Cf. ibid.

[24] Cf. ibid., pp. 287-288, where to substantiate his statement that dialogue, in particular with Hinduism, had already started at the wake of Vatican II, DSA first mentions the special supplement on dialogue and related subjects appearing in *The Clergy Monthly* (today it is called *Vidyajyoti*) from 1952, *Indian Ecclesiastical Studies* from 1962, and a correspondence course on Hinduism from July 1957 till June 1959, published in bookform in 1963. DSA also mentions several Protestant initiatives, such as the foundation of *The Christian Institute for the Study of Religion and Society*, Bangalore; the 4th meeting of the *Indian Christian Theological Conference;* the foundation of *The Indian Christian Theological Association* with as special purpose the study of Christian theology in the Indian context. The *Indian Journal of Dharma* was also to focus on this topic.

[25] Ibid., p. 288: "L'hindouisme représente ... un de plus importants pédagogues (au sens paulinien) religieux de l'humanité et que, donc, pris comme un fait historique, il doit avoir un sens dans l'economie du salut universel." (For translation see: Gerwin van Leeuwen, O.F.M., *Fully Indian - Authentically Christian*, op. cit., p. 271).

[26] Cf. ibid., p. 289.

but separately, (ii) ecumenical studies on Hinduism, made by Catholics and Protestants together, (iii) ecumenical dialogue with Hindus, where Catholics, Protestants as well as Orthodox took part. There was a modest encounter between Protestants and Hindus in Nagpur in 1960, but the first meeting on a broad basis took place in Kerala, where the initiative was taken by Jacobites in 1962. Such move towards dialogue was greatly encouraged by John XXIII, whom Amalor called "the apostle of dialogue with extended hand",[27] and by Vatican II that encouraged the pioneers and confirmed the orthodoxy of their efforts. Paul VI followed the initiative of his predecessor. He established the Secretariat for Non-Christian Religions;[28] and when he came to India at the occasion of the Eucharistic Congress in Bombay (1964), he created a great interest and welcome among Hindu circles. He touched the soul of India with his *namaste* (a very cordial Indian gesture of greeting), his humble visits to the sick and the poor, his appreciative speaking of the true values of the Indian culture by evoking the happy memory of M. Gandhi and quoting the texts from the Upaniṣads on the occasion of his talks and prayers with the members of other religions in his fervent plea for peace. Thus he put into practice what he taught in his encyclical *Ecclesiam Suam* (1964), that is, dialogue is a means to exercise one's apostolic mission, the art of spiritual communion.[29]

Basing himself on the above encyclical and the Pope's praxis in Bombay, Amalor distinguishes the following steps that are to be taken in any dialogue: common human concern, mutual recognition and fraternal love.[30]

### *2.2.1. A true concern for the human: Common language*

The first step in dialogue should be the concern for the human, for all that concerns the quality of human life in this world. All the religions of the world speak a common language, in so as far their ultimate concern and destiny is one and the same, that is, their common search for truth or God and their common concern for the human, namely, salvation.

---

[27] Ibid.: "l'apôtre du dialogue e de la main tendue." (Translation mine).

[28] Today known as Pontifical Council for Interreligious Dialogue.

[29] Cf. DSA, *Destinée*, op. cit., p. 291.

[30] Cf. ibid., pp. 292-293.

This point was well perceived when, on the 3rd of December 1964, the Pope told the representatives of other religions in Bombay that all must begin to work together to build the common future of humankind.

### *2.2.2. Respect and recognition of others as "persons"*

The second step in dialogue is the respectful recognition of the spiritual and moral values in other religions. Dialogue recognizes and respects the partners as persons, with their respective characters and convictions, different from one's own. When one recognizes the partner as the "other", as a "person", one recognizes and respects the "otherness" of the partner, the partners are mutually recognized and treated as "equals".

The partners in dialogue must be treated as equals, not in the sense that all religions are equally true or false or equally good or bad; not in the sense that partners are equally good in character and personality, or they have equally the same grasp of truth and hold the same religious tenets; not in the sense that they adhere to the equally valid essence of what religions mean in human experience and life. If it is so then it would lead to the "equality" of religions and, thereby, destroy the "otherness" of the other and will not recognize the different stages of God's revelation and various human responses to it in different times, cultures and communities in history; it will devalue the all fulfilling and central place of Jesus Christ in the history of salvation. Treating the partners in dialogue as equals means that the partners are capable of contributing to and benefitting from the dialogue: give and take and grow together. It means that other religions are genuinely authentic religions, in search of God and salvation and not a bundle of misguided superstitions or errors or work of the devil.[31] In a genuine dialogue there is no forced conversion, no "dissolution" or "merging" of the other into mine or vice versa, no eclecticism nor syncretism; there is no confrontation, but a communion in their common seeking after truth and sharing of it, journeying towards their common destiny in mutual engagement, understanding and enrichment.[32]

---

[31] See DSA's mind on the point of the "equality" of revelations and religions dealt in detail in the previous chapters, especially, chapters one and two. For this point see also: M. Dhavamony, "The Christian theology of interreligious Dialogue", in: *Studia Missionalia,* vol. 43, op. cit., pp. 62-63.

[32] Cf. DSA, *Approaches,* op cit., p. 44.

*2.2.3. The spirit of dialogue: Fraternal love*

The most important in a dialogue, Amalor considers, is the spirit in which a dialogue is conducted. The encyclical *Ecclesiam Suam* mentions four essential characteristics of dialogue: clarity, amiability, trust, and prudence. But all these characters have a common basis: fraternal love.[33] The encyclical reads: "We must approach one another with our hearts, in mutual understanding, respect and love."[34] The Pope said in Bombay:

> We should not meet one another as simple tourists, but as pilgrims searching for God, not in buildings of stone, but in the hearts of men. This mutual love will animate all our efforts, will unite us with an invisible and indestructible bond with all those who have been gathered in the love of God, and will make us his children, one family.[35]

This does not mean that the Pope was blind or indifferent regarding the various religious expressions as if they were all equal and the same. On the contrary, one must see the reality of religious pluralism in the providence of God and share one's religious experience and convictions with others in the spirit of fraternal love. It is in this spirit of fraternal love that the sharing of one's religious convictions in dialogue becomes meaningful and effective. Amalor considers the spirit of dialogue, that is, the fraternal love, as already a great result of the dialogue.

While reading this important chapter thirteen of his book, *Destinée,* we already grasp the mind of Amalor on the subject. At the very inceptions of the Church's deliberations with dialogue at the time of Vatican II, what seemed concerning most to Amalor in this regard was to establish the *raison d'être* of dialogue and to put his convictions in practice in India. He justifies the initiative and move of the Indian Church towards dialogue,

---

[33] See: DSA, *Destinée,* op. cit., p. 292.

[34] See: Quoted by DSA in: Ibid.: "Nous devons nous rapprocher avec nos cœurs, dans la compréhension mutuelle, l'estime et l'amour." (Translation mine).

[35] See quoted in: Ibid., p. 293: "Nous ne devons pas nous rencontrer comme de simples touristes, mais comme des pèlerins qui vont chercher Dieu, non dans des édifices de pierre, mais dans les cœurs des hommes. C'est cet amour mutuel qui animera tous nos efforts, nous unira par un lien invisible et indestructible à tous ceux qui sont rassemblés dans l'amour di Dieu et fera de nous ses enfants, une seule famille." (For translation see: Gerwin van Leeuwen, O.F.M., *Fully Indian - Authentically Christian,* op. cit., p. 272).

started at some level or other even before the final form of Vatican II. In the conclusion of the chapter, he writes:

> Moreover we should not forget that during the last twenty years a small group of priests in India have been engaged in a dialogue with Hinduism. Up to now they have only received warnings from the Church authorities; they have been victims of suspicion and misunderstanding and were looked upon by the Indian clergy as being 'in the margin of the Church'. All of a sudden the Pope has now put them wholly in the bosom of the Church; he has made the approach and attitude tried by this small group his own. The following fact is symbolic in this connection: a colloquium or seminar on the relation between Christian revelation and the religions of the world did take place from 25-28 November 1964 'in the margin of the Congress', and the Pope has transferred, through what he did in Bombay, this colloquium from 'the margin of the Congress' to the very bosom of the Congress. In our eyes this is a prophetic gesture; that is 'the historical event' about which several Indian newspapers spoke, although they have given it a totally different meaning.[36]

## 3. Conditions for Dialogue

For dialogue to be genuine, effective and permanent, certain preliminary conditions are to be taken into consideration. These are: transparency

[36] See: Ibid., p. 294: "N'oublions pas non plus que, depuis une vingtaine d'années, une petite élite de prêtres en Ind se sont engangés dans un dialogue avec l'hindouisme. Jusqu'ici, ils n'ont reçu de la part des autorités de l'Eglise que des avertissements; ils ont été victimes de soupçons et d'incompréhension et considérés par le clergé indien comme étant 'en marge de l'Eglise'. Or, le Pape les a, tout d'un coup, situés en plein milieu de l'Eglise; il a fait siennes l'attitude et l'approche tentées par ce petit nombre. Le fait suivant est, à cet égard, symbolique: un colloque ou un 'seminaire' sur le rapport entre la Révélation chrétienne et 'les religions du monde' a eu lieu du 25 au 28 novembre 1964, en 'marge du Congrès', et le Pape, par son geste de Bombay, a transféré ce colloque de 'la marge du Congrès' au sein même du Congrès. C'est, a notre avis, un geste prophétique et c'est là 'l'événement historique' dont parlaient plusieurs journaux indiens, bien qu'ils l'aient interprété dans un tout autre sens." (For translation see: Gerwin van Leeuwen, O.F.M., *Fully Indian - Authentically Christian,* op. cit., p. 272).

of *leitmotiv,* openness to the other and openness to truth.[37]

### *3.1. Transparency of Leitmotiv: Fullness of Truth and Life*

The nature of dialogue may differ according to its goal that one follows. Clarity about the goal, therefore, is very much asked for in any dialogue. Dialogue should be free from selfish motives or arrogance. There are no hidden motives or attached strings in dialogue. The goal must be clear, beyond confusion, confrontation and suspicion.

One may easily fall prey to suspicion and exclusion and, thus, impede the process of dialogue. A Hindu or a Buddhist may easily suspect the motive of the Christian or the Muslim, and he/she may be reasonable in doing so. The fact of the centuries of colonial and conquering missionary approach by Christianity, or jihadic approach by Islam in the world in general and India in particular, is not easily forgotten by Hindus and others. The taint of "holy" war and bloodshed cannot be easily wiped out from the minds and hearts of the people. Establishing the clarity of goal or intention, therefore, becomes very important in dialogue.

On the one hand, even after the rightful recognition of dialogue by Vatican II and constant encouragement by the teaching of the Church today, many priests, bishops, religious and lay people still cast a negative attitude to dialogue and would prefer to withdraw from it with the fear of "losing" their Christian identity. Others would like to dialogue with members of other religions on the basis of superiority or inferiority. On the other hand, some members of other religions would aim at a rather vague but universal humanism; while others may try to discover some common moral principles, a universal morality beyond all dogma, ritual and social customs, and from there to come to a 'universal religion'. Radhakrishnan was a great advocate of such a universal religion of the spirit.

Amalor goes beyond all this.[38] He aims at an assumption, an integration or communion of all in Christ -- unity of all people and religions in God through Christ. The understanding of dialogue must be situated in the heart of the mystery of the redemptive incarnation of Christ and the

---

[37] Cf. ibid., pp. 295-301.

[38] Cf. Gerwin van Leeuwen, O.F.M., *Fully Indian - Authentically Christian,* op. cit., p. 273.

catholicity of the Church. It is because Christ has come to recapitulate everything, save everything and take everything -- things, people, religions and ideologies -- along to the final completion in the unity and the fullness of truth and life in God. Christ has come to unite and save not only people, but also all that is human and all that is religious. All the religions of the world are recapitulated in and through Christ.

Christ has saved all and hence the Church has to unite and save all -- not only individual Hindus, but also Hinduism; not only Hinduism but all the religions of the world: Buddhism, Jainism, Sikhism, Sarna, etc.; not only religions and all that is religious but also ideologies, like Communism or Socialism, *dalit* movements, etc., in fact, all that is human. This is the point of departure. The real "dialogical" concern is that of the real Christic concern, that is, the concern for the human being in his/her totality. Thus, "the object of dialogue may be human problems and situations, values and aspirations whether human, religious of Christian. All the three are important, one leading to another."[39]

Dialogue, therefore, concerns itself to the common search of religions for answers to the basic questions of human life and the need to struggle and work together in collaboration and human solidarity, to build a society worthy of human beings, worthy of the kingdom of God that Christ came to established on earth. This is the Church's *leitmotiv* of dialogue. This is the first condition for a successful dialogue, that always calls for the transparency or clarity about its goal.[40]

### *3.2. Openness to the Other: Knowing the Partner and Mutual Respect*

Referring to the Declaration of the Nagpur Theological Conference, Amalor writes: "The basic condition for a genuine dialogue is a spirit of openness and humility and willingness to learn from one another" (cf. no. 25).[41] One of the important factors that determines the quality and effect of inter-religious dialogue is the way the partners perceive each other. That is to say, a true dialogue cannot take place between strangers, not to

---

[39] DSA, *Approaches,* op. cit., p. 28. DSA likes to see the human life it its totality. For him to be concerned about human issues will mean at one and the same time to be concerned about all that is religious and Christian. To be Christian or "religious" is to be human.

[40] Cf. DSA, *Destinée,* op. cit., pp. 295-296.

[41] DSA, "Approach", *op. cit.,* p. 54.

say between enemies. The second important condition for dialogue would, therefore, be that one knows one's partner.

Knowing one's partner implies also knowing oneself, a deeper self-understanding of oneself, one's faith and one's point of view. The question may arise here on the part of the Christian partner, that if he/she possesses the fullness of truth, that is, Christ, how can he/she be a searcher of truth together with the partner from other religion? We would like to answer this mainly on two counts. *Firstly,* Christ is the universal saviour. He is the fullness of God's grace and truth. He is the truth himself (cf. Jn. 14:6). But the experiences of Christ-mystery is not exhausted by Christians alone and their living of the Christian life is not exclusive of others, segregated, but admits communion; it is incomplete and admits progress. The saving mystery of God extends to all and is experienced by all in different ways and expressions. *Secondly,* the "possession", the treasure (Matt. 13:44-45; Col. 2:3), that is, the truth of God, which the Christian has in Christ, is not for his/her sake alone; it is a talent to be used and shared with others (cf. Matt. 25:14-30). A committed Christian, then, cannot but share his/her faith in God and listen to that of the other; he/she cannot but relate himself/herself with the other. This is dialogue (cf. *DH* 3). It is not, however, an enterprise leading to syncretism, eclecticism or fanaticism. It is a "joint venture" of the religions to involve themselves in common concern of seeking and living the truth in the fundamental human concerns of life and death, peace and freedom (cf. *NA* 3).

In dialogue the partners meet each other, as we have seen above, as two different "persons" with their specific religious experience and distinctness, and the effort in dialogue towards uniformity at the cost of diversity is to ignore the other as a person, is to ignore the reality of the other. That can lead only to impoverishment. The other individual or community is often easily and perhaps falsely blamed, or seen as a threat to oneself and killed (cf. Abel in Gen. 4:1-16), or considered as untouchable (cf. Samaritans in Jn. 4:1-30) and condemned as dogs (cf. Gentiles in Mk. 7:27-28). In our own century people of other religions have been considered, especially in the pre-Conciliar period or still today by many, as living in ignorance and sitting in the shadow of death; and their religions as mere human creations, incapable of mediating a relationship with God. With this attitude the 'otherness' of the other is ignored, the common origin and end of all, which is the same God, is not accepted, and, thus, a genuine dialogue is impeded or rendered impossible.

Openness to the other and mutual trust are not based on holding only identical or similar views, nor does it mean the suppression of differences. It is based on commonality in diversity. Dialogue does not suppose only common elements between partners but also takes into account the differences that exist in different religions. It is not a false irenism; neither is it tolerance, refutation, dictating nor self-justification. It is rather self-explanation, listening and learning from others, in mutual openness to the Spirit of God and to one another and to the whole human concern in walking together towards the fullness of truth and life (cf. *DV* 10).

Dialogue, then, has the deepest respect for the 'other'. It does not reduce the other to one's own categories. That will be an epistemological naïveté and ethical impropriety. In dialogue one respects the view of the other and welcomes his/her expressions of faith. This is often not easy, since one may tend to interpose one's ideas on the other and unconsciously stop oneself from listening to the other. True dialogue, then, is a meeting or an encounter of two or more persons with differing views, the primary purpose of which is, for each participant, to learn from the other in mutual openness towards the other, in mutual sharing and enrichment. Dialogue always originates from a sincere and insatiable desire to know the truth more and more. It is, on the part of the Christian partner, to see and recognize the Spirit already operative in others and collaborate with them who are already in search of truth and in collaboration with the Spirit.[42]

Knowing the partner will also imply knowing his or her concrete situation, the real problems and relevant issues. Dialogue is not something abstract, theoretical or bookish. It should be concrete, practical and vital.[43] Dialogue should be on the level of our present situation; it should be existential. For example, when we dialogue with Hinduism, we must know what kind of Hinduism we are dialoguing with. Hinduism is a living movement, constantly in motion, integrating and re-interpreting, rejecting and assimilating, orthodox and modern, philosophical and popular, idealist and realist. We cannot decide with what Hinduism we should start our dialogue, but we should be aware that our partner is a complex person, who is facing a "crisis", a crisis that began at the end of the eighteenth century between the two main groups in Hinduism: (i) those who stress that in spite of all appearances India remains faithful to its spiritual values.

---

[42] Cf. DSA, *Approaches,* op. cit., p. 35.

[43] Cf. ibid., pp. 28-29.

On this level, the suitable topics of dialogue with them would be, for example, the Indian monastic tradition and mysticism; (ii) those with the Westernization and materialistic bend who consider traditional Hindu spirituality as something of the past. Given the case, dialogue should take place not on the core of the vedic religion, but on the melting-point of modern day-to-day life. In other words, it calls for a synthesis of the spiritual and the material. Dialogue will also concern itself with nation-building. The kingdom of God and its realization through inter-religious collaboration will then be the symbol of dialogue, unity and peace, the valuable meeting-point between Christians and Hindus.

Amalor does not consider these two trends in Hinduism as mutually exclusive, but complementary and compatible. It is not an 'either-or', but an 'and-and'. This, he claims, is the sensible opinion of all those who are engaged in an actual dialogue with Hinduism.[44]

### *3.3. Openness to Truth: One God, Many Religions: God, the Converging Point*

Once we know our partner and respect him/her as a person, the next point, on the same line, that would determine the success of a dialogue is to know whether he/she is open for dialogue, and to what level and why? Again we take the example of Hinduism. We ask the question: Is Hinduism open and capable of participating in a dialogue? The answer is both 'yes' and 'no'.

When dialogue is seen as engaging the religions, on the basis of equality, towards a "convergence" of religions in the common search for truth or God, or in a convergence of universal religion or moral system, Hinduism is probably the best partner for dialogue. What we call the 'parliament of religions'[45] is an idea in Hinduism cherished from Akbar and Vivekananda to Tagore and Radhakrishnan.

But the 'no' to dialogue in Hinduism is equally true. Hinduism will not agree to a dialogue as soon as it perceives a superiority or an "over-stepping" attitude in the partner. If the Church pretends to claim to have a monopoly of truth about God, that is, an *exclusive* revelation and

---

[44] Cf. DSA, *Destinée*, op. cit., pp. 298-299. In his footnotes on p. 299, DSA quotes from R. Antoine, J. Neuner, and S. Siauve. Cf. also: Gerwin van Leeuwen, O.F.M., *Fully Indian - Authentically Christian*, op. cit., p. 273.

[45] "Parlement des religions". See: DSA, *Destinée*, op. cit., pp. 299-300.

experience of God in Christ, to designate herself as the only and exclusive means of salvation and, thus, to put her on the throne, though the throne is of Christ, not of the Church, then Christianity becomes a scandal. Then it appears to the other as irrelevant and unwanted and is ranked as an inferior religion whose main concern is "conversion" to Christianity, not to God and his kingdom. Then the dialogue is ruptured and we fall back into a polite hostility and suspicion or "peaceful coexistence", that is, passive coexistence or tolerance. This is the crux of the problem, a major obstacle to dialogue with Hinduism.

Amalor says that the only meeting-point of a true inter-religious dialogue is *God,* and it is *in* God (cf. *NA* 1). "The only point of encounter, of convergence for a true dialogue is in God, when [all] the paths meet at the top of the mountain; till that point there will only be parallels,[46] a coexistence, perhaps at most an inter-existence (mutual interest)."[47] In this quotation we see Amalor hinting at the eschatological convergence of religions in God. Unless the religions are viewed from the vantage point of the providence of God (cf. *AG* 3) and one and the same God as their source and end, there will be embittering "parallelism"; the dialogue will end up in more obstinacy and exclusion; people will then not be united, but divided in the name of God and religion.

In dialogue religions do not borrow from one another but they all actually borrow form the *common source: God.* Thus, when the Church tries to recognize in others the rays of that light which enlightens all humankind, that is, Christ (cf. *NA* 2), she is not trying to complete the

[46] Here the word "parallel" does not mean 'parallelism' of religions. DSA uses this word here in the context of respect and recognition of other religions, so as not to discard them in our common pilgrimage to God. Not to recognize them as religions would be going against the theology of Vatican II, and his theology of God's providence (chapter four). As we have seen earlier, while DSA, in general, does not like to talk about comparisons among religions, he does not accept 'parallelism' or 'equality' (sameness) of religions. That would, in turn, destroy the differences of particular God-experiences in different religious traditions by different people in different social and cultural settings. It will destroy the 'unique' revelation of God in Christ who is for DSA, as we have seen in chapter one, the supreme and definitive sign or medium of God's revelation, the 'Word become flesh'.

[47] DSA, *Destinée,* op. cit., p. 300: "Le seul point de rencontre, de convergence d'une véritable dialogue est en Dieu, comme les routes se rejoignent au sommet de la montagne; jusque-là il n'y a que des parallèles, qu'une coexistence, peut-être au mieux une inter-existence (s'intéresser l'une à l'autre)." (Translation mine; cf. also Gerwin van Leeuwen, O.F.M., *Fully Indian - Authentically Christian,* op. cit., p. 274).

Christian revelation by borrowing from other religions. What she is trying to do is to continually free her *faith* from the limits of its particular form. There are not many truths but the approaches or paths to truth are diverse and varied. Today the religion of Jesus Christ must invite all religions to seek in dialogue, in and through and yet beyond all religions and religious expressions, the one God of all, the God of truth and life preached by Jesus Christ (cf. Jn. 4:24; 8:32; Mk. 10:30). The most dangerous ideology in the Church today would be to imagine that there is but one way of "knowing" and serving God or only one way of interpreting Christ, one model of being the Church and one way of living and being a Christian. In dialogue with other religions, the Spirit being at the basis, the Christian comes to understand how little he/she knows of God, the world and humanity, and the riches of God's mystery in Christ; and, thus, opens himself/herself to unanticipated experiences of the mystery of God, humanity and the world.[48]

## 4. Different Levels of Inter-Religious Dialogue

After having considered the theological bases and some of the basic conditions of dialogue, we now move on to see the different levels of dialogue. A true dialogue embraces the totality of man's life and worship. It should not be a lop-sided dialogue; it must touch the fundamental questions and concerns of human life. It comprises these levels: external, conceptual, and spiritual (God-experience).[49] The Church should enter into dialogue with others at all these levels, in such a way that people belonging to other religions feel at ease and discover in the Church a completion or fulfillment of their religious life and longing.

---

[48] Cf. Felix Machado, "Dialogue in the Year 2000: From Discussion to Dialogue", in: Paul Puthanangady, S.D.B. (ed.), *Church in India: Institution or Movement?,* op. cit., p. 134.

[49] Cf. DSA, *Destinée,* op. cit., p. 301. Since DSA considers the third level, i.e., the spiritual level or the level of God-experience as the most profound level of inter-religious dialogue, we will focus our attention and dwell more on this level. The first and the second levels will be seen rather briefly.

### *4.1. The Level of the Externals*

The first level that presents itself is that of the externals. This will include, when contextualized in India, the indigenization of the Church's social and cultural life; the insertion of the Church in the existential life and concerns of the society, that is, not only at the level of religious field but also at the level of socio-economic and political spheres; the promotion of an indigenous clergy and their formation; etc.

### *4.2. The Level of the Conceptual Expressions*

The second level is that of the conceptual expression. It is particularly the domain of Indian Christian philosophy and theology, terminology and symbol systems. In this regard Amalor refers, among others, to the attempts of Frs. Monchanin, Dandoy, and Johanns.[50] Quoting Johanns, Amalor writes: "The purpose of the articles *To Christ through Vedanta* ..., is to show that we can reconstruct our Catholic philosophy with material borrowed from vedantic systems."[51] It goes without saying that this is a long way and a great challenge. As early as January 1958 about sixty rectors of twenty-three seminaries and scholasticates noted during a meeting at Bangalore:

> The ultimate question of theological studies in India is not a confrontation, neither with the India of the past nor the India of the present. Christianity is not a system that exists side by side other systems, with which it has to be confronted and compared, but it is the universal completion of the human search for the truth.... The result of our attempt should not be a polemic refutation of other systems, but a richer, deeper and more comprehensive presentation of the Christian faith, a presentation that includes truly, visibly and convincingly the treasures of the Indian tradition; we have neither borrowed nor appropriated them from the outside, but the very contact with the Indian world has enabled us to discover in a fresh and deeper manner,

---

[50] Cf. ibid., pp. 302-308.

[51] Ibid., p. 303: "Le but des articles *Vers le Christ par le Védanta,* ...., c'est de montrer que nous pouvons reconstruire notre philosophie catholique avec les matériaux empruntés aux systèmes *védantiques.*" (For translation see: Gerwin van Leeuwen, O.F.M., *Fully Indian - Authentically Christian,* op. cit., p. 274).

the innumerable riches of God and his revelation in Jesus Christ.[52]

Amalor mentions a number of monographies and articles appearing particularly in *The Clergy Monthly Supplement* and *Indian Ecclesiastical Studies* that are pioneering efforts in the field of the development of an original Indian philosophy and theology. He also relates to what has been said that India will soon have her own St. Augustine and St. Thomas Aquinas.[53] In this regard he quotes Fr. Antoine, a Jesuit missionary, who dared say: "The Church of the West does not have the last word on theology or liturgy and, on its long road to the full stature of Christ, the Church will find precious elements of that fullness in Indian spirituality, theology and art."[54] Inter-religious dialogue is, once again, seen here towards the realization of the mystery of Christ in its fullness. The Holy Spirit is working towards it in different religious traditions, in and through their initiatives and united efforts. Amalor also refers to Fr. Daniélou and Fr. Monchanin who feel that India's special contribution in this regard will be the creation of a definite theology of the Holy Spirit.[55] In this regard Amalor points out to yet another aspect of the missionary activity of the Church, that is, the creation and praxis of the "dialogical theology" in the context of religious pluralism today.[56]

---

[52] Ibid., p. 304: "Le problème final des études théologiques en Inde n'est pas la confrontation, ni avec l'Inde du passé ni avec l'Inde de présent. Le christianisme n'est pas un système à côté des autres, avec lesquels il doit être confronté et comparé, mais il est l'accomplissement universel de la recherche humaine vers la vérité.... Le résultat de nos efforts ne doit pas être la réfutation polémique d'autres systèmes, mais une présentation plus riche, plus profonde et plus compréhensive de la foi chrétienne, une présentation qui inclue vraiment, visiblement et avec conviction les trésors de la tradition indienne, non pas comme si nous les avions empruntés ou si nous nous les étions appropriés du dehors, mais parce que le contact avec le monde indien nous fait prendre conscience, d'une façon nouvelle et plus profonde, des richesses incommensurables de Dieu et de sa révélation en Jésus-Christ." (For translation see: Gerwin van Leeuwen, O.F.M., *Fully Indian - Authentically Christian,* op. cit., p. 274).

[53] Cf. ibid., p. 307.

[54] See quoted in: Ibid., p. 308: "L'Eglise d'Occident n'a pas dit le dernier mot en matière de théologie et de liturgie et, dans son acheminement vers la stature parfaite du Christ, l'Eglise trouvera de précieux éléments de maturité dans la spiritualité, la théologie et l'art indiens." (For translation see: Gerwin van Leeuwen, O.F.M., *Fully Indian - Authentically Indian,* op. cit., p. 274).

[55] Cf. ibid.

[56] Cf. ibid.

### *4.3. The Level of God-Experience*

The third level of dialogue is the level of God-experience. It is the deepest and most intimate level of dialogue in an inter-religious quest for truth. Among the different levels at which an inter-religious dialogue can take place, the level of God-experience occupies the pride of place, constituting as it does "the core or the deepest level of every religion."[57] Any attempt to dialogue without a prior experience of God is apt to smack of arrogance and pretentiousness.[58] When we speak of religious experience or God-experience, we are aware of it that authentic religious experience is not the knowledge of any religious doctrine but the encounter of God revealing himself in time and space, here and now. The inevitable paradoxity implied in the self-communicating process of the divine takes us to the experience of the mystery: the mysterious ways of his self-communication, the inexhaustibility of the same and hence the need of keeping ourselves ever open for further revelations from him. This is true, even if Jesus Christ is accepted as the decisive and definitive revelation of the hidden mystery (cf. Heb. 1:1-4).[59] Our faith commitment to the fact of Jesus does not take away the essential structures of "limitation" associated with any revelation. So we say, God reveals himself always "concealing". Christians and others, therefore, must meet together in dialogue as pilgrims in their common quest for God. Amalor bases his "common pilgrimage" thought on the attitude and encouragement of Paul VI during his pilgrimage to Bombay (1964).[60]

On the level of God-experience and witness, we can distinguish between two main schools or trends in Hinduism, which are, to a certain extent, also found in Christianity. These are: the monistic metaphysics, and the *bhakti* school.[61]

---

[57] DSA, "Sharing Worship. Its Relevance in a Multi-Religious Society and in an Inter-Faith Sharing of Life", in: Paul Puthanangady (ed.), *Sharing Worship. Communicatio in Sacris,* op. cit., p. 47.

[58] Cf. DSA, *Preaching the Gospel Today. Main Problems in Mission Lands,* op. cit., pp. 20-21.

[59] See this point treated in detail in chapter one.

[60] Cf. DSA, *Destinée,* op. cit., p. 310. See this point also mentioned above.

[61] We proceed to see these two trends just in brief. Their detailed explanation would be beyond our scope.

*4.3.1. The monistic metaphysical trend*

This trend is best represented by the advaitic (non-dualistic) system of Śankara, resulting in the experience of *tat tvam asi* or *neti neti Brahman.* In its radical form it emphasizes the *indwelling* of the divine in the creature or interiority rather than history or exteriority. It transcends the *māyā* (illusion) and there takes place the union of God (*Brahman*) and the individual soul (*jīva*), experienced and expressed as *aham Brahmāsmi* (self-realization).

*4.3.2. The bhakti trend*

The *bhakti* school is best represented by Rāmanuja and his system of qualified non-duality (*viśiṣṭa advaita*), in which there is a personal God (*Īśvara*) and a relationship of love and devotion (*bhakti*) between this God and the individual.

*4.3.3. The compatibility of advaitic and bhakti trends*

Hinduism is a very complex reality. The Hinduism of the Vedas and its expressions in Purāṇas and the writings of the *ācāryas* (teachers) offer us a rich complexity. For example, the Hinduism of the Dravidian people, surely influenced at least at the latter period by the vedic scriptures, possesses its own specific character. The Hinduism of the *bhakti* poets and Neo-Hinduism have also their own specificities. However, Hinduism is, without going into detail here, generally spoken and understood in its dominant advaitic and bhakti trends. In spite of its high sounding philosophical stand a purely gnostic type of religious experience did not gain much currency in Indian culture; it has always been outbalanced, so to say, in popular terms by the bhakti trend of the common people. Even the mysticism of pure knowledge in non-dualist experience is preceded by the love of God.

The advaitic and bhakti trends of Hindu thought try to unite the transcendence and immanence of God, the Absolute and the 'self', the matter and the spirit, the interiority and the exteriority. When understood in their proper perspectives, these trends of Hinduism may also be recognized in Christianity. There is a danger, however in Hinduism, that one becomes absolute or subordinate to the other, or even at times seen as exclusive of or inferior to the other. In the Christian tradition these trends are seen complementary to each other. Amalor writes:

> In Christian mysticism there are two poles that complement one another: interiorization and exteriorization, closure and opening, immanence and transcendence, anthropocentrism and theocentrism, enstasy and ecstasy. If these elements are complementary, they are, well understood, indispensable for true mysticism. That is why the absence or the reduction of one damages the other and the totality.[62]

The *bhakti* trend, that safeguards the transcendence of a personal God who is at the same time immanent to his devotees, appears to be closer to the Christian understanding and experience. The inter-religious dialogue could start from this platform, taking into account at the same time that the experience and spirituality of God's immanence (self-realization), followed by a number of western mystics too, is also very precious and perhaps the sensitive core of the Hindu tradition. Self-realization is God-realization, for human beings are created in the image and likeness of God and every human being longs in his/her deepest self for God. However, the self-realization in the Hindu tradition, that is, the experience of the self as *aham Brahmāsmi,* which is more of a matter of personal effort, asceticism and self-effacement, differs from the Christian mystique of the self, in which the individual self and the trinitarian God remain distinct persons, even in a most intimate, personal and supreme union. This union (*yoga*) cannot be reached by one's own efforts; first and foremost, man needs the grace of God. God takes the initiative and gives the grace to the individual to realize it.

Because of the one and the same Holy Spirit who is truly present in the one history, we say that grace is already at work in what we are inclined to call "natural mysticism" in Hinduism. Hence, Hinduism with its God-experience of *advaita* (non-duality) or *bhakti* (devotion) and *viśiṣṭa advaita* (qualified non-duality) is not merely a launching pad for

---

62 DSA, *Destinée,* op. cit., p. 319: "Il y a dans la mystique chrétienne deux pôles qui renvoient l'un à l'autre, comme des éléments complémentaires: intériorisation et extériorisation, fermeture et ouverture, immanence et transcendance, homocentrisme et théocentrisme, enstase et extase. Si ces éléments sont complémentaires, ils sont, bien entendu, indispensables pour une vraie mystique. C'est pourqoi l'absence de l'un ou sa diminution sera au détriment de l'autre et de la totalité." (For translation see: Gerwin van Leeuwen, O.F.M., *Fully Indian - Authentically Christian,* op. cit., pp. 275-276).

dialogue, but a valuable road for many to meet and enter into deep communion (*yoga*) with the one true God: Father, Son and the Holy Spirit.[63] Amalor writes: "What happens in the interior of a soul is known to God alone; at the same time it is precisely here that Christianity should open the dialogue with Hinduism. What the Word did for humankind in general,[64] Christianity should do for Hinduism."[65] In this quotation Amalor likes to base the dialogue between Christianity and Hinduism on the principle of the incarnation of the Word.

Dialogue should be based on the model of the mystery of the incarnation of the Word: incarnation, assumption and redemption, that is, God's coming on earth in the person of Christ to "dialogue" with man in order to save him. Following the model of the mystery of the incarnation, the Church, which has herself the experience of immanence and transcendence, should first "incarnate" herself in the Hindu immanence and then carry along this Hindu immanence, by assuming it, to the transcendence of a personal God. In other words, the Church should make God's dialogue with the world in Christ, the salvation in Christ, "enter" in other religions and make them salvific. "Going beyond"[66] or "pilgrimaging"

---

[63] Cf. Gerwin van Leeuwen, O.F.M., *Fully Indian - Authentically Christian,* op. cit., p. 276.

[64] See: DSA, *Destinée,* op. cit., p. 322. DSA describes here the mystical flight of John in his prologue on the incarnation of the Word:

"The Word was with God, and the Word was God" (Jn. 1:1), (transcendence).

"And the Word became flesh and dwelt among us" (Jn. 1:14), (immanence).

"No one has ever seen God; the only Son, who is in the bosom of the Father, he has made him known" (1:18), (immanence and transcendence).

He then quotes from Boismard's *Le Porologue de saint Jean* (Paris, 1953, p. 91): "The Prologue seems to draw a parabole, the basis of which touches the earth and its two branches lose themselves in the infinity of God" [Le prologue semble ainsi dessiner une parabole, dont la base touche la terre et dont les deux branches se perdent dans l'infini de Dieu]. [It does not seem necessary here to cite the passages of the prologue in French. For the translation of Boismard's see: Gerwin van Leeuwen, O.F.M., *Fully Indian - Authentically Christian,* op. cit., p. 289 (reference 71)].

[65] Ibid.: "Quelle que soit la réalité de ce qui se passe, en fait, à l'intérieur d'une âme qui n'est connue que de Dieu, il nous semble que c'est ici que le christianisme doit ouvrir le dialogue avec l'hindouisme. Ce que le Verbe a fait pour l'humanité en général, le christianisme doit le faire pour l'hindouisme." (For translation see: Gerwin van Leeuwen, O.F.M., *Fully Indian - Authentically Christian,* op. cit., p. 276).

[66] See DSA using the term: *Dépassement,* in: Ibid., and so translated by Gerwin van Leeuwen, in: *Fully Indian - Authentically Christian,* op. cit., p. 276.

together ahead, that is, taking Hinduism to its fulfillment in Christ, presupposes that Christianity and Hinduism have first met at a point of convergence. Our convergence here is at a personal God, a creator who gives us grace.

Hinduism will open itself for dialogue on the condition that Christianity shows itself that it is as interior and immanent as Hinduism, as deep as Hinduism in its experience of God in the deepest depths of its being and witnessing. The word "dialogue" implies within itself both, "being" and "doing". It is neither exclusively "being" nor exclusively "doing"; it is both: "being" and "doing", which are identical in God. Hence the inter-religious dialogue should take place in God, at the level of God-experience. Christianity and Hinduism have to meet each other in God, in a deep-level seeking and sharing of truth and their common witness of the experience God in the world. This is the incarnational approach of dialogue.[67]

The God-experience of Hinduism is not only mystical contemplation or cave-asceticism, as it may appear to be or is so predominantly *advaita,* it is, in praxis, both, contemplation and action (devotion, *bhakti*). If it were only contemplation then it would be perhaps asking too much to become monks or mystics to start a dialogue with Hinduism. Amalor gives the example of Fr. Monchanin who was often asked this question: Do we have to be monks or mystics to start a dialogue with Hinduism? Fr. Monchanin denies that one has to be a monk or a mystic. What is required is to know our Christian faith in its *interiority,* because Christian life is actually our dwelling in God and God's dwelling in us (cf. Jn. 17). This interior richness should radiate in all that we Christians do, especially in our dialogue with Hindus.[68]

The three levels of dialogue, we have just seen above, complement one another. The Western analytical mind may see these levels in piecemeal, but the Indian normally sees all these three levels at a glance. Fr. Monchanin, therefore, considered the monastic institution, which by its very nature envelops these three levels, a providential meeting-place between the Church and India. Consequently, says Amalor, hardly anyone has been so 'incarnate'[69] in India as this missionary. He was aware of the

---

[67] Cf. DSA, *Destinée,* op. cit., p. 322.

[68] Cf. ibid., pp. 322-323.

[69] Certainly, the word *incarnate* here is not used in its theological sense as in the mystery

darker side of Hinduism, but in imitation of Christ who took a body of flesh in order to transform it into a temple of the Holy Spirit, Monchanin wanted first to become "incarnate" in Hinduism as it is, in its most specific and deepest God-experience and institution, in order to transform it from within through a passion of the spirit, a noetic crucifixion and a Christic resurrection. Indian Christian monasticism then is a privileged, but not the only, place for dialogue. Fr. Monchanin has been the symbol and prophet of this vision.[70]

Amalor, particularly in his support of the *āśram* movement from its very beginning, showed his faith in the integral Indian vision, embodied by Monchanin. Amalor tried to communicate this to Christian participants and visitors of the NBCLC not only through lectures and their way of living there, but also by inviting persons of other religions to speak and work, and, thus, share their God-experience with others at the Centre. He urged believers of other religions to pray there in their own way, and invited participants and guests of the NBCLC to join their brothers and sisters in the Ramakrishna Ashram in their worship.[71] He continued the same spirit of dialogue and participation in the God-experience of others in the Anjali Ashram. Entering and sharing in the God-experience of others was considered by Amalor as an unambiguous implication of the Conciliar teaching on dialogue, that is, a continuous implication and "incarnation" of the Word in the religions of the world in order to save people as well as their religions.

## 5. Dialogue and Evangelization: A New Form of Missionary Activity

### *5.1. Is Dialogue Evangelization? Difference and Unity*

Though evangelization is distinct from dialogue, there is no conflict between the two. The understanding of dialogue with other religions and

---

of the incarnation of Jesus. I have just used the word used by DSA himself -- *incarné* -- in: Ibid., p. 324 when he writes: 'Par conséquent, nul n'était, on peut dire ... aussi *incarné* en Inde que lui [le Père Monchanin].' The word is used here in the sense of getting oneself involved in the culture of India and in the God-experience of Hinduism.

70 Cf. ibid., pp. 323-324; see also: DSA, *L'Inde à la rencontre du Seigneur,* op. cit., pp. 355-356; id. (ed.), *Indian Christian Spirituality,* op. cit., p. 101.

71 Cf. Gerwin van Leeuwen, O.F.M., *Fully Indian - Authentically Christian,* op. cit., p. 277.

particularly its place in or side by side or even over against evangelization remained for several years a burning question. Even today there seems to be no general agreement over the issue among theologians. Amalor sees it, especially in the context of religious pluralism today, as an integral part of the missionary activity of the Church. He writes: "The mission of the Church with reference to people of other religious traditions can be either dialogue or evangelization or both."[72] Dialogue, as such, "is a new form [or element] of missionary action."[73] Dialogue carried on by a convinced Christian inevitably becomes a form of evangelization.[74]

Before going into further detail, let us just clarify in short these three terms: Evangelization, Proclamation and Dialogue. *Evangelization* or the evangelizing mission of the Church "refers to the mission of the Church in its totality" (DP 8, cf. *NA* 4, *GS* 92). *Proclamation* or announcing "is the communication of the Gospel message, the mystery of salvation realized by God for all in Jesus Christ by the power of the Spirit. It is an invitation to a commitment of faith in Jesus Christ and to entry through baptism in the community of believers which is the Church" (DP 10). Evangelization is indeed the proclamation of the Gospel. In fact, some see these two concepts -- evangelization and proclamation -- as one and the same. While clarifying the concepts, therefore, we mainly dwell on evangelization and dialogue.

The "spirit of dialogue" refers to an "attitude of respect and friendship, which permeates or should permeate all [the] activities constituting the evangelizing mission of the Church" (DP 9). Dialogue belongs to the general evangelizing missionary activity of the Church; it is a new form, a specific and integral but not essential element of evangelization in the context of religious pluralism today. As specific and integral element of evangelization dialogue means all positive and constructive inter-religious relations with individuals and communities of other religions which are

---

[72] DSA, "Approach", *op. cit.*, p. 54.

[73] DSA, *Approaches*, op. cit., p. 28.

[74] Cf. the Patna Workshop Report no. III-3 on "Dialogue with Hindus and Other Religions of India", in: *Light and Life We Seek to Share,* op. cit., p. 326 (point 1), where, for the definition of evangelization, the Workshop Report refers to *AG* 9 and DSA's paper. DSA, in his Orientation Speech at Patna, defines evangelization, we have already seen in chapter two, as 'the proclamation of the Good News, the good news of salvation in Jesus Christ addressed to men, in order to enable them to have faith in him and to have full fellowship with all men'. (See: DSA, "Approach", *op. cit.*, p. 18).

directed at mutual understanding and enrichment, in obedience to truth and respect for freedom. It includes both witness and exploration of one's religious convictions (cf. DP 9).

Teleologically speaking, dialogue and evangelization may mean the same, that is, the salvation of all in God through Christ, but their import and approach are not exactly the same. Dialogue and evangelization are not simply identical. Though the proximate end of evangelization or the mission of the Church may appear or is the conversion of humankind, especially of non-Christians to Christianity; its ultimate end, as we have seen in chapters one and two, is the salvation of all, Christians and others. Conversion is of all and it is *to God* and *by God.* Likewise, the ultimate end of dialogue is none other than salvation and the kingdom of God. However, dialogue does *not* aim at the conversion of others to Christianity, while, of course, it necessarily implies, on the part of the evangelizer, the witness of life -- without which no evangelizing activity whatever can be sincere or credible. While, evangelization, in its broader sense, as we have already seen, is the proclamation of the Gospel, the sharing of one's God-experience in Christ, dialogue is a sharing in what is common and what is different among religions for mutual understanding, collaboration and mutual growth. The partners in dialogue come close to each other and to God, and both are challenged to change to a true *metanoia.* Thus, dialogue does not primarily aim at the conversion of others into an explicit faith in Christ but at the communion of all in God through Christ.

The primary concern of dialogue is the religious tradition as a whole, for example, Hinduism, rather than individual Hindus. Its issues are not limited to religious sphere alone but extend also to the spheres of social and political, to the totality of human problems and concerns, for example, the caste system and untouchability, *dalit* movement, religious fundamentalism, tribal upliftment, education and health, fight against social evils and injustice, thereby, calling the religions, in mutual recognition, respect and understanding, not for their conversion to Christianity but for mutual understanding and collaboration in the common cause and concern of humankind.

Though the concern of evangelization is also religions as a whole, for Christ came to save both individuals and their religious traditions, it may primarily seem to concern itself with individuals or groups of Hindus or Buddhists rather than religions themselves as a whole. Evangelization, in its narrow sense or at least as it was understood and carried out in the past, adopts the approach of 'one way traffic'; it wants only to give, implying conversion and baptism, not to receive, for the Gospel seems to be an exclusive possession of the Church. Seen in this perspective, dialogue does not tend to conversion of one's partner to the religious tradition of the other; rather it tends to a more profound conversion of each to God.[75] It considers the people of other religions as partners, co-citizens and co-pilgrims, walking "together" and "beyond" one's religious tradition to meet others in the common journey of all humankind to God. Thus one's religious tradition becomes a sign, a means, not end, leading to God. It is here that Christ is seen as God's final and full revelation, the supreme sign and the sacrament of God; and the religions are seen as heading towards God -- the God of Jesus Christ -- and, in their united effort, as working for the advent and experience of God's kingdom on earth.

Though the ultimate end of evangelization and of dialogue is one and the same, these are not one and the same. After all, the religions come together in the name of dialogue, not evangelization. This is where lies the difference. However, they are not mutually exclusive; they are interrelated yet not interchangeable. Both have their essential role to play in the total understanding of the Christian faith.

> Interreligious dialogue and proclamation, though not on the same level, are both authentic elements of the Church's evangelizing mission. Both are legitimate and necessary. They are intimately related, but not interchangeable.... The two activities remain distinct but, as experience shows, one and the same local Church, one and the same person, can be diversely engaged in both (DP 77).

Though both these elements of the Church's mission are valid and necessary, proclamation has "permanent priority" (*RM* 44) in the mission of the Church and dialogue "remains oriented towards proclamation" (DP 82).

In his Theological Orientation speech at Patna, referring to the international meeting on evangelization (Nagpur 1971), Amalor states that at Nagpur the participants could not arrive at a wholly satisfactory solution. While some, though they acknowledged that dialogue is valid in itself, considered it a preparation for the proclamation of the Gospel, others thought that such an understanding might arouse misunderstanding and

---

[75] Cf. DSA, *Destinée,* op. cit., p. 300.

suspicion in a country like India, and sought for a theological understanding in terms of polarity and tension between these two activities, which though often connected in praxis, remain theologically distinct. The dialectical tension referred to is that of the Church's existence in the world as eschatological and pilgrim.[76] Amalor emphasizes that dialogue must primarily be understood in terms of the attitude, spirit and mentality of the partners, rather than in terms of contents and issues. Quoting from the Nagpur Declaration, he states:

> Religious dialogue does not necessarily mean that two persons speak about their religious experiences, but rather that they speak as religiously committed persons, with their ultimate commitments and religious outlook, on subjects of common interest (no. 24).[77]

In his report on the 1974 Synod on evangelization in Rome, of which he was one of the two special secretaries, Amalor most clearly brings out his understanding of the relation between dialogue and evangelization. After affirming the presence and action of the Holy Spirit in other religions, he states that dialogue truly belongs to the evangelical mission of the Church in spite of the fact that it is not meant to draw others to the Church, but to mutually share religious and other common concerns with others. He concludes, writing:

> Dialogue is good in itself and be promoted as belonging to the mission of the Church. At the same time, Christians who have experienced Christ and recognized in the Christ-event God's gift of himself to humankind once and for all cannot but proclaim this good news to others. This is what is called evangelization.[78]

---

[76] Cf. DSA, "Approach", *op. cit.*, p. 54. DSA refers to the Workshop Report of the Nagpur Conference.

[77] See: Ibid.

[78] DSA (ed.), *Evangelization of the Modern World,* op. cit., p. 55. In his official report to the Synod (1974) DSA had put the relationship between dialogue and evangelization as follows: As real sharing leads both partners to spiritual growth, mutual edification and genuine conversion to God,

"dialogue is therefore good in itself and an end in itself, as fostering mutual edification and communion; yet it is inseparable from evangelization and does not dispense us from it. Though theologically distinct, evangelization and dialogue make a single whole in the lives of many Christians and it would be difficult to distinguish where the one ends

### *5.2. The Global Concern of Dialogue: Oriented to the Service of the Kingdom*

In his address at the Sedos Symposium (Rome 1969) Amalor gives a wider meaning to dialogue. The whole of human history is a continuous dialogue between God and humankind.[79] The relation between God and humankind has been from the beginning that of "dialogical salvific encounter", culminating in the Jesus Christ event.

In this above perspective dialogue becomes an eloquent proof of solidarity with others, and a necessary means of knowing one another. However, dialogue is not primarily an intellectual exchange, much less a controversy in a polemical tone. It is, in a mutual openness to one another, a listening to God who speaks in and through the experience and witness of the other partner. Amalor writes: "In dialogue each partner listens to God speaking in the self-communication and questioning of his fellow-believers."[80] The partners are to listen to one another because of their pilgrim situation on this earth. It is through common searching and sharing that the partners come closer to the truth. The sharing of one's religious experience and listening of it by the other leads the partners to their spiritual growth and to a kind of deeper *metanoia* or conversion to God. It leads the partners not only to share and participate in the spiritual experience of one another but also enables them to mutual collaboration in areas which include concrete issues and burning questions of the day, be it religious, socio-economic or political.[81]

It has always been very difficult for Christians in general, and Catholics in particular, to accept that they can learn from other religions.

---

and the other begins."

He says that dialogue should be seen in the docility to the Spirit. To fruitfully participate in dialogue Christians must be men and women of the Spirit, committed to their own Christian faith and at the same time open to listen and to learn, because, although God has fully revealed himself in Christ, Christians do not have the monopoly of the Spirit. However, anyone who has really experienced the liberating love of God in Christ, cannot but proclaim this good news to others. [See: Ibid., p. 100; see also: Gerwin van Leeuwen, O.F.M., *Fully Indian - Authentically Christian,* op. cit., p. 290 (reference 87)].

[79] Cf. DSA, *Approaches,* op. cit., p. 28. Here DSA refers to the encyclical *Ecclesiam Suam* without further specification.

[80] DSA (ed.), *Evangelization of the Modern World,* op. cit., pp. 54-55. DSA quotes the Declaration of the Nagpur Conference, no. 27.

[81] Cf. ibid., p. 55.

Vatican II (*LG, GS, AG* and *NA*) has certainly opened their minds and hearts for the values that are present in other religions. Amalor likes to go beyond this, necessitating, thereby, inter-religious dialogue in mutual engagement and enrichment for the full realization of the universality of the mystery of Christ. He writes:

> The Christian wishes to learn of the religious values and experiences of others. The mystery of Christ is universal, yet this universality is at present realized only partially, and therefore the concrete life of the Church, and much more that of the individual is open to continuous enrichment. The partner in dialogue may also be enriched, and the Christian hopes that he may be able to communicate to him something of the richness and strength of faith which is his own.[82]

Dialogue is not a bait to convert the partner, but a sure means of mutual engagement in the common search for truth, as pilgrims in the same world and history, engaged in the realization of the kingdom of God. One needs the humility to be ready to learn from the other in a process of mutual searching, sharing and enrichment. Therefore, every form of collaboration that brings the final eschatological realization of the kingdom of God nearer is worthwhile in itself.

> From the side of the Christian, the dialogue supposes the standpoint of the believer accepting Jesus Christ in faith as God's final and full revelation. It is in this faith that he knows of the bounty of the divine truth and love which from the beginning of the ages is bestowed on all men in many forms. He also knows that the fullness of the mystery of Christ will be revealed only in the end of time when all the treasures of spiritual insights and experiences will be manifest in the glory of Jesus Christ, that therefore, it is his task to grow in the realization of the mystery of Jesus Christ through sharing with others.[83]

Dialogue implies the Church's active participation, not only in the

---

[82] DSA, *Approach*, op. cit., p. 60. In brackets DSA refers to the Special Committee's Statement of the Nagpur International Theological Conference.

[83] Ibid., p. 61. DSA refers to the Special Committee's Statement of the Nagpur Conference.

religious sphere of the other but also in social, cultural and national life and aspirations by the various exchanges and enterprises of human living. Quoting *Ad Gentes,* Amalor writes:

> Just as Christ Himself searched the hearts of men and led them to divine light through truly human conversation [dialogue], so also his disciples, profoundly penetrated by the Spirit of Christ should know the people among whom they live and should establish contact with them. Thus they themselves can learn by sincere and patient dialogue what treasures a bountiful God has distributed among the nations of the earth (no. 11).[84]

The object of dialogue is, therefore, not "bracketed" to religious field; it concerns and deals with human problems and situations, values and aspirations in their entirety -- whether human, religious or Christian. All the three are important, one leading to the other. However, dialogue is not limited to mere mutual knowledge and understanding, social and cultural contacts, exchange of ideas and experiences. It can take the form of collaboration[85] in various activities that bring the kingdom of God nearer, and collaboration is one of the best ways of dialoguing. Some of the fields where collaboration is needed and appreciated are: education, concerted efforts to eradicate famine, hunger and disease, socio-economic projects, promotion of social justice and world peace (cf. *AG* 12).[86] Formerly the Church was inclined to start its own institutions for all these services. Though the Church is justified in having these social institutions and though the advantages are evident, Amalor stresses that the Church should now learn to serve God and his people in prudent collaboration with other agencies and organizations, either private or public, Government or international, other Christian denominational or of other religions (cf. *AG* 12).[87]

Dialogue, then, both in its stricter and wider sense, means for Christ's disciples, as we have already mentioned earlier, to enter more deeply into the mystery of his incarnation. As the Word entered the world and

---

[84] See as quoted in: DSA, *Approaches,* op. cit., p. 28.

[85] The point of inter-religious collaboration will be dealt in detail in the next chapter.

[86] Cf. DSA, *Approaches,* op. cit., p. 29.

[87] Cf. ibid.

assumed the whole humankind by becoming a Jew with the Jews, and started his mission from the heart of his own community, so the community of Jesus' followers should reach out to people of other religions in sincere and total dialogue from within.[88] That is why dialogue begins with an attitude of *togetherness, sympathy* and *solidarity,* not with a superiority/inferiority or competitive complex but with a humble presence of fellow-pilgrims, co-citizens, irrespective of sex, race, nation or religion. Dialogue should, therefore, be carried out with great humility, in a spirit of service in the imitation of Christ who came not to be served but to serve (cf. Mk. 10:45). The Church exists for the world and as such she has to be always at the disposal of the world to render the service it needs, serving and even washing the other's feet in the building up of a new order, worthy of man and expressive of the kingdom of God.[89]

### *5.3. A Sincere and Active Participation of All*

Finally Amalor pleads that such a dialogue is not to be limited to an élite group or to urban areas, but it must gradually extend to all levels and groups, so that every Christian community becomes a community of dialogue with others, and, thus, fosters the universal brotherhood in peace and unity of all humankind, of all religions.[90] Dialogue should be the concern of the whole Church. Local Churches -- lay people, religious and priests -- should be prepared for dialogue in a priority basis; there should

---

[88] The same thought is also brought out in the Conclusions of the Symposium on Mission Theology for Our Times, organized by Sedos, Rome, 27-31 March 1969. DSA belonged to the drafting committee. It reads: "So that a genuine dialogue may be set up and may prove truly fruitful, the fulfillment of several conditions is absolutely necessary.

(a) The missionaries, both priests and lay people, should really and truly enter into the cultures of the non-Christian peoples, so that they may understand them from within and that -- with regard to those whom they are sent -- they may encounter them as they are, even at the level of their own religious experience.

(b) The reality of the existence and history must somehow reproduce within itself the mystery of Christ himself which ... is a dispensation of incarnation, death and resurrection.

(c) The conversion of individual persons must be seen within the larger perspectives of the conversion of entire peoples and the perspective of the salvation of all mankind." (See: DSA, *Approaches,* op. cit., p. 48).

[89] Cf. DSA, *Theology of Development,* op, cit., pp. 25-26; id., *Approaches,* op. cit., p. 29.

[90] Cf. DSA, "Approach", *op. cit.,* p. 55.

be a constant recasting and updating of formation to meet this need. The Indian Church on her part should be enabled to change her attitude from timidity to courage.[91]

One of the target groups in need of such a corrective approach to dialogue is the missionary,[92] notwithstanding his/her full-time involvement in the celebration of sacraments and administration. In this regard, in line with the insistence of Vatican II, Amalor writes that "seminarians should be trained and prepared for dialogue with all religious and secular Indians."[93] Such a training and approach enables them discover God's treasures already present in their countrymen. For this purpose, Amalor suggests the setting up of regional institutes which would also initiate new missionaries and catechists to the study of the language, culture and religious customs of the place.[94]

### *5.4. Pastoral Occasions for Inter-Religious Dialogue*

Amalor writes that the many occasions in which the Church and Christians encounter members of other religions are excellent opportunities for a religious dialogue, whatever the eventual outcome.[95]

#### *5.4.1. The screening of religious films*

The Church in India has long used the projection of religious films for the non-formal religious instruction for Christians. Although primarily meant for Christians, members of other religions also take part as these films are generally screened in public and open grounds. Often these programmes are televised for the public.[96]

---

[91] Cf. DSA, *Inter-Religious Dialogue in India,* op. cit., p. 14.

[92] Cf. DSA, "Workshop on Recent Developments in Catechetics (International Study Week, Manila)", in: *Teaching All Nations* 4 (1967) 3, p. 379.

[93] DSA, "New Theological Approaches in Asia. (With Reference to Religions and Cultures Other than Western Culture and Christianity)", in: *Verbum SVD* 21 (1980) 3 & 4, p. 281.

[94] Cf. DSA, "The Implications of Vatican II for the Mission in Asia", in: *Teaching All Nations* 4 (1967) 3, p. 326.

[95] For example, DSA suggests various levels of dialogue with Hinduism: sensible or external, conceptual and spiritual. Cf. DSA, *Destinée,* op. cit., pp. 301-308.

[96] Cf. DSA, "The Structures of Catechesis in South India and the Regional Centre at

### *5.4.2. Catholic schools and institutes*

Amalor likes to highlight the role of Catholic schools and institutes as occasions of inter-religious dialogue. Dialogue can assume different forms therein: daily prayer sessions at the school assembly common to members of all religions, at which the sacred scriptures of other religions are also to be read; encouraging students to pray in their own religious traditions; a common prayer room and the common celebration of some feasts.[97] Amalor condemned, both for practical and theological reasons, the custom requiring students of other religions to frequent catechism along with Catholic students. For, this would be a gross violation of the religious convictions of others and the exigencies of Christian faith.[98]

### *5.4.3. Āśrams*

The growth of dialogue in India, since Vatican II, owes much to the *āśrams* and the different types of inter-religious centres. Though *āśrams* founded by Catholics have been existing from the 1940s, it was not until the 1970s that they took the establishment of *āśrams* seriously.[99] As a result of the encouragement from various Conferences and Seminars,[100] a number of *āśrams* have been opened by Catholics since 1970. The Anjali Ashram, founded by Amalor at Mysore in 1979, is one of the best among them.[101]

---

Tindivanam", in: *Lumen Vitae* 19 (1964) 4, pp. 747-748; there DSA includes the names of some of the films.

Likewise in the 1980s *Dayāsāgara* (a religious film on Christ) had a much impact also on the people of other religions in India. Often the religious programmes from other religions are also televised which Christians enjoy to watch and learn from them. For example, the TV serials: *Rāmāyaṇa* and *Mahābhārata* in 1987-1988 were watched with much interest and attention by followers of different religions.

97 Cf. DSA, *Inter-Religious Dialogue in India,* op. cit., p. 17.

98 Cf. DSA, "General Problems of Catechetical Formation and Catechesis of Various Age-Groups", in: *Teaching All Nations* 4 (1967) 3, p. 296.

99 Cf. Jose Kuttianimattathil, S.D.B., *Practice and Theology of Interreligious Dialogue,* op. cit., pp. 54-57, 79.

100 For example: *All Indian Seminar: Church in India Today, Bangalore 1969; The International Theological Conference on Evangelization & Dialogue in Asia* (Nagpur 1971), *All India Consultation on Evangelization* (Patna 1973).

101 Jose Kuttianimattathil ranks two best known *āśrams* in India: The Anjali Ashram, and the Christa Prema Seva Ashram. (See: Jose Kuttianimattathil, S.D.B., *Practice and*

*Āśrams* are abodes of prayer, contemplation and service, where all people are welcome to stay and experience dialogue in action.[102] The origin of the Christian *āśram* is to be situated within India's quest for Jesus Christ. Social and religious reformers and pioneers in the struggle for political independence found the *āśram* an ideal which responded to their vision for a new society and an alternative form of living. In this context, dialogue through *āśrams* became a new form of Christian presence, a new way in which the Church came into dialogue and related herself with other religions, especially Hinduism. Today *āśrams* have become an exemplar of on-going dialogue in the encounter of the pilgrim Church with all people and religions.[103]

Amalor's fascination for this form of Indian life and dialogue is reflected in his decision -- after his 15-year tenure at the National Centre (NBCLC) -- to found the Anjali Ashram (Mysore), which became the locus for a fruitful dialogue, unfolding the great possibilities for expressing the Gospel message through the heritage of Indian spirituality.[104]

## 6. Dialogue with Hinduism[105]

The Indian religious scene is multi-faceted. Not only is India a home to many of the major religions of the world, but she also nurtures a number of tribal religions. We limit ourselves here to Hinduism.[106]

---

*Theology of Interreligious Dialogue*, op. cit., p. 80).

102 Cf. DSA, *Inter-Religious Dialogue in India*, op. cit., p. 17. 4 of 13 Indian *Āśrams* engage in inter-religious dialogue. Cf. Cyril De Souza, S.D.B., *Catechesis for India Today*, op. cit., p. 346.

103 Cf. DSA, *Ashram Aikya: Whence and Whither*, NBCLC, Bangalore, [1984], pp. 1-2. *Ashram Aikya* is a fellowship of Indian Christian *Āśrams*.

104 Cf. Paul Puthanangady, "Fr. D.S. Amalorpavadass - Prophet of the Post-Conciliar Church in India", in: *Word and Worship* 23 (1990) 5, p. 171.

105 We do not intend here to enter into the *practice* of inter-religious dialogue with Hinduism. That would be going beyond our scope. Instead, we limit ourselves to the *theology* of inter-religious dialogue. Also we do not go into detail in considering the pros and cons or explanation of the theological issues in dialogue. That would require a separate dissertation. Thus, the religions (Christianity and Hinduism) are not separately dealt here in detail. Our aim is to give their general stand in brief, in so far as they relate themselves to the theology of inter-religious dialogue.

106 DSA mainly dealt with Hinduism.

Within the religious tradition of Hinduism there exists side by side with the official, institutionalized religion of the élite, a more flexible, open or, we can say, a "popular religion"[107] of the many. These may be characterized as two poles of the same religion. Besides, at times, one may witness a practice of a closed and sectarian "religion" of the fundamentalists. Added to these are the class and caste distinctions that cut across religious barriers, adding to the complexity of the religious scene in India. With whom one is to dialogue? These divers factors make the question of the identity of one's partner in a dialogue an important issue.

Let us proceed to identify and consider a dialoguing point with Hinduism in general.

### *6.1. Basis for Dialogue in Hinduism*

#### *6.1.1. The Absolute (Brahman), the basis and unity of all*[108]

Hinduism from the very beginning of its history[109] is in relentless search for the ultimate Being and for the unity (*ṛta*) underlying the multiplicity of realities. The ultimate Reality has been conceived in different ways by Hindus all through their long history.[110] But there is one thread that runs through all their philosophies, theologies and spirituality: the *oneness* of the Absolute or Brahman. Brahman is seen as the source and basis of all multiple realities, the harmonizing reality that brings together all the similar, complementary and even opposing realities (*samanvaya*).[111]

---

[107] By 'popular religion' we mean here, the religiosity of the common people (popular devotion) vis-à-vis the official and institutionalized religion of the élite and intellectuals with its dogmas and doctrines. In Christian theological circles popular religion (popular devotion) is generally understood in contrast to official religion. But such a sharp contrast may not correspond to the experience of most Asian religions who do not have one official central body, e.g., in Hinduism, which determines its doctrines and beliefs. (Cf. Felix Wilfred, "Faith without 'Faith'? Popular Religion - A Challenge to Elitist Theology and Liturgy", in: Paul Puthanangady (ed.), *Popular Devotions in India: Research Seminar,* NBCLC, Bangalore, 1986, pp. 594-596.

[108] Cf. DSA, "A Synthesis of Basic and Constitutive Elements of Indian Christian Spirituality", *op. cit.,* pp. 222, 230-233.

[109] As such Hinduism has no "history"; it is an eternal religion (*sanātana dharma*).

[110] See: M. Dhavamony, *Classical Hinduism,* op. cit., especially chapters two and three (pp. 32-102) where the idea of God and *avatāras* in Hinduism are dealt in detail.

[111] Cf. DSA, "Main Categories of Hindu Philosophy and Spirituality", *op. cit.,* pp. 153-

Brahman is immanent in all the multiple realities and it transcends them all. It is, therefore, perceived in a thousand different ways and can be known not through the logic of the finite mind but through an intuitive experience.[112]

### *6.1.2. Oneness in difference*[113]

The dominant trends of Hinduism have always affirmed the relationships between the Infinite and the finite, God and man, *māyā* and *mukti*, and among the finite beings themselves, in terms of *bhedābheda* (oneness in difference). Hindus, therefore, think that realities are constituted by *samanvaya* (harmony) and their relation is expressed through *bhedābheda*. So the Hindu cannot deny pluralism nor can he or she say that the opposites cannot come together, since reality itself is so constituted. This is the first reason we can say that Hindu religious and philosophical insights lead us to look for harmony where there is diversity and to establish relationships of oneness in difference.[114]

### *6.1.3. Different religions but one common goal*

Hinduism has always accepted not only the factual existence but also the necessity of the different spiritual paths or religions because of the differences of human persons and their spiritual aptitudes.[115] So the religious paths are different. But they find a dynamic oneness because of the one common goal towards which they move.

### *6.1.4. The dialogical nature of humankind, seeking yoga*

Hinduism accepts the human being to be the most important and most significant of all finite beings. This is well seen in the supreme unity (*yoga*) of the *mahāvākya: aham Brahmāsmi*. The human being can

---

155.

[112] Cf. DSA, "A Synthesis of Basic and Constitutive Elements of Indian Christian Spirituality", *op. cit.*, pp. 224-225.

[113] Cf. ibid., pp. 230-233.

[114] See in this respect the principle of Hindu religious tolerance.

[115] Cf. K.N. Mishra and Co., "Call to Harmony through Dialogue", in: *Vidyajyoti* 60 (1996) 4, p. 278.

transcend himself or herself and consciously and freely enter into relations with the Absolute, with others and with the whole of nature. This signifies that Hinduism is dialogical, that it recognizes the universal dialogical nature of the human being.

These philosophical and theological insights of Hinduism have come down to us in different ways and expressions, according to the different traditions of Hinduism. These insights have to be re-interpreted and made effective and fruitful today.[116] Hence, what we conclude is that we cannot accept either the view that "all religions are the same" or that "each religion is totally different from others" as true.

### *6.2. Basis for Dialogue in Christianity*

#### *6.2.1. Oneness of the trinity*

The Christian faith traces the origin of Christianity to the triune God: Father, Son and the Holy Spirit. God's very being is a community of life. This triune God, though identical in nature and essence, is different in persons. Thus the Christian God is an identity in difference; and this God is immanently in mutual dialogue and communion, in constant sharing.

#### *6.2.2. One God, one human family*

Christians believe that every human being is created in the image and likeness of this triune and "dialoguing" God. This is the reason why they affirm that every individual is in dialogue with God and with every other human being because all human beings form one human family.

#### *6.2.3. Jesus Christ, the meeting point*[117]

The centre of Christianity is Jesus Christ, the Son of God. Christian faith affirms that Jesus Christ is both God and man, the two extremes: divinity and humanity, kept in unity in the tension of the personality and mystery of the Son. Jesus Christ is therefore the incarnate "dialogue" of

---

[116] Cf. DSA, *Approaches,* op. cit., pp. 40-44.

[117] See this point already dealt in detail in earlier chapters, especially chapters one and three.

God with humankind; he is also the divine-human bond that brings religions together in dialogue, without destroying their identity and otherness.

### *6.3. Meeting Points Between Hinduism and Christianity*[118]

#### *6.3.1. God always in the history of humankind*[119]

Both Hinduism and Christianity accept that the history of humankind is the history God's dealings with humankind (*līlā*). This is well seen in the Hindu religious legends and myths. Christians on their part call the saving contact of God with the human family in space and time salvation history, accomplished in the mystery of the Jesus Christ event.

Both Hinduism and Christianity, though in different terms, speak of divine-human dialogue in history. The concept or the experience of life and liberation implies a process of dialectics in both Christianity and Hinduism: transcendence and immanence, possession and renunciation, emptiness and fullness, life and sacrifice, death and resurrection.[120] Christians see these realities fully realized in the paschal mystery of Christ. God has fully communicated these realities to the world in the dialectics of the mystery of Jesus' cross or sacrifice (*yajña*) and his resurrection.[121]

The concept of pantheism is perhaps immediately, but wrongly, connected with Hinduism. Amalor says that the experience of the universal presence of God in Hinduism, that is, seeing the all pervading and permeating presence of God in all things, was unfortunately misinterpreted by some Westerners as pantheism and this came to be repeated by Indians later on. It is a wrong interpretation of Hinduism by Westerners.[122] He writes: "The problem is to understand others as they understand themselves rather than attribute to them our wrong understanding. In any case

---

[118] Cf. DSA, "A Synthesis of Basic and Constitutive Elements of Indian Christian Spirituality", *op. cit.*, pp. 221-236.

[119] Cf. DSA, "Biblical World-View and a Renewed Holistic Spirituality", *op. cit.*, pp. 55-56.

[120] Cf. DSA, "A Synthesis of Basic and Constitutive Elements of Indian Christian Spirituality", *op. cit.*, pp. 224-230, 233-234.

[121] Cf. ibid., p. 223.

[122] Cf. ibid., p. 222.

the Hindus do not accept or profess pantheism."[123]

Since God is ineffable and unutterable (*neti neti Brahman*) and therefore cannot be fully communicated through words, Amalor likes to highlight the place and value of interiority and "silence" (*mauna*) in Christianity, and the expression of this ineffable mystery, among others, through the life-style called *āśram*. Again, among others, the concept of *yātrā* (pilgrimage) is found both in Christianity and Hinduism. The word 'pilgrim' Church in Christianity, used in opposition to 'eschatological' Church, is to be used, as it is with the concept of *yātrā* in Hinduism, not only to point out the goal of our movement but also to show the dimension of our human and spiritual life. This requires the grace of *viveka* (discernment), which is of course the work of the Spirit. The pilgrim Church always needs the discernment of the Spirit and her docility to him, especially in the context of dialogue and deliberations with other religions.[124]

### *6.3.2. Dialogue, a salvific relationship with others*

As we have already mentioned, both Hinduism and Christianity speak of the human being as the crown of creation. Christian philosophy thinks of human beings in terms of personality, and personality is constituted in the very act of dialogue. It is the relationship with the other, that is, God and other fellow beings, which gives identity and growth to the person. It is important in this context to see the human person as the immediate[125] centre and meeting point of dialogue, God being the ultimate. The task of human beings to "be fruitful and multiply, and fill the earth and subdue it" (Gen. 1:28), especially in the context of religious pluralism today, constitutes the content and source of dialogue.

### *6.3.3. Dialogue and discipleship*

We are called to follow Jesus. In the gospels we find that Jesus in his own person brought Jews and Gentiles, that is, different cultures, religions and worships, together in truth, faith and love (cf. Jn. 4; *AG* 11). This concept of wholeness and harmony, integrity and totality, is much

---

[123] Ibid., p. 223.

[124] Cf. ibid., pp. 225-226 & 233.

[125] *Immediate* in the sense of proximate, not in the sense of mediate-immediate.

cherished in Hinduism. In following Jesus, therefore, his disciples, should make a valiant attempt to become persons who are agents of unity and peace through dialogue.[126] In this regard one of the best ways of dialogue in action, on the part of Christianity, will be inculturation,[127] thereby, signifying and effecting peace and harmony in our world, where often enough and unfortunately peace and harmony are disturbed in the name of God and religions.

## 7. Concluding Remarks

### *7.1. Dialogical existence of the pilgrim Church: From monological to dialogical*

Today the religions of the world are seen as so many reflections of the one truth, distinct paths to a single goal, God. The Fathers of the Council rightly recognized in other religions the "seeds of the Word" (*AG* 11) and saw "a ray of that truth that enlightens all peoples" (*NA* 2), thereby, attesting that, though the routes taken may be different, there is but one single goal of all humanity and religions to which is directed the deepest aspiration of the human spirit for the full dimension of humanity, fullness of truth and life (cf. *Redemptor Hominis* 11).[128]

The Spirit is present and active in others. The presence of the Spirit affects not only individual persons but the religious traditions themselves (cf. *Redemptoris Missio* 28). It is true that the Spirit manifests himself in a special way in the Church and in her members. Nevertheless, his presence and activity are universal, limited neither by space nor time.

Being ever more aware of the presence and action of the Spirit in others and of her pilgrim nature on earth, the Church is more and more entering into dialogue and collaboration with others. Today the attitude and approach towards other religions is not that of 'monologue' but 'dialogue', an eloquent proof of human solidarity and service to the Spirit and other religions.[129] Thus, the attitude of dialogue may be described as an attempt to establish a 'two-way traffic' hitherto a 'one way street' (pre-

---

[126] Cf. DSA, *Approaches,* op. cit., pp. 28-29.

[127] See the point of inculturation in chapter two.

[128] See in: ND 1038.

[129] Cf. DSA, *Approaches,* op. cit., p. 35.

Vatican II). This fact has been more and more encouraged by the *magisterium* in the Church today. John Paul II, concluding his "Message to the People of Asia" (Manila, 21 February 1981), said:

> All Christians must, therefore, be committed to dialogue with the believers of all religions, so that the mutual understanding and collaboration may grow; so that moral values be strengthened; so that God may be praised in all creation. Ways must be developed to make this dialogue become a reality everywhere, but especially in Asia, the continent that is the cradle of ancient cultures and religions (*RH* 5).[130]

Dialogue makes both partners deeply stirred and challenged to a deeper *metanoia* to God and fellowship with one another. In this regard, Amalor's convocation of the Seminar on Non-Biblical Scriptures (1974) is rightly seen as a major step in dialogue with other religions.[131]

### *7.2. Fruits of dialogue: Mutual enrichment, fullness of truth and life*

Dialogue enriches one's faith. It purifies one's gratuitous assumptions, destroys deep-rooted prejudices and overthrows certain overly narrow conceptions and outlook. It gives the partners a greater understanding of truth and better understanding of one another and leads them to mutual enrichment in their common pilgrimage to God. While listening to the God-experiences of others, one discovers values as well as certain aspects of the divine mystery which might have been better developed or witnessed in other religions than in one's own. Thus, one comes to accept and realize the *one* salvific plan of God for all humankind and his providential ways (cf. *AG* 3) in the realization of this plan in different cultures and religions in history.

Inter-religious dialogue, in seeking the fullness of truth and life, is not to be limited to inter-religious "discussions"; it must be witnessed in action and mutual collaboration. Thus, after considering the theology of dialogue, we proceed to consider the point of inter-religious collaboration in the next chapter.

---

[130] See in: ND 1040.

[131] Cf. Xavier Irudayaraj, "The Pilgrim Church: Inculturation - Dialogue - Liberation", in: Paul Puthanangady, S.D.B. (ed.), *Church in India: Institution of Movement?*, op. cit., pp. 159-160.

# CHAPTER SIX

# INTER-RELIGIOUS COLLABORATION IN THE STRUGGLE FOR A NEW SOCIETY

## 1. Introduction

### *1.1. The divine concern: 'Behold, I make all things new': Restoring the ṛta*

Every age and stage of human history has been marked with the constant struggle of humankind in realizing on earth the challenging words of God: "Behold, I make all things new" (Rev. 21:5). These words refer to the transformation of the world and society and the fulfillment of history, or in the terminology of Hinduism, it is the restoration of *ṛta* (world harmony). In other words, it refers to the realization of the kingdom of God on earth (*Rāmarājya*), among peoples, religions and ideologies of the world. It is a constant struggle till Christ "hands over the kingdom to God the Father, after he has destroyed every [evil] ruler and every authority and power ... that God may be all in all" (1 Cor. 15:24, 28). This is a life-long process wherein man cannot but involve himself if he wants to build a just and humane society, and, in the process, transform and liberate himself.

The Church is called to build a new heaven and a new earth by transforming the world as willed by God (cf. Rev. 21:1). This she can best do not from outside but from within, that is, by identifying and involving herself with the hopes, aspirations and struggles of the world. In getting really involved in the world, committed to the task of building a new human society, the Church shows the fuller dimension of the Christic liberation, revealing thereby that God's plan of love fulfilled in the life, death and resurrection of Jesus, is already being realized in the world. Thus she can proclaim and radiate the light, energies and dynamism that spring from the Gospel in the struggle for a new society, in which she joins the rest of humankind. Following the liberator and Lord of history, she is called not to exist for herself, but for and with others for the fulfillment of God's plan in the world and history (cf. *AG* 9).[1]

The realization of a new society on earth has been the constant concern of God[2] as well as of the peoples, religions and ideologies of the world. This has also been the constant concern of the Church. Though the social teaching of the Church, because of the modern technological advancement with its economic and social complexities today, may seem to be of recent origin, the issue of justice and peace has been constantly encouraged by the *magisterium* of the Church, especially with the thrust of the encyclical letter *Rerum Novarum* of Leo XIII in 1891.[3]

### *1.2. Call for collaboration*

The Church is called to share in the hopes and aspirations of the poor and the rejects of society in the footsteps of the one who though he was rich, yet he made himself poor for the sake of humankind (cf. 2 Cor. 8:9; Phil. 2:6-7). *Lumen Gentium* states: "Just as Christ carried out the work of redemption in poverty and oppression, so the Church is called to follow the same path if she is to communicate the fruits of salvation to all men" (no. 8). Amalor stresses that to do this today in the context of religious pluralism, the Church has to join other people in building new systems and structures in society that promote justice and peace, human dignity, equality and freedom, especially religious freedom, of all men and women.[4] Like leaven that is mixed in with flour (cf. Lk. 13:21), she is to join others in the common struggle of humanity "in dialogue, in solidarity

---

[1] Cf. DSA, *Evangelization of the Modern World,* op. cit., pp. 57-79.

[2] We have seen that history has been the *locus* of God's revelation and action. The historical revelation of God recorded in the Bible shows us that he is the God of truth, justice and steadfast love (cf. Ex. 34:6; Ps. 103:8); and his has always been a liberating action in favour of the "poor". See especially the Books of Exodus, Amos and Jeremiah and the beatitudes.

[3] The importance of *Rerum Novarum* (1891) is seen, among others, in the celebration of the anniversaries of its publication: Pius XI with *Quadragesimo Anno* (1931) for its 40th anniversary; Pius XII with a Radio Message (1941) for its 50th anniversary; John XXIII with *Mater et Magistra* (1961) for its 70th anniversary; Paul VI with *Octogesima Adveniens* (1971) for its 80th anniversary; and John Paul II commemorated its 90th anniversary with *Laborem Exercens* (1981) and its centinary with *Centesimus Annus* (1991). For the social doctrine of the Church in detail see: ND, pp. 287-295.

[4] Cf. DSA, *Evangelization of the Modern World,* op. cit., pp. 58-61.

and collaboration."[5]

While a good social analysis is necessary for any social change, liberation and development, undaunted courage and hope are needed today to fight against the evil forces of the world. The liberating God of the poor (*anawim*) is constantly calling the Church as well as other religions and ideologies of the world, in their radical discipleship to Christ[6] to consciously involve themselves in the creation of a new, liberated society of justice, peace and righteousness. The religions and ideologies of the world are called to work together in order to achieve their common goal. By their very vocation, then, both individually and collectively, they have to proclaim the truth, justice and peace of God on earth. Seeking truth and justice is the common language of all peoples, religions and ideologies of the world; hence to speak this language, understand it and promote it in the world, they need collaboration with one another and with God who is Truth itself (cf. Jn. 4:24), now become flesh in his Son Jesus Christ (cf. Jn. 14:6).

> The new society fondly hoped for will be characterized by a humanizing level of material well-being, with a dignity in social life and a voice in political decision-making; a society in which liberation from all forms of oppression and exploitation will be a permanent feature; a society in which men and women are enabled to live in fraternal community.[7]

Amalor, well known for his trail-blazing contribution to indigenization and inculturation, also manifested, both in his initiatives and writings, his involvement in the transformation of society and his option for the poor, justice and peace. This is well seen in his organizations of different Seminars and Meetings on the issue, for example, the declaration on meeting Marxism of the students of the "All-India Catholic University Federation" (Poonamallee 1970), "The Asian Seminar on Religion and

---

[5] Ibid., p. 58.

[6] Christ is *the* truth of God. There is no doubt today that people of other religions and ideologies can practise a radical discipleship of Christ. Cf. DSA, *Vision of Religious Life in Future and the Future of Religious Life*, NBCLC, Bangalore, 1980, pp. 3-4.

[7] The Final Statement of the Seminar on 'The Indian Church in the Struggle for a New Society', no. 73, in: DSA (ed.), *The Indian Church in the Struggle for a New Society*, NBCLC, Bangalore, 1981, pp. 62-63.

Development" (1973), "National Seminar on Youth Catechesis" (NBCLC 1973), "National Convention of Christian Leaders on the Plight of Christians of Schedule Caste Origin" (1978), and "The Indian Church in the Struggle for a New Society" (1981).[8]

## 2. Theological Underpinnings of the Response to New Society Truth, Justice and Peace

Amalor's response to the issue of social injustice took concrete shape in initiatives such as: conscientization, education, and community building.[9] While Amalor likes to read the Bible from the socio-anthropological context of social justice and peace, he bases his stand on the issue on two key theological realities: Christ, the incarnate Word and liberator;[10] and, the Church, the sacrament of Christ and liberation.[11]

### *2.1. The Bible for the Transformation of Society*

The word of God must transform history and society. It must be the basis of society and the hope of history. It must be relevant to all time and situation.

#### *2.1.1. Dialectics of historical and existential tension*

The relevance of the word of God will, in part, depend on the manner in which this word is proclaimed and interpreted. On the one hand, by taking the Bible as the point of departure, there is every danger of being unduly aprioristic, that is, deducing the significance of life from principles supposedly found in the Bible. On the other hand, by starting from the existential reality of the present, one risks forcing an interpretation, that is,

---

[8] Cf. Cyril De Souza, S.D.B., *Catechesis for India Today,* op. cit., p. 370; also: Gerwin van Leeuwen, O.F.M., *Fully Indian - Authentically Christian,* op. cit., pp. 137-141.

[9] Cf. DSA, *The Church's Mission in India Today: Evangelization and/or Liberation?,* NBCLC, Bangalore, [n. d.], pp. 7 -9.

[10] Cf. the Final Statement (Conclusions) of the Research Seminar on 'The Indian Church in the Struggle for a New Society', in: DSA (ed.), *The Indian Church in the Struggle for a New Society,* op. cit., pp. 54-57.

[11] Cf. ibid., pp. 62-67. DSA sees the Church here as the sacrament of liberation.

creating support in the Bible for a position already assumed.[12]

Amalor solves this dilemma by acknowledging the validity of both forms of God's presence: the Bible as a historical record of God's self-communication (text) and the lived human experience as God's on-going self-communication in the present (existential context). These two "should be related to one another not as a subject towards an object, but as two subjects. They exist in dialectical tension challenging one another."[13]

### *2.1.2. Hermeneutical problems*

The Bible is to be seen as a light, illuminating an opaque, ambiguous and complex reality. Not all hermeneutical approaches are adequate. The objectivist interpretation tries to delink itself from the existential human context and remain at the level of exegesis and critical textual analysis without explicitly passing on to an interpretation of the reality; whereas, the ideological approach is unduly pretextual, using the Bible to justify and legitimate particular ideological options, for example, authoritarianism or colonialism.[14]

An authentic hermeneutics, instead, situates, reads and interprets the Bible in the context of faith. Thus, the Bible becomes an integral part of faith-reflection, faith-interpretation and faith-response, as prophetic word which evokes a commitment. Extrinsic to its faith-context, the Bible becomes an ideological tool of domination.[15]

### *2.1.3. Socio-anthropological concern of the Bible: The Exodus-Pasch pattern*

The anthropological approach to theology lends itself admirably to the task of building a new society. The divine intervention in human history has always been experienced and explained by peoples and religions as the Exodus-Pasch event, of course in their own traditions and

---

[12] Cf. DSA, "Bible Text or Life Situation?", in: *Word-Event* 11 (1981) 5, p. 10.

[13] Ibid.

[14] Cf. DSA, "The Bible in Self-Renewal and Church-Renewal for Service to Society", in: *Word and Worship* 16 (1983) 10, pp. 312-313.

[15] Cf. ibid., p. 312. An example is shown, how the *Magnificat* could be a song of self-satisfaction or a promise of liberation.

terminologies. The Exodus narrative in the Bible represents the liberation story of humankind; it is an event that represents the hope, the aspirations and the struggles of humankind for a new, liberated society. God wills to build a new society with new law and worship by overthrowing the evil structures and injustice in "Egypt": he has *seen* the misery of his people, he has *heard* their cry, he has *known* their suffering and now he has *come* to liberate his people from the chains of injustice and evil structures in the society (cf. Ex.3:7-8). He called Moses and commissioned him to liberate his people -- the responsibility Moses could not shirk (cf. Ex. 3:1-22). Moses, with the help of God, brought the Israelites out of Egypt and they reached the promised land; however, in their long and committed struggle many murmured and died in their doubt and despair on the way (Massah and Meribah, cf. Ex. 17:7). This is the process of new society. Gods's "secular" concern demands man's cooperation. The pasch or the paschal mystery of Christ Jesus is the embodiment of this God's concern for the new society, his kingdom on earth.

### *2.1.4. The liberating Bible for the Indian Society*

The Bible does not give a clear blueprint or a programme of action for the realization of an ideal society, valid for all times and places, but it provides a vision that has to be interpreted and implemented in the concrete Indian situation of an oppressed and exploited people, struggling to overcome the unjust structures that enslave and dehumanize them. In the Bible we notice human situations similar to that of ours,[16] where people aspire and struggle for a just society; they experience God as one who is in their side for the cause of justice and truth. Hence we turn to the Bible for inspiration and orientation. It is in this concrete reality of the world, people and history, the written word of the Bible must become the vivifying and liberating Word of God.

The IV AIBM (All-India Biblical Meeting, NBCLC 1980) proved to be a turning point in the orientation of the biblical apostolate in India. It brought home to the participants the inadequacy of "taking the Bible as neutral to the concrete human situation."[17] In the course of the meeting the

---

[16] See for example, in the Old Testament: Naboth's vineyard grabbed by king Ahab (1 Kg. 21:1-26) and Uriah killed and his wife taken by David (2 Sam. 1-17); and in the New Testament: Jesus' fundamental option for the poor.

[17] DSA, "The Bible and Total Liberation", in: *Word-Event* 11 (1981) 5, p. 28.

very role of the Bible for social liberation was questioned. In response to Amalor's challenge thrown before the participants to give an entirely new orientation to the whole biblical apostolate in the actual reality of India, it was articulated that "the Bible is a liberating word, it has a prophetic character and hence it must serve the cause of social justice and the creation of a new society, the Kingdom of God."[18] In the past the biblical movement had charted its independent course, unaffected by other ecclesial trends such as the thrust for social justice and struggle for a new society. This irrelevance to the Indian situation led to the search for a more contextual approach.[19] In this regard, Amalor referred to the important role that should be played by the Bible in spiritually motivating different groups on the grass-root level of families and those who are involved in conscientization work and Peoples' Movements.

A task force of scripture scholars analyzed the Bible, seeking to identify its primary thrust: whether the new society envisaged therein was an ideal or a reality; whether the Gospel demand referred only to a change of heart or also indirectly involved structural change.[20] They came to the conclusion that the biblical reflection must assure the liberating and prophetic thrust of God's Word, especially in the unjust socio-economic and political structures of the Indian society.[21] The Bible thereby assumes the character of a powerful means of discerning and interpreting God's presence in concrete life situations, evoking a commitment to the transformation of society. It invites people "to pluck up and to pull down, to destroy and to overthrow, to build and to plant" (Jer. 1:10).[22]

The Church's concern and involvement in socio-economic and political spheres is neither a compromise nor a manipulation but a growth

---

[18] DSA (ed.), *Bible for Liberation. Report of the Fourth All-India Biblical Meeting (IV AIBM, 10-15 December, 1980)*, NBCLC, Bangalore, 1980, p. 5.

[19] Cf. DSA, "Introductory Talk. Presentation of the Entire Research Project. Dynamics of the Seminar", in: Id. (ed.), *The Indian Church in the Struggle for a New Society*, op. cit., p. 103.

[20] Cf. DSA, "A Break-through and a Turning Point", in: Id. (ed.), *The Indian Church in the Struggle for a New Society*, op. cit., p. 6.

[21] Cf. DSA, "Introductory Talk. Presentation of the Entire Research Project. Dynamics of the Seminar", in: Id. (ed.), *The Indian Church in the Struggle for a New Society*, op. cit., p. 110.

[22] Cf. DSA, "The Bible in Self-Renewal and Church-Renewal for Service to Society", in: *Word and Worship* 16 (1983) 10, p. 282.

of the Church's understanding of the dynamism of the word of God. In the Indian context, the socio-anthropological reading of the Bible involves: an awareness of poverty, ignorance, oppression, exploitation, enslavement, etc.,[23] and respect for the human person, his/her dignity, rights, subjectivity and personal responsibility.[24] The Word of God should be so interpreted in the context of human reality today that people see in the Bible, as in a mirror, a reflection of their own life-situation. History as human reality has to be interpreted in "its fuller meaning and ultimate fulfillment in the light of God's Word."[25]

Amalor always likes to insist on a blend of the historico-critical method with the empirico-critical method in interpreting the word of God today.[26] This is important for building a new society, whereby the ambiguities of life are illumined and interpreted by the clarifying word of God, which makes the complex simple, the hidden evident and the opaque transparent. The word of God is thereby acknowledged as illuminating the reality of life and evoking a response to pluck up and overthrow the evil and to build a society of justice, peace and righteousness. This response can be a call to the Church, self and societal criticism, the denunciation of enslaving attitudes and systems, etc., effecting, thereby, an integral liberation, the realization of the kingdom of God on earth.[27]

*2.2. Christ Jesus, the Incarnate Word and Liberator: Word and Deed*

In the fullness of time, the liberating Word of God has become flesh in Jesus Christ, and has entered the world in and through a concrete situation and society of Israel. God now continues to transform and renew the face of the earth in and through his Son Jesus Christ (cf. Rev. 21:1-5).

---

[23] Cf. DSA, "The Poor with No Voice and No Power", in: *Concilium* 146 (1981) 6, p. 49.

[24] Cf. DSA, "Socio-Economic Development as an Integral Part of Evangelization in India", in: *Indian Missiolgical Review* 6 (1984) 3, p. 215.

[25] DSA, *Theology of Catechesis,* op. cit., p. 37.

[26] Cf. DSA, "The Bible in Self-Renewal and Church-Renewal for Service to Society", in: *Word-Event* 13 (1983) 3, p. 25.

[27] Cf. DSA, "The Bible and Total Liberation", in: *Word-Event* 11 (1981) 5, p. 28.

*2.2.1. Jesus' vision of a new society: God's kingdom*

Jesus had a vision of a new society, the kingdom of God on earth, of justice, peace and righteousness, comprising all peoples and religions. The kingdom he proclaimed is essentially a kingdom of *relationship* that produces fruits of repentance (cf. Matt. 7:16; Lk. 13:6-9) by turning towards God, which also implies turning towards one's fellow human beings (cf. Matt. 22:37-39). It is a kingdom of fellowship and communion of all who accept the reign of God and his demands. The call of this challenging kingdom is by its very nature communitarian where the option for freedom, equality and justice for all people becomes a necessary condition for belonging to the kingdom. A purely individualistic understanding of God and, consequently, an individualistic practice of religion is incompatible with the kingdom Jesus proclaimed. Thus, as we have already seen earlier, the realization of the kingdom of God, the realization of a new society, becomes a gift and a task, that is, the loving and liberating presence and action of God in Jesus demands human cooperation and acceptance.[28] The love of God for his people transforms men and women and makes them capable of responding to it, by making a clear option for the weak, the oppressed and marginalized as Jesus did. In this way the kingdom has already come in the person of Jesus; it is present and active in the world, wherever and whenever people make a radical option for justice, equality and freedom; and it is -- in the Christic hope and strength -- growing in the world towards its eschatological completion at the fullness of time.[29]

*2.2.2 Christ Jesus: New Moses, new Melchizedek*

In the realization of his vision of a new society of truth, justice and peace, Jesus made, in his "revolutionary" approach, an unambiguous and uncompromising option for the weak and oppressed and stood by them, defying the religious and political authorities and challenging structures that doomed people to poverty and misery. Like Moses in Exodus, he showed to the people the divine discontent over the unjust socio-religious systems of his time and the divine determination for change, truth and justice. Seeing that the greed of the few who were throwing the many into

---

[28] Cf. DSA, "The Bible in Self-Renewal and Church-Renewal for Service to Society", in: *Word-Event* 16 (1983) 3, p. 26.

[29] Cf. DSA, *Approaches*, op. cit., 13.

poverty, hunger and slavery, Jesus, the new Moses, the new covenant, the new law of the Spirit (cf. Acts 3:22-24; 13:39; 2 Cor. 3:14-17; Heb. 3:5-6; Rev. 15:3), the new Melchizedek (cf. Heb. 5:6, 10), denounced injustice of any sort (cf. Lk. 6:20-26; 18:24; Matt. 11:20-24). He challenged the unjust socio-religious structures of his society (cf. Mk. 11:15-17) and continued his liberating activity even at the risk of his life (cf. 13:31-33). His fundamental option for the rejects of the society and his committed action for truth and justice created a movement which the authorities considered subversive (cf. Lk. 23:5), because it had the potential to topple all existing oppressive systems and structures.[30]

In the Pauline letters freedom or liberation is envisaged in holistic terms as involving the whole man and the whole of humanity and the recapitulation of all creation in Christ, and through Christ to God the Father, so that God may be all in all (cf. Eph. 1:3-14; Col. 1:15-20; 1 Cor. 3:23; 15:28). Applying the liberating approach of Jesus to our contemporary world would, then, imply a transformation of structures and humanization of institutions that they may serve the cause of equality of all people and help each person attain his/her full dignity. In other words, the holistic human salvation or re-creation of a new heaven and a new earth, that is, the creation of a new society, will involve the whole gamut of human relationships -- liberation from all alienation, personal and structural, and re-orientation of temporal realities to Christ and through Christ to the kingdom of God.[31] In this manner all creation will be brought under the cosmic Christ and, imbued with his Spirit, people will work with hope for the eschatological fulfillment of God's plan in Christ. Christ Jesus, the incarnate Word, as the proclaimer of this plan and the symbol of its realization, has realized liberation for himself and for all humankind through his resurrection.[32] In and through his words and deeds, Christ has become "the liberator and fulfiller of man."[33]

---

[30] Cf. ibid., pp. 20-22, 36; cf. also the Final Statement of the Seminar on 'The Indian Church in the Struggle for a New Society', no. 82, in: DSA (ed.), *The Indian Church in the Struggle for a New Society*, op. cit., p. 67.

[31] Cf. DSA, "A Synthesis of Basic and Constitutive Elements of Indian Christian Spirituality", *op. cit.*, pp. 229-230.

[32] Cf. DSA, *The Church's Mission in India Today: Evangelization and/or Liberation?*, op. cit., pp. 3-4.

[33] DSA, "A Reflection and Summary of the Part Devoted to Theological Questions", in: Id. (ed.), *Evangelization of the Modern World*, op. cit., p. 32.

### *2.3. The Church, Committed to Christ and the Kingdom: Servant and Sacrament*

With or without the Church, the person of the third millennium is being shaped and a new society is emerging. What part does the Church play in the emergence of the new society, "a new creation" (2 Cor. 5:17)? The risen Lord calls the Church to continue his mission of building a new genuine human society that has been tarnished by sin.

The Church as the 'People of God' is the prophetic witness of the universal quest of people and religions for a new heaven and a new earth, the kingdom of God on earth. In her sincere commitment to Christ, the Church is called to contribute towards the realization of the kingdom of God on earth. She is the servant and sacrament[34] of Christ and of the kingdom of God on earth.

#### *2.3.1. The Church in her prophetic word and deed*

To be the effective sacrament of Christ the liberator, the Church must, as we have seen before, discern the signs of the times, interpret history and manifest the Lord's designs for a new society through her prophetic function: announcing and denouncing.[35] She has to criticize society, denounce its evils, challenge its unfair policies and change its unjust structures. This also involves a positive mobilization of efforts for social change which concretizes the announcement of the Good News and the utopia of a new society. Every human society, no matter how perfect, can be transcended till the eschatological kingdom of God is realized.

The Church is called to commit herself to the transformation of society both in words and deeds. While the rȯle of the Church may be primarily that of an animator, educator or conscientizer to create in people an awareness of their social responsibility and commitment,[36] she is called,

---

[34] See also chapter four for detail on this point: the Church, the servant, sign and sacrament of Christ.

[35] See the Final Statement of the Seminar on 'The Indian Church in the Struggle for a New Society', nos. 71-119, in: DSA (ed.), *The Indian Church in the Struggle for a New Society*, op. cit., pp. 62-77.

[36] Cf. DSA, *The Church's Mission in India Today: Evangelization and/or Liberation?*, op. cit., p. 4. See also: "Holy Father's Concluding Address", in: DSA (ed.), *Evangelization of the Modern World*, op. cit., p. 130.

as did Christ, to identify and involve herself, in genuine solidarity, with the problems, needs and situations of the suffering masses.[37] She is called to embody Christ's all embracing love and effectively present his liberating action in society by her involvement in the common struggle of people for integral liberation. She is called to be the sign and instrument of renovation and "reformation", re-orientation and transformation of people, history and society towards God, towards his kingdom. This mission demands that she embodies within herself, in her own life and structures, the kingdom values of freedom, fellowship and justice. It also demands that she contributes and collaborates with others in the promotion of these values in the ordering of every human society. The struggle for a new society is, therefore, a constitutive element of the Church's evangelizing mission.

> Her specific contribution to a new society will consist in inserting the values of the gospel into human relationships, personal and structural. Negatively this will mean denouncing whatever structures militate against human freedom, fellowship and justice. Positively, it will mean joining with all people of good will in promoting those values in society which Jesus has commissioned the Church to announce.... This would mean that they exercise a continuing vigilance against the erosion of human freedom; that they articulate their ideals in words; that they be 'actors' through a praxis in the ushering in of an ever increasingly human society. All humankind is the Church's arena and a New Society is her agenda. It is at once the privilege and the obligation of the entire people of God to bring about such a society.[38]

The Church needs the spirit of discernment and has the great responsibility of sifting the main issues which affect our society and fixing an order of priority among them. For example, the main areas of struggle in the Indian situation will be: land reform, child labour, bonded labour, the oppressive caste system, the exploitation of the tribals, the élitist

---

[37] Cf. DSA, *The Church's Mission in India Today: Evangelization and/or Liberation?*, op. cit., p. 4.

[38] The Final Statement of the Seminar on 'The Indian Church in the Struggle for a New Society', no. 73, in: DSA (ed.), *The Indian Church in the Struggle for a New Society*, op. cit., pp. 62-63.

educational system, strengthening the *status quo* and the unjust national and international structures, religious riot, bigotry and fundamentalism.[39]

*2.3.2. The Church in her word and worship*

The Church's ministry of the word and worship should be focused on areas of struggle for a new society. The sacramental celebration should breathe its involvement in the real life situation of the people, it should really be a 'life and worship' of the people.

> If the Eucharistic Christ is "Bread broken for a new world", as the 42nd Eucharistic Congress at Lourdes (1981) proclaimed, the whole Eucharistic celebration should breathe our involvement in the struggle to heal all broken persons and to break the structures that are responsible for it. If the Eucharistic Memorial fails to sharpen and deepen our social sensitivity and commitment, it tends to become a mockery of the Lord who struggled till his violent death for the poor and the voiceless.[40]

In this struggle for liberation each section of the Christian community (laity, youth, women, religious, priests and bishops) according to its status in the Church and opportunities in the society is called to play its active and specific role. As the group of religious men and women in the Indian Church is relatively numerous but apparently "closed within walls", there lies a great challenge before them with regard to their insertion and contribution towards creating a more human and just society.

> In virtue of their vocation they should embody the eschatological dimension of the Kingdom and the radicality of the Gospel. They are the group called especially to be most daring, restless and in the vanguard, embodying and ushering in the new society with its values of freedom, fellowship and justice. Having experienced at a deep personal level God's loving choice of them for his mission, they divest themselves of all attachments to goods, persons and preferences so

---

[39] See: Ibid.

[40] The Final Statement of the Seminar on 'The Indian Church in the Struggle for a New Society', no. 82, in: DSA (ed.), *The Indian Church in the Struggle for a New Society,* op. cit., p. 67.

as to freely commit themselves to a community of fellowship that strives for God's justice in the world.... This is their contribution to the full eruption of God's Kingdom in our society.[41]

### *2.3.3. Struggle amidst opposition*

Since the holistic mission of the Church refers also to the temporal spheres, issues of justice and their ramifications have never been alien to her concern. The encyclical *Rerum Novarum* (1891) represents a milestone as far as the modern Church's social issue is concerned.[42] Subsequently, numerous documents have reflected on varying social problems ranging from private property to social justice, world peace, development, human rights, etc., so that the 'social question' has come to embody a definite content. It would not be hyperbole to affirm that the Church stands as one of the most respected institutions for its competent and authoritative interventions in favour of justice and peace, human rights, social and cultural promotion.[43]

To respond to the challenges of the new society the Church needs *a new theology and new structures.* This new theology in the Indian context is most aptly described as 'Indian Theology of Liberation', born out of the Church's struggle side by side with men and women of other religious traditions and ideologies and in the midst of mass poverty.[44] This theology is to be holistic, experiential and concrete, rendering the service of delinking socialism from atheism, developing the spirit of collaboration and more Christian involvement in the great caste and class struggle, based on a holistic approach to reality that is typically Indian -- the well-being of all (*lokasaṁgraha, sarvodaya*).

---

[41] The Final Statement of the Seminar on 'the Indian Church in the Struggle for a New Society', no. 93, in: DSA (ed.), *The Indian Church in the Struggle for a New Society,* op. cit., p. 70.

[42] Cf. Paul Leon, "Changes and Developments in the Social Teaching of the Church Magisterium", in: DSA (ed.), *The Indian Church in the Struggle for a New Society,* op. cit., p. 806.

[43] Cf. Cyril De Souza, S.D.B., *Catechesis for India Today,* op. cit., p. 355.

[44] Cf. Gerwin van Leeuwen, O.F.M., *Fully Indian - Authentically Christian,* op. cit., p. 165.

> Any critical analysis shows that the present pyramidal *Church structures* prevent her from an authentic participation in the world's struggle for a new society. At all levels the decision-making lies in the hands of a few or even a single person and not in those of all the faithful who constitute the Christian community. Although the power and authority of priests and bishops ... are termed 'sacred' and 'spiritual', the very accumulation of all power in the hands of a few facilitates domination tending to stifle all initiatives from below. As long as these feudal structures continue, the institution of different consultative bodies (Synod, Diocesan Pastoral Council, Parish Council) in the wake of Vatican II seems a mere palliative.[45]

All peoples and religions are called to participate in the liberation movement of Christ. Christian groups or communities that are really involved in the struggle for a new society are the proper milieu of such activity; they "deserve all freedom, encouragement and support."[46] The struggle must go on with hope and realism till the fullness of the realization of God's rule upon earth at the fullness of time.

> The cost of Christian discipleship is indeed great (Matt. 10:-), but imbued with the Spirit of Jesus Christ who is the Lord of History and impelled by the conviction that God is the future of man and that He is one with us in our struggle (Ex. 3:-) we forge ahead struggling with the people for full humanity.[47]

## 3. The Indian Reality: A Socio-cultural Analysis and Aspirations

Even a superficial analysis of India's social, economic, political and educational situations would reveal a dismal picture of India where the

---

[45] The Final Statement of the Seminar on 'The Indian Church in the Struggle for a New Society', no. 107, in: DSA (ed.), *The Indian Church in the Struggle for a New society,* op. cit., p. 74.

[46] The Final Statement of the Seminar on 'The Indian Church in the Struggle for a New Society', no. 108, in: Ibid.

[47] See the conclusion of the Final Statement of the Seminar on 'The Indian Church in the Struggle for a New Society', no. 120, in: Ibid., p. 77.

majority live in appalling misery.[48] This poses a challenge to the religious traditions in general, and to the Indian Church in particular, in their struggle for a new society. The situation calls for inter-religious collaboration in building a new society of justice and joy, peace and righteousness.

### *3.1. Need of Social Analysis*

A scientific social analysis is necessary to understand the 'power structure' and the functioning of the 'social mechanism'. Criticizing approaches to social issues that were either 'amateurish' or generic,[49] Amalor felt the need for "a scientific analysis of the world situation and the Indian reality today in socio-economic, political and ideological spheres, both at structural and personal levels and as macro and micro realities."[50]

This concern found practical expressions in the 'Asian Seminar on Religion and Development' (Bangalore 1973), jointly organized by the NBCLC and the International Federation of Institutes for Socio-Religious Research (FERES) of Louvain.[51] It aimed at giving the participants tools of analysis and reflection and at the same time to enable religiously inspired social activists to become aware of the role of religion in Asia, particularly with regard to the transformation of society.[52]

Amalor often quoted statistics and percentages from official documents with a view to obtaining an objective picture of the socio-economic and political reality.[53] This scientific approach brought to his awareness the reality of power structures, social mechanisms and their mutual interaction.[54] At times he remained on a descriptive level, drawing information from the daily papers and highlighting crucial issues. He notes

---

[48] Cf. DSA, *Approach,* op. cit., pp. 62-63.

[49] Cf. DSA, "The Implications of Vatican II for the Mission in Asia", in: *Teaching All Nations* 4 (1967) 3, p. 319.

[50] DSA, *Poverty of the Religious and the Religious as Poor,* op. cit., p. 35.

[51] See: *Word and Worship* 6 (1973) 8, pp. 271-370.

[52] Cf. Gerwin van Leeuwen, O.F.M., *Fully Indian - Authentically Christian,* op. cit., p. 137. According to him the speeches of DSA and S. Kappen at the Seminar may be considered the beginnings of an Indian Theology of liberation.

[53] Cf. DSA, *The Option for the Poor in the Concrete Situation of India and Sri Lanka,* A Redemptoris Publication, Bangalore, 1982, p. 16.

[54] Cf. DSA, *Poverty of the Religious and the Religious as Poor,* op. cit., p. 35.

the issues as

> the spiralling prices, lack of essential commodities, hoarding and profiteering, black-marketing and food adulteration, the parallel economy of black money, the growing gap between the rich and the poor, increased production not resulting in equal distribution to all, the rapid growth of population, unemployment and under-employment, inefficiency and corruption in the whole administration at all levels from top to bottom, harassment of harijans and other weaker sections, in-fights and factions in political parties and consequent political instability, chiefly in the states. The reaction of the people to all this takes the form of 'bandhs' and strikes, including in essential services, violence of all forms, mass looting, communal strife, student indiscipline, break-down of the law and order situation necessitating constant intervention of the police and the army.[55]

Even after fifty years of independence India continues to present a dismal picture. The most glaring fact that sharpens the crisis in the Indian society is the massive, dehumanizing poverty of the vast masses of people. The real causes of this poverty are the unjust structures of the hierarchically stratified layers of society, one lying upon the other. Of India's 690 (1981 census),[56] 300 million live below the 'poverty line', 297 million live on or just above the 'poverty line', 80 million have decent food, clothing and shelter and a meagre 13 million are the rich who can afford almost everything they want.[57] That is to say, nearly half of the population live below the subsistence level, subject to hunger, malnutrition, disease, lacking minimum clothing and shelter.

Poverty is not always caused by lack of wealth. Sometimes it is lack of sharing that is the bigger culprit. When selfishness leads a few individuals to garner all the resources available for themselves, the division of society into rich and poor, haves and have-nots begins. Economic deve-

---

[55] DSA, *Approach,* op. cit., p. 62. See also: S.M. Michael, "Analysis of Society at the Micro-level: The Indian Rural Reality", in: DSA (ed.), *The Indian Church in the Struggle for a New Society,* op. cit., pp. 123-141, for a detailed analysis of the Indian situation.

[56] Today in 1998 it is about 980 million and it is expected to cross 1000 million before the year 2000. (See. *International Herald Tribune,* May 28, 1998, p. 1).

[57] See: Gerwin van Leeuwen, O.F.M., *Fully Indian - Authentically Christian,* op. cit., p. 208.

lopment in itself is not a guarantee of justice and equitable distribution. Besides, while the education system is patterned on the colonial model that leads to dominate people, making them an élitist class and supporting the *status quo,* hopes placed in political parties have been shattered and confidence in Parliamentary Democracy has been shaken.

The causes of these unjust structures are historical, socio-economic and political. The main historical cause was the colonial exploitation, which also undermined the values of the joint family, caste and cooperation network of the village and the values of the Indian ethos at large; while the main structural cause remains the economic system of production, consumption and distribution. The systems, even if well formalized, are oppressive and unjust in execution, incapable of bringing about a change for better, especially since they are backed by vested interests of the dominant. It is the system of the 'big fish in the sea'. By manipulating the economic, political and cultural structures, the international and national élite use their power to maintain their privileged position (*status quo*) and assure a steady drain of resources from the masses who produce them to the few rich élite who enjoy them.

Added to this, the strong and oppressive caste system plays a great role in widening the social gap in India. Though once well-intentioned by the sages of Hinduism for the well-running of society, even supported by M. Gandhi for that matter, the caste system as it is today, with its *stigmata* of untouchability, mutual aversion and oppression, is seen not as a virtue but a vice. While the poor and the rejected struggle for social and political equality, the rich manipulate the socio-political systems and institutions to their own advantage. They oppress the poor, institutionalize and proliferate violence. Such a situation breathes violence and counter-violence.

Amalor says that "the problem is not so much that there is hunger and disease, poverty and misery in the world for many people; as all this is due to injustice and oppression: not simply poverty but injustice [sin]."[58] The oppressed are confronting not just unjust persons and groups but "a systemic evil, structural injustice, organized oppression and institutionalized violence [personal and structural sin]."[59] The cause of all this is obviously the "economic, social and political structures of the country as

---

[58] DSA, "Meditation on Social Awareness", in: Id. (ed.), *Joyful Response to the Challenge of Faith-Formation of Youth,* NBCLC, Bangalore, 1981, p. 356.

[59] DSA, "The Poor with No Voice and No Power", in: *Concilium* 146 (1981) 6, p. 50.

well as sin, man's selfishness and closure."[60]

In this situation, only a structural change can remedy the situation in providing the people development and liberation which are necessarily linked with the emergence of a new society, willed by God. But the chances seem to be bleak and discouraging, because the top 13% have their vested interests in preserving the *status quo.* With the result in the world at large and India in particular the gap between the rich and the poor is increasing.

### *3.2. Basic Needs and Aspirations of the Indian Society*

#### *3.2.1. Liberation and development: Anthropological approach*

When we talk of liberation we always mean "the total liberation of man from sin and all its forces and consequences."[61] The tools of social analysis helped Amalor understand that the relevance of the Good News was closely linked with the critical issue of the relation between religion and development.[62] Human history represents the struggle at both the individual and the collective levels for a total liberation in all dimensions: social, political, economic, cultural, etc., thereby enabling man to develop and fulfill himself integrally.[63]

Advocating a return to the holistic vision of man and society,[64] Amalor strives for an all-embracing understanding of the Church's mission -- salvation of man and the sanctification of the temporal order of society by penetrating and perfecting it with the Gospel.[65]

---

[60] DSA, *The Church's Mission in India Today: Evangelization and/or Liberation?,* op. cit., p. 3.

[61] DSA, *Theology of Development,* op. cit., p. 9.

[62] Cf. DSA, "Editorial", in: *Word and Worship* 6 (1973) 8, p. 271.

[63] Cf. DSA, *Theology of Development,* op. cit., pp. 9-10. Also: *PP* 1.

[64] Cf. DSA, *Our Christian World Vision and Theological Synthesis,* op. cit., pp. 14-17; see also chapter one.

[65] Cf. DSA, *Theology of Development,* op. cit., 8. Also: *AA* 5 & 7.

*3.2.1.1. Anthropological approach*
*Relevant to man and his society*

The key-word, and perhaps the most important clue, towards understanding the anthropological approach of the Church's mission to life, liberation and development and her attitude towards other religions is 'relevance', which is one of the chief concerns of Vatican II.[66] Broadly speaking the anthropological approach to life, liberation and development is the concern of the entire *man,* his entire situation and his relationships. It takes the existential life-situation of man as its point of departure.[67]

Concern for man -- the integral man -- is what makes any approach anthropological, relevant to man and his total concern.[68] While the old vision (pre-Vatican II) stressed God, Church, 'other world' and ignored man, the focus of the new vision (Vatican II) is on man -- his hopes, aspirations, concern and struggles in 'this world'. While in the old ecclesiocentric theology man played a secondary and subordinate role, today "the focus is on man as centre and summit, as master of everything and co-responsible for it, with God."[69] Man and his secularity should be taken seriously and for his own sake, because God who is present in the secular world and history performs his saving action in and through human activities.[70] Hence, such an anthropological focus should be a genuine part of the Church's apostolate -- not merely an attention-getter, nor a bait to lure human beings, nor even a psychological or a pedagogical device -- so that by manifesting Christ in the real situation of man, the Church reveals to man the real truths about his condition and his total vocation (cf. *AG* 8).[71]

In this approach man is seen not as a static essence but in his

---

[66] 'Renewal' or 'updating' was the original motivation of the Council, but it was always in view of relevance.

[67] Cf. DSA, *The Church's Mission as Prophetic and Hermeneutical,* op. cit., pp. 7-8.

[68] Cf. DSA, "Workshop on Recent Developments in Catechetics", in: *Teaching All Nations* 4 (1967) 3, pp. 377-379.

[69] DSA, *Our Christian World Vision,* op. cit., p. 22; see also: Id., *Social Communication,* op. cit., p. 17.

[70] Cf. DSA, "Synthesis of Trends in Catechetical Movement and in Official documents", in: DSA (ed.), *Converging Trends of the Catechetical Movement and Guidelines of Official Documents,* NBCLC, Bangalore, 1979, pp. 52-53.

[71] Cf. DSA, *Purpose,* op. cit., p. 16.

concreteness in a particular context, as one who is "in existence and is constantly in movement",[72] in "becoming".[73] Man is not condemned to his fate, but he has embarked on an adventure of history, both as an individual and in groups, and is desirous of assuming the responsibility for his historical becoming. In this historical adventure all men and women tend towards their total self-fulfillment under the dynamic impulse of creation, engaging their whole being, assessing their vital needs, pooling their resources, becoming conscious of their responsibilities and making heroic efforts so as to work out a better life for themselves and achieve full liberation. This historical adventure involves the transformation of society by man, in the process of which, he himself is transformed. In other words, in order to have a better tomorrow, man himself has to work for the development of the *whole man* and *every man*. Humankind's historical adventure is, thus, essentially in its 'becoming', in its 'struggle' for cooperation with God and collaboration with one another. Such an approach is imperative, "if Christ, His Gospel and His Church are to transform the world, orient history and lead them to fulfillment."[74]

*3.2.1.2. Liberation and development*

On assuming office as Director of the NBCLC (1968), Amalor mainly focused his attention on these current burning issues of the day: evangelization, human development, liberation, and their interrelationships.[75] He also liked to expound the often misinterpreted stance of Vatican II on these issues.[76]

At the 'Zonal Missionary Consultation' (Bombay 1969), the organizers enunciated the theme: "How are education and social work related to the work of evangelization? Are they means to an end or ends in themselves? Do we purposely work for making men Christians or do we want

[72] DSA, *Theology of Catechesis*, op. cit., p. 23.

[73] Ibid.,

[74] DSA, *Theology of Development*, op. cit., p. 23; cf. also: Id., *Approaches*, op. cit., pp. 20-24.

[75] Cf. Gerwin van Leeuwen, O.F.M., *Fully Indian - Authentically Christian*, op. cit., p. 204.

[76] Cf. DSA, *Purpose*, op. cit., p. 6.

nothing more than making men human beings?"[77] This problem had arisen both at the level of theological reflection and missionary praxis, often resulting in simplistic polarization between missionaries and educators, "evangelizers" and social workers. Evangelization was considered a *specific duty* of the Church, whereas development, a dimension of her mission, to some extent optional -- time and personnel permeating. Amalor calls such discussion 'idle academic talk' or even 'an evasion for not facing the reality'.[78]

### *(i) Christian perspective: Integral liberation*

A genuine anthropological approach to evangelization necessarily implies development work towards the integral liberation of man -- individual and communitarian, religious and human. There is a necessary relationship between evangelization and human development because man must be taken as a whole and saved in his totality. All evangelization which is not situated in the milieu of the addressee becomes irrelevant.[79] This issue was hotly debated during the IV Synod of Bishops (Rome 1974) and it was generally agreed that commitment to social justice, the transformation of oppressive structures, human promotion, liberation and development were an integral part of evangelization. The Church must be constantly committed to the transformation of men and society.[80]

In his inaugural key-note address at the International Theological Conference on Evangelization and Dialogue in Asia (Nagpur 1971), Amalor uses for the first time the terms "conscientization" and "liberation".[81] In his theological Orientation Speech to the All-India Consultation

---

[77] DSA, *Theology of Development,* op. cit., p. 5.

[78] Cf. DSA, *Approach,* op. cit., p. 61.

[79] Cf. DSA, *Approaches,* op. cit., pp. 20-24.

[80] Cf. DSA, "A Reflection and Summary of the Part Devoted to Theological Questions", in: Id. (ed.), *Evangelization of the Modern World,* op. cit., 31. See also: "Conclusions of the Symposium on Mission Theology for Our Times", in: Id., *Approaches,* op. cit., pp. 45-51.

[81] See: DSA, *Theology of Evangelization,* op. cit., pp. 6-7; 'Liberation and Development' in the Declaration of the Conference forms a significant section (art. 30-37, in: Ibid., pp. 37-39). See also: Gerwin van Leeuwen, O.F.M., *Fully Indian - Authentically Christian,* op. cit., p. 207.

on Evangelization, Patna (1973), he devotes a whole section to liberation and development, because together with the plurality of religions, the struggle for liberation and development constitutes the Indian reality.[82] He starts with a reference to Sheikh Mujibur Rehman, the Father of Bangladesh, that the world is realistically divided between the oppressors and the oppressed, the rich and the poor. The oppressors dominate and enjoy most of the goods of the world. We are living in a world where 15% of the people enjoy all the benefits of society, while 85% are deprived of them. The topmost 15% are the dominant, the lower 85% are the dominated; many of them are even deprived of the essentials for human survival.[83] The Indian situation, as we have seen above, seems to be worse. In this situation, Christ the liberator should be present. If he is present, Amalor asks the question: "What will He do? What has He done in similar situations? What does He ask of His Church to do now?"[84]

Liberation and development must go hand in hand. We understand by liberation today the total liberation of the whole person, from sin and all its forces and consequences.[85] The forces of sin and its consequences are: massive and stark poverty, hunger, sickness, economic underdevelopment, social injustice, oppression and exploitation of the poor by the rich, discrimination on the ground of sex, race, nationality, religion, war, etc. Liberation, therefore, is always an integral liberation, of both spiritual as well as temporal orders (cf. *GS* 3, 63-64). God's plan for the world is that people of different religions work together to restore the temporal sphere of things, tarnished by sin and selfishness, and develop it fully.

Many elements make up the temporal order: the good things of life and the prosperity of the family, culture, the arts and professions, socio-economic and political affairs, institutions and structures, international relations, and other matters of this kind as well as their development and progress. All of these not only aid in the attainment of human beings' ultimate goal but also possess their own intrinsic value, implanted in them by God (cf. *AA* 7). This is the integral and anthropological approach to liberation and development that the participants of the All-India Seminar

---

[82] Cf. Gerwin van Leeuwen, O.F.M., *Fully Indian - Authentically Christian,* op. cit., p. 207.

[83] Cf. DSA, "Approach", *op. cit.,* p. 55.

[84] Ibid., p. 57.

[85] Cf. DSA, *Theology of Development,* op. cit., p. 9.

on 'The Church in India Today' (1969) echoed in their General Assembly Resolutions: "Our involvement in, and contribution to, the integral development of our country, economic, cultural, social, political, moral and spiritual, is for us, at the same time, a fidelity to our mission as Christians and a service to our motherland, and to the whole of mankind."[86]

It is obvious that work for development and liberation implies the Church's commitment to bring about a radical change in the structures of society.[87] However, there are still many priests, bishops and religious who think that involvement in the developmental work does not belong to their task. Amalor's response to this is a description of the integral salvation which Christ the liberator lived and died for, also for the India of today. Referring to Ephesians 1:3-12, 1 Corinthians 3:23 and 15:29, and later to Isaiah 52 and 53 and Mark 10:41-45, he holds:

> This salvation of the whole man and of all men and a re-creation of a new earth consists in humanization of man in the whole gamut of his relationships within family, social, economic, political and cultural spheres, in liberating him from all forms of alienation, psychological, existential, social, ideological and cosmic and in the redemption of all the realities of the temporal order. In this way, everything will come under the cosmic leadership of Christ, everything will be imbued with his Spirit and oriented to the Creator, towards the eschatological unity and fulfillment of God's Kingdom.[88]

The Church is challenged to be the living sign and instrument of Christ's liberation by her total involvement in the struggles of the common people, her identification with the suffering masses and in her fight against the oppressive structures.

Once again Amalor stresses that Christians should work with others, from within and not from without, for integral human development. The Church has to be the prophet of the day. In this regard, he expects the Church to take seriously Julius Nyerere's well-known speech to the

---

[86] See the General Assembly Resolutions of the *Report of the All-India Seminar on 'The Church in India Today'*, no. IV.1. , in: DSA, *Theology of Development*, op. cit., p. 9.

[87] Cf. DSA, *Approach*, op. cit., p. 63.

[88] Ibid., p. 65.

Chapter of the Maryknoll Sisters:

> The Church should accept that development of peoples means rebellion. Unless we participate actively in the rebellion against those social structures and economic organizations which condemn men to poverty, humiliation and degradation, then the Church will become irrelevant to men.... Unless the Church -- its members and organizations -- express God's love for man by involvement and leadership in constructive protest against the present condition of man, then it will become identified with injustice and persecution.... The development of peoples at this time in man's history must imply a divine discontent and a determination for change. What this amounts to is a call to the Church to recognize the need for social revolution and to play a leading role in it.[89]

*(ii) Indian Perspective: Wholeness (pūrṇam), dharma*

The Indian term for liberation is *mokṣa* or *mukti* which literally mean 'release', release from all that prevents a person from reaching and experiencing the Ultimate Reality (Brahman or Paramātman). To reach that Ultimate Reality one has to be liberated from the endless cycle of birth and re-birth (*saṁsāra*), which manifests itself in persons whose life has been strangled in a meaningless routine, a kind of purposeless drifting, a state of slavery and compulsion, pride, selfishness, brokenness and disharmony (*ajñāna, ahaṁkāra*), a state of merely biological survival or being totally absorbed by mechanical and efficient function without much concern for the fact that society is constituted by men and women, living "persons".[90] Human life is a pilgrimage or journey (*yātrā*) towards reaching and experiencing the Ultimate Reality as life and liberation, that is, one's union with Brahman and with other fellow human beings and the cosmos in an all-round wholeness (*pūrṇam*) and welfare of all (*sarva bhūtahite ratah*), passing through the four-fold goal of life (*puruṣārtha*): *dharma* (social justice), *artha* (wealth), *kāma* (pleasure), and *mokṣa*

---

[89] See: Gerwin van Leeuwen, O.F.M., *Fully Indian - Authentically Christian,* op. cit., pp. 208-209. The speech was delivered by the President of Tanzania to the Chapter of the Maryknoll Sisters at Maryknoll, New York on October 16, 1970. See DSA referring to the speech in: Id., "Approach", *op. cit.,* p. 59.

[90] Cf. DSA, *Poverty of the Religious and the Religious as Poor,* op. cit., pp. 14-15.

(liberation, total freedom). One has to pursue the ultimate and supreme goal, liberation (*mokṣa*), taking into account the three proximate goals of life: social justice (*dharma*), wealth (*artha*) and pleasure (*kāma*) in a relentless quest, as an arrow that leaves its bow to reach its target and realize its purpose, that is, in our case, the realization of self and the Absolute, in the discovery of the one unchanging Reality beyond all forms and names, beneath the changing modes of human consciousness, in the ultimate unity and awareness of all. In short, it is the realization of one's union with God, experienced as *aham Brahmāsmi.* This is the *radicality* of Indian spirituality and the ultimate goal of human life.[91]

The means to reach the highest goal is the practice of *dharma* (social justice) both in the acquisition of wealth and in the enjoyment of pleasure. *Dharma* leads one to the principle of 'sharing', not 'selfishness'. The Mahābhārata enjoins one: "Do not do to others what you do not wish to be done to you; and wish for others what you desire and long for yourself: this is the essence of *dharma*" (5.39.57; 3.198.43). When translated into practice this principle leads one to the performance of one's duty without selfish desire or gain or reward (*niṣkāma karma,* cf. Bhagavad-gītā 5.25; 12.4). Wealth and pleasure are good provided they are in keeping with *dharma.* Amalor writes:

> It is a triptych and hence all the three should be held together as one. Acquisition of wealth and enjoyment of pleasure if *'done with (responsibility and justice) will lead to sharing of oneself and one's goods, to practice of poverty [detachment] and social justice and to*

---

[91] Cf. DSA, "Main Categories of Hindu Philosophy and Spirituality", in: DSA (ed.), *Indian Christian Spirituality,* op. cit., pp. 151-152.

Even though man's 'integral' liberation is advocated in Hinduism; it is generally understood in the 'individual' sense, not in the Christian sense of integral salvation, that is 'total' and 'communitarian'. The concepts of man, matter and God, especially in traditional Hindu philosophy, do not offer a solid basis for integral salvation and development. For example, (i) Man's spiritual self is outside of history; his condition is fixed by caste and *karma.* (ii) Man finds salvation (*mokṣa*) as an individual, without reference to the present world and by escaping the world (matter); the spiritual realm (*paramārthika*) is separated from the social and political (*vyavahārika*). (iii) The world and history are not moving to a final conclusion, but are caught up in an endless cycle of *kalpas* and *yugas.* (iv) The *avatāras* of God do not really suffer and die. These concepts continue to play a negative role in the minds and attitudes of the people. Though modern Hinduism has corrected these attitudes, there is yet much to be done.

*promotion of community fellowship'*. Unrestricted accumulation of wealth and unbridled enjoyment of pleasure should be controlled and subordinated to social justice. In other words, *artha* and *kama* should be so regulated and transcended by *dharma* that they all become conducive to the attainment of *moksha (artha-dharma-kama and moksha)*. One cannot think of possessing wealth or enjoying life independent of the universe, forgetful of society and unconcerned about one's brothers and sisters.[92]

### *3.3. Solidarity and Fellowship: Preferential Option for the Poor*

Solidarity with the poor and the oppressed implies becoming one with them in their on-going struggle for "political independence, economic development, social reform, racial equality, cultural renaissance, updating of religion, cause of justice and peace or international solidarity."[93] A presence of togetherness, sympathy and solidarity, is entirely different from a stifling institutional presence which overpowers with its imposing structures, personnel and means. A genuine solidarity is not the extrinsic 'being there', characteristic of a foreigner or observer, however sympathetic and well-intentioned, but "a presence of fellow-travellers, co-citizens and compatriots, brothers and friends."[94] It is a solidarity that is open to all collectivities, communities and groups whether civic or political, economic or social, cultural or religious. It is not a solidarity in terms of territorial dimensions nor restricted to religious demarcations but a solidarity of human beings, whether Christians or others. It extends freely to the structures and channels of the secular world, to the institutions and agencies of the temporal order in the very mainstream of national life of the country and the world. It is a solidarity from within, a relationship between the Christian community and human group, lived and fostered by fellowship in mutual service and collaboration.[95] *Ad Gentes* states: "The Church through her children, is one with men of every condition, but especially with the poor and the afflicted. On their behalf

---

[92] Ibid., p. 152; also: DSA, *Poverty of the Religious and the Religious as Poor*, op. cit., p. 18.

[93] DSA, *Theology of Development*, op. cit., p. 23.

[94] DSA, *Approaches*, op. cit., p. 26.

[95] Cf. ibid., pp. 26-27. Also: *GS* 1 & 2.

she gladly spends herself (cf. 2 Cor. 12:15). For she shares in their joys and sorrows, knows their longings and problems, suffers with them in throes of death" (no. 12).[96]

Christianity is not first of all and essentially a philosophy, a code of ethics, a doctrinal system. It is, above all, "a life of relationship and fellowship among persons: with God and with one another, animated by charity. The relationship of love among men is a sign and proof of man's relationship with God in love."[97] The Christian solidarity and collaboration must be inspired and nourished by charity and respect (cf. *AG* 11). This charity should be spontaneous, selfless and sacrificing, universal and open, springing from the heart and concretely expressed. It must flow towards others from the very love God has poured into their hearts through his Spirit, in their sincere witness to Christ and the Church (cf. Jn. 13:35).

### *3.4. A New Society: Rāmarājya*

The hope and constant struggle for the kingdom of God is also found in Indian religious traditions. In Hinduism it is symbolized by Rāmarājya, the kingdom of God, of justice, peace, love and righteousness. M. Gandhi spoke of the kingdom of God (Rāmarājya) as the ideal society.

This Rāmarājya is a gift and a task. It is attained through the grace of God and human cooperation. The Bhagavad-gītā is the ideal enshrinement of this hope for Rāmarājya expressed in its cosmic conflictual perspective of *dharma* (justice) and *adharma* (injustice) in society. While the principle of *avatāra* in Kṛṣṇa insists on the need of God's grace,[98] it also asks Arjuna for human cooperation to fight for justice, peace and righteousness (cf. Mahābhārata). God's grace is needed in the realization of Rāmarājya on earth. The Bhagavad-gītā reads:

> Out of your gracious favour for me you have uttered the highest mystery, namely, 'what pertains to Self' (11.1).
> I cannot find my bearings, I cannot find a refuge; have mercy, God of gods, home of the universe (11.25).
> And so I bow to you, prostrate my body, crave grace of you, my Lord

---

[96] See as quoted by DSA in: Ibid., p. 27.

[97] Ibid., pp. 27-28.

[98] Cf. M. Dhavamony, *Classical Hinduism*, op. cit., 457-465.

adorable (11.44).
Thinking on me you will surmount all dangers by my grace (18.58).

The above concept is crystal clear when Kṛṣṇa states:

> For whenever righteousness withers away, and lawlessness raises its head, then do I generate myself on earth.
> For the protection of the good, for the destruction of the wicked, for the setting up of righteousness, I come into being age after age (BG 4.7-8).

The doctrine of the many and repeated *avatāras* of God (Kṛṣṇa, Rāma) shows the eschatological completion of the kingdom of God (Rāmarājya).

The closeness of God to human beings through grace is realized not only historically and spiritually but also typically and sacramentally. Popular festivals like Dusaharā, Durgā Pūjā, Holī and Dīpāvalī, bear witness to the on-going conflict between *dharma* and *adharma* in society and the final hope of the triumph of *dharma* over *adharma*. The victory of good over evil is seen as a present reality, to be reached through a struggle from which no one can escape. The establishment of *dharma* over *adharma* indicates a building up of a society of righteousness, peace and prosperity, justice and brotherhood. The hope of the triumph of good over evil is eternalized in the Indian ethos as *'satyameva jayate'* ('truth will prevail'), be it in the social reform or political independence. Any attempt to motivate the Indian people for a 'new society' must seriously take into account this burning hope and aspiration of the people.[99]

### *3.5. Need of Collaboration in Building a New Society*

Such being the case of the Indian society, if the Church and other religious traditions of India want to be faithful to God and his cause of truth and justice in the society, then they cannot but actively enter into the society, to give it a new orientation of hope and liberation. This requires well organized programmes and undertakings, mutual understanding and sincere collaboration. Religions must come out to collaborate also with the

---

[99] Cf. DSA, "A Synthesis of Basic and Constitutive Elements of Indian Christian Spirituality", *op. cit.*, pp. 230-233.

development programmes proposed and undertaken by Government and non-governmental organizations, institutions and agencies (cf. *AG* 12). Work for development and liberation implies a commitment to effect a radical change in structures of society, and if need be, a change also in the structures of religious institutions, their concerns and priorities.[100]

### *3.5.1. Christian perspective: Global concern*

Collaboration in the creation of a new society by social change should be patterned on the Christian vision, that is, global and all-inclusive concern, and not constrained by institutionalism and exclusivism. It should aim at creating a better society, comprising a global, open community of men and women of different religious traditions of the world.[101] In this regard, the Church must learn to collaborate more and more with others. Some of the fields where collaboration is needed and most appreciated are, as we have seen earlier: education, concerted efforts to eradicate famine, hunger and disease, projects and enterprises for socio-economic development, moral values and freedom, social justice and world peace (cf. *AG* 12).[102]

> Hitherto much of this work was carried out chiefly and under the auspices and through the institutions of the Church. Though the Church is justified in having institutions and though the advantages are many, we have more and more to serve through other institutions and agencies.... 'In this activity', the Decree advises, 'the faithful should be eager to offer their prudent aid to projects sponsored by public and private organizations, by Government, by international agencies, by various Christian communities and even by non-Christian religions' (*AG* 12d).[103]

---

[100] Cf. DSA, *Approach,* op. cit., p. 63. See also: Desmond De Souza, "Handicaps of the Church to Gear Her Mission to Creating a New Society", in: DSA (ed.), *The Indian Church in the Struggle for a New Society,* op. cit., pp. 165-168, who said that "the mutual influence between the structures of society and those of the Church" prevent her from fulfilling her mission.

[101] Cf. DSA, "New Theological Approaches in Asia", in: *Verbum SVD* 21 (1980) 314, pp. 301-302.

[102] Cf. DSA, *Approaches,* op. cit., p. 29.

[103] Ibid.

No genuine commitment to development and liberation on the part of anyone is genuine and valid unless it is translated into what is known as 'conscientization and commitment'.[104] The issues of justice, peace and development are the living concerns, not only of the Church but of all religions and ideologies of the world. Hence there arises the need for collaboration among the religions and ideologies of the world.

*3.5.2. Indian perspective: Ṛta, dharma, karma*

Once again Amalor likes to base his theology of collaboration for social justice, harmony, solidarity and liberation on the concept of *mokṣa* through *ṛta* (harmony), *dharma* (social justice) and *niṣkāma karma* (selfless service). According to the Vedas the universe is a structured, harmonious and well-ordered totality (*ṛta*). The harmony of the universe is the model of just order in society (*dharma*) and personal integrity through an awareness of self, others and God. Real social solidarity (*lokasaṁgraha*) among the inhabitants of the world reflects the eternal cosmic harmony (*ṛta*), and social concern is an essential human responsibility in view of a just human society and the welfare of all (*sarvodaya, lokasevā*). Every human person is called to enter into this cosmic order, maintain it and contribute to it through the practice of social and cultic duties (*dharma* and *karma*). Whenever and wherever this social order is broken, there prevails *adharma* (injustice) and society is in disharmony. The harmony is to be restored. Amalor writes:

> Whenever and wherever this social order is disturbed *adharma* prevails and society is in disharmony with *ṛta,* one should change it and restore the harmony by practice of *dharma* and the performance of his duties in a disinterested way (*nishkama karma*). This is poverty or detachment, and social solidarity (*lokasamgraha*), this is justice, this is sharing and communion with others. This is also the core and origin of *karma marga.* This is humanization and liberation of all peoples, all become brothers and sisters, ushering in of a *dharmic* (just), human and fraternal society of sharing and realizing *moksha* hereafter and even already here and now.

To understand it better we need to situate this ideal in the Hindu

---

[104] Cf. DSA, *Approach,* op, cit., p. 69. Amalor refers to Paulo Freire.

world-view which is expressed through a triptych: *rta, dharma* and *atman:* cosmic harmony or ecological balance of the universe, social order, or a just society and personal wholeness and integrity. This defines and emphasizes *man's integrity and totality as covering individual (or personal), communitarian and cosmic dimensions.* Man's salvation or self-realization cannot be realized in an isolated, individualistic or selfish manner but should be social and universal in perspective and concern.[105]

In the Upaniṣadic world-view the unity and totality of the Reality is also expressed by the pair: *Brahman* or *Paramātman,* as the ultimate ground of being, and *Ātman* or *Jīvātman* as the subjective reality or consciousness; both the all-pervading Spirit (*Brahman*) and the indwelling Spirit (*Ātman*) are to be experienced as one. "The awareness of the one leads to the awareness of the other in a dialectical relationship. Salvation or *moksha* is connected with the attainment of that state when one transcends all dualism and arrives at an awareness of the identity of both."[106] This one reality is also experienced and described as *Saccidānanda* (*sat, cit, ānanda:* reality, awareness, bliss). In Christian circles this triad is sometimes used for the Trinity, in whom also there is no duality.[107] This is the basis of action and contemplation, religion and politics.

This transcendence of duality forms an important basis for overcoming the tension between action and contemplation with which both the Hindu and the Christian sages wrestled for centuries. Through one's action and involvement in the world one becomes aware of Brahman as the one all-pervading Reality, residing at one and the same time within and in the world.[108] Thus, Amalor writes that human beings require two things for salvation: "Communion with Brahman by being aware of him as the one Reality; and meditation of the world and our involvement with the world by our action without which one cannot become aware of Brahman."[109]

---

[105] DSA, "Main Categories of Hindu Philosophy and Spirituality", *op. cit.*, p. 154; also: Id., *Poverty of the Religious and the Religious as Poor,* op. cit., p. 26.

[106] DSA, "Main Categories of Hindu Philosophy and Spirituality", *op. cit.*, p. 155.

[107] DSA, *Towards Indigenization in the Liturgy,* op. cit., p. 96.

[108] This view was much cherished by M. Gandhi and Rabindranath Tagore.

[109] DSA, "Karma Marga and Spirituality of All-Round Presence and Awareness: Solution to a Problem both Ancient and Modern, Hindu and Christian", in: Id. (ed.), *Indian Christian Spirituality,* op. cit., p. 175.

It is in this holistic Indian thought he relates with Hinduism the two-fold mission of the Church: "Salvation of men and transformation of the temporal order by Gospel values (cf. *GS* 14, 34, 36, 39; *AA* 2)."[110] At this moment the Indian Church in collaboration with others is called to embody and contribute to a radically new type of society where the needs of all will replace the profit of a few, cooperation will prevail over competition, quality over quantity, truth and justice over evil, love over hatred, and where the human dignity and equality of opportunities will be open to all. Besides, the openness of each person to the other will foster openness to the Absolute, to the dimension of the Transcendence.

As optimistic as ever of the gradual realization of a new society, Amalor calls on all men and women, Christians and others, young and adults, "to become aware of themselves and their life-situation, to become involved in it by committed action in common, to enter into a process that will lead people to a more human development and to the building up of communities at all levels and to reach thereby human maturity and adult-hood and attain the community's common goals of total liberation and integral development."[111] Can the Indian Church search for the well-spring of this new society in her Judeo-Christian past and in her Indian ethos?

## 4. The Response of the Indian Church

The Church in India in recent times was called upon to evolve a response to concrete situations of social injustice, in the articulation of which Amalor played an important role.[112]

The CBCI's concern for social justice dates back to the early years of its existence (1945). One of the expressions of its concern was the celebration of a 'Social Justice Sunday'.[113] However, in 1945 the question of social justice meant mainly fighting Communism.[114] Vatican II marked

---

[110] Ibid., p. 176.

[111] DSA, *Community Education of Faith through Non-Formal Education,* NBCLC, Bangalore, 1979, p. 12.

[112] Cf. Cyril De Souza, S.D.B., *Catechesis for India Today,* op. cit., p. 352.

[113] Cf. Paul Puthanangady, "Pastoral Planning at the CBCI Level. An Evaluation", in: *Word and Worship* 25 (1992) 4, p. 161.

[114] Cf. Cyril De Souza, S.D.B., *Catechesis for India Today,* op. cit., p. 354 (footnote 8).

the beginning of a new awareness on the part of the Church regarding her role and involvement in the earthly well-being and development of humankind. In response to this the CBCI established a 'Commission for Social Action'.

The realization of the social teaching of the Church inevitably calls for social analysis of society, interpretation of history and the contextualization of theology. Contextualization of theology would be, therefore, a faith response to the challenges posed by the massive poverty, injustice and oppression of the poor and the powerless. Such theology is popularly called 'Liberation Theology'.[115]

We proceed to briefly dwell upon some of the important Seminars that Amalor organized or animated, which seem important regarding the issue.[116]

### *4.1. The Asian Seminar on Religion and Development (16 July - 4 August 1973): Social Thrust of the Church and Other Religions*

This Seminar was jointly organized by the NBCLC, Bangalore, and FERES (the International Federation of Institutes for Socio-Religious Research, Louvain). The idea was to give a tool of analysis and reflection to religiously inspired social activists on the role of religion in the transformation of society and at the same time to discover together the role of religion in Asia and particularly in India.[117]

The combination of education and research was a particular feature of this Seminar. The Seminar was divided into three courses. In the first course, while reading and reflecting on the social teaching of the Church, Canon Houtart and Prof. Matthes (from FERES) showed the inevitable relation between theology and sociology, faith and social situation. Theology must use the tools of social analysis. They showed the relation between religion and society and the role of religion and Church in different types of societies. In the second course, Surindar Singh Suri

---

[115] Cf. Roger Haight, "Liberation Theology", in: J. Komonchak and Co. (eds), *The New Dictionary of Theology,* op. cit., pp. 570-571.

[116] Some of the Seminars, organized and animated by DSA, have already been mentioned earlier; here we proceed to see a little more about them.

[117] There were fifty participants from India, thirty from other Asian countries, and some others from abroad (Louvain). See: Gerwin van Leeuwen, O.F.M., *Fully Indian - Authentically Christian,* op. cit., p. 137.

(from Friends' World College, Bangalore) critically analyzed the socio-economic, political and cultural situation of India and Asia; and finally Dr. S. Kappen (from the Centre for Social Reconstruction, Madras) and Amalor gave a general theology of the Asian reality, redefined the Church's mission in the fast changing Asian situation and showed that the proclamation of the Gospel implies a radical social and political commitment.

The outcome of the seminar was admirably far reaching, especially in the field of conscientization, development and pedagogy for social change. In its critical analysis of society, the Seminar discovered the usefulness of the Marxian approach to the analysis of social reality. In its Final Statement it reads:

> As we progressed in our critical analysis of society and of the inevitability of surfacing latent conflicts, we discovered the usefulness of the Marxian approach to the analysis of social reality. From experience we know that there is a tendency to marginalize and brand as Communists those Christians who become involved in conscientization and organization for radical social change even if they do not adopt an atheistic ideology. In the light of the Gospel, the message of liberation and source of our faith, we do not oppose this tendency, but declare that we should as a Christian Body, take a more positive approach towards our Marxist brethren at the social, political and ideological levels (no. 8).[118]

Persons from other religions and secular ideologies also cooperated in the Seminar. Thus all learned that they can be inspired by the values found in the religious scriptures and traditions of others.[119] The Church's development work in cooperation with political or religious groups must serve to increase the power of the people and not seek to extend her own power. Priests must get involved as conscientizers and catalysts, if necessary, even organize the oppressed; the formation of the clergy and religious has to be developed in that spirit. Adequate exposure programmes are to help future priests and religious during their years of

---

[118] See quoted by Gerwin van Leeuwen in: Id., *Fully Indian - Authentically Christian*, op. cit., p. 138.

[119] Cf. the Statement of the Asian Seminar on Religion and Development, no. 9.

formation so that their commitment and ideological reflection may flow from involvement in and analysis of the existential situation. In this regard Amalor seems to be more radical and emphasizing. He says:

> Thus our seminaries, theological institutes and renewal centres can no more be places where routine, stale and abstract theology will be taught in the name of orthodoxy, where mediocrity and dullness will prevail, and from where colourless and spiritless men will emerge as theologians and prophets. But they must be like the heights of Carmel where the one carried away by the spirit of Yahweh will be a scourge and challenge to Ahab and to the prophets of Baal, and where, as at the cave of Horeb, the one filled with great zeal for Yahweh will have reassuring encounter with God and will feel impelled to return to the social reality to continue to prophesy at the risk of one's own life. From this double experience will gush forth vigorous and stimulating words of a new theology for the new times.[120]

A faulty analysis does not become true by looking at it with the eyes of faith. A sincere and effective involvement of religions in the process of social change needs the tools of correct, factual and critical social analysis. Critical social analysis implies involvement and identification. In this regard, it is to "die to the educated and dominant elite class, in order to experience *resurrection* on the side of the victimized masses. The challenge is clear, but it is also very disturbing to all of us."[121]

The impact of this Seminar was great. Till the Seminar began, says Fr. H. Volken, the tools of analysis were hardly brought to bear upon Christian life and pastoral planning in India. The Seminar was a kind of shock-treatment for many, because it impelled the Church to make her prophetic impact on society. Only recently religious groups began to act prophetically and critically with regard to dominant groups in society and

---

[120] See: Gerwin van Leeuwen, O.F.M., *Fully Indian - Authentically Christian,* op. cit., p. 140, where Fr. H. Volken, S.J., at that time Director of the Training Centre of the Indian Social Institute, Bangalore, quotes DSA in evaluating the Asian Seminar on Religion and Development. See also: *Word and Worship* 6 (1973) 8, a 'special number' on the Seminar, pp. 311-315.

[121] See: Gerwin van Leeuwen, O.F.M., *Fully Indian - Authentically Christian,* op. cit., p. 141, where Gerwin van Leeuwen quotes Paulo Freire whom DSA often referred in his writings.

to take the side of the poor. The theologians readily admitted that they needed the empirical sciences to know the Asian reality. They saw the interaction between the human sciences and theology as the need of the hour.[122]

Christ has come to liberate people from sin; he has come to establish a new society of justice, peace and love. The Church, as the sacrament of Christ today, cannot become true to her call in liberating people and building a new society unless she begins to wake to the social reality and collaborate with others. A long struggle has begun, not only in India and Asia but all over the world. The struggle still goes on till the eschatological culmination of human history in God through Christ. The Seminar, in its Statement, concludes modestly but full of hope:

> We are aware of our human condition as pilgrim people that is journeying towards the realization of the Kingdom of God as the eschatological goal of mankind. This journey entails an ongoing dialectical process of liberation and alienation, involvement and detachment. The Kingdom already present in this process of liberation cannot be identified with any particular society, historical period or ideology. It will emerge in its fullness at the culmination of human history.[123]

This Seminar gave the orientation to and provided the tools for a soul-searching reflection on the mission of the Church, especially in building a new society in the particular social and religious reality of India, which found its culmination in the fourth Research Seminar: *The Indian Church in the Struggle for a New society* (1981).

---

[122] Cf. ibid., pp. 139-141.

[123] See: *Word and Worship* 6 (1973) 8, a 'special number' on the Asian Seminar on Religion and Development (1973): Statement no. 13, last para.

### *4.2. Interdisciplinary Research Seminar on 'The Indian Church in the Struggle for a New Society' (19-24 October 1981)*[124]

One among the various tasks entrusted to the National Centre is to organize an in-depth study on the theme 'Kingdom of God' with its implications for the mission of the Church in India and biblical apostolate in particular in view of social change and social justice. The IV All-India Biblical Meeting, held at the NBCLC (10-15 December 1980), decided on a new orientation in biblical apostolate for the decade (1980-1990) to set in relief the prophetic and liberating character of God's Word and to permeate biblical apostolate with it. The Catholic Biblical Association of India (CBAI) which met on the afternoon of 15 December 1980, wanted to revitalize itself and undertake more challenging projects, particularly research in the Indian social reality, approaches and scientific methods towards it. It aimed at bringing out the social dimension of the Bible. Besides, the CBCI Commission for Labour in the process of its national survey on domestic workers wanted a study of the type to inspire and orientate the lay leaders and animators of the Workers' Movement. Amalor was unanimously elected coordinator of the project and organizer of the next seminar on the issue. He convened a research seminar on *The Indian Church in the Struggle for a New Society,* combining the three agencies of the project (NBCLC, CBAI, and the CBCI Commission for Labour). With its due preparation, the Seminar took place at the NBCLC from 19-24 October 1981.[125]

The Seminar brought together about a hundred people for a comprehensive and systematic study of the social *magisterium.* The participants analyzed "the historical background and context of the entire period, the sociological methods followed by the Popes, the basis of their social teaching (philosophical and historical or the data of social sciences), the approach to social questions from the micro to the macro dimensions, the correspondence between the world's concerns and the Church's concerns,

---

[124] A full report of all the research papers, short comments and proceedings of the meeting, including the Final Statement, is published by DSA, in: Id. (ed.), *The Indian Church in the Struggle for a New Society,* op. cit.; the Report and the Statement may also be obtained separately from the research paper of George Soares Prabhu, entitled *The Kingdom of God. Jesus' Vision of a New Society,* edited by DSA, Bangalore, 1981.

[125] There were 96 participants: 2 bishops, 52 priests, 6 religious brothers, 15 sisters and 21 lay persons. See: Gerwin van Leeuwen, O.F.M., *Fully Indian - Authentically Christian,* op. cit., p. 158.

etc."[126] These magisterial pronouncements were studied in their implications for the local reality with a view to reformulating the mission of the Church in India.

### *4.2.1. The rationale of the Seminar*

Today there are in India individuals and groups (lay people, religious and priests, students and workers) who are progressively involved in actions for development and justice, hoping to create a more just society. Christians among them are convinced that by getting actively involved they are working for the realization and manifestation of God's kingdom ushered in by Jesus Christ.

Such Christians and Christian action groups, however, feel often marginalized and even ignored by the official Church authorities. The situation worsens, because many in the Church do not know or are not convinced of the new understanding of the Church's mission in the world. This causes a lot of tension in the Church. That is a why a clear understanding of what is meant by the kingdom of God in the New Testament and the Vatican II Council's understanding of the Church's involvement in society, her mission and struggles for justice, peace and liberation, for the full and final coming of the kingdom was seen urgent. Hence a project of research, community reflection, leading to practical strategy for liberation was imperative, so that more and more Christians would become inspired to participate wholeheartedly or be confirmed in their conviction in the great struggle for liberation, the building of a new, more human and just society.[127]

### *4.2.2. Seeing the main points of the Seminar*

The Seminar was aimed at asking the participants to build up genuine human communities and to make a firm option in favour of the poor. The research was not limited to socio-political and historical areas with an emphasis on social analysis, scriptural studies and an examination of

---

[126] DSA, "A Break-through and a Turning Point", in: Id. (ed.), *The Indian Church in the Struggle for a New Society,* op. cit., p. 7.

[127] Cf. DSA (ed.), *The Indian Church in the Struggle for a New Society,* op. cit., pp. 17-18; see also: Gerwin van Leeuwen, O.F.M., *Fully Indian - Authentically Christian,* op. cit., pp. 156-167.

relevant documents of the *magisterium,* but also included papers and reflections on Indology, theology, liturgy, spirituality and catechetics. It wanted to reflect the Indian social situation from within, from an Indian perspective, and make its contribution to the Indian society as well as to the world at large.

The synthesis of the *socio-political and historical* studies pictured the Church in India as a Church in a society where power and wealth are unequally distributed. On the one hand, there is injustice and oppression in the society; on the other, the Church is over-clericalized and appears as rich and cosy Church amidst the poor and suffering people, where lay people and particularly women play only subordinate roles; her theologies and spiritualities nurture and reflect the concerns of the rich and the West. She, then, presents herself as an institution that is "one of maintenance, adjustment, support and compromise rather than one of confrontation, conflict and radical challenge."[128] The Seminar felt that grass-root level groups, working for a radical transformation of society from a Christian inspiration, are the hope for the future. It was stressed that cultural analysis should complement social analysis.

The synthesis of *Indology* showed that there are various currents in the Indian religious culture that offer an Indian approach to liberation; hence the Indian Church should exploit her own resources and make a unique contribution to a fuller understanding of liberation.

The Indologists felt that a secularistic socialism is not going to deliver the goods in India. We should work for a socialism imbued with the concept of *dharma* and animated by integral humanism.[129]

The synthesis of the *biblical* studies brought out that the Bible, depending on the circumstances in which particular books have been written, calls for a change both of heart and of structures. The Bible scholars analyzed the vision of a new society at work in the Bible and felt that belonging to the kingdom of God meant making a radical option for the poor.[130]

The synthesis on the *social teaching of the magisterium* noted an evolution in the social doctrine of the universal Church and the Church in

---

[128] See: General Report of the event, by C. Amritha Raj, in: DSA (ed.), *The Indian Church in the Struggle for a New Society,* op. cit., p. 35.

[129] See the whole summary of T.M. Manickam, C.M.I., in: Ibid., pp. 986-990.

[130] See the full summary by A. Mariaselvam in: Ibid., pp. 981-984.

India. It showed that from 1974 the emphasis shifted to caution, stressing the spiritual and discouraging direct involvement and action for justice, and a growing apprehension about groups working with the people for justice. They came to the conclusion that the Church's denunciation of evil in society should also include her own structures and institutions. The Church in India should not be over-dependent on Rome with regard to the solution of her local problems.[131]

The synthesis on *liturgy, spirituality, theology and catechetics* pointed out the need to work for a liturgy that springs from the people's struggle for liberation. In this regard they also noted that Christian *āśrams* can promote justice by offering inspiration and formation and by working for justice in their Hindu environment.[132]

Gerwin van Leeuwen observes that "the very fact that there was not even one paper explicitly dealing with theology showed the indifference and suspicion of a number of theologians; all the same a new approach to theologizing arose from the very dynamics of the Seminar."[133] However, the theologians considered the pilgrim model most suitable for a Church involved in the struggle for a new society. The basic ecclesial communities (BEC/BCC) are its cells and agents for action and involvement in building up a new society.[134]

### *4.3. The National Convention of Christian Leaders on the Plight of Christians of Scheduled Caste Origin (15-19 June 1978)*

The creation of a just and human society occupies the first place in the four-fold major thrust of the NBCLC as envisaged by Amalor. It states: "Commitment to *social justice* and struggle for liberation in view of creating a new society: free, just, human, fraternal, egalitarian, sharing and participatory."[135] It is in this perspective of a struggle for social justice and integral liberation that the plight of Christians of Scheduled Caste

[131] See the full summary by Felix Wilfred in: Ibid., pp. 985-987.

[132] See the full summary by Gerwin van Leeuwen, O.F.M., in: Ibid., pp. 998-1001.

[133] Gerwin van Leeuwen, O.F.M., *Fully Indian - Authentically Christian,* op. cit., p. 159.

[134] Cf. ibid., p. 160.

[135] See: DSA, *NBCLC Campus. Milieu of God-Experience. An Artistic Synthesis of Spirituality,* op. cit., p. 6. The other three major thrusts deal with 'inter-religious dialogue and cooperation', 'inculturation', and the development of 'an authentic Indian Christian Spirituality' (see: Ibid). See also chapter two.

Origin (CSCO) draws the attention of the Indian Church and challenges her to committed action in her firm option for the poor.

God and man can and should be distinguished, but man can and should never be separated from God. The love and worship of God inevitably calls for the love and service of man (cf. Mk. 12:28-34). But in the Indian society, the Scheduled Castes are being discriminated in the name of God and religion. The Scheduled Caste Christians are victims of double discrimination and injustice: originally based on caste -- discriminated against in the social, economic and political areas; and subsequently based on religion -- discriminated against for being Christians, that is, they miss the privileges and provisions made for those belonging to the Scheduled Castes, because now they have become Christians or are converted to other minority religions. In order to deal with their problem a National Convention was organized at the NBCLC in 1978.

*4.3.1. The participants*

Originally the initiative to organize the Convention was taken by the Joint Committee of the CBCI and the AICU (All-India Catholic Union), but in January 1978 it was felt that all the Churches from different denominations could be involved. Thus, the NCCI (National Christian Council of India) was contacted and from March 1978 onwards it became a truly ecumenical venture for the cause of justice.[136]

The Convention was in many ways unique. Besides Christians from most states and from different denominations, associations of the Scheduled Caste Christians and other interested groups and movements came for the first time together at the national level to work for a common cause. All were determined not only to share and discuss, but to arrive at effective follow-up actions.

*4.3.2. The main deliberations*

Though the Convention dealt with only one section of the people, that is, the struggle for justice for the Christians of the Scheduled Caste Origin, it was situated within the global concern for justice and liberation. The

---

[136] Cf. Gerwin van Leeuwen, O.F.M., *Fully Indian - Authentically Christian,* op. cit., pp. 175-176.

participants deliberated that it is a gross injustice to discriminate against a section of the people in a secular state on the basis of religion. This is a flagrant violation of the fundamental rights guaranteed by the Indian Constitution, namely, freedom of conscience, religion and speech.

On the basis of caste, it said that Christians as such have no caste system. Yet Christians of Scheduled Caste Origin have suffered and continue to suffer from the oppressive caste system.

The Convention aimed at addressing the Central Government for the redress of grievances and for rendering of justice to this section of people on a permanent basis. It aimed at nothing short of an amendment of the Constitution (Scheduled Castes) Order no. 19 of 10 August 1950, para 3.[137]

The work of the Convention culminated in a "Statement of Recommendations" and a "Message to the Churches", approved by the whole Convention. While the "Message to the Churches" underlined the just and unjust structural dimensions of society, it also affirmed the mission of the Church in terms of struggle for justice. It stated:

> We do recognize that the principalities and powers of this world continue to alienate man from man, and perpetuate structures which allow oppression of man by man in the name of caste, class, sex and religion. We believe that such oppression is a violation of God's will and negation of the work of Christ. Therefore we pledge to be true to the mission of the Church and fight against all such oppression and for the human dignity for all.[138]

While the Convention raised its voice against the unjust structures of society, it also humbly acknowledged to see the Christians of Scheduled Caste Origin being marginalized even in the Church. It boldly resolved that all forms of discrimination and segregation against the Christians of Scheduled Caste Origin in the Church must be overcome by really accepting them as equals. In order to realize this, it advocated, besides their conscientization and mobilization, inter-caste marriages, adequate representation of theirs in the Church bodies, making special reservations

---

[137] Cf. *Word and Worship* 11 (1978) 7, p. 288. The Indian Constitution guarantees the equality of all its citizens; there is no discrimination because of one's creed, caste, sex or social status.

[138] See: "Message to the Churches", in: Ibid., p. 293.

for them in Christian institutions and encouraging their children to join seminaries and convents.[139]

Finally, the Convention stated that the Church's fidelity to Christ, the liberator, and her commitment to truth and justice will be seen in the measure that she becomes the instrument of Christ in bringing about a new society, based on the Gospel values of justice, freedom and love. Thereby, the participants resolved to intensify their struggle, however hard and prolonged it may be, for the eradication of discrimination against the Scheduled Caste Christians as the first step in the realization of the larger objective of a just society. In this struggle they looked for collaboration with all men and women of good will, irrespective of their caste and creed.[140]

One of the palpable results of this Convention was that under the able guidance and animation of Amalor the representatives and friends of Scheduled Caste Christian Associations, working in various states, resolved to form a national level federation of such associations in order to wage and forge ahead in collaboration in the future the struggle for their common cause and aspirations.[141]

The cause of the Scheduled Caste Christians is never a communal issue. It is a human problem and is directly connected with justice for all and for each section of the population. The whole Church is called to rally round this common cause of justice for all and launch a united front of action with others -- in view of a just and human society, willed by God.

## 5. A Secular Society: Secularization, Religion and Politics

### *5.1. India: A Secular State*

According to its Constitution India is a secular state. The Preamble of the Constitution defines India as a sovereign secular, socialist, democratic and republic state and guarantees all its citizens equal rights of social, economic and political justice, freedom of thought and speech,

---

[139] Cf. the Statement of the National Convention on 'Christians of Scheduled Caste Origin', nos. 6-7.

[140] Cf. *Word and Worship* 11 (1978) 7, p. 300.

[141] Cf. Gerwin van Leeuwen, O.F.M., *Fully Indian - Authentically Christian,* op. cit., p. 176.

faith and worship. While it upholds the unity of the nation and the equality and dignity of every person, it abolishes castes and privileges. All citizens have the right to equality, freedom and justice, that is, all discrimination based on *religion,* race, caste, sex or place of birth has been abolished (cf. articles 14-16, 19, 25-26, 28-30).[142]

### *5.2. Secularization*

Generally speaking, the term 'secularization' denotes a process of separating the religious from political, legal, economic and other institutions, for example, the removal of religious control over land and governments. Peter Berger describes it as

> the process by which sectors of society and culture are removed from the domination of religious institutions and symbols..... This implies that secularization is more than a social-structural process. It affects the totality of cultural life and ideation and may be observed in the decline of religious contents in arts, in philosophy, in literature and, most of all, in the rise of *science as an autonomous, thoroughly secular perspective of the world...* without the benefit of religious interpretation.[143]

While the primitive, "non-secular" people stood by a supra-empirical interpretation of the reality in which they lived and saw it as *datum* ('given'), as divine creation, "secular" people, come of age today, hold that the realities of the world, especially the socio-political realities, are not divine creation but cultural and man-made situations which can be challenged and transformed. In the course of history, with the help of reason, science and technology, people have begun to understand the world and themselves better and act accordingly. The primitive "faith" and

---

[142] See: DSA, *Destinée,* op. cit., p. 120. The very first meaning of 'secular', on which everyone agrees, is that India -- unlike many of her neighbours and some Western countries -- does not have a state religion; nor there is, in the name of secularization, the suppression of religions.

[143] Peter L. Berger, *The Social Reality of Religion,* Middlesex, 1973, p. 113. In U.S.A. this book appeared as *The Sacred Canopy.* (See quoted by Gerwin van Leeuwen, O.F.M. in explaining the mind of DSA, in: Id., *Fully Indian - Authentically Christian,* op. cit., p. 293).

often superstitious interpretation of the world and society has been superseded today, however, not negating faith and supra-empirical reality, by a "secular and scientific" interpretation of the same. This is what we mean by the process of secularization which, as E. Schillebeeckx rightly observes, "is given with the growth of humanity itself. In this respect, the process of secularization is clearly a positive achievement."[144]

When we talk about secularization we do not mean *secularism*. Secularization and secularism do not mean the same. "Secularization, rightly understood, acknowledges the 'proper autonomy' of earthly realities (*GS* 36) without endangering the ultimate orientation and thrust of all human activity."[145] While secularization, which can also be called 'modernization', does not negate the supra-empirical reality, secularism, as an ideology, holds that human persons alone are responsible for the universe in which we live and there is nothing beyond this scientifically observable or empirical reality; the empirical world is the only world which exist; man's knowledge is based solely upon observable phenomena; hence, "faith" and religion can be dismissed.[146]

However, if the process of secularization is not followed in its proper spirit and intent it may lead to secularism, to the negation of the beyond, God, religion and spiritual order. But a healthy secularity will always lead to the affirmation of the here and now, the concern for society and the temporal order, the importance of reason and rationality combined with faith and acceptance of man's responsibility for his destiny and that of the world. Such an approach will lead the Church and other religions to the purification, personalization and universalization of faith. In a secularized society, then, the Church and other religions are challenged to become creative and show their concern for the world and give to the world such a united, powerful and prophetic witness that people are led to seek the kingdom of God and its justice, and, thus, discover the mystery of the divine in a healthy secularity.[147]

---

144 E. Schillebeeckx, *God, the Future of Man,* London, 1969, p. 68. (See quoted by Gerwin van Leeuwen while explaining the mind of DSA, in: Id., *Fully Indian - Authentically Christian,* op. cit., pp. 293-294).

145 DSA, *Approaches,* op. cit., p. 51.

146 Cf. Gerwin van Leeuwen, O.F.M., *Fully Indian - Authentically Christian,* op. cit., pp. 293-294. We do not go into detail in explaining the terms, in so far only a short explanation serves our purpose.

147 DSA (ed.), *Evangelization of the Modern World,* op. cit., pp. 56-57 & 93-94.

### *5.3. The Divine Concern for the Secular: Incarnational Approach*

Though Amalor hardly ever explicitly takes up the question of secularization, "religious secularity" is one of his main concerns.[148] A healthy concern for the secular is one of the main tenets of his biblical or Vatican II world vision, which forms the background of his whole theology. In what he calls the pre-Vatican II or dichotomic world vision, the secular belongs to what is dark and evil. But in his holistic or Vatican II vision the secular is something precious in the eyes of God. God has created it; he is concerned about it and has saved it in and through his Son Jesus Christ. God has "so loved the world that he gave his only Son, so that everyone who believes in him may not perish but may have eternal life" (Jn. 3:16). In the mystery of the incarnation the Word has became flesh; God has entered the world and history in the person of Jesus, has assumed everything and saved everything; and the Holy Spirit is continuously working for the sanctification of the world. This is in short the incarnational approach of divine concern for the secular. The Church finds her entity in this divine concern for the secular; she is called to share in the divine mission for the transformation of the world.

In spite of all ambiguity and deviations such a vision gives followers of Christ a very positive though critical attitude towards creation and history, the temporal order and the secular life. It enables them to see God's on-going concern for the secular in and through historical events and developments, leading the world, history and humanity to their final destiny: communion (*yoga*) in its fullness with God. This communion is a process where man is called to collaborate with God in and through his knowledge (*jñāna*), action (*karma*) and his social and cultic duties (*dharma, bhakti*).[149]

In the middle of the twentieth century both the Church and Hinduism in India had to respond to the inevitable challenge of secularization, not only because of the rise and great strides of modern sciences but also because, on the one hand, the event of Vatican II in the Church, and on the other hand, India's newly acquired independence forced everyone to come to terms with the tremendous implications of the secularization process. Neutrality became impossible. At this juncture, inspired by the biblical

---

[148] Cf. Gerwin van Leeuwen, O.F.M., *Fully Indian - Authentically Christian*, op. cit., p. 305.

[149] Cf. DSA, *Social Communication*, op. cit., pp. 27-28.

teaching on creation, incarnation and Christian hope and guided, though sometimes reluctantly,[150] by thinkers like Teilhard de Chardin and K. Rahner, Amalor took a clear stand of the "melting pot" -- the unity of the spiritual and the material.[151] In building up a new society people of different religions and idealogies should rejoice to see that they can follow the example of Jesus who worked as an artisan. In the exercise of their earthly activities, then, people are called to gather their human, domestic, professional, social and technical enterprises into one vital synthesis with religious values in Christ, under whose supreme direction all things are harmonized unto God's glory (cf. *GS* 34, 43).[152] In this context, Amalor speaks of the civilization of man, which should be both material and spiritual. He writes:

> The duty of a spiritual civilization like that of India is, therefore, to incarnate itself in this technical-material world in order to give it a soul, to purify and redeem it, ... why should we fear and condemn the technical civilization? Like Christ and in Him, it is by accepting this world that we will save it. This is the task of all lay Christians, but very particularly and urgently the task assigned to spiritual India till the coming of the new heavens and new earth, for which we hope.[153]

Basing himself on sound biblical and theological grounds, Amalor rejects dualism and dichotomy. While an unhealthy verticality or *verticalism* may lead people to a life and worship of a 'purely other-worldly' nature, an unhealthy secularity may easily lead them into exclusive *horizontalism,* devoid of transcendence and supernatural, which does not sufficiently express the reality of God's presence and action in temporal

---

[150] So says Gerwin van Leeuwen, see: Id., *Fully Indian - Authentically Christian,* op. cit., p. 307.

[151] Cf. DSA, *Destinée,* op. cit., pp. 66; also see chapter two.

[152] Cf. ibid., p. 69-70.

[153] DSA, *Destinée,* op. cit., p. 70: "Le devoir d'une civilisation spirituelle comme celle de l'Inde est donc de s'incarner dans ce monde technico-matériel pour lui donner une âme, pour le purifier et le rachter, ... pourquoi craindre et condamner la civilisation technique? Comme le Christ et en Lui, c'est en assumant ce monde que nous le souverons. C'est la tâche de tous le chrétiens laïcs, c'est très spécialement, et de façon urgente, la tâche assignée à l'Inde spirituelle, jusqu'à l'avènement des cieux nouveaux et de la terre nouvelle que nous espérons." (For translation see: Gerwin van Leeuwen, O.F.M., *Fully Indian - Authentically Christian,* op. cit., p. 308).

realities. Religion and development must go hand in hand. In the process of secularization and modernization, India cannot do away with the religious ethos of her people.

### *5.4. Secularization and Indigenization*

In the context of religion and development, Amalor would rather term the concept of secularization as 'indigenization'.[154] Indigenization, as we have already seen earlier, does not mean anti-modernization, living in the past. Due to the interaction with past, present and future, indigenization or inculturation, like culture, is a complex and dynamic process. Hence indigenization will always mean an on-going change and evolution, open to influence by both assimilating new elements and values and rejecting some others and, thereby, realizing a fresh, vital and dynamic synthesis of the spiritual and the material that is needed for a new society.[155]

Now in order to realize the importance of Amalor's understanding of secularization and his emphasis on healthy secularity, that is, what we call now, indigenization, we have to take into account the ethos of the Indian religious traditions, especially Hinduism and Islam, towards secularization. The Research Seminar on 'The Church in the Struggle for a New Society' (1981), organized and animated by Amalor, has clearly brought out that India's religions which up to now have generally hallowed and legitimized the existing unjust structures, possess within themselves the prophetic, constitutive and inspiring imperatives for a new and better society, provided they are properly and authentically interpreted.[156] In the Christian tradition this prophetic thrust is symbolized by the biblical vision of the 'kingdom of God', while in the Indian traditions it is the challenge

---

[154] Cf. DSA, *Gospel and Culture,* op. cit., pp. 58-62. While the term 'Sanskritization' can be described as a process whereby the lower castes may try to emulate the ways of the higher castes, the terms 'westernization' or 'modernization' or 'secularization', though they may all ultimately aim at the development of 'society, culture and religion', somehow or other do not carry the exact concept we are talking about in our context, i.e., the combination of religion and development; besides, these terms may be easily misunderstood or misinterpreted. In this case what seems most adequate is the term 'indigenization' or 'inculturation' which covers the totality of human development and liberation -- religious, social, economic, political, cultural, national and international.

[155] Cf. Ibid., p. 59.

[156] Cf. Gerwin van Leeuwen, O.F.M., *Fully Indian - Authentically Christian,* op. cit., p. 297.

of establishing an integral humanism through a holistic world-view. This challenging vision of religions will be realized only when the religious legitimization of the existing oppressive structures in society and culture has ceased to exist, that is, when the process of secularization and liberation has borne its fruit. A proper and authentic understanding of religions will remove the "enslaving" function of religions in society and will free them to exercise a liberating function in building a new and better society; else the world will opt for anti-religious movements, like Communism, and the freedom of faith, speech and expression will be curtailed in one way or the other.[157]

### *5.5. Islam and Secularization*

Islam is generally known for its conservatism. However, the onslaught of modern science today has forced Islam in one way or the other in the tension between conservatism and secularization, be it Iran or India. Robert Casper distinguishes three Muslim reactions that manifest a threefold impact of secularization on Islam: conservatism, reformism, and modernism, and observes that a person may be conservative in one field and modern in another.[158]

The conservative trend rejects all secularization and modernization. It holds that all the evil and the inferiority of the Muslim countries comes from abandoning the pure doctrine of the Qu'rān and the old Islamic customs and traditions. The golden age of the first three centuries of Islam must be restored by eliminating radically all innovations introduced since then, and more specially all traces of the corrupt influence of the West. The strict union of state and religion must be restored.

This sort of conservative reaction is seen in the fundamentalism of Khomeini and his associates. It is also found in India. They are radically anti-secularization and even reject the whole concept of a secular state. How they feel threatened and insecure particularly by the Hindu ethos in a secular and democratic India is clear from the highly emotional speech of Syed Badrdduja in the Indian Parliament on 28 April 1966:

> Secularism is a snare and delusion, it is fraud and deception.... Secularism! Thy name is hypocrisy, thy name is treachery ... thy

---

[157] Cf. ibid., pp. 297-298.

[158] See: Ibid., pp. 298-300.

> name is wanton encroachment upon the fundamental rights of the citizens ... thy name is exploitation of the minorities particularly of the Muslim minority.[159]

A. Abdul Gaffar once said: "It is an irony of fate that the country which believes in spiritual values of life and the maintenance of her spiritual heritage should have chosen to call herself secular."[160]

While among the reformists in India there is moderate and eclecticist acceptance of secularization, the trend of modernism is mainly found among the younger Muslims in India, especially in university circles and highly westernized townships. However, this group is relatively small and, hence, secularization among the Muslims in India is not so obvious.

### *5.6. Hinduism and Secularization*

Two of India's greatest statesmen show two typically different ways in which India should react to secularization and shape her future: Jawaharlal Nehru and S. Radhakrishnan. J. Nehru, the first Prime Minister of the post-independent India (1947), for whom religion consisted in national technicho-material prosperity and who believed in the primacy of material values over spiritual for present day India, wrote:

> We have to get rid of that narrowing religious outlook, that obsession with the supernatural and unprovable metaphysical speculations, that loosening of the mind's discipline in religious ceremonials and mystical emotionalism, which come in the way of our understanding of ourselves and the world. India must lessen her religiosity and turn to science. She must get rid of the exclusiveness in thought and social habit which has become a life prison to her, stunting her spirit and preventing her growth. The day to day religion of the Orthodox Hindus is more concerned with what to eat and what not to eat, who to eat with and from whom to keep away than with spiritual values.[161]

Whereas, S. Radhakrishnan was firmly committed to the primacy of spiritual values in the renaissance of Indian society. He believed in the

---

[159] See quoted in: Ibid., p. 298.

[160] See quoted in: Ibid., p. 314 (reference 28).

[161] See quoted in: Ibid., op. cit., pp. 300-301.

scientific knowledge, yet admitted its limitation and proposed the concept of 'intuition' for the knowledge of the 'inner truth'. He wrote in the 1970s:

> We are today in one of the creative periods of Hinduism. We are beginning to look upon our ancient faith with fresh eyes. We feel that our society is in a condition of unstable equilibrium. There is much wood that is dead and diseased that has to be cleared away. Leaders of Hindu thought and practice are convinced that the times require not a surrender of the basic principles of Hinduism, but a restatement of them with special reference to the needs of a more complex and mobile social order. Such an attempt will only be a repetition of a process which has occurred a number of times.[162]

Hinduism and Indian culture are something unique: there is openness, adaptation as well rejection. They have the ability to receive and absorb the best from others and reject the rest. That is why they have survived and continue to thrive and grow, maintaining their identity. We may distinguish three different reactions of Hinduism to the increasing influence of science and secularization in the 19th century: total abandonment, total rejection, and adaptation.[163]

The trend of *total abandonment* is the total abandonment of the previously held Hindu beliefs, in order to foster secularization and modernization. This relatively small group, which is now on the increase, is convinced that the previously held Hindu beliefs cannot come to terms with Western thought, therefore, a complete break with the orthodox faith is the only possibility for secularization. Its counterpart in Hinduism is seen in *total rejection* of the scientific way of thinking. The Arya Samaj, founded by Dayanand Sarasvati in 1875 and still influential and powerful, is the embodiment of this response of the total rejection of secularization. This group is all for *Hindutva;* the Hindu heritage is as good or even better than what others have to offer; hence Hinduism must go back to the past. The third reaction to secularization can be termed *adaptation* or the trend

---

[162] S. Radhakrishnan, *The Hindu View of Life,* London, 1971 (16th ed.), p. 72. See quoted in: Gerwin van Leeuwen, O.F.M., *Fully Indian - Authentically Christian,* op. cit., p. 301.

[163] Cf. Gerwin van Leeuwen, O.F.M., *Fully Indian - Authentically Christian,* op. cit., pp. 300-305.

of social and religious reforms. Vivekananda and Aurobindo were the pioneers of this school of thought, while Brahmo Samaj, founded by Raja Ram Mohan Roy in 1828, was its first embodiment. After the death of R. M. Roy, Debendranath Tagore led the Samaj away from R. M. Roy's deism to a more theistic outlook. The third important figure of the Samaj, Keshub Chunder Sen, inclining himself more to Christianity, added a third source to the Samaj: 'divine revelation through history'. This enabled him to give still greater importance to science. He said: "Science will be your religion ... above the Vedas, above the Bible. Astronomy, Geology, Botany and Chemistry, Anatomy and Psychology are the living Scriptures of the God of Nature, just as Philosophy, Logic and Ethics are the Scriptures of the God of the Soul."[164]

M. Gandhi, painfully aware of the poverty of the Indian masses due to the Western colonial and industrial expansion was certainly critical of modern science and technology and rationalism. He may seem, and is often misunderstood by others, to be against reforms and secularization in the society. It is not true. What he was against was not the process of secularization but the unjust social and political systems and structures of the British system in India at that time. He was not against the British, as such, but the unjust and oppressive British rule in India. He hated sin, not the sinner. He proclaimed *swarāja* (self-rule), *swadeśī* (home-made goods) and *swatantratā* (independence). He boycotted foreign goods, not because he was against foreign goods or technology as such, but at that time and situation he wanted his people to really work with their own hands, appreciate their won products, so that they do not become slaves and dependent for their livelihood on others, on the unjust socio-economic and political structures. He wrote: "India is essentially *karmabhūmi* [land of duty] in contradiction to *bhogabhūmi* [land of enjoyment]."[165] His movement of *carkhā* (cloth spinning wheel) and *khādi* (cotton clothes) was the time-bound technique of opting for just means for a just end, justice and independence, that met the needs and struggles of the majority of poor, illiterate and rural Indians of that time for their just cause of liberation of self and society. Thus we say that M. Gandhi was not against secularization; he was for the process of "science and secularization with a soul". Thus, deeply religious and deeply committed to social reforms, M. Gandhi

---

[164] See quoted in: Ibid., op. cit., p. 302.

[165] *Young India,* 5. 2. 25.

remains a great inspiration for those who hold that men and women are responsible for the course of history, for social and economic change, justice and equality. Even J. Nehru, in his "atheistic" approach to secularization, could not do away with the philosophy of M. Gandhi. J. Nehru said: "At the basis of everything ... lies the heritage of Gandhi who is dear to us and who still directs our thinking. We cannot realize all that Gandhi said, because the world evolves and in a new world the conditions are different, but what is essential in his philosophy always inspires our way of thinking."[166]

Such a trend is well seen in the manifestos of the political parties today. They cannot secure seats in parliaments if they do away religion in the name of development. The best example can be quoted here is the CPI (M or ML), Communist party of India (Marxist or Marxist-Leninist), which, unlike its neighbour (China), must allow freedom of faith and religion, if it likes to remain under the Indian Constitution, or at least not be rejected altogether by the Indian people; hence it believes in a modified Communism.[167] In this regard, many also hold that M. Gandhi would never have become 'the Father of the nation', a 'hero of humanity'[168], if he deeply religious himself, had not succeeded in touching India's religious soul and in giving her future a religious foundation. Today everyone knows it that in a secular India religious affiliations play a great role and often exert a decisive influence on such 'secular' matters as voting and government and other appointments.

Besides all that we have said above, the majority of the Indian population lives in villages. A major part of the population is still illiterate, yet highly religious. Given the case, religions should play an important role in bringing about social change; they should really become agents for indigenization, for a new society. It is here that Amalor says that India is

---

[166] DSA, *Destinée,* op. cit., p. 64: "Au fond de tout ... reste l'héritage de M. Gandhi qui nous est cher et qui gouverne notre pensée. Nous ne pouvons pas réaliser tous ce que Gandhi a dit, car le monde évolue et les conditions sont différentes dans un monde nouveau, mais ce qui et essential dans sa philosophie inspire toujours notre manière de penser." (For translation see: Gerwin van Leeuwen, O.F.M., *Fully Indian - Authentically Christian,* op. cit., p. 306).

[167] At present two of the Indian states are under the Communist governments: West Bengal and Kerala.

[168] So was called M. Gandhi by John Paul II. See: John Paul II, *The Pope Speaks to India,* St. Paul Publications, Bombay, 1986, p. 16.

waiting for a saviour, Christ and Christianity. Christianity must play an important role in the struggle for a new society, in collaboration with others.[169] Liturgies and religious celebrations, then, must be animated by the divine concern for the secular -- for the consecration of the world, of history and of the realities of human existence, so that the temporal order may be oriented to its creator and may contribute to humankind's salvation.[170] The liturgy will always be relevant to man in so far as it is an re-enactment or actualization of the mystery of the Christ event in the hopes, aspirations and struggles of humankind, particularized or "secularized" in local communities or societies.

### *5.7. Participation in Politics*

The promotion of development and liberation or bringing about the required changes in the unjust structures of society implies a participation in politics, though other forms of involvement should not be neglected.[171] It is in this context Amalor establishes the need for 'conscientization' of all those committed to liberation and nation-building. Conscientization is the process whereby one learns to perceive the social, economic, cultural and religious contradictions and begins to take action against the oppressive elements in one's environment through critical involvement, total identification and committed action in favour of the poor, the destitute, the outcaste, the victimized and the voiceless. This new type of participation in nation-building calls for a total identification with Christ, his cross and his cause of a new life of justice, freedom, equality and solidarity of all human beings. However, it is far from being a romance; at times it leads to risking one's life, personal security and facing failures. The two constituents of the Indian reality: its rich and living religious heritage, and its struggle for development and liberation are not contrary and mutually exclusive concerns of India. Amalor says that the concern for development is a modern expression of India's age-old spiritual quest for life and

---

[169] Cf. DSA, *Destinée,* op. cit., pp. 65-87. See also chapter two.

[170] Cf. DSA, *Towards Indigenization in the Liturgy,* op. cit., pp. 168-171.

[171] It is to be noted here that in India wherever the Church (Christians) has stepped in there is development, equality and justice: e.g., education, health and social work. The Church's involvement in politics, so far, is to be deplored. She must participate in politics, that is, prepare people for it, encourage them and conscientize them for a better politics, better society.

liberation (*mokṣa/mukti*).[172]

Amalor clearly holds the issues of spiritual liberation and material development together. In this regard he stands in the tradition of M. Gandhi who in his commitment to social justice and India's independence never failed to appeal to the 'religious soul' of the Indian people. He knew that the people he led were formed for centuries by the great epics: Rāmāyaṇa and Mahābhārata, and interpreted their struggle for justice and peace as the war at Kurukṣetra (battle ground) of the Bhagavad-gītā.[173] He never saw a dichotomy between politics and religion. He aimed for an integral liberation of man, that necessarily includes his social, economic, religious and political aspects.[174]

Amalor was convinced of the Gandhian approach that the deepest ground for a radical commitment to radical change and social justice is to be found in religion. In this context, then, social change, development and liberation will include the concept of indigenization or inculturation which, as we have already seen in chapter two, means

> solidarity with men and involvement with all issues and problems, and entry into the dynamism and adventure of human history with all that they imply, and in all that they demand. It ... is a concern for the contemporary reality and integrated in the culture and life of today's man.[175]

### *5.8. Building a Human Community: A Common Project of All Religions*

Amalor's thought on the struggle for a new society is in keeping with the tenor of *Populorum Progressio:* the total liberation and development

---

[172] Cf. DSA, *Approach,* op. cit., pp. 69-72.

[173] Cf. Gerwin van Leeuwen, O.F.M., *Fully Indian - Authentically Christian,* op. cit., p. 211.

[174] For example M. Gandhi says: "I could not be leading a religious life unless I identified myself with the whole of mankind and that I could not do so unless I took part in politics. The whole gamut of man's activities today constitutes an indivisible whole. You cannot divide social, economic and purely religious work into watertight compartments". See quoted in: R.K. Prabhu and U.R. Rao (eds), *The Mind of Mahatma Gandhi,* London, 1945, p. 71. See the Gandhian approach to development and liberation dealt in detail by DSA and others in: DSA (ed.), *The Indian Church in the Struggle for a New Society,* op. cit., pp. 299-330.

[175] DSA, *Gospel and Culture,* op. cit., p. 59.

of man and society -- individual and communitarian. Gerwin van Leeuwen comments on Amalor's concern for development: "To follow Jesus Christ who radically opted for the poor means to fight consistently and effectively the structural causes of injustice and thus to contribute to the building of a new society by inserting the Gospel values into all human relationships, personal and structural."[176] In this endeavour Amalor calls for universal communion and joint action among men and women, whether they be Christians, Hindus, Muslims, Communists or Atheists.[177]

Amalor, in and through his writings and seminars, facilitated the struggle for social justice towards the realization of a new society. It was his basic conviction that "... what is basically Christian is its prophetic character. Christ, the Word of God, enlightens and reveals, judges and interprets man and his existence. So also the Church in every aspect of Her mission should be prophetic, should be a proclamation and interpretation of our experiences."[178] To realize her mission in the context of religious pluralism today the Church cannot but collaborate with others.

Amalor deplores to see the gap between the 'word and deed' of the Church, that in spite of the many social encyclicals and *Gaudium et Spes* no. 1 which he calls "a marvellous charter of full solidarity",[179] the Church often merely indulges in words; her deeds lag so much behind that her speaking and preaching appears hypocritical. He writes:

> The institutional Church thus appears as having vested interests, as being one with the established order [*status quo*]. The Church seems clearly as an institution not for development but for retardation, injustice and exploitation. The Church in this way is a counter-sign; it appears to the common man as holding back the currents of liberation, development and progress.[180]

He quotes Ashok Mehta: "If you, Christians, really believe that the agony of Christ is extended in the sufferings of the masses, you must show it in

---

[176] Gerwin van Leeuwen, O.F.M., *Fully Indian - Authentically Christian*, op. cit., p. 108.

[177] Cf. DSA, "Approach", *op. cit.*, p. 44.

[178] DSA, *Liturgy Relevant to Life*, NBCLC, Bangalore, [1975], p. 11.

[179] DSA, *Theology of Development*, op. cit., p. 16.

[180] Ibid., p. 17.

action."[181]

Amalor feels that despite her faith in the incarnation, the Church has not fully accepted God's incarnational and *theandrical* pedagogy, for she may still consider preaching the Word and administrating the sacraments somewhat higher than working in great solidarity and fellowship with and for people of other religions and ideologies, fostering warm and genuine human relationships, building communities where all can be themselves, experiencing togetherness, sympathy and solidarity, and promoting selfless service, dialogue and collaboration.[182]

Christ's disciples have to join their fellow pilgrims in whatever helps towards building a new heaven and new earth. Amalor stresses that the refusal to work with others for the common well-being, taking up the vital and burning issues of human existence at all levels, makes the Church a counter-sign; while joining hands in solidarity and collaboration with others is already announcing the good news of salvation and working for the emergence of a new society.[183] He whole heartedly subscribes to the statement of the Seminar on 'The Church in India Today' on the promotion of an integral development by joining the mainstream of India's development:

> A new spirit has to animate us: one that is open to every human value, to all that is good and noble in our people, our history and tradition, in our age. We seek to cooperate genuinely with other Christians, believers of other religions and persons who value this common cause. We Christians in India resolve: 1) to commit ourselves once again to work wholeheartedly and without reserve for the common good of our country. We rededicate ourselves to serve the people of India so that we may enjoy freedom and the opportunity to live a decent human life, liberated from hunger, illiteracy, poverty and other social evil....[184]

---

[181] Ibid., p. 31.

[182] Cf. DSA, *Approaches,* op. cit., pp. 25-29; also: Id., *Theology of Development,* op. cit., 24-25; *LG* 4.

[183] Cf. Gerwin van Leeuwen, O.F.M., *Fully Indian - Authentically Indian,* op. cit., p. 206.

[184] See the General Assembly Resolutions of the Seminar on 'The Church in India Today', no. IV.1., in: Gerwin van Leeuwen, O.F.M., *Fully Indian - Authentically Christian,* op. cit., p. 206.

This commitment to development and liberation must always be placed in its concrete historical context. If Christ, his Gospel and his Church are to transform the world, orient history and society and lead them to fulfillment, they have to enter into the adventure of the process of liberation in historical movement.

The announcement of Christ and his Gospel will not be a revelation of God unless it is first and foremost a revelation of man, an interpretation of his human existence and an answer to his problems and aspirations. It is then that Christ will become necessary and appear to every person and society as the Word that has been expected, an intelligible word, a word that serves as the key to all the rest of human existence and aspiration.[185]

In this regard there is much to be done by the Church. Formerly the Church must have adopted an attitude of "untouchability", considering others as sinners and, thus, abstaining herself from working with and for others. In such a case it is natural for Hindus and others in India to regard the Church as a disinterested, arrogant and selfish-motivated institution, and the Christians as outsiders. Following Christ, the king, the priest and the prophet -- who is always interested in man and his society-- will mean, therefore, getting involved in human society, in order to transform it. This is a mission to be fulfilled not only by the Church and individuals but by all peoples and religions; it is the common project of the whole humanity[186] -- "the historical adventure [which] is essentially mankind's becoming, *devnir.*"[187]

## 6. Conclusion

### *6.1. The coming of the kingdom, the creation of 'a new heaven and a new earth': Not ideal, it is real*

The kingdom of God is not an abstract idea; it is real and challenging. For this Christ was born, lived, died and rose again. He says that the coming of the kingdom of God is not merely to be expected at the end of time but is to be lived and experienced here and now (cf. Lk. 17:21).

---

[185] Cf. DSA, *Theology of Development,* op. cit., pp. 23-29.

[186] Cf. DSA, *Approaches,* op. cit., p. 29.

[187] Ibid., p. 19.

The kingdom[188] and the liberation proclaimed and practised by Jesus should neither be "spiritualized" nor merely "eschatologized". It is to be lived with others in concrete human societies, working for it in an attitude of healthy secularity and with the hope of its completion at the fullness of time. The 'this-worldly' character, that is, the 'social thrust' of Jesus' preaching of the kingdom and building a new society should not be blunted nor should it be so unilaterally emphasized as to make it exclusive of its 'eschatological' character. The kingdom and the liberation are both historical and heavenly, this-worldly and other-worldly, spiritual and material, personal and social. The Bible must be read and interpreted in concrete historical and social contexts,[189] so that peoples and nations, inspired and strengthened by the Spirit of God, engage themselves for the realization of a new heaven and new earth, willed by God (cf. Rev. 21:1-5).

### *6.2. God's constant concern for human society*

History is the milieu and medium of God's revelation. God always reveals himself through the medium of history and society. That is to say, in other words, that God has constant concern for every human being and every human society, every age and stage of mankind's history. This concern of God for the secular, his saving will and activity, is fully revealed and realized in his Son Jesus Christ.

The realization of a new society entails a tremendous two-fold task, that is, to work for a structural change towards a more human and just society and at the same time foster the sense of the spiritual and the transcendent, the integration of the spiritual and the material. India has not yet achieved such integration and wholeness, but it is the firm hope and strong desire of Amalor that, with her rich religious and cultural heritage and her determination to hold the spiritual and the material, the sacred and the secular together, and in a concerted effort of inter-religious lead, action

---

188 When DSA speaks about 'the kingdom', he is particularly indebted to two outstanding, scholarly articles by George M. Soares Prabhu: 'The Kingdom of God: Jesus' Vision of a New Society' and 'Good News to the Poor! The Social Implications of the Message of Jesus'; they are published in: DSA (ed.), *The Indian Church in the Struggle for a New Society,* op. cit., pp. 579-608 & 609-626. See: Gerwin van Leeuwen, O.F.M., *Fully Indian - Authentically Christian,* op. cit., p. 222 (reference 107).

189 Cf. DSA, *Poverty of the Religious and the Religious as Poor,* op. cit., p. 48.

and collaboration, she is marching ahead to attain her success and set an example to the world.[190]

People and societies are to be liberated. Liberated society is the need and desire of every people. The realization of this end requires a conscious collaboration among peoples and religions of the world. Religious traditions are not monolithic entities, they have a global responsibility for the world, the entire humanity; they are agents for social change, secularization and development: the total liberation of man. People of different religions, nations and ideologies are in a common pilgrimage (*yātrā*), but often along different paths, to their common goal, God and his the kingdom (Rāmarājya). This common pilgrimage of history and humankind is energized by the Spirit; and where the Spirit is, there is life and freedom (cf. Lk. 4:18-19; Rom. 8:6; 2 Cor. 3:6,17).

---

190 Cf. DSA, *NBCLC Campus. Milieu of God-Experience. A Artistic Synthesis of Spirituality,* op. cit., pp. 26-27; id., *Approaches,* op. cit., pp. 24-33; id. , "A Synthesis of Basic and Constitutive Elements of Indian Christian Spirituality", *op. cit.,* pp. 229-233; also: Gerwin van Leeuwen, O.F.M., *Fully Indian - Authentically Christian,* op. cit., p. 312.

GENERAL CONCLUSION: EVALUATION AND PROPOSALS

God unfolds his presence and plan in our historical context inviting us to transform it in an on-going process and make it move towards its full realization of the kingdom of God. The context of religious pluralism in which we find ourselves today is itself a medium of God's revelatory presence. The inter-religious tensions, conflicts and call for dialogue and collaboration, the joys and sorrows, the aspirations and needs, movements and searches of contemporary society are not just an accidental context of God's word but the very milieu of his active presence among us (cf. *GS* 4, 11, 44, etc.).

As we come to the end of the dissertation, it seems more useful, by way of conclusion, to evaluate the theological stand of Amalor and suggest some proposals which have emerged along the way. Hence the conclusion comprises three main points: evaluation, proposals, and résumé. All these points will be seen within the radius of the thesis.

## 1. An Evaluation

"Fr. Amalor considered his life as part of a movement. Whatever he did: the NBCLC, the Chair and Department of Christianity in Mysore University, the Anjali Ashram, were not mere institutions, but movements."[1] These words of Paul Puthanangady are an apt prelude to evaluating Amalor.

The influence of Amalor transcends national boundaries. Admittedly his theological vision and approach had a particular relevance to the Indian reality, but the theological content and attitudes enunciated by him are expressive of universal significance and, as such, valid in themselves. This partly explains the fact of his much-sought after participation at international meetings,[2] at some of which he had the honour of delivering

---

[1] These are the concluding words of the mortuary letter of Amalor on June 1, 1990, by Paul Puthanangady, Director of the NBCLC. See: Cyril De Souza, S.D.B., *Catechesis for India Today,* op. cit., p. 375.

[2] "Sixth International Catechetical Study Week" (Medellin 1968), "International Missionary Conference" (Lyon 1972), "International Ecumenical Colloquium" (Rome 1980), etc.

the key-note address,[3] and a series of conferences.[4] Furthermore he was invited to contribute articles to international reviews[5] and publications of acknowledged academic repute.[6]

The foundational principles which gained Amalor recognition of international standing go to his successful dexterity and diffusion of the new vision of Vatican II. Any theology to be adequate calls for an appropriate approach and explanation. The pitfalls and general ineffectiveness of the pre-Vatican II theology, especially with regard to other religions, can largely be attributed to a defective approach of fear, suspicion and superficiality. Vatican II broke new ground by advocating a return to the Bible and a genuine concern for man and respect for his role in the history of salvation.[7]

Let us proceed to evaluate Amalor in a triple perspective: his theological stand, merits and his contribution.

### *1.1. His Theological Stand*

#### *1.1.1. An evolving shift in his theological vision: Cosmic vision, cosmic revelation*

A study of Amalor's publications points to a gradually evolving shift in his theological vision. A perusal of his earlier publications which treat of biblical themes shows that Amalor had already (1957) drawn inspiration from the 'kerigmatic' shift of emphasis from content or text of the Bible to context, that is, the anthropological or existential application of

---

[3] "World Congress of Catechetics" (Rome 1971), "International Theological Conference" (Nagpur 1971), "World Catholic Federation for the Biblical Apostolate" (Malta 1979), etc.

[4] "National Catechetical Seminar of Australia" (1973), "National Catechetical Congress of Malta" (1978), etc.

[5] *Concilium* (1978) & (1981), *Studia Liturgica* (1990), etc.

[6] See: "Missionary Adaptation", in: The Catholic University of America (eds), *New Catholic Encyclopedia,* vol. XVII, McGraw-Hill Book Company, New York 1979, pp. 426-427; "Church and Culture", in: J. Komonchak and Co. (eds), Glacier Inc., Wilmington, 1987, pp. 201-206; etc. (See all this in: Cyril De Souza, S.D.B., *Catechesis for India Today,* op. cit., p. 382).

[7] Cf. DSA, "The Implication of Vatican II for the Mission of Asia", in: *Teaching All Nations* 4 (1967) 3, pp. 320-321; id., *Theology of Evangelization,* op. cit., pp. 22-25.

the Bible, that was steadily gaining popularity in India.[8]

*L'Inde à la rencontre du Seigneur* (1964) is indubitably a watershed in the development of his thought. It constitutes a line of division separating Amalor's more mature and anthropological approach from his earlier publications.[9] From 1964, he had definitively opted for anthropological approach in his theologizing. In Vatican II he found himself confirmed; and in the subsequent period he nuanced his presentation and emphasized his concepts in the light of the Vatican II deliberations and contemporary theological awareness.[10]

### *1.1.2. The prophetic mission of the Word: From ministry within to mission outside*

There is a noticeable evolution in Amalor's understanding of the prophetic ministry of the Word and its corresponding missionary task of the Church as a continuation of the mission of Christ on earth, both ministries within the Church and with regard to other religions and wider society.

#### *1.1.2.1. The Word and the ministry within*

Initially (1964), Amalor considered the prophetic mission of the Word solely to the proclamation of the Word with the purpose of making known God's plan of salvation and preaching of the Gospel;[11] subsequently (1971), there is an added element: this proclamation should invite a

---

[8] Cf. Cyril De Souza, S.D.B., *Catechesis for India Today,* op. cit., pp. 387-388. It is to be noted that at this time the *Institut Catholique de Paris,* where DSA was studying at that time, was moving away from a content-base kerigmatic approach to an anthropological approach in theology and catechetics.

[9] Cf. ibid., p. 385. DSA's earlier publications are (in Tamil): *Why do I suffer?* (the problem of evil), Pondicherry 1957; *The Royal Priesthood,* Madurai 1957; *The Heavenly Jerusalem* (the biblical theme 'temple'), Madurai 1957; *The Day of the Lord* (the biblical themes 'rest', 'joy', and 'hope'), Madurai 1958; *The Lord is my shepherd,* Madurai 1958; *The Spouse,* Nagercoil, 1958; *The Missionary Spirit in the Bible,* Madurai 1959; and some articles in French: "Les évêques de mission et le Concile", in: *Illustré Missionnaire* 13 (1963) 6, pp. 103-109; "L'Église au Pays Tamoul", in: *Missions Etrangères de Paris* (1963) n. 129, pp. 23-28; etc.

[10] Cf. Cyril De Souza, S.D.B., *Catechesis for India Today,* op. cit., p. 389.

[11] Cf. DSA, *L'Inde à la rencontre du Seigneur,* op. cit., pp. 47-48.

human response to and acceptance of God's call.[12] This acceptance (1973), should effect a transformation of self and society, even at personal risk (1977).[13] When he finalized his 'new' global vision of the reality of God, man, the world and the Church (1980),[14] his perspective underwent a qualitative leap with the prophetic ministry of the Word being characterized as a way of animating every action in the Church (1984): theologizing, evangelization, dialogue, catechesis, preaching, liturgical celebrations, socio-political commitments, etc.[15]

*1.1.2.2. The Word and missionary task outside*

Writing in 1963-1964 (French articles),[16] Amalor had already touched upon the anthropological concern of the Word. In these articles he expounded the social, cultural, economic and ecclesial aspects of India in general and Tamil Nadu in particular. The missionary task of the Church for him in the context of religious pluralism (1969-1970) meant mutual respect and recognition, solidarity, dialogue and collaboration.[17] He called the religions and ideologies of the world in their common struggle towards realizing the kingdom of God on earth and man's integral liberation.[18] The kingdom of God involves (1972) 'actualizing' the reign of Christ and his Spirit in the universe and leading the humankind, history and creation to God through Christ.[19]

---

[12] Cf. DSA, *Theology of Catechesis,* op. cit., p. 9.

[13] Cf. DSA, "Meaning and Role of Charismatic Renewal in India Today - Its Challenge", in: *Word and Worship* 10 (1977) 2, p. 94.

[14] See: DSA, *Our Christian World Vision and Theological Synthesis,* NBCLC, Bangalore, 1980.

[15] Cf. DSA, "Experience of the Word", in: *Word and Worship* 17 (1984) 8, p. 261.

[16] See: DSA, "Le Pays Tamoul", in: *Missions Etrangères de Paris* (1963) no. 128, pp. 35-38; id., "L'Église au Pays Tamoul", in: *Missions Etrangères de Paris* (1963) no. 129, pp. 23-28; id., "A l'écoute des Pauvres en Inde", in: *Informations Catholiques Internationales* (1964) no. 229, pp. 34-40.

[17] See in general: DSA, *Destinée,* (Paris 1967); id., *Approaches,* (Bangalore, 1st print in 1970).

[18] See: DSA (ed.), *The Indian Church in the Struggle for a New Society* (Bangalore 1981).

[19] Cf. DSA, *Approaches,* op. cit., p. 33.

### *1.1.3. Revelation and its on-going actualization*

Amalor initially (1969) understood revelation as the action of God in the events of our history, culminating in a personal and community encounter;[20] subsequently (1971), he qualified it as personalist and social, concrete and relevant, historical and existential, actual and dynamic.[21] He finally arrived at a global understanding of revelation "in terms personal and personalist, communitarian and social, concrete, existential and historical, actual and on-going, dynamic, relevant and transforming, implying personal commitment, discovery from within and involvement in the whole process."[22]

The word 'revelation' which earlier smacked of content-based intellectualism, is replaced by more existential expressions, such as: on-going and universal divine communication to all people and all times, human response, assimilation and involvement in the transformation of the self and society.

### *1.1.4. Accepting the evolution: Divine happening greater than individual experiences*

The evolution of the vision of Amalor was not merely a theological fad or novelty, 'deliberately assumed' by him, but rather a 'happening' in his life: openness to the Spirit and to the reality around him. His personal charisma, his sensitivity to people and their socio-economic, political, cultural and religious contexts had their say in this process. Amalor himself claimed that living his dialogic encounter with living men and living religions helped him grow in the awareness that he was involved in an on-going process of God which was much greater than himself (Amalor). He believed that though every individual God-experience, individually or as a community, may be a true experience of God, but God as he is in himself and his cosmic plan cannot be "confined" to individual experiences and expressions, concepts and categories. In Amalor's own words, quoted and commented by T. Emprayil, we read: "'A Christian experience does not experience the whole Experience.' It grows. Just as 'my experience of the Reality today is richer than St. Paul's, everyday brings with me new

---

[20] Cf. DSA, *Theology of Development,* op. cit., p. 15.

[21] Cf. *Theology of Catechesis,* op. cit., p. 17.

[22] DSA, *The Church's Mission as Prophetic and Hermeneutical,* op. cit., p. 3.

everyday brings with me new experiences and new awareness.'"[23]

Amalor was quite successful in implementing his vision. He did it by coordinating, planning, drafting, experimenting (e.g., Indian rite liturgy), evaluating, revising, publishing and diffusing.

### *1.1.5. The bases of his theologizing: Theological and anthropological*

#### *1.1.5.1. Theological basis*

Amalor's theological perspective is mainly based on these three points: an adequate world vision, an up-dated theology of revelation, and a deeper understanding of faith.

(i) It is very important to have an adequate vision of God, man, the world and the Church in any theologizing and pastoral approach. A prophet should have a vision. Amalor had a penetrating, critical and radical vision with which he could feel, dream and imagine the future of the Church and the Church of the future. He felt the alienation of the Church in India with regard to its relevance, especially in the context of religious pluralism. He wanted to rectify the approach of the Church with his new world vision that resulted in inculturation. Jacob Theckanath writes: "More than anyone else in the recent past he has contributed to the cause of inculturation in India. His name is synonymous with inculturation."[24] However, inculturation made him a sign of contradiction. He was loved because of it, and he was viciously attacked for it by those opposed to inculturation. He accepted the attacks for the love of Christ, love of the Church and his love for the rich social and religious cultures of India.[25]

The very first talk Amalor used to give in all his seminars was on 'world vision', aimed at stimulating participants evaluate their own world vision.[26] With the help of illustrations in contrasting the 'old' and the 'new' visions, he highlighted the interrelationships among these four factors: God, man, the world, and the Church. They should not be dichotomized or opposed, but integrated, so as to form a single whole in mutual

---

[23] See quoted by: Thomas Emprayil, *The Emerging Theology of Religions*, Vincentian Publications, Rewa, 1980, p. 103. The source of the quote is not given.

[24] Jacob Theckanath, "Methodology and Spirituality for Pastoral Action", in: Paul Puthanangady, S.D.B. (ed.), *Church in India: Institution or Movement?*, op. cit., p. 163.

[25] Cf. ibid.

[26] Cf. ibid., p. 162.

solidarity and collaboration.

(ii) An adequate understanding of God's revelation, as we have just seen above, calls for a human response that is personal as well as communitarian, social, concrete, existential and historical, dynamic, on-going and transforming.

Since the revelation is indirect and mediate, it requires a medium of communication, namely, 'signs', which are inclusive of words and deeds (cf. *DV* 2). Such a revelation, realized in the events of one's life-situations and experiences is expressed through signs, of which Jesus Christ is the greatest.[27] God's self-communication, which is interpersonal, takes place in human life and history and hence the need for an on-going understanding of the process.[28] The on-going revelation demands on-going human response.

This understanding of revelation earned Amalor both bouquets and brickbats. While the resolutions of the English-speaking group at the 'World Catechetical Congress' (Rome 1971) accepted the view of Amalor, some others raised a hue and cry against his view and his unwarranted assertion.[29] Today it is accepted in the Church.

(iii) A corresponding understanding of faith is the third element of Amalor's theological basis. This is the faith in the Word of God, made flesh in Jesus who lived, died and rose to become the universal Christ, the Lord of all. This faith is a personal encounter with the living God in and through Jesus Christ in the midst of our life; a loving acceptance of him by a loving surrender of one's whole being to him and an unreserved commitment to live according to his word in an awareness and acknowledgement of one's belonging to him.[30]

### *1.1.5.2. Anthropological basis*

The anthropological approach of theologizing acknowledges human dignity in a holistic sense, involving: sincere sympathy, a sense of solidarity, a sharing rapport and genuine acceptance -- leading to the integral

---

[27] Cf. DSA, *Theology of Catechesis,* op. cit., pp. 20-22.

[28] Cf. ibid., p. 21.

[29] Cf. Gerwin van Leeuwen, O.F.M., *Fully Indian - Authentically Christian,* op. cit., p. 59; Cyril De Souza, S.D.B., *Catechesis for India Today,* op. cit., p. 405.

[30] Cf. DSA, *The Church's Mission as Prophetic and Hermeneutical,* op. cit., p. 5.

liberation of the whole humankind.[31] The main focus of the anthropological approach is that of 'relevance'. Since the signs through which revelation takes place are often ambiguous and ambivalent, the Church must interpret it, in order to make it relevant to each community and culture of the world. Human experiences should be taken into consideration in theologizing,[32] catechizing,[33] evangelizing[34] and in the process of inculturation.[35]

Aided by the human sciences, this approach considers man not as a static essence but in his triple dynamism towards fulfillment: the vital dynamism of personality development, the dynamism of intense group living, and the dynamism of history, moving towards its fulfillment.[36]

### *1.2. His Merits*

#### *1.2.1. Pioneer and prophet of the post-Conciliar period*

Thorough as he was with the Conciliar insights, Amalor based himself on the vision, used the theological underpinnings and followed the guidelines furnished by the Council. Gerwin van Leeuwen calls him a "pioneer of the post-Conciliar renewal."[37] Amalor embodied the teaching of Vatican II wholeheartedly and as Director of the NBCLC became "the motor and soul of the Vatican II renewal in the Indian Church."[38] He did it through his all-round concern of the ecclesial life: theology, liturgy, catechetics, inculturation, evangelization, biblical apostolate, etc.

His was an action oriented theology and a Church of service and action, renewal and relevance. Jacob Theckanath writes: "Fr. Amalor synthesized, developed and communicated the Vatican II methodology for

---

[31] Cf. DSA, *Approaches,* op. cit., pp. 20-24.

[32] Cf. DSA, *Approach,* op. cit., pp. 18-20.

[33] Cf. DSA, "General Orientations for the Redaction of Catechetical Material", in: *Word and Worship* 2 (1968) 4, pp. 144-145.

[34] Cf. DSA, *Preaching the Gospel Today. Main Problems in Mission Lands,* op cit., pp. 12-14.

[35] Cf. DSA, *Gospel and Culture,* op. cit., pp. 27-28.

[36] Cf. DSA, *Theology of Catechesis,* op. cit., p. 23.

[37] See: Gerwin van Leeuwen, O.F.M., "D.S. Amalorpavadass Pioneer of Post-Conciliar Renewal", in: *Vidyajyoti* 54 (1990) 9, p. 481.

[38] Gerwin van Leeuwen, *Fully Indian - Authentically Christian,* op. cit., p. 307.

the renewal of the Church and society. He spelt out the theology of an anthropological, incarnational or human approach that should be followed in all the activities of the Church...."[39]

Paul Puthanangady too sees Amalor as a prophet of the post-Conciliar Church in India. He writes:

> Fr. D.S. Amalorpavadass was one of those men raised up by God in the post Vatican II period in order to facilitate the Church in the fulfillment of the pastoral mission. His methodology ... was based on a world vision that made her [Church] look at reality in such a way, that she found herself as the servant of God who was active in history. It made her listen to God ... in order to meet the exigencies of such a response. It is for this reason I would like to say without hesitation that the pastoral vision of Vatican II began to become a concrete reality in India through the ministry of Fr. D.S. Amalorpavadass, the prophet of the post-Vatican II Church in India."[40]

*1.2.2. A Spirit-led man and a man of prophetic vision*

Jacob Theckanath writes: "In animating the renewal movement Fr. Amalor attuned himself to the Spirit. He was a man who listened with intense interiority to the promptings of the Spirit. He was Spirit-guided."[41] This fact is well displayed as Amalor put it in writing in the booklet of the NBCLC which he used to distribute to the various groups that came into it. The booklet reads:

> Ultimately, it is the spirit of the council -- the Spirit of Pentecost that is permeating us, one and all, though at different degrees and varying speeds. The power of the Spirit and the might of God's Word are evidently at work in the Church of God in India, and lead the renewal movement. Against this background the prospects of the future cannot but be bright. We know ... that the Spirit will continue to operate

---

[39] Jacob Theckanath, "Methodology and Spirituality for Pastoral Action", in: Paul Puthanangady, S.D.B. (ed.), *Church in India: Institution or Movement?*, op. cit., p. 164.

[40] Paul Puthanangady, "Amalor's Contribution for a Pastorally Oriented Church in India", in: Id. (ed.), *Church in India: Institution or movement?*, op. cit., pp. 63-64.

[41] Jacob Theckanath, "Methodology and Spirituality for Pastoral Action", in: Paul Puthanangady, S.D.B. (ed.), *Church In India: Institution or Movement?*, op. cit., p. 163.

> through us. We pray and hope that we may continue to be Spirit-permeated, Spirit charged, Spirit-led, Spirit recognizing, Spirit-experiencing and Spirit-sharing....[42]

It was his great sensitivity to the Spirit that prompted Amalor to quickly join with any new movement that contributed to the renewal and growth of the Church and society. For example, the movement of the laity through the All-India Catholic Union (AICU), the *āśram* movement, the charismatic movement, women movement, liberation movement and the inter-religious movements in India. He also founded the Christian Renewal Movement of India (CRMI).[43]

With an unusual perceptiveness, he could see the presence, action and movement of the Spirit in India, a land of diverse religions and cultures. He called India a land of the Spirit: "In all modesty we could state that no other country, no other people has so deeply and universally experienced the Spirit and expressed this experience in its religious literature, religious practices, worship and prayer as India."[44]

Being a Christian necessarily implies experiencing the Spirit in various ways in the signs of the times. It is the assurance and the "consolation of the Spirit"[45] that gives the Church to go forward in her uncharted ways of the third millennium. God through the power of the Word and the creativity of the Spirit continues to inspire the hearts of men and women as they read the scriptures of the world and lead them to their destiny.[46] He does so in a baffling variety of forms, leading the Church to her future amidst the religions and ideologies of the world.[47]

### *1.3. His Contribution*

Amalor's contribution stands out in full relief only when situated in the context of his country, time and situation in which he theologizes,

---

[42] See quoted in: Ibid.

[43] Cf. ibid., pp. 164-165.

[44] DSA, "Meaning and Role of the Charismatic Renewal in India Today: Its Challenges", in: *Word and Worship* 10 (1977) 2, p. 90.

[45] Ibid., p. 98.

[46] In this regard see the research seminar on Non-Biblical Scriptures (Bangalore 1974), organized and animated by DSA.

[47] Cf. DSA, *Approaches*, op. cit., p. 14ff.

especially the renewal and mission of Church during and just after Vatican II amidst the ancient and living religions and cultures of India, which in turn need to be inserted in the impetus of the wider theological movement.

### *1.3.1. Lay leadership of service in the Church and society*

In his enthusiastic renewal movement of the Church in India and in his effort to enhancing the lay participation in the Church, he started the project *Jagruti* (awareness, conscientization) through the movements like AICU (All-India Catholic Union, the only officially recognized all-India Catholic organization for lay people) and CRMI (Christian Renewal Movement of India) -- all for building up the body of Christ (cf. *AA* 2; *AG* 21; *LG* 31, 32) and the service of society.

In this regard as seen needed and suited to the Indian reality, Amalor repeatedly raised the issue of the lay catechists and did not rest until decisions were taken at an all-India level. Through his efforts, the Second All-India Catechetical Meeting (1971) made concrete recommendations regarding the training, appointment and remuneration of lay catechists.[48]

He defined the role of a catechist as that of a pedagogue (*guru*). A catechist is the one who has experienced God by means of a genuine inter-personal relationship and fellowship. He guides others to the same experience by a testimony of words and deeds in concrete life-situations. He plays the role of a prophet by interpreting God's on-going revelation in the events and experiences of his group; and in that, he becomes himself the very sign of God's revelation.[49]

Not that everything was rosy. Amalor was often misunderstood. Given the variety of outlooks, avocations and expectations it was no wonder that quite a few lay people misunderstood him. They had even dragged his name to the court of law. Even some bishops had banned his entry into their dioceses. But nothing deterred him. He forgave them all. He would not even speak apologetically of his own programmes of the Church's renewal and revitalization. He carried on his mission of renewal

---

[48] Cf. "Recommendations Made at the II All-India Catechetical Meeting, January 1971", in: DSA (ed.), *Report of the Third All-India Catechetical Meeting,* NBCLC, Bangalore, 1976, pp. 336-337.

[49] Cf. DSA, *Practical Conclusions and Obvious Consequences of Revelation-Faith and Christian World Vision for Our Pastorale and Spirituality,* NBCLC, Bangalore, 1978, p. 11.

in the Church and of self as enthusiastically as he could. No wonder, with his undaunted lead and dedicated service, he proved himself a true leader, a *guru*. This explains how a number of people, laity, clergy, religious, besides listening to him in seminars, conferences and in his writings, thronged to Anjali Ashram and sought his guidance to get God-experience and live with him in touch of the God-experience.

Thus, the force he created through the various ways was indeed a spiritual force, a force which could be at the service of the society and the Church.[50]

### *1.3.2. Church at the service of society*

Amalor never saw the Church as set apart from society. The Church exists in and for society as an instrument of transformation -- transformation of self, of society and of nature. Hence she must join the aspirations and daily struggles of people and nations. Paul Puthanangady writes:

> The response of the Church in India to Jesus Christ cannot be isolated from national struggle. It was necessary to find a method of integration between the mission of the Church and the struggle of emerging India. One of those who have contributed to find a methodology suited to this historical situation, I feel, is Fr. D.S. Amalorpavadass. His contribution to build up an Indian Church in a free India will be recognized by the Church historians of India.[51]

### *1. 3.3. Inculturation of the Church: Renewal, relevancy, revitalization*

Amalor has been outstanding in his insistence on inculturation in all areas of his ecclesial concern. This is seen in his general theologizing, lectures and writings. Inculturation follows the principle of the incarnation. His theology can be called an explicit redemptive incarnational theology, because it begins with the significance of the incarnation, life, death, resurrection and cosmic reign of Christ.

---

[50] A. Pushparajan, "Amalor the Animator of a Lay Church in India", in: Paul Puthanangady, S.D.B. (ed.)., *Church in India: Institution or Movement?*, op. cit., pp. 74-83.

[51] Paul Puthanangady, "Amalor's Contribution for a Pastorally Oriented Church in India", in: Id. (ed.), *Church in India: Institution or Movement?*, op. cit., p. 72.

The mystery of the incarnation of Christ implies the inculturation of the Church in a particular cultural and religious milieu, so that her preaching of the *good news* becomes relevant to the needs and aspirations of the people she serves. Inculturation "implies that the gospel message was received in a culturally and socially conditioned form. A very consistent type of explicit incarnational theology is found in Amalorpavadass."[52]

Amalor's dedication to inculturation has also been highlighted by Sergio Torres. His association with Amalor goes back to their common membership in the 'Ecumenical Association of Third World Theologians' (EATWOT) since its formal inauguration in Dar-es-Salaam (1976).[53] Torres acknowledges his indebtedness to Amalor for highlighting the salient points of a theological approach to inculturation, among which there figure both 'ancient religious traditions' and 'development and liberation'.[54] Further, there is the originality of the methodology Amalor employed and followed: the need to be consciously involved in reality and actively participate in the concerns and task of contemporary society.[55] His was not a sectorial inculturation, but a global one so that the entire Church be so rooted in the context as to become an authentic Local Church. We can attest with assurance that, by deftly combining Christ's message with the Indian ethos, Amalor has responded to one of the vital challenges confronting the Indian Church.

### *1.3.4. Inspiration to develop an Indian Christian Spirituality*

Not only did Amalor show how much God's providence is at work in other religions and in particular in India's main religion, Hinduism, and how active the presence of the Spirit is in the Hiṇdu scriptures, traditions and religious disciplines; much clearer did he manifest his conviction in the way he tried to develop and promote an Indian Christian Spirituality.

One's teaching and preaching must go with one's lifestyle. He

---

[52] A. Mookenthottam, M.S.F.S., *Indian Theological Tendencies,* op. cit., p. 168.

[53] Cf. Sergio Torres, "The Inculturation of the Gospel in the Latin American Continent", in: Russell Chandran (ed.), *Third World Theologies in Dialogue,* op. cit., pp. 19-20.

[54] Cf. DSA, "The Indian Universe of a New Theology", in: Sergio Torres and Virginia Fabellla (eds), *The Emergent Gospel. Theology from the Underside of History,* Orbis Books, Maryknoll, 1979, pp. 135-156.

[55] See: DSA, "New Theological Approaches in Asia", in: *Verbum SVD* 21 (1980) 3 & 4, p. 294.

worked very hard to establish the Department of Christianity at the Mysore University, of which he became the first head (1979). According to the Indian Spirituality *being* is more important than *doing.* He combined this academic success with a life style. This was his deep conviction that teaching Christianity at the University should be integrated with an experience of Christian life in action and inter-religious dialogue at the level of God-experience, for which the Ashram in a Hindu setting is most suitable. The Anjali Ashram bears witness to this fact.

### *1.3.5. Towards the creation of an Indian Christian Theology: Local Church, local theology*

The Church as a mystery is an event in the life of a people in history;[56] and theology is a reflection of Christians upon their faith and their Christian experience in a particular time and culture.[57] Hence only Christian communities which are involved in the actual life, aspirations and struggles of the contemporary world and which take active responsibility within their society or community can best fashion the theology that is relevant to them. This idea upholds the emergence of Local Churches and local theologies.[58] In this regard Amalor always appreciated and worked for the emergence of the Indian Local Church and consequently, Indian Christian Theology.[59]

No doubt, with its rich cultural and religious background the emergence and impact of Indian Theology is ever gaining ground in the Indian Church in particular and the universal Church at large. The appreciation and attempts are being launched from both Catholic and other Christian denominational circles. In this regard the two recent articles of M. Dhavamony are worth quoting here: "Indian Christian Theological Method" and "Indian Christian Theology".[60] Also, besides teaching other religions in major seminaries which is seen obligatory in India, some seminaries, where it is possible, add and organize interfaith study tours

---

[56] Cf. DSA, "Approach", *op. cit.,* p. 65.

[57] Cf. DSA, *Theology of Evangelization,* op. cit., p. 18.

[58] Cf. ibid.

[59] See chapter two.

[60] See both these articles subsequently appearing in: *Studia Missionalia,* vol. 45, op. cit., pp. 57-94 & pp. 95-117.

and excursions in their study curriculum; for example, visit to sister Churches, mosques and temples, and "participating" in their prayers and *pūjās* (religious celebrations), inviting other religious leaders and professors in seminaries for classes and talks, etc.[61]

Though the appreciation of Indian Theology is ever on the rise in the Church, at least among the Indian theologians, it has not always been without some apparent problems, particularly in explaining the socio-religious reality from the Indian religious concepts and categories. While some of the concepts seem to be outmoded as 'caste system', a number of them have extensive, different and yet deep significance, for example, *avatāra* and *saṁsāra*. The function of concepts is to convey ideas. Some of the Indian concepts need to be redefined in Christian categories.

### *1.3.5.1. Problem of truth and a Christocentric approach*

India's age long quest for the Absolute along with its idea of tolerance has posed the problem of theocentrism and Christocentrism in Indian Theology. While theocentrism has the merit of developing a Christian advaitic theology, it has the disadvantage of overlooking the human, social, secular and historical dimensions of life which have serious consequences on a developing country. While, in an advaitic context (Śankara), the universality and transcendence of Jesus Christ, Jesus of history who is constituted the cosmic Christ, and the history itself tend to disappear in the Absolute Godhead, too great an emphasis laid on the social and secular aspect of man and history runs the risk of separating Jesus from his Trinitarian relationship with the Godhead; it runs the risk of diluting the divine saving mystery of God realized through Jesus Christ and his Gospel.

The problem of reconciling the primacy of the Absolute with Christocentrism remains. Amalor reconciles these two trends: theocentrism through Christ. A. Mookenthottam writes, "Indian Catholic theology in general, with the exception of Amalorpavadass, shows a predominantly theocentric approach."[62]

---

[61] For example, besides visiting Churches of other denominations, I had the opportunity to visit some of the famous mosques and temples in India, in order to see their religious life, prayers and *pūjās* or religious celebrations, etc., arranged and organized by St. Albert's College, Ranchi. This is a part of the study curriculum of the seminary.

[62] A. Mookenthottam, M.S.F.S., *Indian Theological Tendencies,* op. cit. p. 173.

Jesus Christ is the fullness of God's revelation; he is the fullness of God's grace and truth (cf. Jn. 1:14); he "is the image of the invisible God, the firstborn of all creation" (Col. 1:15). God has created the world, loved it and saved it in and through Christ (cf. Jn. 3:16; Col. 1:16).

*1.3.5.2. Relevance of his theology: Unity of faith and pluralism of theology*

Convinced that God manifests himself to human beings in the concrete historical and cultural situations, Amalor felt that the Church in India in her theology, mission and evangelization should likewise take into account the Indian reality, characterized by: (i) an ancient cultural heritage; (ii) age-old religious traditions; and (iii) stark social injustice.[63]

When the Church is actively involved in making her theology relevant to the local reality there cannot but emerge a pluralism of theology in the Church, but always in the unity of faith.[64]

*1.3.5.3. Giving an identity to the Indian Church*

Because of his love and appreciation of the rich Indian religious culture and his active involvement in the indigenization of the Church in India, Amalor surely stands among the few who have helped articulate the identity of the Indian Church. Felix Machado writes:

> Among a few people who have helped the Church in India articulate Her identity is Dr. Amalorpavadass. Although India is said to have made no significant impact in Her contribution to Church's theology, Dr. Amalor was a pioneer in giving certain direction to the question of Indian Identity. From the very beginning of his impressive involvement in Church's life, Dr. Amalor recognized the fact that the Church in India is privileged to be in a unique situation of being surrounded by many religions and is challenged at the same time, by dehumanizing poverty.... He was convinced that the Church

63 Cf. Paul Puthanangady, "Pastoral Planning at the CBCI Level", in: *Word and Worship* 25 (1992) 4, pp. 160-161. These three characteristics were already indicated by the CBCI in 1966.

64 See chapter two.

would discover Her authentic identity not in isolation but in being in dialogue with her surrounding reality.[65]

There is no gainsaying the fact that Amalor was one of the prime movers of the pastoral renewal in India, especially during his tenure of the NBCLC (1967-1982). The efforts of Amalor has witnessed a marvellous renewal in the all-round renewal of the Church in India. His was a multi-pronged strategy: theology, catechetics, liturgy, biblical apostolate, new society, mission, evangelization, etc. He suitably translated the teachings of the Church, both universal and local, and gave ample importance to the declarations and statements of various ecclesial consultations and meetings into a valid form of ministry of the Word for India.

Transformation is effected with greater ease when individuals and small groups are involved; orders from top is often resented. From this point of view, the achievement of Amalor is all the more remarkable because the renewal movement in theology and catechetics was initiated from the National Centre.[66] Yet he was able to make it a collaborative enterprise, a team work, involving the entire Church, laity, clergy, religious, catechists, youth, and also people from other religions and ideologies. It was necessary for Amalor and his collaborators to take into account all the cultural, linguistic and religious diversities of India. He had close liaisons with sister Churches.

Amalor personally assimilated the Vatican II theological trends, and taking into account at every step the Indian ethos, reformulated and contextualized them. He was convinced that any relevant theology, missionary activity or ecclesial ministry to be relevant, should be contextualized. It is here he saw the importance of the Local Church and, thereby, worked hard for the emergence and implementation of an Indian Christian Theology and an Indian Christian Spirituality that require original thinking and application of the Indian concepts, cultures and belief systems in keeping with the catholicity of the Church. He was 'catholic' in his openness and readiness to assimilate experiences and knowledge no matter their source -- 'Indian' or 'foreign'. He combined Christ's message with the Indian spirit. It speaks volume for his gifts of analysis and synthesis

---

[65] Felix Machado, "Dialogue in the Year 2000: From Discussion to Dialogue", in: Paul Puthanangady, S.D.B. (ed.), *Church in India: Institution or Movement?,* op. cit., p. 126.

[66] Cf. Cyril De Souza, S.D.B., *Catechesis for India Today,* op. cit., p. 376.

that he was dexterously able to weave all these different strands into a remarkably new orientation towards the creation of an Indian Theology. He was not copying trends practised elsewhere, but consciously presented these trends in view of the Indian situation, especially in the context of religious and cultural pluralism.

It is important to keep in mind that Amalor was not primarily an "academician", proposing new theories, but a pastorally-oriented person involved in the all-round renewal of the Church in India in the post-Conciliar period. Though he is much acclaimed in the field of inculturation, also in the fields of catechetics, liturgy, evangelization, he never claimed to be the creator of an original theological system, but he was a creative promoter of Vatican II renewal, especially in liturgy and catechesis.

The "originality" of Amalor's theological thought is its *relevance* to India. In fact, he is acknowledged "not much as a radically creative theologian, [but] as a theologian who, steeped in Indian culture and sensitive to Indian reality, was able to penetrate and grasp the great insights of many other theologians from diverse cultural backgrounds and the major perspectives of Vatican II theology."[67]

### *1.4. A Word of Observation*

Having said all this, what could be said as a word of observation is this:

(i) Amalor's keen interest in promoting the Vatican II renewal in the Church at times led him to caricature the contrast between the 'old' and the 'new' approaches of the Church. This tendency can be seen in his simplistic description of the absence of concern for man in the past,[68] the earlier methods of evangelization[69] and especially the old vision of reality.[70] However, when it came to expounding his ideas on inculturation, he seems to have been aware of the difficulties involved in receiving the Vatican II vision. Hence he constantly referred to the practical, emotional and psychological difficulties in accepting the post-Conciliar insights,

---

[67] P.M. Meagher, "Book Reviews", in: *Vidyajyoti* 54 (1990) 12, p. 657.

[68] See: DSA, *L'Inde à la recontre du Seigneur,* op. cit., pp. 272-277.

[69] See: DSA, *Approach,* op. cit., pp. 42-48.

[70] See: DSA, *Our Christian World Vision,* op. cit., pp. 9-12.

especially with regard to the understanding of the world religions. This realism was at times lacking in his treatment of other subjects.[71]

(ii) Since Amalor was well acquainted with the documents of Vatican II, his literary output abounds with Conciliar references. However, this is not equally true of other ecclesiastical documents -- whether emanating from the universal or local Church. From a methodical point of view, Amalor's commendable grasp of contemporary theological culture is evident in his two earlier major works: *L'Inde à la rencontre du Seigneur* (1964) and *Destinée de l'Église dans l'Inde d'aujoud'hui* (1967).[72] In course of time, this scientific rigour in identifying sources was not all that apparent.[73] This may be because, as we have pointed out above, what he published later was not so much of an academic intent but pastorally based, mostly the outcome of seminars, conferences and meetings.

The Indian Church is still reeling under the impact of Amalor's death. While it is true that his publications can be listed, his seminars and conferences can be counted, the full significance of his contribution is still in the process of being discovered. His research seminars on themes both challenging and *avant-garde* in general and his method of right attitude for right approach towards other religions in particular will bear fruit in the years to come.

## 2. Proposals

### *2.1. One Reality but Plurality of Experiences and Expressions*

We cannot find any religion starting with an abstract idea of God. God always reveals himself to man in history (cf. Heb. 1:1-2), and hence the experience (*anubhava*) of God by each religion is historically and culturally conditioned. It is the experience of the divine that conceives God as duality (*dvaita*) or non-duality (*advaita*) or a God of worship (*bhakti*), or as Yahweh, a tribal God of Hebrews, showing them the way

---

[71] Cf. Cyril De Souza, S.D.B., *Catechesis for India Today*, op. cit., p. 407.

[72] R. Rossignol commends DSA for the amazing amount of documentation to substantiate his key assertions; see: Raymond Rossignol, "Book Reviews", in: *Word and Worship* 6 (1969) 13, p. 672.

[73] Cf. Cyril De Souza, S.D.B., *Catechesis for India Today*, op. cit., p. 407.

through the desert, who was considered the universal creator of heaven and earth only after their settlement in Palestine as an agricultural people. God does not reveal himself through alien "images", concepts, categories and situations; neither can he be "defined" by human concepts and categories. The plurality of religions is the outcome of different experiences and expressions of the same reality, God.

God is an ineffable mystery. Man, left to himself, cannot grasp the fullness of the divine reality as it is in itself. Hence, there arises the need of divine revelation. God has been, in his salvific plan and providence, revealing himself to all mankind at different times and traditions. For Christians God is triune: Father, Son and Holy Spirit. In the fullness of time God's Word (*śabda, kalimat*), by the power of the Holy Spirit, has became incarnate to redeem all mankind in the person of Jesus Christ. The Holy Spirit continues the work of Christ in the Church and in the world. All peoples and religions are called to fully participate in the divine life. Yet they cannot fully participate in the divine life unless and until there is a fullness of revelation and fullness of response. In Christ, because of the mystery of incarnation, is found the fullness God's revelation and fullness of mankind's redemption.

### *2.2. Unity of the plurality of Experiences in God*

The pluralism of religions is easier to understand if we consider religion not primarily as a creed or an institution, but as a symbolic structure that mediates a living relationship between the individual and his/her community and God. Thus pluralism of religions is seen basically as a pluralism of one's response to and relationship with God. While taking into account the double freedom of the divine and of the human, this view gives religions a dynamic orientation towards their final unity and fulfillment in God. The affirmation that God is one and has one plan of salvation for all humanity implies that these relationships are oriented to a unity that is rooted in God and that it has to be achieved in and through dialogue and collaboration.[74]

The unity of religions is possible only when we recognize the Spirit of God working in others and respect the experience and expressions of

[74] Cf. Xavier Irudayaraj, "One God and Many Religions", in: *Indian Missiological Review* 18 (1996) 2, p. 6.

one another and, thus, come together to mutually share our experiences in order to grow together and reach our common destiny, namely, God (cf. *NA* 1), in and through his Son Jesus Christ (cf. 1 Cor. 15:28).

### *2.3. Missio Dei and the Challenges of the Third Millennium*

There is but one mission in the world, the *missio Dei:* mission of the Father and the Son and the Spirit. Christian mission is the continuation of Christ's mission on earth. The evangelization of the Church in the modern world finds its *raison d'être* in the will of God who wishes all men to be saved through his Son Jesus Christ (cf. 1 Tim. 2:4-5). The Church as the sacrament of Christ is called to carry out the *mission manifesto* of Jesus (cf. Lk. 4:16-18; Matt. 11:4-5), that is, a programme and service of human liberation, accomplished with the power of the Spirit, in the very certitude of the *missio Dei.* It is a mission of witness unto death. "Woe to me if I do not proclaim the gospel," says Paul (1 Cor. 9:16).

What is the future of the Church amidst the pluralism of religions and ideologies in the world today? K. Rahner says, "The Church is the sacrament of the unplanned future, because the future is no other than the eternal incomprehensibility of God."[75] The Church (ecclesia - from the Greek *ek-kalo,* to be called together by God) is the community of those who have accepted to become God's kingdom as inaugurated by and exemplified in the person of Jesus Christ. The kingdom itself is built by the Father and the Son and the Holy Spirit. Therefore to reduce the mission of the Church to merely human mission would endanger the mission in the third millennium.

There are vast areas in the world with no effective Christian presence, especially in Asia; and with the rise and renaissance of religions and cultures today it seems most unlikely that Asia will be a Christian continent. As the second millennium after Christ's coming draws near to an end, and as the Decade of Evangelization from December 25, 1990 to December 25, 2000 is already at its last days of completion, it is time for the Church to bear witness to Christ, present him as the universal saviour to the world, guard the deposit of faith and examine herself and her missionary motivation and method as she enters into uncharted third

---

[75] See quoted in: W. Bühlmann, *The Church of the Future,* Orbis Books, Maryknoll, New York, 1986, p. 191. Cf. Anthony Packiasamy, "The New Evangelization 2000: Concept, Context and Need", in: *Indian Theological Studies* 32 (1995) 4, p. 352.

millennium, its challenges and fears, knowing that "it is not we who are principal agents of the Church's mission, but Jesus Christ and his mission" (*RM* 36). Jesus repeats the same words of mission he commissioned to his Apostles two thousand years ago: "As the Father has sent me, so I send you" (Jn. 20:21).

Even though Asian religions that consider themselves to be religiously self-sufficient, self-satisfied and, therefore, saved and saving, Christian mission enjoys two major advantages: the transparency and witnessing of the missionaries with their selfless dedication (*niṣkāma karma*), and the person of Jesus Christ who has an immense appeal to the people of Asia.[76]

### *2.4. Facing the Challenges on the Indian Scene*

The problem, especially with regard to evangelization on the Indian scene arises on three levels: (i) the relation between the Church and other religions; (ii) the relation between the Catholic Church and other sister Churches; and (iii) the relation between the universal and the local Church.

(i) The Church's claim to be the universal sacrament of salvation is challenged by other religions. All the religions of the world promise salvation in and within them. The world and the religions seem to be divided in the name of God. While Buddhism and Islam are by their nature missionary religions, Hinduism too has lately assumed a missionary character. The renaissance of religions and secularism demands a response more than the simple proclamation of the Word.

(ii) The question of "domination-dependence" between the Catholic Church and sister Churches goes on. The Church and Christians seem to be divided in the name of Christ. The validity of the Catholic Church's institutions, dogmas, doctrines and their formulations to present Christ to the world relevantly and effectively is questioned by sister Churches. It is sad to see Christians from sister Churches (Protestants) in India at times out in their mission to convert and "save" Catholics.

(iii) On the level of the relation between the universal Church and local Churches some have the fear that the pyramidal Church, already put

---

[76] Cf. Sebastian Karotemprel, "The Shape of Christian Mission in the Third Millennium", in: *Indian Missiological Review* 18 (1996) 2, pp. 71-72.

aside by Vatican II, still exists in some form or other. At times there seems to be a complaint that the lack of understanding of the indigenous cultures, concepts and categories, with the anxiety to keeping the purity of doctrine and unity of the Church, is effectively checking the progress of evangelization and the Church.[77]

Besides, on the national or local level, the alien character of the Church in India, the socio-cultural integration of the Church in an evolving society and the problem of an Indian rite need solutions which will help the Church to bear effective witness to Christ.

The task of effectively integrating various aspects of evangelization such as salvation, liberation, dialogue, development, service, personality, community and secularization is not yet fully achieved. There is much to be done in this regard, for which the Church has to work in dialogue and collaboration with others. The Church is ever called to commit herself to Christ with deeper faith and hope.

### *2.5. Right Attitude, Right Approach*

Even after a long history of missionary presence in India,[78] Christianity has not gained much ground here, at least in terms of number. What would be the reasons? One of the main reasons is the impact of other religions on the people. The salvific impact of other religions may be seen as the first deterring factor to Christianity in India. The "salvific appeal" of Christianity is already met by other religions; they too promise salvation. Besides, the colonizing "coercions" and wars have produced a wrong impression of Christianity to many an Indian mind.

Looking at history nobody can deny the fact that while religions have been the means of peace and salvation, the world has fought many wars in the name of God and religions. God has been often misunderstood and religions misinterpreted and practised wrongly. Mutual ignorance, misunderstanding and prejudice among religions, improper missionary motivation and method have caused a great havoc in history. What is required today is to have a right attitude and a right approach to other religions.

---

[77] Cf. A. Mookenthottam, M.S.F.S., *Indian Theological Tendencies,* op. cit., 176.

[78] According to a tradition, Christianity was brought to India by St. Thomas the Apostle, in the second half of the first century of the Common Era. See: A. M. Mundadan, *Sixteenth Century Traditions of St. Thomas Christians,* Dharmaram College Studies, no. 5, Dharmaram College, Bangalore, 1970, pp. 81-82.

## *2.6. Inter-Religious Dialogue and Global Responsibility*

The human race is one. Christians are first of all human persons, and members of the human community. This community because of its special experience of God in Christ does not find itself separate from the rest of human beings, forming a class apart, having to live in a world of its own. On the contrary, their experience of Christ in the very midst of individual and collective existence awakens them to their task of "everyday dialogue" in life with others at both micro and macro levels -- officially or unofficially, individually or collectively, internally or externally.[79] Religions and ideologies of the world, if they are to truly serve the world today, they must assume a global concern and global responsibility, in dialogue and mutual collaboration, for the peace and salvation of the world. In this regard, Hans Küng writes: "No human life together without a world ethic for the nations; no peace among the nations without peace among the religions; no peace among the religions without dialogue among the religions."[80]

The need in India of an inter-religious dialogue that goes beyond sharing of religious experiences and beyond the dialogue of every day praxis should also address itself to the concern for the political reality of India, today threatened and thwarted by many issues arising in the name of religion like riots, hatred, violence and killings. Not only sin and violence must be done away with, but also the causes of sin and violence. In a country like India the causes of riots, violence and killings are very often communally based and often politically patronized. Dialogue, if it be honestly self-critical and ready to creatively solve historical and religious problems, can contribute to the democratic process of rebuilding the nation at a moment when its existence as a secular state is endangered. What seems to be most needed in this regard is a politically based dialogue -- 'a dialogue for democracy' -- a democracy that can secure its citizens political as well as religious freedom.[81]

A theologian in dialogue is called to accept the many as the many,

---

[79] Cf. Hans Küng, *Global Responsibility: In Search of a New World Ethic,* SCM Press Ltd., London, 1991, p. 138; DSA, *Main Problems in Preaching the Gospel Today. Main Problems in Mission Lands,* op. cit., pp. 13-14.

[80] Hans Küng, *Global Responsibility: In Search of a New World Ethic,* op. cit., p. 138.

[81] Cf. Felix Wilfred, "Inter-Religious Dialogue as a Political Question", in: *Vidyajyoti* 60 (1996) 6, pp. 361-374.

which means to respect other religions in their own otherness. It is not merely a tolerant and anarchic pluralism but a unitive and creative pluralism.[82]

*2.7. A Biblical Perspective: Not Conquest but Collaboration*

The early faith experience of Israel had its foundation in their liberation from the Egyptian domination. Their constant confession was that they were "brought out of Egypt" by their God Yahweh (Num. 23:22; 24:8; Deut. 26:8; Ex. 20:2; Judg. 6:13). The relationship between Yahweh and Israel had its political overtones. Israel did need a protector having been humiliated by the Egyptian rulers. Their relationship with Yahweh took the form of a covenant that demanded the true worship of Yahweh and no other gods. Its basic tenet was that Yahweh was absolute: "I am the Lord your God, who brought you out of the land of Egypt, out of the house of slavery; you shall have no other gods before me" (Ex. 20:2-3).

Israel's faith in their liberator God was their main strength on conquering any nation, and they could not permit the existence of any other god who for them was a symbol of slavery. Their zeal for Yahweh was so intense and their attitude towards other deities so uncompromising that they took to a total annihilation of the local deities. But even at this early stage of total exclusivism, some people of Israel did experience a syncretism at the popular level. Baal was the god of the land believed to be controlling its fertility. Observing certain days and seasons in the cultivation of the land was in fact part of the Baal worship. The Israelites who were also given to agriculture fell in line with such observances, and in this sense they bound themselves to the gods of the land, without in any way turning away from Yahweh. The former Canaanite shrines like Bethel, Shechem and Gilgal were rededicated to Yahweh and festivals of pilgrimages were introduced after the manner of the Canaanites (cf. Ex. 34:22-23). Even some of the Israelite children seemed to have been named after Baal with such names as Jerubbaal (Judg. 6:32), Meribbaal (1 Chr. 8:34), and Ishbaal (2 Sam. 2:8). At Shechem worship was offered to Baal-berith (Baal-of-the-Covenant) (Judg. 9:4).

The spirit of compromise that crept in among the Israelites was

[82] Cf. Xavier Irudayaraj, "One God and Many Religions", in: *Indian Missiological Review* 18 (1996) 2, pp. 4-5.

basically a feeling that Yahweh and Baal could not be mutually Exclusive.[83] Later on exclusivism was challenged by the Yahwist writer who reminded Israel that her being chosen by him from so many other nations, meant that she should be the agent of his blessings upon all the families of the earth (cf. Gen. 12:1-3; 17:18; 22:18; 26:4; 28:14). This vision of the Yahwist was later elaborated by Isaiah with the proclamation that Israel is the light of the nations (cf. Is. 42:6; 49:6; 58:8; etc.). Isaiah turned the severe and exclusive notion of Yahweh into a benevolent and inclusive one (cf. Is. 19:16-25). In Isaiah 19:25 Yahweh is seen as imparting his blessing upon all peoples and religions, saying, "Blessed be Egypt my people, and Assyria the work of my hands, and Israel my heritage."

To be chosen, therefore, is to be sought out for mission, for service (cf. Is. 41:8-9; 43:10). The title servant is now given to Israel: "You are my servant, Israel, in whom I will be glorified" (Is. 49:3). Israel has now to fulfill a mission and glorify Yahweh. She has to bring "justice to the nations" (Is. 42:1), she has to be a light to the nations. She is sent to "open the eyes that are blind, to bring out the prisoners from the dungeon, from the prison those who sit in darkness" (Is. 42:6-7), that is, she is sent to liberate people and nations from bondage. Israel has to mediate God's salvation to the ends of the earth, and that too, not by conquest or compulsion, but through a prophetic and kenotic approach of a humble servant (Is. 50:6; 53:10-13).

This has also been the understanding of Jesus -- his is a service of a humble servant of God's universal salvific will and action (cf. Lk. 2:33; 4:18; Is. 42:6; 49:6). The gospels, especially of Mark, present Jesus in his relationship to non-Jewish religions. For example, Jesus is presented as opening his mission activity to a variety of people from Galilee, Judea, Jerusalem, Idumea and beyond Jordan, Tyre and Sidon, making no distinction whatever (cf. Mk. 3:7-12). Jesus went beyond the confines of the Jewish territory to serve the Gentiles (cf. Mk. 5:1-20); he healed the daughter of a Syrophoenician woman (cf. Mk. 24-31).[84] He respected the

---

[83] Cf. S.J. Anthonysamy, "Christian Mission in the context of Many Religions Today: A Biblical Perspective", in: *Indian Missiological Review* 18 (1996) 2, pp. 9-11.

[84] The story of the Syrophoenician woman should be read in the context of the Jew-Gentile polemics. Old hard-core exclusivism had still not perished; it was in fact being revived in a subtle manner. It was claimed that the Jew should come first, and then only the Greek (cf. Rom. 1:16; 2:9-10). Jesus would not like to be part of such religious distinctions.

religion of the woman, which made her humbly profess God's providence to the whole creation (cf. Mk. 7:28). The religion of Jesus is a religion of service -- service to God and fellow human beings.

Following the example of Jesus, the Church is called to go beyond the Christian "territories" of experience and expressions, concepts and categories, and recognize the "faith" of others and the working of the Spirit of God in them. Unfortunately and sadly, this was not the case in the long history of the Church until the Vatican II Council humbly accepted others as religions and recognized the salvific presence and action of the Spirit in them.

### *2.8. The Resurrection of Jesus, the Rallying Point: A New World Order*

Christianity seen exclusively as a religion which focuses attention on laws, obedience, sin, cross, propitiation and judgement misses the depth and freshness of the Gospel. The cross of Jesus is to be seen as a symbol of hope and victory (Easter Sunday) than a mere object of *propitiation* to appease the terribly offended God (Good Friday). The emphasis laid on Jesus' *love* for God and humankind makes the cross ever radiant, sublime, appealing to the suffering humanity of today as the symbol of hope and liberation.

What is particularly appealing to the Indian religious outlook familiar with the *śakti* (divine power) that raises the dead is the new order brought about by the constitution of Jesus as the Son of God through the resurrection (cf. Rom. 1:4). The conquest of death and the introduction of everlasting life in and through Christ is to be seen in the spirit of the Vedic prayer: "From the unreal lead me to the real; from darkness lead me to light; from death lead me to immortality" (Bṛh. Up. 1.3.28).

Jesus' resurrection is not merely a happy ending imagined for an unjust tragedy, but rather the triumph of the spirit over the flesh, a new order over the old, and a declaration of what the authentic condition of human beings should be.[85]

[85] Cf. John B. Chethimattam, "The Challenge of Evangelization in India at the Threshold of the Third Millennium", in: *Jeevadhara* 16 (1986) 155, pp. 337-338.

## *2.9. Religious Pluralism and a Constant Search for Jesus*

One wonders why it took Christians so long to recognize the presence of God in other religions. Yet a serious study of religions has engaged Christian theologians today in a search for the "historical" Jesus and his unique saving role, his divinity, as never before. The world's largest literature ever been written and still being written on a single person is on Jesus Christ and his saving role in the world.

To see the unique role of Jesus Christ in the history of salvation, some thinkers have not only distinguished Jesus Christ from the Jesus of history but actually have separated him from the Jesus of Nazareth. Whether it is the 'Logos Jesus Christ' of John (Epilogue) or the Pauline image: 'the first born of all creation' (Col. 1:15) and the beloved 'Son' (Col. 1:13), Christ becomes for some more an idea than a name for the person of Jesus of Nazareth. The particularity of the real Jesus is a scandal for them and in various ways his human face is forgotten. But it is the same historical person of Jesus of Nazareth who is constituted as Christ in his resurrection. He is one and the same person -- Jesus the Christ (cf. Acts 2:36).[86]

It is true that Christ is the Alpha and the Omega (Rev. 22:12-13; *GS* 45). He is the same for all times -- "the same yesterday and today and forever" (Heb. 13:8). But this "sameness" of Jesus is often misunderstood: often it is applied to or identified with the customs and cultures of a community, consisting of concepts, categories, life-style, etc. Christ transcends all times and cultures. What is same in Jesus for all times and traditions is that he is the Son of God, who has come in the world to save the world. Hence this sameness -- God's saving Word become flesh in his Son Jesus -- should be applied and appropriated by all peoples, times, traditions and cultures. To do this what is required is a constant search and longing for Jesus, interpretation and re-interpretation of his saving message to all times and traditions.

Jesus is the *new covenant* (Lk. 22:20; 1 Cor. 11:25; Heb. 9:15; cf. Jer. 31-34) between God and humanity; he is the promised word of God fulfilled; he is the *term* towards which the whole human history is moving; he is the climatic and definitive revelation of God in and within the one history of salvation. Thus, we say that there is only *one* God and *one* salvation history that comprises all peoples and religions, all times and

---

[86] Cf. J. Dupuis, *Jesus Christ at the Encounter of World Religions,* op. cit., pp. 178-190.

cultures.[87] The religions of the world are called to follow God through Christ, led by the Spirit. "To be in touch with Christ, we must first have been touched by the Holy Spirit."[88] This is the salvific mystery of the triune God, the mystery of the new creation in Christ. St. Irenæus writes:

> Baptism gives us the grace of new birth in God the Father, through his Son, in the Holy Spirit. For those who hear God's Spirit are led to the Word, that is, to the Son, and the Son presents them to the Father, and the Father confers incorruptibility on them. And it is impossible to see God's Son without the Spirit, and no one can approach the Father without the Son, for the knowledge of the Father is the Son, and knowledge of God's Son is obtained through the Holy Spirit.[89]

## 3. Résumé

(i) The divine plan for humanity is one, but multifaceted and ongoing (cf. *NA* 1). The Triune God who is always in communication and communion within himself has been revealing himself in diverse ways to diverse peoples and cultures at different times. That God spoke in many and various ways before speaking through his Son (cf. Heb. 1:1-2) is not incidental; nor is the rich and varied, the plural character of God's self-manifestation merely a thing of the past. The decisiveness of the Son's advent in the flesh in Jesus Christ does not cancel the universal presence and action of the Word and the Spirit in other religions. Instead, the coming of Jesus Christ is seen as the confirmation of God's saving presence and action in other religions as preparation for Christ and his Church and their consummation in and through Christ. Religious pluralism in principle rests on the immensity and ineffable mystery of God who is spirit, love and truth, and is ever present and active in creation, leading it to its consummation. (Chapter one).

---

[87] Cf. DSA (ed.), *Non-Biblical Scriptures - Theological Understanding,* op. cit., pp. 24-25.

[88] *CCC,* 683.

[89] See: St. Irenæus, *Dem. ap. 7:* SCh 62, 41-42, as cited in: *CCC,* 683.

(ii) The Church is the people of God, who put their faith and hope in Christ and his Gospel. While it is true that the Holy Spirit who resides in the whole community (*sensus fidei* or *sensus fidelium,* cf. *LG* 12) is the theological basis for the authority of the Church in matters of faith and morals, the Church can never be reduced to its mere visible institutions and structures. The mystery of the Church transcends all these external manifestations and expressions to such an extent that it can influence those outside the visible boundaries of the Catholic Church.[90] This new vision has prompted the Vatican II Council to accept the ecclesial reality of the sister Churches; to recognize other religious traditions as religions and see the presence and activity of the Spirit in them; and consider the Church not as identical to the kingdom but as the servant and sacrament of the kingdom.

By recognizing the salvific values and positive aspects in other religions, the Church does not diminish her indispensable role of proclaiming the *Good News* in the world. On the contrary, it implies the Church to become what she is primarily meant to be, that is, the sacrament of unity of all peoples in God (cf. *LG* 1).

Jesus does not reject any culture, any human condition; he should be "born" in every culture. The Church's theology must be relevant; it must reflect the reality of the people. The great challenge of evangelization today is to make people reflect on the contribution Jesus and his Gospel can make with respect to salvation in their own socio-political, cultural and religious context. To do this, the Church has to enter into dialogue with her fellow countrymen in their actual concerns. She has to show new forms of solidarity and new images of social bond with the poor, involving herself in the authentic human experiences of the people where the Spirit of God is actually present, inviting all people and nations to recognize the new spiritual reality made available to them in Jesus Christ. (Chapter two).

(iii) The Jesus Christ event is "constitutive" of universal salvation. It means that the person of Jesus Christ and the whole Christ event (OT and NT, from promise to fulfillment) are constitutive of salvation -- in particular, in and though his life, death and resurrection Jesus has realized the absolute saving will of God. Put in other words, the humanity of Jesus Christ is the sacrament of God's universal will to save. God's universal

---

[90] Cf. Kuncheria Pathil, "Theology of the Role of the Laity in Vatican II", in: *Jeevadhara* 16 (1986) 154, p. 255.

saving will and word (*śabda, kalimat*) displayed in the past through varied ways and means has been now fully realized in the incarnate Word, Jesus Christ (cf. Heb. 1:1-2). Jesus Christ is, then, the continuation, confirmation and consummation of the universal saving will of God in every stage of history. The uniqueness of Jesus Christ lies, therefore, in the uniqueness of God's execution of his saving will. The Jesus Christ event is, therefore, "constitutive" of God's absolute saving will and action in history.

Thus, the historical event of God becoming flesh marks the deepest and most decisive engagement of God with humanity; it establishes with humankind a bond of union that can never be severed. This event, in the order of God's will and execution, is necessary for humankind, and is marked by the particularity of the historical happening.

The person of Jesus Christ unites human history. He is the unity of God's saving will and activity. The "transhistorical" or the cosmic character of Jesus Christ is "limited", so to say, by its insertion in history, without which its singular significance, density and 'trans-historicity' would vanish. The Jesus Christ event is, thus, at once particular in time and universal in meaning and application (concrete and universal), and as such, "singular unique", yet *related* to all other divine manifestations to humankind in the one history of salvation. All history and all religious traditions and their aspirations, then, are related to Christ as their head for their completion.

The historical event of Jesus Christ does not in any way overshadow the eschatological convergence of religions in God at the fullness of time, instead Christ is constituted the Lord -- to unite all things in heaven and on earth (cf. Eph. 1:10) in the unity of faith and knowledge of truth (cf. Eph. 4:13) and to hand over to God everything -- where God will be all in all (cf. 1 Cor. 15:24, 28). It is in this sense we say that all salvation comes from Christ the head through the Church which is his Body (cf. *LG* 14).[91] The Church is, then, seen as the sacrament of Christ and his universal salvation (cf. *LG* 48). The Church is at the service of God's kingdom brought about by his Son Jesus Christ. She is sent out to bring people and nations to that *faith* in God without which it is impossible to please him and be saved (cf. Heb. 11:6; *AG* 7).[92] This is the faith in Jesus Christ. His

---

[91] Cf. also: *CCC,* 846.

[92] Cf. also: *CCC,* 848.

saving presence and action are operative and effective everywhere and at all times. (Chapters three and four).

(iv) Almost three decades had elapsed since the Second World War. Now one could think and theologize in terms of not confrontation but dialogue and collaboration. Vatican II (1962-1965) saw the Church as the sacrament of unity of all mankind (cf. *LG* 1). It was a call launched to all Christians to help them read "the signs of the time" (*GS* 4).

*Nostra Aetate* (1965), as well as the encyclical letter of Paul VI *Ecclesiam Suam* during the Council (1964), officially provided a new step in the Roman Catholic Church towards dialogue with other religions. *Nostra Aetate* was meant to mobilize the commitment of Christians in building the kingdom of God, inaugurated by Christ. Its declaration was not a point of arrival or an achievement accomplished; rather, it was a point of departure, a challenge set before all Christians to go for dialogue with others so that the words of Jesus, "that all may be one" (Jn. 17:11) may be fulfilled. Thus *Nostra Aetate* created a point of departure, a new culture of dialogue in the Church. Later, John Paul II saw the declaration (*NA*) as presenting a map of various religions and said that the universal awareness by the Church as the sacrament of unity and peace is to be formed in dialogue (cf. *RH* 11). Dialogue is avowed to be a movement inspired and assisted by the Holy Spirit, and no one can stop what comes from God (cf. Acts 5:38-39). (Chapter five).

(v) The reading of the Bible makes clear cut demand on social justice. The covenant which is central to the Old Testament prescribes social justice as the precondition for love of God. God is seen to be on the side of the poor, the marginalized and the oppressed. It does not mean thereby that he is against all non-poor. It only means that God shows his concern first and foremost for those people in whom humanity is most endangered. He is on the side of the poor for the whole of humanity, not against the rest of humanity.

Likewise, for Jesus no authority (Temple, Torah or Sabbath) was too great to be contradicted. He fought against any authority, social or religious, that was offensive to human dignity and endangered the cause of justice and peace. His teaching was a call to conversion to a 'God-and-neighbour-centered life' and the establishment of God's kingdom on earth. He announced a programme of social reversal to make the least and last first and important (cf. Mk. 10:31). The riches and resources of the world are meant for all; they are to be shared among all (cf. Lk. 3:11; 12:33).

Jesus' stand on political liberation was also clear. For him power was seen displayed in humble service to God and humankind. He was against éliticism, discrimination and inequalities; he wanted love of all, including enemies, and genuine human freedom. He chose rather to die in order to affirm human freedom and the values of the kingdom of God than to compromise with evil and injustice.

This aspect became the sole theme of justice in the world of the synod of Bishops (1971). The change the Church wants is not merely attitudinal and personal, but social as well. It requires a sincerity of purpose and integrity of life, change of heart and change of society. Change of structures without the change of heart is a materialistic and collective illusion and the so called change of self or person without the change of structures is an idealistic and liberalistic illusion. We need both kinds of changes in order to respond fully to the vital needs of our society today.[93] The mission of the Church is not simply to announce the Gospel but also to organize the poor and the oppressed into liberation struggles for justice and thereby bring back their lost dignity of human persons, created in the image and likeness of God.[94] It is not enough only to *pray* for the kingdom to 'come on earth as it is in heaven', the Church has to *work* for it.

In other words, Christians and others in a multi-religious society have to work together for the realization of the kingdom of God on earth.[95] It is a challenge for the Church, collectively and individually, to assume her role and responsibility in the transformation of the world. This is what, referring to Deuteronomy 30:15-16, John Paul II in his recent visit to Poland (31 May-10 June 1997) appealed to the thousands of people gathered there: "Do not be afraid to take up responsibilities in society: face the world courageously."[96] (Chapter six).

The Church has witnessed a succession of theologies in the interpretation of the relation between Christianity and other religions. Once

---

[93] Cf. A. Pushparajan, "Social Justice from the Point of View of Christian Tradition", in: *Indian Theological Studies* 32 (1995) 4, p. 336.

[94] Cf. ibid., p. 333.

[95] Cf. S.J. Samartha, *One Christ - Many Religions. (Toward a Revised Christology)*, Orbis Books, Maryknoll, New York, 1994 (2nd edition, its 1st edition in 1991), pp. 58-65.

[96] See: *L'Osservatore Romano*, (Italian edition), 2-3 Giugno 1997, p. 10: "Non abbiate paura di assumervi le responsibilità della vita sociale: andate con coraggio verso il mondo." (Translation mine).

'crisis' theology dominated the scene; then came the theology of 'fulfillment' only to be supplanted by the theology of 'mutual fulfillment', 'eschatological fulfillment', 'cross fertilization', etc. While these theologies may differ among themselves in their approach to other religions, they try to meet the challenges posed by the reality of religious pluralism in the world in general and India in particular. A synthetic view-point of different paradigms of theology of religions (Christocentrism, theocentrism, regnocetrism) are to be seen in mutual relationship and reciprocal implication in a Christian theology of religions. "To separate these various aspects from each other is to fall short of the complexity and richness of the Christian experience."[97]

This leads us to conclude that "between God's coming in Christ and the final consummation of all things, theology as pilgrim is on the way to the ultimate mystery of God."[98] Amalor's theology is a Christocentric and inclusive theology that proceeds from the centrality of the Jesus Christ event in the one and universal salvific plan of God.[99] Christ is the saviour of all. The Spirit of Christ is present and active in other religions, leading them through the Church, the universal sacrament of salvation (cf. *LG* 8, 48), to the eschatological pleroma and sovereignty of Christ, and through Christ to God the Father (cf. 1 Cor. 15:28).[100] This is, what we call, the 'inclusive paradigm' in the Christian theology of other religions, where, as such, we do not speak in terms of exclusion or inclusion of other religious figures or traditions but their *completion* in Christ, their recapitulation (*anakephalaiósis*) in Christ. The Spirit is certainly leading the Church and other religions through Christ to the fullness of truth and their common unity in God (cf. Jn. 14:26; *NA* 1).

---

[97] J. Dupuis, *Toward a Christian Theology of Religious Pluralism,* Orbis Books, Maryknoll, New York, 1997, p. 385.

[98] M. Dhavamony, "Indian Christian Theology", in: *Studia Missionalia,* vol. 45, op. cit., p. 111; cf. also: DSA, *Approaches,* op. cit., p. 8.

[99] Cf. DSA, *Approaches,* op. cit., pp. 11, 33; id., *Approach,* op. cit., pp. 27-28; Gavin D'Costa, *Theology and Religious Pluralism: The Challenge of Other Religions,* Basil Blackwell, Oxford, 1986 (see in general).

[100] Cf. DSA, *Approaches,* op. cit., pp. 11, 33-44; see also the Declaration of the Nagpur Conference, no. 16, in: Id., *Theology of Evangelization,* op. cit., p. 33.

# BIBLIOGRAPHY

Although this is a study of Amalor's theological understanding of other religions, yet in this list I have also included other significant publications of his that are not directly dealing with other religions. It is because his publications are of a varied nature and it is practically impossible to give an order of importance, because the key issues and insights return in many publications.

Especially two existing lists[1] helped me make this collection. I have arranged the whole bibliography into three main divisions: (a) Primary Sources, (b) Secondary Sources, and (c) Other Works Consulted. These are in turn further subdivided, especially into books and articles. The "Primary Sources" is arranged according to chronological order. In the "Secondary Sources" and "Other Works Consulted" I have followed the alphabetical order, except for the subdivisions of Curial and Papal Documents which follow the chronological order.

The writings of Amalor: his publications, articles in various periodicals, his contributions in his edited books and his audio-visual cassettes form the primary sources; and writings on Amalor form the secondary sources.

## A. Primary Sources: Amalor's Publications, Articles and Cassettes

### 1. Publications (Books, Brochures and Pamphlets)


*The Heavenly Jerusalem* (the biblical theme 'temple'), [in Tamil], Madurai: De Nobili Press, 1957.

*The Royal Priesthood,* [in Tamil], Madurai: De Nobili Press, 1957.

*Why do I suffer?* (the problem of evil), [in Tamil], Pondicherry: Mission Press, 1957.

*The Day of the Lord* (the biblical themes: 'rest', 'joy' and 'hope'), [in Tamil], Madurai: De Nobili Press, 1958.

*The Lord is my Shepherd* (the biblical theme 'pastor'), [in Tamil], Madurai: De Nobili Press, 1958.

*The Spouse* (the biblical theme 'spouse'), [in Tamil], Nagercoil: Assisi Press, 1958.

*The Missionary Spirit in the Bible* (biblical themes: 'vocation', 'election'), [in Tamil], Madurai: De Nobili Press, 1959.

*L'Inde à la rencontre du Seigneur,* Paris: Éd. Spes, 1964.

*Destinée de l'Église dans l'Inde d'aujourd'hui,* Paris: Fayard-Mame, 1967.


[1] See in: Gerwin van Leeuwen, O.F.M., *Fully Indian - Authentically Christian,* NBCLC, Bangalore, 1990, pp. 344-353; and Cyril De Souza, S.D.B., *Catechesis for India Today,* Kristu Jyoti Publications, Bangalore, 1994, pp. 421-470.

1.1. Mission Theology Series

*Theology of Development.* (A Lecture delivered at the Second Missionary Zonal Consultation held in Bombay from 20th to 23rd September 1969), Bangalore: NCLC, 1969 (reprinted in 1972, 1979).[2]

*Mission Theology for Our Times*, Bangalore: NBCLC, 1969 (reprinted in 1970).

*The Theology of "Indirect Evangelization"*, Bangalore: NCLC (NBCLC), 1970.

*Purpose and Motivation of Missionary Activity*, Bangalore: NBCLC, 1970 (reprinted in 1976).

*Approaches in Our Apostolate Among the Followers of Other Religions*, Bangalore: NBCLC, 1970 (reprinted in 1976, 1978).

*Theology of Evangelization in the Indian Context*, Bangalore: NBCLC, 1971 (reprinted in 1973, 1976, 1984).

*Theology of Catechesis.* (Key-note Address delivered at the World Congress of Catechetics, Rome, September 1971), Bangalore: NBCLC, 1971 (revised and reprinted in 1973).

*Adult Catechumenate and Church Renewal*, Bangalore: NBCLC, 1971.

*Efforts made in the Roman Catholic Church towards Indigenization*, Bangalore: NBCLC, 1971.

*Towards Indigenization in the Liturgy*, Bangalore: NBCLC, 1971 (reprinted in 1973, 1975).

*Approach, Meaning and Horizon of Evangelization.* (The Theological Orientation Speech delivered at the All India Consultation on Evangelization at Patna, 3-8 October 1973), Bangalore: NBCLC, 1973.

*Preaching the Gospel Today. Main Problems in Mission Lands.* (A Speech delivered at the International Missionary Conference, Lyon, 9-12 November 1972), Bangalore: NBCLC, 1973.

*Gospel and Culture. Evangelization and Inculturation*, Bangalore: NBCLC, 1978 (reprinted in 1985).

*Vision of Religious Life in Future and the Future of Religious Life*, Bangalore: NBCLC, 1980.

*Image of a Religious Brother in a Declericalized Church*, Bangalore: NBCLC, 1981.

*Poverty of the Religious in the Indian Context and Biblical Tradition*, Bangalore:NBCLC, 1982.

*Poverty of the Religious and the Religious as Poor*, Bangalore: NBCLC, 1982 (reprinted in 1984).

*The Option for the Poor in the Concrete Situation of India and Sri Lanka*, Bangalore: A Redemptoris Publication, 1982.

*The Bible in Self-Renewal and Church-Renewal for Service to Society*, Bangalore: NBCLC, 1984.

*Social Communication and Christian Communion. Reality, Theology, Pedagogy and Spirituality of Communication*, Bangalore: NBCLC, 1984.

---

[2] In the bibliography we have shown the years of the first publication of the books as well as (when there are) the years of their reprints/editions. A particular year of publication is indicated when referred to in the dissertation.

*Vision, Thrust and Policy for Evangelization. (Concrete Proposals for the Function of the CBCI Commission)*, Bangalore: NBCLC, 1985.

1.2. Liturgical Renewal and Spirituality Series

*Community Building*, Bangalore: NBCLC, 1975 (reprinted in 1978).
*NBCLC Campus. Milieu of God-Experience. An Artistic Synthesis of Spirituality*, Bangalore: NBCLC, 1982.
*Samdhya -- Initiation and Experience*, Bangalore: NBCLC, 1984.
*Ashram Aikya: Whence and Whither*, Bangalore: NBCLC, [1984].

1.3. Ecumenical Movement Series

*Relation between the Catholic Church and the World Council of Churches*, Bangalore: NBCLC, 1976.
*Ecumenism in Perspective*, Bangalore: NBCLC, 1976.

1.4. NBCLC Seminar and Leaflet Series[3]

*A Review of Life on the Exercise of Authority.*
*A Short Initiation to the Liturgy of the Hours.*
*Basic Christian Prayer or Biblical Prayer.*
*Basic Structure of Liturgical Action.*
*Bible Meditation.*
*Bibliography for Youth Catechesis.*
*Common Confession and General Absolution.*
*Family Catechesis.*
*Initiation to the Eucharist in Small Groups.*
*Initiation to Dhyana: An Indian Form of Meditation.*
*Inter-Religious Dialogue in India.*
*Introducing the 'God-with-Us' Catechetical Series.*
*Liturgy Relevant to Life: Meaningful and Experiential Celebration:*
*A First Approach: Starting from the Reformed Liturgy such as we find in the revised Rites/Books.*
*Liturgy Relevant to Life:*
*B Second Approach: Starting from the group or community which celebrates the Liturgy and its life-situation which needs to be interpreted, proclaimed and celebrated.*
*Liturgy Relevant to Life:*
*C Third Approach: Starting from the socio-cultural-religious traditions which*

[3] Since many of the booklets and leaflets of this series are regularly used for seminars and courses at the NBCLC and diocesan seminars, conducted by NBCLC teams, there have been several reprints, often without mentioning the year of their publication or reprint. Hence we refrain here from indicating the year of publication and the number of reprints. (See also done so: Gerwin van Leeuwen, O.F.M., *Fully Indian - Authentically Christian*, op. cit., p. 346). All the booklets and leaflets of this series have been published by the NBCLC, Bangalore.

*furnish the signs and symbols, language and thought-patterns, through which one can express the mystery of our salvation (indigenous form of worship).*
*Man, Centre and Summit of the Universe, Medium and Milieu of Relevance.*
*Our Christian World Vision and Theological Synthesis.*
*Pastorale of First Communion and Confession.*
*Practical Conclusions and Obvious Consequences of Revelation-Faith and the Christian World Vision for the Pastorale and Spirituality.*
*Prayer and Activity within a New World Vision.*
*Religious Life.*
*Renewal of the Sacrament of Penance: Sacrament of Conversion and Reconciliation.*
*The Catechetical Pedagogy for the Youth.*
*The Church's Mission as Prophetic and Hermeneutical.*
*The Church's Mission in India Today: Evangelization and/or Liberation?*
*Towards Indigenization in the Liturgy.*

2. Articles

"Catechetical Refresher Course in India", in: *Asia* 12 (1960) 7, pp. 699-703.
"St. Paul, Model of Catechists", in: *The Clergy Monthly Supplement* 5 (1961) 6, pp. 225-235.
"Imparting the Mission to Catechists", in: *Good Tidings* 1 (1962) 3, pp. 60-62.
"Le Mouvement Liturgique en Inde", in: *Paroisse et Liturgie* 45 (1963) 8, pp. 785-798.
"L'Église au Pays Tamoul", in: *Missions Étrangères de Paris* (1963) no. 129, pp. 23-28.
"Le Pays Tamoul", in: *Missions Étrangères de Paris* (1963) no.128, pp. 35-38.
"Les Évêques de Mission et le Concile", in: *Illustré Missionnaire* 13 (1963) 6, pp. 103-109.
"Les Vicaires Laïcs du Missionnaire", in: *Les Missions Catholiques* (1963) no. 95, pp. 259-286.
"Les Vicaires Laïcs du Tamilnad", in: *Informations Catholiques Internationales* [9] (1963) no. 204, pp. 25-31.
"Liturgical Formation of Catechists at Tindivanam", in: *Epiphanie. Bulletin de Documentation des Missions Étrangères de Paris* (1963) no. 12, pp. 397-411; also in: *Teaching All Nation* 1 (1964) 2, pp. 316-328.
"A l'écoute des Pauvres en Inde", in: *Informations Catholiques Internationales* [10] (1964) no. 229, pp. 34-40.
"Conditions d'un Dialogue avec l'Hindouisme", in: *Les Missions Catholiques* (1964) no. 96, pp. 41-72.
"The Catechetical Movement in South India and the Regional Centre of Tindivanam", in: *Lumen Vitae* 19 (1964) 1, pp. 147-156.
"The Structures of Catechesis in South India and the Regional Centre at Tindivanam", in: *Lumen Vitae* 19 (1964) 4, pp. 744-749.
"Approche de l'Hindouisme", in: *Au Service du Maître de la Maison* (1965) no. 199, pp. 42-46.
"Indigenous Expressions in Cathedrals", in: *Bangalore Theological Forum* (United Theological College, Bangalore), 1965, pp. 26-40.
"The Implementation of the Liturgical Constitution and the Instruction in Tamilnad,

South India", in: *Teaching All Nations* 2 (1965) 4, pp. 469-473.
"The Meaning of Advent", in: *Witness unto Christ* 1 (1965) 6, pp. 122-127.
"Tindivanam Missions Katechetisches Zentrum für Südindien", in: *Missions und Religionswissenschaft* 49 (1965) 1, pp. 1-16.
"Una Chiesa Sannyasi?", in: *Selezione Missionaria* 12 (1965), pp. 122-131.
"Vocations en Inde", in: *Ensemble* 1965 (1965), pp. 14-15.
"Pastoral formation of Priests", in: *The Clergy Monthly Supplement* 8 (1966) 2, pp. 66-76.
"Lifelong Formation of the Clergy", in: *Teaching All Nations* 4 (1967) 1, pp. 43-59.
"General Problems of Catechetical Formation and Catechesis of Various Age-Groups", in: *Teaching All Nations* 4 (1967) 3, pp. 294-299.
"Sacred Silence", in: *Word and Worship* 1 (1967) 5, pp. 165-170.
"The Implication of Vatican II for the Missions in Asia", in: *Teaching All Nations* 4 (1967) 3, pp. 319-326.
"Workshop on Recent developments in Catechetics (International Study Week, Manila)", in: *Teaching All Nations* 4 (1967) 3, pp. 377-379; also published in: *Good Tidings* 6 (1967) 4 & 5, pp. 117-118, 143.
"General Orientation for the Redaction of Catechetical Material", in: *Word and Worship* 2 (1968) 4, pp. 134-146 & 2 (1968) 5, pp. 186-190.
"Discovery of the Relevance of Catholic Private Schools", in: *Word and Worship* 2 (1969) 6, pp. 220-229.
"Liturgy and Catechetics in India Today", in: *Teaching All Nations* 6 (1969) 4, pp. 373-388; also published under the title: "Liturgy and Catechetics in the All India Seminar on the Church in India Today", in: *Word and Worship* 3 (1970) 1, pp. 19-32.
"Suggestions for a Reform of the Existing Institutions and Shaping a New Pastoral Policy", in: *Word and Worship* 2 (1969) 8, pp. 321-325.
"World Day of Peace", in: *Word and Worship* 2 (1969) 7, pp. 259-267.
"Decisions on the Liturgy at the Ordinary General Meeting of the Catholic Bishops' Conference of India, Ernakulam, 7-16 January, 1970", in: *Word and Worship* 3 (1970) 3, pp. 89-100.
"Is Latin still the Language of the Liturgy?", in: *Word and Worship* 3 (1970) 1, pp. 35-36.
"Les Novices Indiennes - erreurs et vérité", in: *Peuples du Monde - Magazine de la Mission Universelle* (1970) no. 35, pp. 15-17.
"Liturgical Information", in: *Word and Worship* 3 (1970) 3, pp. 123-126.
"Editorial [First Holy Communion]", in: *Word and Worship* 4 (1971) 4, pp. 149-151.
"National Biblical Centre", in: *Word and Worship* 4 (1971) 6, pp. 254-255.
"VIII National Seminar on Holy Scripture (April, 1971) [Editorial]", in: *Word and Worship* 4 (1971) 9, p. 383.
"Inaugural Key-Note Address: The Theology of Evangelization in the Indian Context", in: M. Dhavamony (ed.), *Evangelization, Dialogue and Development. Selected Papers of the International Theological Conference, Nagpur (India) 1971*, Roma: Università Gregoriana Editrice, 1972, pp. 21-39.
"The Apostolate to Non-Christians", in: *Foundations of Mission Theology*, edited by SEDOS, translated by John Drury, Maryknoll Documentation Series, New York: Orbis Books, 1972, pp. 63-90.
"Approach, Meaning and Horizon of Evangelization", in: The Church Extension Commission (eds), *Light and Life We Seek to Share. (The All India Consultation*

*on Evangelization held under the auspices of the Church Extension Commission of the CBCI at Patna, 3-8 October 1973),* Bangalore: The Church Extension Commission, 1973, pp. 18-83.

"Catechetics and Indian Approach", in: George Gispert-Sauch (ed.), *God's Word among Men. Paper in honour of Fr. Joseph Putz,* Delhi: *Vidyajyoti,* 1973, pp. 361-378.

"Christianity and Development", in: *IDOC Bulletin* 14 (1973), pp. 9-11.

"Een schets van de Theologische Grondslag van de Indigenisatie: de Missie van de Kerk en het Proces van de Indigenisatie", in: *Wereld en Zending* 2 (1973), pp. 289-296.

"Evangelization: Two Approaches", in: *Living Light* 10 (1973) 4, pp. 497-502.

"Le Centre National de Bangalore", in: *Les Oasis de l'Esprit. Dossier Parole et Mission* (1973) 6, pp. 55-61.

"Liturgy Relevant to Life", in: *Word and Worship* 6 (1973) 7, pp. 233-242.

"Catechists and Evangelization", in: *Word and Worship* 7 (1974) 3, pp. 128-131.

"International Association of Mission Studies (IAMS)", in: *Word and Worship* 7 (1974) 9, pp. 343-344.

"Le Monde n'a pas besoin de Nouvelles Exhortations de l'Église", in: *Informations Catholiques Internationales* [20] (1974) no. 468 & 469, pp. 23-24.

"Prayer and Activity within a New World Vision", in: *Word and Worship* 7 (1974) 10, pp. 375-382.

"Research Seminar on Non-Biblical Scriptures", in: *Word and Worship* 7 (1974) 3, pp. 132-134.

"Indigenous Expressions in Cathedrals", in: *The Indian Journal of Theology* 24 (1975) 1, pp. 24-40.

"Non-Biblical Scriptures in Christian Experience: A Problem?", in: *Word and Worship* 8 (1975) 2, pp. 150-158.

"A Survey of the Catholic Hospital System in India", in: *Word and Worship* 9 (1976) 7, pp. 366-367.

"Catechists in our Time. Especially for Children and the Youth", in: *Word and Worship* 9 (1976) 8, pp. 406-407.

"Pastoral Approach for the Religious Formation of Youth", in: *Word and Worship* 9 (1976) 8, pp. 422-428.

"A Quality Document of the CBCI. Extraordinary Meeting of the CBCI, January 1977", in: *Word and Worship* 10 (1977) 3, pp. 152-154.

"Des Institutions Différentes suivant les Pays", in: *Informations Catholiques Internationales* [23] (1977) no. 250, pp. 38-41.

"Dialog zwischen den Religionen in Indien", in: *Lebendiges Zeugnis* 32 (1977) 4, pp. 19-34.

"Ecumenical Dialogue of Third World Theologians", in: *Indian Theological Studies* 14 (1977) 1, pp. 403-421.

"Meaning and Role of the Charismatic Renewal in India Today - Its Challenges", in: *Word and Worship* 10 (1977) 2, pp. 88-99.

"The Nature, Content and Approach of Mission Studies. An Asian Presentation", in: *IAMS News Letter* 10 (1977) 3, pp. 59-78.

"Trends of the Catechetical Movement in India and its New Orientation", in: *Word and Worship* 10 (1977) 1, pp. 3-8.

"A Review of Life. On the Exercise of Authority", in: *Word and Worship* 11 (1978) 3, pp. 135-137.

"Books for College Catechesis", in: *Word and Worship* 11 (1978) 8, pp. 343-344.
"Evangelization and Culture", in: *Concilium* 114 (1978) 4, pp. 61-71.
"Gospel and Culture V: Some practical Implications and Conclusions", in: *Word and Worship* 11 (1978) 7, pp. 262-266.
"The Indian Universe of a New Theology", in: Sergio Torres and Virginia Fabella (eds), *The Emergent Gospel. Theology from the Underside of History. Papers from the Ecumenical Dialogue of Third World Theologians, Dar es Salaam, August 5-12, 1976,* New York: Orbis Books, 1978, pp. 137-156.
"Mission as Revelation", in: *The Biblical Apostolate* 8 (1978) 32, pp. 135-144.
"National Convention on Christians of Scheduled Caste Origin. What is the Convention About?", in: *Word and Worship* 11 (1978) 7, pp. 284-289.
"The Leadership of the Indian Hierarchy - Through the Biennial Plenary of the CBCI", in: *Word and Worship* 11 (1978) 2, pp. 42-49.
"Vision and Understanding of Religious Life in Future, with Reference to Formation and Collaboration", in: CRI Permanent Secretariat (eds), *Meeting of the Asian Conference of Major Superiors, Bangalore, 27 Feb.--4 March 1978,* Delhi: CRI Permanent Secretariat, 1978, pp. 48-63.
"Family Catechesis", in: *Word and Worship* 12 (1979) 9, pp. 345-351.
"Missionary Adaptation", in: The Catholic University of America (eds), *New Catholic Encyclopedia,* vol. 17, New York: McGraw-Hill Book Company, 1979, pp. 426-427.
"No Turning Back", in: *Word and Worship* 12 (1979) 10, pp. 378-390.
"A Chair of Christianity. In the University of Mysore", in: *Word and Worship* 13 (1980) 6, pp. 193-197.
"Evangelization in the Context of India", in: *Indian Theological Studies* 17 (1980) 2, pp. 97-119.
"Indian Culture", in: *Word and Worship* 13 (1980) 10, pp. 313-325.
"New Theological Approaches in Asia. (With Reference to Religions and Cultures other than Western Culture and Christianity)", in: *Verbum SVD* 21 (1980) 3 & 4, pp. 279-302.
"Religious Life as a Relentless Quest for Freedom", in: *Word and Worship* 13 (1980) 8, pp. 237-249.
"The Ecumenical - Climate and Mood - Today", in: *Word and Worship* 13 (1980) 6, pp. 181-185.
"A New Impetus for Evangelization 'Your Kingdom Come'", in: *Word and Worship* 14 (1981) 1, pp. 1-11.
"An Unprecedent and Extraordinary Development. A Department of Christianity in the University of Mysore", in: *Word and Worship* 14 (1981) 7, pp. 251-256.
"Bible Text or Life Situation", in: *Word-Event* 11 (1981) 5, pp. 10, 29.
"Responsibility, Sharing, Eucharist. A Communication and Testimony from Asia", in: Congrès Eucharistique International, *Symposium International du Congrès Eucharistique,* Toulouse, Université Paul-Sabatier, 1981, S.03 English (Mimeographed), pp. 1-10.
"Situating the Basic Christian Community in the Church's Mission and the Renewal Movement", in: *Word and Worship* 14 (1981) 7, pp. 217-225.
"The Bible and Total Liberation", in: *Word-Event* 11 (1981) 5, pp. 28-29.

"The Core and Source of Dialogue", in: Joseph Pathrapankal (ed.), *Religions and Man. World Conference of Religions,* Cochin: Chavara Cultural Centre, [1981], pp. 125-128.

"The Poor with no Voice and Power", in: *Concilium* 146 (1981) 6, 45-52.

"The Poor with Reference to the Reality of the Third World/Asia/India. Poverty and Ignorance, Exploitation and Oppression, Injustice and Dependence", in: *Word and Worship* 14 (1981) 4, pp. 127-134.

"The Church as a Community of Faith in the Asian Context. (A Position Paper presented at the Third Plenary Assembly of the Federation of Asian Bishops' Conferences, Lux Mundi Seminary, Sampran, Thailand, 20-27 October 1982)", in: *FABC Papers* (1982) no. 30, pp. 1-28.

"Various Contemporary Challenges to a Common Confession of Faith", in: G.J. Békés and H. Meyer (eds), *Confessio Fidei. International Ecumenical Colloquium, 3-8 November 1980, Rome, Studia Anselmiana 81,* Rome: Pontificio Ateneo S. Anselmo, 1982, pp. 151-158.

"Dialogue Between Third World Theologians and First World Theologians. Geneva, 5-13 January 1983", in: *Word and Worship* 16 (1983) 2, pp. 63-65.

"Die Katechese als ein Schritt auf dem Weg zu Gott. Ein Erfahrungsbericht aus Indien", in: *Missio - Pastoral* (1983) 3, pp. 19-21.

"Inculturation: Christian Visual Symbols", in: *Sonolux Information* 10 (September 1983), pp. 6-10.

"Interpreting the Word", in: *Word-Event* 13 (1983) 3, pp. 21-23.

"The Bible in Self-Renewal and Church-Renewal for Service to Society", in: *Word and Worship* 16 (1983) 9, pp. 277-285; and 16 (1983) 10, pp. 312-317; and published with the same title also in: *Word-Event* 13 (1983) 3, pp. 24-28.

"Experience of the Word. Welcome and Introductory Speech to the III Plenary Assembly of WCFBA", in: *Word and Worship* 17 (1984) 8, pp. 258-267.

"Religious Life in the Indian Context", in: Brother John (ed.), *National Assembly. POC, Ernakulam, 5-9 January 1984,* New Delhi: CRI Secretariat, 1984, pp. 11-37.

"Socio-Economic Development as an Integral Part of Evangelization in India", in: *Indian Missiological Review* 6 (1984) 3, pp. 214-220.

"Would that All were Prophets, WCFBA Plenary Assembly", in: *Word and Worship* 17 (1984) 6, pp. 185-193.

"Approach and Process of Theologizing in India Today", in: Felix Wilfred (ed.), *Theological Education in India today. The Statement, Papers and Proceedings of the Eighth Annual Meeting of the Indian Theological Association, Pariyaram, Kerala, December 28-31, 1984,* Bangalore: Asian Trading Corporation, 1985, pp. 109-110.

"Church and Culture", in: Joseph Komonchak and Co. (eds), *The New Dictionary of Theology,* Wilmington: Glacier Inc., 1987, pp. 201-206.

"Orientation/Guidelines for the Revision of the 'God-with-Us' Series and Other Catechisms", in: Paul Puthanangady (ed.), *Catechesis for the India of Tomorrow. Report of the Seventh All India Catechetical Meeting (VII AICM), 1st-6th December 1985,* Bangalore: NBCLC, 1987, pp. 134-145.

"Sharing Worship. Its Relevance in a Multi-Religious Society and in an Inter-Faith Sharing of Life (Key-note Address)", in: Paul Puthanangady (ed.), *Sharing Worship. Communicatio in Sacris,* Bangalore: NBCLC, 1988, pp. 35-38.

"Towards a Theology of Peace. An Indian Approach, Understanding and Experience of

Peace", in: *Indian Theological Studies* 26 (1989) 3, pp. 197-214.
"Cultural Challenge to Mission", in: *Voices from the Third World* 13 (1990) 2, pp. 89-114.
"Knowledge and Wisdom for Service", in: *Word and Worship* 23 (1990) 4, pp. 154-160.
"Theological Reflections on Inculturation", in: *Studia Liturgica* 20 (1990) 1, pp. 36-54 & 20 (1990) 2, pp. 116-136.
"Ugadi. Kannada New Year", in: *Word and Worship* 23 (1990) 3, pp. 112-116.

3. Publications Edited by Amalor[4]

3.1. Research

*Asian Seminar on Religion and Development,* Bangalore: NBCLC, 1973.
→Also published in: *Word and Worship* 6 (1973) 8, pp. 271-370 (special number).
*Non-Biblical Scriptures - Theological Understanding, Liturgical Role and Pastoral Use,* (reprint of *Word and Worship,* March 1975), Bangalore: NBCLC, 1975.
*Research Seminar on Non-Biblical Scriptures,* Bangalore: NBCLC, 1975.
*Ministries in the Church in India. Research Seminar and Pastoral Consultation,* Delhi: CBCI Centre, [1976].
*Statement on Non-Biblical Scriptures - Theological Understanding, Liturgical Role and Pastoral Use,* Bangalore: NBCLC, 1976.
*Theological and Pastoral Statements on the Renewal of Ministries in the Church,* Bangalore: NBCLC, 1976 (reprinted in 1978).
*Statement of the Research Seminar 'The Indian Church in the Struggle for a New Society',* Bangalore: NBCLC, 1981.
*The Indian Church in the Struggle for a New Society* (All the Research Papers and Workshop Reports of the Research Seminar), Bangalore: NBCLC, 1981 (pp. 1104).
*The Indian Church in the Struggle for a New Society* (General Report and Statement of the Research Seminar), Bangalore: NBCLC, 1981.
*The Kingdom of God. Jesus' Vision of a New Society* (by George Soares Prabhu, s.j.), Bangalore: NBCLC, 1981.

3.2. Mission Theology Series

*Adult Catechumenate and Church Renewal,* Bangalore: NBCLC, 1970 (reprinted in 1973).
*Evangelization of the Modern World (Synod of Bishops, Rome, 1974),* Bangalore: NBCLC, 1975 (reprinted in 1977).

3.3. Ecumenical Movement Series

*Nairobi Assembly of the World Council of Churches 1975,* Bangalore: NBCLC, 1976.

---

[4] Whenever an edited book of Amalor is referred to in the body of the dissertation, the particular work of Amalor (or of others) in the book is cited in the footnote. Hence we refrain here from indicating the particular writings of Amalor in his edited books.

3.4. Liturgical Renewal and Spirituality Series

*Bishops and Priests, Leaders of Liturgical Renewal* (by Paul Puthanangady, s.d.b.), Bangalore: NBCLC, 1973.

*Texts for the Office of Readings:*

*I Advent and Christmas*, Bangalore: NBCLC, 1973.

*II Lent*, Bangalore: NBCLC, 1973.

*III Holy Week and Easter*, Bangalore: NBCLC, 1977.

*Bhajans* (Text in various languages, but Roman script, with English translation, several editions), Bangalore: NBCLC, 1975 & 1977, 1978, 1980 (supplement).

*Praying Seminar*, Bangalore: NBCLC, 1976.

*Charismatic Renewal in India.* (A reprint of the special number of *Word and Worship*, February 1977), Bangalore: NBCLC, 1977 (reprinted in 1980).

*Church from the Roots. Basic Ecclesial Communities* (by José Marins & team), Bangalore: NBCLC, 1981.

*Indian Christian Spirituality*, Bangalore: NBCLC, 1982.

3.5. Reports, Statements and Pastoral Guidelines in the Areas, Particularly Entrusted to the NBCLC

3.5.1. Biblical Apostolate

*Biblical Movement in India*, Bangalore: NBCLC, 1971.

*First All-India Biblical Meeting, 8-10 April 1973*, Bangalore: NBCLC, [1973].

*Proclaiming the Word of God in Audio-Visual (AV) Language*, Bangalore: NBCLC, 1973.

*Second All-India Biblical Meeting, 6-12 April 1975*, Bangalore: NBCLC, 1975.

*Statement of the Second All-India Biblical Meeting*, Bangalore: NBCLC, 1975.

*The Word of the Lord in India. A Five Year Progress in Biblical Apostolate, 1971-1975*, Bangalore: National Biblical Centre, 1976.

*A Bible Festival of India. Report of the III All-India Biblical Meeting*, Bangalore: NBCLC, 1977.

*Biblical Movement in India. (A Seven-Year Report of Biblical Apostolate in India, 1971-1978)*, Bangalore: NBCLC, 1978.

*Statement of the III All-India Biblical Meeting, 11-17 December 1977*, Bangalore: NBCLC, 1978.

*Apocrypha, Demoted and Retrieved*, Bangalore: NBCLC, 1979.

*Guidelines for the Bible Sunday*, Bangalore: NBCLC, 1979.

*Third All-India Biblical Meeting (1977).* A Complete Report, Bangalore: NBCLC, 1979.

*Bible for Liberation. A Report of the IV All-India Biblical Meeting (1980)*, Bangalore: NBCLC, 1980.

*Statement of the IV All-India Biblical Meeting, 9-15 December 1980*, Bangalore: NBCLC, 1980.

3.5.2. Catechetical Movement Series

*Catechists' Training Schools in India*, Bangalore: NBCLC, 1970 (reprinted in 1971).

*Catechetical Progress in the Dioceses of India (1968-1970)*, Bangalore: NBCLC, 1971.

*First All-India Catechetical Meeting (Bangalore, 25-27 November 1967)*, Bangalore: NBCLC, 1971.
*Report of the II All-India Catechetical Meeting (27th Dec. 1970 to 3rd Jan. 1971)*, Bangalore: NBCLC, 1971.
*A Decade of Catechetical Renewal in India (1966-1976)*, Bangalore: NBCLC, 1976.
*Report of the III All-India Catechetical Meeting (11-17 December 1973)*, Bangalore: NBCLC, 1976.
*Catechetics in our Time. A Service Document for the 1977 Synod of Bishops*, Prepared by the IV All-India Catechetical Meeting (AICM), Bangalore: NBCLC, 1977.
*Report of the IV All-India Catechetical Meeting (5-10 December 1976)*, Bangalore: NBCLC, 1977.
*An Audio-Visual Programme for Catechesis*, Bangalore: NBCLC, 1978.
*Adult Catechesis*, Bangalore: NBCLC, 1979.
*Community Education of Faith through Non-Formal Education*, Bangalore: NBCLC, 1979.
*Converging Trends of the Catechetical Movement and Guidelines of Official Documents*, Bangalore: NBCLC, 1979.
*Moving with the Spirit. Report of the V All-India Catechetical Meeting (11-17 December 1978)*, Bangalore: NBCLC, 1979.
*Joyful Response to the Challenge of Faith-Formation of Youth*, Bangalore: NBCLC, 1981.
*Pilgrims of Hope. Statement of the VI All-India Catechetical Meeting (1981)*, Bangalore: NBCLC, 1982.

3.5.3. Liturgical Renewal Series

*Post-Vatican Liturgical Renewal in India, vol. 1 (1963-1968)*, Bangalore: NCLC, 1968.
*Report of the First All-India Liturgical Meeting (20-22 February 1968)*, Bangalore: NCLC, 1968.
*Five Years of Liturgical Progress in India (1967-1972)*, Bangalore: NBCLC, 1972.
*Liturgy in Major Seminaries*, Bangalore: NBCLC, 1973.
*Post-Vatican Liturgical Renewal in India, vol. 2 (1968-1971)*, Bangalore: NBCLC, 1973.
*Post-Vatican Liturgical Renewal in India at All Levels During a Decade, vol. 3 (1971-1973)*, Bangalore: NBCLC, 1976.
*Guidelines for the Celebration of Social Justice Sunday*, Bangalore: NBCLC, 1978. *Mass for Social Justice Sunday*, Bangalore: NBCLC, 1978.
*Post-Vatican Liturgical Renewal in India, vol. 4 (1974-1976)*, Bangalore: NBCLC, 1978.
*Report of the Official Meeting of the CBCI Commission for Liturgy (NBCLC, 26-28 October 1977)*, Bangalore: NBCLC, 1978.
*Guidelines for Liturgical Translation of the Psalms into Indian Languages*, Bangalore: NBCLC, 1979.
*No Turning Back.* (Report on the Liturgy. Agenda for the General Meeting of the CBCI, Ranchi, October 1979), Bangalore: NBCLC, 1979.
*Statements of Facts on the First Stage of Liturgical Indigenization* (with appendices), Bangalore: NBCLC, 1979.

### 3.6. Statements of Consultations and Meetings[5]

*CBCI Study Committee's Statement on the Renewal of the Ministries in the Church (March 1975),* Bangalore: NBCLC, 1975.
*Statement of the Ecumenical Dialogue of the Third World Theologians (EATWOT)* (Dar-es-Salaam, August 1976), Bangalore: NBCLC, 1976.
*Statement by the 300 Participants of the National Seminar for Educators of Youth (May 1976),* Bangalore: NBCLC, 1976.
*Message to the People of God by the Synod of Bishops (Rome 1977),* Bangalore: NBCLC, 1977.
*Message to the Churches from the National Convention of Christian Leaders on the Plight of Christians of Scheduled Caste Origin (June 1978),* Bangalore: NBCLC, 1978.
*Statement of the National Seminar for Lay Leaders on Leadership of the Laity in the World and in the Church (May 1977),* Bangalore: NBCLC, 1977.
*Statement of the First All-India Consultation on Ashrams (June 1978),* Bangalore: NBCLC, 1978.
*Statement of the Plenary Assemble of WCFBA (Malta 1978),* Bangalore: NBCLC, 1978.
*Statement on Inculturation of Religious Life* (by the General Assembly of CRI, Women's Section, March 1976), Bangalore: NBCLC, 1978.
*Statement and Resolutions of the National Convention of Christian Leaders on the Plight of Christians of Scheduled Caste Origin (June 1978),* Bangalore: NBCLC, 1978.
*The Churches and Justice to Christians of Scheduled Caste Origin* (by Samuel Ryan, s.j.), Bangalore: NBCLC, 1978.
*The Emergence of African Theologies* (EATWOT) (Accra, Ghana, December 1977), Bangalore: NBCLC, 1978.
*The Story of 30 Years' Struggle for Justice for Christians of Scheduled Caste Origin,* Bangalore: NBCLC, 1978.
*Statement of the Asian Theological Conference* (EATWOT) (Colombo, Sri Lanka, January 1979), Bangalore: NBCLC, 1979.
*The Policy Statement of the Government of India on Adult Education,* Bangalore: NBCLC, 1979.
*Statement of the Ecumenical Association of the Third World Theologians (Fourth EATWOT Conference, San Paulo, Brazil, February - March 1980),* Bangalore: NBCLC, 1982.

### 3.7. General

*NBCLC at the Service of the Church in India* (a booklet on the Centre), Bangalore: NBCLC, 1975 (reprinted in 1976, 1977, 1978, 1980).
*Directory of the NBCLC, 1980,* Bangalore: NBCLC, 1980.
*NBCLC: Inculturation Pamphlet* Series no. 16.

---

5 Apart from the statements of the All-India and similar meetings at the NBCLC that have already been mentioned, DSA also edited and published these statements.

3.8. Audio-Visual Publications

*Vita Slide Series for Adult Catechesis:* 18 themes, 657 slides, and commentary, Bangalore: NBCLC, 1977.
*Jyoti Slide Series.* A Collection of 340 slides on 27 topics, Bangalore: NBCLC, 1978.
*Saccidananda Slide Series.* A set of 70 slides on an Indian order of the Mass and a cassette with commentary, Bangalore: NBCLC, 1980.

4. Audio Cassettes of Amalor

Although these cassettes have been recorded during his life time (1932-1990), the mass diffusion of the cassettes materialized only later.
*Conversion in the Context of Dialogue,* Mysore: Guru Vani, 1991. Duration: 1 hr.
*Education as a Process of Liberation,* Mysore: Guru Vani, 1991. Duration: 1 hr.
*Evangelization in the Context of India,* Mysore: Guru Vani, 1991. Duration: 1 hr.
*Sannyasa - Religious Life,* Mysore: Guru Vani, 1991. Duration: 1 hr.

## B. Secondary Sources: Writings on Amalor

1. Books

Chandran, Russell (ed.), *Third World Theologies in Dialogue. Essays in Memory of D.S. Amalorpavadass,* Bangalore: EATWOT, 1991.
De Souza, Cyril, s.d.b., *Catechesis for India Today. An Appraisal of the Proposal of D.S. Amalorpavadass,* Bangalore: Kristu Jyoti Publications, 1994.
Mookenthottam, Antony, m.s.f.s., *Indian Theological Tendencies. Approaches and Problems for Further Research as Seen in the Works of Some Leading Indian Theologians,* Berne: Peter Lang, 1978. (Regarding Amalor see: pp. 81-94, 167-174, 306-307 & 317-318).
Njaralakkatt, George, *D.S. Amalorpavadass: His Concepts of Catechetics and His Role in the Catechetical Renewal in India After the II Vatican Council,* Rome: Pontifical Salesian University, 1986 (unpublished).
Puthanangady, Paul (ed.), *Church in India: Institution or Movement? A Tribute to the Memory of Fr. D.S. Amalorpavadass, Founder-Director of NBCLC, on the First Anniversary of his Mahasamadhi, 25th May, 1990--25th May, 1991),* Bangalore: NBCLC, 1991.
Van Leeuwen, Gerwin, o.f.m., *Fully Indian - Authentically Christian. A Study of the First Fifteen Years of the NBCLC (1967-1982), Bangalore - India, in the Light of the Theology of its Founder, D.S. Amalorpavadass,* Bangalore: NBCLC, 1990.

2. Articles

Camps, Arnulf, "Theologie de Inkulturation: Duraisamy Simon Amalorpavadass", in: Hans Waldenfels (ed.), *Theologen der Dritten Welt,* München: C.H. Beck, 1982, pp. 129-140.
Chandran, Russell, "Rev. Fr. D.S. Amalorpavadass 1932-1990", in: *Mission Studies* 8 (1991) 1, pp. 104-106.

Hirudayam, Ignatius, "The Amalorpavadass I Knew", in: *The New Leader* 80 (1990) 12, pp. 6-8.

"In Memorial", in: *Catholic Biblical Federation. Bulletin Dei Verbum* 4 (1990) 17, p. 11.

Puthanangady, Paul, "Fr. D.S. Amalorpavadass - Prophet of the Post-Conciliar Church in India", in: *Word and Worship* 23 (1990) 5, pp. 169-172.

---------, "Fr. D.S. Amalorpavadass: Prophet of the Post-Conciliar Church in India, Passed away on Friday, 25 May, 1990", in: *The Examiner* 141 (1990) 23, pp. 621-622.

Shai, Jyoti, "Fr. Amalor in an Artist's View", in: *Word and Worship* 23 (1990) 5, p. 173.

Vallamatam, John, "Le P. D.S. Amalorpavadass: une perte pour l'Église", in: *Ecos de la Rue du Bac* (1990), pp. 269-271.

Van Leeuwen, Gerwin, "In Memoriam. D.S. Amalorpavadass, 1932-1990", in: *Exchange* 19 (1990) 2, pp. 172-174.

---------, "D.S. Amalorpavadass Pioneer of Post-Conciliar Renewal", in: *Vidyajyoti* 54 (1990) 9, pp. 481-493.

---------, "D.S. Amalorpavadass and the Uniqueness of Christ", in: *Word and Worship* 23 (1990) 5, pp. 175-187.

## C. Other Works Consulted

### 1. Basic Texts

*Catechism of the Catholic Church*, New York: Doubleday, Image Book, 1995. Flannery, Austin (ed.), *Vatican Council II: The Conciliar and Post Conciliar Documents*, Bombay: St. Paul Publications, 1987.

*The Holy Bible*. (New Revised Standard Version: Catholic Edition), London: Geoffrey Chapman, 1993.

### 2. Dictionaries

Brown, Raymond E. and Co. (eds), *The New Jerome Biblical Commentary* (student edition), London: Geoffrey Chapman, 1996 (reprint. Its first print in 1989).

Komonchak, Joseph A. and Co. (eds), *The New Dictionary of Theology*, Wilmington: Glacier Inc., 1987.

Latourelle, René and Rino Fisichella (eds), *Dictionary of Fundamental Theology*, New York: Crossroad, 1994.

Leon-Dufour, X. (ed.), *Dictionary of Biblical Theology* (English translation by G. Chapman), London: Cassell Publishers Ltd., 1972 (reprint).

Neil, William, *One Volume Bible Commentary*, London: Hodder and Stoughton, 1973 (second edition. Its first edition in 1962).

O'Collins, Gerald, s.j. and Edward G. Farrugia, s.j., *A Concise Dictionary of Theology*, New York: Paulist Press, 1991.

### 3. Curial Documents

Secretariatus pro non Christianis, *The Attitude of the Church Towards the Followers of*

*Other Religions. Reflections and Orientations on Dialogue and Mission,* Vatican City: Vatican Polyglot Press, 1984.

Statement of the Pontifical Secretariat for Non-Christians, *Dialogue and Mission,* "Attitudes of the Catholic Church Towards the Followers of Other Religions", in: *AAS* 84, 1984, pp. 816-828.

Pontifical Council for Inter-Religious Dialogue, *Guidelines for Dialogue Between Christians and Muslims,* 2nd edition (prepared by Maurice Borrmans and translated by R. Marston Seight), Interreligious Documents, no. 1, New York: Paulist Press, 1990.

Statement of the Pontifical Council for Inter-Religious Dialogue and Congregation for the Evangelization of Peoples, *Dialogue and Proclamation,* in: *Bulletin (Bulletin Pontificium Concilium pro Dialogo inter Religiones)* 26, no. 2, 1991, pp. 210-250. (From 1994/1 onwards the review is known as *Pro Dialogo*).

Pontifical Biblical Commission, *The Interpretation of the Bible in the Church: Address of His Holiness Pope John Paul II and Documents of the Pontifical Biblical Commission,* Città del Vaticano: Libreria Editrice Vaticana, 1993.

*Christianity and the World Religions,* Città del Vaticano: Libreria Editrice Vaticana, 1997.

4. Papal Documents, Discourses, Encyclicals and Apostolic Exhortations

Leo XIII, Encyclical Letter *Rerum Novarum* (1891), in: *AAS* 23 (1890-1891), pp. 641-670.

John XXIII, Encyclical Letter *Mater et Magistra* (1961), in: *AAS* 53 (1961), pp. 401-464.

---------, Encyclical Letter *Pacem in Terris* (1963), in: *AAS* 55 (1963), pp. 257- 304.

Paul VI, Encyclical Letter *Ecclesiam Suam* (1964), in: *AAS* 56 (1964), pp. 650-653.

---------, His Discourses during his visit to India in 1964, in: *AAS* 57 (1965), pp. 116-138.

---------, Encyclical Letter *Populorum Progressio* (1967), in: *AAS* 59 (1967), pp. 257-299.

---------, Apostolic Letter *Octogesima Adveniens* (1971), in: *AAS* 63 (1971), pp. 401-441.

---------, Apostolic Exhortation *Evangelii Nuntiandi* (1975), in: *AAS* 68 (1976), pp. 1-76. All English translation, from J.A. Coleman, s.j., *One Hundred Years of Catholic Social Thought,* Maryknoll, New York: Orbis Books, 1991.

John Paul II, Encyclical Letter *Redemptor Hominis* (1979), in: *AAS* 71 (1979), pp. 257-324.

---------, John Paul II, Apostolic Letter *Laborem Exercens* (1981), in: *AAS* 73 (1981), pp. 577-647.

---------, "Address of the Pope at the Conclusion of the Plenary Assembly of the Secretariat", in: *AAS* 76 (1984), pp. 709-712.

---------, His Discourses during his visit to India in 1986, in: *AAS* 78 (1986), pp. 737-782.

---------, "Pope's Christmas Address to the Roman Curia (22 December 1986): The World Situation Constitutes a Pressing Appeal for the Spirit of Assisi", in: *AAS* 79 (1987), pp. 1082-1090.

---------, Encyclical Letter *Sollicitudo Rei Socialis* (1987), in: *AAS* 80 (1988), pp. 513-586.

---------, Encyclical Letter *Redemptoris Missio* (1990), in: *AAS* 83 (1991), pp. 249-340.

---------, Encyclical Letter *Centesimus Annus* (1991), in: *AAS* 83 (1991), pp. 793-867. All English translations: Libreria Editrice Vaticana.

5. Seminars, Conferences and CBCI Commission for Dialogue and Ecumenism

Catholic Bishops' Conference of India, *All India Seminar: Church in India Today, Bangalore 1969,* Delhi: CBCI Centre, n.d.

---------, *Light and Life We Seek to Share: All India Consultation on Evangelization, Held Under the Auspices of the Church Extension Commission of the Catholic Bishops' Conference of India at Navajyoti Niketan, Kurji, Patna, 3-8 October, 1973,* Bangalore: The Church Extension Commission, 1973.

CBCI Dialogue Commission, *Guidelines for Inter-Religious Dialogue* (revised draft), Varanasi: CBCI Dialogue Commission, 1977.

---------, *Guidelines for a Dialogue Between Muslims and Christians* (Indian edition), Cochin: K.C.M. Press, 1979.

CBCI Commission for Dialogue and Ecumenism, *Guidelines for Inter-Religious Dialogue,* 2nd revised edition, Delhi: CBCI Centre, 1989.

6. Books

Amaladoss, Michael, *Walking Together: The Practice of Inter-Religious Dialogue,* Jesuit Theological Forum Reflections, no. 7, Anand: Gujarat Sahitya Prakash, 1992.

---------, *Towards Fullness - Searching for an Integral Spirituality. (Lectures in Memory of Fr. D.S. Amalorpavadass - 1932-1990),* Bangalore: NBCLC, 1994.

Amaladoss, Michael, T.K. John, and G. Gispert-Sauch (eds), *Theologizing in India. Selection of Papers Presented at the Seminar Held in Poona on October 26-30, 1978,* Bangalore: Theological Publications in India, 1981.

Ayakara, Thomas A. (ed.), *Meeting of Religions: New Orientations and Perspectives,* Bangalore: Dharmaram Publications, 1978.

Borg, Markus J., *Jesus, a New Vision: Spirit, Culture, and Life of Discipleship,* San Francesco: Harper & Row, 1987.

Bosch, David, *Transforming Mission. Paradigm Shifts in Theology of Mission,* Maryknoll, New York: Orbis Books, 1991.

Boyd, Robin H.S., *India and the Latin Captivity of the Church: The Cultural Context of the Gospel,* Cambridge: Cambridge University Press, 1974.

---------, *Kristadvaita. A Theology for India,* Madras: Christian Literature Society, 1977.

Braybrooke, Markus, *The Undiscovered Christ: A Review of Recent Developments in the Christian Approaches to Hinduism,* Madras: Christian Literature Society, 1973.

Bühlmann, Walbert, *All have the Same God,* Slough: St. Paul Publications, 1979.

---------, *The Search for God. En Encounter with the Peoples and Religions of Asia,* Maryknoll, New York: Orbis Books, 1980.

---------, *The Chosen Peoples,* Slough: St. Paul Publications, and Maryknoll, New York: Orbis Books, 1982.

---------, *The Church of the Future,* Maryknoll, New York: Orbis Books, 1986.

Camps, Arnulf, *Partners in Dialogue: Christianity and World Religions,* Maryknoll, New York: Orbis Books, 1983.

Cohn-Sherbok, Rabbi Dan, *On Earth as it is in Heaven. Jews, Christians, and Liberation Theology,* Maryknoll, New York: Orbis Books, 1987.

Congar, Yves, *I Believe in the Holy Spirit,* 3 Vols., London: Geoffrey Chapman, 1983.

---------, *The Word and the Spirit,* London, Geoffrey Chapman, 1986.

Covell, Ralph R., *Confucius, the Buddha and Christ,* Maryknoll, New York: Orbis Books, 1985.

Cragg, Keneth, *The Christ and the Faiths: Theology in Cross-Reference,* London: SPCK, 1986.

Cullman, Oscar, *Christ et le Temps,* Neuchâtel: Delachaux & Niestlé, 1957.

Cuttat, Jacques-Albert, *The Encounter of Religions. A Dialogue between the West and the Orient with an Essay on the Prayer of Jesus* (Translated by Pierre de Fontnouvelle with Evis McGrew), Tournai: Desclée Company, 1960.

---------, *The Spiritual Dialogue of East and West,* Delhi: Max Müller Bhavan Publications, 1961.

---------, *Expérience chrétienne et spiritualité orientale,* Burges: Desclée de Brouwer, 1967.

Cyriac, M.V., *Meeting of Religions,* Madras: Dialogue Series, 1983.

Daniélou, Jean, *Holy Pagans in the Old Testament,* London: Longmans, Green and Co., 1957.

---------, *The Lord of History. Reflections on the Inner Meaning of History,* London: Longmans, 1958.

---------, *The Salvation of the Nations,* Notre Dame: University of Notre Dame Press, 1962.

D'Costa, Gavin, *Theology and Religious Pluralism: The Challenge of Other Religions,* Oxford: Basil Blackwell, 1986.

--------- (ed.), *Christian Uniqueness Reconsidered. The Myth of Pluralistic Theology of Religions,* Maryknoll, New York: Orbis Books, 1990.

Desrochers, John, *Christ the Liberator,* Bangalore: The Centre for Social Action, 1977.

Dhavamony, Mariasusai (ed.), *Evangelization, Dialogue and Development. Selected Papers of the International Theological Conference, Nagpur (India) 1971,* Documenta Missionalia - 5, Roma: Università Gregoriana Editrice, 1972.

---------, *Phenomenology of Religion,* Documenta Missionalia - 7, Roma: Università Gregoriana Editrice, 1973.

---------, *Classical Hinduism,* Documenta Missionalia - 15, Roma: Università Gregoriana Editrice, 1982.

---------, *Christian Theology of Inculturation,* Documenta Missionalia - 24, Roma: Editrice Pontificia Università Gregoriana, 1997.

---------, *La Spiritualité Hindou,* Paris: Beauchesne, 1997.

---------, *Christian Theology of Religions. A Systematic Reflection on the Christian Understanding of World Religions,* Berne, Berlin, Frankfort/M, New York, Paris, Wien: Peter Lang, 1998.

Dulles, Avery, *Revelation Theology,* New York: Herder and Herder, 1969.

---------, *Models of the Church,* London: Macmillan, 1974.

---------, *Models of Revelation,* Garden City, New York: Doubleday, 1983.

---------, *Models of the Church* (expanded edition), New York: Doubleday, Image Books, 1987.

Dupuis, Jacques, *Jesus Christ at the Encounter of World Religions* (translated from the French by Robert R. Barr), Maryknoll, New York: Orbis Books, 1991.

---------, (ed.), *The Christian Faith in the Doctrinal Documents of the Catholic Church* (sixth revised and enlarged edition), New York: Alba House, 1996 (by special arrangement with "Theological Publications in India").

---------, *Toward a Christian Theology of Religious Pluralism,* Maryknoll, New York: Orbis Books, 1997.

Emprayil, Thomas, *The Emerging Theology of Religions. The Contribution of the Catholic Church in India,* Rewa: Vincentian Publications, 1980.

Farquhar, John N., *The Crown of Hinduism,* London: Oxford University Press, 1915.

Fuellenbach, John, s.v.d., *Hermeneutics, Marxism and Liberation Theology,* Manila: Divine Word Publications, 1989.

---------, *The Kingdom of God. The Message of Jesus Christ Today,* Maryknoll, New York: Orbis Books, 1995.

Gandhi, M.K., *An Autobiography or the Story of my Experiments with Truth,* Ahmedabad: Navajivan Publishing House, 1927 (reprint in 1966).

---------, *The Removal of Untouchability,* Ahmedabad: Navajivan Publishing House, 1954 (reprinted in 1959).

George, S.K., *Gandhi's Challenge to Christianity,* Ahmedabad: Navajivan Publishing House, 1957.

Gort, J.D., *On Sharing Religious Experience: Possibility of Interfaith Mutuality,* Grand Rapids, Mich.: Eerdmans, 1992.

Gottwald, Norman K. (ed.), *The Bible and Liberation. Political and Social Hermeneutics,* Maryknoll, New York: Orbis Books, 1984 (second print. Its first print in 1983).

Griffiths, Bede, *The Marriage of East and West,* London: Collins, 1982.

---------, *The Cosmic Revelation,* Bangalore: Asian Trading Corporation, 1985.

---------, *Christ in India,* Bangalore: Asian Trading Corporation, 1986.

Heim, S.M., *Is Christ the Only Way? Christian Faith in a Pluralistic World,* Valley Forge: Judson Press, 1986.

Hick, John, *God and the Universe of Faiths: Essays in the Philosophy of Religion,* London: Macmillan, 1973.

---------, (ed.), *The Myth of God Incarnate,* London: SCM Press, 1977.

---------, *God has Many Names,* London: Macmillan, 1980.

---------, *Problems of Religious Pluralism,* London: Macmillan, 1985.

Hooker, Roger, *Themes in Hinduism and Christianity: A Comparative Study,* Frankfurt am Main: Verlag Peter Lang, 1989.

Jackson, Paul (ed.), *The Muslims of India: Beliefs and Practices,* Bangalore: Theological Publications in India, 1988.

John Paul II, *The Pope Speaks to India,* Bombay: St. Paul's Publications, 1986.

Karotemprel, Sebastian (ed.), *Following Christ in Mission: A Foundational Course in Missiology,* Bombay: Pauline Publications, 1995.

Knitter, Paul F., *No Other Name? A Critical Survey of Christian Attitudes Towards the World Religions,* Maryknoll, New York: Orbis Books, 1974.

Küng, Hans, *Global Responsibility: In Search of a New World Ethic* (translated from the German by John Bowden), London: SCM Press Ltd., 1991.

Kuttianimattathil, Jose, s.d.b., *Practice and Theology of Interreligious Dialogue. A Critical Study of the Indian Christian Attempts Since Vatican II,* Bangalore: Kristu Jyoti Publications, 1995.

Latourelle, R. (ed.), *Vatican II, Assessment and Perspectives* (Twenty-five Years After Vatican II), 3 volumes, New York: Paulist Press, 1989.

Mathew, K.M. (ed.), *Manorama Yearbook 1994,* Kottayam: Malayala Manorama (English edition, issue yearly).

--------- (ed.), *Manorama Yearbook 1997,* Kottayam: Malayala Manorama (English edition, issue yearly).

Monis, John, *"Liberated society": Gandhian and Christian Vision. Comparative Study,* Documenta Missionalia - 23, Roma: Editrice Pontificia Università Gregoriana, 1996.

Mookenthottam, Antony, m.s.f.s., *Indian Theological Tendencies. Approaches and Problems for Further Research as Seen in the Works of Some Leading Indian Theologians,* Berne: Peter Lang, 1978.

Mundadan, A. Mathias, *Sixteenth Century Traditions of St. Thomas Christians,* Dharmaram College studies, no. 5, Bangalore: Dharmaram College, 1970.

Neuner, Joseph (ed.), *Christian Revelation and World Religions,* London: Burns and Oates, 1967.

Panikkar, Raimundo, *The Unknown Christ of Hinduism,* London: Darton, Longman and Todd, 1964.

---------, *Salvation in Christ: Concreteness and Universality. The Supername,* California, Santa Barbara, 1972.

---------, *The Unknown Christ of Hinduism: Towards an Ecumenical Christophany* (Revised enlarged edition), London: Darton, Longman and Todd, 1981.

Parrinder, Geoffrey, *Upanishads, Gītā and Bible. A Comparative Study of Hindu and Christian Scriptures,* London: Faber and Faber, 1962.

Pathil, Kuncheria, c.m.i. (ed.), *Religious Pluralism. An Indian Christian Perspective. The Papers and Statements of the Twelfth and Thirteenth Annual Meetings of the Indian Theological Association, 1988, 1989,* Delhi: ISPCK, 1991.

Pinto, Joseph Prasad, *Inculturation through Basis Communities: An Indian Perspective,* Bangalore: Asian Trading Corporation, 1985.

Power, John, s.m.a., *Mission Theology Today,* Maryknoll, New York: Orbis Books, 1971.

Prabhu, R.K. and U.R. Rao (eds), *The Mind of Mahatma Gandhi,* Ahmedabad: Navajivan Publishing House, 1969 (reprint).

Pushparajan, A. (ed.), *Challenges to Religious Pluralism,* Madurai Archdiocese: The Commission for Dialogue, 1994.

Puthanangady, Paul (ed.), *Popular Devotions in India: Research Seminar,* Bangalore: NBCLC, 1986.

--------- (ed.), *Sharing Worship. Communicatio in Sacris,* Bangalore: NBCLC, 1988.

Radhakrishnan, S., *The Hindu View of Life,* London: Allen and Unwin, 1926.

---------, *Eastern Religions and Western Thought,* London: Allen and Unwin, 1939.

Rahner, Karl, *Inspiration in the Bible,* Quaestiones Disputatae 1, New York: Herder and Herder, 1961.

Ratzinger, Cardinal Joseph (Sacred Congregation for the Doctrine of the Faith), *Instruction on Certain Aspects of 'Theology of Liberation',* Vatican City: Vatican Polyglot Press, 1984.

Roest Crollius, Ary A., *The Word in the Experience of Revelation in Qu'rān and Hindu Scriptures,* Documenta Missionalia - 8, Roma: Università Gregoriana Editrice, 1974.

---------, *Scienze delle Religioni: Introduzione allo Studio delle Religioni. (Parte I: Introduzione Generale - Religioni Indiane),* Roma: Editrice Pontificia Università Gregoriana, 1994.

Roest Crollius, A., and T. Nkéramihigo, *What is so New About Inculturation?*, Roma: Editrice Pontificia Università Gregoriana, 1991 (first reprint. Its first edition in 1984).

Rosales, G.B., and C.G. Arévalo (eds), *For All the Peoples of Asia: Federation of Asian Bishops' Conferences Documents from 1970-1991*, Maryknoll, New York: Orbis Books and Philippines: Quezon City, 1992.

Samartha, S.J., *The Hindu Response to the Unbound Christ*, Madras: Christian Literature Society, 1974.

---------, *One Christ - Many Religions. Towards a Revised Christology*, Maryknoll, New York: Orbis Books, 1994 (second Indian edition).

Schillebeeckx, E., *The Mission of the Church*, London: Sheed and Ward, 1973.

Schlette, Heinz R., *Towards a Theology of Religions*, New York: Herder and Herder, 1966.

Scullion, John, s.j., *The Theology of Inspiration*, Cork: The Mercier Press, 1970.

SEDOS (ed.), *Foundations of Mission Theology* (translated by John Drury), Maryknoll Documentation Series, New York: Orbis Books, 1972.

Singh, Herbert Jai (ed.), *Inter-Religious Dialogue*, Bangalore: CISRS, 1967.

Soares-Prabhu, George, *Inculturation, Liberation, Dialogue*, Pune: Jnanadeepa, 1984.

Staffner, Hans, *The Open Door: A Christian Approach to the World Religions*, Bangalore: Asian Trading Corporation, 1978.

---------, *The Significance of Jesus Christ in Asia*, Anand: Gujarat Sahitya Prakash, 1985.

---------, *Jesus Christ and the Hindu Community: Is a Synthesis of Hinduism and Christianity Possible?*, Anand: Gujarat Sahitya Prakash, 1988.

---------, *Dialogue: Stimulating Contacts with Hindus*, Anand: Gujarat Sahitya Prakash, 1993.

Swearer, Donald, *Dialogue: The Key to Understanding Other Religions*, Philadelphia: Westminster Press, 1977.

*The Doctrine of Tenrikyo*, Tenrikyo Church Headquarters (Tenri, Nara, Japan), 1995 (second printing).

*The Upaniṣads* (in two parts: Part I and Part II), translated by F. Max Müller, New York: Dover Publications, Inc., 1962. (This new Dover edition, first published in 1962, is an unabridged and unaltered republication of the work first published by the Clarendon Press, Oxford. The *Upaniṣads*, Part I, first published in 1879, is Volume I of the "Sacred Books of the East" edited by F. Max Müller and Part II, first published in 1884, is Volume XV of the same series).

Thomas, M.M., *Risking Christ for Christ's Sake: Towards an Ecumenical Theology of Pluralism*, Geneva: WCC Publications, 1987.

Thottakara, Augustine (ed.), *Dialogical Dynamics of Religions*, Rome: Centre for Indian and Inter-Religious Studies and Bangalore: Dharmaram Publications, 1993.

Tillich, Paul, *Christianity and the Encounter of World Religions*, New York: Columbia, 1963.

---------, *The Future of Religions*, New York: Harper and Row, 1966.

Tracy, David, and John B. Cobb (eds), *Talking about God: Doing Theology in the Context of Modern Pluralism*, New York: Seabury Press, 1983.

Troeltsch, Ernst, *The Absoluteness of Christianity and the History of Religions*, Richmond: John Knox Press, 1971.

Van Beeck, Franz Josef, *God Encountered: A Contemporary Catholic Systematic Theology. Vol. 2/1 - The Revelation of the Glory (Introduction and Part I: Fundamental Theology)*, Minnesota: M.G. Book, The Liturgical Press, 1993.

Vandana, *Find Your Roots and Take Wings. Three Essays. Spiritual Formation for the East and the West*, Bangalore: Asian Trading Corporation, 1991.

Van Exem A., *The Religious System of the Munda Tribe*, Ranchi: Satya Bharati, 1982.

Veliath, Dominic, s.d.b. (ed.), *Towards an Indian Christian Spirituality in a Pluralistic Context. Papers and Statement of the Indian Theological Association, Fourteenth Annual Meeting, December 28-31, 1990, Ishvani Kendra (Pune)*, Bangalore: Dharmaram Publications, 1993.

Vempeny, Ishanand, *Inspiration in Non-Biblical Scriptures*, Bangalore: Theological Publications in India, 1973.

---------, *Kṛṣṇa and Christ. In the Light of the Fundamental Concepts and Themes of the Bhagavad Gītā and the New Testament*, Anand: Gujarat Sahitya Prakash, 1988.

Viviano, Benedict T., *The Kingdom of God in History*, Wilmington, Del.: Michael Glazier, 1988.

Von Balthasar, Hans Urs, *A Theology of History*, London: Sheed and Ward, 1964.

Vroome, H., *No Other Gods: Christian Belief in Dialogue with Buddhism, Hinduism, and Islam*, Mich.: Eerdmans, 1996.

Whaling, Frank, *Christian Theology and World Religions: A Global Approach*, London: Marshall Pickering, 1986.

Zaehner, R.C., *The Bhagavad-Gītā* (With a Commentary based on the Original Sources), New York: Oxford University Press, 1981 (original 1973).

---------, *Hindu Scriptures* (translated and edited by R.C. Zaehner), Calcutta: Rupa & Co., 1992 (first published: London, 1966).

7. Articles

Anthonysamy, S.J., "Christian Mission in the Context of Many Religions Today: A Biblical Perspective", in: *Indian Missiological Review* 18 (1996) 2, pp. 9-19.

Antoine, R., "Dialogue", in: *All India Seminar: Church in India Today, Bangalore 1969* (Catholic Bishops' Conference of India), New Delhi: CBCI Centre, n.d., pp. 105-108.

Bevans, Stephen, "Inculturation of Theology in Asia. The Federation of Asian Bishops' Conferences, 1970-1995", in: *Studia Missionalia*, vol. 45, Roma: Editrice Pontificia Università Gregoriana, 1996, pp. 1-23.

Chethimattam, John B., "The Challenges of Evangelization in India at the Threshold of the Third Millennium", in: *Jeevadhara* 16 (1986) 155, pp. 329-347.

Daniélou, Jean, "Non-Christian Religions and Salvation", in: *Foundations of Mission Theology*, edited by SEDOS, translated by John Drury, Maryknoll Documentation Series, New York: Orbis Books, 1972, pp. 54-59.

D'Costa, Gavin, "Christian Theology and Other Religions: An Evaluation of John Hick and Paul Knitter", in: *Studia Missionalia*, vol. 42, Roma: Editrice Pontificia Università Gregoriana, 1993, pp. 161-178.

Dhavamony, Mariasusai, "The Religious Quest of Hinduism", in: *Studia Missionalia*, vol. 15, Roma: Pontificia Università Gregoriana, 1966, pp. 65-82.

---------, "Revelation in the History of Religions (Introductory Essay)", in: *Studia Missionalia,* vol. 20, Rome: Gregorian University Press, 1971, pp. 9-15.
---------, "Revelation in Hinduism", in: *Studia Missionalia,* vol. 20, Rome: Gregorian University Press, 1971, pp. 163-189.
---------, "Christian Approaches to Hinduism: Points of Contact and Difficulties", in: *Gregorianum* 53, no. 1 (1972), pp. 89-116.
---------, "Hindu Incarnations", in: *Studia Missionalia,* vol. 21, Rome: Gregorian University Press, 1972, pp. 127-169.
---------, "Meditation in the History of Religions", in: *Studia Missionalia,* vol. 21, Rome: Gregorian University Press, 1972, pp. 9-20.
---------, "Evangelization and Dialogue", in: *Light and Life We Seek to Share: All-India Consultation on Evangelization, Held Under the Auspices of the Church Extension Commission of the Catholic Bishops' Conference of India at Navajyoti Niketan, Kurji, Patna, 3-8 October, 1973,* Bangalore: The Church Extension Commission, 1973, pp. 140-151.
---------, "Self-Understanding of World Religions as Religion", *Gregorianum* 54, no. 1 (1973), pp. 91-130.
---------, "Scientific Study of Religions and Dialogue", in: *Bulletin Secretariatus pro non Christianis* 10, no. 2 (1975), 319-327.
---------, "Typology of Hindu Mysticism", in: *Studia Missionalia,* vol. 26, Rome: Gregorian University Press, 1977, pp. 237-285.
---------, "Classical Patterns of Hindu Salvation", in: *Studia Missionalia,* vol. 29, Rome: Gregorian University Press, 1980, pp. 209-271.
---------, "Ways of Salvation in Hinduism", in: *Studia Missionalia,* vol. 30, Rome: Gregorian University Press, 1981, pp. 307-349.
---------, "The Holy Spirit in Hinduism", in: *Credo in Spiritum Sanctum, Atti del Congresso Teologico Internationale di Pneumatologia,* Estrato: Libreria Editrice Vaticana, 1982, pp. 1426-1435.
---------, "Evangelization and Dialogue in Vatican II and in the 1974 Synod", in: René Latourelle (ed.), *Vatican II: Assessment and Perspectives,* vol. 3, New York: Paulist Press, 1989, pp. 264-281.
---------, "The Hindu Way to Peace", in: *Studia Missionalia,* vol. 38, Roma: Editrice Pontificia Università Gregoriana, 1989, pp. 195-218.
---------, "Today's Challenge: Salvation Offered by Non-Christian Religions", in: *La Salvezza Oggi,* Congresso Internationale di Missiologia, Studia Urbaniana 34, Roma, 1989, pp. 81-100.
---------, "Hindu Hospitality and Tolerance", in: *Studia Missionalia,* vol. 39, Roma: Editrice Pontificia Università Gregoriana, 1990, pp. 303-320.
---------, "Mother Teresa's Mission of Love for the Poorest of the Poor", in: *Studia Missionalia,* vol. 39, Roma: Editrice Pontificia Università Gregoriana, 1990, pp. 135-158.
---------, "The Cosmic Christ and World Religions", in: *Studia Missionalia,* vol. 42, Roma: Editrice Pontificia Università Gregoriana, 1993, pp. 179-225.
---------, "The Christian theology of interreligious Dialogue", in: *Studia Missionalia,* vol. 43, Roma: Editrice Pontificia Università Gregoriana, 1994, pp. 61-93.
---------, "The Christian Theology of Inculturation", in: *Studia Missionalia,* vol. 44, Roma: Editrice Pontificia Università Gregoriana, 1995, pp. 1-43.

---------, "Indian Christian Theological Method", in: *Studia Missionalia,* vol. 45, Roma: Editrice Pontificia Università Gregoriana, 1996, pp. 57-94.

---------, "Indian Christian Theology", in: *Studia Missionalia,* vol. 45, Roma: Editrice Pontificia Università Gregoriana, 1996, pp. 95-117.

---------, "Modern Hinduism", in: *For a Dialogue with Hinduism,* Secretariat for Non-Christians, Roma: Editrice Ancora, n.d., pp. 67-96.

---------, "The Hindu-Christian Dialogue", in: *For a Dialogue with Hinduism, Secretariatus pro non Christianis,* Milano - Roma: Editrice Ancora, n.d., pp. 97-108.

Dupuis, Jacques, "Knowing Christ through the Christian Experience", in: *The Indian Journal of Theology* 18 (1969) 1, pp. 54-64.

---------, "The Presence of Christ in Hinduism", in: *The Clergy Monthly* 34 (1970) 4, pp. 141-148.

---------, "The Use of Non-Christian Scriptures in Christian Worship in India", in: *Studia Missionalia,* vol. 23, Rome: Gregorian University Press, 1974, pp. 127-143.

---------, "Five Years of Theological Reflection in India", in: *Indian Theological Studies* 14 (1977) 1, pp. 91-114.

---------, "The Kingdom of God and World Religions", in: *Vidyajyoti* 51 (1987) 11, pp. 530-544.

---------, "World Religions in God's Salvific Design n Pope John Paul II's Discourse to the Roman Curia (22 December, 1986)", in: *Seminarium* 27 (1987) 1-2, pp. 29-41.

---------, "Evangelization and Kingdom Values: The Church and the 'Others'", in: *Indian Missiological Review* 14 (1992) 2, pp. 4-22.

Duraisingh, Christopher, "World Religions and the Christian Claim for the Uniqueness of Jesus Christ", in: *The Indian Journal of Theology* 30 (1981) 3-4, pp. 168-185.

FABC, "Asian Bishops' Seminar: Christian Presence among Muslims in Asia", in: *Bulletin Secretariatus pro non Christianis* 19, no. 1 (1984), pp. 29-48.

---------, "BIRA III, Papers", in: *Bulletin Secretarius pro non Christianis* 18, no. 2 (1983), pp. 135-178.

Faruqi, I.H. Azad, "Living Together in World Community", in: *Islam and the Modern Age* 17 (1996) 2, pp. 66-72.

Gispert-Sauch, G., "Sacred Scriptures in Indian Religions", in: *Vidyajyoti* 39 (1975) 5, pp. 217-222.

Irudayaraj, Xavier, "One God and Many Religions", in: *Indian Missiological Review* 18 (1996) 2, pp. 4-8.

Jackson, Paul, "Christian-Muslim Dialogue in India", in: *Studia Missionalia,* vol. 43, Roma: Editrice Pontificia Università Gregoriana, 1994, pp. 159-176.

Kilgallen, John J., "Acts 17, 22-31: An example of interreligious Dialogue", in: *Studia Missionalia,* vol. 43, Roma: Editrice Pontificia Università Gregoriana, 1994, pp. 43-60.

Karotemprel, Sebastian, "The Shape of Christian Mission in the Third Millennium", in: *Indian Missiological Review* 18 (1996) 2, pp. 63-77.

Kottukapally, Joseph, "Evangelization and Liberation in Today's Multi-religious Context", in: *Indian Missiological Review* 18 (1996) 1, pp. 18-35.

Machado, Felix, "*Nostra Aetate* and Universal Awareness of the Church", in: *Indian Missiological Review* 18 (1996) 2, pp. 40-47.

Martinez, Ernest R., "The Identity of Jesus in Mark", in: *Communio* 1 (1974) 4, pp. 323-342.

Meagher, P.M., "Book Reviews (Indian Scene)", in: *Vidyajyoti* 54 (1990) 12, pp. 656-657.

---------, "Jesus of History and Jesus of Faith", in: *Jeevadhara* 16 (1986) 152, pp. 107-118.

Mishra, K.N., A. Pushparajan, and Ignatius Puthiadam, "Call to Harmony through Dialogue", in: *Vidyajyoti* 60 (1996) 4, pp. 275-281.

Packiasamy, Anthony, "The New Evangelization 2000: Concept, Context and Need", in: *Indian Theological Studies* 32 (1995) 4, pp. 339-352.

Parappally, Jacob, "Interreligious Dialogue: A Sharing of Hope", in: *Jeevadhara* 16 (1986) 155, pp. 367-377.

Pathil, Kuncheria, "Theology of the Role of the Laity in Vatican II", in: *Jeevadhara* 16 (1986) 154, pp. 247-263.

Phan, Peter C., "The Christ of Asia. An Essay on Jesus as the Eldest Son and Ancestor", in: *Studia Missionalia,* vol. 45, Roma: Editrice Pontificia Università Gregoriana, 1996, pp. 25-55.

Pushparajan, A., "Social Justice from the Point of View of Christian Tradition", in: *Indian Theological Studies* 32 (1995) 4, pp. 321-338.

Puthanangady, Paul, "Pastoral Planning at the CBCI Level", in: *Word and Worship* 25 (1992) 4, pp. 154-167.

Rahner, Karl, "Christianity and the Non-Christian Religions", in: *Theological Investigations,* vol. 5, London: Darton, Longman and Todd, 1966, pp. 115-134.

---------, "History of the World and Salvation History", in: *Theological Investigations,* vol. 5, London: Darton, Longman and Todd, 1966, pp. 97-114.

---------, "Anonymous Christians", in: *Theological Investigations,* vol. 6, London: Darton, Longman and Todd, 1969, pp. 390-398.

---------, "One Mediator and Many Religions", in: *Theological Investigations,* vol. 9, London: Darton, Longman and Todd, 1972, pp. 169-186.

---------, "Church, Churches and Religions", in: *Theological Investigations,* vol. 10, London: Darton, Longman and Todd, 1973, pp. 30-49.

---------, "Anonymous Christianity and the Missionary Task of the Church", in: *Theological Investigation,* vol. 12, London: Darton, Longman and Todd, 1974, pp. 161-178.

---------, "The One Christ and the Universality of Salvation", in: *Theological Investigations,* vol. 16, London: Darton, Longman and Todd, 1979, pp. 199-224.

---------, "Jesus Christ in the Non-Christian Religions", in: *Theological Investigations,* vol. 17, London: Darton, Longman and Todd, 1981, pp. 39-50.

---------, "On the Importance of the Non-Christian Religions for Salvation", in: *Theological Investigations,* vol. 18, London: Darton, Longman and Todd, 1984, pp. 288-295.

---------, "Christianity's Absolute Claim", in: *Theological Investigations,* vol. 21, London: Darton, Longman and Todd, 1988, pp. 171-184.

Ratzinger, Joseph, "Der christliche Glaube und die Weltreligionen", in: *Got in Welt,* II Festschrift Karl Rahner, 1964, pp. 287-305.

Reinhardt, Klaus, "In What way is Jesus Christ Unique", in: *Communio* 1 (1974) 4, pp. 343-364.

Rossano, P., "The Bible and the Non-Christian Religions", in: *Bulletin Secretariatus pro non Christianis* 2, no. 4 (1967), pp. 18-28.

Rossignol, Raymond, "Book Reviews", in: *Word and Worship* 6 (1969) 13, pp. 669-673.

Saldanha, Julian, "Development and the Need of a New Humanism", in: *Indian Missiological Review* 18 (1996) 4, pp. 75-82.

Vadakumpadan, Paul, "Development through Evangelization, Evangelization through Development: The Experience of the North East", in: *Indian Missiological Review* 18 (1996) 4, pp. 66-74.

Von Balthasar, Hans Urs, "Editorial: Buddhism - An Approach to Dialogue", in: *Communio* 15 (1988) 4, pp. 403-410.

Wilfred, Felix, "Inculturation as a Hermeneutical Problem", in: *Vidyajyoti* 52 (1988) 9, pp. 422-436.

---------, "Inter-Religious Dialogue as a Political Question", in: *Vidyajyoti* 60 (1996) 6, pp. 361-374.

8. Some Other Periodicals and News Magazines

*Harijan,* 7.4.47. [An English weekly journal (1933-1956) founded by M. Gandhi and published under the auspices of Harijan Sevak Sangh, Poona, and from 1942 by the Navajivan Trust, Ahmedabad].

*International Herald Tribune,* May 28, 1998, p. 1.

*L'Osservatore Romano* (English edition), January 29, 1990, p. 3.

*L'Osservatore Romano* (Italian edition), 2-3 Giugno, 1997, p. 10.

*The New Leader* 109 (1996) 5, p. 24.

*The New Leader* 111 (1998) 3, pp. 4-5.

*Young India,* 5.2.25. (An English weekly journal published from Ahmedabad, and as bi-weekly from Bombay).

# GLOSSARY OF HINDI AND SANSKRIT TERMS[1]

| | |
|---|---|
| *ācārya* | master, teacher, head of an *āśram*. |
| *ādmī* (H) | the human being. |
| *advaita* | non-dual; a term used in non-dualist systems in reference to the Absolute (*Brahman*) who is without a second; often used also to designate non-dualism. |
| *aham Brahmāsmi* | I am Brahman". |
| *ahaṁkāra* | pride; refusal of God. |
| *ahimsā* | non-injury; the desire and endeavour to live and act at all times in such a way as to cause no injury to others but instead benefit. The meaning is very comprehensive, including non-injury to people's thoughts and feelings as well as to their bodies and possessions; and non-injury by speech, thought and action. It has a positive connotation, meaning benevolent love to all living beings. |
| *ānanda* | bliss or joy; a characteristic of supreme consciousness. |
| *āndolana* (H) | movement. |
| *anubhava* | experience; perception which is direct, immediate and existentially possessed. |
| *anugraha* | God's grace, favour. |
| *ārati* | worship offered by waving of flames. |
| *artha* | object, aim, wealth. |
| *āśram* | hermitage. |
| *āśrama* | stage of life. |
| *ātman* | soul, being. |
| *Ātman* | the Absolute; the Supreme Spirit; the ground of all that exists in the world and the ultimate Self of all selves or souls. |
| *avatāra* | descent of God, especially of Viṣṇu, to save the universe from disaster, to uphold righteousness, to reward the good, to punish the evil, finally to show the right path to liberation and to aid humankind with grace. |
| *avidyā* | ignorance; the primordial ignorance, the fundamental cause of humankind's phenomenal existence and its imperfections. |
| *bhagavān* | Lord, God. |
| *bhajan* | hymn. |
| *bhakta* | devotee, God-lover. |
| *bhakti* | in the religious usage the term conveys the meaning of choosing God as one's part, worshipping, adoring and loving him. The religious attitude connotes the notion of a personal God to whom love and devotion are shown. The term |

[1] We have preferred this glossary for its attempt to include not only the classical meaning of the terms but also their present day significance. The specific Hindi terms are indicated with (H). This is a selective glossary limited to the dissertation.

| | |
|---|---|
| | expresses interpersonal relationships of loyalty, service, reverence, love -- interpersonal participation and communion between God and man in mutual love and surrender. |
| *bhakti mārga* | the path of loving devotion. |
| *bhakti yoga* | the discipline of love. |
| *bhogabhūmi* (H) | land of enjoyment. |
| *bhūdāna-grāmadāna* (H) | gift of land and village, a movement started by Vinobha Bhave for the cause of the poor. |
| *Brahman* | the Absolute; the Supreme Being; the ground of all that exists in the world. |
| *brahmacāri(n)* | one who undergoes religious studentship, who practises continence. |
| *brāhmin* | one who belongs to the priestly caste. |
| *buddha* | awakened one. |
| *Buddha* | lord Gautama Buddha. |
| *celā* (H) | disciple. |
| *cit* | the mind, spirit, consciousness. |
| *dalit* (H) | a person belonging to the oppressed class in India. |
| *Daridranārāyaṇa* | God of the poor; God in the form of the poor. |
| *darśan* | sight; entering the presence of God; spiritual perception of God; encounter. |
| *darśana* | philosophical system or point of view. |
| *devdāsī* | a temple girl. |
| *devī* | goddess. |
| *dharma* | what is right; law; religious and social duty; duty of one's state of life; norm of religious and social life; merit; the form of things as they are and the power that keeps them as they are; religion. |
| *dharma-śāstra* | law book. |
| *dhyāna* | meditation; continuous mental effort to concentrate on one object. |
| *Divālī/Dīpāvalī* | Hindu festival of lights. |
| *guha* | cave; the inner centre of human beings. |
| *guru* | preceptor, spiritual master. |
| *gurukula* | residence of the spiritual master. |
| *harijan* | people of God; the untouchables. |
| *Īśvara* | Lord, God. |
| *jagat* | world. |
| *jagatguru* | teacher of the world. |
| *jāti* | caste or class. |
| *jīva* | a living being; principle of life. |
| *jīvātma* | individual self. |
| *jīvanmukta* | one who is liberated while being embodied. |
| *jīvanmukti* | state of having attained liberation while in this life. |
| *jñāna* | true knowledge; spiritual insight into the true nature of the self and of the Supreme Being; there are two kinds of *jñāna:* the lower and higher -- the lower consists of the knowledge of the |

Veda and all the sciences, arts; the higher is that by which one realizes one's true relationship to the Supreme Being.

*jñāna mārga* — the path of knowledge.

*jñāna-yoga* — the discipline of knowledge.

*kāma* — desire; passion; lust.

*karma* — willed activity; result of such an activity; the law of *karma* means that every individual reaps the reward of his/her own efforts and actions, both good and bad. It implies also that the state in which we are now is the outcome of our past actions. *Karma* is of three kinds: what one is now doing; what is one now receiving or what from the past is now fructifying, and what one has in storage for the future.

*karmabhūmi* (H) — land of duty.

*karma mārga* — the path of action, effort.

*karma-yoga* — discipline of action; moral-spiritual realm.

*khādi* — handspun and handwoven cotton cloth.

*koṣa* — layer; sheath; division.

*kṣatriya* — the warrior class/caste.

*līlā* — sport of the gods.

*lokasaṁgraha* — well-being of the world, world maintenance.

*mahātmā/mahatma* — one who is a 'great soul'.

*mahāvākya* — great sentence.

*mārga* — path, way.

*maṭh* — monastery.

*māyā* — the creative power of God; ignorance.

*mokṣa* — liberation; release; the final and spiritual attainment of the human being, which consists either in realizing one's identity with the Absolute or in being united with the personal God.

*mukti* — liberation, release, salvation.

*nāma-rūpa* — 'name and form'; the world of phenomenon.

*neti, neti* — not this, not this/that; apophatism.

*nirguṇa* — without qualities.

*nirvāṇa* — dissolution of self-delusion.

*niṣkāma karma* — action without selfish desire, or disinterested activity.

*Om śānti, śānti!* — Om peace, peace! May God grant peace!

*paramātman* — the Supreme *ātman,* God.

*parameśvara* — Supreme Lord.

*prakṛti* — nature; primordial matter.

*pramāṇa* — means of valid knowledge.

*prasāda* — divine grace.

*pūjā* — worship, adoration.

*purāṇa* — works of mythology, ancient tale.

*puruṣa* — man, the primordial person.

*puruṣārtha* — goal of human life.

*Rāmarājya* — kingdom of the lord *Rāma.*

*ṛṣi* — seer.

*ṛta* — the eternal order, law of the world.

| | |
|---|---|
| *sab bhāī bhāī* (H) | all are brothers; fellowship and brotherhood among all religions. |
| *śabda* | sound, verbal testimony. |
| *saccidānanda* | existence-consciousness-bliss; the nature of the Supreme Being. |
| *sadguru* | the Supreme Master. |
| *sādhana* | spiritual discipline; means. |
| *sādhu* | a wandering monk, ascetic. |
| *saguṇa* | with qualities. |
| *saṁsāra* | cycle of "rebirth", bondage. |
| *saṁskāra* | sacramental rites of Hinduism. |
| *sannyāsa* | renunciation, life of total renunciation. |
| *sannyāsi(n)* | one who has renounced everything. |
| *śānti (shanti)* | peace; tranquillity of the mind and body. |
| *sarvadharma-samabhāva* | a position that considers all religions as equal. |
| *sarvodaya* | a movement inspired by M. Gandhi that strives for the up-liftment of all. |
| *sat* | existence; reality; the true. |
| *satya* | truth. |
| *satyāgraha* | holding on to truth even in the most testing of times. |
| *satyameva jayate* | truth will prevail. |
| *sevā* | service. |
| *śiṣya* | disciple. |
| *Smṛti* | secondary scripture; what is remembered and handed on. |
| *Śruti* | primary scripture; what has been heard, the Vedic revelation, the revealed and absolutely valid scripture. |
| *śuddha* | pure; undefiled. |
| *śuddhikaraṇa* | purification. |
| *śūdra* | a member of the lowest caste. |
| *sūtra* | short aphorism. |
| *svabhāva* | true nature; character. |
| *svarga* | heaven. |
| *tapas* | austerity. |
| *varṇa* | colour; caste. |
| *vijñāna* | knowledge; science. |
| *viśiṣṭa* | qualified. |
| *viveka* | discernment. |
| *yajña* | sacrifice. |
| *yātrā* | pilgrimage, journey. |
| *yoga* | spiritual exercise; the discipline of unifying body and mind; integration; union; join. |
| *yuga* | world period. |

INDEX

As the name of Amalor appears practically on every page of the book, it has generally not been indexed. We include in this index the names of only those persons and authors who have been cited or referred to in the text or in the footnotes, and not all the names of the authors found in the bibliography.

Riproduzione anastatica: 21 marzo 1999
Finito di stampare nel mese di marzo dallo Stab. Tipolit. Ugo Quintily S.p.A. - Roma